THE
ABC-CLIO
COMPANION TO

*Women's
Progress
in
America*

Women's progress in the United States has often been tied to major economic turmoil such as world wars. This African American, photographed in Daytona Beach, Florida, in 1943, became a welder during World War II.

THE
ABC-CLIO
COMPANION TO

Women's Progress in America

Elizabeth Frost-Knappman

With the assistance of
Sarah Kurian

ABC-CLIO

Copyright © 1994 by Elizabeth Frost-Knappman

Library of Congress Cataloging-in-Publication Data

Frost-Knappman, Elizabeth.
    The ABC-CLIO companion to women's progress in america / Elizabeth Frost-Knappman, with the assistance of Sarah Kurian.
       p. cm. — (ABC-CLIO companions to key issues in American history and life)
    Includes bibliographical references and index.
    1. Women—United States—History—Encyclopedias. 2. Women's rights—United States—Encyclopedias. I. Kurian, Sarah.
  II. Title. III. Series.
  HQ1410.F76 1994 305.4'0973—dc20 94-9355

ISBN 0-87436-667-4 (alk. paper)

01 00 99 98 97 96 95 94   10 9 8 7 6 5 4 3 2 1 (hc)

ABC-CLIO, Inc.
130 Cremona Drive, P.O. Box 1911
Santa Barbara, California 93116-1911

This book is printed on acid-free paper ∞ .
Manufactured in the United States of America

For Kathryn Cullen-DuPont

ABC-CLIO Companions to Key Issues in American History and Life

The ABC-CLIO Companion to the American Labor Movement
Paul F. Taylor

The ABC-CLIO Companion to the Civil Rights Movement
Mark Grossman

The ABC-CLIO Companion to Women in the Workplace
Dorothy Schneider and Carl J. Schneider

The ABC-CLIO Companion to Women's Progress in America
Elizabeth Frost-Knappman

Forthcoming

The ABC-CLIO Companion to the American Peace Movement
Christine A. Lunardini

The ABC-CLIO Companion to the Computer Revolution
Paul E. Ceruzzi

The ABC-CLIO Companion to the Environmental Movement
Mark Grossman

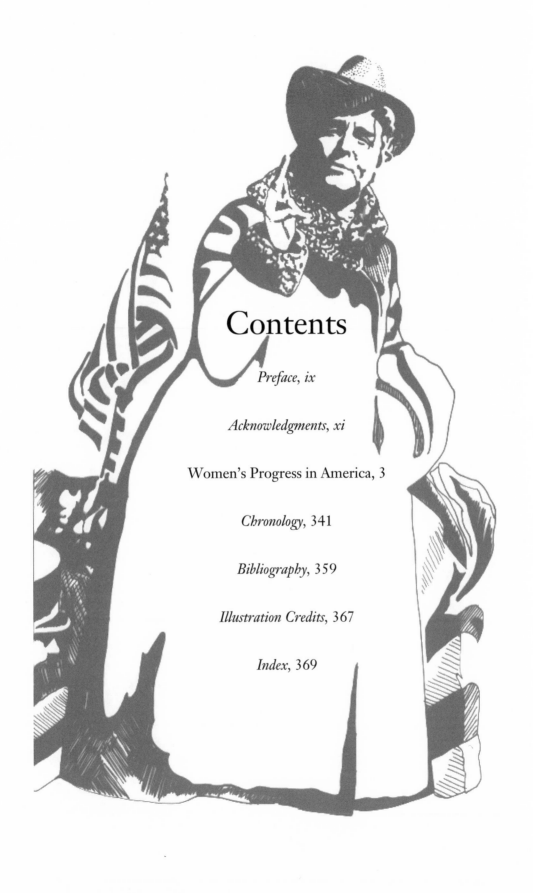

Contents

Preface, ix

Acknowledgments, xi

Women's Progress in America, 3

Chronology, 341

Bibliography, 359

Illustration Credits, 367

Index, 369

Preface

American women have struggled for equality with men for over two centuries. Their quest for the vote alone took 72 years, dating from the Seneca Falls Convention of 1848 to the passage of the nineteenth Amendment in 1920. Ninety-three years elapsed between the introduction of the first equal pay bill for working women and the passage of the Equal Pay Act of 1963. Despite this long history, the legal, economic, and educational conditions of women have changed more rapidly in the last 20 years than in the prior 200. The year 1992 witnessed a record number of women elected to Congress: their percentage increased by 200 percent in the U.S. Senate and by 68 percent in the House of Representatives (although in real numbers they held only 6 out of 100 senate seats and 48 out of 435 house seats).

I became interested in this fascinating quest for equal status in society in 1988, while researching the book *History of Women's Suffrage in America*. That work traced the nineteenth-century campaign for the vote and aroused my curiosity about women's public achievements since the founding of the colonies in 1607. As I reviewed the laws, court cases, organizations, publications, and lives of women and men who helped to advance the position of women in society, I found how sparse the documentation was for the colonial and early nationalist periods, in comparison to the voluminous data for the nineteenth and twentieth centuries. For,

unlike Anne Bradstreet, few seventeenth-century women published poetry books or, like Anne Hutchinson, risked their lives to attack Puritan orthodoxy. I have tried to emphasize these early dramatic accomplishments, but not, I hope, at the expense of the contemporary period.

Included here are women whose achievements were unusual for their time, such as colonial printer Ann Timothy, poet Phillis Wheatley, and lawyer Myra Bradwell. At the suggestion of my editor, I have occasionally included a topic to balance another, such as the Code Napoléon to highlight the Common Law. Rarely have I included entries for events that set back the course of women's progress, and space does not permit the inclusion of women's private acts of courage and achievement—those women who participated in wars dating back to the Revolution, went on strike for equal pay when their families relied on their income, donated to women's schools and colleges, struggled to control their own property rights, ran businesses when they could not legally make contracts, sat on juries, and won custody of their children when the laws were stacked against them. What this book does do is record the public milestones of women's history, emphasizing those people who either self-consciously championed women's rights or pioneered the way for others. For those who do not find a key figure or event, I apologize.

Acknowledgments

The author would like to express appreciation to Sarah Kurian for her invaluable help with this book. Thanks are also due to the following people: Susan Brainard of New England Publishing Associates for her patient assistance with computer operations and help compiling the chronology and bibliography; Lois Nadel and Pam Crum of the Chester Book Company for tracking down hard-to-find and long out-of-print volumes; Gloria Eustis and the staff of the Chester Public Library for cheerful and skillful research; Amy Collins for careful fact-checking; Heather Cameron and Sallie Greenwood of ABC-CLIO for commissioning this book and adding valuable editorial suggestions; Edward William Knappman for assuming additional responsibilities while I completed my research; Amanda Lee Frost Knappman for inspiring me with her study of Alice Paul; and, finally, to Kathryn Cullen-DuPont for her friendship, interest, and generous sharing of ideas, which greatly enriched this book.

THE
ABC-CLIO
COMPANION TO

Women's Progress in America

Abolition Movement

The women's rights movement of the nineteenth century had its roots in the campaign to end slavery. A landmark event best illustrates this: On Wednesday, 21 February 1838, Angelina Grimké, called Devil-ina by a hostile press, delivered a speech to the Massachusetts legislature, becoming the first woman to address a U.S. legislative body. She and her older sister, Sarah Grimké, were early leaders of the abolition movement. On 21 February they represented the 20,000 Massachusetts women who had signed petitions to end slavery. Attendance was extraordinary, and when Angelina Grimké rose to her feet, she inspired tears as well as hisses. Soberly dressed in Quaker grey, she questioned why women should not be admitted to the political arena from which they were arbitrarily excluded.

Because [slavery] is a political subject, it has often been tauntingly said, that women had nothing to do with it. Are we aliens because we are women? Are we bereft of citizenship because we are mothers, wives and daughters of a mighty people? Have women *no* country—no interests staked in public weal—no liabilities in common peril—no partnership in a nation's guilt and shame? ... If so, then may we well hide our faces in the dust, and cover ourselves with sackcloth and ashes. This dominion of women should be resigned—the sooner the better; in the age which is approaching she should be something more—she should be a citizen.

What makes this event so remarkable is that, in 1838, women could neither vote nor run for office. They were excluded from all colleges except Oberlin (Mount Holyoke being a seminary at this time). Only the Quakers allowed women to speak out in public or to participate in church affairs. Respectable females did not dare express their opinions about political topics publicly for fear they would be threatened, ridiculed, or even mobbed. When Frances Wright gave a public lecture in 1828, she was jeered and called a freak.

Even in the abolition movement of the 1820s and early 1830s, women had no real power and were unable to vote at leadership meetings. Male abolitionists, with the exception of William Lloyd Garrison and a few others, rejected them. When abolitionists met in 1833 to organize the American Anti-Slavery Society, they denied women membership. As late as 1840, women delegates were refused recognition at the World's Anti-Slavery Convention in London.

In this social climate, the Grimké sisters, who were upper-class southern women, became the first female antislavery agents in America. Other women soon followed. Some middle-class women saw a link between women's freedom and the freedom of slaves. Many early female activists, particularly those in the Northeast, were related to male abolitionists. They organized female antislavery societies, such as the Philadelphia Female Anti-Slavery Society founded by Lucretia Mott in 1833. Through their participation in antislavery societies, women learned to organize, hold public meetings, raise money, and gather petitions.

By 1837, petitioning the government was the abolition movement's foremost activity because of the large number of women in the movement and the fact that petitioning was the only form of political expression open to them. By the time of the Seneca Falls Convention in 1848, many women were dedicated abolitionists, ready to apply the ideal of natural rights to women as well as to enslaved men.

3

See also American Anti-Slavery Society; Female Antislavery Societies; Garrison, William Lloyd; Grimké, Angelina; Grimké, Sarah; Petitions; Philadelphia Female Anti-Slavery Society; Seneca Falls Convention; World's Anti-Slavery Convention.

Abortion

English custom held that abortion was an ethical issue only after the mother detected fetal movement, or quickening, which usually occurs during the fourth month of pregnancy. In colonial America, ministers exhorted women that to abort their "fruit of the womb" was equivalent to murder. Yet abortions were neither forbidden by written law nor prosecuted under the common law so that women used herbal abortifacients and even more primitive abortion techniques to end their pregnancies, while midwives and male doctors used intrusive procedures. During the eighteenth century, American women used coitus interruptus, abstinence, and abortion to limit family size. In the nineteenth century, a decline in the birth rate was achieved without any advance in contraceptive knowledge at all: withdrawal, douche, rhythm, and abstinence were the only *recommended* means of birth control, but abortion remained a remedy for unwanted pregnancy. Marie Costa writes that from 1800 to 1900, the fertility rate for European-American women dropped from 7.04 to 3.56 offspring, due mainly to the increased use of abortion. By 1850, abortionists were advertising in circulars, newspapers, and other media. During the first half of the nineteenth century, most of their clients were single. Later in the 1800s, an increasing number of married women sought abortions.

Around 1830, some states began to declare abortion illegal after the fourth month of pregnancy. These included Connecticut (1821), Missouri (1827), and Illinois (1827). By 1840, abortion was restricted by law in ten of the 26 states. According to the *Handbook of American Women's History*, "the movement to establish abortion as both criminal and sinful was led by male physicians as part of a crusade from the 1860s to the 1880s to outlaw all forms of contracep-

tion." From shortly after its founding in 1847 until the 1880s, the American Medical Association kept up a public campaign against abortion, playing up fears about the drop in fertility of native white women. Yet magazines and newspapers continued to accept advertisements from abortionists, and the rate of abortion soared. During the period 1800–1830, one abortion was performed for every 30 live births; by midcentury, the ratio was one abortion for every five to six live births; and by 1880, one in every five live births was terminated by abortion.

By the early twentieth century birth control advocate Margaret Sanger served as nurse and midwife to working-class women, recording their widespread fear of pregnancy. Mothers begged her to perform abortions and provide information about contraceptives. Methods of abortion included leaping off tables, rolling around on the floor, massaging one's stomach, drinking nausea-inducing potions, and inserting blunt instruments into the vagina. Historian Ellen Chesler cites a small study of immigrants on the Lower East Side of New York in 1917 that indicated only one-third knew of any form of birth control besides abortion. Doctors bemoaned the frequency with which middle-class women resorted to abortion. During the 1920s and 1930s, women used more reliable methods of birth control, including the condom, diaphragm, and a more accurate rhythm method; still, self-induced abortions continued. Although there are no reliable numbers on home abortions, one study estimates that, during the 1920s, one in two pregnancies ended in abortion. In 1961, between 200,000 and 1.2 million women underwent an abortion. Nevertheless, by 1965, the laws in all 50 states prohibited abortion, restricting its use to life-threatening situations. In some states, women succeeded in modifying these laws to make exceptions for rape, incest, or fetal deformity. However, as legal historian Joan Huff has shown, inadequate access to contraception and abortion confined women in certain "strongholds of disability." In the 1970s, feminists fought all restrictions on abortionists, resulting in the U.S. Supreme Court's landmark *Roe v. Wade* decision in 1973, which invalidated all state laws that prohibited abortion during the first 12 weeks after conception. As a result of this and other legal decisions, "the right of a woman," in the words of Barron's *Law Dictionary* (1991), "to have an abortion during the early stages of her pregnancy without criminal sanctions applied to her or those who perform the abortion and to have it free of unreasonable government restraint, has now been established as part of a constitutional right of personal privacy." Recently, the Court has begun to reexamine a woman's right to abortion. The Hyde Amendment, upheld by the Supreme Court in 1980 in *Harris v. McCrae*, restricted Medicaid payments for abortion, and the Court's *Webster v. Reproductive Health Services* (1989) upheld a state statute that prohibited the use of public staff and facilities in abortions. In *Planned Parenthood v. Casey* (1992), Pennsylvania was permitted to regulate abortion as long as it did not unfairly burden women. The Freedom of Access to Clinic Entrances Bill passed the U.S. Senate on 16 November 1993 and the House of Representatives on 18 November 1993; the bill seeks to protect women's access to abortion clinics by prohibiting bombings, arson, and blockades at clinics as well as threats and acts of violence against medical staff performing abortions. An abortion rights bill has not yet been passed by either body.

See also American Law Institute Abortion Laws; Blackmun, Harry; Clergy Consultation Service on Abortion; *Doe v. Bolton;* Jane; National Abortion Rights Action League; *People v. Belous; Planned Parenthood of Central Missouri v. Danforth; Planned Parenthood of Southeastern Pennsylvania v. Casey;* Redstockings; *Roe v. Wade; Webster v. Reproductive Health Services.*

Abzug, Bella Savitzy (1920–)

Bella Abzug, the first Jewish woman to be sent to Congress, was born in the Bronx, New York, on 24 July 1920. A lawyer and unconventional politician, she is well known for speaking out about many unpopular ideas and causes.

Abzug attended public schools in the Bronx and later worked in her father's store in Manhattan, The Live and Let Live Meat Market. In 1942 she received her B.A. from Hunter College and in 1944 married Martin Abzug. At Columbia Law School Abzug became the editor of the *Columbia Law Review.* After graduating Abzug was admitted to the New York Bar in 1947 and practiced until 1970. A specialist in labor issues, she represented the first rank-and-file longshoreman strikers and many other unions. Much of her work for civil rights and civil liberties clients was done *pro bono.*

Abzug also worked as a lawyer for the Civil Rights Congress and the American Civil Liberties Union. One of her most famous cases was that of Willie McGee, a black man executed in Mississippi in 1951 for the rape of a white woman. In her appeals, Abzug pointed to the exclusion of African Americans from juries and to the exclusive use of the death penalty for African Americans convicted of rape. Abzug also represented a number of New York schoolteachers and writers accused by Senator Joseph McCarthy of being communists.

During the 1960s Abzug became active in the peace, antinuclear, and women's movements and gained national attention as a supporter of the feminist movement. In 1961 she founded and chaired the National Women's Political Caucus.

In 1970, Abzug competed for and was elected to the U.S. House of Representatives from New York City's 19th District where through 1976 she served in office. While there she ran for the U.S. Senate against Daniel Patrick Moynihan, an election she lost. Soon after, she attempted to defeat Edward Koch in the Democratic mayoral primary in New York City, again losing. She continued to appear in headline news throughout the 1970s as a peace activist and staunch supporter of the women's movement. President Jimmy Carter appointed her co-chair of the National Advisory Committee for Women in 1978. The committee had a full agenda and was very demanding concerning future prospects, yet after the first meetings, President Carter dismissed Abzug from the committee, to the dismay of her fellow workers. Several members, including the co-chair, resigned from the group and the public outcries were noticeable for some time concerning the action taken by the president.

Today Abzug, the mother of two daughters, remains active as a commentator and writer on political and women's issues. She is the author of *Gender Gap: Bella Abzug's Guide to Political Power for Women* (1984).

See also National Women's Political Caucus.

Act To Confirm Certain Conveyances and Directing the Manner of Proving Deeds To Be Recorded

In 1771, New York enacted a law that strengthened a married woman's right to her own property, which generally came under the control of her husband after marriage. After passage of An Act to Confirm Certain Conveyances and Directing the Manner of Proving Deeds to be Recorded, a husband could not sell or mortgage his wife's property unless she signed the deed and testified to a judge, in a private examination, that she agreed to the transaction. This ensured that husbands did not coerce their wives into signing away the wives' property, a very real possibility. The rights of married women in New York were strengthened by the New York Married Woman's Property Act of 1848 and the New York Married Woman's Property Act of 1860.

See also Coercion; New York Married Woman's Property Act (1848); New York Married Woman's Property Act (1860).

Adams, Abigail Smith (1744–1818)

Abigail Adams, who left 2,000 extant letters, was one of the outstanding women of her generation. She was born 11 November 1744 in Weymouth, Massachusetts, and, like most women of her time, had no formal schooling, though in his first mention of her in his diary (she was 14 years old), John Adams described her as a "wit." On 25 October 1764, she married Adams and over the next decade she gave birth to their five children.

The family lived in Braintree (now Quincy), Massachusetts, and Boston. However, in 1774 John Adams left Boston for Philadelphia, where he became a delegate to the first Continental Congress. John and Abigail would not live together again, except for brief periods, until 1784. Their long separations encouraged Abigail Adams's genius for letter writing, and her most famous reports of people, news, and events date from this period.

In her letters, Abigail Adams called for independence from England earlier than was fashionable. She also was a proponent of women's rights. In a 1776 letter to her husband, she implored him to include a women's rights plank in the Declaration of Independence: "Remember the Ladies, and be more generous and favorable to them than your ancestors. Do not put such unlimited power into the hands of the Husbands. Remember all men would be tyrants if they could." In another letter, she criticized the unfairness of denying girls the educational opportunities offered to boys. And throughout her long life, in both word and deed, she opposed the practice of slavery.

Adams directed the household's dairy and farming operations, from home and abroad, so skillfully that some say she saved her family from poverty. In 1797 she became first lady, occupying an unfinished White House. The president discussed political problems with Adams, asked her help in drafting quasi-official letters, and according to historian Page Smith, treated her as a "minister without portfolio." By 1797 inflation had eaten into the president's salary, so that entertaining was a drain. Yet the first lady managed the family's finances so efficiently that the Adamses saved money in addition to fulfilling social obligations.

Although Adams lived to see her son, John Quincy Adams, become President James Monroe's secretary of state, she died on 28 October 1818 in Braintree, before he was elected president.

See also Adams, John Quincy.

Adams, Hannah (1755–1831)

Hannah Adams was the first American woman to earn a living solely by writing. Born 2 October 1755 in Medfield, Massachusetts, she lacked formal schooling but inherited a love of books from her studious (but impoverished) father. A collector of historical material, in 1784 she compiled her first book, *An Alphabetical Compendium of the Various Sects which Have Appeared from the Beginning of the Christian Era*. It was eventually profitable, going through three American and three British editions. The success fueled her ambition to make a living as a writer, and in 1799 she published *Summary History of New England*. Because the income from those two books was small, friends contributed to her financial support. Several books followed, including *The Truth and Excellence of the Christian Religion Exhibited* (1804), *History of the Jews* (1812), and *Letters on the Gospels* (1824). Adams died in Brookline, Massachusetts, on 15 December 1831. Her *Memoir of Miss Hannah Adams, Written by Herself* was issued the following year.

Adams, John Quincy (1767–1848)

Eldest son of John Adams, second president of the United States, and Abigail Adams, John Quincy Adams was the nation's sixth chief executive. During his years in Congress (1831–1848), he became a champion of the right of women to petition the government.

Adams was born 11 July 1767 in Braintree (now Quincy), Massachusetts. Educated in Europe (1778–1780) and at Harvard (1787), Adams was admitted to the bar in 1790, becoming a lawyer and statesman. In 1802 he was elected to the Massachusetts state senate and went to the U.S. Senate the following year. Although Adams lost his bid for reelection in 1808, he represented America abroad, helping to negotiate the Treaty of Ghent, which was signed 24 December 1814. In 1817, he returned to the United States to become President James Monroe's secretary of state. He became president in 1825, after a split electoral vote threw the election into the House of Representatives. Adams's presidency was marred by the hostility of the followers of Andrew Jackson, and he lost reelection to Jackson in 1828.

In 1830 Adams was elected to the House of Representatives. His years of service as a congressman (1831–1848) are, in terms of domestic issues, the most remarkable of his career. He was a courageous voice against slavery and advocate of what was then the sole political right of women: to sign or gather signatures on petitions.

Adams's staunch defense of the right of citizens to petition the government is illustrated by events of the 1830s. In 1834, the American Anti-Slavery Society launched a petition drive to end slavery in Washington, D.C. The campaign was phenomenally successful; thousands of petitions flooded Congress. But Southern congressmen forced passage of a gag rule that effectively shelved the petitions. In addition, Congressman Howard of Maryland criticized women who ventured into the public sphere to circulate the petitions. In a series of speeches that earned him the sobriquet "Old Man Eloquent," Adams defended the right of women to exercise their basic political right. He argued, "Why does it follow that women are fitted for nothing but the cares of domestic life, for bearing children and cooking the food of a family, devoting all their time to the domestic circle—to promoting the immediate personal comfort of their husbands, brothers, and sons?" He even questioned the idea that women had no right to vote.

In 1837, when the number of petitions peaked, Adams was threatened with censure by his congressional colleagues, but he successfully defended himself. Gradually his tenacity and courage won over the majority, and, by 1844, Adams's motion to replace the Gag Rules was passed 108 to 80. On 21 February 1848, Adams fell unconscious to the floor of the House. He died two days later.

See also Abolition Movement; Adams, Abigail; Female Antislavery Societies; Garrison, William Lloyd; Petitions.

Adams v. Kellogg

In 1788, the Supreme Court of Errors of Connecticut allowed Mary Kellogg to make

7

a will leaving property from a previous marriage to her present husband. But her brother and heir-at-law went to court, arguing that, under common law, married women were not allowed to make a will leaving real property. In a decision that strengthened the rights of married women in the state, the court upheld Mary Kellogg's will, allowing the property to go to her husband as she had wished.

Addams, Jane (1860–1935)

Nobel Peace Prize recipient, settlement house founder, pacifist, and suffragist, Jane Addams was one of this country's most important reformers. She was born 6 September 1860 in Cedarville, Illinois. When Addams was two years old her mother died, and the little girl became intensely attached to her father. In 1877 she enrolled in the Rockford (Illinois) Female Seminary, forgoing her preference, Smith College, in deference to her father. Upon his death in 1881,

Jane Addams

the year of her graduation, Addams enrolled in the Woman's Medical College of Pennsylvania, but left after a few months.

Addams traveled to Europe with her stepmother (1883–1885) and returned there with former classmate Ellen Gates Starr two years later. In 1888 the women visited Toynbee Hall, a settlement house in the East End of London. When they returned to the United States, they bought an abandoned mansion, once owned by Charles J. Hull, in a Chicago immigrant slum. Addams and Starr moved into Hull House in September 1889 and a few years later the settlement house was offering arts-and-crafts classes and education and job programs, as well as a nursery, playground, boardinghouse, dispensary, gallery, theater, and music school.

By 1910 more than 400 settlement houses had attracted thousands of young people, a majority of them women, who organized literary evenings, art classes, and kindergartens for the poor. By 1915, the reformers were beginning to lobby legislators, organize unions, and promote international peace. They championed the Factory Inspection Act, the first juvenile court, the first mother pension act, the eight-hour workday for women, workmen's compensation, tenement housing regulations, an end to sweatshop work conditions, and the promotion of organized labor. As Suzanne Lebsock has written, "Settlement workers took the domestic and public spheres . . . that were cast as mutually exclusive . . . and rolled them into one." (Chafe, 1991)

In 1907, Addams joined the Chicago municipal women's suffrage campaign and served as the first vice-president of the National American Woman Suffrage Association (1911–1914). In 1913 she attended the International Woman Suffrage Alliance meeting in Budapest, Hungary. Among her many other offices were chair of the Woman's Peace Party (1915), chair of the International Congress of Women at The Hague (1915), and first president of the Women's International League for Peace and Freedom (1919). Addams shared the 1931 Nobel Peace Prize with Nicholas

M. Butler, an educator, philosopher, and pacifist, donating her share of the prize money to the Women's International League for Peace and Freedom. Her many publications on social reform include *Democracy and Social Ethics* (1902), *The Spirit of Youth and the City Streets* (1909), *Twenty Years at Hull House* (1910), and *The Second Twenty Years at Hull House* (1930). *Newer Ideals of Peace* (1907), and *Peace and Bread in Time of War* (1922) reflect her views on pacifism. Her travels, lectures, and concern for the poor continued until her death in Chicago on 21 May 1935.

See also Jane Club; Settlement House Movement; Woman's Peace Party.

Adkins v. Children's Hospital

In *Adkins v. Children's Hospital* (1923), a conservative Supreme Court under the leadership of Justice George Sutherland overturned a Washington, D.C., minimum-wage law for women. The Court found that the law's interference with a woman's right to bargain with her employer on the subject of wages was unconstitutional. Earlier decisions had declared that women's unique need for protection took precedence over the principle of bargaining freedom in contracts. However, the Court declared that the Nineteenth Amendment put men and women on an equal footing and made such protective laws unnecessary. The decision blocked the success of the drive for protective legislation.

See also *Bowe v. Colgate-Palmolive Co.*; Fourteenth Amendment; *Muller v. State of Oregon; United States v. Libbey-Owens; Weeks v. Southern Bell Telephone and Telegraph Co.; West Coast Hotel v. Parrish.*

Adultery

In colonial America, adultery was one of the most serious offences a woman could commit, inviting stern penalties. Historian Mary P. Ryan writes that adultery was punished by death six times in the history of the colonies. Carol Hymowitz and Michaele Weissman point out that women who bore children out of wedlock were sentenced to public whippings, brandings, and fines. Extramarital sex was widely believed to be more offensive in women than in men, although some religious communities tried to treat adulterers of either sex equally, forcing them to confess their sins in church. In fact, adultery was defined as sex with a married woman. Married men who had sexual union with a single woman were charged with fornication, a lesser crime. In the South, the most successful complaint for divorce was a wife's adultery; the first private divorces granted in Maryland (1790) and Virginia (1803) were to men whose wives gave birth to mulatto babies.

Historian Eleanor Flexner writes that, even as the twentieth century began, the greatest inequities everywhere were in the realm of divorce. Minnesota, for instance, required that a woman divorced for adultery forfeit even such real estate as had been her own property; Pennsylvania forbade her disposal of it, if she continued to live with the man with whom she had committed adultery, after divorce. In neither state was a man so penalized. According to Barron's *Law Dictionary* (1991), most states today view adultery as an offense if either sexual partner is married. However, some states have kept the common law notion that adultery has taken place *only* if the woman is married.

See also Divorce.

Akeley, Mary Lee Jobe (1878–1966)

Akeley was a photographer and mountaineer, the leader of six expeditions to the Canadian Northwest. In honor of her explorations and first ascents, the Canadian government named Mount Jobe after her. She was born Mary Leonore Jobe 29 January 1878 on a farm in Tappan, Ohio. She received the equivalent of a B.A. from Scio College (later Mount Union College) in 1897 and entered Bryn Mawr in 1901 for two years of graduate work. Jobe earned an M.A. from Columbia College in 1909, while teaching at Normal College of the City of New York (now Hunter College), a post she held until 1916.

Mary Lee Jobe Akeley, American explorer and mountaineer, photographed in about 1917, wears clothing collected during expeditions to the Canadian west.

Although Jobe had made earlier trips to Canada, by 1913 she had developed a serious interest in exploring the Canadian Northwest. She mapped the headwaters of the Fraser River and made the first attempt to scale Mount Sir Alexander, one of Canada's highest mountains. By the time Jobe met taxidermist Carl Akeley in 1918, she was recognized as an outstanding explorer of British Columbia. Jobe married Akeley in 1924 and later accompanied him to Africa to collect specimens for the Great African Hall of the American Museum of Natural History.

When Carl Akeley died in 1926, she took over as the expedition's leader, mapping large areas of Kenya, the Belgian Congo (Zaire), and Tanganyika (Tanzania). Returning to New York in 1927, she became a special advisor to the Great African Hall (renamed the Akeley Hall for her husband in 1936), a position she held until 1938. In 1947 the Belgian government commissioned her to survey Congolese wildlife sanctuaries and parks, and her subsequent films and collections helped alert the world to Africa's vanishing species.

Carl Akeley's biographer, Penelope Bodry-Sanders, has described Mary Akeley as "a powerful, independent, and assertive woman who had . . . been made a Fellow of the Royal Geographical Society of London only two years after the society was opened to female enrollment." A crusader for parks, game preserves, and the rights of native people to maintain their customs, Akeley remained intellectually and physically active until just before her death in Stonington, Connecticut, on 19 July 1966.

Akron Convention

At a women's rights convention in Akron, Ohio, Sojourner Truth electrified the audience with her now-famous "And Ain't I a Woman?" speech. The convention was held 28–29 May 1851. More men attended this than any other convention for women's rights; many were clergymen who had come to heckle. Despite pleas to convention president Frances D. Gage that Truth not be permitted to speak, Gage allowed Truth to take the podium after one day's wait. Nearly six feet tall, with a proud carriage and a gaze that made her seem to Gage "like one in a dream," Truth came down the aisle of the church toward the pulpit in a white dress and white turban, covered by a bonnet, amidst whispers of "Go to it, darky!" and "Woman's rights and niggers!" So hostile was the crowd that Gage was unable to recognize her formally. So that day Truth either sat crouched against the wall or busily sold her autobiography, *Narrative of Sojourner Truth*, during intermission.

But the next day, despite hissing opposition, Gage asked Truth to speak.

The crowd hushed when Truth finally reached the pulpit. Laying her bonnet at her feet, she turned her attention to a clergyman who had just mocked women as being too weak and helpless to be entrusted with the vote. In a powerful voice, she said, "That man over there says women need to be helped into carriages, and lifted over ditches, and to have the best place everywhere. Nobody ever helps me into carriages or over puddles, or gives me the best place—and ain't I a woman?" By the time she was finished, the audience was in tears. In the words of Frances D. Gage, "Amid roars of applause, she returned to her corner, leaving more than one of us with streaming eyes, and hearts beating with gratitude." Hundreds rushed up to shake hands with Sojourner Truth and to congratulate the "glorious old mother."

See also Gage, Frances; Truth, Sojourner.

Alcott, Louisa May (1832–1888)

Louisa May Alcott is best remembered as the creator of Jo March, the articulate, independent heroine of the novel *Little Women*. Alcott was born 29 November 1832 in Germantown, Pennsylvania. She was educated by her father, transcendentalist Amos Bronson Alcott, at home and in his Temple School in Boston. Bronson Alcott was unable to support his family on the income from his schools and other projects, so Louisa worked as a servant, seamstress, and teacher.

In 1851, Alcott began publishing poems, stories, and sketches—all pseudononymously. In 1854, her first book, *Flower Fables*, appeared, and by 1860, she was contributing regularly to popular magazines. During the Civil War, Alcott served as a volunteer nurse (1862–1863). Her letters home served as the inspiration for her first popular book, *Hospital Sketches* (1863). When typhoid fever forced her to leave nursing, she went to work on her first novel, *Moods* (1864).

The novel that made her famous, *Little Women*, was published in two installments in 1868 and 1869, selling 60,000 copies in its first year. In the novel, Jo March unconventionally ignores the "ladylike" behavior prescribed for girls at that time. She is neither domestically inclined nor modest and self-effacing. Eventually Alcott sold about 270 works, including *Little Men* (1871) and *Eight Cousins* (1875). Her strongly feminist novel *Work* (1873) harshly criticized traditional women's employment of the mid-nineteenth century.

Not satisfied with a life of celebrity, Louisa May Alcott became involved in the temperance and women's suffrage movements. She tried to interest the women of Concord, Massachusetts, in voting and in 1879 was the first woman in town to register to vote on school and tax issues. Women's rights were always important to Alcott, as they were to her parents, and she promoted feminist principles throughout her life. Louisa May Alcott died in Boston, unmarried, at the age of 55 on 6 March 1888.

Alcuin

Alcuin (1798), Charles Brockden Brown's first novel, has been called America's first indigenous feminist work. In it, Brown presents a powerful argument for the rights of women. A young man, Alcuin, engages in conversation with a married woman, Mrs. Carter. She teaches him about the true nature of marriage, which she opposes "because it renders the female a slave to the man" and "leaves a woman destitute of prop-

erty." Mrs. Carter explains, "The will of her husband is the criterion of all her duties. All merit is comprised of unlimited obedience. She will be most applauded when she smiles with most perseverance on her oppressor, and when, with the undistinguishing attachment of a dog, no caprice or cruelty shall be able to estrange her affection." Even the American government, thought to be the freest in the world, disenfranchised women: "We are excluded from all political rights without the least ceremony. Lawmakers thought as little of comprehending us in their code of liberty, as if we were pigs, or sheep." In a remarkable resolution for the time, the novel ends with a fantasy of what society would be like if women were truly equal to men.

Alice Paul Picket
See National Woman's Party.

Alliance for Displaced Homemakers/National Displaced Homemakers Network

The Alliance for Displaced Homemakers (founded in 1974 and replaced by the National Displaced Homemakers' Network in 1978) gave feminists renewed respect for housewives. The group's long-term goal was to persuade both men and women to regard homemaking and child rearing as occupations. Its immediate, practical goal was to find work for, or otherwise help, women who could suddenly no longer rely on their husbands for financial support. Tish Sommers and Laurie Shields, two such women, founded the alliance. In 1975, with some state funding, they established a program in California to give displaced homemakers job training and guidance. Shields traveled widely in the United States to advise other groups who were seeking state funding for similar programs. Despite opposition from some conservative groups, the alliance secured federal funds to found centers where such programs could be conducted. Between 1982 and 1984, these programs experienced serious setbacks because the Reagan Administration reduced their funding. In 1984, however, Congress resuscitated the centers. (As of 1991, they are still in existence.) Shields and Sommers went on to organize the Older Women's League.

See also Older Women's League.

Amalgamated Clothing Workers of America (ACWA)

Women workers were unwelcome in trade unions before 1930. One exception was the Amalgamated Clothing Workers of America (ACWA). Founded in 1914 by Bessie Abramowitz and her future husband, Sidney Hillman, the ACWA organized workers by industry rather than craft. By doing so, ACWA gained prominence over the United Garment Workers, which ignored the rank and file. The ACWA was one of the first unions in the United States to provide members with health care, housing, adult education, scholarships, and day-care centers. With the International Ladies' Garment Workers' Union (ILGWU), it fought for better conditions in sweatshops during the early twentieth century.

By 1920, as a result of the success of both unions, nearly one-half of all women laborers in the clothing industries were organized. (The ACWA then had 66,000 women members; the ILGWU, 65,000.) Yet even in this progressive union, there was discrimination: the ACWA sanctioned lower wages for women throughout the 1930s, when half of its members were female. According to historian Eleanor Flexner (1975), at a time when the ACWA had 289,000 female members in a total membership of 386,000, only two of its 17 board members were women. In 1976 the ACWA merged with the Textile Workers Union of America to form the Amalgamated Clothing and Textile Workers Union. In 1992, the union's total membership was 236,000, of which 70–75 percent were women. Of 24 board members, five were women in 1993.

See also International Ladies' Garment Workers' Union.

American Anti-Slavery Society

The American Anti-Slavery Society was formed in 1833 by William Lloyd Garrison and the brothers Arthur and Lewis Tappan, and its activities were entwined with those of female reformers. Only four women were permitted to attend the society's founding meeting in 1833, the male organizers specifying that females were to be "listeners and spectators," not full participants. In response, one of the four women attendees, Lucretia Mott, established the Philadelphia Female Anti-Slavery Society (1833).

However, the American Anti-Slavery Society did introduce women to political life, hiring agents such as Lucretia Mott, Sara and Angelina Grimké, and Abbey Kelley (Foster) to organize and give lectures. When the Grimké sisters became agents for the American Anti-Slavery Society in 1836, they first spoke to gatherings of women only. But, in 1837, for the first time, they addressed "mixed audiences" of men and women, inviting a storm of criticism, as the first southern women to speak in public. The sisters came to believe that if could not act politically, "then may we well be termed 'the white slaves of the North.' " Garrison, who sponsored and financed them, agreed, taking the then-unpopular position that women's rights were as important as abolition. Until then, the abolitionists were a united group.

But, between 1839 and 1840, divisions emerged in the society over the role of women and the group's participation in electoral politics. Garrison believed in the political equality of women; he supported their right to vote and speak before abolition societies and their activities as lecturing agents. A pacifist, he also opposed all governments based on force. These positions offended various groups within the society. Things came to a head in 1840, when Abigail Kelley Foster was elected to the society's business committee leading conservatives, such as James Birney, to form a new political party, called the Liberty party. Theodore Weld and the Tappan brothers also left the American Anti-Slavery Society, founding the American and Foreign Anti-Slavery Society.

Both Garrison's and the Tappans' anti-slavery groups sent delegates to London in 1840 to attend the World's Anti-Slavery Convention. There, Garrison refused to take his seat because the female delegates from the United States, which included the Quaker minister Lucretia Mott, were excluded. The membership of the American Anti-Slavery Society peaked that year at 300,000.

In 1841 Garrison was elected president of the organization, a post he held until emancipation. Although the membership was reduced, women participated fully. At the end of the Civil War, Garrison announced the end of his abolitionist work and advised that the American Anti-Slavery Society be dissolved. But the group carried on under the leadership of Wendell Phillips until 1870.

See also Grimké, Angelina Emily; Grimké, Sarah Moore; Mott, Lucretia; Philadelphia Female Anti-Slavery Society; Weld, Theodore.

American Association of University Women (AAUW)

The origin of the American Association of University Women (AAUW) dates to the founding of the Association of Collegiate Alumnae (ACA) in 1882, shortly after the first generation of Vassar, Wellesley, and Smith students graduated. The organization was founded by Marion Talbot with Alice Freeman Palmer, Alice Hayes, Ellen Swallow Richards, and 13 other first-generation college graduates. The ACA sponsored research refuting the widely held view that college education ruined women's health; in addition, the ACA fought discrimination, granted scholarships to women, and provided a haven for graduates who found society unresponsive to their professional aspirations. Indeed, the group's original function was to ease the transition for women who graduated from college only to be offered jobs as underpaid teachers. In addition, by reaching out to settlement houses and consumer advocacy groups after World War I, the organization became important in the drive to secure fundamental rights for women, such as equal pay for equal work. The ACA merged with the Western Association of Collegiate Women in 1883 and with the Southern Association of College Women in 1921, to form the AAUW. Through its efforts, money was made available to improve the salaries of women professors, build women's dormitories, hire female faculty, and lobby for women's issues.

Today, the AAUW's membership is close to 140,000, with chapters in every state. The organization is composed of three corporations: the Educational Foundation, the Legal Advocacy Fund, and the Association. Its current activities focus on advancement of women through advocacy and encouraging lifelong learning. It engages in research, lobbies Congress, and conducts study and action programs on women's topics. One of these studies, commissioned by the Educational Foundation, received widespread attention when it was made public in 1992. Called "How Schools Shortchange Girls," the study indicates that two decades after the passage of Title IX, which prohibits discrimination on the basis of sex in federally funded school programs, girls receive less attention by classroom teachers than boys do. In response to the study, a package of nine bills on gender equity (H.R. 1793) was introduced into the House of Representatives in 1993. The bill package calls for the establishment of an office of women's equity in the Department of Education, equity training for teachers, efforts to improve girls' achievement in math and science, and the eliminations of sexual harassment in schools.

See also Title IX of the 1972 Higher Education Act.

American Birth Control League (ABCL)

The American Birth Control League (ABCL) was the forerunner to the Planned Parenthood Federation. The ABCL was formed in 1921 by the merger of the National Birth Control League and the Voluntary Parenthood League. Under the leadership of Margaret Sanger, it was incorporated after extensive lobbying of officials in New York State in 1922. The league worked to legalize contraception and to educate doctors and the public about birth control. Sanger established the nation's first medically staffed birth control clinic in Brooklyn in 1916, and in the following year was arrested and sent to a workhouse for 30 days. She appealed, and the New York Court of Appeals, supported by public opinion, ruled that doctors could advise patients about birth control. After this ruling, Sanger formed the ABCL to push for legislation that would exempt doctors from laws prohibiting the distribution of contraceptives.

To run the American Birth Control League, Margaret Sanger expanded the board and staff of her magazine, the *Birth Control Review*. Sanger headed the American Birth Control League board, with Juliet Rublee as vice-president, Frances Ackerman as treasurer, and Anne Kennedy as executive director. Sanger's biographer, Ellen Chesler, records that during its first year the league distributed 75,000 pamphlets, 300,000 letters, 12 different books about contraception, and 15,000 to 30,000 copies of *Birth Control Review*. The league had 18,000 paid members and 132,000 other inquirers, with a budget of $38,000. In 1925 its Motherhood Department answered 30,000 letters from women who wrote, often in despair, to request birth control information. The average ABCL member was an upper-middle-class 35-year-old housewife, white, native-born, and Protestant. The membership was 50 percent Republican, 8 percent Socialist, and most members were married to a college graduate. Males, mostly professionals and academics, made up 17 percent of the members.

Sanger wanted to set up, via local groups, birth control clinics throughout the country and was able to establish ABCL offices in nine states. These offices, however, drained money from headquarters, and to compensate this loss the main office set up a national council of wealthy women in 1925. Chesler notes that of 250 members, one-half were listed in *Who's Who*. Even so, interest in organized birth control took hold only

gradually. The League's major achievements until this time were the acquisition of state affiliates and the slow organization of local clinics.

In June 1926 Sanger announced her leave of absence from the ABCL to study for an international conference scheduled in Geneva in 1927. When she returned to New York in 1928 to resume the presidency, she found the board's wishes and her own were not always in accord, and in June 1923 she resigned as president. Eleanor Jones was appointed her permanent replacement.

During the mid-1920s, the ABCL's legislative strategy had become the dominant one within the birth control movement. In 1936 the group's efforts resulted in the Supreme Court's *United States v. One Package* decision, which permitted the mailing of contraceptives by doctors.

In 1937 the league officially endorsed the use of contraception for the prevention of disease. Then, in 1939, after one year of negotiation, Margaret Sanger reunited with the ABCL under the umbrella of the new Birth Control Federation of America. After rejoining the group, Sanger was still unhappy with the ABCL, calling its members "drawing room lizards."

In 1942 the ABCL changed its name to Planned Parenthood Federation of America and chose to advocate child spacing, not limitation, with the hope that such a program would be more acceptable to the general public.

See also Birth Control; Contraception; *Eisenstadt v. Baird*; *Griswold v. Connecticut*; National Birth Control League; Planned Parenthood Federation of America; *Planned Parenthood of Central Missouri v. Danforth*; Sanger, Margaret; *United States v. One Package*.

American Civil Liberties Union (ACLU)

The American Civil Liberties Union (ACLU) created two projects to assist in women's struggle for equality: the Women's Rights Project (WRP), which focuses on general issues of equality, and the Reproductive Freedom Project (RFP), which focuses on abortion rights. These projects, taken together, have made the ACLU one of the women's movement's greatest assets in legal battles.

The WRP got its impetus from the ACLU's success in the historic 1971 Supreme Court decision *Reed v. Reed,* in which the Court treated gender discrimination as a type of classification that must be viewed with a fair amount of suspicion and must be scrutinized more carefully than other laws. (Future Supreme Court Justice Ruth Bader Ginsburg was the attorney arguing the ACLU's case.) The *Reed* decision encouraged the ACLU to explore ways to use the Constitution's guarantee of equal protection as a means of advancing women's rights. Among the ACLU's other triumphs are the *Frontiero* case, which raised the issue of women's rights under the due process and equal protection clauses of the Constitution, and the 1975 *Weinberger v. Wiesenfeld* case, in which the Court ruled against sex discrimination in the awarding of social security benefits and promised greater scrutiny of instances of gender bias in social security and welfare issues. The WRP, based in New York City, receives financial support from the Ford Foundation and from other foundations. The group maintains an office in Richmond, Virginia, to handle nonlegal work, such as increasing public awareness of women's issues and encouraging feminist activism on a local level.

The demands made on the WRP for assistance in abortion-related cases and the reluctance of some WRP backers to become involved in abortion rights led the ACLU to establish the RFP in 1974. The financial support for its establishment came primarily from John D. Rockefeller III. The RFP takes legal action to maintain abortion rights, lobbies on the federal and state level, undertakes media campaigns, gives endorsements to pro-choice Supreme Court nominees, and provides information on abortion-related matters. Its concerns include all aspects of reproductive freedom, including Medicaid funding for abortion, restricted by the Hyde Amendment; infringement of fetal rights upon mothers' rights, even apart from abortion issues (for example, limitations on the behaviors and freedom of pregnant women); and the new restrictions on abortion introduced in some state legislatures after the *Webster v. Reproductive Health Services* decision in 1989. The RFP has continued the tradition of dedicated pro-choice activism maintained by the ACLU even prior to the establishment of the WRP. It has become a magnet for pro-choice support, as well as one of the more prominent projects with the ACLU.

See also Abortion; *Frontiero v. Richardson; Reed v. Reed; Webster v. Reproductive Health Services.*

American Equal Rights Association

The American Equal Rights Association was formed shortly after the Civil War to reunite the abolition and women's rights activists who had divided over the issue of whether suffrage for African-American men should take precedence over women's suffrage. The association held that suffrage should be universal, that is, extended to both African Americans and women. The association was formed at the eleventh National Woman's Rights Convention, organized by Susan B. Anthony and Elizabeth Cady Stanton. The convention was held 10 May 1866 at the Church of the Puritans, Union Square, in New York City. Theodore Tilton, who had been trying for a year to reunite the divided abolitionists and women's rights activists, suggested the merger as a means of allowing both groups to press for universal suffrage. Although many women favored the motion to declare women's suffrage a component of universal suffrage, others thought the goal was unattainable and believed that, in terms of suffrage, the aftermath of the Civil War should be the "Negro's hour." During the convention, Susan B. Anthony said, in a speech recorded by the editors of the *History of Woman Suffrage,* Volume Two, "We . . . wish to broaden our Woman's Rights platform, and make it in *name*—what it ever has been in *spirit*—a Human Rights platform. . . . As women we can no longer *seem* to claim for ourselves what we do not for others—nor can we work in two separate movements to get the ballots for the two disfranchised classes—the negro and woman—since to do so must be at double cost of time, energy, and money." When the vote was taken, the Eleventh National Woman's Rights Convention decided to become the American Equal Rights Association.

Just three years after its founding, the group split over the same issue that had brought it together. At a May 1869 meeting of the association, Stanton called for immediate action on a women's suffrage amendment. Her call split the association into two factions. The more radical faction, led by Stanton and Anthony, founded the National Woman Suffrage Association. The second wing, led by Lucy Stone, was the American Woman Suffrage Association. Those two groups merged again in 1890 to form the National American Woman Suffrage Association.

See also American Anti-Slavery Society; American Woman Suffrage Association; Anthony, Susan B.; Kansas Campaign; National American Woman Suffrage Association.

American Federation of Labor (AFL)

From the demise of the Knights of Labor in 1890 to the 1960s, American labor unions were uninterested in organizing women. A good example of this is the American Federation of Labor (AFL), founded by Samuel Gompers in 1881 as the Federation of Organized Trades and Labor Unions. Under Gompers's leadership, the AFL became the most significant labor organization in America. However, by organizing unions according to craft, the AFL ignored women and minorities, most of whom were unskilled. In addition, AFL affiliates barred women from membership. The organization's first female delegate was Mary Burke, elected in 1890, but her proposed resolution to authorize women to mobilize other women on behalf of the AFL met with mixed results.

In 1892 the AFL appointed Mary E. Kenney for five months to mobilize women workers for the AFL; she organized women in New York and Massachusetts. Although occasional resolutions from the national headquarters urged the admission of women, local unions continued to refuse to accept them. Many of the union's conservative officials thought women were too difficult to organize, too impermanent in the work force, and too poor to pay dues. Not until 1903 did the AFL approve the establishment of the National Women's Trade Union League. Even the merger with the Congress of Industrial Organizations (CIO) in 1955 did little to rectify the problem. Although there are still few women in positions of leadership, the AFL-CIO more recently has been a positive force in matters of gender equity.

See also Amalgamated Clothing Workers of America; International Ladies' Garment Workers' Union; Knights of Labor; Women's Trade Union League.

American Federation of State, County and Municipal Employees v. State of Washington

This 1981 lawsuit was an effort to achieve pay equity, or equal pay for jobs of comparable worth. In 1973, at the request of the American Federation of State, County and Municipal Employees of Washington (AFSCME), Governor Don Evans commissioned a study to evaluate the differences in pay among predominantly male and predominantly female jobs. The study revealed a 20 percent discrepancy in pay favoring men, and the report recommended raises for women. However, Evans's successor, Dixy Lee Ray, refused to grant the pay raises, and the AFSCME sued the state. U.S. District Court Judge Jack Tanner ordered the state to pay the women ten years of back pay. Although the appeals court overturned the decision and the case was eventually settled out of court, Judge Tanner's decision prompted government administrations across the nation to take the issue of pay equity more seriously.

See also Comparable Worth; Ray, Dixy Lee.

American Law Institute Abortion Laws

In response to the controversy over abortions, the American Law Institute (ALI) made the following suggestion in its 1959 Model Penal Code: Abortion should be permitted not only when it threatened the life of the mother but when her health and well-being might be damaged, when she was a victim of rape or incest, or when birth defects were probable. This suggestion was adopted in some states that reformed their abortion laws in the years before the 1973 *Roe v. Wade* decision, which legalized abortion nationwide. Laws based on the ALI code are called ALI-type abortion laws.

See also Abortion; *Doe v. Bolton; People v. Belous; Roe v. Wade.*

American Woman Suffrage Association (AWSA)

Just three years after the American Equal Rights Association united abolitionists and women's rights activists in a push for universal suffrage, the association split over the same issue that had divided the groups in the first place: whether women should wait for suffrage until after it had been granted to African-American men. The bitter division lasted 20 years after the Fifteenth Amendment was ratified. Lucy Stone organized the Boston-based American Woman Suffrage Association (AWSA) in November 1869, in opposition to the more radical National Woman Suffrage Association, which Elizabeth Cady Stanton and Susan B. Anthony organized earlier that year. Only representatives from established suffrage groups were invited to the AWSA convention, a departure from tradition. More conservative than the NWSA, the AWSA supported the Fifteenth Amendment, campaigning for women's suffrage on state and local levels. On 8 January 1870, the AWSA began publishing *Woman's Journal*, edited by Lucy Stone with her husband, Henry Blackwell, and Mary Livermore. The *Woman's Journal* became the most important feminist publication of its day. In 1890, the AWSA and the NWSA merged to form the National American Woman Suffrage Association.

See also American Equal Rights Association; National American Woman Suffrage Association; National Woman Suffrage Association; Stone, Lucy.

American Women

See Citizens' Advisory Council on the Status of Women; President's Commission on the Status of Women.

American Women's Himalayan Expedition (1978)

In 1978, an expedition of women, led by Arlene Blum, made the first American ascent of the world's tenth highest mountain, 26,545-foot Annapurna in Nepal. Although the expedition was a success when Irene Miller and Vera Komarkova reached the summit with two sherpas, it was also marked by tragedy when Vera Watson and Alsion Chadwick-Onyszkiewicz died in a fall on their attempt to reach the summit. The purpose of the expedition, in addition to climbing the mountain, was to give women an opportunity to gain high-altitude mountaineering experience in the Himalayas. This objective was met when members participated in and organized subsequent expeditions to the world's highest peaks, including Dhaulagiri, Ama Dablam, Cho Oyu, and Mount Everest. Arlene Blum subsequently published her account of the Annapurna expedition in the book *Annapurna: A Woman's Place.*

Anita Hill Case

Anita Hill's allegations against Supreme Court nominee Clarence Thomas raised the issue of sexual harassment to a national level in October 1991. Thirty-five-year-old Anita Hill had worked for Clarence Thomas from 1981 to 1983 at the Department of Education and later at the Equal Employment Opportunity Commission. Hill claimed that while she worked for Thomas, she was sexually harassed by him on several occasions, by which she meant he discussed with her sex acts and his own sexual prowess.

Hill's involvement in the confirmation hearings began in July 1991, after Clarence Thomas had been nominated for associate justice of the Supreme Court by President George Bush. An old law school friend and lawyer at the Federal Communications Commission, Gary Phillips, called Hill and during their conversation asked her what she thought about the news of her old boss, Clarence Thomas. Hill said Thomas had sexually harassed her while she worked for him.

Rumors about Hill and Thomas soon began to circulate throughout Washington, and in mid-August Hill was contacted by various aides and Senate staffers who asked her about the alleged incidents. Meanwhile, the confirmation hearing continued. On 17 September 1991 Senators Joseph Biden, Howard Metzenbaum, and Ted Kennedy were informed of the matter. However, Hill did not want her name attached to the allegations she had made. On 19 September, eight days prior to Thomas's confirmation vote, Hill called Washington to ask about the progress of her charges. She was then told that members of the committee would not be notified of these claims against Thomas unless Hill officially used her name to support them. On 23 September, after agonizing over the decision, Hill faxed a signed statement to the committee authorizing an FBI investigation, but still insisting upon public anonymity. On 26 September, one day before the vote, Hill was contacted and told that unless she went public, using her name, the charges would not be circulated to all members of the committee. Hill retreated. The vote came on 27 September: a 7 to 7 split on Thomas's nomination.

The media became aware of the Hill-Thomas affair on 6 October, and the story broke wide open. National Public Radio and *Newsday* both asked for Hill's story, and the allegation against Clarence Thomas became public knowledge. Due to the serious nature of the allegations, the Senate canceled the next vote on Thomas's confirmation. Instead, public hearings were set on the charges filed by Anita Hill.

The televised hearings were held on 11 and 12 October, astonishing the nation. Clarence Thomas denied that he ever sexually harassed Anita Hill, then refused to be cross-examined or listen to Hill's testimony. Anita Hill offered a detailed account of the events. She claimed Thomas frequently bothered her for dates, openly discussed sex and his sexual prowess, and graphically described pornographic movies. Both Hill and Thomas had many credible references. The hearings ended with no objective truth, both parties irreconcilable, and neither side admitting perjury. Clarence Thomas was seated as the 106th associate justice of the Supreme Court on 1 November 1991.

After Hill's charges became public, at least six former female government employees admitted that Clarence Thomas had made sexual comments to them. Only one publicly made these claims, never testifying.

Today many people admire the courage of Anita Hill for making these charges publicly. A symbol for many women, she may be the inspiration for many to report illegal conduct in the workplace, for since the hearings, the Equal Employment Opportunity Commission has reported a substantial increase in complaints of sexual harassment on the job.

Anthony, Susan Brownell (1820–1906)

With Elizabeth Cady Stanton, Susan B. Anthony was the most important women's leader of the nineteenth century. Daughter of a cotton manufacturer, Anthony was born 15 February 1820 in Adams, Massachusetts. Anthony's father was a Quaker who gave his daughter a fine education. He wrote to a friend, "What an absurd notion that women have no intellectual and moral faculties sufficient for anything but domestic concerns." Although Anthony did not experience discrimination by her father, she did see the results of women's inequality under the law firsthand. In 1838, when her father's cotton mill collapsed, everything the family owned was sold to pay his debts, including the teenager's clothes and gifts her grandmother had given to her mother, Lucy. A few years later Daniel Anthony lost another mill. Legally, his creditors could have claimed Lucy's inheritance, but her parents, anticipating the possibility, left their estate to her brother, Joshua. When Daniel found a farm to buy, Joshua purchased it for him, but kept the title in his name. After the passage of the Married Woman's Property Act of 1848, New York allowed a married woman to keep her own property, so Joshua transferred the farm to Lucy.

Anthony taught school for 15 years, and her interest in women's rights sprang, in

Susan B. Anthony

part, from having to make do with a salary of about $10 per month, while male teachers earned that much each week. She taught at a Quaker seminary at New Rochelle, New York; from 1846 to 1849 she was headmistress of the Female Department at Canajoharie Academy, also in New York.

Anthony's public life began in 1852 with her interest in the temperance movement. At that time, a woman could not divorce her husband on the grounds of drunkenness. The wife of an alcoholic who squandered the family's money was without recourse. He had custody of her children and full control over her earnings. So, like other women who wanted to stop the free flow of liquor, Anthony became a member of the Rochester Daughters of Temperance, traveling as a delegate to temperance meetings in New York State. That year the Sons of Temperance held a meeting in Albany to which they invited delegates from the Daughters. The Rochester group appointed Anthony as its representative. The convention accepted her credentials, but when she attempted to speak to a motion, the president told her "the sisters were not invited to speak but to listen and learn." Anthony left at once. Most of the other women remained, calling Anthony and her three or four supporters "bold, meddlesome disturbers." Anthony found a lecture room at the Hudson Street Presbyterian Church in which to hold meeting, then went to see Thurlow Weed, editor of the *Evening Journal*, who publicized her treatment by the Sons of Temperance. The New York State Temperance Society was founded soon after.

During her temperance work, Anthony met Amelia Bloomer, founder of the first feminist journal, *The Lily*. Bloomer popularized an outfit consisting of loose-fitting Turkish pants covered by a knee-length skirt, which came to be known as the Bloomer costume. She invited Anthony to her home in Seneca Falls, and during the visit Anthony met Elizabeth Cady Stanton. They were briefly introduced on a street corner as Anthony was rushing to a temperance meeting and Stanton was out strolling in her Bloomer outfit. The two liked each other immediately, and began a friendship and political association that would last 50 years. Stanton encouraged Anthony's interest in women's suffrage, and Anthony soon became a leader in the movement.

In addition to suffrage, Anthony championed women's labor issues, property and divorce rights, and the end of slavery. Beginning in 1854 she traveled door to door, sometimes in the freezing cold, to obtain signatures needed to expand the New York Married Woman's Property Act of 1848, a goal finally achieved in 1860. Her petitions urged that women be allowed to assume custody of their children in case of divorce, control their own earnings, and vote. She described some of her experiences in a letter to her family dated 11 January 1856.

Just emerged from a long line of snow-drifts and stopped at this little country tavern, supped and am now roasting over a hot stove. Oh, Oh, what an experience! No trains running and we have had a thirty-six-mile ride in a sleigh. Once we seemed lost in a drift full fifteen feet deep. The driver went on ahead to a house, and there we sat shivering. When he returned we found he had gone over a fence into a field, so we had to dismount and plough through the snow after the sleigh; then we reseated ourselves, but oh, the poor horses!

At times, after long hours of travel, she would find only a dozen people waiting to hear her speak.

Beginning in 1856 Anthony was the principal New York agent of William Lloyd Garrison's American Anti-Slavery Society. She organized and led many reform organizations, often with Stanton. These included the National Woman's Loyal League, which championed emancipation; the American Equal Rights Association; the Working Women's Association; and the National Woman Suffrage Association. In addition, Anthony and Stanton published a newspaper, *The Revolution*, whose mission statement declared: "The True Republic—

21

men, their rights and nothing more; women—their rights and nothing less."

In 1866 Anthony handed Congress petitions, bearing thousands of signatures, urging that women be granted the vote. She campaigned vigorously, though unsuccessfully, to change the wording of the Fourteenth Amendment to give both women and African-American men the right to vote. In a test of the amendment, she cast a ballot in the presidential election of 1872 in Rochester, New York. She was arrested but, before she came to trial the following year, she voted in another election. She was found guilty and fined $100. The judge, who had written the verdict before the trial, did not object when she refused to pay the fine.

Anthony traveled widely—alone and with Stanton. In 1867 she went to Kansas to campaign for suffrage, later traveling to California in 1871, Michigan in 1874, and Colorado in 1877. Because of her reform activities, Anthony was burned in effigy, attacked by mobs, and ridiculed by the press. Although the newspapers often depicted her as a tough, plain, humorless spinster, her friends appreciated her warmth and humor. At the end of her career, Anthony was acclaimed throughout the United States. She died at home in Rochester on 13 March 1906. The Nineteenth Amendment, sometimes called the Anthony Amendment, was adopted 14 years later. In 1979, the woman known as Aunt Susan became the first woman to have her likeness appear on U.S. currency, the dollar coin.

See also American Anti-Slavery Society; American Equal Rights Association; Kansas Campaign; National Woman Suffrage Association; National Woman's Loyal League; Nineteenth Amendment; Petitions; *The Revolution*; Stanton, Elizabeth Cady.

Antiabortion Clause of the 1988 Civil Rights Restoration Act

The antiabortion clause of the Civil Rights Restoration Act (CRRA) stated that, in order to receive federal funds, educational institutions could not be required to provide access or funding for abortions. Some colleges and universities had been required,

under Title IX of the Higher Education Act (1972), to provide coverage for pregnancy and abortion as part of health insurance for students and faculty. Supporters of the CRRA made a three-year attempt to have the clause taken out. Despite the initial dismay of feminists that such a clause could be added to a significant civil rights bill, they eventually endorsed it. The bill passed, over Ronald Reagan's veto, in 1988.

See also Title IX of the 1972 Higher Education Act.

Apgar, Virginia (1909–1974)

Virginia Apgar developed a simple procedure to evaluate the health of a newborn within one minute of birth. The Apgar Score measures a baby's vital signs (color, pulse, reflexes, muscle tone, and respiration) to determine if medical attention is needed and is used throughout the world. Apgar was born 7 June 1909 in Westfield, New Jersey. She graduated from Mount Holyoke College in 1929. Four years later she received an M.D. from Columbia University's College of Physicians and Surgeons—a most unusual accomplishment for a woman at that time. She interned at Columbia-Presbyterian Medical Center in surgery, a specialty that attracted even fewer women. Eventually, she decided that a woman could not support herself in surgery and turned to the new specialty of anesthesiology. She completed her residency at the University of Wisconsin and Bellevue Hospital in New York (1935–1937).

In 1938 she became director of anesthesiology at Columbia-Presbyterian, the first woman to head a department there. In 1949 she became Columbia University's first full professor of anesthesiology, the first woman to hold a full professorship on the university's medical faculty. In 1952 she developed the Apgar Score. In 1959 Apgar left Columbia to attend Johns Hopkins University, where she received a master's degree in public health at the age of 49. She then joined the National Foundation–March of Dimes and spent the rest of her life trying to raise public awareness about birth defects. A beloved lecturer and professor of pediatrics, Apgar was the first woman to receive the Gold Medal for Distinguished Achievement in Medicine from the Alumni Association of the Columbia College of Physicians and Surgeons. The recipient of many other awards and honors, Apgar maintained a lifelong devotion to infant and maternal health. She died 7 August 1974 in New York City.

Arendt, Hannah (1906–1975)

Hannah Arendt, the first woman to hold full professorial rank at Princeton University, was born 14 October 1906 in Hanover, Germany. She earned a doctorate in philosophy in 1929 at the University of Heidelberg. During Hitler's rise, she was arrested for being a Jew, but fled to France, where she continued her studies and assisted Jewish orphans. Arrested again during the German occupation of France, she escaped to the United States in 1941. Living in New York, she wrote essays for Jewish magazines. She also taught history at Brooklyn College and was director of research at the Conference on Jewish Relations.

From 1946 to 1948 Arendt was an editor at Schocken Books. In the 1940s she also worked for *Partisan Review, The Nation,* and other publications. *The Origins of Totalitarianism,* published in 1951 (the year she became a U.S. citizen), was the first significant work on totalitarianism published after World War II. In it, she held that mass society was the precursor of totalitarianism, and that communism and Nazism were similar. Her next book, *The Human Condition,* was published in 1958. The year after it appeared she became the first female full professor at Princeton University, holding the title Visiting Professor of Political Science. At Princeton, she delivered the lectures that were later collected in *On Revolution* (1963).

From 1963 to 1967, Arendt was professor of political science at the University of Chicago. During this time she produced *Eichmann in Jerusalem: A Report on the Banality of Evil* (1964), which was based on articles she had written for *The New Yorker.* This controversial book portrayed S.S. General Adolf Eichmann, planner of the Nazi program for exterminating the Jews, as an average bureaucrat, not a psychopath, and it blamed Jewish leaders for forsaking their fellow Jews. The book cost her many friends, yet she continued to write essays and books on unconventional topics during the 1960s, including *Men in Dark Times* (1968), *On Violence* (1970), and *Crises of the Republic* (1972). Having accepted, in 1967, a teaching position at the New School for Social Research, her lectures formed the basis of *The Life of the Mind* (1979), which was edited by Mary McCarthy and published after Arendt's death. Arendt died 4 December 1975 in New York City.

Association of Collegiate Alumnae

See American Association of University Women.

Association of Working Girls Societies

In 1884, the first Working Girls Club was founded by 12 factory workers in a Tenth Avenue slum with the help of Grace Dodge, a wealthy, religious young woman with a desire to educate. The following year, enough of these self-improvement societies had been formed in New York to organize the Association of Working Girls Societies, which soon spread to many large cities in the East and Midwest. Some of the clubs had their own residences, with educational classes, libraries, medical care, and physical fitness programs, and produced a monthly magazine, *Far and Near.* Ultimately, the clubs were unable to advance the position of women in the labor force, and they gradually disappeared, poor health and poverty proving stronger than the self-help impulses that brought the groups together.

Atkinson, Ti-Grace

A radical feminist leader, Ti-Grace Atkinson was most active in the women's liberation movement of the 1960s and 1970s.

23

President of the New York chapter of the National Organization for Women (NOW), she resigned over policy differences. (NOW refused to become less hierarchical or to name men as its enemies.) Joining other radical feminists in 1968, she founded The Feminists and cofounded Human Rights for Women, Inc. She argued that women, as a class, were oppressed by men, who used romantic notions of love to prevent female solidarity. As a result, women willingly embraced the institutions that oppressed them, such as marriage and religion. Women needed to break all ties with men and their values, forming separate institutions controlled solely by women. Atkinson published *The Institution of Sexual Intercourse* (1968) and a collection of essays and speeches, *Amazon Odyssey* (1974). She continues to work for feminist causes.

See also The Feminists; National Organization for Women.

Avery, Rachel G. Foster (1858–1919)

Rachel Foster Avery, a close friend of Susan B. Anthony, was a leader in the women's suffrage movement. She was born 30 December 1858, in Pittsburgh, to Quaker parents who supported the causes of abolition and women's suffrage. The earliest suffrage meetings in the city were said to be held in her parents' home. She traveled widely and studied political economy at the University of Zurich (1885). Active at a young age in the Citizens Suffrage Association, in 1879 Foster attended the National Woman Suffrage Association (NWSA) convention, where she met Susan B. Anthony. By the following year, she had been elected the organization's corresponding secretary. In this capacity she directed the 1882 suffrage campaign in Nebraska. Later she planned the Kansas suffrage campaigns (1887 and 1892).

She was a close personal friend and confidant of Susan B. Anthony and over the years assumed many of Anthony's responsibilities in various organizations. Foster married Cyrus Avery in 1888, an act that worried Susan B. Anthony, who feared it would lessen her friend's dedication to feminism. To provide financial security for Anthony in her old age, Rachel Avery solicited donations, which she pooled with her own money to purchase an annuity. She broke with Anthony temporarily to lobby against Elizabeth Cady Stanton's *The Woman's Bible* (1895) because she feared it would turn religious women away from the movement. Avery was active in several suffrage organizations. She helped to establish the International Council of Women and served as its secretary from 1889 to 1893. In 1890, she supported the merger of the National Woman Suffrage Association and the American Woman Suffrage Association, and she served as the first vice-president of the resulting organization, the National American Woman Suffrage Association, from 1907 until 1910. Avery was corresponding secretary of the National Council of Women (1891–1894), secretary of the Committee of the World's Congress of Representative Women (1893), the International Council of Women (1888–1893), and the International Woman Suffrage Alliance (1904–1909). In 1908 she headed the Pennsylvania Woman Suffrage Association, revitalizing the cause of women's suffrage in that state. Avery died in Philadelphia on 26 October 1919, before the Nineteenth Amendment was ratified.

See also Anthony, Susan B.; Stanton, Elizabeth Cady; *The Woman's Bible.*

24

The Baby M Case

On 6 February 1985, Mary Beth Whitehead signed a legal contract agreeing to be a surrogate mother for William and Elizabeth Stern of New Jersey. Elizabeth Stern had health problems that might worsen if she became pregnant. Whitehead was contracted and assumed all medical risks, for which she was to be paid $10,000, if the baby was born healthy. After several attempts at artificial insemination, Mary Beth Whitehead conceived on 2 July 1985. A baby girl was born on 27 March 1986, and Whitehead decided she wanted to keep the child she felt was rightfully hers.

For the first week of the baby's life, the Sterns traded the baby back and forth with Whitehead. The Sterns named her Melissa while Whitehead called her Sara. On 5 May 1986, the Bergen County Family Court awarded temporary custody to the Sterns. On the following day, Whitehead fled to Florida, taking the baby with her. Four months later, the FBI and private investigators located Whitehead and forced her to return Baby M to the Sterns. The court battle had begun.

The New Jersey Superior Court decision was rendered on 31 March 1987 as Judge Harvey Sorkow ended all of Mary Beth Whitehead's maternal rights to the child. In his statement he said he felt the necessity of choosing between a parent's rights and a child's welfare and that he felt strongly that the child's welfare must come first. The child legally belonged to William and Elizabeth Stern.

Ten months later, on 2 February 1988, the case was heard before the New Jersey Supreme Court. Speaking for the court, Justice Robert Wilentz issued the ruling that reversed the first decision, reinstating Whitehead's maternal rights, making the original adoption of Baby M by Elizabeth Stern invalid. Thus Baby M became the daughter of Mary Beth Whitehead and William Stern. Custody was given to William Stern and visitation rights were established following the same procedures as in divorce cases.

The Baby M case raised many moral and legal issues, with much focus put upon the reproductive rights of women and men. Legal questions arose: does the biological mother have more rights than the biological father? Are women's bodies now marketable commodities? Feminists felt that a woman has a right to control her own body, and that if that right is lost, other rights (legal abortion, pay equity) would also be lost. Throughout this case, the judges, mental health experts, and others stated that Mary Beth Whitehead was not Baby M's "real" mother, but only a surrogate, and that the baby's real mother was her father, William Stern. Others felt that the baby was being treated as a piece of property rather than a human being.

The case has paved the way to similar cases receiving a court hearing in the future. Today surrogacy has become a common term, an answer for many infertile couples, with different laws upheld in each state. In New Jersey, surrogacy contracts are only allowed if "the surrogate mother volunteers, without any payment, to act as a surrogate and is given the right to change her mind and to assert her parental rights." By 1992, 16 states had passed legislation that strictly limits or forbids commercial surrogacy contracts.

Bache, Sarah Franklin (1743–1808)

Born 11 September 1743, Sarah Franklin Bache was the daughter of Benjamin Franklin and Deborah Read. During the American Revolution, while her husband, Richard Bache, served as postmaster general, Sarah Bache and fellow Philadelphian Esther De

Berdt Reed raised money to make shirts for soldiers. By 4 July 1780, the women had raised $300,000 in continental paper currency from 1,645 people to make 2,000 linen shirts. According to historian Eleanor Flexner, this contribution foreshadowed the Sanitary Commission of the Civil War and later the Red Cross. After her mother's death in 1744, Bache served as her father's representative in America; from 1785 until his death in 1790 she served as his official hostess. She also helped her husband maintain their farm near Bristol, Pennsylvania. Bache died in Philadelphia on 5 October 1808.

See also Red Cross; Reed, Esther De Berdt; Sanitary Commission.

Bagley, Sarah G. (fl. 1835–1847)

Sarah Bagley was the United States' first recognized female trade union leader. Her date of birth is unknown, but her birthplace was probably Meredith, New Hampshire. In 1836 she started work at the Hamilton Manufacturing Company, a cotton mill in Lowell, Massachusetts. She later moved to the Middlesex Factory. In 1844, after management repeatedly sped up machine operation, lengthened the workday, and cut wages, Bagley began to campaign for a law to limit the workday to ten hours. This led her to oppose Harriet Farley, editor of the operators' magazine *Lowell Offering,* who believed that the mills offered better housing and education than other factories. In fact, as historian Eleanor Flexner points out, average wages were approximately two dollars per week plus board. Women slept six to a room, and long hours left little time for enlightenment.

In December 1844, Bagley and four other operatives met to plan a strategy for winning a ten-hour workday. In January 1845 they formed the Lowell Female Labor Reform Association, an auxiliary of the New England Workingmen's Association, with Bagley as its president. The group grew quickly and soon collected 2,000 signatures on petitions demanding the ten-hour workday. On 13 February 1845, the first U.S.

government investigation of labor conditions began, with Bagley and other operators testifying that working conditions had worsened their health. Despite their testimony, the committee recommended that no ten-hour day legislation be initiated.

Growing ever more dissatisfied with labor conditions, Bagley publicly attacked the textile mills and, in an Independence Day address in 1845, criticized Farley for not publishing Bagley's articles in the *Lowell Offering.* Next month, in an article in the *Lowell Express,* she called Farley "the mouthpiece of the corporations." That year Bagley was appointed corresponding secretary of the New England Workingmen's Association and frequently contributed to its journal, *Voice of Industry.* The *Voice of Industry* competed with the more conservative *Lowell Offering,* which folded in late 1845 because of Bagley's more popular labor movement. At the same time, Bagley formed the Industrial Reform Lyceum, which brought activists to Lowell to speak.

Bagley helped to spearhead a second drive for the ten-hour workday in 1846. This attempt also failed. Bagley's health declined, and in 1846 she found work as a telegraph operator—the first female telegraph operator in the country. The date and place of her death are unknown.

See also Farley, Harriet; Female Labor Reform Associations; Lowell Female Labor Reform Association; *Lowell Offering; Voice of Industry.*

Barnard College

Barnard College was founded during a period of mounting pressure on men's universities to admit women. The new college was named in honor of Frederick Augustus Barnard, a scientist and professor and the tenth president of Columbia College (1864–1889). Columbia College had long refused to admit women as degree candidates but permitted them to attend certain classes. As president of the college, Barnard worked to extend education to women. On 12 July 1882, at the Twentieth Annual Convocation of the University of the State of New York at Albany, Barnard presented a paper entitled, "Should American Colleges Be Open to American Women as Well as to Men?" in which he remarked, "existing colleges shall be opened to women because they exist, because they possess the means of doing the work desired, and because the right to receive an education, liberal in the highest sense, belongs to women no less than to men." The next year Columbia established a separate course of study, called the Collegiate Course, for women. The course allowed women to earn certificates of graduation from Columbia if they passed various tests. Shortly after Barnard's death on 27 April 1889, Barnard College for Women was established, with the collegiate course under its purview. Because there were so few academically trained women at the time, Columbia's professors also taught at Barnard. Gradually the college began to hire its own teachers. Barnard was incorporated into the Columbia University system in 1900.

Barney, Nora Stanton Blatch (1883–1971)

Nora Barney was the first female member of the American Society of Civil Engineers (ASCE). She was born 30 September 1883, in Basingstoke, England. Her mother was Harriot Stanton Blatch and her maternal grandmother was Elizabeth Cady Stanton. Her family moved to New York City during the 1890s, and Nora graduated from the Horace Mann School. She entered Cornell University, where she organized a women's suffrage club and graduated in 1905, the first woman to receive a degree in civil engineering from the school. That year she became a junior member of ASCE and worked as a draftsman from 1905 to 1906. In 1908 she married Lee de Forest; however, they divorced four years later. Barney worked as assistant engineer and chief draftsman for the Radley Steel Construction Company and as an assistant engineer for the New York Public Service Commission. In 1916, she unsuccessfully sued ASCE for dropping her after she passed the age limit for junior status. From 1909 to 1917 she worked to win the vote for women in New York. As a member of the Women's Political Union, Barney edited its publication, *Women's Political World.* In 1919, she married Morgan Barney and the couple moved to Greenwich, Connecticut. There, Nora Barney began a new business in home construction. She made her living in real estate development and continued to work for peace, equal rights, and world government until her death in Greenwich on 18 January 1971.

Barton, Clara (1821–1912)

Clara Barton, founder of the American Red Cross, was a lifelong feminist who supported the vote for women and equal pay for equal work. She was born Clarissa Harlowe Barton on 25 December 1821 in Oxford, Massachusetts. Between the ages of 11 and 13, she helped to care for an ill older brother, an experience that probably shaped her future work as a nurse. In 1839 she began a career in teaching, but returned to her own schooling, attending the Liberal Institute in Clinton, New York (1850–1851). The following year she established one of the first public schools in New Jersey at Bordentown. Soon the school became so large that the town refused to let a woman direct it, and Barton chose to resign rather than report to a male superior. She went to Washington, D.C., to work at the Patent Office, becoming one of the first female civil servants appointed in the United States (1854–1857).

At the outbreak of the Civil War, Barton volunteered to help Massachusetts soldiers in Washington, D.C. Moved by the lack of supplies at the Battle of Bull Run, she purchased and solicited supplies through newspaper advertisements, bringing in medicine, bandages, and food, which Barton stored in her rooms. In 1862, she and a friend began to distribute the supplies to hospitals and battlefields in Maryland and Virginia, transporting the supplies by mule team. Barton's activities were separate from the U.S. Sanitary Commission, a voluntary group made up of representatives of voluntary aid associations, and independent of the military bureaucracy. This independence, and

Clara Barton

contacts she had made in her earlier career as a civil servant, allowed her to instigate government probes into the medical neglect of soldiers in the field. In June 1864, Barton was appointed superintendent of nurses for the Army of the James. In 1865, with a few subordinates, she set up an office in Annapolis, Maryland, from which she traced thousands of missing men, identifying 12,000–13,000 of their graves. From 1866 to 1868, she supplemented her missing persons work with hundreds of lectures about wartime conditions.

The strain of travel throughout the North and West undermined Barton's health, and by 1869 she was advised to vacation in Europe. While in Geneva, she discovered that the United States had refused to sign the 1864 Geneva Treaty, which had formed the International Red Cross. She joined the organization's efforts in the Franco-Prussian War, distributing funds raised in the United States and establishing a sewing workshop in Strasbourg for female victims of the war.

After returning to the United States, Barton began five years of lobbying for the nation's participation in the International Red Cross. Her effort focused on nonwar emergency relief, such as for natural disasters. She was unable to interest either President Ulysses S. Grant or President Rutherford B. Hayes. However, President James Garfield supported her, and his successor, President Chester Arthur, signed the Geneva Treaty in 1882. Barton did not wait for the signing of the treaty to found the American Association of the Red Cross; she formed the organization in her Washington, D.C., home on 21 May 1881. After the official proclamation of its founding, on 16 July 1882, the organization elected Barton as its first president, a post she held until 1904. In 1893, the organization changed its name to the American National Red Cross. Barton remained active in Red Cross activities well into old age. During her seventies, she could be found in the field, feeding the hungry and housing orphans during the Spanish-American War. She wrote many pamphlets about the Red

Cross and an autobiography, *The Story of My Childhood* (1907). A lifelong supporter of equal rights for women, including the vote and pay equity, Barton died in Glen Echo, Maryland, on 12 April 1912.

See also Red Cross.

Beale v. King and Woolford

In *Beale v. King and Woolford* (Maryland, 1797), a chancery court strengthened a married woman's right to her own property, which, under common law, fell under the control of her husband at marriage. A prenuptial contract written by Ann Woolford and her husband, Levin, before their marriage, permitted Ann Woolford to will her own property to her children by previous marriages. However, when she fell mortally ill, Levin denied her the means of making the will, forcing her to execute it secretly. After she died, Levin contested the will, claiming their prenuptial agreement was executed without trustees and therefore invalid. The Chancery Court of Maryland disagreed, allowing the marriage agreement to stand, thereby validating the will. It was the first decision supporting a marriage settlement without trustees made in Maryland.

See also Chancery Courts; Common Law; Equity Law; *Feme Covert*.

Beard, Mary Ritter (1876–1958)

Mary Beard, a pioneer in the field of women's studies, is best known for her book *Woman as Force in History*, in which she disputed the traditional theory that women existed on the fringe of history. Born 5 August 1876 in Indianapolis, Indiana, Ritter began her studies at DePauw University at the age of 16. There she met Charles Beard, her future husband and collaborator. She graduated from DePauw in 1897 and married three years later. Active in the women's suffrage movement, from 1910 to 1912 she edited *The Woman Voter*, which was published by the Woman Suffrage party of New York. In addition to the many historical works she produced with her husband, Beard was a distinguished author in her own right. Twenty years after their publication, her accounts of women's history were still considered pioneering works in the field of women's studies. These works include *Women's Work in Municipalities* (1915), *A Short History of the American Labor Movement* (1920), *On Understanding Women* (1931), and *America through Women's Eyes* (1933). In a short review of the *Encyclopaedia Brittannica* (1942), she criticized the publication's treatment of women. However, her most significant book, published when Beard was 70 years old, was *Woman as Force in History* (1946). In it, Beard challenged the idea that women throughout history have been subject to men and have had little influence on the course of civilization. She leveled an important critique of eighteenth-century English jurist Sir William Blackstone, who claimed that the legal existence of women was "suspended" during marriage. Beard argued that Blackstone oversimplified British jurisprudence, giving too much weight to common law and not enough to equity law, that is, law as defined by a judge rather than precedent. This misreading had important consequences because women had more standing under equity law than they did under common law. Beard continued to write for another decade; *The Force of Women in Japanese History* was published in 1953, when Beard was almost 80 years old. Beard died 14 August 1958 in Phoenix, Arizona.

Beecher, Catharine Esther (1800–1878)

A study in contrasts, Catharine Beecher espoused conservative views about the role of women but worked to broaden women's educational opportunities. She was born 6 September 1800 on Long Island (New York), into one of the nineteenth century's most notable families. She was the eldest daughter of Lyman Beecher and the sister of Harriet Beecher Stowe, Henry Ward Beecher, and Edward Beecher. Her half sister was Isabella Beecher Hooker. Growing up in Litchfield, Connecticut, she was "hindered by her sex from receiving much formal education," according to Robert McHenry.

She attended schools for fashionable young ladies and studied Latin, mathematics, and philosophy at home. In 1821 she became a teacher. Two years later she established the Hartford Female Seminary (1823–1831), which offered instruction in teaching, domestic science, and calisthenics. In 1832 she and her father moved to Cincinnati, Ohio, where she established the Western Female Institute. The institute closed after five years, and she turned her energies to creating educational opportunities for women in the Midwest. Her lectures and writings persuaded 500 female teachers to make their way west. In 1852 Beecher founded the American Woman's Educational Association, which opened teacher-training schools in Wisconsin, Iowa, and Illinois. Beecher's educational philosophy put her at odds with pioneers of women's rights, such as Angelina Grimké. In *An Essay on Slavery and Abolitionism, with Reference to the Duty of American Females* (1837), addressed to Angelina Grimké, Beecher argued that women belonged at home, out of the public sphere, where they could tend to their children. Concerned that working women would be exploited by employers, Beecher felt that women should be educated only to perform their homemaking duties within their domestic sphere. This, she thought, was an improvement over toiling ten or more hours a day for a pittance in the textile factories. *The Evils Suffered by American Women and American Children* (1846) discussed this problem. On the issue of women's suffrage, Catharine Beecher and Harriet Beecher Stowe were at odds with Henry Ward Beecher and Isabella Beecher Hooker, firmly opposing the vote for women. Yet Catharine's Beecher's life contradicted her ideas: never married, she was part of the spirit of reform concerning women's education, and she supported herself by her writing and lectures. Her many books include *The Duty of American Women to Their Country* (1845); *A Treatise on Domestic Economy* (1841) and its sequel, *The Domestic Receipt Book* (1846); and *Physiology and Calisthenics for Schools and Families* (1856). In *The American Woman's Home* (1869), a revision of her

1841 volume *A Treatise on Domestic Economy*, she collected information on cooking, sewing, health, and other matters that every proper housewife should know. This book, prepared with the help of Harriet Beecher Stowe, was a popular title, reflecting the professional attitude of women regarding their domestic roles. Some of Catharine Beecher's other books include *Woman Suffrage and Woman's Profession* (1871) and *Educational Reminiscences and Suggestions* (1874). Catharine Beecher died 12 May 1878 in Elmira, New York, and is honored today more for her educational advancement of women than for her conservative philosophy.

See also Stowe, Harriet Beecher; *A Treatise on Domestic Economy*.

Belmont, Alva Erskine Smith Vanderbilt (1853–1933)

Suffragist, socialite, and an authority on architecture, Alva Belmont was born 17 January 1853 in Mobile, Alabama. The family moved to France after the Civil War, where Alva was educated. In 1875 she married William Vanderbilt and shocked society by divorcing him for adultery in 1895. One year later Alva married Oliver Belmont. She devoted a great deal of her fortune to the women's suffrage campaign. In 1909, a year following the death of her husband, she founded the Political Equality Association and served as its president. During the New York City shirtwaist makers' strike of 1909–1910, she gave money and time to the New York Women's Trade Union League. In 1912, Belmont marched in the Women's Political Union parade in New York City, "a few steps ahead of Rebecca Goldstein, who runs a sewing machine in a shirtwaist shop," according to one newspaper. In 1913, she served on the executive board of the Congressional Union for Woman Suffrage and of the National Woman's Party (NWP) after 1917. Elected that organization's president in 1921, she recruited the young Clare Boothe (Luce). She donated the historic Sewall-Belmont House to the NWP, and the mansion still serves as the party's headquarters. At The Hague Conference on the Codification of International Law in 1930, Belmont represented the NWP in opposing legal restrictions against women in international law. She died 26 January 1933 in Paris.

See also National Woman's Party.

Benevolent Societies

Perhaps the earliest women's organizations in the United States were the female benevolent societies. They allowed women to engage in social welfare activities outside the home, provided them with company, and enabled them to collect money, chair meetings, and network. As early as the 1790s, African-American women formed organizations for mutual aid. They provided a form of insurance for their members, taking money contributed by individuals and doling it out to those in need. According to historian Dorothy Sterling, one of the oldest of these groups was Philadelphia's Female Benevolent Society of St. Thomas, formed in 1793. Another early group was the African Female Benevolent Society of Newport, Rhode Island, formed in 1809 by dissatisfied members of the African Benevolent Society, which allowed only men to vote or hold office. Records of the earliest benevolent societies have not been found, but reports do exist from groups founded in 1821. For example, transactions recorded in the Daughters of Africa Order Book (1821–1829) show money paid to the sick, loans for funerals, and other expenses.

Between 1800 and 1860, the number of female benevolent societies grew, spreading throughout the United States. For example, at the turn of the century, Isabella Graham founded the Society for the Relief of Widows with Small Children in New York. The Boston Female Missionary Society was founded in 1800. Women formed orphanages, charity schools, and homes for the poor. The Female Missionary Society had a chapter in New York State that, in 1818, had activities in 46 towns. One group of women in Boston helped 10,000 families, giving away $22,000 from 1812 to 1842.

Women's interest in abolition, temperance, and suffrage emerged from their tradition of benevolence, which was an accepted part of the "woman's sphere" in the 1800s. It would later be said that women's contributions during the Progressive Era and their involvement in the profession of social work originated in the benevolent societies of the nineteenth century.

See also Voluntarism; Women's Clubs.

Benoit (Samuelson), Joan (1957–)

Joan Benoit made history by winning the gold medal in the first Olympic Games marathon for women in Los Angeles in 1984. Born 16 May 1957 in Cape Elizabeth, Maine, she was a senior at Bowdoin College in her home state when she won the 1979 Boston Marathon with a winning time of 2:35:15. In 1983 she won the Boston Marathon again, this time setting the world's record at 2:22:42. But it is for her performance at the 1984 Olympic Games, where for the first time in modern history women ran the marathon, that she will be remembered. Only 17 days before the event she underwent surgery on her right knee, making her participation in the event doubtful. Despite the surgery, she ran the third-best time ever for a woman, beating the world champion, Norwegian Grete Waitz. For her achievement, Benoit received many honors and awards, and, since 1984, she has continued to compete in numerous races.

Bethune, Mary McLeod

See National Association of Colored Women; National Council of Negro Women.

Bethune v. Beresford

The chancery court's ruling in *Bethune v. Beresford* (South Carolina, 1790) illustrates how seriously South Carolina judges considered the possibility of husbands' coercion of their wives when it came to the control of the wives' property. In this case a debtor tried to convince his wife to use her property as collateral to get credit. The wife consented, but later tried to invalidate her agreement, claiming she was not truly a free agent. As Marylynn Salmon records, the wife argued that "the natural affection a woman entertains for her husband is so great that at his request, and to ward off difficulties, she would join him in many transactions which might tend to injure her unless protected by the court." The court agreed that, although there was no sign of force, the wife had to be protected from her own actions, as she was not a "free agent."

See also Coercion.

Biden, Joseph

See Violence.

Bird, Caroline (1915–)

Feminist and journalist Caroline Bird was born 15 April 1915 in New York City. Her

Joan Benoit wins the first Olympic marathon for women at Los Angeles, California, in 1984.

book *Born Female* (1970) documented the unequal status and lower pay of women in the work place during the sixties. She pointed out that young women needed higher grades than men to be accepted by colleges, were relegated to low-paying, sex-segregated industries after graduation, faced lower top-pay ceilings than men, and were disqualified for a number of high-paying jobs because of their gender. Bird was the historian of the United Nations' International Women's Year (1975) and the National Women's Conference in Houston, Texas (1977). Her works include *Everything a Woman Needs To Know To Get Paid What She's Worth* (1973), *Enterprising Women* (1976), *What Women Want* (1979), *The Two-Paycheck Marriage* (1979), *The Good Years* (1983), and *Second Careers: New Ways To Work after Fifty* (1992).

Birth Control

The term *birth control* was coined around 1914 by Otto Bobstein, a friend of Margaret Sanger. Sanger used it because of its simplicity. But the desire to limit family size is as old as the nation itself.

Eighteenth-century capitalism freed large numbers of men from the constant struggle to survive, giving them the chance to pursue, writes historian Gerda Lerner (1979), "liberty, opportunity, and upward mobility as something belonging to them by right." The same is not strictly true of women, for whom only freedom from the necessity to reproduce as many children as possible, ensuring that some will survive, can provide such opportunities.

In the broadest sense of the term—meaning any method of controlling reproduction, including abstinence and abortion—women have been knowledgeable about birth control since early times. Colonial women used the age-old practices of withdrawal, sexual abstinence, and induced abortion to limit births. Even in the nineteenth century, birth control techniques were not much more advanced, consisting of withdrawal, sponges, chemical douches, potions, and rhythm. The first publication of the need for and means of contraception in the United States was Robert Dale Owen's *Moral Physiology; or a Brief and Plain Treatise on the Population Question* (1831). This was followed by the first printed work on birth control by a physician, *Fruits of Philosophy; or the Private Companion of Young Married People* (1839), by Dr. Charles Knowlton.

The fertility of white women dropped "from 7.04 in 1800 to 5.42 in 1850 to 3.56 in 1900," according to Lerner. This drop occurred despite the fact that nineteenth-century feminists opposed contraception, believing it to be a means for men to indulge themselves at women's expense. Instead, they argued that men should engage in sex infrequently and that women should refuse to have sex with their husbands or even refuse to marry. Harriet Martineau and Ann Wheeler were among the few feminists of the era who championed contraception. But women were not the only ones to advocate infrequent sex. Victorian medical opinion held that ejaculation wasted men's vital energies, which were located in the semen. Doctors and marriage manuals, therefore, variously recommended that men have sex no more often than once every 21 months, once a month, 19 times in a lifetime, and so forth. Women, it was presumed, had no real sex drive. It all added up to a conscious attempt to abstain from sex and bear fewer children, which was remarkably successful.

Historian Mary P. Ryan writes that the largest advertisement in an antebellum newspaper was likely to be for "female pills" that would prevent pregnancy and a headache at the same time. This widespread dissemination of birth control information ended after the Civil War, when reformer Anthony Comstock, founder of the Society of the Suppression of Vice in New York, campaigned to ban all sexually explicit materials. In 1873, he persuaded Congress to pass a bill strengthening a 1872 law making it illegal to circulate obscene materials through the United States post office. The law defined birth control materials as obscene. Similar state statutes followed, ultimately confusing the courts as to what obscenity really meant, with the result that, in the words of Joan Hoff, "enforcement remained highly idiosyncratic and only as effective as fanatics like Comstock could make it." After the passage of the antiobscenity laws, contraception remained underground until birth control advocate Margaret Sanger made it a public issue. She deliberately violated the Comstock law in 1913, when an article she wrote on syphilis was deemed unmailable by the post office. Undaunted, Sanger continued her work as a pioneer in the birth control movement, coining the phrase *birth control* and founding the American Birth Control League in 1921.

Ever since, women's view of birth control has taken a revolutionary turn. Popular discussion about sex was at unprecedented levels from 1915 to 1930, writes historian William H. Chafe. And from 1910 to 1930, the sexually liberated flapper seized the public's imagination. The technology of contraception improved with the refinement of the condom and diaphragm. By the twenties, roughly 70 to 80 percent of upper- and middle-class women used a fairly reliable means of birth control. A decade later, one-third of poorer women were also using some method of birth control. And by the 1950s most women used contraception regularly. The widespread use of contraceptives occurred even though the Comstock law was not revised to exclude the ban on birth control information until 1971.

By the 1970s, the widespread availability of oral contraceptives provided women with more power than ever before in controlling their family size. Barrier methods include the condom (for men and women), diaphragm, vaginal sponge, and spermicides. Hormonal methods of birth control, from "the pill" to the "morning after" contraceptive are becoming more available, with experimental contraceptive implants being tried out for wider use. Surgical methods, such as tubal ligation for women and vasectomy for men, are widely used.

In 1973, the year of the *Roe v. Wade* decision, most young mothers reported that 2.8 was the number of children they hoped

to bear. By 1990, according to the Gallup Poll, 63 percent of women felt the ideal number of children was two or fewer. These mothers were bearing their last child before they were 25, and their children (41 percent were aged three to five) were in nursery school or preschool. Limiting family size and having children early meant that these women could enter the work force much sooner than mothers before them—after only ten years of full-time child care. As historian Ellen Chesler has put it, "birth control has fundamentally altered private life and public policy . . . no idea of modern times, save perhaps for arms control, more directly challenges human destiny."

See also Abortion; American Birth Control League; *Birth Control Review*; Birth Rate; Comstock Act; Contraception; National Birth Control League; Owen, Robert Dale; Planned Parenthood Federation of America; Sanger, Margaret.

Birth Control Review

Published between 1917 and 1940, The *Birth Control Review* was a periodical devoted to the issues surrounding birth control, although it did not include specific information about contraceptives themselves. Started by Margaret Sanger and Frederick Blossom, an influential socialist and birth control advocate, the *Review* attempted to avoid an extremist image. It reported on regional birth control associations and provided a forum for discussion and debate among a number of prominent writers and thinkers of the day, including H. G. Wells and Havelock Ellis.

See also Sanger, Margaret.

Birth Rate

The falling birth rate among American women has changed the course of history, redistributing power and liberating one-half of the population. The number of children borne by seventeenth-century American women was one of the highest in world history. Colonial women bore children at a rate of 50–57 live births per 1,000

The July 1919 cover of the Birth Control Review.

population, compared to the present-day figure of 14 live births per 1,000. Colonial mothers bore an average of six to eight children, doubling the population every 20 years. According to historian Mary P. Ryan, the typical colonial mother cared for an infant for 20 years and spent almost 40 years rearing children. She rarely survived more than a few years after the marriage of her youngest child.

By the late eighteenth century, perhaps because of the decline of subsistence agriculture and the postponement of marriage, the nation's birth rate decreased. One study of wealthy members of the Society of Friends in Philadelphia, New York, and Salem reveals that the number of births by Quaker women declined by an average of 1.4 in this period, as the result of their conscious choice to have smaller families. As the Victorian era progressed, writes Ryan, the "average fertility rate of white women [fell] from 7.04 children in 1800 to 5.21 in 1860," the consequence of individual restraint. Couples decided to have fewer children at greater intervals. Men practiced coitus interruptus on a regular basis, because it was expensive to rear children, especially in the cities, and because Victorian medical opinion discouraged frequent sex. Between 1860 and 1890, the birth rate among native-born white women dropped still further to 20 percent without any improvement in birth-control methods. While in 1860 native-born white women bore an average of five children, by 1890 the figure was four children or less. Immigrant women typically bore two or three more children than native-born white women. Yet, by mid-century a declining birth rate was typical of rural, urban, eastern, and western families. In urban middle-class communities such as Detroit or Chicago, women were having fewer than four children by the 1870s. It is speculated that women were told it was unseemly to be passionate and therefore insisted on long periods of sexual abstinence. Male doctors advised couples that sex once a month, or whenever they wanted to conceive, was sufficient. Some women abstained from inter-

course for months, even years, on the advice of doctors.

By the turn of the century, it was the fashion to have small families, especially among the well-off. Yet fertility among working-class women also declined. By 1910 the average native-born married woman gave birth to 3.4 children; for foreign-born women the comparable figure was 4.3 births. The birth rate plummeted again during the 1920s; while sexual mores became more tolerant, contraceptive methods became more advanced. The Depression led to even more widespread use of contraception, perhaps leading to the federal legalization of birth control in 1936 for the first time since 1872.

The birth rate bottomed out in 1932, reaching a low that would not be achieved again until the late 1960s. After the 1960s, the birth rate dropped again. By the 1970s, according to the U.S. Census Bureau, for the first time in U.S. history, most mothers thought the perfect family size was 2.8 children, barely the rate of replacement. According to the Gallup Poll, the percentage of women since 1936 who thought the ideal family size was two children or fewer was as follows: 34 percent (1936), 27 percent (1947), 29 percent (1953), 19 percent (1957), 48 percent (1973), 55 percent (1980), and 63 percent (1990).

See also Abortion; Birth Control; Contraception.

Blackmun, Harry Andrews (1908–)

Harry Blackmun, considered a conservative judge, became a champion of women's reproductive freedom. Blackmun wrote the landmark 1973 Supreme Court decision in *Roe v. Wade*, which relegalized abortion, and he wrote a stinging criticism of fellow Supreme Court justices in his dissent of the 1989 decision in *Webster v. Reproductive Health Services*. Blackmun was born 12 November 1908, in Nashville, Illinois. He received a bachelor's degree in 1929 and his law degree in 1932 from Harvard. From 1934 to 1950 he practiced law in Minneapolis, and from 1942 to 1949 he taught at the

St. Paul College of Law and the University of Minnesota Law School. Blackmun was named to the U.S. Court of Appeals for the Eighth Circuit in 1959 and in 1970 was appointed to the Supreme Court by President Richard Nixon. In his dissent of the Court's decision in *Webster v. Reproductive Services*, Blackmun wrote,

Although today, no less than yesterday, the Constitution and the decisions of this Court prohibit a state from enacting laws that inhibit women from the meaningful exercise of that right, a plurality of this Court implicitly invites every state legislature to enact more and more restrictive abortion regulations in order to provoke more and more test cases, in the hope that sometime down the line the Court will return the law of procreative freedom to the severe limitations that generally prevailed in this country before January 22, 1973. Never in my memory has a plurality announced a judgment of this Court that so foments disregard for the law and for our standing decisions. Nor in my memory has plurality gone about its business in such a deceptive fashion. At every level of its review, from its effort to read the real meaning out of the Missouri statutes to its intended evisceration of precedents and its deafening silence about the constitutional protections that it would jettison, the plurality obscures the portent of its analysis. With feigned restraint, the plurality announces that its analysis leaves Roe "undisturbed," albeit "modif[ied] and narrow[ed]." But this disclaimer is totally meaningless. The plurality opinion is filled with winks and nods and knowing glances to those who would do away with Roe explicitly, but turns a stone face to anyone in search of what the plurality conceives as the scope of a woman's right under the due process clause to terminate a pregnancy free from the coercive and brooding influence of the State. The simple truth is that Roe would not survive the plu-

rality's analysis, and that the plurality provides no substitute for Roe's protective umbrella. I fear for the future. I fear for the liberty and equality of the millions of women who have lived and come of age in the 16 years since Roe was decided. I fear for the integrity of, and public esteem for, this Court.

See also Planned Parenthood of Southeastern Pennsylvania v. Casey; Roe v. Wade; Webster v. Reproductive Health Services.

Blackwell, Alice Stone (1857–1950)

Alice Stone Blackwell was instrumental in reuniting two branches of the women's suffrage movement 20 years after a bitter dispute divided the movement. Blackwell, the daughter of suffrage leaders Lucy Stone and Henry Brown Blackwell, was born 14 September 1857 in Orange, New Jersey. An aunt, Elizabeth Blackwell, was the first

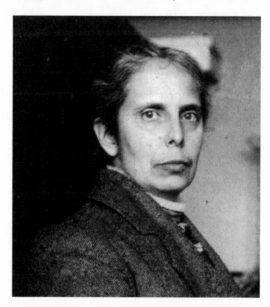

Alice Blackwell

woman doctor of modern times, and another aunt, Antoinette Brown Blackwell, was the country's first female ordained minister. After graduating from Boston University with honors in 1881, Blackwell became an editor of her mother's feminist publication, *Woman's Journal*, produced by the

American Woman Suffrage Association. She was instrumental in merging that group with its rival, the National Woman Suffrage Association, to form the National American Woman Suffrage Association (1890). Blackwell became recording secretary of the newly merged organization, holding that position until 1918. From 1887 to 1905 she edited and circulated to newspapers the "Woman's Column," a series of suffrage news articles, while at the same time shouldering most of the editorial burdens of putting out the *Woman's Journal*. Following the death of her mother in 1893, Blackwell became increasingly interested in other causes. She was active in the Woman's Christian Temperance Union, the National Women's Trade Union League, the National Association for the Advancement of Colored People, the American Peace Society, and the Massachusetts League of Women Voters. Her one romantic involvement, in 1893, with an Armenian theological student, who told her of the Turkish persecution of his people, led to her lifelong interest in helping the Armenian immigrant community. She managed a service to find jobs for refugees and translated and published their poetry. She also published the verse of other oppressed peoples. Her works include *Armenian Poems* (1896), *Songs of Russia* (1916), *Songs of Grief and Gladness* (Yiddish poetry, 1908), and *Spanish-American Poets* (1929). She edited a book that criticized czarist Russia, *The Little Grandmother of the Russian Revolution: Reminiscences and Letters of Catherine Breshkovsky* (1917), and wrote a biography of her mother, *Lucy Stone* (1930). Blackwell died 15 March 1950 in Cambridge, Massachusetts.

See also American Woman Suffrage Association; Blackwell, Elizabeth; National American Woman Suffrage Association; Stone, Lucy.

Blackwell, Antoinette Louisa Brown (1825–1921)

Clergywoman and reformer Antoinette Blackwell was born 20 May 1825 in Henrietta, New York. At the age of nine she publicly stated her faith, convincing the local Congregational church to accept her as a member. Attending Oberlin Collegiate Institute, she was among the first women to complete the literary, or nondegree, course in 1847. Her friend and ally there was abolitionist and suffragist Lucy Stone. After completing the literary course, Antoinette Brown wanted to take Oberlin's theological course of study, but Stone, along with Brown's family and professors, objected. She did complete the theological course of study in 1850, but the college refused to award her a divinity degree because she was a woman. In 1908 Oberlin finally awarded her the divinity degree, 58 years after she earned it. For three years after completing her theological course work, she was a traveling lecturer, addressing abolition, temperance, and women's rights. She was occasionally invited to preach at progressive churches, including the Unitarian churches of Thomas Wentworth Higginson and Theodore Parker. In 1853 she attempted to speak at the World's Temperance Convention in New York. Despite her growing reputation and the fact that she was an accredited delegate, the other delegates shouted her down because of her sex. Ignoring the opposition of her fellow clergymen, she was ordained a minister of the First Congregational Church in South Butler and Savannah, New York, on 15 September 1853, becoming the first formally appointed female pastor in the country. Ten months later, in July 1854, she resigned her pastorate and became a Unitarian. Two years later she married Samuel C. Blackwell, brother of Elizabeth Blackwell and brother-in-law of Lucy Stone. After her marriage, Antoinette Blackwell withdrew from public life to study social and physical sciences. However, at the first congress of the Association for the Advancement of Women (1873), she delivered a paper in which she discussed her belief that women should maintain interests outside of the home and that paid part-time work and domestic assistance from husbands were essential to this end. In 1878 she resumed lecturing for about two years; during that interval she supported Lucy Stone's leadership of the American Woman Suffrage Association, contributed to *Woman's Journal*, and served as vice-president of the Association for the Advancement of Women. Blackwell wrote several books, including *Shadows of Our Social System* (1856), which collected articles she wrote for the *New York Tribune* about her work in slums and prisons, and *The Sexes throughout Nature* (1875), which discussed the implications of Darwinian theory for feminism. Her other books include *Studies in General Science* (1869), *The Philosophy of Individuality* (1893), and *The Making of the Universe* (1914). She also wrote a novel, *The Island Neighbors* (1902), and a book of poetry, *Sea Drift; or, Tribute to the Ocean* (1902). Blackwell died in Elizabeth, New Jersey, on 5 November 1921, one year after exercising her right to vote.

See also Stone, Lucy.

Blackwell, Elizabeth (1821–1910)

Elizabeth Blackwell was the first woman doctor of modern times. Born on 3 February 1821 in Countership, England, she was one of 11 siblings. Her sister Emily also became a doctor, and two of her brothers married feminists: Samuel to Antoinette Brown Blackwell, America's first woman minister, and Henry to suffragist Lucy Stowe. Their father, Samuel Blackwell, was a Dissenter, and the children of Dissenters could not attend school, so Elizabeth and her brothers and sisters were tutored on an equal basis at home.

The Blackwells moved to the United States in 1832, settling in New York City, where they became friendly with William Lloyd Garrison and were active abolitionists. Three years later, the family moved to Jersey City, and, in 1838, to Cincinnati, in search of greater prosperity. There, Samuel Blackwell died, his family left destitute.

For four years, Elizabeth, her mother, and two of her sisters ran a school to help support the family. Leaving to teach in Henderson, Kentucky, Elizabeth returned to Cincinnati after one year, where she decided to study for her medical degree. She studied medicine privately in North and South Carolina from 1845 to 1847, and taught school at the same time. In 1847, she left for

Philadelphia, where she tried to enroll in medical school. Although she was adequately prepared, she was turned down by every school in the city because of her gender, as well as by Bowdoin, Harvard, and Yale.

Nevertheless, Blackwell kept up her medical studies privately, and applied for admission at several rural medical schools. One of them, Geneva College in New York State, finally accepted her. She learned, however, that her good fortune was accidental, for the administrators had allowed the students to decide on her admission, and they had approved her, believing her application to be a practical joke played on them by another school.

Blackwell began her studies at Geneva in November 1847 and soon found herself ignored, thought to be immoral, and even barred from classroom demonstrations. But, gradually, her fellow students, following the leadership of one of her professors, grew to respect her. She graduated from Geneva in 1849, following several months of practical experience at Philadelphia Hospital. Although she was now a naturalized American citizen, Blackwell left for England, then continued to France in search of further training. But the only position she could find was that of a student midwife at a state institution in Paris. Unfortunately, even this modest training soon came to an end, as she became ill after treating a sick child, losing the sight in one eye, and ending her hopes of becoming a surgeon.

In 1850, Blackwell returned to London, where she studied at St. Bartholomew's Hospital. The following year, she returned to New York, hoping to begin practicing medicine. Yet all doors were closed to her: city hospitals would not hire her, and landlords refused to rent her consulting rooms. As a result, Blackwell was forced to spend what few funds she possessed to buy a house. Finding herself isolated from her colleagues, she adopted a seven-year-old orphan, Katharine Barry, in 1854.

Unable to attract patients, Blackwell gave lectures on hygiene, which were published in 1852 as *The Laws of Life, with Special*

39

Reference to the Physical Education of Girls. Many Quaker women attended these lectures, and from them came Blackwell's first patients. In 1853, the "female physician" (as she was referred to) opened a dispensary in a poor section of New York, where she ministered to 200 women in 12 months. This dispensary was eventually developed into the New York Infirmary for Women and Children. In 1856, Elizabeth was joined in her practice by her sister, Dr. Emily Blackwell, and a friend, Dr. Marie E. Zakrzewska, who would later found the New England Hospital for Women and Children in Boston.

In 1858, Elizabeth Blackwell traveled back to England, where she worked for one year. Before returning to the United States in 1859, she had become the first woman to be entered in the medical register of the United Kingdom.

At the outbreak of the Civil War, Blackwell called a meeting at her infirmary to discuss how to care for the soldiers. Soon after, the Women's Central Association for Relief was formed, at Cooper Union; this association developed into the U.S. Sanitary Commission, for which both sisters trained nurses.

In 1868, Blackwell founded the Woman's Medical College of the New York Infirmary, where she established rigorous entrance exams ten years before they were required by law. Women could now obtain the necessary practical experience in medicine, and in a school with high standards. The medical college existed until 1899, when Cornell University Medical School in New York began admitting women.

In 1869, Elizabeth Blackwell returned to England, opening a practice in London. In 1871, she formed the National Health Society, and four years later was made chair of gynecology in the New Hospital and London School of Medicine for Women. After one year, however, she fell ill and retired to Hastings with her daughter. Using the town as a base, she traveled and wrote. In 1878, she published *Counsel to Parents on the Moral Education of Their Children* and, in 1884, *The Human Element in Sex*, works considered

inflammatory for their time. Elizabeth Blackwell died in 1910 in Argyllshire, Scotland.

See also Stone, Lucy

Blatch, Harriot Eaton Stanton (1856–1940)

Harriot Stanton Blatch brought fresh energy to the feminist movement from 1910 to 1915. She was born 20 January 1856 in Seneca Falls, New York, the daughter of women's rights leader Elizabeth Cady Stanton and lawyer and abolitionist Henry Stanton. Her parents sent her to private schools and she graduated from Vassar in 1878. She worked with her mother and Susan B. Anthony to compile the *History of Woman Suffrage*, contributing the chapter about Lucy Stone and the American Woman Suffrage Association, over the objections of her mother and Anthony, who were leaders of the rival National Woman Suffrage Association. Her essay was published in Volume 2 in 1881 and would later help to reconcile the two groups. One year later she married William Blatch, with whom she moved to England in 1902. The Blatches returned to the United States and Harriot picked up her relations with suffrage leaders.

In 1907, five years after her mother's death, in an effort to reinvigorate the suffrage movement, Blatch formed the Equality League of Self-Supporting Women, which later became the Women's Political Union (1910). This organization's most influential members were its many female factory workers, who had never before shared the values of the suffrage campaign. The Women's Political Union eventually merged with the more radical Congressional Union for Woman Suffrage in 1916. During World War I, Blatch served as head of the Food Administration Speakers Bureau and as director of the Woman's Land Army. She wrote *Mobilizing Woman-Power* (1918), which exhorted women to become involved in the war effort and in humanitarian efforts after the war, and *A Woman's Point of View* (1920), which detailed the horrible causes and effects of the war and advo-

40

cated women's role in preventing future wars. Her autobiography, *Challenging Years* (with Alma Lutz) was published in 1940. With her brother, Theodore Stanton, she edited *Elizabeth Cady Stanton, as Revealed in Her Letters, Diary and Reminiscences* (1922). Blatch died 20 November 1940 in Greenwich, Connecticut.

See also Congressional Union for Woman Suffrage; Equality League of Self-Supporting Women; *History of Woman Suffrage;* Stanton, Elizabeth Cady.

Bloomer, Amelia Jenks (1818–1894)

Reformer and editor Amelia Bloomer is best remembered for popularizing the Bloomer costume, pantaloons worn under a bell-shaped knee-length skirt. She was born 27 May 1818, in Homer, New York, and attended local schools. After graduation she taught school one year and worked as a tutor and governess. In 1840 she married Dexter C. Bloomer (omitting the word "obey" from the ceremony), editor of the Seneca County *Courier*, and they moved to Seneca Falls. She soon became interested in public affairs, writing articles for various newspapers and becoming an early member of a local temperance society. Bloomer attended the Seneca Falls Convention in 1848 and the following year launched a temperance and women's rights newspaper called *The Lily*. In *The Lily*, Bloomer defended Elizabeth Cady Stanton's right to wear full Turkish pantaloons and a short skirt. This article brought publicity to *The Lily* and made the Bloomer costume a feminist cause. Bloomer adopted the costume herself, but after six or eight years gave it up. Although the costume gave women greater freedom of movement, Bloomer felt that it distracted people from the more important issues of suffrage and women's property rights. Bloomer continued to publish *The Lily* in Seneca Falls, where she was also the deputy postmistress (Dexter Bloomer had been appointed postmaster in 1849). In 1852 she spoke in favor of women divorcing husbands for drunkenness, and by 1853 she was very active in the women's movement. In the same year Bloomer moved the paper to Mount Ver-

non, Ohio, where she helped her husband publish the *Western Home Visitor* and became a leader in getting women to set type. In 1855 she and her husband moved to Council Bluffs, Iowa, and there *The Lily* was sold. By 1871 she was president of the Iowa Woman Suffrage Association, for which she lectured and wrote articles, continuing her reform activities until her death in Council Bluffs on 30 December 1894.

See also Bloomers; *The Lily*.

Amelia Bloomer, photographed in about 1850, wears attire considered scandalous for the time.

Bloomers

The Bloomer costume caused an enormous public outcry when it was first worn in the mid-nineteenth century. The outfit consisted of ballooning trousers worn under a

41

knee-length skirt. In 1850 Elizabeth Smith Miller, a cousin of Elizabeth Cady Stanton, made a Bloomer costume modeled after one she saw the actress Fanny Kemble wearing in Europe the previous year. Lydia Sayer Hasbrouk also wore a version of the costume that year. Miller felt that the contemporary style of women's clothes—yards of heavy skirts and suffocating bodices and stays—kept women helpless and weak. Such clothing could be dangerous when descending stairs, and the petticoats, which could weigh up to 12 pounds, made movement difficult. Stanton, in a letter to Miller (5 August 1851), described one Bloomer costume as "a short green tunic not reaching to the knee, and white linen drilling trousers made à la masculine." Farm wives, pioneer women, and skaters wore Bloomer costumes, but feminists, including Stanton, Lucy Stone, and Paulina Wright Davis, led the way. People reacted with great hostility, considering the outfit indecent. In a 4 June 1851 letter to Miller, Stanton described how she was jeered by street urchins who "hissed and sung and screamed 'breeches' with the greatest vim."

See also Bloomer, Amelia Jenks.

Bly, Nellie
See Seaman, Elizabeth Cochrane.

Bona Fide Occupational Qualification (BFOQ)
Title VII of the 1964 Civil Rights Act, known as the Equal Employment Opportunity section, forbids discrimination by private employers, employment agencies, and unions on the basis of race, color, religion, national origin, or sex. Title VII actually took effect beginning 2 July 1965. Strictly speaking, Title VII does not prohibit sex discrimination entirely, because it does permit a narrow category of exemptions for cases in which sex can be considered a bona fide occupational qualification (BFOQ) for a job. The BFOQ means that exemptions can be granted when the need to have a worker of a particular sex can be justified.

For example, sex can be considered a BFOQ for modeling women's clothes or acting in female roles because, realistically, a man could not be expected to be suitable for such work. Over the years, the courts have given an increasingly narrow interpretation, as feminists would favor, to the BFOQ exception.

See also Title VII of the 1964 Civil Rights Act.

Bookbinding
During the early 1900s, women in bookbinding were a sharp contrast to other working women. Better educated and American-born, they constituted one-half of all bindery workers. Twenty-five percent of female bookbinders were unionized; few other woman workers were as strongly organized. Women were members of 24 affiliated locals of the International Brotherhood of Bookbinders in 1910, with their most noted local being the Women Bookbinders Local 43 of New York City.

Another powerful local was organized in Chicago by Mary Kenney O'Sullivan (1864–1943). O'Sullivan first worked at a printing and bindery factory in Hannibal, Missouri. After moving to Chicago in the late 1880s, O'Sullivan became angered by the unclean, impoverished conditions in which working-class people lived. In response she joined and soon led the Chicago Women's Bindery Workers' Union No. 2703 of the American Federation of Labor. Elected as a delegate to the Chicago Trades and Labor Assembly, she became friendly with Jane Addams, who subsequently let female binders meet at Hull House. Addams paid for and distributed advertisements promoting the union.

See also Addams, Jane; Jane Club.

Boston Equal Suffrage Association for Good Government
Founded in Massachusetts in 1901, the Boston Equal Suffrage Association for Good Government was particularly successful in drawing support for suffrage from new

quarters. Its innovative strategies included door-to-door campaigning in all parts of the city, conducting impromptu meetings, and giving speeches at the stops on a trolley line. Despite the youth of many of the group's participants, its success inspired a great deal of enthusiasm.

Boston Marriage

Boston marriage was a late Victorian term for women who lived together for economic or sexual reasons. As a practical matter, sharing a household with another woman enabled a woman to keep a job, whereas heterosexual marriage frequently resulted in the loss of employment. Male and female spheres were so separate during the late nineteenth century that bonding among women was common.

Boston Women's Health Book Collective

The Boston Women's Health Book Collective, formed in 1970, is one of the leading forces in the feminist health movement. The collective grew out of a women's health workshop at a 1969 Boston Woman's Conference at Emmanuel College. The workshop generated so much interest that some of its attendees decided to meet for further talks. The group researched women's health issues and released their findings in a booklet published by the New England Free Press (at the collective's expense). That booklet evolved into *Our Bodies, Ourselves*—one of the most helpful books to emerge from the women's movement. It offers easy-to-understand medical information as well as personal stories and a discussion of the impacts of the American economic system on women's health. The book has sold millions of copies in several languages. Its success caused the group to incorporate, and profits from the book have enabled the group to support a variety of women's health causes. In 1984 the collective produced *The New Our Bodies, Ourselves*, and in 1987, *Ourselves Growing Older*.

Bourke-White, Margaret (1904–1971)

Photographer Margaret Bourke-White, who created art from such unlikely subjects as industry and war, was one of the earliest female war correspondents. She was born Margaret White on 14 June 1904 in New York City. While in college she added her mother's maiden name to her own last name.

In 1927, Bourke-White graduated from Cornell University and began to establish her reputation as a photographer of industrial and architectural subjects—an unusual occupation for a woman at the time. An associate editor of *Fortune* from its creation in 1929 until 1933, Bourke-White also published numerous books based on her trips to the Soviet Union, including: *Eyes on Russia* (1931), *Red Republic* (1934), and *U.S.S.R., a Portfolio of Photographs* (1934). In 1936, she became the first woman to join the photo staff of the new magazine *Life*. She worked for the magazine as an editor for the next 33 years. With writer Erskine Caldwell she published a book on the poverty of Southern sharecroppers, *You Have Seen Their Faces* (1937). The two also collaborated on *North of the Danube* (1939) and *Say, Is This the U.S.A.?* (1941). The couple married in 1939 but divorced three years later. After 1939, Bourke-White traveled to Europe, Asia, and the Soviet Union. After Pearl Harbor, she became the first woman to be accredited as a war correspondent to the army air force. In that capacity, she covered the war throughout England, North Africa, and Europe for both the air force and *Life*.

Since she was not permitted to travel with men who flew missions from England, Bourke-White traveled by ship to North Africa, surviving a torpedo attack along the way. She covered the North African and Italian campaigns, as well as the siege of Moscow, from the front. In 1944, she photographed the opening of Buchenwald and other concentration camps. Her war photos were published in *Dear Fatherland, Rest Quietly* (1946). After the war, Bourke-White traveled to India and South Africa, and then resumed her role as a war correspondent during the Korean War. Her other books

Maragret Bourke-White

include *Shooting the Russian War* (1942), *They Called It Purple Heart Valley* (1944), *Halfway to Freedom: A Study of the New India* (1949), *A Report on the American Jesuits* (1956), and *Portrait of Myself* (1963). Bourke-White developed Parkinson's Disease, which rendered her less professionally active in the middle 1950s, but she remained on the staff of *Life* until 1969. She died in Stamford, Connecticut, on 27 August 1971, only two years after formally retiring from the magazine.

Bowe v. Colgate-Palmolive Co.

Bowe v. Colgate-Palmolive Co. (1969) was a test of whether or not a private company (rather than a state) could deny women jobs that required lifting certain weights. Although a lower court ruled that Title VII of the 1964 Civil Rights Act could permit such restrictions, the U.S. Court of Appeals reversed the lower court's decision, ruling that women could not be excluded by weight-lifting restrictions and that such restrictions must apply to all employees if they are to be valid under Title VII.

See also Bona Fide Occupational Qualification; Title VII of the 1964 Civil Rights Act; Human Rights for Women, Inc.

Boyd, Belle (1844–1900)

Isabelle (Belle) Boyd was a Confederate heroine, well known for her activities as a spy during the Civil War. Born 9 May 1844 in Martinsburg, Virginia (now West Virginia), she attended Mount Washington Female College in Baltimore from 1856 to 1860. At the outbreak of the Civil War, she returned to Virginia to raise money for the Confederacy. In 1861 when federal troops arrived, the 17-year-old Boyd killed a Union soldier who entered her home. She had developed and maintained such good relations with Union officers (all the while collecting information from them) that she went unpunished. So successful was she at espionage that she became a courier for Confederate generals P. G. T. Beauregard and Thomas J. Jackson.

In 1862, as Jackson prepared to retake Union-held Front Royal, Virginia, Boyd rode 15 miles on horseback to deliver information she had gathered about Union

Spy Belle Boyd, dressed in a Confederate uniform, lectured widely about her Civil War experiences.

armies. Some credit her, perhaps apocryphally, with risking her life to deliver to General Jackson information that permitted him to save the bridges of Front Royal. She was arrested on several occasions, becoming a heroine as a consequence. In 1864, while sailing from Wilmington, North Carolina, to England with hidden messages for Confederate agents there, her ship was captured by a Union ship. Boyd was sent to Canada under threat of death should she return to the United States. Nevertheless she made her way to London to give her final report as a spy. The captain of the Union ship followed her there and they were married; he died two years later. In 1865 the famous spy published her memoirs, *Belle Boyd, in Camp and Prison*. She returned to the United States, where, in 1868, she appeared on the stage in *The Honeymoon*. Still later she gave lectures to earn a living; she died while on tour, in Kilbourn (now Wisconsin Dells), Wisconsin, on 11 June 1900.

Bra Burners
See Miss America Protest.

Bradstreet, Anne (1612–1672)
Born in 1612, Bradstreet sailed for America at the age of 18, accompanied by her husband, Simon Bradstreet, and her parents. Members of John Winthrop's party, they were the first settlers on Massachusetts Bay. Aboard the ship, her father was made deputy governor of the Massachusetts Bay Company; her husband was already an assistant in the company. A mother of eight and helpmate to her husband and father, she also wrote poetry. Her poems were first printed in England under the title *The Tenth Muse Lately Sprung Up in America* (1650). The manuscript had been transported there by her brother-in-law, the Rev. John Woodbridge, without her knowledge. This publication was a great achievement for a woman at that time. However Anne Bradstreet's reputation rests on a second volume of poems, *Several Poems Compiled with Great Variety of Wit and Learning*, published in

America in 1678, six years after her death in North Andover on 16 September 1672.

Bradwell v. State of Illinois
The first women's rights case to be brought before the U.S. Supreme Court, *Bradwell v. State of Illinois* (1873), was also the first to use the Fourteenth Amendment to challenge job classification by sex. After Myra Bradwell passed an examination for the Chicago bar, the state of Illinois refused to grant her a license because she was a married woman "who was not competent to perform such duties as making contracts." Bradwell, founder and editor of the influential *Chicago Legal News* and president of a publishing house, was widely respected for her legal scholarship and quite used to making contracts. Indeed, she had been granted a state charter to do so. In her suit, Bradwell argued that the privileges and immunities clause of the Fourteenth Amendment, which describes the rights citizens have by virtue of their citizenship, protects the basic rights of Americans from such onerous state laws.

This argument was similar to the one posed in the Slaughter-House Cases (Louisiana, 1873), which was ruled upon by the Court the day before the Bradwell case. This causes some confusion over which case was the first to pose women's rights and Fourteenth Amendment questions. Although Bradwell went to the Supreme Court two weeks before the Slaughter-House Cases, the Court ruled on the Slaughter-House Cases one day before it ruled on the Bradwell case, hence the latter's fame as the court's first interpretation of the Fourteenth Amendment. In both cases, the Supreme Court destroyed the privileges and immunities argument. Writing the majority opinion, Justice Miller contended that the right to practice law was not a right of citizenship under the Fourteenth Amendment. In his concurring opinion, Justice Joseph P. Bradley fell back on Blackstone-inspired common-law precedents that said married women had no legal existence apart from their husbands:

The claim that, under the Fourteenth Amendment of the Constitution, which declares that no state shall make or enforce any law which shall abridge the privileges and immunities of citizens of the United States, and the statute law of Illinois, or the common law prevailing in that state, can no longer be set up as a barrier against the rights of females to pursue any lawful employment for a livelihood (the practice of law included), assumes that it is one of the privileges and immunities of women as citizens to engage in any and every profession, occupation or employment in civil life. It certainly cannot be affirmed, as a historical fact, that this has ever been established as one of the fundamental privileges and immunities of the sex. On the contrary, the civil law, as well as nature herself, has always recognized a wide difference in the respective spheres and destinies of man and woman. Man is, or should be, woman's protector and defender. The natural and proper timidity and delicacy which belongs to the female sex evidently unfits it for many of the occupations of civil life. The constitution of the family organization, which is founded in the divine ordinance, as well as the nature of things, indicates the domestic sphere as that which properly belongs to the domain and functions of womanhood. The harmony, not to say identity, of interests and views which belong or should belong to the family institution, is repugnant to the idea of a woman adopting a distinct and independent career from that of her husband. So firmly fixed was this sentiment in the founders of the common law that it became a maxim of that system of jurisprudence that a woman had no legal existence separate from her husband, who was regarded as her head and representative in the social state. . . . The paramount destiny and mission of woman are to fulfill the noble and benign offices of wife and mother. This is the law of the Creator. And the rules of civil society must be adopted to the general constitution of things, and cannot be based upon exceptional cases.

The same arguments in both the Bradwell and Slaughter-House cases were eventually applied under the equal protection clause of the Fourteenth Amendment and stood as an example for similar claims in the future.

See also Fourteenth Amendment.

Brant, Mary (c. 1736–1796)

Born c. 1736, Mary Brant was an American Indian leader. She was the daughter of a Mohawk *sachem* (religious leader) and sister to the well-known Mohawk warrior Joseph Brant. Her common-law marriage to Sir William Johnson, superintendent of Indian affairs for the northern colonies and a hero of the French and Indian War, gave her wealth and influence, which she used to assist her husband in smoothing relations with various Indian nations. Upon Johnson's death in 1774, she became a trader to support their nine children. Her eldest son, Peter, a Loyalist (like the rest of the family), is thought to have captured Ethan Allen in Montreal in 1775. During the American Revolution, Brant passed information on American troop movements to the British and supplied them with ammunition. Her influence "was decisive in bringing the entire Iroquois nation into the British camp," according to Robert McHenry. After the revolution, she settled with other Loyalists in Ontario, Canada, where she died 16 April 1796, a pensioner of the British government.

Bread and Roses

Bread and Roses was a short-lived organization linking small feminist collectives at the beginning of the 1970s. Established in Boston in 1969, Bread and Roses identified itself as a "socialist revolutionary" organization and did not limit its attention to efforts dealing solely with women's rights. Some of its activities included participation in protests against the Vietnam War, feminist theater projects, and efforts to spread the ideas of the women's liberation movement. The group died out in the early 1970s.

Brent, Margaret (c. 1601–1671)

Margaret Brent was the first woman in the colonies to demand the right to vote. Born c. 1601, Brent emigrated from England in 1638 with her sister, two brothers, and their servants to the Catholic colony of Maryland, settling in St. Mary's City, the capital. She and her sister were granted 70.5 acres, called the Sisters Freehold; this was the first land grant made to women in Maryland. She became one of the few colonial female landowners and one of the few women of the period to manage her own affairs. The proprietor of the colony, Lord Baltimore, later increased her allotment, and Brent enlarged it further through business deals and family transactions until she was one of the colony's major landowners.

Through her various dealings in the colony, Brent became so trusted by Lord Baltimore's brother, Governor Leonard Calvert, that on his deathbed the governor named Brent executor of his will. Brent's major responsibility as executor of the Calvert estate was to pay off soldiers that the governor had imported from Virginia to quell a Protestant uprising (1644–1646). The governor had pledged his estate—and the estate of his brother, Lord Baltimore—to pay the soldiers, but there was some delay and the soldiers grew restive. Brent used her power as Calvert's executor (and by extension Calvert's power of attorney to act for Lord Baltimore) to liquidate Calvert's estate and to sell some of Lord Baltimore's cattle to raise the money. In 1648, she amazed the House of Burgesses by insisting that she be granted a double vote, one recognizing her power of attorney on behalf of Lord Baltimore and one for herself, to which she would have been entitled as a male freeholder. When her request was denied, she demanded that all proceedings of the council be declared invalid. Lord Baltimore later

condemned her for having sold his holdings to pay the soldiers. Brent moved to Westmoreland County, Virginia, where she died in 1671.

Brooks, Gwendolyn (1917–)

Poet Gwendolyn Brooks is the first African-American woman to win a Pulitzer Prize. Brooks was born 7 June 1917 in Topeka, Kansas. She grew up in Chicago and studied at Wilson Junior College, from which she graduated in 1936.

Brooks wrote her first poem at the age of 13; by the time she reached her twenties, her work was appearing in *Harper's, Yale Review, The Saturday Review of Literature,* and other literary publications. In 1945, the year her first book of poems, *A Street in Bronzeville,* was published, *Mademoiselle* magazine named her one of "Ten Women of 1945." Her second book of poems, *Annie Allen,* won the Pulitzer Prize in 1950. During the 1950s Brooks wrote a novel, *Maude Martha* (1953), and an illustrated collection of poems for children, *Bronzeville for Boys and Girls* (1956). *The Bean Eaters,* a collection of poems reflecting some of the bitterness of the civil rights period, was published in 1960.

After publishing the poem *In the Mecca* (1968), Brooks decided to publish her works only with small presses owned by African Americans. That year she was chosen to succeed Carl Sandburg as poet laureate of Illinois. Her other books include: *Selected Poems* (1963), *Riot* (1969), *Family Pictures* (1970), *Aloneness* (1971), *Report from Part One* (1972), *The Tiger Wore White Gloves* (1974), *Beckonings* (1975), *Primer for Blacks* (1980), *To Disembark* (1981), *The Near-Johannesburg Boy and Other Poems* (1986), and *Winnie* (1988).

Brooks has been a Guggenheim Fellow and has taught at several midwestern colleges and universities, among them the University of Wisconsin, Columbia College (Chicago), and Elmhurst College. In 1976, she became the first African-American woman appointed to the National Institute of Arts and Letters; in 1985, she became the first African-American woman to be named poetry consultant to the Library of Congress, the U.S. equivalent of poet laureate. In 1988, Brooks was named to the National Women's Hall of Fame. The following year, she won the Frost Medal of the Poetry Society of America and the Lifetime Achievement Award of the National Endowment for the Arts. In 1990, Chicago State University endowed the Gwendolyn Brooks Chair in Creative Writing.

Brown (Blackwell), Antoinette Louisa
See Blackwell, Antoinette Louisa.

Brown, Hallie Quinn (1850–1949)
Hallie Brown was a leader in the colored women's clubs of the early twentieth century. She was born 10 March 1850, the child of former slaves, in Philadelphia, where she remained until the family moved to Chatham, Ontario, in 1864. She was educated at Wilburforce University (Ohio). After graduating in 1873, she taught elementary school in Mississippi and South Carolina. From 1885 to 1887, Brown served as dean of Allen University in Columbia, South Carolina; during summers, she studied at the Chautauqua Lecture School, from which she graduated in 1886. Returning to Ohio in 1887, she worked as a lecturer and teacher, traveling widely. She returned to the South in 1892 to become principal of the Tuskegee Institute under Booker T. Washington. In 1893, she was appointed professor of elocution at Wilburforce University. Also that year, she became the major promoter of the Colored Women's League, which in 1896 merged with other organizations to become the National Association of Colored Women. From 1894 to 1899 Brown traveled extensively in Europe, lecturing on African-American life. She twice appeared before Queen Victoria and, in 1895, spoke at the World's Woman's Christian Temperance Union in London. In 1899, Brown was a representative from the United States at a meeting of the International Congress of Women, also held in London. From 1905 to 1912, Brown served as president of the Ohio State Federation of Colored Women's Clubs; she went on to become president of the National Association of Colored Women from 1920 to 1924. Under her leadership the association worked to preserve the Washington, D.C., home of Frederick Douglass.

Brown also participated in party politics. Earlier in the decade, she was vice-president of the Ohio Council of Republican Women. She addressed the party's national convention in 1924 and helped to organize African-American women to elect Calvin Coolidge. She also wrote several books, including *Bits and Odds: A Choice Selection of Recitations* (1880), *First Lessons in Public Speaking* (1920), *Homespun Heroines and Other Women of Distinction* (1926), and *Pen Pictures of Pioneers of Wilberforce* (1937). Brown died 16 September 1949 in Wilburforce.

Brown, Olympia (1835–1926)
Olympia Brown was a Universalist minister, the first woman ordained by full denominational authority. (Antoinette Brown Blackwell, the first American woman to become an ordained minister, was ordained by the autonomous authority of a single congregation.) Brown was born 5 January 1835 in Prairie Ronde, Michigan. Denied admission to the University of Michigan because of her gender, she attended Mount Holyoke and Antioch College, graduating from the latter in 1860. After helping with the arrangements to have Antoinette Brown Blackwell preach at Antioch—the first woman Brown had seen preach—Brown decided to become a minister herself. She entered the St. Lawrence University theological school and was ordained in 1863. She married John Henry Willis in 1873 but continued to use her maiden name. In 1866, Susan B. Anthony invited Brown to attend a suffrage meeting; Brown became a champion of women's rights and a charter member of the American Equal Rights Association. In 1868, she organized a convention in Boston that led to the formation of the New England Woman Suffrage Association. Brown continued her suffrage activity after the

family moved to Wisconsin so that Brown could accept pastorship of a church in Racine. From 1884 to 1912, she served as president of the Wisconsin Woman Suffrage Association. In 1887, she unsuccessfully sued election officials in the city of Racine for having denied her the vote. That year she resigned her pastorate to work for suffrage.

Olympia Brown

In addition to her activities in Wisconsin, Brown maintained her commitment to suffrage on a national level, becoming vice-president of the National Woman Suffrage Association (NWSA) in 1884. However, her commitment was to a suffrage amendment to the Constitution, rather than the state-by-state suffrage amendments for which the NWSA worked. To promote the amendment, she helped form the Federal Suffrage Association in Chicago in 1892. She served as its vice-president until 1902, when the group was reorganized and renamed the Federal Equality Association (FEA). A year later she was named president of the association, serving in that capacity until 1920. Brown was also a member of the Congressional Union for Woman Suffrage. In 1917, while in her eighties, she picketed the White House with the National Woman's Party, passing out literature holding President Woodrow Wilson re-

sponsible for the failure to pass a federal suffrage amendment.

From 1893 to 1900 Brown managed *The Racine Times*, a newspaper owned by her husband. She authored *Acquaintances, Old and New, among Reformers* (1911). A lifelong feminist, Brown was involved in reform activities until her death in Baltimore, Maryland, on 23 October 1926.

Brown and Sharp Manufacturing Case
In 1942, the National War Labor Board (NWLB) ruled that the Brown and Sharp Manufacturing Company could not pay women only four-fifths what it paid men for the same work. The NWLB supported giving women equal pay for the same quantity and quality of work in similarly difficult jobs, thus echoing a view expressed by the government's War Manpower Commission. The NWLB also stated that women should be able to feel confident that they will not experience discrimination in pay.
See also Equal Pay Act.

Brownmiller, Susan (1935–)
Born 15 February 1935 in Brooklyn, New York, journalist Susan Brownmiller is best known for her ground-breaking book *Against Our Will: Men, Women, and Rape* (1975), which traces rape through history, concluding it is an act of oppression. Brownmiller also helped to establish the New York Radical Feminists in 1969. She is the author of *Femininity* (1984) and *Waverly Place* (1989).

Bryn Mawr
Bryn Mawr college was established in Bryn Mawr, Pennsylvania, as a women's college in 1885 by a group of Pennsylvania and Baltimore Quakers. Twenty-eight-year-old Martha Carey Thomas became its first dean; she was named president of the college in 1894. Thomas was one of the first graduates of Cornell University and one of the very few women to travel to Europe to receive her doctorate. (In 1882 she became the first

foreigner, and the first woman, to obtain a Ph.D. degree from the University of Zurich.)

Thomas galvanized the educational community by setting Bryn Mawr's standards as high as Harvard's. Her entrance requirements were demanding, and applicants had to pass strict examinations. From its founding, Bryn Mawr offered resident fellowships for women to undertake graduate work—the earliest such grants available to women. In 1921 Thomas and Hilda Smith, an instructor at Bryn Mawr and a member of the National Women's Trade Union League (NWTUL), used money from NWTUL to open the Bryn Mawr Summer School for Workers. The school was part of a plan by contemporary female reformers to effect social change by training women unionists in the skills they would need to assume leadership positions in unions. Each summer about 60 women workers spent six to eight weeks at Bryn Mawr, studying economics, history, and politics. While some women felt uncomfortable with the lifestyle and values of the college, others enjoyed the program. Although it encouraged other such programs, the school yielded no immediate, tangible progress for most female industrial workers, who, unlike the participants in this program, were for the most part not unionized. The financial difficulties of the 1930s forced the school to close.

See also Thomas, Martha Carey.

Bryn Mawr Summer School for Women Workers
See Bryn Mawr; Camp Jane Addams.

Buck, Pearl Sydenstricker (1892–1973)
Pearl Buck was the first American woman to win the Nobel Prize for Literature, as well as being a tireless worker on behalf of disadvantaged children. Her novel about peasant life in China, *The Good Earth*, won both the Pulitzer Prize (1932) and the Nobel Prize (1938). She was born 26 June 1892 in Hillsboro, West Virginia. Her father was a

Presbyterian missionary in China, and Pearl was reared there, educated in Chenchiang, China, by her parents and a Chinese tutor. At the age of 15 she attended a boarding school in Shanghai, entering Randolph-Macon Woman's College in Virginia two years later. Graduating in 1914, she taught psychology at the college for one year before returning to China. In 1917 she married John Lossing Buck. In 1922 she began writing short pieces about China, and by 1931 had written two novels, including the Pulitzer Prize–winning novel, *The Good Earth*.

Pearl Buck

For extended periods between 1915 and 1930, Buck taught English in various Chinese schools and universities, returning to the United States to receive an M.A. in English from Cornell University in 1926. Her first novel, *East Wind, West Wind*, was published in 1930; it was followed by *The*

Good Earth (1931), *Sons* (1932), and *A House Divided* (1935). Some of her other titles include the stories of her parents, *The Exile* and *Fighting Angel* (both in 1936). She produced about 40 novels and many collections of short stories. In 1941, she established the East and West Association to promote international peace, disbanding it in 1951 due to pressures from anticommunists. The mother of six adopted children, in 1949 Buck founded the Asian-American adoption agency Welcome House and the Pearl S. Buck Foundation to help abandoned children in Asia. Between 1945 and 1953, Buck published five novels set in America in which she used the pen name "John Sedges," so that male critics would treat her seriously. *The Townsman* (1945) was the first of these novels. A lifelong advocate for women's rights, Buck died in Danby, Vermont, on 6 March 1973.

Burial of Traditional Womanhood

The Burial of Traditional Womanhood was a protest within a protest. It is often blamed for widening the gap within the radical women's movement. In 1968, to protest the Vietnam War, the Jeanette Rankin Brigade, a network of women's antiwar organizations, held a demonstration and convention in Washington, D.C.; thousands of women attended. Because some of the women explained their objection to the war in terms of their traditional roles as helpless but devoted wives and mothers, they themselves drew protest from some radical feminists, who were angered by the perpetuation of such images. The angry radicals, led by the New York Radical Women and similar groups, arranged a mock funeral of an effigy they labeled "Traditional Womanhood." The protest was held at Arlington National Cemetery; the speakers decried old-fashioned values. Their message was well received by many women, although it fueled the debate within the radical women's movement about how much emphasis should be placed on social rather than political concerns.

Burns, Lucy (1866–1966)

Lucy Burns, a redheaded Irish American, was jailed for more months than any other women's suffrage leader. She was born 28 July 1866 in Brooklyn, New York. She attended Vassar, where she was a top scholar, graduating in 1902. Burns pursued graduate studies at Yale University from 1902 to 1903, an unusual feat for a woman of her day. One year later, she began teaching English at Brooklyn's Erasmus Hall High School, where she remained until 1906. That year she traveled to Germany to study languages at the University of Berlin (1906–1908), and the University of Bonn (1908–1909). In 1909 she began doctorate work at Oxford. In England, Burns met Emmeline and Christabel Pankhurst, with whom she campaigned for women's suffrage in Great Britain and through whom she met Alice Paul. When Burns returned to the United States in 1912, she joined Paul to orchestrate a campaign for a women's suffrage amendment to the Constitution. Their national approach conflicted with the state-by-state strategy that dominated the women's movement at that time, advocated by the National American Woman Suffrage Association. In 1913, Burns and Paul organized the Congressional Union for Woman Suffrage to work toward national suffrage. Burns edited the Congressional Union newspaper, *The Suffragist.* The Congressional Union's successor, after 1916, was the National Woman's Party (NWP), for which Paul was the strategist and Burns the organizer. The NWP adopted a confrontational strategy, and from 1913 to 1919 Burns was arrested for a variety of suffrage activities, including chalking ads for the vote on the streets of Washington, D.C. In 1917, after her arrest for picketing the White House, she went on a 19-day hunger strike and was force-fed. With Paul, Burns can be credited with providing the impetus for congressional approval of the Nineteenth Amendment. Soon after its approval, Burns tired of reform activities. She spent the last 25 years of her life pursuing personal interests and raising her niece after the child's mother, Burns's sister, died.

A religious woman, Burns maintained close ties to the Catholic church until her death in Brooklyn on 22 December 1966.

See also Congressional Union for Woman Suffrage; National Woman's Party; Nineteenth Amendment; Paul, Alice.

Business and Professional Women

During the twentieth century the careers of business and professional women have exhibited dramatic change. Following World War I, the type of work women performed changed: Millions of white-collar jobs, such as typing and stenography, opened up for young women, many of whom had high school educations. Overall, however, women's low economic status and inability to break into traditionally male occupations remained unchanged. According to historian William H.Chafe, the period from 1920 to 1940 saw only a slight change in status for professional women; during these years the proportion of women who worked in professions barely increased, from 11 percent to 14.2 percent. Three out of four female college graduates continued to enter traditionally female professions, such as nursing, social work, and teaching. These occupations offered little opportunity for advancement. The proportion of architects and lawyers who were women, writes Chafe, was constant at less than 3 percent from 1910 to 1930; during the same period, the number of female doctors declined by more than 25 percent, from 9,015 to 6,825.

As of 1970, women's participation in the key professions—doctors, lawyers, scientists, engineers, clergy, dentists, biologists, chemists, mathematicians, physicists, and college professors—had not significantly changed since the turn of the century. Their numbers in business management were equally stagnant. Since the 1970s, social scientists, such as Cynthia Fuchs Epstein,

have documented the many reasons for sex segregation in the professions. These reasons include employer discrimination, public policy, family demands, and government policy. However, according to economists Claudia Goldin, Francine Blau, and June O'Neill, women were big economic winners in the 1980s, gaining almost as much in that single decade as they had during the 80 years between 1890 and 1970. For example, women in economics with doctorate degrees earned 95–99 percent of the amount their male peers earned during this time. In addition, the number of women in law and medical schools significantly increased, from under 10 percent in the late 1970s to more than 30 percent in the late 1980s. Additional evidence of the breakdown of sex segregation in the professions can be found in college graduating classes: women earn more than one-third of all professional degrees today, up from 6 percent in 1971. In 1960, about 80 percent of college-educated women went into the traditionally female careers of teaching, nursing, social service, and civil service; by the end of the 1980s this figure fell below 30 percent. In the early 1990s, 30 percent of working women are professionals or managers—the same proportion as men. Although just 3 percent of top executives are women, they make up one-half the accountants and one-sixth of all doctors.

Increasing opportunities for women have encouraged their ambition and success in fields where once only men were thought to have an interest. The work force is still segregated by sex, but women have taken on all types of traditional male jobs, particularly professional ones, making solid gains in the 1980s that are likely to be maintained and strengthened by the year 2000, when women will account for one-half of the work force.

Cable Act

The Cable Act of 1922 and its revision in 1930–1931 together granted married women citizenship status independent of their husbands' status. Previously, a woman's citizenship depended entirely on her husband's—that is, a woman's citizenship was always made to conform, if necessary, to that of her husband. This meant that immigrant women would not apply for citizenship individually, female U.S. citizens who married foreigners could be reclassified as aliens, and immigrant or alien women who married a U.S. citizen would become U.S. citizens by virtue of their marriage.

The champions of the Cable Act, many of whom were members of the Women's Joint Congressional Committee, were essentially concerned with the portions of the immigration policy that were damaging to women, and not the fact that women could gain citizenship through marriage. For this reason, the provisions of the original Cable Act were only concerned with certain women who were victimized by immigration laws as they stood: those who married foreigners. Under the 1922 Cable Act, those women would now be reclassified as naturalized citizens (rather than aliens, as they would have before—but still not as native citizens). The only exception to this was that female U.S. citizens who married Asian men were still forced to accept alien status. (The Cable Act of 1922 therefore reproduced the racist ideology of contemporary immigration laws, which did not allow Asians to become naturalized citizens.)

To some extent, the 1922 Cable Act reflected the principle behind the suffrage movement, that is, a person's privileges of citizenship should not be determined by gender. However, it was only with the 1930–1931 revision of the Cable Act that that principle found its fullest expression. The original Cable Act was flawed because it

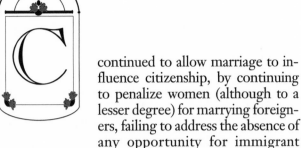

continued to allow marriage to influence citizenship, by continuing to penalize women (although to a lesser degree) for marrying foreigners, failing to address the absence of any opportunity for immigrant women to apply for citizenship individually, maintaining the policy of granting immigrant women citizenship because of marriage to a U.S. citizen, and because of the racist exemption of American wives of Asian men from an improvement in their citizenship status. So, while women's citizenship had ceased to be completely dependent upon their husbands', it had not yet become completely independent.

The revision of the Cable Act in 1930–1931 corrected all the defects in the original law by making the citizenship of wives absolutely independent of their husbands' citizenship; this in turn made the race of a woman's husband irrelevant to her citizenship. This time there were no exemptions based on the race of the husband: female citizens of the United States who married Asian men, like those who married men of other races, were permitted to retain their U.S. citizenship.

Camp Jane Addams

Located at Bear Mountain, New York, Camp Jane Addams was the first of 28 summer camps for poor, single women established throughout the country in 1933 and 1934. Young women who attended the camps studied health, homemaking, education for workers, crafts, and career training. In addition to education, the women received a small allowance. Some women were able to find jobs after completing the program. The camps were considered combined federal and state agencies under the Federal Emergency Relief Administration that came into being during the Great Depression in the thirties. Hilda Smith, one of

55

the founders of the Bryn Mawr Summer School for Women Workers, was in charge of setting up the camps.

The camps had been proposed by First Lady Eleanor Roosevelt and Labor Secretary Frances Perkins, following Mrs. Roosevelt's White House Conference on Resident Schools for Unemployed Women. Roosevelt and Perkins had originally conceived of the camps as a female counterpart to the all-male Civilian Conservation Corps, which accepted married as well as single men and required them to work on public projects for wages (rather than granting them allowances). However, the idea of such camps for married women, as well as single women, outraged the public because of the prospect of removing wives from the home. Nevertheless, Eleanor Roosevelt continued to champion the cause of women's camps in some form. Although their value was largely symbolic, the camps (especially Camp Jane Addams, with which she had been personally involved) were a source of pride to Mrs. Roosevelt.

See also Roosevelt, Eleanor.

Carroll v. Warren

Carroll v. Warren (Maryland, 1736) was one of the earliest known cases to examine the requirement that the court privately question a married woman before the sale or transfer of her real property by her husband to make sure she had not been coerced into the sale by her spouse. Under Maryland law, a married woman had to sign a deed in order to transfer her property to another person. In this respect, Maryland law differed from that of most other colonies, in which a married woman's personal property automatically transferred to her husband by virtue of the marriage.

To protect a wife from her husband's coercion, a 1674 law required that a judge privately question the woman to convey her property "without being induced by any Force or Threat used by her Husband, or through Fear of his Displeasure." In this case, Sarah Curtis inherited a great deal of property from her first marriage. In 1711,

her second husband, Michael Curtis, deceived her into signing a deed for the transfer of that property. Evidently, Sarah thought the property was to be leased, not sold. After Sarah Curtis's death, her heir, John Warren, claimed that the property belonged to him because Sarah's consent was fraudulently obtained. He claimed Sarah never meant to give away her right and title to the land. The court of chancery, an equity court, ruled in favor of the heir, declaring that the rules for conveying a married woman's estate had not been strictly followed. This decision acknowledged that married women had some control over conveying their own property.

See also Bethune v. Beresford; Coercion; Married Women's Property Acts.

Carson, Rachel Louise (1907–1964)

Rachel Carson was an influential biologist and nature writer at a time when few women felt encouraged to study or work in science. Born 27 May 1907 in Springdale, Pennsylvania, Carson loved nature from her youth. She entered Pennsylvania College for Women intending to become a writer, but switched to biology, doing so at a time when the number of women in such professions was so small as to be considered deviant. After graduating in 1929, she entered Johns Hopkins University, where she received an M.A. in 1932. In 1931 she began teaching at the University of Maryland, and from 1929 to 1936 she also taught at the Johns Hopkins summer school, while pursuing postgraduate studies at the Marine Biology Laboratory in Woods Hole, Massachusetts.

In 1936 she was hired as an aquatic biologist by the U.S. Bureau of Fisheries, where she worked until 1952. While at the bureau, she wrote *Under the Sea-Wind* (1941) and *The Sea around Us* (1951). The latter book won the National Book Award and was translated into 32 languages. She followed that book with *Edge of the Sea* (1955). However, it was her last work, *Silent Spring* (1962), for which she is best remembered. In it she charged that overuse of chemical pesticides and herbicides could permanently upset the earth's ecological balance. A life-long advocate of the environment, she continued to focus public attention on the widespread use of the pesticide DDT until her death 14 April 1964 in Silver Spring, Maryland.

Casey Hayden–Mary King Paper

Casey Hayden and Mary King were staff members of the Student Nonviolent Coordinating Committee (SNCC), a civil rights group that was part of the New Left movement of the 1960s. In 1965, they wrote a paper that exposed the sex bias within that organization and distributed the unsigned paper at a staff retreat. The paper infuriated some of the men and became one of the catalysts of the women's liberation movement. Hayden and King noted that women often were given the less desirable jobs in the SNCC and that the issue of women's status in the organization was treated with contempt, reflecting a belief in male superiority.

In 1965 Hayden and King expanded some of their ideas in a memo to women activists. The memo discussed the conflict between the ideology of the New Left and the sex bias it exhibited. The memo was published the following year as "Sex and Caste" in the feminist magazine *Liberation*.

Casket Girls

In 1728, the India Company of France sent young women to Louisiana to marry settlers, as so few women inhabited the colonies. The women brought their possessions in wooden trunks, hence their sobriquet *filles á la cassette*. But unlike earlier arrivals, most of whom were prostitutes released from houses of correction ("Correction Girls"), the Casket Girls had a reputation for virtue and were cared for by nuns until husbands could be found for them. Later generations would think a person descended from a Casket Girl held high status.

Catt, Carrie Clinton Lane Chapman (1859–1947)

In the pantheon of woman suffragists, Carrie Chapman Catt stands beside Susan B. Anthony and Alice Paul as the woman most responsible for passage and ratification of the Nineteenth Amendment. She was born 9 January 1859 in Ripon, Wisconsin, and worked her way through Iowa State College at a time when this was highly unusual, even for an unmarried woman. After graduating in 1880, she worked in a law office and became principal of a high school in Mason City, Iowa (1881). Two years later she was appointed superintendent of schools, one of the first female superintendents in the country. She married Leo Chapman, publisher of the *Mason City Republican*, in 1885; he died the following year.

By 1887, having worked briefly as a reporter, Chapman joined the Iowa Woman Suffrage Association and became an organizer. She joined the newly organized National American Woman Suffrage Association (NAWSA) in 1890. A prenuptial agreement with her second husband, George Catt, stipulated that she would spend four months a year on suffrage work. In 1895, Catt suggested the NAWSA set up an organizational committee to direct the efforts of suffragists around the country. Catt served as chairman of the committee, participating in 20 hearings before Congress on a proposed women's suffrage amendment to the Constitution. In 1900, Susan B. Anthony chose Catt to succeed her as president of the NAWSA, a position Catt held for four years. She gave it up because of her husband's illness and because she was becoming more involved in international suffrage efforts. Catt was one of the founders of the International Woman Suffrage Alliance (later the International Alliance of Women), founded in Berlin in 1904, serving as president of the alliance until 1923. At the beginning of World War I, Catt, Jane Addams, and others formed the Woman's Peace Party. However, Catt believed that suffrage should not be put on hold during the war. From 1913 to 1915, she led New York's high-profile but unsuccessful campaign for the vote.

Catt was reelected president of NAWSA in 1915. She held this position for the rest of her life, using it to influence the group to adopt her Winning Plan. The plan attacked the suffrage issue at both state and national levels. In a post-convention meeting of the Executive Council at NAWSA's 1916 convention, Catt unveiled her strategy for getting the Nineteenth Amendment submitted by Congress and ratified by the respective legislatures. She assigned specific tasks to each of the 36 states, pledging NAWSA's officers to secrecy. Her specific instructions were: "We should win . . . a few more states before the Federal Amendment gets up to the legislatures. . . . A southern state should be selected and made ready for a campaign, and the solid front of the 'anti' South broken as soon as possible. Some break in the solid 'anti' East should be made too. . . . By 1920, when the next national party platforms will be adopted, we should have won Iowa, South Dakota, North Dakota, Nebraska, New York, Maine and a southern state." The plan would prove successful.

In 1919, before the Nineteenth Amendment was ratified, Catt began to pave the way for the founding of the League of Women Voters, an organization to educate the newly enfranchised women voters. After ratification of the Nineteenth Amendment, the NAWSA became the League of Women Voters, and Catt served as its honorary president until her death. Her other reform activities included the founding of the Committee on the Cause and Cure of War (1925), support of the League of Nations, and aid to Jewish refugees in Germany. Her books include *Woman Suffrage and Politics* (1933) and *Why Wars Must Cease* (1935). Catt died in New Rochelle, New York, on 9 March 1947.

See also Addams, Jane; Anthony, Susan B.; International Woman Suffrage Alliance; League of Women Voters; National American Woman Suffrage Association; Nineteenth Amendment; Winning Plan; Woman's Peace Party.

Cell 16

To many women's liberationists, Cell 16 appeared to be the most militant group in the women's liberation movement. Founded in the summer of 1968 by Roxanne Dunbar, Cell 16 (first called the Female Liberation Front, or Female Liberation) advocated celibacy, separatism, and karate. The emphasis on karate (as a form of self-defense) came in response to discussions about women's vulnerability to physical and cultural assault. As part of its rejection of traditional femininity, Cell 16 developed a look that became widely imitated throughout the women's liberation movement: short hair, combat boots, khaki pants, and work shirts. The group's ideas were widely publicized through its periodical, *No More Fun and Games: A Journal of Female Liberation*, one of the first radical feminist publications.

As a self-styled elite, vanguard group, Cell 16 deliberately remained small, and it avoided the divisive ideological conflicts that troubled other groups by demanding ideological conformity as a prerequisite for membership. Dunbar acted as de facto leader and spokesperson despite the group's official adoption of a nonhierarchical style of organization. While it deplored masculine values, Cell 16 did not at first develop a uniquely feminist worldview. Instead, it expanded Marxist philosophy to explain the supremacy of man within the family by describing women as an oppressed class within the family. Dunbar criticized the New Left as being too little committed to Marxist teachings, and she urged women to remain active within the broader left-wing movement. One area of Dunbar's teaching, which was based on undiluted feminism, was the subject of pornography: Dunbar was a pioneer in antipornography feminist theory and described pornography as an outgrowth of masculine power, equating it with violence itself.

Dunbar left the group in 1970. From that time until its dissolution in 1973, Cell 16 tended to emphasize distinctly feminist rather than Marxist values, and it proclaimed that unity among women was already a reality. The development of a female-centric view at this time was actually quite ironic because, in the same time period (beginning in 1969), for unrelated reasons, Cell 16 was secretly infiltrated by female members of the Young Socialist Alliance (YSA), which had formulated a plan for infiltrating a number of different feminist groups. The YSA members eventually left, but not until after they had gained access to key Cell 16 resources. Members of Cell 16 were discouraged and disillusioned, which brought about the dissolution of the group. The YSA members established a socialist feminist organization, calling itself Female Liberation, the original name of Cell 16. For a time, the YSA's Female Liberation was the only major feminist organization in Boston.

Center for the American Woman in Politics (CAWP)

In 1972, Rutgers University established the Center for the American Woman in Politics (CAWP) to analyze the treatment of women in political life. Its surveys did a great deal to expose the sexism in politics and to highlight the fact that women voters have a distinct agenda and therefore tend to develop a greater sensitivity and loyalty to women's issues. The CAWP seeks to link female politicians from both parties and from various regions and to reinforce concerns about women's issues in the minds of female politicians. It has had considerable success in creating a political base for women as well as addressing their immediate concerns.

See also National Women's Political Caucus.

Chancery Courts

Chancery refers to jurisprudence that takes place in a court of equity. During the colonial period, it was exercised, as it was under British law, by a chancellor. In contrast to common law, which is defined by precedent, equity law is determined by the courts. Chancery courts not only dealt with equity law but administered trust estates, often deciding cases in which women owned property separately from their husbands. These "separate" estates evolved in England as an

exception to the common law principle that the husband controlled his wife's property and served the needs of the wealthy. Over the years the chancery used marriage settlements to expand women's property rights, but the common law courts refused to enforce them. Hence, a dual system developed for establishing the rights of married women: under one, women held equal property rights to men; under the other, none at all. Opposed by Puritans and Quakers as disruptive of family harmony, the chancery courts were not established by the colonies of Connecticut, Massachusetts, or Pennsylvania. However, chancery courts were found in New York, Maryland, Virginia, and South Carolina, indicating support for women's right to separate estates. The chancery, or equity, courts gave married women the rights to own, devise, convey, and manage property. This was, in the words of legal scholar Marilynn Salmon, "a radical breakthrough for women. It was the most significant change in the legal status of women until the advent of the married women's property acts of the nineteenth century." But for the majority of women, such protection was inaccessible, since the rules were not defined by statutes, and few had the knowledge or money to fight in court for their rights.

See also Doctrine of Agency; Doctrine of Intentions; Doctrine of Necessities; Equity Law.

Chapman, Maria Weston (1806–1885)

Maria Chapman was an author and a leading abolitionist. She was born 25 July 1806 in Weymouth, Massachusetts, but was educated in England. In 1828, she moved back to the United States and became "lady principal" of a girls' school in Boston. After marrying Henry G. Chapman in 1830, she left the school. Influenced by reformer William Lloyd Garrison, the Chapmans became abolitionists, a highly unpopular act at the time. In 1832, Maria Chapman helped organize the Boston Female Anti-Slavery Society, which gathered signatures for petitions demanding the end of slavery in the District of Columbia, and which favored the education of free African-American men and women in Boston. When William Lloyd Garrison was threatened by a mob while trying to address the Boston Female Anti-Slavery Society in 1835, Chapman calmly moved the meeting to her home. Later, she became a leader of the Massachusetts Anti-Slavery Society and worked as an editor on Garrison's *The Liberator*. In 1836, Chapman published *Songs of the Free and Hymns of Christian Freedom*. She welcomed Sarah and Angelina Grimké to New England in 1837 and publicized their antislavery lectures. In May 1838, in Philadelphia, she spoke at the second national female antislavery convention while a mob (which next day burned down the hall) raged outside. The next year she tried to influence the Boston Female Anti-Slavery Society to back the Garrison wing of the antislavery movement. Her publication, *Right and Wrong in Massachusetts* (1839), concerned the subsequent split among the abolitionists.

In 1840, Chapman became an executive board member of the American Anti-Slavery Society, assisting Garrison with its journal, *National Anti-Slavery Standard*. Four years later she became the journal's coeditor, an unusual position for a woman. From 1839 to 1846 she edited *Liberty Bell*, an annual gift book, the proceeds from the sale of which supported abolition work. From 1839 to 1842 she edited *Non-Resistant*, the publication of Garrison's New England Non-Resistance Society. Chapman lived in Paris from 1848 to 1855. Upon her return to Boston she published *How Can I Help Abolish Slavery?* (1855). After the Emancipation Proclamation and the passage of the Thirteenth Amendment, Chapman joined Garrison in wanting to disband the antislavery societies. However, the societies continued advocating the rights of African Americans. Chapman died in Weymouth on 12 July 1885.

See also Female Antislavery Societies; Garrison, William Lloyd.

Chesler, Phyllis (1940–)

Psychologist Phyllis Chesler's *Women and Madness* (1972) was one of the most influen-

tial works to emerge from the women's liberation movement. The book argues that sex-role stereotypes cause much of what society calls mental illness. Both men in general and male therapists criticize women's independent and assertive behavior, maintaining a double standard for men's and women's health. Women who are strong, assertive, or ambitious are considered abnormal, even mad. Likewise, normal feminine behavior is considered sick in a male, which leads the man to depression and mental illness. The book rapidly became influential in the women's movement, selling more than 1.5 million copies. Chesler also wrote *Women, Money and Power* (1976), *About Men* (1978), *With Child* (1979), and *Sacred Bond: The Legacy of Baby M.* (1988).

Chesnut, Mary Boykin Miller (1823–1886)

Mary Chesnut, a diarist, is one of the few female authors from the Civil War period whose nonfiction is still considered important today. Born 31 March 1823, near Camden, South Carolina, she attended a girls school in Charleston. In 1840 she married James Chesnut, who became a senator and aide to Confederate General P. G. T. Beauregard. She traveled with her husband, a general in command of the South Carolina reserves, and knew many of the Confederacy leaders. Yet Mary Chesnut was critical of southern faults and deplored slavery. Her diary, which she began when South Carolina seceded from the Union, is valued by historians for its intelligent detail of observation. Chesnut died in Camden 22 November 1886, leaving her diary to a friend. Portions of the diary were published in 1903 and 1949. The authoritative version, *Mary Chesnut's Civil War* (1981), edited by C. Vann Woodward, won the Pulitzer Prize in 1982. Filled with unguarded comments, including how women of both races felt about one another, Chesnut's diary is a standard reference about plantation life during the Civil War.

Chicago, Judy (1939–)

Judy Chicago, the feminist artist, cofounded the Woman's Building in Los Angeles and helped to bring female imagery into the art. Born Judy Cohen on 20 June 1939 in Chicago, she received her B.A. in 1962 and M.A. in 1964 from U.C.L.A. In 1970, she changed her name as a symbol of resistance to male authority. Chicago established the women's art program at Fresno State College in California and, in 1972, helped mount "Womanhouse" in Los Angeles, a show that attracted 10,000 people. Also in that year, she organized a nationwide conference for women artists. In 1973, Chicago set up the Woman's Building, providing space for theater groups and exhibition areas for writers, painters, etc.

Judy Chicago

Chicago's most famous piece is *The Dinner Party*, in which images of the vagina and flowers are combined in a work of 39 china plates on textile runners covering an open, triangular table. Her *Heritage Floor* features 2,300 porcelain tiles bearing the names of 999 women of history; more than 250 women and men worked on this project. *The Birth Project*, a series of tapestry works celebrating birth and assembled by a team of women artists, was exhibited in 1984. She is the author of several books about her work, including *The Dinner Party* (1979), *Through the Flower* (1975), and *The Birth Project* (1985).

See also Feminist Art Program.

Child, Lydia Maria Francis (1802–1880)

Lydia Child, a best-selling author, risked her reputation to support abolition. She was born 11 February 1802, in Medford, Massachusetts. The daughter of abolitionists, she had some schooling and also taught school before publishing her first book, *Hobomok* (1824), a re-creation of early life in the Salem and Plymouth colonies. Her second book, *The Rebels, or Boston before the Revolution*, was published in 1825. From 1825 to 1828, she ran a private school in Watertown, Massachusetts, and launched the nation's first children's magazine, *Juvenile Miscellany* (1826). In 1828 she married David L. Child, through whom she met, in 1831, the great abolitionist William Lloyd Garrison. By this time Child had become well known for her best-selling books of advice, including *The Frugal Housewife* (1829) and *The Mother's Books* (1831).

She sacrificed her reputation as a writer when she turned her attention to the reform of slavery laws, publishing *An Appeal in Favor of That Class of Americans Called Africans* (1833). Among other things, the book called for the education of African Americans. It created an uproar. Child's membership in the Boston Athenaeum was rescinded because of the publication, the *Juvenile Miscellany* folded, and sales of her books plummeted. Nevertheless, the *Appeal* brought new attention to the issue of slavery. In 1836, her novel *Philothea* restored some of her prior success. Four years later she was elected to the executive committee of the American Anti-Slavery Society. Lydia Child edited the organization's weekly New York periodical, the *National Anti-Slavery*

Standard, from 1841 to 1843, and her husband edited it the following year.

Between 1843 and 1845 Child wrote a series of columns for a Boston newspaper, collected in two volumes of *Letters from New York*, which were very widely read. Ever the activist, Child attempted in 1859 to minister to John Brown in prison after his raid on Harper's Ferry. Again she became the center of public debate. Her response was to publish *The Duty of Disobedience to the Fugitive Slave Act, The Patriarchal Institution*, and *The Right Way, the Safe Way*, all in 1860. In 1861 she edited *Incidents in the Life of a Slave Girl*, a book of the memories of ex-slave Harriet Jacobs. Child edited three volumes of *Flowers for Children* (1844–1847), and wrote *Fact and Fiction* (1846), *The Progress of Religious Ideas through Successive Ages* (1855), *Autumnal Leaves* (1857), *The Freedman's Book* (1865), *An Appeal for the Indians* (1868), and *Aspirations of the World* (1878). Though she did not write directly about women's issues or contribute to any women's organization, Child advocated greater equality between the sexes. After a lifetime of acting on her beliefs despite public opinion, Child died in Wayland, Massachusetts, on 20 October 1880.

Child Custody

Historically, under common law, fathers automatically gained custody of their children after a divorce. This unfairness surrounding child custody law was among the specific grievances cited in 1848 by the women of Seneca Falls in the Declaration of Rights and Sentiments. However, changes in custody law began with *Commonwealth v. Addicks* (1813), when a Pennsylvania court first raised the "tender-years doctrine," giving a mother temporary custody while upholding the idea that the father had primary rights to the child. By 1860, New Jersey had codified the doctrine, so that prepubescent children would be placed with the mother unless she was unfit. With *McKim v. McKim* (1879), which established the "best-interests-of-the-child" doctrine, courts began treating women as separate

legal entities from their husbands, seeing them as best able to care for the emotional needs of their offspring. By the turn of the century, most separated or divorced mothers received custody of their children. Today, statutes in many states mandate some form of joint custody. In addition, more men are fighting for custodial rights to their children. According to Phyllis Chesler's book *Sacred Bond*, between 10 and 15 percent of all divorces now involve a major custody battle. In 1986, the New York State Task Force on Women and the Courts published a study on sex bias in courtrooms, concluding that when fathers contest custody, "they win as often as mothers do." This opinion is supported by a study published in the *Family Law Quarterly* (1984) and by research conducted by Phyllis Chesler (1986) showing that fathers now win custody 62 to 70 percent of the time, when they contest custody at trial. Nonetheless, most young children are still awarded to mothers, who are, however, seeing their incomes decline due to no-fault divorce laws while their financial burdens increase. Within the last decade judges have also opened their eyes to the existence of nontraditional families, such as homosexual couples, interpreting what is in the best interests of the child in a broader way than ever before.

See also The Baby M Case; Declaration of Sentiments; Divorce; Seneca Falls Convention.

Child Support

In colonial America fathers were theoretically obliged to support their offspring. In reality, men often escaped the arm of the law, leaving mothers to support their children alone. Throughout American history, child support payments awarded by the courts have been insubstantial and difficult to collect. However, by the mid-twentieth century, reforms were underway. The Revised Uniform Reciprocal Enforcement of Support Act was passed by Congress in 1968 and adopted in 35 states. It has helped mothers collect child support payments across state lines by filing a simple petition in their home states. If payment is not forthcoming, the court can order a contempt citation and, ultimately, a jail sentence.

Yet, despite such laws, the 1975 International Women's Commission reported that only 44 percent of divorced mothers were awarded child support by the courts. Further, less than half of these women received their support regularly. Court-awarded payments were usually less than enough to provide one-half of a child's support. Most states still hold men responsible for child support. Nevertheless, according to legal historian Joan Hoff, of the 78 percent of all divorced women with children who were awarded child support in 1985, only 48 percent received the full amount; 25.8 percent received partial payment; and 26 percent none at all. Hoff goes on to report that although the average amount each woman received was $2,538, courts are less generous when ordering child support to mothers who are poor or never married.

In 1984, Congress passed the Child Support Enforcement Amendments to help women secure court-ordered child support payments. The amendments, part of Title IV-D of the Social Security Act, have helped to prosecute delinquent fathers across state lines; they require states receiving federal welfare funds to enforce court-ordered child support payments. Despite these attempts, children still suffer because of delinquent child support payments or inadequate awards, and public policy has not adequately addressed this problem. As of 1994, hundreds of child support cases were turned over to the Internal Revenue Service under a pilot project to collect money from delinquent parents. The project applies to child support cases with an average debt of $21,000. President Bill Clinton hopes that under his proposed welfare reform legislation sweeping improvements can also be made in the child support enforcement system.

Chisholm, Shirley St. Hill (1924–)

Former congresswoman Shirley S. Chisholm is the first African-American woman elected to Congress, as well as the first African American and the first woman to serve on the House Rules Committee. She was born 30 November 1924 in Brooklyn, New York, and spent her childhood in Barbados, where she learned to read at the age of three and one-half. Chisholm returned to the United States to attend high school and then enrolled in Brooklyn College. She graduated cum laude with a degree

Shirley Chisolm

in sociology in 1945, later earning an M.A. in education from Columbia University. In 1949 she married Conrad Q. Chisholm. Four years later, she became the head of a primary school in the Bronxville section of Brooklyn. The next year she became director of the Hamilton-Madison Child Care Center, a position she held until 1959. In 1964, Chisholm was elected to represent Brooklyn in the state assembly, becoming the first African-American woman to represent the district. There, she supported education bills for young and college-bound children. (She was reelected in 1965 and 1966.) In 1968, she ran successfully for the

U.S. House of Representatives, joining the House Education and Labor Committee in 1971. In Congress, she fought for increased welfare for the poor, a cut in defense spending, and encouraged women to enter politics. In 1972, she made an unsuccessful bid for the Democratic party presidential nomination and, in 1976, began serving on the House Rules Committee. In 1983 Chisholm became a professor at Mount Holyoke College. She is the author of *Unbought and Unbossed* (1970) and *The Good Fight* (1973).

See also National Women's Political Caucus.

Chodorow, Nancy (1944–)

Born 20 January 1944 in New York City, sociologist Nancy Chodorow wrote one of the twentieth century's most important works on motherhood and the development of personality, *The Reproduction of Mothering: Psychoanalysis and the Sociology of Gender* (1978). In it, she argues that women's exclusive role as mother creates a "psychology of male dominance and fear of women in men." It also leads to an unequal society in which women perform the less valued domestic work and men perform the highly valued public work. In *The Reproduction of Mothering*, Chodorow also analyzes the process of separating from the mother, which is different for girls and boys. Among her conclusions is that men and women must share parental responsibilities for the health of their children.

Chopin, Kate O'Flaherty (1851–1904)

Kate Chopin is best remembered for *The Awakening*, a novel that horrified its readers with its account of a woman's mixed-race affair and suicide. Chopin was born 8 February 1851 in St. Louis, Missouri, the daughter of Irishman Thomas O'Flaherty and Eliza Faris, of Creole background. In 1870 she married Oscar Chopin and went with him to New Orleans. There, she gave birth to six children. In 1882, after her husband's death, she returned to St. Louis, where at the age of 37 she began her career

as a writer. Her first novel, *At Fault* (1890), was followed by more than 100 short stories, some of which were collected in *Bayou Folk* (1894) and *A Night in Acadie* (1897). In 1899 Chopin published her second novel, *The Awakening*, which is considered her best work. Set in the Creole society of New Orleans, it is the story of Edna Pontellier's sexual and artistic strivings. After witnessing a friend's painful experience giving birth and being abandoned by her Creole lover, Pontellier drowns herself. Critical reaction was severe: condemned by many readers and reviewers as moral poison, the book was banned from libraries, and Chopin was rejected by many of her former acquaintances. She died in St. Louis on 22 August 1904.

Citizens' Advisory Council on the Status of Women

In December 1961 President John F. Kennedy created the President's Commission on the Status of Women, or the Kennedy Commission. The commission's report, *American Women*, suggested that Kennedy establish a Citizens' Advisory Council on the Status of Women made up of 20 private citizens. Kennedy acted quickly on the suggestion, authorizing the advisory council just days before his assassination. In conjunction with the Interdepartmental Commission on the Status of Women (also established by Kennedy), the advisory council sponsored national conferences of state commissions on the status of women and published progress reports on women's issues. In 1965, an advisory council paper submitted to the Equal Employment Opportunity Commission urged that, except in very rare cases, employers should not be permitted to discriminate. The paper also favored outlawing sex-segregated want-ad columns. In 1966, the council established task forces in the areas of health and welfare, Social Security and taxes, labor standards, and family law and policy. Over the years, some of the council's other proposals have included legalization of abortion, sex-blind alimony laws, equal property rights for wives, passage of the Equal Rights Amendment, the treatment of pregnancy as merely a temporary disability, and equal rights for illegitimate children. The establishment of the council was one of the greatest achievements of the President's Commission on the Status of Women. Perhaps because it was comprised of private citizens, it was able to make bold recommendations, which could not have originated from a body of government officials. The council survived until 1977, when it was replaced by a similar body (which lasted only until the administration of Ronald Reagan came into power).

See also Citizens' Advisory Council on the Status of Women; President's Commission on the Status of Women.

City of Akron v. Akron Center for Reproductive Health

In 1983, in *City of Akron v. Akron Center for Reproductive Health*, the U.S. Supreme Court overturned an Akron, Ohio, ordinance that required abortions after the first trimester be performed in hospitals and that women be forced to wait 24 hours before having an abortion. The Akron decision, unlike some Supreme Court decisions in the preceding years, endorsed *Roe v. Wade*. The decision outraged antiabortion activists.

See also Abortion; *Planned Parenthood of Central Missouri v. Danforth; Planned Parenthood of Southeastern Pennsylvania v. Casey; Roe v. Wade; Webster v. Reproductive Health Services.*

Civil Rights Act of 1964

See Title VII of the 1964 Civil Rights Act.

Civil Rights Restoration Act of 1988 Antiabortion Clause

See Antiabortion Clause of the 1988 Civil Rights Restoration Act.

Claflin, Tennessee Celeste (1845–1923)

Tennessee Claflin and her sister Victoria (1838–1927) were renowned in their day as the "Queens of Finance." As the country's first "lady brokers," the sisters made history by founding the brokerage firm of Woodhull, Claflin & Co. Their newspaper, *Woodhull & Claflin's Weekly*, was devoted to feminism, spiritualism, the same moral code for men and women, free love, liberalized divorce laws, legalized prostitution, and dress and tax reform.

Tennie Celeste Claflin was born 26 October 1845 in Homer, Ohio, and would later take the name Tennessee, a compound of Tennie and her middle initial C. She was educated intermittently as her family moved about the Midwest, selling elixirs and psychic cures. Her sense of showmanship and ability to arrange séances for her sister Victoria helped to establish the family fortune-telling show. At 15 Victoria married Dr. Canning Woodhull, whose name she used after their divorce in 1864. As adults, the sisters continued the family tradition.

In 1870, the sisters established their brokerage firm in New York, which was backed by Commodore Cornelius Vanderbilt. Though successful at first, the business was damaged by the sisters' public lives. In 1871, Woodhull announced for president and began to publish *Woodhull & Claflin's Weekly*. On 2 November 1872, a special issue of the *Weekly* revealed that Henry Ward Beecher, the most famous preacher of his day and an ardent suffragist, had dozens of mistresses, among them Elizabeth ("Lib") Tilton, the wife of his best friend, Theodore Tilton, another suffragist. Under the notorious Comstock Act, the post office refused to mail the magazine, and the sisters were arrested for attempting to mail obscene materials; both were acquitted seven months later.

In 1877, Claflin and Woodhull moved to England. There, in 1885, Claflin married Francis Cook; the following year she became Lady Cook. With her sister she wrote *The Human Body, the Temple of God* (1890). Her shrewdness and flair for publicity ensured an audience for her unconventional ideas. She died in London on 18 January 1923.

See also Woodhull, Victoria.

65

Clarke, James Freeman (1810–1888)

James Freeman Clarke was a clergyman and social reformer. He was born 4 April 1810, in Hanover, New Hampshire, and attended Harvard Divinity School. Ordained in Boston, 21 July 1833, he left to head a Unitarian congregation in Louisville, Kentucky, which was then a slave state. There, Clarke immediately began working for the abolition of slavery. In 1840, he returned to Boston, where he founded the Church of the Disciples, which brought together women and men whose goal was to apply the ideals of Christianity to contemporary social problems. Clarke served as minister of the church from 1841 to 1850, later teaching at Harvard from 1867 to 1871. Clarke was a courageous reformer on the leading moral questions of the time, believing in the broadest application of human rights. He believed that the woman's sphere should be extended to the public arena. In *Woman Suffrage Leaflet 2, No. 14*, published 15 February 1889, he wrote, "One of the most important of the reforms proposed at the present time is that which shall give the suffrage to women. It is not merely a political question, but a social question, a moral question, and a religious question." A poet as well as a scholar, Clarke's best-known work is *Ten Great Religions* (1871–1883). He died 8 June 1888.

Clay, Laura (1849–1941)

Suffrage leader Laura Clay was born 9 February 1849 in White Hall, Kentucky. Her father, a relative of Henry Clay, founded the first antislavery newspaper in Kentucky, *True American*. Laura Clay attended Sayre Institute, graduating in 1865. She briefly attended the University of Michigan (1880) and the State College of Kentucky (1885–1886). She was introduced to the women's movement by her older sister, Mary Clay Herrick, who formed the first women's suffrage club in Kentucky. In 1881, Clay was elected president of the newly formed Kentucky Woman Suffrage Association, a position she held until 1912. (The organization was renamed the Kentucky Equal Rights Association in 1888.) Under her guidance the group succeeded in repealing several Kentucky laws that discriminated against women, including those that denied married women the right to own separate estates or make wills. In 1895 Clay joined the board of the National American Woman Suffrage Association (NAWSA), but in 1911 she was not reelected, in part due to her opposition to the drive for a federal suffrage amendment. For years, the national organization supported winning suffrage through state action, a position that encouraged Southerners in the belief that the vote for women would help maintain white supremacy. But the policy changed with the rise of Carrie Chapman and Anna Howard Shaw to the leadership of the NAWSA. In 1913, Clay became vice-president of the Southern States Woman Suffrage Conference, a group that worked for state suffrage. During the next two years she lobbied against an amendment to the Constitution in favor of a law that allowed women to vote in congressional elections if they met the voter requirements of their state. Such a law was proposed in Congress but failed to pass. This issue estranged her from the mainstream women's suffrage movement.

In addition to her suffrage activities, Clay was an early advocate of separate courts for juvenile offenders. Also active in other political arenas, Clay was a member of the Woman's Peace Party from 1915 to 1917. At the age of 74, Clay ran unsuccessfully for the Tennessee senate, and in 1928 she campaigned for Democratic presidential candidate Alfred E. Smith. In 1933, at the age of 84, she was elected to the Tennessee convention that ratified the Twenty-first Amendment, which repealed Prohibition. Clay devoted the last decade of her life to expanding the opportunities for women in churches and universities. She died in Lexington on 29 June 1941.

See also Catt, Carrie Clinton Lane Chapman; Shaw, Anna Howard.

Clergy Consultation Service on Abortion

The Rev. Howard Moody, a New York City minister, founded the Clergy Consultation Service on Abortion in 1967. At the time of its founding, the organization comprised 22 ministers and rabbis who offered free advice and assistance to women seeking abortions. In the years following the group's founding, the Rev. Moody organized a national network of clergy referral services with 1,000 counselors in 24 states. With most abortions illegal at the time, all persons doing referrals risked arrest. The greatest contribution of the Clergy Consultation Service was perhaps the degree of respectability it lent the movement to legalize abortion. The service ended with the 1973 *Roe v. Wade* decision.

See also Abortion; *Roe v. Wade*.

Clerical Work

At the turn of the twentieth century, almost all working women were domestics, farm workers, teachers, or factory operators. But by the 1930s, the number of female clerical workers dramatically increased. In 1920, according to historian William Chafe, 500,000 women—mostly white, single, and middle class—worked as stenographers, typists, or file clerks. This was the first time, according to labor historian Alice Kessler-Harris, that the percentage of women working in white-collar jobs (25.6) was higher than the percentage in manufacturing (23.8), domestic service (23.8), or farm labor (12.9). By 1930, the number of female clerical workers had climbed to about two million, and by 1940 clerical work had become the dominant category of employment for white women.

Wars create paperwork, and the federal government creates most of that paperwork, so it is not surprising that, between 1940 and 1945, the number of female clerical workers employed by the federal government doubled, constituting 38 percent of all federal employees by 1945. In the years following World War II, greater numbers of women than ever before joined the labor force—in sex-segregated jobs, such as clerical work. Between 1940 and 1960, according to Chafe, the number of working women doubled, and the median age of female workers was 41. The number of working mothers jumped 400 percent, from 1.5 million in 1940 to 6.6 million in 1960. Although, before World War II, most married working women belonged to the working class, by 1960 middle-class married women were just as likely to be employed. The expansion of white-collar work was partly responsible for the revolution in female employment. Some historians argue that women were unable to advance in these jobs, accepting low pay for white-collar status. Other historians point out that female clerical workers displayed a stronger commitment to stay in the work force than ever before in U.S. history, remaining for longer and longer periods after marriage; this in itself, they say, constitutes progress.

See also Business and Professional Women; Domestic Service.

Clinton, Hillary Rodham (1947–)

Hillary Rodham Clinton holds the most powerful post ever assigned to a president's wife: chair of the President's Task Force on National Health Reform. She was born 26 October 1947 in Chicago. By the time she was 16 years old, she had organized a neighborhood Olympics, child care for migrant workers, and a voter registration project. Rodham attended Wellesley College, where she was president of the student government and the first student to speak at a commencement (1969), for which she was pictured in *Life*. She attended law school at Yale, where she was an editor of *The Yale Review of Law and Social Action*.

After receiving a law degree in 1973, she worked in Washington, D.C., as a staff attorney for the Children's Defense Fund, a nonprofit organization that protects the rights of children. She worked for the National Women's Education Fund and served as counsel on the House Judiciary Committee that considered the impeachment of

President Richard Nixon. In 1974, she left Washington to join her law school classmate Bill Clinton, who was teaching law at the University of Arkansas. There, she taught law and ran a legal aid clinic. The two were married in 1975. In 1977, she founded the Arkansas Advocates for Children and Families.

The following year, Bill Clinton was elected governor of Arkansas. After the couple's move to the state capital, Rodham joined the prestigious Rose Law Firm, of which she later became a partner. Twice she has been named one of "The 100 Most Influential Lawyers in America" by the *National Law Journal* (1988 and 1991). In 1980, she gave birth to the couple's daughter, Chelsea. From 1983 to 1984, she chaired the board of directors of the Arkansas Education Standards Committee, whose work led to new accreditation standards for Arkansas public schools that were later replicated elsewhere throughout the nation.

Rodham maintained her interest in children's rights, chairing the Board of the Children's Defense Fund from 1986 to 1992. She also served on the boards of the Children's Television Workshop and the Child Action Campaign. Between 1987 and 1992, she was chair of the American Bar Association's Commission on Women in the Profession. Yet, despite her accomplishments, Hillary Rodham Clinton's career and abilities became an issue for some Americans during her husband's campaign for president of the United States. After President Bill Clinton was inaugurated on 20 January 1993, Hillary Rodham Clinton set up her office in the West Wing of the White House, near the president's senior staff advisors. This was a departure from tradition; other first ladies established their offices in the East Wing.

On 25 January 1993, President Clinton appointed his wife to chair the President's Task Force on National Health Reform, saying, "She's better at organizing and leading people from a complex beginning to a certain end than anybody I've ever worked with in my life." However, Hillary Rodham Clinton's impact on the job of first lady cannot be fully evaluated by historians until Bill Clinton completes his term of office.

Coalition for Women's Appointments
See National Women's Political Caucus.

Code Napoléon
The first code of French civil law was called the Code Civil des Français. Made law 31 March 1804, it was renamed Code Napoléon in 1807 and has had various names since (for example, after 1870 it was called the Code Civil). The great accomplishment of the Code Napoléon was its blending of ancient French law with that of the French Revolution (1789). It reformed laws governing the individual, real property, inheritance, and mortgages. The clarity of its provisions and the spirit of equality that inspired them made the code a model for other nations. However, the code's creators could not foresee the revolutionary changes in economic and social relations that took place in the nineteenth century. Provisions that dealt with the legal relations between the sexes were discriminatory: for example, a married woman's property and earnings belonged to her husband. In French-dominated Louisiana, the discriminatory provisions meant that, as historian Eleanor Flexner points out, "a married woman did not even have legal title to the clothes she wore." Nevertheless a somewhat reformed Code Napoléon remains the basis of the law in Continental Europe and Louisiana.
See also Common Law; Divorce.

Coercion
A recognized legal problem during the seventeenth and eighteenth centuries, coercion was the practice of husbands forcing their wives to execute deeds to property jointly owned, although controlled by the husband. Because the practice was a familiar one, courts sought ways to protect women. The

most important protective measure was private questioning of the wife by a justice, during which the wife could withdraw her consent if she had been coerced by her husband. In many regions the courts gradually strengthened the formal procedures regulating a wife's consent.

See also Bethune v. Beresford; Carroll v. Warren; Flanagan's Lessee v. Young.

Collar Trade

The most common home-manufacturing trade for women in the nineteenth century was sewing for the ready-made clothing industry. Manufacturers delivered raw materials to women in their homes and later picked up the finished products. In the early nineteenth century, native-born white women worked in this industry, but by mid-century the work was considered less respectable and was done only by the poorest women. In large cities, such as New York and Chicago, companies bought up blocks of tenements and leased them to workers. Women and children labored in these sweatshops for starvation wages.

Troy, New York, was the Collar and Cuff Capital of the United States. During the late nineteenth century, the Troy Collar Laundry Union (TCLU) was formed for women who made, laundered, and ironed detachable collars for men's shirts. Under the leadership of Kate Mullaney, the union became the best-known women's union of its day. In 1866, it won a wage increase of $6 per week, a 75 percent increase. That year, the union also donated $1,000 to the striking Iron Molders' Union. In 1868, Mullaney became assistant secretary of the National Labor Union. In 1869 the TCLU struck again and, to pressure the manufacturers, formed a cooperative laundry operated by union members. The collective failed, and the union went into a rapid decline. Factors contributing to the union's failure were the introduction of paper collars and a sudden loss of support and money from male unions, which were also in disarray. In 1870 the union was dissolved.

College Equal Suffrage League
See Park, Maud May Wood.

Committee for Abortion Rights and against Sterilization Abuse (CARASA)

The Committee for Abortion Rights and against Sterilization Abuse (CARASA) was formed in 1977 in New York City by radical and socialist feminists. In 1978, in conjunction with the National Women's Health Network, CARASA persuaded New York City to develop sterilization guidelines that were tougher than the guidelines released by the Department of Health, Education and Welfare (HEW) in 1974. As a direct result of CARASA lobbying efforts, HEW revised its guidelines to be more like the stricter New York City guidelines. CARASA is still active.

The problem of sterilization abuse is one with which many white women are unfamiliar, but one which women of color maintain is not uncommon, even in modern times. Some activists charge that it is particularly serious in the South. Supplying incorrect information is one of the principal methods of coercing women to be sterilized. Specifically, these misrepresentations include exaggerations of the physical dangers of a future pregnancy; the claim that if a woman failed to agree to sterilization, welfare benefits would be lost; and the characterization of the effects of the operation as not necessarily permanent. An incident occurred in Alabama in 1973 that involved the improper sterilization of two African-American minor sisters without the informed consent of their mother. This led to a class action suit on behalf of the many individuals who claimed to be victims of sterilization abuse. The original (1974) HEW guidelines were formulated in response to this event; these guidelines required (1) a three-day waiting period between the signing of consent and the performing of the operation, and (2) informing the woman of the permanent nature of the surgery's results. However, lack of sufficient enforcement and the absence of a requirement that women be able to comprehend consent forms made revisions in the guidelines necessary.

Common Law

In the seventeenth century, English common law prevailed in the American colonies. Derived from broad principles of justice and common sense, rather than rules, common law is the system of law on which the U.S. legal codes are based. Under common law married women had no more rights than children or idiots. A married couple was considered one person under the law, and that person was the husband. A married woman could own no property or money—including her own wages—and could not inherit. She could not make contracts, nor sue or be sued. She had no right to custody of her children. A wife could not even buy or sell anything without her husband's permission. After marriage, a wife became what was called a *feme covert* (one protected—"covered"—by her husband). In 1632, *The Lawes Resolutions of Women Rights; or The Lawes Provision for Women* explained the term as follows:

When a small brooke or little river incorporateth with Rhodanus, Humber or the Thames, the poor rivulet looseth its name, it is carried and recarried with the new associate, it beareth no sway, it possesseth nothing during coverture. A woman as soon as she is married, is called *covert*, in Latin, *nupta*, that is, *veiled*, as it were, clouded and overshadowed. . . . To a married woman, her new self is her superior, her companion, her master.

By contrast a single woman, or *feme sole*, retained her property rights but, against all logic, had no political rights.

Common law did offer one major protection to married women: a widow's dower right to one-third of her husband's property; however, after the American Revolution this protection eroded. During the 1830s, as the economy worsened and women became more publicly active, women's inability to control property became increasingly unpopular. When a dead man's assets were collected to pay his debts, a wife's property was seized as well, and increasing numbers of widows were suddenly left on the dole. Their dependence on public alms gave men a reason to revise the law, as did fathers' desires to preserve their daughters' inheritance, and states began to pass laws giving married women control over property they brought into a marriage or earned after it. The New York Married Woman's Property Act of 1848 is perhaps the best known.

In the first quarter of the twentieth century, some remnants of the common law served to discriminate against women. For instance, some states allowed husbands to control a wife's earnings, excluded women from juries, made women responsible for children born out of wedlock, and limited a widow's inheritance to one-third of her husband's estate. It took the better part of the century for these laws to be eradicated.

See also Beale v. King and Woolford; Chancery Courts; Code Napoléon; *Feme Covert; Feme Sole;* Married Women's Property Acts; New York Married Woman's Property Act (1848).

Commonwealth v. Jane Daniels

Commonwealth v. Jane Daniels (Pennsylvania, 1968) outlawed sex discrimination in the sentencing of female criminals. In 1966 Jane Daniels was convicted of robbery. Sentenced under Pennsylvania's Muncy Act (1913), which in effect caused women to receive longer prison terms than men for the same criminal offense, Daniels received a longer sentence than her male partner in the robbery. The Pennsylvania Superior Court upheld her sentence in 1967, but the following year the Pennsylvania Supreme Court overruled the lower court decisions and overturned the Muncy Act as well. As a result, the prison terms of many women who were sentenced under the Muncy Act were reviewed. The case was one of the earliest and most celebrated successes in the drive for the equitable treatment of women in the criminal justice system.

Comparable Worth

Feminists introduced the concept of comparable worth during the 1970s in an attempt to correct persistent sex-based pay inequities. They pointed out that discrimination against women resulted not only in paying women less than men for identical work (a problem that was remedied with legislation in the 1960s) but has also resulted in lower wages in female-dominated professions than in male-dominated professions, even when the professions demand equivalent levels of skill. These professions include teaching, nursing, office, and retail work. A comparable male-dominated profession would be vocational teaching.

Advocates of comparable worth have proposed adjusting wages through legislation, thereby generating a great deal of controversy. Opponents of such proposals say they interfere in what should be a free market, point to individual responsibility for choosing a career, and claim that occupations cannot be compared or assigned absolute worth. Advocates of comparable worth, on the other hand, point to societal limitations and pressures that steer women toward lower paying jobs, cite the effectiveness of job evaluation systems, and point out that employers themselves sometimes interfere with free market principles in determining wages. In establishing pay equity, employers assign a numerical value to skills and other factors required to do a given job and compare these to rankings for other positions. Equal pay is established for each job with the same score. New Mexico, Washington, Connecticut, Idaho, Iowa, and Minnesota have enacted pay equity legislation, as have various municipalities, such as Los Angeles. Nonetheless, the concept remains a controversial one.

See also American Federation of State, County and Municipal Employees v. State of Washington; Brown and Sharp Manufacturing Case.

Complex Marriage

See Noyes, John Humphrey; Utopian Communities.

Comstock, Ada Louise (1876–1973)

The first full-time president of Radcliffe College, Ada Louise Comstock was born 11 December 1876 in Moorhead, Minnesota. She received a bachelor's degree from Smith College in 1897 (after attending the University of Minnesota from 1892 to 1894) and a master's degree from Columbia University in 1899. From 1900 to 1912 she taught at the University of Minnesota, becoming, in 1907, the first dean of women and the school's only female administrator. In 1912 she became the first dean of Smith College; although she headed the college admirably as acting president (1917–1918), she was denied the title of president because she was a woman. However, she continued at Smith until 1923, when she was appointed president of Radcliffe College. Comstock built a close relationship with Harvard, drawing upon Harvard's ranks of professors to teach at Radcliffe and instituting joint projects. In addition, she instituted programs that transformed Radcliffe from a small women's college to a major national university.

Comstock was active in public as well as educational affairs. In 1921, she became the first president of the American Association of University Women, a position she held until 1923. In 1929, she became the only woman on the National Commission of Law Observance (the Wickersham Commission), which, among other things, called for modification of the Eighteenth Amendment. In 1941, she joined the National Committee for Planned Parenthood. In 1943, one week after retiring from Radcliffe, she married Yale scholar Wallace Notestein. Over her lifetime, Comstock fought sex discrimination in its many forms, including jury duty, education, or the work place. She served as a role model for college-educated women. She died in New Haven on 12 December 1973.

Comstock, Elizabeth Leslie Rous (1815–1891)

Elizabeth Rous Comstock was one of the most renowned Quaker women of the nineteenth century. Born 30 October 1815 in Maidenhead, England, she taught in Quaker schools before her marriage to Leslie Wright (1848), who died three years after their marriage. In 1854 she moved to Canada, where she was a shopkeeper. There she met and married John T. Comstock (1858), moving with him to his home in Rollin, Michigan, a station on the Underground Railroad. Elizabeth Comstock soon became a minister who advocated abolition, and her gift for preaching made her a popular speaker throughout Michigan. She also advocated temperance, women's rights, peace, prison reform, and other causes. In 1864, she and several other Quakers met with President Lincoln in an encounter that evolved into a Quaker-style prayer meeting in which the president participated. Throughout the Civil War, Comstock aided sick and imprisoned slaves. Later she raised money for freed men and women, serving for two years as secretary of the Kansas Freedmen's Relief Association. Comstock spearheaded an early form of "home mission" welfare, which benefited impoverished women and children in the growing cities. In 1885 she moved to Union Springs, New York, where she died 3 August 1891.

See also Abolition Movement.

Comstock Act

After the Civil War, a conservative shift in public opinion led to the passage of the Comstock Act (1873), which used the post office to suppress the circulation of "obscene" materials. The Comstock Act stifled the dissemination of information about birth control and contraception, including advertisements in newspapers. Anthony Comstock, after whom the law was named, was born in New Canaan, Connecticut, in 1844, and joined the Union Army to take the place of his younger brother. In 1872 he won the backing of the YMCA in a crusade against pornography. Founder of the New York Society for the Suppression of Vice, and a special investigator for the New York City post office, Comstock originated a drive in New York for the suppression of vice, securing in 1869 a statewide law that prohibited traffic in abortion and birth control. In persuading Congress in 1873 to pass the federal obscenity law, he displayed piles of pornography, contraceptives, and abortifacients, tying them to "immorality." His efforts resulted in the trial (1873) of Victoria Woodhull and Tennessee Claflin for attempting to mail issues of *Woodhull & Claflin's Weekly* in which they exposed an affair between Henry Ward Beecher and Elizabeth Tilton and led to the arrest of Margaret Sanger (1916) for distributing birth control information. Spoofing Comstock's efforts, George Bernard Shaw coined the term comstockery. In 1936, Margaret Sanger's Committee on Federal Legislation for Birth Control succeeded *(United States v. One Package)* in revising the law to permit doctors to import and prescribe contraceptive devices. This paved the way for the American Medical Association's decision (1937) that birth control is a medical service that

Anthony Comstock

could be taught in schools of medicine. But not until 1971 was this notorious law rewritten to remove the specific mention of birth control material.

See also Birth Control; Claflin, Tennessee; Contraception; Sanger, Margaret; Woodhull, Victoria.

Congress To Unite Women

On 1–3 May 1969, the Congress To Unite Women was held in New York City, its aim to create a unified women's liberation movement. Moderate to radical women's groups attended, from the National Organization for Women to the Redstockings. The resolutions passed by groups at the conference included passage of the Equal Rights Amendment, free child care centers, and repeal of abortion laws. Despite its noble aim, the women's movement could not overcome its internal divisions, and the second Congress To Unite Women, held in 1970, was a failure.

Congressional Union for Woman Suffrage

In 1913, Alice Paul and Lucy Burns established the Congressional Union for Woman Suffrage, a national organization to work solely for a suffrage amendment to the Constitution. The Congressional Union, as it was called, published a weekly newspaper, *The Suffragist.* Paul was the union's chair and Burns was its organizer. The Congressional Union advocated an immediate campaign for an amendment to the Constitution, but the national suffrage leadership, believing that state-by-state referenda constituted a better strategy, eventually removed Paul as chair of the National Association's Congressional Committee. The successor to the Congressional Union was the National Woman's Party, which campaigned against Democratic congressional candidates regardless of their position on women's suffrage (for the leadership's failure to pass a federal suffrage amendment) and, in 1916, opposed President Wilson's bid for reelection.

See also Burns, Lucy; National Woman's Party; Nineteenth Amendment; Paul, Alice.

Consciousness Raising

The consciousness-raising group was an invention of the second wave of twentieth-century feminism and was particularly popular among radical feminists during the 1970s. Consciousness raising sought to unite women by exposing their common feelings and experiences. A small group of women would gather to discuss sexual relationships, sex-based characteristics of their upbringing, and other topics. Consciousness raising has been characterized by some feminists as excessively introspective and self-absorbed, and it has been accused of leading to passivity. Actually, it has always been intended to lead to political involvement and has, in fact, led to tangible results in the form of protests and speak-outs. The most notable of these was the protest of the treatment of women as sex objects at the 1968 Miss American pageant. (Issues of sexuality were of special concern to consciousness-raising groups because accounts of sexual mistreatment were quite common whenever participants discussed their personal lives. Consciousness-raising groups were the first to show that there was a political dimension to issues of sexuality.)

Contraband Relief Association

As the Civil War progressed, many former slaves traveled to the North. Called contrabands, they were placed under the jurisdiction of the Union army. Although free, they were without education or possessions. Elizabeth Keckley, a former slave who was employed by First Lady Mary Lincoln during the war, was so distressed about the difficulties the contrabands faced that she addressed the congregation of an African-American church to suggest that freed men and women unite to help the contrabands. She became president of the newly created Contraband Relief Association of D.C. and raised large amounts of money, including

73

$200 from the first lady. When African Americans were finally allowed to join the army, the Contraband Relief Association expanded its mission to include soldiers and changed its name to Freedmen and Soldiers' Relief Association of Washington.

Contraception

Contraception, writes historian Linda Gordon, refers to methods that permit sex without pregnancy. In this sense, contraception was poorly practiced in colonial America, which had one of the highest birth rates in history. Because so few physicians and midwives understood fertility and the mechanics of conception, herbal teas and douching with potions that were sometimes poisonous were all too common. Eighteenth-century Americans used withdrawal and self-induced abortion to control reproduction, and a few of the very wealthy understood the use of condoms made of skin or gut, which they used as prophylactics. However, withdrawal was likely the most common contraceptive practice. In 1837 Charles Goodyear discovered a technique that made rubber more pliable, leading to the cheap manufacture of condoms. Two decades later his published inventories listed the rubber pessary, a plug preventing insemination. Rubber diaphragms, in use in Europe from the late nineteenth century, became legal in the United States by doctors' prescription after a civil disobedience campaign in the 1920s by feminists championing the legalization of contraceptive devices. The Depression of the 1930s brought about even greater use of contraception among middle-class women and men, and in 1936 for the first time, contraception became legal. Historically, the methods for preventing conception have included the rhythm method; barrier methods (spermicides, condoms, diaphragms vaginal sponges, and cervical caps); hormonal methods (the Pill and "morning-after" contraceptives); and surgery (tubal ligation or vasectomy).

See also Abortion; Birth Control; Birth Rate.

Corbin, Margaret Cochran (1751–c. 1800)

Margaret Corbin, born 12 November 1751, was the first woman to fight as a soldier during the American Revolution. Her husband, John Corbin, joined the militia during the American Revolution. After he was posted at Fort Washington, she joined the encampment there. In 1776, during a battle, John Corbin was killed, and his wife took over his post until she was wounded. As a result of her wounds she lost the use of one arm. As an impoverished invalid, she petitioned and was awarded stipends by the Pennsylvania Supreme Council, the Continental Congress, and the Board of War. The stipends amounted to one-half of the pay of a soldier in service, plus allowances for clothing and liquor. Margaret Corbin died around 1800 in Westmoreland County, Pennsylvania.

Corset

The clothing that women wore in the nineteenth century in part reflected the restraint that women had to exhibit around men. Corsets fashionable in the first half of the nineteenth century best illustrate this. Made of silk or cotton and ribbed with steel or bone straps, they fastened in front with hooks, buttons, or laces. When laced tightly, breathing became very difficult; this caused the fainting of many nineteenth-century women. Also, when laced too tightly, the corset could dislocate the kidneys, liver, and other organs. The flapper period of the 1920s liberated women from such restrictive clothing.

Coutts v. Greenbow

In *Coutts v. Greenbow* (Virginia, 1811), a chancery court showed support for women's property rights. Reuben Coutts, a doctor, lived with a woman for many years, during which time they had a number of children. When they finally married, Coutts established a jointure (estate in property secured to a wife as part of a marriage settlement) and made provisions for his children. But after his death, his creditors sued his estate, arguing that debtors could not make a binding marriage settlement. Neither, they held, could the rights of children born out of wedlock hold up against creditors. But some courts recognized the unfairness of permitting a married woman's own estate (property either real or personal) to be used to pay a husband's debt. The Virginia court was one of these. It dismissed both points and held that "marriage of itself is a sufficient consideration for a settlement; not marriage and a previous chastity." To the court, the most important consideration was Coutts's desire to leave property to his wife in consideration of their marriage. As the economy became depressed in the nineteenth century, courts became even more willing to grant all women independent property rights.

See also Equity Law; *Flanagan's Lessee v. Young; Gregory v. Paul; Helms v. Franciscus.*

Coverture
See Common Law.

Craig v. Boren
The significance of the Supreme Court decision in *Craig v. Boren* (1976) was not the ruling itself but the principle it established for examining laws that classify individuals on the basis of gender. The case challenged an Oklahoma law that attempted to combat drunk driving by requiring males to wait three years longer than females, until their twenty-first birthday, to purchase 3.2 percent alcohol beer. The state argued that young men are more likely than young women to drive while drunk, and it presented documents proving that more than ten times as many males as females between the ages of 18 and 20 were arrested for drunk driving.

In finding the statute unconstitutional, the Court recognized a new standard for judging laws that incorporate a gender-based classification, as this law did. According to the new standard, gender classifications must be "substantially related" to an "important governmental objective."

Previously, there were only two standards by which the courts could judge classification-type laws: Strict scrutiny was applied to suspect laws and minimal scrutiny was applied to ordinary laws. Suspect laws include those that incorporate race-based classifications. A suspect law may stand only if it survives strict scrutiny, that is, if the state can show a compelling or overriding need for the law and also can show that the race-based classification is necessary for the law to serve its purpose. For an ordinary law, the state need only show that the law is reasonably related to a valid government objective. Most laws are judged by the latter standard and most survive it.

Significantly, the Court did not consider gender-based classification suspect, as it does race-based classification. Instead, it declared that the intermediate standard was operating in previous cases although it had not been articulated. By developing and articulating this intermediate level of strictness for gender-based classifications, the Court granted a considerable victory to those battling sex discrimination.

Crandall, Prudence (1803–1890)
Prudence Crandall faced down a community's hate to bring education to African-American girls. Crandall was born 3 September 1803 in Rhode Island. Crandall, whose parents were Quakers, was educated at the New England Friends' Boarding School in Providence. She taught school briefly in Plainfield, Connecticut, before moving to Canterbury. There, in 1831, she opened a private girls' school called the Canterbury Female Boarding School, among the state's best.

When Crandall admitted the daughter of a local African-American farmer, the town became outraged, and she became the focus of much hatred and controversy. Crandall closed the school and announced that, in its place, she would open a boarding school for African-American women who wished to be teachers. The school opened in April 1833. The townspeople stopped food shipments to the school and refused to allow its students to attend the town Congregational church. When their attempts to force Crandall to close the school failed, the town persuaded the state legislature to pass a law that required the permission of town authorities before any school could be opened to nonresident African Americans. Crandall kept her school open and was arrested, jailed, and tried. Although a lower court convicted her, the court of appeals reversed her conviction because of a technicality. Nevertheless, mob violence and arson eventually forced Crandall to close the school in September 1834.

A month earlier she had married Calvin Philleo, a Baptist minister, and the couple moved to Illinois. After Philleo died in 1874, she moved to Elks Falls, Kansas. In 1886, the Connecticut legislature granted her a small pension as compensation for their outlawing of her school more than five decades earlier. She died 28 January 1890 in Elks Falls.

See also Education.

Crater's Raiders

Crater's Raiders was a small but influential lobbying group that is credited with securing congressional approval of the Equal Rights Amendment (ERA) in 1972. The group was named for Flora Crater, who had chaired the National Organization for Women's (NOW) National Ad Hoc Committee for the Equal Rights Amendment. In December 1970, when the ad hoc committee was dissolved, Crater and some of the committee members formed their own group. The group members became central figures in a lobbying effort for the ERA, working independently of any government capacity. Congressional approval of the ERA has been attributed to the determination and skilled lobbying of this group. The group's efforts included collecting information and publishing a newsletter, *The Woman Activist*. The group disbanded in March 1972 after the Senate approved the ERA.

See also Equal Rights Amendment; Women United.

Cullom Bill

The Cullom Bill, which declared polygamy as practiced in Utah Territory illegal, was introduced in Congress in 1869–1870. Male Mormon leaders claimed that Mormon women endorsed polygamy; in 1870, the franchise was extended to women in order that they might have a means of demonstrating support to a hostile Congress, thus dissuading Congress from acting against the institution. To gain votes against it, Mormons in Utah granted women suffrage in 1870. The Cullom Bill passed in the House but failed to win Senate approval. In 1887 Congress passed the Edmunds-Tucker Act, which outlawed polygamy and revoked women's suffrage in Utah. This was immediately denounced as penalizing the women of the territory but not the men. Utah women did not regain their right to vote until 1896, when Utah became a state under a constitution that prohibited polygamy.

See also Frontier Women.

Cult of Domesticity

The cult of domesticity, a nineteenth-century concept, romanticized family life and a woman's roles within it. Historian Linda Kerber suggests it might have been a response to the disruption of domestic life that occurred during the American Revolution. Whatever its origin, by the 1840s and 1850s the concept had political implications. The ideal of the female-centered, middle-class home was held up for the rest of the world to emulate. From press to pulpit women were charged with upholding moral virtues, such as self-sacrifice and purity, for the good of society. The major consequence was to isolate women in the domestic sphere in contrast to the public sphere of men. Poor women, who lacked the opportunity to conform to middle-class mores, nonetheless passed on the concepts to their daughters, perhaps diverting their economic and social grievances.

Curtis, George William (1824–1892)

George Curtis, with wit and insight, defended women's right to higher education. Born 24 February 1824, Curtis became the political editor of *Harper's Weekly* shortly before the Civil War, and he used the position to shape public opinion during the war. A leader of civil service reform, Curtis rejected several offers from the Republicans to run for office. In 1890, he gave the address at the celebration of the twenty-fifth anniversary of Vassar College. In the address, entitled "The Higher Education of Women," Curtis said:

> . . . if any skeptic should ask, 'But can delicate woman endure the hardship of a college course of study?' it is a woman who ingeniously turns the flank of the questioner . . . 'I would like you to take thirteen hundred young men, and lace them up, and hang ten to twenty pounds of clothes upon their waists, perch them on three-inch heels, cover their heads with ripples, chignons, rats, and mice, and stick ten thousand hairpins into their scalps. If they can stand all this they will stand a little Latin and Greek.

Curtis died on Staten Island on 31 August 1892.

Cutler, Hannah Maria Conant Tracy (1815–1896)

Hannah Cutler, writer and women's rights activist, is best known for her efforts to reform married women's legal rights. She was born 25 December 1815 in Becket, Massachusetts. She began her schooling at the Becket public school. After her family moved to Rochester, Ohio, in 1831, she heard that the coeducational Oberlin Collegiate Institute was opening. She wanted to apply, but her father objected to coeducation. At the age of 18 she married John Martin Tracy, who died 20 years later at the hands of a mob while he was attempting to help escaped slaves. After her husband's death Cutler returned to her parents' home and began writing for local newspapers. She also taught school, ran a boardinghouse, and attended Oberlin (1847–1848). There she became friends with Lucy Stone. Later, while matron of the Ohio Deaf and Dumb Asylum in Columbus, Ohio, she met Frances Dana Barker Gage. She continued her reporting, contributing to the *Ohio Cultivator* a popular advice column, "Letters to Housekeepers," as well as an advice column for teenage farm girls.

The *Ohio Cultivator* championed women's rights, and she became swept up in the movement. She was one of the organizers of the Woman's Temperance Society in Rochester. In 1851, she was a delegate to the World's Peace Congress in London, where she lectured on women's rights and introduced the Bloomer costume. In 1852 she married Colonel Samuel Cutler. That year she was elected president of the Ohio Woman's Rights Association. Shortly thereafter, the family moved to Dwight, Illinois, where Cutler managed the family farm and taught her children at home. In 1859 and 1860 she successfully campaigned in New York, Illinois, and Ohio for laws to protect married women's legal rights. In 1868, at the age of 53, Cutler enrolled in the Women's Medical College in Cleveland. She earned an M.D. in February 1869 and practiced homeopathic medicine for the rest of her life. She also remained involved in the women's rights movement. After working with Stone to organize the American Woman Suffrage Association (1869), Cutler served as its president (1870–1871). She participated in her last suffrage campaign in 1873, when she lectured and circulated petitions throughout Ohio. Cutler's many books include *Woman as She Was, Is, and Should Be* (1846), *Phillipia, or a Woman's Question* (1886), and *The Fortunes of Michael Doyle, or Home Rule for Ireland* (1886). She died in Ocean Springs, Mississippi, on 11 February 1896.

See also American Woman Suffrage Association.

Dame Schools

Dame schools were private schools taught by women, or school dames. Dame schools were one type of private school that emerged in larger towns a generation or two after colonists began to settle in America. Dame schools taught both boys and girls to read, and some offered classes in needlework, French, religion, and the like.

See also Education.

Daughters of Bilitis (DOB)

A club for lesbians, the Daughters of Bilitis (DOB) was founded in 1955 by a small group of women in San Francisco. Its purpose was to provide a place where women did not have to conceal their lesbianism. Del Martin and Phyllis Lyon, a lesbian couple who were to become leaders among feminist lesbians in the 1970s, organized the group. In its first year of existence a dispute arose about the issue of secrecy, and those who favored maintaining absolute secrecy outside the group left. The organization then began to work with other homosexual groups to change the public's view of homosexuality. As part of the effort, the group held monthly meetings that were open to the public. The group has opened chapters in various cities. The liberal activism of the 1960s and 1970s added, somewhat ironically, a new dimension to the role of organizations such as DOB: when lesbian feminists encountered opposition within women's groups and other gay rights groups, lesbian feminist activists found refuge not only from persecution in society as a whole but from the intolerance of many of their fellow activists.

In 1968, Martin and Lyon joined the National Organization for Women (NOW). Martin was elected to an office of a regional branch of NOW; later, she urged NOW to endorse lesbian rights. Martin and Lyon, authors of the book *Lesbian/Woman*, have contributed to the understanding of lesbianism as a sexual choice and as a choice of a woman-centered lifestyle.

Daughters of Liberty

Before and during the American Revolution, women fought the British by refusing to drink tea, boycotting merchants who violated nonimportation resolutions, buying only domestic products, gathering food and clothing for Washington's soldiers, and making and using homespun cloth. The women were sometimes loosely organized in groups called the Daughters of Liberty, which were affiliated with the Sons of Liberty under Samuel Adams. Between 1768 and 1769, throughout the colonies, women in groups of 15 or 20 held spinning bees in the homes of clergy or friends, spinning yarn for the host. They tried to assist the boycott of British goods by spinning and making clothes and by buying only domestic. The graduating classes of Rhode Island and Harvard wore, on at least two occasions, clothing produced by these spinning bees. During the war, women led by Esther Reed embarked on a large-scale effort to make clothes for Washington's soldiers. In addition to direct action, women practiced among themselves political measures they observed among men: the signing of resolutions and pledges. Various groups of women signed pledges to avoid using imported tea, and more than 50 women signed a resolution that endorsed other resolutions passed by the Nonimportation Association in 1774. In these ways, women participated in the public life of the colonies and expressed their revolutionary and political zeal.

See also Bache, Sarah Franklin; Edenton Proclamation; Reed, Esther.

Daughters of St. Crispin

The Daughters of St. Crispin, formed by shoemakers in Lynn, Massachusetts, was the first national women's trade union in the United States. An affiliate of the Knights of St. Crispin, the Daughters was started in about 1868. It had its founding convention as a national union on 28 July 1869 in Lynn. When the Baltimore Daughters, founded in 1871, were fired for their membership, their brother Knights went on strike in sympathy. The Daughters of St. Crispin, led by Carrie Wilson, lobbied for a ten-hour workday, equal pay for equal work, and other labor issues, such as keeping their work in factories instead of letting it be done outside, where piecework rates were cheaper. By 1876, the Daughters of St. Crispin was once again a local organization, but consistent female labor activity continued through the eighties and nineties.

Daughters of Temperance

The Daughters of Temperance was responsible, albeit indirectly, for involving Susan B. Anthony in the women's rights movement. Anthony's first reform project was temperance. In 1852, the Rochester Daughters of Temperance selected Anthony to represent the local group at a mass meeting of the Sons of Temperance. Anthony attended the meeting, but when she rose to speak she was told, "The sisters were not invited to speak but to listen and learn." Anthony and a few other women immediately left and formed another temperance group. With this experience, Anthony began to understand that without the vote women could not effect reform. Notwithstanding Anthony's defection, the Daughters of Temperance became one of the largest female societies of the period, with more than 30,000 members.

See also Anthony, Susan B.; National Woman's Christian Temperance Union; Temperance.

Davis, Paulina Kellogg Wright (1813–1876)

Paulina Wright Davis was a nineteenth-century reformer, active in the antislavery, temperance, and women's suffrage movements. Born 7 August 1813 in Bloomfield, New York, she hoped to become a missionary but gave up the goal in 1833 when she married Francis Wright. The couple became active in reform circles and in October 1835 they helped to organize an antislavery convention in Utica, New York, a dangerous act that resulted in a retaliatory attack made by a mob on their house. In the 1830s, Paulina Wright and Ernestine Rose circulated petitions asking the New York legislature for a married woman's property law. Wright became independently wealthy after the death of her husband in 1845, and for a few years after his death, she lectured on health and hygiene. In 1849 Wright married Thomas Davis, a Rhode Island jewelry maker and politician, and the following year she began to campaign for women's rights. She helped to organize the first National Woman's Rights Convention in Worcester, Massachusetts, and published one of the first women's rights periodicals, *The Una* (1853–1855). In 1868 Wright helped organize the New England Woman Suffrage Association and a Rhode Island suffrage association, serving as president of the latter until 1870. When the women's suffrage movement split in 1869, Davis was one of the few New England women to side with the National Woman Suffrage Association. Davis died 24 August 1876 in Providence, Rhode Island.

See also Married Women's Property Acts; National Woman Suffrage Association; New York Married Woman's Property Act (1848).

D.C. Women's Liberation Movement

The D.C. Women's Liberation Movement was a small group of women organized in Washington, D.C., after the 1968 Jeanette Rankin Brigade protest. The members of this radical group were experienced activists who had solid ties to the capital's leftist establishment; they formed a largely homogeneous group because many of the members were associated with the Institute for Policy Studies, a left-wing organization based in Washington, D.C. The group apparently was highly exclusive. This prevented it from becoming a large-scale organization but fostered a unique closeness and solidarity among its members. The D.C. Women's Liberation Movement attempted to unify various strands of feminist thought by placing equal emphasis on a separatist method of fighting male oppression and continued participation in the New Left's effort to change the economic system.

Debs, Eugene Victor (1855–1926)

Born 5 November 1855 in Terre Haute, Indiana, Debs was a socialist leader, advocate of industrial unions, and pacifist. His beginnings in labor reform and socialism date to 1875, when he founded the Terre Haute lodge of the Brotherhood of Locomotive Firemen. While jailed on a strike-related offense, he became a socialist. In 1901, his Social Democratic party merged with the labor reform arm of the Socialist Labor party to form the Socialist party. Debs was nominated for president of the United States six times, once by the Social Democratic Party (1900) and five times by the Socialist Party (1900, 1904, 1908, 1912, and 1920). The last time he ran for president, while in prison for violating the Espionage Act, Debs received 900,000 votes—more than he had received in any previous election.

Debs supported the feminist cause as part of his general struggle for social justice. He expressed his views in "Woman—Comrade and Equal," in which he said,

The London Saturday Review in a recent review brutally said: "Man's superiority is shown by his ability to keep woman in subjection." . . . [This sentiment] is embodied and embedded in the cruel system under which we live, the criminal system which grinds children to profits in the mills, which in the sweatshops saps women of their power to mother a race of decent men, which traps the innocent and true-hearted, making them worse than slaves in worse than all that has been said of hell. It finds expression in premiers hiding

from petticoated agitators, in presidents ignoring the pleading of the mothers of men, in the clubbing and jailing of suffragists; in Wall Street gamblers and brigands cackling from their piles of loot at the demands of justice. It is expressed in laws which rank mothers and daughters as idiots and criminals. It writes, beside the declaration that men should rebel against taxation without representation, that women should submit to taxation without representation. It makes property the god that men worship, and says that woman shall have no property rights. Instead of that, she herself is counted as property, living by sufferance of the man who doles out the pittance that she uses.

Debs died on 20 October 1926 in Elmhurst, Illinois.

Declaration of Rights for Women

The absence of negative public reaction to a publicity stunt staged by Susan B. Anthony and four other women in 1876 was a sign that some progress in women's rights had taken place since the Seneca Falls Convention 28 years beforehand. In 1876, the centennial of the United States was celebrated in Philadelphia. The National Woman Suffrage Association hoped to use this event to bring women together and to publicize the unequal status of women. The NWSA prepared a declaration of women's rights, which requested civil and political rights for women in keeping with the spirit of 1776. The group requested permission to read the document during the Fourth of July celebration at Independence Hall but were turned down. Instead, the group was given five tickets to the event. At the celebration, when the audience rose to its feet to greet the guest speaker, five women marched across the stage: Susan B. Anthony, Matilda Joslyn Gage, Phoebe Couzins, Lillie Devereux Blake, and Sara Andrews. Anthony thrust a three-foot scroll at the chairman of the festivities, Thomas W. Ferry. He grasped it, and the women quickly left the hall, scattering handbills bearing the declaration as they went. By taking the scroll, Ferry made the declaration an official part of the event. At a bandstand outside Independence Hall, Anthony read the declaration to a large crowd, ending with "We ask justice, we ask equality, we ask that all civil and political rights that belong to citizens of the United States, be guaranteed to us and our daughters forever." The declaration demanded that women be seated on juries, that there be no taxation without representation (an allusion to suffrage), and that the word *male* be stricken from state constitutions and judicial codes. It is worth noting that while the 1848 Declaration of Sentiments attacked men, the 1876 declaration targeted the state.

See also Anthony, Susan B.; Declaration of Sentiments.

Declaration of Sentiments

When planning the first women's rights convention, to be held on 19–20 July 1848 in Seneca Falls, New York, Elizabeth Cady Stanton thought a manifesto was needed to argue the case for women's rights. She suggested modeling it on the Declaration of Independence, linking women's rights with the principles of the republic and stating women's complaints against men in much the same way the colonists stated their grievances to King George. Together, the convention planners drafted a declaration of sentiments, which Stanton read at the convention. The declaration read,

> We hold these truths to be self-evident: that all men and women are created equal. . . .
>
> He [man] has never permitted her to exercise her inalienable right to elective franchise.
>
> He has compelled her to submit to laws, in the formation of which she has no voice. . . .
>
> He has made her, if married, in the eye of the law, civilly dead. . . .
>
> He has so framed the laws of divorce, as to what shall be the proper

causes, and in case of separation, to whom the guardianship of the children shall be given, as to be wholly regardless of the happiness of women. . . .

> He has denied her the facilities for obtaining a thorough education, all colleges being closed against her.
>
> He allows her in Church, as well as State, but a subordinate position. . . .
>
> He has usurped the perogative of Jehovah himself, claiming it as his right to assign for her a sphere of action, when that belongs to her conscience and to her God.

After the declaration came 12 resolutions, including the right to speak and teach in all religious assemblies, and to equal opportunities in commerce, trade, the professions, and education. All were readily accepted by the convention, except for the ninth resolution, which called for the vote. This resolution was so controversial that Henry Stanton, a supporter of women's rights, left town rather than attend the convention at which it would be proposed. Elizabeth Cady Stanton and Frederick Douglass gave strident speeches defending the resolution, and it was approved by a small margin.

See also Declaration of Rights for Women; Douglass, Frederick; Seneca Falls Convention; Stanton, Elizabeth Cady.

Defense Advisory Committee on Women in the Services (DACOWITS)

The Defense Advisory Committee on Women in the Services (DACOWITS) counsels and otherwise assists the secretary of defense on issues pertaining to military women. DACOWITS was created by the military in the 1950s in response to the urging of women activists to appoint women to emergency war committees during the Korean War. The primary purpose of DACOWITS at the time of its creation was to encourage female enlistment by making parents feel that their daughters would be well treated; female enlistment, however, did not increase at that time as much as it was hoped that it would. Through DACOWITS, dozens of women gained, at least nominally, a voice in the formation of some policies. Initially, the overall value of DACOWITS was essentially in its symbolic demonstration of the military's interest in women's issues.

Improvements in the status of women in the military since the 1950s have not eliminated the need for DACOWITS as a voice in support of opportunities for military women. In April 1989, DACOWITS issued a recommendation, later rejected by the army, to experiment with the use of women in certain combat jobs, and in April 1991, DACOWITS recommended the repeal of laws excluding women from combat in the air force and navy.

Deloria, Ella Cara (1888–1971)

The studies of Ella Deloria, linguist and anthropologist, provide invaluable information about the language and culture of her native people, the Dakota. Deloria was born 30 January 1888 on the Yankton reservation in South Dakota. Some four years after her graduation from Columbia University (1915), the noted anthropologist and linguist Franz Boas urged her to devote herself to the study of the Dakota language. Deloria took his advice, working with Boas until his death in 1942 and continuing with Ruth Benedict until her death six years later. As part of her research, Deloria traveled to various reservations to interview elders about the Dakota way of life. *Dakota Texts* (1932) collected some of the Dakota myths and stories. *Dakota Grammar* (1941) was coauthored by Deloria and Boas. *Speaking of Indians* (1944) described Indian life for a general audience. Deloria researched and wrote about the Dakotas until her death on 12 February 1971 in Tripp, South Dakota.

Dewey, John (1859–1952)

Noted philosopher and educator John Dewey was born 20 October 1859 in Burlington, Vermont. He received a B.A.

from the University of Vermont in 1879 and a Ph.D. from Johns Hopkins University in 1884. After teaching philosophy for several years, Dewey became the head of the University of Chicago's philosophy department (1894–1904) and its school of education (1902–1904). A strong advocate of women's rights, he was a mentor of feminists and of men who supported women's rights, such as Thorstein Veblen, W. I. Thomas, and George Herbert Mead. Dewey was progressive in educational theory, believing that coeducation benefited both boys and girls. In 1902, Dewey convinced the president of the University of Chicago to embrace coeducation, stating, "The kind of man that will be kept from the University simply because he will have to associate upon equal terms with his equals is not the kind the University wants or needs." In 1904 Dewey joined the faculty of Columbia University, where he helped found the Men's League for Woman Suffrage with the help of his assistant in the philosophy department, Max Eastman. His article "Is Co-Education Injurious to Girls?," published in the *Ladies' Home Journal* (28 June 1911), detailed the benefits of coeducation: "What are the intellectual effects of co-education? Well, it has at least forever laid at rest one old bugaboo—the notion of the inherent mental inferiority of the female sex." Among his many books are *The School and Society* (1899), *Democracy and Education* (1916), *Experience and Nature* (1925), *Art as Experience* (1934), and *Logic: The Theory of Inquiry* (1938). The leading light in American education of his day, Dewey died 1 June 1952 in New York City.

Dickinson, Anna Elizabeth (1842–1932)

An orator and would-be playwright, Anna Dickinson was perhaps the first woman to address the U.S. Congress. She was born 28 October 1842 in Philadelphia. Growing up in poverty, she received only about six years of schooling, and went to work at the age of 15. Yet at the age of 14 she wrote an article for William Lloyd Garrison's antislavery paper, *The Liberator*. She made her first

83

speech at the age of 17, before the Pennsylvania Anti-Slavery Society, and other speaking engagements soon followed. In 1861, she spoke in Philadelphia about "The Rights and Wrongs of Women," achieving such success that she was asked to speak throughout New England. That year she began to work at the U.S. Mint, but she was fired because in one of her speeches she accused Gen. George B. McClellan of treason. After this she devoted her life to public speaking. She spoke out on the rights of African Americans, the emancipation of women, prison reform, and public aid for the poor.

In 1863, Dickinson spoke on behalf of Republican candidates in New Hampshire and Connecticut. Her speeches were so instrumental in local Republican victories that Republican congressmen invited her to speak at the Capitol in 1864, before an audience that included President Abraham Lincoln and Mrs. Lincoln. Dickinson wrote several books, including *What Answer?* (1868), about interracial marriage, and *A Paying Investment* (1876), about various reforms, such as the need for universal, compulsory education. Her memoir, *A Ragged Rester (of People, Places and Opinions)*, was published in 1879. Dickinson was famous for her passionate oratory and sarcasm.

For several years after the Civil War she was a star on the lecture circuit. She spoke on a number of topics, usually as a critic of social ills. Among the issues she addressed was the need for women's political and economic rights, but she did not align herself with the suffrage movement. As interest in public lectures declined during the last quarter of the century, Dickinson turned to writing plays and acting, but after several terrible reviews, she retired. In 1888, the Republicans called her out of retirement to speak on the campaign circuit. However, her fiery denunciations of other candidates became so extreme that the Republicans distanced themselves from her. In 1891, signs of mental deterioration and paranoia led to her involuntary commitment to a mental hospital in Pennsylvania. Upon her release she sued those who had had her committed, and she was judged sane in 1897. During the last

40 years of her life she lived quietly in the home of two friends. She died on 22 October 1932 in Goshen, New York.

Orator Anna Dickinson wrote, "The world belongs to those who take it."

Dickinson, Emily (1830–1886)

Emily Dickinson, thought by many to be the greatest woman poet in the English language, was born on 10 December 1830 in Amherst, Massachusetts. Emily Dickinson graduated from Amherst Academy after six years of study, later attending Mount Holyoke Female Seminary in South Hadley, Massachusetts, for one year. But her unhappiness at being away from home led her to return to her parents' house in 1848, where she remained until her death. From student days, she wrote occasional verse, eventually penning 1,776 poems, most of them sent to women. Of these, 267 were sent to her sister-in-law, Susan Gilbert Dickinson, whom some scholars believe was Emily's muse. By 1858, she had started recopying her poems and binding them into packets, perhaps for posterity. In 1861, her "closest earthly friend," the Rev. Charles Wadsworth, left Amherst for San Francisco. The separation prompted the writing of a great many poems by Dickinson, 366 composed in the following year alone. The month that Wadsworth left, Dickinson wrote to Thomas Wentworth Higginson, editor of *The Atlantic Monthly*, asking him to read her work. He did so, counseling against publication, but continued to correspond with her for 20 years. Dickinson became more reclusive, occasionally refusing to see old friends when they came to visit, and preferring to remain in her bedroom, where she read and wrote poems and carried on her correspondences with Higginson, Wadsworth, and other friends. Although her father's death in 1874 and her mother's paralysis in 1875 required Emily's assistance, draining her energy, she nonetheless fell deeply in love during this time with Judge Otis P. Lind, although they never married. His death in 1884, not long after the death of her eight-year-old nephew, resulted in Emily's collapse. By 1885, her condition (diagnosed as Bright's disease) worsened, and she died in Amherst on 15 May 1886, at the age of 55.

Few of her poems were ever published during her lifetime, but upon her death, her neatly organized packets of poems were found in her dresser, destined for a far larger readership. In 1890, her sister Lavinia convinced a dubious Higginson and Mabel Loomis Todd to help publish them in a small book, *Poems by Emily Dickinson.* The book received unfavorable criticism but sold sufficiently to lead to the publication of *Poems: Second Series* (1891), and *Poems: Third Series* (1896). By 1945, nearly all of her poems were in print, and her place as quite possibly the country's greatest poet well established.

See also Higginson, Thomas Wentworth.

Divorce

Divorce was unusual in colonial America. Before it could be granted, the party seeking the divorce had to present signed petitions accompanied by written proof of the date the couple was married. The most frequent petitioners were women whose husbands had abandoned them. Couples who wanted to separate had three options. The first was divorce *a vinculo matrimonii*, or absolute divorce, which permitted remarriage. This type of divorce was rare; only Massachusetts and Connecticut granted it and only for adultery, cruelty, desertion, and "absence without word." The second option was divorce *a mensa et thoro*, separation from bed and board. This type of divorce was more common but did not permit remarriage. The third option was the private divorce agreement, in which couples divided their property and lived apart. In some communities, a local form of divorce was the "wife sale." In this symbolic ritual, the sale was prearranged, with the buyer being a lover or relative of the wife. On some occasions the woman was actually placed in a halter and auctioned. This custom may have developed as a reaction to the limited options available to unhappy couples.

During the colonial period, only Massachusetts and Connecticut passed laws permitting absolute divorce, presumably influenced by the Puritans, who believed divorce to be a civil, not a religious, contract. Yet, except for Connecticut, every colony granted separation from bed and board for bigamy, adultery, cruelty, and failure to support. After independence, many of the new states reformed their divorce laws, with an actual increase in the number of men suing their wives for desertion. But divorce remained rare in the South, and absent in South Carolina.

By the late nineteenth century divorce had become more difficult to obtain, as legislators came under pressure from influential individuals, such as Horace Greeley, who thought the laws were too liberal. At this time, divorce laws were most restrictive in the Mid-Atlantic states (New York to South Carolina) and least restrictive in the West. Passage of more liberal divorce laws became a key demand of some suffrage leaders, such as Elizabeth Cady Stanton. By 1859, Indiana passed a bill, introduced by Robert Dale Own, that broadened the grounds for divorce beyond adultery. Now drunkenness, cruelty, and abandonment could be grounds for divorce.

New York followed suit with the introduction of a similar bill in 1860. Elizabeth Cady Stanton addressed the legislature and drew a good deal of criticism for her efforts. The bill was defeated in the Senate by four votes.

For many years, Stanton was the only woman in the United States who wrote and spoke on the subject of divorce. In 1860, she decided that divorce would be the theme of her speech before the Tenth National Woman's Rights Convention in New York. On hearing this, Lucy Stone immediately sent word that she would not appear with Stanton on the program. Speaking for more than an hour, Stanton compared the status of women with that of the enslaved and urged the legislature to make marriage more difficult and divorce easier. Most shocking, Stanton demanded divorce for reasons of simple incompatibility. This triggered a fight that lasted for an entire session. Horace Greeley and Wendell Phillips joined the majority against Stanton, arguing that her speech and resolutions should not be recorded. So provocative was the topic that Lucy Stone preferred to see it treated separately along with infanticide, abortion, and similar subjects. Stanton was seated next to the Rev. Samuel Longfellow (brother of Henry Wadsworth Longfellow), who whispered to her, "Nevertheless, you are right, and the convention will sustain you." Ernestine Rose and Susan B. Anthony eventually supported her, yet the resolutions were tabled and recorded.

Even at the turn of the century, women suffered the burdens of discrimination more acutely than men when they were divorced, especially if they committed adultery. In Minnesota, women divorced for adultery were required to forfeit their own real estate; Pennsylvania denied a woman the right to dispose of real estate if she continued to live with her lover after her divorce. But men were not so penalized.

Yet, various studies, such as one by the U.S. Census Bureau, indicate a rise in the divorce rate between 1886 and 1906: in 1886, the number of divorces was more than 25,000; by 1906 that number had climbed to more than 72,000, a much higher rate than in other countries that kept such statistics. Within the nation's 49 jurisdictions, 85 percent allowed divorce for desertion, adultery, or cruelty. Of the 945,625 divorces reported from this period, 78 percent were granted for desertion (39 percent), adultery (22 percent), or cruelty (16 percent). Overall, the family as an institution was weakened in the late nineteenth and early twentieth century, with 200 divorces occurring per 100,000 married couples between 1808 and 1902. This was equivalent to one divorce annually for each 1,400 people.

Throughout the twentieth century, divorce has been a major social issue, with the rate turning sharply upward from 1960 to the mid-1980s. By the mid-1980s, according to Ada P. Kahn and Dr. Linda Hughey Holt, there were approximately 5 divorces per 1,000 people in the United States, compared with 2.5 per 1,000 in Canada and Australia and about 3.2 per 1,000 in the United Kingdom. Also at this time, all but two states had some type of no-fault divorce law on their books, meaning that no grounds were needed to dissolve the marriage. No-fault divorce, which originated in California in 1969, is based on the erroneous assumption that housewives long out of the job market can easily become self-supporting. What happens is that men's standard of living rises in the first year following divorce, while women's and children's declines. Legal scholar Marcia Boumil thinks that today the divorce rate may be stabilizing, perhaps due to a weak economy, resulting in people not being able to afford separate housing, but statistics are not yet conclusive.

See also Adultery; Child Custody; Doctrine of Necessities; Greeley, Horace; Stone, Lucy.

Dix, Dorothea Lynde (1802–1887)

Dorothea Dix, renowned for advocating the reform of treatment of the mentally ill, was born 4 April 1802 in Hampden, Maine. She left an impoverished and unhappy home at the age of 12 to live in Boston with her grandmother. Two years later, she opened her own school for small children in Worcester, Massachusetts. By 1821, she had returned to Boston and opened a dame school for young girls at her grandmother's home. Soon she opened a charity school for poor children called The Hope, also on her grandmother's estate.

Dix worked incessantly, teaching at both schools and studying to stay ahead of her pupils. When deteriorating health forced her to stop teaching, she turned to writing—producing eight books in five years. The books reveal her appreciation and understanding of the outdoor world and her deeply religious nature. *Conversations on Common Things* (1824) was a popular science textbook. *Hymns for Children* (1825), a poetry anthology, appears to include some of her own poems. Her other books include *Evening Hours* (1825), *Meditations for Private Hours* (1828), and *The Garland of Flora* (1829). She attended the Unitarian church of the great reformer Dr. William Ellery Channing, who would become one of her mentors, and worked for three years as the summer governess to his children.

In 1831 Dix established another school for girls in Boston. But, five years later, she contracted tuberculosis and was forced to close the school. She traveled to England, where she lived for about two years. Here, she became friendly with a number of influential reformers, perhaps including Dr. Samuel Tuke, son of the founder of a progressive institution for the mentally ill. Still in poor health, Dix returned to the United States, where she learned that she had inherited from her grandmother enough money to support her for a lifetime. Though ill, Dix was not inactive, spending several years traveling and reading about mental illness.

The turning point in Dix's life came in March 1841, when she began to teach a Sunday school class for female inmates of the East Cambridge (Massachusetts) jail. There, she learned that although many inmates were suffering from mental illness, they were imprisoned without heat or light, and without regard to age or gender. Some were naked, chained to walls, and beaten. Dix investigated the conditions of the jail and brought her discoveries to the attention of the local court, which resulted in some reform. Encouraged by Channing, Horace Mann, and philanthropist Samuel Gridley

Howe, she embarked on an 18-month survey of conditions in every jail and poorhouse in Massachusetts. She found that some inmates were chained to walls and many lived without light, heat, or adequate toilet facilities. Others were crammed into pens, stalls, cages, and cellars. Many were beaten. However, her research also unearthed examples of progressive treatment. Her address to the Massachusetts legislature in January 1843 convinced it to enlarge an asylum in Worcester. Dix then surveyed the institu-

Dorothea Dix

tions of Rhode Island, New York, New Jersey, Kentucky, Pennsylvania, Maryland, Ohio, Illinois, Mississippi, Alabama, Tennessee, North Carolina, and other states. Her reports led to improvements in facilities and, in 15 states, to financing for the construction of state hospitals for the insane. She played a direct role in the founding of 32 state mental institutions in the United States, which grew from 13 in 1843 to 123 by 1880.

Applying her knowledge of prison conditions to convicts, she wrote *Remarks on Prisons and Prison Discipline in the United States* (1845), which recommended the separation of different types of offenders, among other reforms. By 1847 she had traveled from Nova Scotia to the Gulf of Mexico, visiting 18 state penitentiaries, 300 county jails and houses of correction, and more than 500 almshouses; by 1854, she had secured congressional approval of a bill designating 12 million acres of public lands as a federal land trust to benefit the insane, deaf, mute, and blind. The measure was vetoed by President Franklin Pierce. Following that defeat she returned to Europe, ostensibly to rest, but carrying out investigations of asylums, jails, and poorhouses in Scotland, France, Turkey, Russia, and Italy.

In 1861, during the Civil War, when she was almost 60, Dix was appointed superintendent of Union army nurses, a job for which she was ill suited because of the managerial responsibilities it entailed and because of her dictatorial style. For example, she established standards for all volunteer nurses, and she fired volunteer nurses who had been accepted without her approval. According to historian Eleanor Flexner, Dix required the nurses to be "over thirty, plain, not wasp-waisted, strong enough to turn a grown man over in bed, and willing to do the most menial work." Dix forced improvements in army medical services, such as setting up and staffing infirmaries in churches and schools, cleaning up established hospitals, and stockpiling medical supplies. She held the post until 1866, despite intense disputes and a transfer of some of her power, particularly over nurse recruitment, to the surgeon general. After the war she returned to her more primary interest, investigating hospitals and prisons and working for reform. Dix died on 18 July 1887 in a hospital that she had founded in Trenton, New Jersey. Throughout her life, she sympathized with the cause of women's rights, although she never strayed from her primary interest, the reform of living conditions for the mentally ill.

See also Sanitary Commission.

Doctrine of Agency
In colonial America, married women could not enter into contracts or else the docu-

ments could be deemed illegal. There were a few ways around this, however. One was called the doctrine of agency. If a woman's husband gave his tacit agreement that his wife was acting as his agent, some courts, acting under this doctrine, allowed women to buy property or sign leases. The doctrine of agency was based on the concept that the wife was acting as an agent for her husband.

Doctrine of Intentions
In the early nineteenth century certain court decisions, such as *Coutts v. Greenhow* (Virginia, 1811), strengthened married women's property rights. By midcentury, most chancery courts had concluded that all married women were entitled to separate property, and they began to make it easier for women to inherit separate estates by will or deed. In the early part of the century, the person bestowing a gift had to do so in a technically precise way, using specific words or phrases, such as "to her sole and separate use." As the requirements relaxed, a donor could, merely by indicating intent, give property to a woman, not her husband. This was the case in *Lowndes v. Champneys* (1821), when the chancellor explained that technical language wasn't necessary to create a separate estate for a wife, only clear intent that the gift was for her. The doctrine of intentions meant that if a person expressed a desire to give property to a woman, that property would be hers; the doctrine did away with the need for trustees and other legal requirements in bestowing the gift.

See also Chancery Courts; *Coutts v. Greenhow;* Equity Law; *Feme Covert; Johnson v. Thompson.*

Doctrine of Necessities
The legal doctrine of necessities permitted married women whose husbands had deserted them to charge their husbands' estate for food, clothing, and other household essentials. A wife's actions were viewed as if she were the agent for her husband. Colonial courts looked favorably upon suits against a

husband's estate that were brought by creditors who, on credit, supplied married women with goods. If a husband did not pay these bills, his property could be seized. The longer a man was away, the greater the power his wife had to make contracts, the courts reasoning that, as years went by, wives needed more power to contract for household necessities. Gradually, the law was broadened to cover other business transactions undertaken by wives. Legal scholar Marilynn Salman cites an 1818 Connecticut case, *Rotch v. Miles*, in which a husband who had deserted his wife was ordered to pay her debts when he returned to the state, including those she had incurred during the course of her operation and ultimate rental of a boarding house. In these ways, the courts, throughout the eighteenth and early nineteenth century, used the doctrine of necessities to help women. However, women forfeited the support of their husbands if they were found to have committed adultery or deserted the family home.

See also Chancery Courts; Equity Law; *Feme Covert*.

Dodge Study
See Project on the Psychology of Women.

Doe v. Bolton
In *Doe v. Bolton* (1973), the Supreme Court struck down Georgia's abortion law, which was modeled on the 1959 American Law Institute (ALI) Model Penal Code. The Supreme Court treated *Doe v. Bolton* as a companion case to *Roe v. Wade* and ruled on both cases 22 January 1973. For that reason, *Roe v. Wade* is sometimes used to refer to both cases.

Mary Doe was a pregnant young woman who lacked the financial resources to support a child, and who, as a former mental patient, had been told to avoid having children. She sought an abortion, but the process for obtaining it was extremely difficult. When the local public hospital refused to perform the abortion, Doe turned to the Legal Aid Society, which listed her as a potential participant in a class action lawsuit to challenge the Georgia law. Doe agreed to participate, although a court ruling would probably be too late to help her. In July 1970, a lower court found the Georgia abortion law unconstitutional because it violated the right to privacy in medical treatment. The state appealed and the case went to the U.S. Supreme Court.

Attorney Margie Hames argued that the Georgia law violated the due process clause of the Fourteenth Amendment because it denied people the right to seek, and others to give, medical care, both of which are liberties guaranteed by the Constitution. The opposing argument (in *Roe v. Wade* as well) defended the state's interest in restricting abortion and declared that the case was moot because Doe was no longer pregnant, and stated that pregnant women are inherently incapable of victory in legal battles over abortion since it takes more than nine months for a case to progress through the court and, therefore, no pregnant woman who filed a suit would still be pregnant by the time the case reached the Supreme Court.

The Court's ruling in *Doe v. Bolton* overturned all ALI-type abortion laws because they interfered with medical decisions. It struck down requirements that first-trimester abortions be performed in hospitals, that women get the approval of hospital boards or other doctors before having an abortion, and that only residents of a particular state could obtain abortions in that state. Chief Justice Warren Burger, in a concurring opinion, called attention to the fact that the decision does not entitle women to abortion on demand but gives the physician the right to decide whether an abortion is appropriate—and, of course, each woman has the right to choose her own physician. Equally important is the Court's interpretation of the word *person* as it is used in the Constitution; the Court defined the word to exclude the unborn. This definition came into play in later suits involving restrictions on and funding for abortions.

See also Abortion; American Law Institute Abortion Laws; *People v. Belous; Roe v. Wade*.

Domestic Service

In the early seventeenth century, according to historian Alice Kessler-Harris, only one group of American women could be considered wage earners: domestic servants. Many worked as indentured servants. While men were sometimes offered land or training to encourage them to fulfill their terms of indenture, women were offered no equivalent incentives. More than half of the white immigrants to the colonies were indentured servants, women and men alike agreeing to work for four to seven years to repay the cost of their passage. Females might learn to spin and weave, but other benefits were limited to room and board, the cost of passage, £3 a year spending money, and a suit of clothes when the term of servitude ended. Overall, male servants outnumbered female servants during the colonial period.

During the eighteenth century, the growth of commerce combined with a more stratified economy to restrict the practice of indenture, and men and women began to earn wages as domestic servants in the homes of the rich. According to Kessler-Harris, male servants were valued more than females. Before the American Revolution, men were paid as much as 40–50 percent more than women. For example, in 1748 female servants in Philadelphia earned £8–10 annually, or 50 percent of what male servants earned. Yet, throughout the century, capitalism provided an increasing number of new jobs for men outside domestic service, so that by 1851 only 10 percent of servants were male, while more rural and immigrant females moved in to take their place.

The nineteenth century saw a growth in domestic service, with the new servant being a young, single woman who worked in a small urban household. She washed, cooked, cleaned, ironed, mended, and cared for children. She worked on average 11–12 hours a day, seven days a week. By 1890, the coun-

Women of Black River Falls, Wisconsin, circa 1890, pose with items signifying their domestic duties: a broom and dustpan, a box of laundry starch, a pie pan and crust, dishes, apples, and a child.

try's 1.5 million domestics accounted for 60 percent of all working women. They lived at their places of employment, earning a pittance beyond room and board. More than 30 percent of the domestics were immigrants; in some states, such as Massachusetts, the figure was 60 percent.

With the coming of the twentieth century, domestic service began to shrink. By 1900 women made up one-fifth of the nation's work force, but of the five million women at work, less than half—about two million—were domestic maids, nurses, laundresses, or cooks. As early as 1910, domestic service accounted for only 25 percent of all wage-earning women's jobs. In the South, most domestics were African Americans. In the North, most were recent immigrants. In 1919, writes Angela Davis, when the southern leaders of the National Association for the Advancement of Colored People drew up their list of grievances, the terms and conditions of domestic service were first on their list.

Yet, by the 1930s domestic jobs were performed primarily by African-American women. Over time, this changed as newer immigrants moved into these jobs. By 1991, according to the Bureau of Labor statistics (Employment and Earnings), African-American and Hispanic workers constituted 21 percent each of all private household help. But one aspect of domestic service remains unchanged: the overwhelming majority of servants, cleaners, and child care workers are women (in 1991, 96 percent), who take such jobs because of lack of education, limited job opportunities and skills, or discrimination.

See also Indentured Servitude.

Domestic Violence
See Violence.

Douglass, Frederick (c. 1817–1895)
Frederick Douglass was a good friend of the suffrage movement. Self-taught, he became one of the nineteenth century's finest speakers. Born about February 1817 in Tuckahoe,

Maryland, he barely knew his mother, an enslaved woman, or his father, possibly her master. The child was reared until the age of six by his grandmother, and then was forced to live at the plantation manager's house. At the age of eight he was sent to work as a servant in Baltimore. There, with money he earned secretly by blackening boots, he bought his first book, the *Columbian Orator*. Soon he learned to write free passes for escaped slaves. In 1833, he was sent to work as a field hand in St. Michaels, Maryland. Douglass attempted an unsuccessful escape in 1836, for which he was jailed, and a successful escape to New York City, disguised as a sailor, in 1838. He then moved to New Bedford, Massachusetts, where he changed his name from Frederick Augustus Washington Bailey to Frederick Douglass at the suggestion of a friend who admired Sir Walter Scott's *Lady of the Lake*. He worked for three years as a day laborer in New Bedford.

His fortunes changed in 1841, when he made an impromptu speech at a meeting of the Massachusetts Anti-Slavery Society meeting. The society immediately hired him to act as a speaker. For the next four years Douglass traveled throughout the North, speaking out against slavery. To end speculation that he was an impostor, he authored the first of three autobiographies, *Narrative of the Life of Frederick Douglass, an American Slave* (1845). Fearing he might be recaptured, he left the United States for the United Kingdom, where he lectured in Ireland, Scotland, and England to enlist British sympathy for the U.S. abolition cause (1845–1847). Sympathizers raised £150 to legally secure his manumission. No longer subject to the Fugitive Slave Law, he returned to the United States.

Beginning in 1847, Douglass published the abolition movement's most important newspaper, the *North Star* (after 1851, renamed *Frederick Douglass's Paper*) in Rochester, New York. This paper, which continued for 16 years, was the first to be published by an African American in the United States and supported the first women's rights convention at Seneca Falls,

New York (1848). At the convention, his passionate speech in support of women's suffrage persuaded delegates to approve a controversial resolution calling for the vote. He said, "We hold woman to be equally entitled to all we claim for man. We go farther, and express our conviction that all political rights which it is expedient for man to exercise, it is equally so for women." For his bravery he endured the taunts of the press, which labeled him a hermaphrodite and an Aunt Nancy Man. After the Civil War, Douglass disagreed with Elizabeth Cady Stanton and some other suffragists about whether African-American men should get the vote before women, but he will always be remembered for supporting equal treatment for women when it was highly unpopular to do so.

Douglass was a popular lecturer after the Civil War and filled a number of government posts until 1891. He died on 20 February 1895 in Washington, D.C.

See also Abolition Movement; Seneca Falls Convention.

Dove, Rita Frances (1952–)

On 18 May 1993 Rita Frances Dove was named as the first African-American poet laureate. At 40 years of age, she was also the youngest person to hold the position. Born in Akron, Ohio, on 28 August 1952, Dove received her B.A. degree from Miami University in Oxford, Ohio, in 1973. She went on to earn her M.F.A. from the University of Iowa in 1977. Formerly a teacher at Arizona State University, she has also been a member of the University of Virginia faculty since 1989.

Dove has achieved numerous honors and awards throughout her career. She was writer-in-residence at Tuskegee Institute in Tuskegee, Alabama, in 1982 and winner of the Guggenheim Fellowship in 1983. She won the Pulitzer Prize for poetry for *Thomas and Beulah* in 1987, making her the first African-American woman to win since Gwendolyn Brooks in 1950. Other honors include the Ohio Governor's Award in 1988 and induction into the Ohio Women's Hall of Fame in 1991. Her poetry is published in *The Yellow House on the Corner* (1980), *Museum* (1983), *Fifth Sunday* (1985), *Thomas and Beulah* (1985), and *Grace Notes* (1989); in 1992 she published a collection of short stories, *Through the Ivory Gate*.

Dove's position as poet laureate was commemorated on 7 October 1993, when she read from her poetry at the Library of Congress's annual literary series. Dove lives with her husband, German writer Fred Viebahn, and their daughter, Aviva, in Charlottesville, Virginia.

Dower

A dower is a life estate to which a wife is entitled upon the death of her husband. Originally, under common law, it was a way of compensating widows for the loss of their property at marriage. The colonial widow's right to one-third of her husband's real estate and personal property was acknowledged before other claims to his estate were made. If a couple had no children, a widow could claim one-half of her husband's estate. Dower was her minimum right. If a man died intestate, by the dower rule, a widow could claim her "third" in court. However, she could not sell or mortgage her dower, as it represented a life interest only and had to be passed on to her heirs at death. Neither could a woman damage or diminish the value of her late husband's estate. Legal historian Marilynn Salman notes that some colonies had restrictions against cutting down trees, opening mines, or failing to keep up buildings. Only if a man devised real property to his wife, specifically free from such restrictions, would she not be responsible for such maintenance. Dower was a critical means of providing security to women who had no other legal means of providing for their financial well-being. After the American Revolution, courts reduced this protection to the extent that some scholars have argued that the erosion of dower rights was the most important legal development affecting women of the early republic. By the mid-nineteenth century, the Married Women's Property Acts, passed by many states, helped women gain control of their inheritance and other property.

See also Common Law; *Feme Covert*; Married Women's Property Acts.

Duniway, Abigail Jane Scott (1834–1915)

Abigail Duniway, a newspaper publisher and lecturer, was founder of the Oregon Equal Suffrage Association. She was born 22 October 1834 near Groveland, Illinois. She received little education, having been born into a farming family that migrated by wagon to Oregon in 1852. Her mother and a brother died along the way. The family made its home in Lafayette, Oregon, and Abigail taught school until her marriage to Benjamin C. Duniway in 1853. For the next ten years she farmed with her husband, bore four children, and wrote the first novel to emerge from the Pacific Northwest, *Captain Gray's Company* (1859).

In 1862, her husband lost the family farm after a friend defaulted on debts that Benjamin Duniway had endorsed. Abigail Duniway took to heart the lesson she learned about the limits of a wife's property rights. Soon after losing the farm, Benjamin Duniway was injured in an accident. To support the family, Abigail Duniway ran a boarding school in Lafayette and later taught in Albany, Oregon. In 1871, still resenting the loss of her farm, she moved to Portland and began publishing a weekly newspaper, *New Northwest*, dedicated to women's rights and suffrage. Before long Duniway was lecturing throughout the Northwest for suffrage. She founded the Oregon Equal Suffrage Association in 1873; through her efforts, the Oregon legislature passed a number of laws reforming married women's property rights. She was instrumental in gaining women's suffrage in Washington Territory (1883), but her attempts were frustrated in Oregon. After the state legislature approved an amendment to the state constitution giving women the vote, the amendment was defeated at the poll (1884).

In 1887, Duniway stopped publication of *New Northwest*, and the family moved to a

Abigail Duniway registers for the 5 November 1912 Oregon election, the first in which women were allowed to vote.

farm in Idaho. Several years later the family returned to Portland, and in 1895 Duniway became editor of the weekly *Pacific Empire*, which she used as a platform for suffrage. Although she is considered instrumental in the successful campaign for suffrage in Idaho the following year, success in Oregon eluded her until 1912. Duniway moved away from the policies of the National Woman Suffrage Association over time, skeptical of its demonstrations and speechmaking, and opposed to its linkage of suffrage and prohibition. She resigned as president of the state organization in 1905. When Oregon finally wrote women's suffrage into the state constitution, Duniway was confined to a wheelchair. Yet, she was asked to write the suffrage proclamation and given the honor of signing it with the governor. She soon became the first registered woman voter in the state of Oregon. Duniway was honorary president of the Oregon Federation of Women's Clubs and president of the Portland Woman's Club. Among her several books are a collection of poems, *My Musings* (1875), a long poem entitled *David and Anna Matson* (1876), and an autobiography, *Path Breaking: An Autobiographical History of the Equal Suffrage Movement in the Pacific Coast States* (1914). Duniway died on 11 October 1915 in Portland.

Duston, Hannah Emerson (1657–1736?)

Hannah Duston was one of a number of colonial women who were kidnapped by Native Americans. Her escape made her a hero of King William's War. She was born 23 December 1657 in Haverhill, Massachusetts, and at the age of 20 married Thomas Duston. During King William's War, the governor of Canada instigated attacks by Native Americans on colonial settlements. In one such attack, on 15 March 1697, Duston and at least one other woman were taken captive and forced to march toward Canada. After witnessing the murder of her baby along the way, and after being warned that the women would have to run a gauntlet naked when they arrived at their final desti-

nation, she became determined to escape. Soon they reached an encampment along the way, where a young boy who had been kidnapped 18 months earlier was being held captive. On 30 March 1697, Duston killed nine of her captors as they slept. She led the party away from the camp, but returned to scalp the dead as proof of her ordeal. Then she and the other two colonists made their way back to Haverhill. The date of Duston's death is unknown but is believed to be early 1736.

See also Rowlandson, Mary White.

Dworkin, Andrea (1946–)

Andrea Dworkin was born in Camden, New Jersey, on 26 September 1946. With Catharine MacKinnon, Dworkin drafted a city ordinance for Minneapolis (1983) that was the first antipornography law in the United States to oppose pornography on the grounds that it violates women's civil rights. The law was based on a novel argument that, because pornography violates women's civil rights, women who are harmed by pornography should be permitted to sue its makers and distributors for sex discrimination. The Minneapolis law and others like it failed judicial challenges. Many feminists even opposed it, fearing that local law enforcement agencies would use it to stifle feminist writings. Dworkin was an editor of *Ms.* magazine and has written a number of works about male violence and sexuality. Among her works are *Man Hating* (1974), *Our Blood* (1976), *The New Woman's Broken Heart* (1979), *Pornography: Men Possessing Women* (1981), *Right-Wing Women* (1983), *Ice and Fire* (1986), *Intercourse* (1987), *Mercy* (1991), and *Women Hating: A Radical Look at Sexuality* (1991).

Dyer, Mary Barrett (?–1660)

Mary Dyer has been long remembered for giving her life to challenge Boston's anti-Quaker laws. There are scanty records of her early years; she was probably born in Somerset, England, but her date of birth is not known. She married William Dyer in London in 1633, and the couple sailed to America in about 1635. They settled in Massachusetts and became followers of Anne Hutchinson, supporting her belief that the spirit of God rests within each individual. For supporting Hutchinson, the Dyers were excommunicated and banished from Massachusetts Colony. They followed Hutchinson to Rhode Island, where William Dyer was one of the founders of Portsmouth.

In 1652 the Dyers returned to England, and Mary Dyer became a member of the Society of Friends, or Quakers. Upon her return to New England in 1657, she began doing missionary work for the Quakers. The previous year, Massachusetts Colony had adopted anti-Quaker laws. Dyer was imprisoned in Boston in 1657 and banished from New Haven in 1658. The following year,

while visiting two Quakers imprisoned in Boston, she was jailed under a 1658 law that exiled Quakers on penalty of death. Determined to challenge the law, Dyer and other Quakers returned to Boston several times. Once, she was sentenced to death with the two Quakers she had visited in the Boston prison. The two men were hanged, but Dyer was granted a last-minute reprieve. In May 1660 she once again returned to Boston. On 1 June, after refusing to agree to banishment, she was publicly hanged. A heroine in the struggle for religious liberty, Dyer is honored by a statue at the State House in Boston. The statue was authorized in 1959 by the Massachusetts General Court, the same court that had sentenced her to death 300 years before.

See also Hutchinson, Anne; Society of Friends.

Earhart, Amelia Mary (1897–1937)

Amelia Earhart was the first woman to fly across the Atlantic, becoming a role model for a generation of women who wanted to break through the boundaries set for them by society. She was born on 24 July 1897 in Atchinson, Kansas. She grew up in Kansas City, a girl fond of the outdoors, completing high school in Chicago in 1916. Her father's alcoholism caused hard times for the family, but an inheritance from her grandmother enabled Earhart to enter Ogontz School in Rydal, Pennsylvania, in 1916. She left the school about one year later to become an army nurse in Canada during World War I.

After one year at Columbia University (1919), Earhart followed her parents to California. Over their objections she learned to fly from one of the nation's first female pilots, Neta Snook. At the age of 25, Earhart pawned her belongings to buy her first plane in July 1922, a Kinner Canary. She flew the barnstorming circuit in southern California and set a world's altitude record for women at 14,000 feet. By 1924 her parents' marriage had ended in divorce; that year she and her mother moved to Medford, Massachusetts. Earhart resumed her medical studies for a time, taught briefly, and became a social worker.

Earhart became the first woman to fly across the Atlantic in 1928. Publisher George Putnam chose her to take the place of Amy Phipps Guest, who had to drop out because of opposition from her family. The flight was made 17–18 June, with Wilmer Stultz as pilot, Lou Gordon as mechanic, and Earhart keeping the log. For this she was hailed as a feminist heroine, called Lady Lindy and First Lady of the Air. Within the year Earhart became aviation editor of *Cosmopolitan* and published a book about her flight, *20 Hours, 40 Minutes* (1929). She was a founder and the first president of the Ninety-Nines, an international organization for female pilots (1929). She also was vice-president (1928–1931) of Luddington Airlines, Inc., which flew passengers in the eastern United States.

In 1931, Earhart married Putnam with the understanding that she would keep her maiden name and continue to fly. During 22 and 23 May 1932, she became the first woman to fly solo across the Atlantic, traveling from Newfoundland to Ireland in a record-breaking 14 hours, 56 minutes. This flight also made her the first person to fly across the Atlantic twice. For the feat she was awarded the Distinguished Flying Cross (from Congress), the cross of the French Legion of Honor, the National Geographic Society Gold Medal, and the Harmon International Trophy. In 1935, she made the first solo flight from Honolulu to the United States mainland and the first nonstop flight from Mexico City to New York.

On 2 July 1937, during an around-the-world flight, Earhart's plane went down in the middle of the Pacific while en route from New Guinea to tiny Howland Island. Until recently no traces of her or the plane were found. But on 16 March 1992, the *New York Times* reported that the International Group of Historic Aircraft Recovery found a sheet of metal from Earhart's plane on Niku-Maroro Island, halfway between New Guinea and Hawaii. In addition to her first book, Earhart wrote *The Fun of It* (1932) and *Last Flight* (1937), which was published by her husband after her disappearance.

Eastman, Crystal (1881–1928)

Feminist and socialist, Crystal Eastman was born on 25 June 1881 in Marlborough, Massachusetts. Her mother was a preacher and advocate of women's rights near Elmira, New York, where Eastman was reared. She received her early education in Elmira and graduated from Vassar College in 1903. The following year she took her master's degree from Columbia University, and in 1907 she received a law degree from New York University Law School. Three years later she published *Work Accidents and the Law* (1910), which provided some impetus for the passage of workers' compensation laws. As secretary of the New York State Employers' Liability Commission, of which she was the only female member, she worked to secure passage of the New York workers' compensation bill.

Eastman championed birth control, world peace, and, in the words of historian Howard Zinn, "new ways of men and women living together and retaining their independence, different from traditional marriage." In 1913 she joined Alice Paul, Lucy Burns, and others to found the Congressional Union for Woman Suffrage. Eastman was also a member of Heterodoxy, a feminist group that thought the focus of the suffragists was too narrow and whose members included Charlotte Perkins Gilman. In 1917 she became managing editor of *Liberator*, a magazine published by her brother, socialist Max Eastman. Two years later, she and other feminists organized New York City's Feminist Congress. When World War I broke out, she participated in the founding of the Civil Liberties Bureau, which aided conscientious objectors.

Eastman lived her beliefs. Through two marriages she retained her maiden name. When she divorced her first husband, Wallace Benedict, in 1916 (after five years of marriage), she refused to accept alimony. Shortly after the divorce she married her second husband, Walter Fuller, an Englishman. In 1921 the couple moved to England, where Eastman founded the London bureau of the National Woman's Party. In 1927, in poor health, she returned to the United States without her husband; a month later she learned of his unexpected death. A year later, on 8 July 1928, Eastman died of a kidney disease in Erie, Pennsylvania.

See also Congressional Union for Woman Suffrage; Gilman, Charlotte Perkins; National Woman's Party.

Ecofeminism

The ecofeminist movement represents the merger of environmental and feminist concerns. A feminist-sponsored conference on the environment, following the 1980 Three Mile Island nuclear plant accident near Harrisburg, Pennsylvania, was the first organized ecofeminist activity, and the WomanEarth Institute was the first national group. The concept of ecofeminism has expanded to mean an objection to all types of domination—racial, sexual, environmental, and of species.

Edenton Proclamation

In October 1774, in Edenton, North Carolina, 51 women met to sign an agreement endorsing the Nonimportation Association resolves of that year. The women wrote a petition that stated their inability to "be indifferent on any occasion that appears nearly to affect the peace and happiness of our country." This assertive act, by which women claimed a right and duty to participate in the politics of the day, met with ridicule. A British cartoonist drew the "Edenton Ladies' Tea Party" as a laughable affair. Despite this, many women throughout the colonies protested privately, by not purchasing imported goods, and publicly, by signing petitions and gathering in meetings.

See also Daughters of Liberty.

Edmonds, Sarah Emma Evelyn (1841–1898)

Sarah Edmonds disguised herself as a man to serve as a soldier in the Civil War. Born Sarah Edmonson in December 1841, in New Brunswick, she received little education, and she ran away from home during the 1850s. She supported herself by selling Bibles, of necessity dressed as a man and using the name Frank Thompson. She gravitated west to Flint, Michigan. When the Civil War broke out, she used her salesman's name to enlist in a volunteer infantry company organized by a friend. She fooled some—but not all—of her fellow soldiers.

A British cartoon ridicules women of North Carolina's first capital who, on 25 October 1774, boldly declared that they would not drink tea or use English-made goods "untill such time that all Acts which tend to Enslave this our Native Country shall be repealed."

Nevertheless, she served with Company F of the 2nd Michigan Regiment of Volunteer Infantry in the first battle of Bull Run and was active during the Peninsular campaign of May–July 1862 and in the battle at Fredericksburg. Once she "disguised" her-self as a woman to spy behind Confederate lines. In 1863 she deserted, ostensibly for her health, but her diaries indicate that she had fallen in love with a soldier from another regiment who resigned from the army the same day she deserted. Apparently nothing came of this interest. Moving to Ohio and taking the name Sarah Edmonds, she became a nurse for the U.S. Christian Commission. Edmonds wrote a best-selling, fictionalized account of her adventures entitled *Nurse and Spy in the Union Army* (1865). In 1867, she married Linus Seelye and devoted herself to caring for their family of five children. In July 1884, Congress granted her a veteran's pension of $12 per month under the name Sarah E. E. Seelye, alias Frank Thompson. Shortly before her death Edmonds became the only woman admitted into the Grand Army of the Republic as a regular. She died 5 September 1898 in La Porte, Texas.

Edmunds-Tucker Act
See Cullom Bill.

Education
Until the 1970s American women have had far fewer educational opportunities than men. Social pressures have dictated that maternal obligations come first, followed by duties as wives. Outside interests have come in a poor third. Press and pulpit reinforced this order early in the country's history. On September 1791, in an "Oration upon Female Education, Pronounced by a Member of One of the Public Schools in Boston" a speaker explained,

> . . . while the *sons* of our citizens are cultivating their minds, and preparing them for the arduous, important, and many employments which America offers to the industrious, their *daughters* are gaining that knowledge, which will enable them to become amiable sisters, virtuous children; and, in the event, to assume [maternal] characters, more interesting to the public, and more endearing to themselves.

During the colonial period, women's brains were thought to be smaller than those of men. According to writer Carol Tavris, this belief persisted as late as the nineteenth century, when medical illustrations portrayed women with tiny skulls and large pelvises. Because women were thought to have small brains, it was believed that they could not master courses in science or math. During the colonial and early national periods, many daughters of the wealthy were taught only sewing, painting, and singing. The Rev. John Cosens Ogden wrote in *The Female Guide* (1793), "Every man, by the Constitution, is born with an equal right to be elected to the highest office, And every woman, is born with an equal right to be the wife of the most eminent man."

Scottish-born Frances Wright, the first woman to lecture to mixed audiences of men and women in the United States, wrote in *Views of Society and Manners in America* (1821), "Hitherto the education of women has been but slightly attended to." In fact, there were no advanced educational opportunities for women until 1821, when Emma Willard opened the Troy Female Seminary in Troy, New York. Barred from observing the teaching methods used in men's schools, Willard was resourceful: She carved cones and pyramids out of turnips and potatoes to demonstrate solid geometry. Parents were shocked to see their daughters drawing the human circulatory system on the blackboard—so shocked that cardboard covers were pasted over textbook pages depicting human anatomy. Nonetheless, although the curriculum was inferior to that offered to boys, a more challenging curriculum was at last being offered to girls. Between 1821 and 1872, more than 12,000 women attended the Troy Female Seminary, and many alumnae went on to start their own schools.

If education in the early years of the republic was inferior for white girls, for African-American women it was nonexistent. In the South it was against the law to teach slaves to read. Nevertheless, a few children of freed men and women went to schools founded by African-American women in South Carolina, Georgia, and Louisiana. In the North, many African-American children were denied access to public schools. As late as 1837, there was no school open to African-American children in Michigan. In

Ohio during the 1840s, African Americans were taxed for schools they could not attend. African-American girls, by virtue of their color and gender, were thought to be the least educable of all children. Early in 1833, Prudence Crandall had tried to teach African-American girls in Canterbury, Connecticut. She was jailed, stoned, and turned away by doctors and shopkeepers. When all else failed, the state passed a law that required town approval for any school that taught nonresident African Americans.

Despite the obstacles, education was the first area in which European-American women achieved some measure of equality with men. This advance was effected in large measure by the entry of New England women into the labor market, beginning with the textile mills in Lowell, Massachusetts, and the resulting need for an educated work force.

From 1823 to 1831 Catharine Beecher headed the Hartford Female Seminary, which offered women education in teaching, domestic science, and calisthenics. Beecher believed that there would soon be a surplus of females in the East because of the westward migration of so many men. She thought that these women would have to earn their living in dirty factories with long hours and low wages. Therefore, Beecher insisted, women should be either educated to teach or to perform domestic skills in a more professional way. In addition, she believed that a woman should be educated as rigorously for housework as a man might be for law or medicine. Her *Treatise on Domestic Economy* (1841) was a best-selling reference on home management.

Oberlin College, America's first coeducational institution, was founded in 1833. It admitted both sexes from the start, but only to its full course in 1837. That year, Mary Lyon opened Mount Holyoke Female Seminary in South Hadley, Massachusetts, for the first time making higher education available to girls of middle income. Lyon traveled throughout New England to raise money for her school at a time when such behavior was considered out of bounds. At this time, the Midwest offered women the

best opportunities for higher learning. In 1852 Ohio's Antioch College became coeducational, the second institution of higher education to do so after Oberlin (1833). In 1862, the Morrill Land Grant Act provided federal land for the establishment of coeducational agricultural and mechanical (A & M) colleges in each state that had remained within the Union. The states were to sell the land and use that money to endow at least the college that would teach engineering, agriculture, and home economics, as well as academic subjects. The proliferation of these colleges in the West and Midwest advanced women's education in the aftermath of the Civil War. As the century progressed, college officials attempted to make the curricula of women's schools equal to that of men's schools. Established in 1885, Bryn Mawr, under the leadership of M. Carey Thomas, offered a curriculum as difficult as Harvard's. And Radcliff, founded in 1878 and chartered in 1893 as a full-fledged institution of college rank, required students to fulfill Harvard's entrance requirements.

The education of women was improving. In New England, before the American Revolution, the literacy rate for women was one-half that of men; the 1850 federal census indicated equal, universal literacy skills among white, native-born women and men of that region. Hunter College, the first college to offer free education to women in the United States, opened in 1870. By 1900, educational opportunities for women had increased significantly. That year, 58 percent of the nation's high school enrollment was female, 40,000 women were enrolled in college, there were 30,000 female college alumnae, and one-third of all college students were women. By 1937, the figure neared 40 percent. In 1900, women earned 19 percent of all college degrees awarded. That figure rose to 41 percent just before World War II, although it declined in the 1950s. Until the mid-1960s, when the number of female college graduates regained earlier levels, the education of girls took second place to that of boys. According to sociologist Cynthia Fuchs Epstein, nearly 14 percent of women, compared to 9 percent of men, who scored high on the 1957 National Merit Scholarship tests dropped out of school.

The 1967 *Statistical Abstract of the United States* showed that, in 1965, a total of 1,303,00 boys graduated from high school as compared to 1,337,000 girls—but 317,669 boys graduated from college as compared to 217,362 girls. The National Center for Educational Statistics "Summary Report on Bachelor's and Higher Degrees Conferred during the Year 1964–65" showed that far fewer women than men reached the higher rungs of the educational ladder. Fewer women applied to medical school than had applied 15 years earlier; 93.1 percent of men and 6.9 percent of women received doctorates in law; 99.5 percent of men and .05 percent of women received doctorates in engineering; and 88 percent of men and 12 percent of women received doctorates in the biological sciences. In 1965 women received only one of every 11 doctorates awarded in the United States.

By 1970 the content of girls' education, from primary school through college, was nearly comparable with that of boys. However, although more girls than boys graduated from high school, more men than women received college degrees, with women only 41 percent of all college students. By 1988 women had moved up the educational ladder. Their percentages in law and medical schools increased from less than 10 percent in 1977 to 30 percent or more in 1988.

Figures from the U.S. Department of Labor's National Center for Education Statistics show that in 1991 approximately 42 percent of students studying law and 35 percent of those studying medicine were women. In 1992–1993, 39.4 percent of all medical students were female. In 1993, 67 percent of female high school graduates went to college, according to educator Diane Ravitch. This compares to 58 percent of male high school graduates. And women today make up 55 percent of all undergraduates, receiving 54 percent of all bachelor's degrees; females are 59 percent of all master's degree students, earning 53 percent of

all master's degrees; and women today earn more than 39 percent of all professional degrees. In addition, an American Council on Education study released in early 1994 showed that more women are earning doctoral degrees than ever before—making up 44 percent of Ph.D. recipients, whereas they made up only 36 percent in 1982—while the number of male doctoral recipients has dropped. During the last 25 years, masses of women have clearly demonstrated a desire for and excellence in higher learning once thought beyond them.

See also Beecher, Catharine; Bryn Mawr, Crandall, Prudence; Dewey, John; Hunter College; Lyon, Mary; Mount Holyoke College; Oberlin College; Thomas, Martha Carey; Troy Female Seminary, Willard, Emma.

Eisenstadt v. Baird

The Massachusetts "Crimes against Chastity" law was the subject of the 1972 *Eisenstadt v. Baird* decision. This law made it illegal to give unmarried people contraceptives and required married people to purchase contraceptives only from doctors or by doctors' prescriptions. Bill Baird, an advocate of birth control rights, challenged the law by distributing contraceptive foam to a dozen unmarried female students during a lecture at Boston University. Baird was convicted and imprisoned. The Supreme Court found the Crimes against Chastity law unconstitutional because, by discriminating against unmarried people, it violated the equal protection guarantee of the Fourteenth Amendment. The Court recognized that the right to privacy is of paramount importance in issues relating to childbearing. This endorsement of the right to privacy helped to build the foundation of the *Roe v. Wade* decision.

See also Doe v. Bolton; Griswold v. Connecticut; Roe v. Wade.

Emerson, Ralph Waldo (1803–1882)

Philosopher, founder of the Transcendentalist movement, essayist, poet, and women's rights advocate, Ralph Waldo Emerson was born 25 May 1803 in Boston, Massachusetts. In 1817 he entered Harvard

College, graduating in 1821. Dissatisfied after three years of teaching in a Boston girls' school, he entered Harvard's divinity school in 1826; by 1829 he had become a minister at the Second Church (Unitarian) of Boston, the year he married Ellen Tucker. She died in 1831, an event that left him deeply depressed and in poor health. (He would remarry in 1835.) He resigned from the pastorate in 1832.

Emerson traveled to Europe, where he met Coleridge, Carlyle, Wordsworth, and other men of letters. During the return voyage he wrote, "A man contains all that is needful to his government within himself" and "The highest revelation is that God is in every man." This was the essence of the philosophy of Transcendentalism, a belief shared by feminist writer Margaret Fuller, whom he met in 1836. With her and other transcendentalists he edited *The Dial* (1840–1844), a quarterly journal of poetry and philosophy that became a respected example of American letters. Emerson's essays and poems established his reputation in America and Europe, and his activity as a lecturer increased. "The American Scholar," an address delivered at Harvard in August 1837, called for independence and realism in American intellectual life. In addition to lecturing, Emerson continued to preach, though not affiliated with any church, until 1847.

An active abolitionist, Emerson also championed the rights of women. On 20 September 1855 he delivered a speech in Boston entitled "Woman: A Lecture Read before the Woman's Rights Convention." In language that was strong for the time, he said,

Let the laws be purged of every barbarous remainder, every barbarous impediment to women. Let the public donations for education be equally shared by them, let them enter a school as freely as a church, let them have and hold and give their property as men do theirs;—and in a few years it will easily appear whether they wish a voice in making the laws that are to govern

them. If you do refuse them a vote, you will also refuse to tax them. . . . No representation, no tax.

Among Emerson's many publications are *Nature* (1836), *Essays: First Series* (1841), *Essays: Second Series* (1844), *Representative Men* (1850), *English Traits* (1856), *The Conduct of Life* (1860), *Society and Solitude* (1870), *Letters and Social Aims* (1876), and posthumously, *Natural History of the Intellect* (1893), *Journals of Ralph Waldo Emerson* (1909–1914), and *Letters of Ralph Waldo Emerson* (1939). In a letter to Carlyle, Emerson called himself "half a bard." His collections of poetry are *Poems* (1846) and *May-Day and Other Pieces* (1867). He died in Concord on 27 April 1882.

See also Fuller, Margaret.

EMILY's List

Beginning in 1984, feminists created the political action committee (PAC) EMILY's List to raise money for female, pro-women candidates. The acronym EMILY stands for Early Money Is Like Yeast. EMILY's List offers money and other types of assistance to female Democratic congressional candidates. Careful analysis had revealed that receiving money from traditional PACs was difficult for women, particularly in the early stages of fund raising. Many women could not survive primary elections because they lacked financial backing. To correct the situation, EMILY's List was created.

Equal Credit Opportunity Act (ECOA)

The Equal Credit Opportunity Act of 1974 bans sex discrimination and discrimination based on marital status in granting credit. It applies to banks, credit card companies, home finance and home mortgage lenders, and retail stores. The law resulted from an investigation into the accessibility of credit conducted by the National Commission on Consumer Finance in 1972. The commission's hearings exposed widespread sex discrimination in the credit industry. The following year, conservative Republican Senator William Brock of Tennessee sponsored one of several credit antidiscrimination bills. The bill, drafted by Brock's aide, feminist Emily Card, became the Equal Credit Opportunity Act (ECOA). Passed in 1974, the ECOA was a noncontroversial bill that passed unanimously in the Senate and got only one dissenting vote in the House. The Federal Reserve Board drew up the ECOA regulations. The final regulations came out in 1976, after women's groups and the credit industry wrangled over various provisions. The effectiveness of the ECOA is unclear, and few complaints have been filed under it.

Equal Pay Act

The Equal Pay Act of 1963 states that women and men must receive the same pay for equal work, that is, an identical amount of work performed under identical conditions. The first federal law prohibiting sex discrimination by private businesses, the act was actually an amendment to the 1938 Fair Labor Standards Act, which required that men be given some of the same work place protections that were given to women. Because of this, it extended the exemptions written into that act, and executive, professional, and administrative employees were not originally covered by the equal pay provisions. The act is enforced by the Wage and Hour and Public Contracts Division of the Department of Labor.

See also Brown and Sharp Manufacturing Case; President's Commission on the Status of Women.

Equal Rights Amendment (ERA)

The Equal Rights Amendment (ERA) was drafted by renowned suffragist Alice Paul and introduced in Congress in 1923. Changed slightly in 1944, it reads as follows:

Section 1: Equality of rights under the law shall not be denied or abridged by the United States or by any state on account of sex.

Section 2: The Congress shall have power to enforce, by appropriate legislation, the provisions of this article.

Section 3: This amendment shall take effect two years after the date of ratification.

In 1970, Congresswoman Martha Griffiths brought an end to an almost 50-year period in which the ERA had been buried in the House Judiciary Committee files. She forced the amendment onto the House floor for a vote using an unusual method, a discharge petition. The amendment was approved on 10 August 1970 by a vote of 352 to 15, after an hour's debate (the limit for discharge petition bills), in the full House's first action on the amendment since 1923.

The scheduling of the Senate hearings on the ERA that year came about as a result of the action of Wilma Scott Heide (then chair of the National Organization for Women [NOW] board of directors), who, in February 1970, along with roughly 20 other women, had disrupted Senate hearings on a constitutional amendment to enfranchise 18-year-olds with a demand for Senate hearings on the ERA. From 5 to 7 May 1970, the Senate held its first ERA hearings since 1956: the ERA hearings of the Senate Subcommittee on Constitutional Amendments. The subcommittee gave the ERA a favorable report. From 9 to 15 September 1970, the Senate Judiciary Committee motivated by the House passage of the ERA, held hearings on both the version passed by the House and a substitute motion proposed by anti-ERA Senator Sam Ervin (D-NC). Debate on the floor of the Senate began in October. At this stage, the Senate could not pass the ERA with wording that was acceptable to feminists. This made it necessary to reintroduce the ERA in both houses with the reconvening of Congress in January 1971. California Representative Don Edwards's subcommittee in the House Judiciary Committee sent the ERA to the full Judiciary Committee after holding hearings on it in March 1971 and giving it a favorable report. In October, the ERA reached the floor of the House and, on 12 October 1971, the House passed the ERA by a vote of 354 to 23. Indiana Senator Birch Bayh reintroduced the ERA in the Senate and, on 28 February 1972, the Senate Judiciary Committee, in response to pressure from feminist lobbyists, finally approved the ERA after a long delay, 15 to 1. In March, debate on the floor of the Senate began and, on 22 March, the Senate passed the ERA by a vote of 84 to 8. In both the Senate and the House versions, feminists were successful in keeping the amendment free of riders that could dilute its impact, or even destroy its impact completely; however, they had agreed to accept a seven-year limit for ratification by the states, a time period that would eventually prove insufficient.

By 1973, through the efforts of many groups and individuals, 30 states had ratified the amendment. Only eight more states were needed. At this point, a conservative backlash forced some states to rescind ratification. At the Republican Convention in 1980, presidential candidate Ronald Reagan forced the party to break with tradition by dropping the ERA plank from its platform. Without enough states to endorse it, on 30 June 1982, the ERA failed to become part of the Constitution.

Some historians have pointed out that the original success of feminists in securing Congressional passage of the ERA was due to the fact that the Congressional debate stressed technical aspects of legal theory, which were less controversial than the social issues that would emerge during the ratification process. Some of the controversy surrounding the ERA pertained to its potential consequences for the draft, alimony and child custody laws, and the sex segregation of public bathrooms and other facilities. In addition, conservatives were able to link the ERA to even more controversial causes that were not inherently related to it or even endorsed by most feminists of the day. However, although the defeat of the ERA can be primarily attributed to right-wing mobilization in opposition to it, a lack of passion for the ERA on the part of even many nonconservative women may have also contributed to the failure to ratify the amendment. Many radical women were obviously unwilling to participate in the existing political system to any degree, but more significantly, many women of color perceived the ERA as an issue relevant only to the needs of middle- and upper-class white women, and felt that some of the energy directed at winning its passage should have been spent battling racial discrimination.

Equal Rights Party

The Equal Rights Party was a small political party active between 1884 and 1888 that agitated for women's suffrage; an end to the sale of liquor; national legislation regarding marriage, divorce, and property; and peace. Suffrage leader Belva G. Lockwood ran for president on the party's ticket in 1884 and again in 1888. However, the Equal Rights Party did not receive much support even from suffrage groups, capturing at its height 2,000 votes.

See also Lockwood, Belva.

Equal Suffrage Amendment

See Nineteenth Amendment.

Equality League of Self-Supporting Women

The Equality League of Self-Supporting Women (which in 1910 changed its name to Women's Political Union in order to embrace a wider group of women) was founded in 1907 by Harriot Stanton Blatch. This organization enjoyed the support of women from both the working class and middle class and sought to politicize the suffrage issue, as well as to educate the public about women's issues. Its effective methods included addressing politicians, contacting labor unions, and handing out leaflets near polling sites. In 1917, the Women's Political Union and the Congressional Union together formed the National Woman's Party.

See also Blatch, Harriot Easton Stanton.

Equity Law

Equity law is law decided by a judge, based on the judge's sense of fairness rather than precedent, upon which common law is based. The concept originated in English common law in reaction to the inability of common law courts to provide a remedy for every injury. Equity law modified common law by introducing the concept of a wife's separate estate, independent of her husband. Common law allowed a married woman no such right: Any property she brought to the marriage or inherited or earned afterward automatically became the property of her husband.

Until the passage of various states' married woman's property acts during the nineteenth century, equity law brought about the most important legal changes in the status of women. It is interesting to note that common law extended property rights to unmarried women. Equity law extended those rights to married women as well. Under equity law, a prenuptial contract could itemize the property a woman brought with her into marriage. Wives could bring lawsuits against husbands who failed to uphold such contracts. Equity law's protection was far from complete, however. The courts construed prenuptial contracts narrowly, and most women could not afford to go to court. Hence married women generally endured civil death under the common law.

In England, equity law protected married women in another way. When a husband asked for the court's help to gain possession of personal property owned by his wife but due and recoverable from others, he was made to set up a fund for his family's maintenance. This was called the wife's equity to a settlement, and courts enforced similar provisions in America.

In England, equity law was dispensed by the Court of Chancery. In the colonies, some colonies enacted the radical legal change of eliminating the chancery courts. Connecticut, Massachusetts, and Pennsylvania refused to establish separate courts of equity. New York, Maryland, Virginia, and South Carolina retained them. Some legislative bodies, such as the General Assembly

of Connecticut, sat as a court of equity. Today, equity jurisdiction rests with the same courts that have jurisdiction over statutory and common law.

See also Chancery Courts; Common Law; *Coutts v. Greenhow; Feme Covert; Feme Sole.*

Ewing v. Smith

In *Ewing v. Smith* (1811), a South Carolina court of appeals held that a married woman with her own property must be privately questioned by a judge before she and her husband could lease or sell her property. This was in order to protect married women from coercion by their husbands. The court broke with English tradition, which allowed married women to act as if they were single and to avoid private exams when they transferred their property rights. In South Carolina, the courts were more careful about protecting married women's property rights than the courts in the North.

See also Coercion; *Harvey and Wife v. Pecks; Watson v. Bailey.*

Executive Order 11375

Executive Order 11375 banned sex discrimination by federal contractors and subcontractors, and by federal employees. An executive order is a directive issued by the president that carries the force of law—for the federal government only. This power is broader than it may appear because, in addition to governing the federal bureaucracy, it may be applied to any institution or company that receives more than $10,000 in federal funds through contracts (including grants) and the subcontractors of those companies. Executive Order 11375, which prohibits sex discrimination, was issued by President Lyndon B. Johnson on 13 October 1967. It is actually an amendment to a previous order, Executive Order 11246, which prohibited race discrimination. That order was issued by President Johnson on 24 September 1965. For this reason, Executive Order 11375 is often referred to as "Executive Order 11246 as amended." Although issued in 1967, the order did not go into effect until 1968.

Executive Order 11375 contains two sections: one applying to federal contractors and subcontractors and the other dealing with federal employees. The section that deals with federal contractors and subcontractors is enforced by the Department of Labor's Office of Federal Contract Compliance (OFCC), which was created in 1965 with the original executive order on race discrimination. As part of its effort, the Department of Labor issued sex discrimination guidelines in 1970. The section of the executive order that deals with federal employees was enforced by the Civil Service Commission until 1 January 1979, when the Merit System Protection Board and the Office of Personnel Management replaced the commission. In 1971, the Labor Department issued Revised Order Number 4, which established regulations pertaining to the executive order. Unlike the executive order, Revised Order Number 4 actually prescribed specific antidiscrimination measures. Additional regulations were placed on federal contractors with 50 or more employees and more than $50,000 in contracts. Revised Order Number 4 required that these larger firms put together and enforce written affirmative action plans, including goals for hiring women and timetables for achieving those goals. The order required not only the abolition of current discriminatory practices but also required bona fide attempts to redress the lingering consequences of previous discrimination. Like the executive order itself, Revised Order Number 4 was not fully enforced under the administration of Ronald Reagan.

See also Federally Employed Women.

Factory Girls' Album and Operatives' Advocate

The *Factory Girls' Album and Operatives' Advocate* was one of the early magazines set up by women factory operators in the New England Mills. It began publication in Exeter, New Hampshire, in 1846 and was edited entirely by an association of females who worked in the factories. Like other publications that followed the demise of the *Lowell Offering* in 1845, the *Factory Girls' Album and Operatives' Advocate* demolished some of the myths surrounding factory life by describing actual working conditions. Operatives used such publications to point out that manufacturers and workers had opposite interests when it came to pay, hours, and working conditions. As Philip S. Foner writes, "This note of class consciousness was sounded in many forms, including poetry. . . . " From the *Factory Girls' Album and Operatives' Advocate* emerged the Female Labor Reform Association, an early trade union.

See also Factory System; *Lowell Offering.*

Factory System

During the early nineteenth century, thousands of New England women aged 17 to 22 left their parents' farms, where they had been responsible for spinning and weaving, to find work in mill towns such as Lowell, Massachusetts, and Waltham, Massachusetts. More has been written about these young women than any other pre–Civil War labor group because they left so many letters, diaries, and magazine articles. Single and white, by 1831 they made up almost 40,000 of the 58,000 workers in the textile industry. As historian Catherine Clinton writes, "As late as 1850—despite the large influx of male immigrants—women represented 24 percent of the total number of all manufacturing workers because of cotton's first rank among American industries."

The origin of the factory system in America dates to 1789, when Samuel Slater, a mechanic who memorized the closely guarded British plans for spinning machines, came to America. The following year, Slater supervised the construction of the first Arkwright spinning machine in Pawtucket, Rhode Island. In addition to imitating the British machinery, the Pawtucket mills copied the British system of labor, which employed families—especially those with many young children—to work the machines for long hours. Labor historian Philip S. Foner records in his book *The Factory Girls* that, after visiting Pawtucket in 1801, educator Josiah Quincy felt pity for "these little creatures, plying in a contracted room, among flyers and coggs, at an age when nature requires for them air, space, and sports. There was a dull dejection in the countenances of all of them." Others agreed with Quincy, and opposition to child labor gradually spread.

The Waltham system, introduced in 1813, presented an alternative to child labor. The system made use of power looms and united spinning and weaving under one roof. The Waltham system, like the Pawtucket system, was copied from the British. In 1815, the first U.S. patent for a power loom went to Cabot Lowell (for whom the famous mill town was later named), and a factory based on the new devices was running in Waltham. Because the machines were difficult for children to tend, the factories hired young adult females. Women worked as spinners or weavers while children worked as doffers, replacing used bobbins. According to historian Sarah M. Evans, "By the 1830s the work force in the Lowell, Massachusetts, mills—the heart of America's textile production and of the industrial revolution itself—were almost exclusively young, native-born women."

During the nineteenth century young women such as this shoe vamper in Lynn, Massachusetts, worked in textile mills and in shoe factories.

Textile mills dotted New England wherever there was a river to power them. They drew women and girls from Massachusetts, New Hampshire, Vermont, and Maine. The women earned spending money and had more independence in the cities than they had on their father's farms. They were disciplined, inexpensive, and no competition for the existing skilled workmen. They worked 12 to 13 hours a day, six days a week. Average wages were two dollars per week plus room and board—one-third to one-half the wages paid to men, who generally became supervisors. Yet these wages represented the greatest amount of money women could earn in the 1830s. Teaching, sewing, and domestic work—the only other jobs for which women were hired—paid far less. The women and children workers lived in company boardinghouses under strict rules and the watchful eye of company-paid matrons.

Women workers, called operators, worked until they married, which they generally did later in life than women outside the factories. Likewise, they bore children later in life. Many of the operators eagerly sought education. So strong was their desire for self-improvement that after a 12- to 13-hour day they would read or meet in study groups until bedtime. They attended lectures and church meetings. In the 1830s and 1840s, for example, mill girls made up two-thirds of the Lowell Lyceum audiences.

As the century progressed, the nature of work in the mills changed. By the late 1830s, machines were more efficient and processes were faster. Workers earned less while working more. During the 1837 depression, prices fell and wages were cut. Women oversaw more machines, working longer hours at lower wages. After the Irish famine of 1846, poor Irish immigrants replaced native-born women. The increase in immigrant workers was swift: in 1845 as many as 90 percent of the operatives were New Englanders; five years later 50 percent were Irish.

Because of the textile industry, women played a major role in the pre–Civil War economy: 60 percent of U.S. exports in 1860 relied upon cotton, which was harvested by African-American men and women in the South and processed by European-American women in the North. Indeed, textiles led the way in the nation's factory manufacturing boom, with women constituting a critical source of cheap labor. Although the replacement of home production by the factory system brought about a gradual separation of the work spheres of married men and women, for white women it created an impetus for additional education, postponed marriage, and fuller participation in the nation's economy.

See also Bagley, Sarah; *Factory Girls' Album and Operatives' Advocate;* Farley, Harriet; Female Labor Reform Associations; Lowell Female Labor Reform Association; *Lowell Offering; Voice of Industry.*

Fair Labor Standards Act

The Fair Labor Standards Act (1938), also called the Wages and Hours Law, established a minimum wage of 40 cents per hour and a maximum workweek of 40 hours. It extended to men benefits women had already won. The act prohibited employing children under the age of 16 and restricted the hiring of 16- to 18-year-olds to nonhazardous occupations. The law applied only to enterprises that engaged in or affected interstate commerce, and it specifically exempted many other occupations, such as domestic, seasonal, agricultural, and professional jobs.

Passage of the law should have resolved one of the most divisive issues within the women's movement: protective legislation. However, certain reformers, such as those in the National Consumers' League, believed that women were physically, economically, and socially a separate class from men and therefore required special treatment, while a smaller group of feminists, including members of the National Woman's Party, contended that women—given a level playing field—could achieve equality with men in all areas of public policy. In particular, these feminists believed that equality could be achieved only through an amendment to the Constitution that guaranteed equal rights to women. These two groups

111

remained at odds for years. Reformers who favored protective legislation supported the New Deal, which adopted many of their programs but played a negative role when it came to the Equal Rights Amendment.

See also Equal Rights Amendment; National Consumers' League; National Woman's Party; Protective Legislation.

Family Violence Prevention and Services Act

Enacted in 1984, the Family Violence Prevention and Services Act provides funds to shelters and other services for battered women and victims of family violence. The law also requires states to allow a batterer to be evicted from the home. Earlier in 1984, Congress created a crime victims' fund made up of federal criminals' forfeitures and fines. The family violence act specifies that a portion of the money in the crime victims' fund be given to battered women's shelters. The Reagan administration opposed the bill but endorsed the feminist position that batterers should be evicted. Hence, only states that permit the eviction of a batterer are eligible for funding under this law.

See also Violence.

Farley, Harriet (1813–1907)

Harriet Farley, a textile mill operator who became editor of the *Lowell Offering*, one of the first operators' magazines, eventually lost her audience because she refused to acknowledge labor strife in the pages of the magazine. Her date of birth is not certain but is believed to be 18 February 1813. Born in Claremont, New Hampshire, she was reared in Atkinson, New Hampshire, where she was educated at a school headed by her father. In 1837 she went to Lowell, Massachusetts, to work in a textile mill. There she eagerly attended nightly literary societies and improvement circles. In 1842 she left the mill to assume editorship of the *Lowell Offering*, a post she held until the magazine folded eight years later. Harriot Curtis, known by her pen name Mina Myrtle, was Farley's coeditor.

As editor Farley shunned controversial subjects in favor of inspirational poetry, letters, and stories that reflected the intelligence and culture of the workers. Even during the 1840s, when the battle was raging for shorter hours, higher wages, and better working conditions, Farley refused to publish discussions of the actual working conditions of the operatives. In 1845 the *Lowell Offering*—under attack from Sarah Bagley—succumbed to a competing labor paper, the *Voice of Industry*. In contrast to the *Lowell Offering*, the *Voice of Industry* adopted an adversarial stance toward the mill owners. The 7 November 1845 issue proclaimed, "The press has been too long monopolized by the capitalist nonproducers, party demagogues and speculators, to the exclusion of the people, whose rights are as dear and valid."

In 1847, after the struggle for a ten-hour day failed, Farley revived the *Lowell Offering* as the *New England Offering*. However, the paper had lost its audience and ceased publication in 1850. Farley then moved to New York, where she contributed to *Godey's Lady's Book*. A collection of her writings from the *Lowell Offering* appeared in *Shells from the Strand of the Sea of Genius* (1847). Farley also wrote a children's book, *Happy Days at Hazel Nook* (1853). After her marriage to John Intaglio Donlevy in 1854, she stopped writing for almost 20 years. After his death in 1872, she picked up her pen once again to write *Fancy's Frolics* (1880). Farley died 12 November 1907 in New York City.

See also Bagley, Sarah; Factory System; Lowell Female Labor Reform Association; *Lowell Offering*; *Voice of Industry*.

Federal Women's Program

See Federally Employed Women.

Federally Employed Women (FEW)

Federally Employed Women (FEW) was created in 1968 to push for equal opportunity for women employed by the U.S. government. According to the group's founder, Daisy Fields, the idea to create the group resulted from government executive training sessions that highlighted the scarcity of advancement opportunities for women in the federal government.

The FEW's target was the Civil Service Commission, which was responsible for enforcing the portion of Executive Order 11375 that banned discrimination among employees of the federal government. To do that, the commission wrote guidelines for judging sex discrimination complaints and established the Federal Women's Program to expedite the handling of those complaints.

For each agency of the federal government, the Federal Women's Program appointed a coordinator who was responsible for eliminating sex discrimination and proposing a plan to hire and promote women in that agency.

The FEW was extremely dissatisfied with the Federal Women's Program. The FEW claimed that the program had nominal support from the Civil Service Commission because the commission was more interested in fighting race discrimination than sex discrimination. The FEW suggested that the complaint process should be handled by an independent body, so that federal employees would not feel too intimidated to express their grievances. The FEW also tried to instill in women the confidence to file complaints. By doing so it antagonized some federal workers, but overall it sensitized people to the issue of sex discrimination in the federal government. The FEW, which is still in existence, is based in Washington, D.C., but has chapters in some cities in which the government is the main employer. The Civil Service Commission was dissolved in 1979; the Office of Personnel Management has taken over its functions.

See also Executive Order 11375.

Felton, Rebecca Ann Latimer (1835–1930)

Rebecca Felton was the first woman to take a seat in the U.S. Senate, although she acquired the seat as a lark and served no more than a few moments. She was born 10 June 1835 near Decatur, Georgia, and graduated in 1852 from the Madison (Georgia) Female College. The following year she married and moved with her husband, Dr. William H. Felton, to Cartersville, Georgia. Their home was ruined during the Civil War.

During the 1870s the Feltons became interested in public affairs. William Felton successfully ran for Congress as an independent in 1874, 1876, and 1878; Rebecca Felton served as his press secretary and campaign manager. After his defeat in 1880 and return to Cartersville in 1881, she helped him to establish and run a local paper. In 1884, William Felton began to serve the first of three terms in the state legislature, and Rebecca Felton again stepped in to draft bills, write speeches, and devise strategy.

William Felton retired from politics in 1894, after two unsuccessful campaigns to regain his seat in Congress. Rebecca Felton continued to champion prison reform, temperance, women's suffrage, the admission of women to the state university, and vocational education for poor white girls. Despite her interests in reform, Felton was a racist who advocated lynching, ostensibly to teach African-American rapists a lesson. She also wrote articles denouncing Catholics and Jews and was a strict isolationist. As a columnist for the *Atlanta Journal* (1899–1927), a delegate to the Progressive Republican National Convention (1912), and popular speech maker, she became the most influential woman in Georgia.

In 1920, Felton used her popularity to encourage voters to elect the racist Thomas E. Watson to the Senate. Watson died just before finishing his term, and the governor of Georgia appointed Felton to fill Watson's seat. Because Congress had already adjourned and a newly elected senator would take Watson's seat in the next session, the appointment was honorary. But the wily 87-year-old Felton convinced Senator-elect Walter George to wait a short time before presenting his credentials. So it happened that on 21 November 1922, Felton became the first woman to take a seat on the floor of the Senate. The next day, after being sworn in as a junior senator, she turned her seat over to George. Felton wrote three books: *My Memoirs of Georgia Politics* (1911), *Country Life in Georgia in the Days of My Youth* (1919), and *The Romantic Story of a Georgia Woman* (1930). She died 24 January 1930 in Atlanta.

See also La Follette, Belle Case.

Female Antislavery Societies

Women in antislavery societies learned to conduct meetings, circulate petitions, engage in public speaking, travel independently and widely, and raise funds. Later, women's rights activists used these skills in their fight for equality.

The first female antislavery society was formed in Boston in 1832, and became an auxiliary of the American Anti-Slavery Society, under William Lloyd Garrison. In 1833, Lucretia Mott and several other women who were excluded from membership in the American Anti-Slavery Society established the Philadelphia Female Anti-Slavery Society. Unsure of their organizational skills, the women asked a freedman to preside over their first meeting. As part of its effort to fight slavery, the group promoted the establishment of other female antislavery societies.

At the time women had few, if any, political rights. Even the right to petition the government was not universally acknowledged. Among the earliest achievements of the female antislavery societies were securing for women the right to circulate petitions and demonstrating that they could do so effectively. In the 1834 American Anti-Slavery Society petition campaign to abolish slavery in Washington, D.C., female antislavery societies collected thousands of signatures. When congressmen questioned women's right to petition the government, former president John Quincy Adams passionately defended that right. Today the National Archives holds petitions bearing hundreds of thousands of signatures collected between 1834 and 1843, proof of women's desire to exercise what was, at the time, their only political right.

The courage of female abolitionists was also seen in Boston. In 1835, when word spread that abolitionist William Lloyd Garrison was to speak before the Boston Female Anti-Slavery Society, men stormed the building where the women were meeting. Although Garrison escaped out a back door, he was later captured and paraded through the streets by a rope. To protect the African-American members of the society, each white woman took a black woman by the hand and walked to safety.

By 1837, the women were strong enough to hold their first National Female Anti-Slavery Society Convention in New York City, and 12 states sent 81 delegates. A second national convention was held the following year. And this time, the women ran their own meetings.

See also Abolition Movement; Adams, John Quincy; American Anti-Slavery Society; Anthony, Susan B.; Garrison, William Lloyd; Grimké, Angelina Emily; Grimké, Sarah Moore; Petitions; Philadelphia Female Anti-Slavery Society.

Female Labor Reform Associations

In 1845, Sarah Bagley and other mill operators formed the Lowell Female Labor Reform Association to work for a ten-hour day. Soon, through Bagley's efforts, female labor reform associations sprang up in Manchester, New Hampshire; Dover, New Hampshire; and Fall River, Massachusetts. The groups staged labor rallies and fought wage cuts and work speedups. They affiliated with the New England Workingmen's Association, championing a ten-hour workday. This early alliance between working men and women was a fairly equal one, with women attending meetings and speaking publicly. But by 1848, the association began losing members. Without sufficient money or time, the female labor associations, as well as the New England labor movement as a whole, went into decline.

See also Bagley, Sarah; Lowell Female Labor Reform Association; *Voice of Industry*.

Feme Covert

The old French word *feme* (modern *femme*) occurs in legal parlance as *feme covert*, a married woman; that is, one protected or covered by her husband. English common law regulated marriage according to the concept of *coverture*, the merging of a woman's property and identity with those of her husband. Thus, the married couple became, in the eyes of the law, one person. The rule that husband and wife cannot testify against each other in court derives from this concept of unity. But the benefits were one-sided, for only the wife merged with the husband. Historian Eleanor Flexner, quoting *The Lawes Resolutions of Women's Rights; or The Lawes Provision for Women* (London, 1632), cites the following interpretation of the term *coverture:* "When a small brooke or little river incorporateth with Rhodanus, Humber or the Thames, the poor rivulet looseth its name, it is carried and recarried with the new associate, it beareth no sway, it possesseth nothing during coverture."

Under English common law, which was widely adopted in the colonies, coverture meant legal disabilities for married women. A woman's entire personal property passed absolutely to her husband at marriage. Her real estate went to her husband for him to manage and to reap the profits. If she received an inheritance, even if she had a child eligible to inherit it, still her husband, upon her death, could hold her estate as a tenant for his lifetime. She had neither the right to her own wages nor the right to sue in court, sign contracts, or have custody of her own children. Under English common law a man could not grant or give anything to his wife, because the two were one. And if any contracts existed before marriage, they became invalid afterward.

Although, technically, a wife was merged with her husband, she could also be considered one of his vassals, so that she was sometimes immune from punishment for a crime committed in front of her husband, and not held responsible for his debts. While equity courts modified the rules of common law by introducing the notion of separate estates (that is, property given to the wife that creditors could not claim), in practice, most women were too poor or ignorant to avail

themselves of this option and hence suffered civil death upon marriage.

See also Common Law; Equity Law; *Feme Sole;* Married Women's Property Acts.

Feme Sole

The term *feme sole*, in English common law, refers to a single woman or widow. A *feme sole*, while considered of inferior status to a *feme covert*, or married woman, actually had more legal rights than her married counterpart. She had full rights to her own property and wages and could engage in business. Also, she could act as an administrator of an estate and make contracts. Widows had a somewhat different status under English common laws. For instance, they came under the protection of church and state instead of fathers or brothers. But both groups had more legal and economic autonomy than their married contemporaries, a condition that remained unchanged into the twentieth century.

See also Common Law; *Feme Covert.*

Feme Sole Trader

In colonial America, a single woman who operated a business was called a *feme sole* trader. Such a woman could make contracts, enter into lawsuits, and otherwise engage in commerce. (Married women could own businesses only with the consent of their husbands.) In 1718, the Pennsylvania General Assembly passed a law that allowed women whose husbands did not support them (such as mariners or husbands who had deserted their wives) to act as *femes soles* traders. In South Carolina, an act for better securing the payment of debts (1712) held *femes soles* traders responsible for their debts. The law was enacted because some single women fraudulently claimed that they were married and therefore not responsible for paying their business bills. The new statute benefited all businesswomen, because it made people less afraid to buy from or sell to them. Abigail Stoneman became a *feme sole* trader, opening several inns and coffeehouses in Rhode Island, New York, and Massachusetts. In

1772–1773 she became the only woman licensed to sell liquor in Newport, Rhode Island.

See also Common Law; Equity Law; *Feme Sole*.

The Feminine Mystique

Regarded by many as the book that launched the second wave (1960–1990) of twentieth-century feminism, Betty Friedan's 1963 best-seller, *The Feminine Mystique*, addressed the feelings of emptiness that many middle-class housewives experienced. Friedan's premise for *The Feminine Mystique* developed out of a survey she conducted on the effects of higher education on the satisfaction among housewives. She attributed the unhappiness of housewives—"the problem that has no name"—to what she called the "feminine mystique," a tenet that women should be content with marriage and parenting and should not seek opportunities for fulfillment outside the home. Although millions of women experienced the dissatisfaction that Friedan described, no one had so far been able to articulate this feeling and to identify the culprit: the cultural canons that dictated that even educated women must devote themselves entirely to domestic life. Previously, women who had raised any objections to this social code were labeled neurotic and accused of being bad mothers and sexually unfulfilled. Especially because the Second World War had briefly offered many women some opportunities to do work outside the home (to help meet the demands made on the country by the war), the attempt to accept a life of housework was particularly difficult. Without proper identification of the problem and with high social costs to expressing any discontent, women had been suppressing their frustrations for years. The publication of *The Feminine Mystique* allowed the release of the frustration, which came with explosive force. With women rebelling en masse, they could no longer be intimidated into keeping silent about their anger. Shortly, they started pressing for demands pertaining to issues not directly dealt with in the book.

See also Friedan, Betty; National Organization for Women; President's Commission on the Status of Women.

Feminist Art Program (FAP)

Judy Chicago and Miriam Schapiro founded the Feminist Art Program (FAP) at the California Institute of the Arts in Valencia in 1971. The program offered a feminist alternative to the art establishment. It instilled in participants a new sense of confidence about women's creative capacity and the suitability of women's experiences as subjects for art. Although the FAP did not survive the 1970s, it fueled discussions about the qualities of uniquely female art.

See also Judy Chicago.

The Feminist Press

Founded by Florence Howe in 1970, the purpose of the Feminist Press is to rediscover women's written works and heritage. Among the oldest feminist publishers, The Feminist Press has published titles by Charlotte Perkins Gilman and Zora Neale Hurston. In 1986, the publishing company affiliated with the City University of New York.

See also Gilman, Charlotte Perkins; Hurston, Zora Neale; KNOW.

The Feminists

The prominent and radical feminist Ti-Grace Atkinson formed The Feminists after a heated dispute over issues of leadership within the National Organization for Women (NOW). Atkinson left NOW on 17 October 1968 to found the October 17th Movement, later known as The Feminists. One of the best-known radical feminist groups, The Feminists favored a nonhierarchical organization and rotated responsibilities among all group members. The group's vocal opposition to the institution of marriage resulted in a much-publicized demonstration in 1969 in which it stormed the New York City marriage license bureau. The group lasted until 1973.

See also Atkinson, Ti-Grace; Radical Feminism.

Feminization of Poverty

In February 1978, sociologist Diana Pearce coined the term *feminization of poverty* in an article entitled "The Feminization of Poverty: Women, Work, and Welfare," which appeared in *Urban and Social Change Review*. Pearce pointed out that almost two-thirds of all poor adults in the United States were women. She suggested that the increase in the number of single mothers, who are very often in a precarious financial situation, was one of the main causes of the problem. Furthermore, according to Pearce, the plight and numbers of single mothers were greatly responsible for leaving women as a group, in her view, in a worse financial situation in the late 1970s than they had been in 20 years before. This implies that the gains made by feminists since then in the area of equal employment opportunity had been offset by the enormous dimensions of this problem. The introduction of the term drew much attention to the problem, and since then feminists have specifically targeted their efforts at the causes of impoverishment of single mothers.

Fenwick, Millicent Vernon Hammond (1910–1992)

Millicent Fenwick was named the first American envoy to the United Nations Food and Agriculture Organization in Rome in 1982. Born in New York City on 25 February 1910, Millicent Vernon Hammond attended Foxcroft School in Virginia, but left to accompany her father when he began serving as the American ambassador to Spain under President Calvin Coolidge. Even though Millicent never received a high school diploma or college degree, she was well educated, studying at Columbia University and the New School for Social Research. She spoke fluent French, Italian, and Spanish.

Millicent became involved in a scandalous affair with married entrepreneur Hugh Fenwick. They were married in 1934 and divorced four years later, leaving Millicent Fenwick with her husband's staggering debts and two children to raise.

At age 64, Fenwick became a renowned Republican congresswoman, representing New Jersey's Fifth Congressional District from 1975 though 1982. In her first race, her political rival was Thomas H. Kean, who eventually went on to become governor. Known as the Katherine Hepburn of politics, Fenwick's lively personality and eloquent manner prompted the creation of cartoon character "Representative Lacey Davenport" for Garry Trudeau's Doonesbury comic strip. Fenwick won the support of her peers on various issues, but on several occasions she differed with the Republican party and its leadership. She refused to support President Ford's B-1 bomber and also disagreed with his strip-mining regulations bill. While serving in Congress, she criticized special-interest groups and power brokers, including Democratic Representative Wayne Hays, the chairman of the House Administration Committee. Hays even threatened to refuse to sign staff paychecks for Fenwick unless she quieted down. Fenwick's strong beliefs included support of legal aid, food, consumer protection, and abortions for the poor.

Fenwick lost her bid for the 1982 U.S. Senate race against Democratic millionaire Frank Lautenberg. She lost by a narrow margin, but stood firm on her principle of being politically independent, refusing to accept campaign donations from political action committees or lobbyist groups.

After the election loss, Fenwick accepted an appointment from President Ronald Reagan as the first American envoy to the United Nations Food and Agriculture Organization in Rome. She remained in the post until her retirement in 1987. Fenwick died at her Bernardsville, New Jersey, home on 16 September 1992.

Ferber, Edna (1885–1968)

Born 15 August 1885 in Kalamazoo, Michigan, Edna Ferber, who fictionalized strong, assertive women, grew up in Appleton, Wisconsin. She graduated from high school in 1902 but had no money to attend college. Instead she took a job as a reporter for the

Appleton Daily Crescent, becoming the paper's first female reporter. Two years later she moved to the *Milwaukee Journal,* but after two years she collapsed under the strain of overwork. Turning to fiction, she published her first story in *Everybody's Magazine* (1910) and her first novel, *Dawn O'Hara* (1911). Her magazine stories were as numerous as they were popular, and were soon being collected in book form. Her first collection, *Buttered Side Down* (1912), was followed by *Roast Beef Medium* (1913), *Emma McChesney & Co.* (1915), and *Fanny Herself* (1917), *Cheerful—By Request* (1918), *Half Portions* (1919), *The Girls* (1921), *Gigolo* (1922), *Mother Knows Best* (1927), and *One Basket* (1947). In 1916, the Emma McChesney character was played on Broadway by Ethel Barrymore in *Our Mrs. McChesney.* In 1919, Ferber began her career as a playwright, collaborating once (unsuccessfully) with George M. Cohen and, beginning in 1924, with George Kaufman. The Ferber-Kaufman team produced *The Royal Family* (1927) and *Dinner at Eight* (1932). Ferber's best-selling novel, *So Big* (1924), won the 1925 Pulitzer Prize. In the 1940s and 1950s several of her books were made into films, including *Giant* (published in 1952 and filmed in 1956). Ferber wrote two autobiographies, *A Peculiar Treasure* (1939) and *A Kind of Magic* (1963). She died 16 April 1968 in New York City. Her novel *Showboat* (1926) was made into a musical and revived on Broadway in 1994.

Fern, Fanny
See Parton, Sarah Willis Payson.

Ferraro, Geraldine Anne (1935–)
Geraldine Ferraro was the first woman (and Italian American) to campaign for vice-president of the United States as the candidate of a major political party. She was also the first woman to chair the Democratic party's national platform committee. Born 26 August 1935, in Newburgh, New York, she was the youngest child of Dominic and Antonetta Ferraro. When she was eight years old her father died. Her mother moved the family to New York City and went to work in a garment factory. In 1956, Ferraro graduated from Marymount Manhattan College and became an elementary schoolteacher. While working she attended law school at night, obtaining a J.D. degree from Fordham University in 1960. Shortly after graduating, she married John A. Zaccaro and spent the next 14 years caring for their three children, intermittently doing legal work. In 1974 Ferraro was appointed assistant district attorney in Queens. She served until 1978, leaving, in part, because she was paid less than her male colleagues. That year she was admitted to practice before the Supreme Court and was elected to the House of Representatives from the Ninth District (Queens). Her district, which had never before sent a woman to Congress, reelected her in 1980 and 1982.

During the early 1980s, Ferraro became increasingly aware of the problems women faced in education and employment. She fought for the Economic Equity Act (1981), which was intended to accomplish many of the goals of the defeated Equal Rights Amendment. In 1984, she became the first woman to chair the national platform committee of the Democratic party. A few months later, she was selected to share the presidential ticket with Walter Mondale. They were defeated by Republicans Ronald Reagan and George Bush. In 1992, she ran in the New York State Democratic primary for the Senate, but was defeated by Robert Abrams, after which she became a member of the U.S. delegation to the United Nations World Conference on Human Rights (1993). Her 1993 book *Changing History: Women, Power and Politics,* a collection of essays and speeches, showed Ferraro to be an advocate of children, females, and those who face discrimination, as well as a speaker unafraid to condemn publicly (Helsinki Committee) the rape of women and girls in Bosnia-Herzegovina.

Fifteenth Amendment
The Fifteenth Amendment to the Constitution (1870) prohibits states from depriving

citizens of the right to vote "on account of race, color, or previous condition of servitude." It does what the Fourteenth Amendment does not: It prohibits, rather than merely penalizes, the withholding of suffrage from African-American men. Elizabeth Cady Stanton and Susan B. Anthony denounced the amendment because it excluded women. In 1869, the year that Congress approved the amendment, Anthony and Stanton left the American Equal Rights Association to organize the National Woman Suffrage Association, which was devoted solely to women's suffrage. Anthony and Stanton turned their attention to changing the Fifteenth Amendment. Just as they had wanted a one-word deletion from the Fourteenth Amendment—changing *male citizen* to *citizen*—they now wanted a one-word addition to the fifteenth—"on account of race, color, *sex*, or previous condition of servitude." Another contingent of suffragists made ratification of the Fifteenth Amendment a higher priority than women's suffrage. They believed that enfranchising African-American men was an achievable goal that would promote the women's cause. They also thought it was proper for African-American men to receive the vote before women; they considered Stanton and Anthony racist for opposing the amendment. These suffragists, led by Lucy Stone, formed the American Woman Suffrage Association. The fight over the Fifteenth Amendment split what had been an antislavery and suffragist movement, but that division led to the creation, for the first time in history, of a truly independent women's movement.

See also American Equal Rights Association; American Woman Suffrage Association; National Woman Suffrage Association.

Finkbine, Sherri

The heavily publicized case of Sherri Finkbine brought national attention to the abortion debate, especially to the question of the personhood of a fetus. In 1962 Sherri Finkbine, an Arizona mother, was pregnant with her fifth child. She learned that Thalidomide, a sleeping pill she had been taking, caused birth defects. Her obstetrician arranged for her to have an immediate abortion. Finkbine, in an attempt to warn other women, contacted the local newspaper. The paper published an article that described Finkbine's predicament and the problems with Thalidomide. The day the article appeared—the same day Finkbine's abortion was to take place—the hospital canceled the procedure. Finkbine's doctor tried unsuccessfully to pressure the hospital to perform the abortion, going so far as to apply for a court order. Finkbine eventually had her abortion in Sweden.

Firestone, Shulamith (1945–)

A radical feminist writer, Shulamith Firestone was one of the first influential organizers of the women's liberation movement in the United States. Firestone was born in Ottawa, Ontario, in 1945. As a student at the Chicago Art Institute, she became involved in the civil rights and anti–Vietnam War movements. In 1967, she and Pam Allen organized New York City's first women's group, Radical Women. In 1969, Firestone and Ellen Willis cofounded the radical group Redstockings—one of the first organizations to champion and use consciousness-raising. That same year, editor Anne Koedt and Firestone became cofounders of *Notes from the First Year*, a feminist journal. In December 1969, Koedt and Firestone coedited a manifesto, "Politics of the Ego," and "Organizing Principles" to use in a large-scale radical feminist movement. The idea was to coordinate consciousness-raising, theory, and action. In 1969, these principles were introduced to a small group of women (about 40) in New York, who eventually became known as the New York Radical Feminists. In 1970, Firestone's prominence increased with her book, *The Dialectic of Sex: The Case for Feminist Revolution*, a highly controversial work. In the book, Firestone sets forth a radical analysis of the sex/class system and the case for feminist revolution.

See also Redstockings.

Flanagan's Lessee v. Young

In 1782, Maryland jurists decided that the transfer of a married woman's property by her husband was invalid because court officers had not signed on the face of the deed that they had observed her private acknowledgment that she consented to the transfer. Maryland courts, unlike those farther north, were very careful to protect married women from their husbands' coercion in cases involving the conveyance of the wives' property.

See also Coercion; *Coutts v. Greenhow, Gregory v. Paul; Helms v. Franciscus.*

Flapper

The term *flapper* refers to a young woman of the 1920s who adopted a cosmopolitan, sexually liberated lifestyle, possibly as a reaction to the deprivations of World War I. Flappers took great pride in their carefree and unorthodox manner, breaking many of the traditional stereotypes of womanhood and the social canons of women's behavior. Flappers adopted a distinctive look: They

John Held, Jr.'s cover for the 18 February 1926 issue of Life *captures the spirit of flappers—young women of the 1920s who bobbed their hair, elevated their hems, and danced the night away.*

were extremely thin, and they wore makeup, short hair, and a style of knee-length dress with a dropped waist.

The obvious changes in the behavior and morals of the day included greater sexual experimentation and, as a result, greater tolerance of women's sexual desires. But the flapper was more a product or reflection of this new attitude than the cause of it. The new sexual freedom could be more accurately attributed to other social shifts: first, the growth in the female labor force, which gave single women a new level of economic independence (although they were still in many ways far from full equality with men in the work force) and a greater degree of control over their lifestyle choices; second, a growing acceptance of the use of contraceptive devices, reducing the danger of unwanted pregnancy.

Flappers' opposition to traditionalism arose from their fun-loving nature; they were generally not serious-minded individuals who were seeking to endorse social change. They did not seek to alter social roles or structures, and eventually adopted many elements of the conventional lives of their mothers, such as marriage, motherhood, and restriction to domestic life. In any case, flappers constituted only a small percentage of the women in their generation, and, although their entertaining behavior attracted considerable admiration from the public, it would have been unlikely that they could have effected change in the area of the woman's homemaking role.

Flynn, Elizabeth Gurley (1890–1964)

Elizabeth Gurley Flynn, commonly known as Gurley Flynn, was a radical socialist and the first leader of the American wing of the Communist party. She was born 7 August 1890 in Concord, New Hampshire. Both of her working-class parents were socialists. She joined the Industrial Workers of the World (IWW) in 1906, the same year that her career as an activist and labor agitator began. That year, at the age of 16, she spoke on the topic of women at the Harlem Socialist

120

Elizabeth Gurley Flynn, whose dedication to labor personified the ideals of the Industrial Workers of the World, inspired IWW leader Joe Hill to compose "The Rebel Girl" in 1915.

Club. By 1907 she was a regular speaker for the Socialist Labor party, Socialist party, and the IWW. At the age of 17, she left school to join an IWW speaking tour at the sugges- tion of iron workers' organizer John Archibald Jones. They married the following year but divorced in 1920 because Flynn refused to give up her work.

She soon became a nationally recognized IWW speaker and organizer. Through her efforts and those of Margaret Sanger, the Lawrence, Massachusetts, strike of 1912 received national publicity. Sanger had arranged for children of the strikers to live in New York City during the strike. When police tried to keep the children from boarding a train to New York, Congress threatened to investigate.

In 1918, Flynn was a founder of the Workers' Defense Union (WDU), which defended immigrant workers threatened with deportation; this group also publicized the Sacco and Vanzetti trial. Flynn served as the WDU's secretary until 1922. After the WDU merged with the International Labor Defense, Flynn served as chair of the ILD (1926–1930). She was also a founding member of the American Civil Liberties Union (1920).

In 1926, Flynn suffered a bout of heart disease and curtailed most of her activities for ten years. In 1936 she resumed a full schedule, joining the Communist party and becoming a columnist for the party's paper, the *Daily Worker*. She remained a Communist for the rest of her life. In 1942 she ran for a seat in the New York legislature, campaigning on women's issues. Flynn was arrested in 1951 for violating the Smith Act, which prohibits advocating the overthrow of the government by force. She was convicted and jailed in Alderson, West Virginia, from January 1955 to May 1957. In 1961 she became the first female chairman of the American branch of the Communist party, a post she retained until her death. In 1962 the state department revoked her passport under the McCarran Act, which denied entry into the United States to supporters of totalitarianism. She and historian Herbert Aptheker took the case to the Supreme Court in 1964 (*Aptheker v. Secretary of State*). They won the case, and Flynn applied for a passport to travel to the Soviet Union. She died 5 September 1964 in Moscow, where she was given a state funeral. Her autobiography, published in 1955 as *I Speak My Own Piece*, was reprinted under the title *The Rebel Girl* in 1973.

See also Industrial Workers of the World; Strikes.

Foster, Abigail Kelley (1810–1887)

Abigail Kelley Foster was a fiery reform speaker who broke taboos by traveling with Frederick Douglass and Erasmus Darwin Hudson to lecture for the American Anti-Slavery Society (1842–1845). Born 15 January 1810, in Pelham, Massachusetts, she was reared near Worcester, Massachusetts, as a Quaker. She was educated in Quaker schools and taught at one in Lynn, Massachusetts. Recruited to the abolitionist cause by William Lloyd Garrison, she served as secretary of the Lynn Female Anti-Slavery Society (1837–1838). She attended the first and second national women's antislavery conventions in New York City (1837) and in Philadelphia (1838). At the second convention she made her first speech to a mixed audience; the next day a mob burned the hall in which the group met. At the urging of abolitionists, Kelley agreed to quit her teaching job and became a lecturer. In September 1838, she helped Garrison found the New England Non-Resistant Society.

During the late 1830s, abolitionists disagreed about the role of women in their organizations. At the 1840 convention of the American Anti-Slavery Society, Kelley was elected to the group's business committee. Conservatives in the group so strongly objected that they left to form their own group. As a traveling lecturer, with Douglass and Hudson, Kelley suffered from the sexual innuendoes of critics, who referred to their "traveling seraglio." One of her fellow abolitionist lecturers was Stephen H. Foster, whom she married in 1845. Together the two lectured for abolition reform until 1861, adding women's rights to their addresses in the 1850s. She died 14 January 1887 in Worcester, Massachusetts.

See also American Anti-Slavery Society; Female Antislavery Societies.

Fourteenth Amendment

Women's rights litigation, agree legal thinkers from Leslie Friedman Goldstein to

Sandra Day O'Connor, is as old as the Fourteenth Amendment, which has been used as the basis of sex-based challenges to laws relating to hiring, promotions, maternity leave, seniority, pension rights, and disability insurance. The Fourteenth Amendment to the Constitution was introduced into Congress in 1865. It was passed to the states for ratification in 1866 and was adopted in 1868. The amendment establishes the basis of American citizenship and forbids states to deprive any person of life, liberty, or property without due process of law. Specifically, it contains three clauses that have been used to argue the most significant constitutional litigation of the twentieth century. They are: (1) No state shall make or enforce any law which shall abridge the privileges or immunities of citizens of the United States; (2) Nor shall any state deprive any person of life, liberty, or property without due process of laws; (3) Nor deny any person within its jurisdiction the equal protection of the laws. The latter provision, commonly referred to as the equal protection clause, has been a major weapon of both women and African Americans in their struggle for equality ever since.

By tying states' representation in the House of Representatives to the number of their male voters, the Fourteenth Amendment forced the former Confederate states to grant suffrage to freedmen or face reduced representation in Congress. The Republican party adopted the amendment in its platform for the Congressional elections of 1866. The American Anti-Slavery Society, to which the women's movement looked for leadership, supported it, believing that African-American male suffrage should come before that of women. In an 1865 letter to abolitionist Wendell Phillips, who that year became head of the American Anti-Slavery Society, Elizabeth Cady Stanton asked, "Do you believe the African race is composed entirely of males?" Phillips told women's suffragists, "One question at a time. This hour belongs to the Negro."

Before the Civil War, state laws denied women the right to vote. The Constitution, while not mentioning women, uses the gender-neutral terms "person" and "citizen." As Sandra Day O'Connor writes in *Women, Politics and the Constitution*, "There was, as far as we know, no disagreement that representation in Congress should be based on the whole free population, women as well as men." The Constitution, however, left to the states the qualification of voters and women were not deemed qualified. The Fourteenth Amendment, for the first time, inserted the word *male* into the Constitution, denying women the constitutional right to vote as well. In the section on the right to vote, the term *male citizen* was used rather than the established term *the people* or *citizens*. The implication was that women were not citizens, and it meant that women would need another amendment to the Constitution to be able to vote in federal elections. This brought about an argument among feminists that would eventually lead to a split in the women's suffrage movement, with Elizabeth Cady Stanton, Susan B. Anthony, and other feminists abandoning both the abolitionists and the Republican party in 1869, over the Fifteenth Amendment.

The first women's rights case to reach the U.S. Supreme Court was *Bradwell v. Illinois* (1873), in which Myra Bradwell challenged Illinois's refusal to allow her to practice law because of her sex, basing her argument on the privileges and immunities clause. In *Miner v. Happersett* (1875), the only case concerning women's right to vote to reach the Court in the 1870s, Virginia Miner used the same clause of the Fourteenth Amendment to argue that women could vote in state as well as federal elections. After these unsuccessful attempts at winning equal citizenship with men through the privileges and immunities clause, women turned to the equal protection clause, where they had greater success. After World War II, the Court shifted in its view of the Fourteenth Amendment and began using it to eliminate "invidious" distinctions or classifications (e.g., race). But the same logic was not applied to women until 1971.

A new wave in interpreting the Fourteenth Amendment as it pertained to women came in the 1971 case of *Reed v. Reed,* which declared it was arbitrary for Idaho to classify women as being less worthy than men to serve as administrators of estates. Increasingly, the Court was interpreting the Fourteenth Amendment in ways that invalidated many discriminatory laws. The due process clause was used in *Griswold v. Connecticut* (1965) to convey a basic right to privacy. Later, in *Roe v. Wade* and *Doe v. Bolton*, both decided in 1973, the appellants argued a right of personal "liberty" in the due process clause. Women's rights litigation was also strengthened in the case of *Phillips v. Martin-Marietta Corp.* Here, the Supreme Court began to implement the sex discrimination provisions of Title VII of the Civil Rights Act of 1964. In *Frontiero v. Richardson* (1973) the Court struck down a federal law that determined the dependency status of a spouse of an armed services member according to gender. In *Weinberger v. Wiesenfeld* (1975) it declared unconstitutional a Social Security Act provision that paid benefits to widows but not widowers. In *Stanton v. Stanton* it overruled a state law requiring divorced fathers to support their sons until age 21, but daughters until 18. *Craig v. Boren* (1976) overturned a state law requiring men to be 21, women 18, in order to buy beer. In *Orr v. Orr* (1979), a state law requiring men, not women, to pay alimony was overturned. In *Kirchberg v. Feenstra* (1981) a state law was overruled allowing husbands the right to manage and sell jointly owned property without the wife's consent.

Enforcement of the equal protection clause also can be seen in such cases as *Pittsburgh Press v. Human Relations Commission* (1973) and *Johnson v. Transportation Agency* (1978). The number of such cases declined in the 1980s, with more recent cases involving interpretations of Title VII (*Meritor Savings Bank v. Vinson* in 1986), or First Amendment controversies (*Hishon v. King & Spalding* in 1984).

Overall, the Fourteenth Amendment has been inexorably bound to the struggle for women's social, as well as legal, rights, and has been used to help women gain equal rights of citizenship from the vote to protec-

tion from sexual harassment. Since 1971 the Supreme Court has heard more than 50 cases regarding sex discrimination under the equal protection clause of the Fourteenth Amendment.

See also *Adkins v. Children's Hospital;* Anthony, Susan B.; *Bradwell v. State of Illinois; Doe v. Bolton;* Fifteenth Amendment; Ginsburg, Ruth Bader; *Griswold v. Connecticut; Minor v. Happersett; Muller v. State of Oregon; Personnel Administrator of Massachusetts v. Feeney; Phillips v. Martin-Marietta Corp.; Pittsburgh Press v. Human Relations Commission; Reed v. Reed; Roe v. Wade;* Stanton, Elizabeth Cady; Weddington, Sarah.

Fowler, Lydia Folger (1822–1879)

Lydia Fowler was a physician, reformer, and lecturer. She was born 5 May 1822 in Nantucket, Massachusetts. She began her career in 1847 as a traveling lecturer, speaking to women about hygiene, physiology, and anatomy. In November 1849, she enrolled in the Central Medical College in Syracuse, New York, and, in June 1850, became the second woman (after Elizabeth Blackwell) in the United States to receive a medical degree. In 1851, she became professor of midwifery and diseases of women and children at the college. From 1852 to 1860 she practiced medicine in New York City. Fowler was a strong advocate of female physicians, believing that modesty prevented many women from submitting to examinations by male physicians. Fowler also contributed to other reform movements: In January 1852 she served as delegate to the New York Daughters of Temperance and was president of the women's temperance meeting in New York City. During the following year, she lectured with Clarina Nichols. In 1863 she moved to London, where she served as honorary secretary of the Woman's British Temperance Society. Fowler published several books, among them *Familiar Lessons on Physiology* (1847), *Familiar Lessons on Phrenology* (1847), *Familiar Lessons on Astronomy* (1848), and *Nora: The Lost and Redeemed* (1863), a temperance novel. A collection of her child care lectures, *The Pet of the Household and How To Save It,* was published in 1865. Fowler died 26 January 1879 in London.

See also Nichols, Clarina Irene Howard.

Franklin, Ann Smith (1696–1763)

Ann Franklin was perhaps the first female printer in colonial America. She was born 2 October 1696 in Boston. In 1723 she married James Franklin, a brother of Benjamin Franklin. The family settled in Newport, Rhode Island, where James Franklin established a newspaper and printing business. After her husband's death in 1735, Ann Franklin took over the business. Her first published work was *The Rhode-Island Almanac for the Year, 1737.* Later, she printed *Acts and Laws of 1745* for the Rhode Island General Assembly. Remembered as a superb typesetter, she raised her daughters to be excellent compositors. Her son, James, took over the business in 1748, but Franklin remained active in it until 1757. When her son died in 1762, the 65-year-old Franklin resumed publishing the newspaper. That arrangement lasted only a few months because of her declining health. She died 18 April 1763 in Newport.

See also Goddard, Mary Katherine; Goddard, Sarah Updike; Green, Anne Catherine Hoof; Timothy, Ann Donovan.

Freedom of Choice Act

The Freedom of Choice Act, if passed by Congress, would prohibit states from enacting laws restricting most abortions (except for limited circumstances). The bill was first introduced in 1989 after the Supreme Court's decision in the *Webster v. Reproductive Health Services* case. The ruling allowed states more flexibility in regulating abortions, thereby inviting them to test the limits of the former *Roe v. Wade* decision by passing abortion restrictions. This action prompted many states to pass stricter laws concerning abortion; requiring minors to notify parents or obtain permission before having an abortion, or making a woman go through a 24-hour waiting period before an abortion could be performed. As each court decision increased these restrictions, Democratic leaders in the House and Senate attempted to pass legislation that would guarantee a woman's right to have an abortion. The number of votes was never guaranteed for this legislation to overcome the anticipated veto from former president George Bush.

On 29 June 1992 the Supreme Court established a neutral ground on this subject. The action came after a ruling in *Planned Parenthood of Southeastern Pennsylvania v. Casey.* The Court upheld restrictions on abortion in Pennsylvania but also approved the woman's right to have an abortion.

With the election of Bill Clinton as president in 1992, the outlook for abortion rights improved, as he promised to support such legislation. The House Judiciary Subcommittee on Civil and Constitutional Rights approved the Freedom of Choice Act (H25), by voice vote on 18 March 1993. Opponents say this act will surely help to erode present state laws currently regulating abortion that the Supreme Court has upheld for the last several years. Proponents say that the act will help to clarify and define the 1973 *Roe* decision, which legalized abortion.

The House Bill (H25) and the Senate Bill (S25) for the Freedom of Choice Act differ on some points. They agree on one issue: if passed, the Freedom of Choice Act will protect the reproductive rights of women throughout the United States. This legislation is one of many abortion issues facing members of the House and Senate. Federal funding of abortion for various people comes under separate bills for future consideration.

Friedan, Betty Naomi Goldstein (1921–)

Betty Friedan's 1963 best-seller, *The Feminine Mystique,* sparked the second wave of the women's movement. Born 14 February 1921, in Peoria, Illinois, and a summa cum laude graduate of Smith College (1942), Betty Goldstein attended graduate school at the University of California, Berkeley. Unsure of her direction after graduation, she held various jobs until 1947, when she married Carl Friedan. For the next ten years she cared for her family in the suburbs of New York City while working as a freelance writer.

In 1957, by circulating a questionnaire among her Smith classmates, Friedan learned that they, like her, were dissatisfied with their lives. This research formed the basis of *The Feminine Mystique*. Its premise is that educated suburban woman in the post–World War II period lived restricted lives as wives and mothers, and the media's romanticization of traditional feminine roles gave these women a sense of unreality and unease.

Friedan was a founder of the National Organization for Women (NOW) in 1966 and served as its president for four years, working to end sex-segregated employment advertisements, to increase the number of women in government, and for the establishment of child care centers and the legalization of abortion. She was an organizer of the national Women's Strike for Equality (26 August 1970), which championed equal jobs for women and child care and abortion rights. In 1971, with Gloria Steinem, Shirley Chisholm, and Bella Abzug, Friedan established the National Women's Political Caucus to place women in government posts. She also contributed to the establishment of the First Women's Bank in 1973 and called the International Feminist Congress in that year. In 1974, she joined an economic think tank for women in South Carolina.

In addition to *The Feminine Mystique*, Friedan has written *It Changed My Life: Writings on the Women's Movement* (1976), *The Second Stage* (1981), and *The Fountain of Age* (1993). In *The Second Stage* she argues that, in their attempts to be the same as men, women may have gone too far, postponing or forgoing childbirth for a career and later regretting the decision. She also urges men to cooperate with housework and child rearing. Her emphasis on worldwide equality for all people separated her to some extent from NOW. Nonetheless, she remains an influential voice for changing women's roles in the United States.

See also The Feminine Mystique; National Organization for Women; National Women's Political Caucus; Women's Strike for Equality.

Frontier Women

Popular culture associates the American frontier with the Far West. But the eastern frontier was the first to be conquered. From there, men and women pushed toward the Pacific. By the 1840s, emigrants had crossed the Mississippi River, spurred on by the discovery of gold in 1848 in California. The Homestead Act of 1862 and similar laws encouraged more pioneers to struggle across Wyoming, Nevada, California, and south to the Mexico border. The years of heaviest migration were 1841–1867: During that period, 350,000 people traveled to California and Oregon. With the completion of the transcontinental railroad in 1869, moving to the West became easier. By 1880, according to historian Julie Roy Jeffrey, "that half of the continent which 40 years earlier had contained less than 1 percent of the nation's people boasted over 20 percent of the population." By 1893 the frontier was declared closed.

Most of the female settlers in the West were young married women. At first they were scarce: in 1865 California had 3 men for every woman, Washington had 4 to 1, Nevada 8 to 1, and Colorado 20 to 1. Emigrant women rode on wagons (covered and uncovered) or trudged beside them for months at a time. They hunted, cleared land, felled trees, built shelters, and preserved food. Despite their hard work, often on a par with men, women valued—and were valued for—their traditional roles. They bore children, nursed the sick, cooked over open fires, wove, sewed, and washed clothes. Their concern about the preservation of their families contributed to their desire for reform and culture in the wilderness. These efforts to civilize the frontier brought women into conflict with men, particularly when the women fought the liquor, gambling, and prostitution interests.

A minority of women fought for the right to vote. In 1867, the Kansas legislature announced a November election on suffrage for women and African-American men. Suffrage leaders Lucy Stone and Henry Blackwell traveled to Kansas at the end of March. To address people throughout the state they climbed hills, dashed down ravines, forded creeks, and ferried rivers. Women's suffrage supporters transported them around the state, and they spoke to large audiences. "We have crowded meetings everywhere," the elated Stone wrote to Susan B. Anthony. Despite the crowds, the Kansas campaign ended in defeat for women. In Utah Territory women's suffrage was enacted in February 1870, albeit as a tactic to preserve polygamy. Wyoming Territory permitted women to vote for the first time on 6 September 1870. By 1914 women had the vote in ten of the 11 western states, no eastern states, and only one midwestern state (Illinois, 1913).

The attempt to bring Prohibition to the West disrupted relations between the sexes. In the late nineteenth century, drunkenness was more pervasive in the West than in the East. In 1888 there was one saloon in California for every 16 voters. San Francisco had 31 bars for every church. Many saw liquor as a serious threat to families and social order. Women organized to fight the liquor interests, marching on saloons, making speeches, and going to jail. Their efforts incurred the wrath of the liquor interests and had serious repercussions: fearing that women would vote for prohibitionist candidates, the liquor lobby became an intractable opponent of women's suffrage.

Many writers have pointed to the early enfranchisement of women and the number of coeducational colleges in the West as an indication of the greater liberty accorded women there. But a closer study reveals that the vote was often granted to women for secondary, and often conservative, reasons. In Utah, women were granted suffrage to fight a Congressional ban on polygamy. In Wyoming, suffrage was used to attract stable settlers. Other rights, such as the right to sit on juries or hold office, would not come to women, east or west, until the twentieth century. For example, Wyoming stopped

allowing women to sit on juries in 1870 on the basis that jury duty had no relation to suffrage. Wyoming women did not regain that right until 1950. To be fair, women share the blame for their lack of rights. For most women, campaigning for political rights took a back seat to organizing for religious or charitable purposes or supporting reforms that would improve family life.

See also Cullom Bill; Kansas Campaign; Temperance; Wyoming Territory.

Frontiero v. Richardson

In *Frontiero v. Richardson* (1973) the Supreme Court studied sex discrimination in the light of the Constitution's guarantee of equal protection. Sharon Frontiero, an air force lieutenant, was married to a college student. Although male officers received extra money for housing and extra medical benefits when they married, women did not unless they could prove that their husbands were dependents. Because Frontiero's husband was a veteran and received a small GI benefit, she could not demonstrate that he was her dependent. Frontiero's case was founded on the charge that the unequal treatment of men and women's spouses was in violation of the Fifth Amendment due process clause and the Fourteenth Amendment equal protection clause. In deciding in Frontiero's favor, the justices handed down an extremely complicated ruling, relying heavily on statistics, which discussed the progress made by women in the work force, and maintained that this reflected public acceptance of women as breadwinners. The Court was still unwilling, however, to disfavor sex-based classifications to the same degree as race-based classifications.

See also Ginsburg, Ruth Bader.

Fuller, Margaret (1810–1850)

Margaret Fuller, critic, intellectual, and transcendentalist, was a leading literary figure of her day. She was born 23 May 1810 in Cambridgeport, Massachusetts, and was educated by her father. He was a severe taskmaster and overwork damaged her

127

health. At the age of six she started to read Latin; as an older child, Shakespeare, Cervantes, and Molière were her favorite authors. As a young woman she learned German to read Goethe, Schiller, and other masters. In 1835, after her father died, she went to Boston, where she taught languages in a school run by Bronson Alcott, Louisa May Alcott's father. In 1837, she became principal teacher at the Green Street school in Providence, Rhode Island. She stayed there until 1839, when she began to live in various places near Boston and became friendly with Ralph Waldo Emerson, Nathaniel Hawthorne, W. H. Channing, and other intellectuals of the day.

Emerson met Fuller in 1836 and described her this way:

> She was then twenty-six years old. She had a face and frame that would indicate fulness and tenacity of life. She was rather under the middle height; her complexion was fair, with strong fair hair.... Her extreme plainness, a trick of incessantly opening and shutting her eyelids, the nasal tone of her voice, all repelled; and I said to myself we shall never get far.

He was wrong. Emerson became one of Fuller's closest friends and was captivated by her mind and empathy. From 1839 to 1844 Fuller conducted her famous Conversations, group discussions with women on my-thology, art, ethics, education, and women's rights. In 1840 she was among the group of transcendentalists that began *The Dial*, a literary and philosophical journal. Fuller served as editor of *The Dial* until 1842. She also helped to establish Brook Farm, the transcendentalist community in West Roxbury, Massachusetts.

Fuller wrote two books between 1844 and 1845. *Summer on the Lakes* (1844) won her a position at the *New York Tribune* as a literary critic. *Woman in the Nineteenth Century* (1845) became a feminist classic with considerable influence on the 1848 Seneca Falls women's rights convention. In 1846, some of her articles on contemporary authors were collected in *Papers on Literature and Art*. That year Fuller became the *Tribune*'s foreign correspondent, traveling to England, France, and Italy. In 1849, she married the marquis Giovanni Angelo Ossoli in Italy and the two became active in the revolution of 1848–1849. When the revolutionary Roman republic was overthrown in July 1849, the two fled to Rieti and then to Florence, where Margaret Fuller Ossoli began work on a history of the Roman revolution. The following year she sailed for the United States with her husband and infant son. On 19 July 1850, within a few miles of the U.S. coast, the ship ran aground and the family perished.

See also Emerson, Ralph Waldo; *Woman in the Nineteenth Century*.

Gage, Frances Dana Barker (1808–1884)

Women's rights activist and author Frances Barker was born 12 October 1808 in Union Township, Ohio. She received little formal education but read constantly. At the age of 21 she married James L. Gage; the couple had eight children. Through her reading she developed an interest in reform issues, including abolition, women's rights, and temperance. Under the name Aunt Fanny she wrote for the Ladies' Department of the *Ohio Cultivator*. She also began lecturing, building some local notoriety.

In 1850, she petitioned the Ohio state legislature to omit the words *white* and *male* from the state constitution, which was then being drafted. The following year she presided over a statewide women's rights convention in Akron, Ohio, and, in 1853, over the national convention in Cleveland. It was she who introduced Sojourner Truth, who delivered her famous "And Ain't I a Woman?" speech. In 1853 the Gages moved to St. Louis, Missouri, where Frances contributed pieces to various newspapers and collaborated with Elizabeth Cady Stanton and Susan B. Anthony on women's rights issues. In 1857 three fires, possibly set by opponents of Gage's reform activities, destroyed the family home. Soon after the fires, the Gages left Missouri for Illinois, returning to Ohio in 1860. In Columbus, Ohio, Gage became associate editor of the *Ohio Cultivator* and of the weekly *Field Notes*.

During the Civil War, Gage went to South Carolina, where she cared for 500 freed men and women on Parris Island. She returned to Ohio after hearing that her husband had fallen ill. After his death in 1863, she turned to lecturing to raise money for the former slaves. Gage was a featured speaker at the May 1866 meeting of the eleventh National Woman's Rights Convention, which voted to become the American Equal Rights Association. In 1867 she published a temperance novel, *Elsie Magoon*, and a collection of poetry, *Poems*. Gage died 10 November 1884 in Greenwich, Connecticut.

See also Akron Convention; American Equal Rights Association; Truth, Sojourner; Women's Rights Conventions.

Gage, Matilda Joslyn (1826–1898)

Matilda Gage is best remembered for collaborating with Susan B. Anthony and Elizabeth Cady Stanton on the first three volumes of the six-volume *History of Woman Suffrage*. She was born 25 March 1826 in Cicero, New York. Educated at home by her father, she studied Greek and math, among other subjects not generally taught to girls at the time. In 1841 she entered the Clinton Liberal Institute, where she completed her formal education. In 1845 she married Henry H. Gage, and the couple moved to Fayetteville, New York. In September 1852, she gave her first public speech at the third National Woman's Rights Convention in Syracuse, New York. Although public speaking was difficult for her, she became a dedicated lecturer for the suffrage cause.

Gage was active in suffrage organizations. She became a member of the National Woman Suffrage Association (NWSA) from the date of its founding in 1869, contributed to its newspaper, *The Revolution*, edited its newsletter, *National Citizen and Ballot Box* (1878–1881), and became a member of its first advisory council. In 1869, Gage served as secretary and vice-president of the New York State Woman Suffrage Association, going on to become president of that association (1869–1879). She was also president of NWSA between 1875 and 1876. In 1880, she lobbied the Republican, Democratic, and Greenback-Labor parties to influence them to add woman suffrage to their platforms. In 1890 she formed the Woman's National Liberal Union, a more radical group than the NWSA. Her break followed several years of political differences with the older group, and reflected Gage's belief that the Church was a vehicle for male supremacist ideology.

Gage authored a number of books. In *Woman, Church and State* (1893), she argued that religion was responsible for the widespread belief that women were inferior to men. She also wrote several pamphlets, including *Woman as Inventor* (1870) and *Who Planned the Tennessee Campaign of 1862?* (1880). Her work with Elizabeth Cady Stanton and Susan B. Anthony produced the first three volumes of the *History of Woman Suffrage* (1881–1886). Gage wrote, but was too ill to deliver, a speech to the fiftieth anniversary convention of the women's rights movement in Washington, D.C., in February 1898. She died 18 March 1898 in Chicago.

See also History of Woman Suffrage; National Woman Suffrage Association.

Garlick v. Strong

In *Garlick v. Strong* (1832), a New York chancery court ruled that married women could prevent their husbands from transferring the wives' property by withholding consent to the transfer. Mrs. Garlick complained that her husband had broken an agreement concerning the sale of her property. The agreement was that if Mrs. Garlick suspended her dower rights—a life estate to which a woman is entitled upon the death of her husband—then Mr. Garlick would set aside half of the proceeds from the sale as a fund to support the family if he died. Mr. Garlick later reneged and argued that married couples could not enter into such bargains because the bargains would make titles to property questionable. But the court agreed with Mrs. Garlick that women had the right to withhold their consent to the transfer of their property.

See also Dower; *Griffith v. Griffith; Kempe's Lessee v. Kennedy et al.*

Garrison, William Lloyd (1805–1879)

William Lloyd Garrison, a radical abolitionist and ardent supporter of women's rights, was also a pacifist and religious reformer considered by some to be an extremist. He was born 12 December 1805 in Newburyport, Massachusetts. His father, a sea captain, left home when Garrison was a child, never to return. Garrison's mother encouraged him to be a shoemaker. Dissatisfied with that trade, he turned to cabinetmaking. This did not suit him either, and in 1818 he was indentured to the publisher of the *Newburyport Herald.* This work he loved. He soon became a compositor and later a writer. In 1826 he became editor of a local paper, the *Free Press.* When the paper failed, Garrison went to Boston, where he became the editor of the *National Philanthropist,* the nation's first paper to champion total abstinence from liquor. In 1828 he founded the Bennington, Vermont, *Journal of the Times,* which supported John Quincy Adams for president.

Benjamin Lundy, a Quaker opposed to slavery, enlisted Garrison in the abolition movement. Lundy was the publisher of *The Genius of Universal Emancipation,* a Baltimore emancipation journal. In an effort to recruit Garrison as editor of the journal, Lundy walked through the winter snows from Boston to Bennington, a distance of 125 miles, an anecdote recorded in the eleventh edition (1910–1911) of *The Encyclopaedia Britannica.* Garrison joined Lundy in Baltimore in 1829. Eventually the two separated over whether emancipation should be gradual or immediate, with Garrison taking the latter view. Garrison was jailed for libeling a slave trader in an article that appeared in the *Genius of Universal Emancipation.* He was released after Arthur Tappan, a New York philanthropist and abolitionist, paid his fine. Garrison returned to Boston where, on 1 January 1831, without one dollar of capital, he published the first issue of *The Liberator,* an emancipation paper. He edited the paper for the next 35 years, until after ratification of the Thirteenth Amendment.

Garrison opposed war, yet he believed that if slavery was not ended by peaceful means, then violence was inevitable. He advocated the use of "moral suasion," or an appeal to Americans' religious conscience, to end slavery. This view imbued the first society established under Garrison's auspices, the New England Anti-Slavery Society (1831). In 1833, he joined with the brothers Arthur Tappan (who had bailed him out of jail in 1830) and Lewis Tappan to create the American Anti-Slavery Society. The group's declaration of principles and purposes, which Garrison wrote, called for immediate emancipation. In 1835 he tried to address the Boston Female Anti-Slavery Society, but a mob captured him and paraded him through town at the end of a rope. Rescued at the last moment, Garrison was jailed for his own protection and spirited out of the city.

Garrison strongly advocated the political equality of the sexes. He supported the full participation of women in all antislavery societies, allowing them to vote, speak in meetings, and lecture as agents. His unbending, assertive support for women was partly responsible for splitting the abolition movement in two. In May 1840 the American Anti-Slavery Society split. The Tappan brothers and others who opposed women's rights left to form the American and Foreign Anti-Slavery Society. Other reformers, who sided with Garrison on the question of women's rights but disagreed with his extremist views on religion and politics, left to form the Liberty party.

At the 1840 World's Anti-Slavery Convention in London, Garrison refused to take his seat as a delegate because the convention would not accept the credentials of the American female delegates. Scheduled to be the key speaker, instead he sat silently with the women behind a curtain for the ten days of the conference. Later he wrote, "After battling so many long years for the liberty of African slaves, I can take no part in a convention that strikes down the most sacred rights of all women."

In 1843 the Massachusetts Anti-Slavery Society, under Garrison's leadership, declared the Constitution "a covenant with death and an agreement with hell." He wrote to the 1850 Woman's Rights Convention, "I doubt whether a more important movement has ever been launched . . . than this in regard to the equality of the sexes." In a speech before the fourth National Woman's Rights Convention in Cleveland (1853), Garrison blamed the oppression of women on the "intelligent wickedness" of men, claiming, "As man has monopolized for generations, all the rights which belong to woman, it has not been accidental, not through ignorance on his part; but I believe that man has done this through calculation, actuated by a spirit of pride, a desire for domination which has made him degrade woman in her own eyes, and thereby tend to make her a mere vassal."

On 4 July 1854, Garrison burned the Constitution before a group in Framingham, Massachusetts, saying "So perish all compromises with tyranny!" He believed that, because the national government was constitutionally bound to aid in the capture of fugitive slaves and repress their attempts to win freedom, endorsing these policies amounted to compromise with tyranny. At the end of the Civil War, Garrison called for the dissolution of the American Anti-Slavery Society (1865). When the society refused to disband, he quit. Garrison died in New York on 24 May 1879. His published works include *Thoughts on African Colonization* (1832), *Sonnets and Other Poems* (1843), and *Selections from His Writings and Speeches* (1852).

See also Abolition Movement; American Anti-Slavery Society; Female Antislavery Societies; World's Anti-Slavery Convention.

Gender Gap

Although suffragists predicted that women would eventually vote as a unit, the gender gap was not identified as a phenomenon until the 1980 presidential election. That election revealed a strong correlation between gender and support of a candidate: Ronald Reagan's support among women was 10 percent less than among men. The gender gap, by creating the impression that women would vote as a bloc, empowered women in the early 1980s to press for their demands with a threat of political retaliation. For this reason a variety of feminist bills were passed in the early 1980s, and the phenomenon may have contributed to the selection of Geraldine Ferraro as Walter Mondale's running mate in the 1984 presidential campaign. With the 1984 election the gender gap seemed to have disappeared. But during the 1988 presidential election, there was a five- to six-point difference in the voting behavior of men and women. In 1992, 47 percent of women compared to 41 percent of men chose Bill Clinton over George Bush.

See also Ferraro, Geraldine.

General Federation of Women's Clubs

The widespread desire for self-improvement in the nineteenth and twentieth centuries resulted in the establishment of women's clubs, which gradually moved away from cultural pursuits to reform activities. In 1890, reading societies throughout the United States organized to form the General Federation of Women's Clubs (GFWC). In a few years, members became involved in civic affairs and educational and sanitary reform. Historians Carl J. Schneider and Dorothy Schneider record that at one point the GFWC asked each club in the country to report all working children under age 14. The Florida clubs were appalled by the number of Cuban children working in the sugar mills and immediately began lobbying for protective legislation. By 1900 the clubs had begun financing sanitary housing in slums, urging the restructuring of the judicial system for juveniles, and endorsing child labor legislation. Women such as Mary Wood of New Hampshire worked to improve the conditions of store clerks and promote public health nursing. Members elected presidents with strong reformist zeal, like Sarah Sophia Decker of Colorado, who fought for the conservation and reform of the civil service.

By the 1920s, the GFWC had retrenched to promote more conservative goals. However, during the 1960s, the group strongly supported the Equal Rights Amendment.

See also Equal Rights Amendment; Nathan, Maud.

Gilligan, Carol (1936–)

Carol Gilligan is known for Project on the Psychology of Women and the Development of Girls at Harvard University, which seeks ways to help girls weather the crisis of adolescence. Born in 1936 in New York City, she attended Swarthmore College and received her Ph.D. in clinical pyschology from Harvard. After a period of activism in the peace and civil rights movements of the 1960s and 1970s, she began teaching at Harvard, where she is now a professor of education. As of 1992, she was one of the few tenured female professors at Harvard.

Gilligan's book, *In a Different Voice: Psychological Theory and Women's Development* (1982), made her reputation, but also caused a furor among academics by suggesting that girls differed from boys in their psychological development. In another area of research, Gilligan headed a team of faculty and students in the Dodge Study, also known as the Project on the Psychology of Women. This was a five-year study of trends in the self-confidence of adolescent girls. Gilligan's study of the role of gender in psychological development and maturation is one of the few landmark psychological studies that includes females. Most other models of healthy development are based on males.

Gilligan also led pioneering research about gender differentiation in the area of ethics. In three research studies Gilligan found that ethical distinctions made by women differ from those made by men. Previous theories interpreted the ability to reason from abstract principles as the highest stage of moral development. But Gilligan believes that women respond more often in the "care voice" and men in the "justice voice." One way of responding is no higher or lower than the other; they are simply different, Gilligan says.

Some feminists, such as Carol Tavris, author of *The Mismeasure of Woman* (1992), have questioned Gilligan's theory, arguing that its popularity does not rest on its scientific merit. According to Tavris, new research indicates that men and women use both care-based reasoning and justice-based reasoning in making decisions. However, Tavris concedes that Gilligan has broadened the notion of moral reasoning with the concept of the ethic of caring.

As well as *In a Different Voice*, Gilligan has written eight other books, including *Women, Girls and Psychotherapy: Reframing Resistance* (1991), and *Making Connections: The Relational Worlds of Adolescent Girls at Emma Willard School* (1989).

See also Project on the Psychology of Women.

Gilman, Charlotte Anna Perkins Stetson (1860–1935)

Feminist writer Charlotte Perkins Gilman was a leading intellectual of the early women's movement. She was born 3 July 1860 in Hartford, Connecticut, growing up in poverty because her father, a member of the prominent Beecher clan, abandoned his family soon after her birth. Consequently the family moved 19 times in 18 years. Charlotte received a spotty education that included a brief period of study at the Rhode Island School of Design. Married to artist Charles D. Stetson in 1884, she soon fell ill with depression, presumably over her married state and domestic responsibilities. Her symptoms disappeared during a solitary trip to California in 1885. Three years later she and her daughter moved to Pasadena, California, where she began writing poems and stories for publication.

In January 1892 her horror story, "The Yellow Wall-Paper," was published in *New England Magazine.* Today a feminist classic, it tells the story of a well-off housewife who becomes insane due to her life of domesticity. The narrator, ill and imprisoned in her bedroom, a former nursery, comes to believe that she sees a woman, then many women, trapped behind the patterned bars of the room's yellow wallpaper. The women are trying to creep from behind the barred paper

to freedom. Soon, the narrator joins them, dimly perceiving that theirs is the situation of all women. The story so offended the editor of *The Atlantic Monthly*, to whom it was originally submitted, that he wrote, "I could not forgive myself if I made others as miserable as I have made myself!"

A collection of poems, *In This Our World* (1893), brought her a small following, and in 1894 she coedited the *Impress*, the publication of the Pacific Coast Woman's Press Association. In 1894 she divorced Stetson and moved to San Francisco. Soon after the divorce Stetson married his ex-wife's best friend. Despite this, Charlotte sent their daughter to live with Stetson and his new wife, causing a scandal. Nonetheless, she went on to make a career in writing and public speaking, particularly on the topics of reform of working conditions and the equal treatment of women.

After a brief stay at Jane Addams's Hull House in 1895, Charlotte Stetson was a

Charlotte Anna Perkins Stetson Gilman in 1900

133

delegate (1896) to the International Socialist and Labor Congress in London. Her *Women and Economics* (1898)—a devastating critique of sexual and economic relations between the sexes—called for the economic equality of women. She had come to believe that child rearing and housework should not be the sole responsibility of the solitary housewife but should be performed by those best suited for the chores. She called for communal nurseries and kitchens so that women could be free to work outside the home; she later elaborated on these ideas in her *Concerning Children* (1900) and *The Home* (1903). *Human Work* (1904) further extended her arguments about the sexual division of labor.

In 1900 Charlotte married her cousin, George H. Gilman. The couple lived in New York City until 1922, when they moved to Norwich, Connecticut. During this period Charlotte Gilman wrote *What Diantha Did* (1910), *The Crux* (1911), and *Moving the Mountain* (1911). In 1909 she launched a feminist magazine, *Forerunner*. In a 1915 issue of the magazine, she published "Herland," a fantasy about a female utopia. "Herland" is a humorous story about three men who happen to discover the utopia and learn to appreciate women as human beings, not merely as members of the other sex. Also in 1915, Perkins Gilman joined Jane Addams and other women's leaders to found the Woman's Peace Party. She wrote *His Religion and Hers* (1923) and *The Living of Charlotte Perkins Gilman* (1935). In 1932, she learned she had cancer. After her husband's unexpected death in 1934, she moved to Pasadena to live with her daughter's family. There, because she did not want to be a burden, she committed suicide by using chloroform on 17 August 1935.

See also Woman's Peace Party.

Ginsburg, Ruth Bader (1933–)

Ruth Bader Ginsburg, whose litigation on behalf of women's rights transformed the legal landscape of the 1970s, is the second woman to serve on the Supreme Court. Ginsburg was nominated by President Bill Clinton on 14 June 1993, approved by the Senate on 3 August, and sworn in on 10 August.

Ruth Bader was born in Brooklyn, New York, in 1933 and graduated from James Madison High School. She attended Cornell University, graduating Phi Beta Kappa in 1954. That year, she also married Martin D. Ginsburg. In 1956, the mother of a 14-month-old daughter, Ginsburg became one of only nine women in the 400-person first-year class at Harvard Law School, where she was a member of the *Harvard Law Review*. However, she did not graduate from Harvard, moving instead to New York City and transferring to Columbia University. She received her J.D. in 1959, the first person to be a member of both the Harvard and Columbia law reviews.

After graduating, Ginsburg interviewed at a number of law firms, but, unlike her male colleagues, she could not find a job as a lawyer because of her gender. When a professor recommended her as a law clerk to Supreme Court Justice Felix Frankfurter, the justice commented that he was not ready to hire a female for the job. Eventually, she was hired by Edmund L. Palmieri of the U.S. District Court for the Southern District of New York.

After clerking for Palmieri, Ginsburg became research associate, then associate director, for the Columbia Law School Project on International Procedure. She authored books and articles on the Swedish and Scandinavian legal systems.

Ginsburg taught at Rutgers University between 1963 and 1972; she was made a full professor in 1969. In 1972, she joined the Columbia Law School faculty, teaching, among other courses, Sex-Based Discrimination. In 1977, *Time* magazine selected her as one of ten outstanding law professors in the United States. In 1979, Ginsburg received the Society of American Law Teachers annual Outstanding Teacher of Law award. She would later become the first female to be tenured at Columbia's law schools.

While at Columbia, Ginsburg founded and directed the Women's Rights Project of the American Civil Liberties Union. She also brought landmark discrimination cases before the U.S. Supreme Court and played a role in winning every 1970s Supreme Court case that invalidated laws that discriminated on the basis of gender. Because of these cases, Ginsburg is called the "Thurgood Marshall of the Women's Movement." In six of these gender discrimination cases, she presented the oral arguments; in five cases she prevailed. The cases were *Frontiero v. Richardson* (1975), in which she won for women in the armed services equal benefits with men for their dependents; *Weinberger v. Wiesenfeld* (1975), which invalidated a provision of the Social Security Act that granted survivor benefits to widows with minor children but not to widowers with minor children; *Edwards v. Healy* (1975), in which the Court vindicated Ginsburg's position in *Taylor v. Louisiana*, challenging a Louisiana law that exempted women from jury service automatically, unless they made a written statement that they wished to serve; and *Califano v. Missouri* (1979), which struck down a Missouri law that exempted women from jury service upon request, on the grounds that the law violated the criminal defendants' right to a jury drawn from a fair cross-section of the community.

Ginsburg's other most significant cases were the historic *Reed v. Reed* (1971), which Ginsburg coauthored, and which declared unconstitutional an Idaho statute that stated that between persons "equally entitled" to administer a descendant's estate, "males must be preferred to females." This was the first time the Court had struck down a gender-based classification as inconsistent with the equal protection clause of the Fourteenth Amendment. In *Moritz v. Commissioner of Internal Revenue* (1973), which Ginsburg personally argued before the Court of Appeals, the Supreme Court for the first time held a provision of the Internal Revenue Code to be unconstitutional. The provision had granted tax deductions to daughters and married sons, but not to unmarried sons, who cared for an elderly, infirm parent. *Struck v. Secretary of Defense* (1972) involved a U.S. Air Force rule that mandated the discharge of pregnant air force officers. After Ginsburg filed her Brief for Petitioner, the air force agreed to allow Captain Struck to serve and they changed the rule under challenge. *Kahn v. Shevin* (1974) was Ginsburg's sole defeat in a Supreme Court oral argument. In this case, the Court upheld an 1885 Florida law that provided a real property tax exemption for widows but not for widowers. Finally, in *Owens v. Brown* (1978), the Court held that a federal statute that prohibited female members of the navy from being given sea duty was unconstitutional. Ginsburg had represented the plaintiff in the U.S. District Court.

In 1980, receiving the American Bar Association's highest rating for a prospective judge, Ginsburg was nominated by Jimmy Carter to the federal bench. In her 13 years on the Appeals Court, she won a reputation as the mediator between the court's warring liberal and conservative factions.

After President Clinton nominated Ginsburg to the Supreme Court, some women's groups, such as National Abortion Rights League, criticized Ginsburg for some of her comments over the years questioning some aspects of the 1973 *Roe v. Wade* decision. They specifically cited her spring 1993 James Madison Lecture at New York University School of Law, in which she said the decision was too sweeping and may have contributed to the 20 years of bitter debate that followed. Ginsburg argued that it was unwise for the Court to impose a detailed formula telling states how to regulate abortion in each of the trimesters. Instead, she said, the justices should have simply overturned the Texas law. But after her testimony at the Senate confirmation hearings, Ginsburg had won over all but the most ideological of opponents.

Ginsburg's awards include the 1980 Barnard College annual Woman of Achievement award and the ABA's Margaret Brent Women Lawyers of Achievement award (1993).

See also *Frontiero v. Richardson; Reed v. Reed.*

Girl Scouts of the U.S.A.

The forerunner of the Girl Scouts was the Girl Guides, founded in England in 1909. Established in 1912 in Savannah, Georgia, by Juliette Gordon Low and renamed the Girl Scouts in 1913, the organization was one of the first volunteer societies for young females in the nation. By 1921 there were Girl Scout organizations in every state. Like many women of her day, Low opposed women's suffrage. Nevertheless, she wanted to offer girls greater opportunities and to encourage them to participate in outdoor activities. Today, with 332 local councils, the organization is the largest volunteer organization of women in the world. By 1993 almost 60 million girls and women had belonged to the organization. Although the group still emphasizes citizenship and outdoor activities, its focus is now on urban girls.

In 1993 Girl Scouts of the U.S.A. had nearly three million members participating in community and outdoor activities.

Goddard, Mary Katherine
(1738–1816)

Mary Katherine Goddard was a printer, publisher, and probably America's first female postmaster. She was born 16 June 1738, in Groton or New London, Connecticut. In 1765 she and her widowed mother, printer Sarah Goddard, took over a printing business and newspaper founded by her brother, William. In 1768, they sold the business and joined William Goddard in Philadelphia, where Mary Goddard helped her brother to publish the *Pennsylvania Chronicle.* In 1773 William Goddard made another move, this time to Baltimore, Maryland, leaving Mary Katherine to run the business he left behind. In 1774, she sold the newspaper and moved to Baltimore to take over her brother's weekly, the *Maryland Journal; and the Baltimore Advertiser.* Her role as publisher was formally acknowledged on the masthead in 1775. That year she became Baltimore's postmaster, probably the first female postmaster in America. (Her brother had established the colonial postal system.) Two years later, Goddard printed the first copy of the Declaration of Independence that included the names of the signers. She held the position of postmaster until 1789, when she was replaced because the job had been expanded to include traveling, which was considered improper for a woman. More than 200 businessmen supported her petition to retain her job to no avail. Goddard quarreled with her brother in 1784 and left the printing business but continued to manage a bookstore she had opened. She operated the bookstore until 1809 or 1810. She died 12 August 1816 in Baltimore.

See also Franklin, Ann Smith; Goddard, Sarah Updike; Green, Ann Catherine Hoof; Timothy, Ann Donovan.

Goddard, Sarah Updike
(c. 1700–1770)

Colonial printer and mother of publisher Mary Katherine Goddard, Sarah Updike was born c. 1700 near Wickford, Rhode Island. She received a well-rounded education at home and in 1735 married Dr. Giles Goddard, who died in 1757. They had two children who lived to adulthood, Mary Katherine and William. In 1762,

136

Sarah provided her son with money to launch the *Providence Gazette*, the first print shop and newspaper in Providence, Rhode Island. Sarah and her daughter Mary Katherine moved to Providence that same year, to work in the print shop. Three years later, William suspended publication of the newspaper and left the printing business under his mother's management. That year mother and daughter published *West's Almanack*. The following year they revived the *Providence Gazette* under the name of Sarah Goddard, making her Providence's second printer. She ran the newspaper as well as a bookstore and bindery until 1768, when she sold the business and joined her son in Philadelphia, where he was publishing the *Philadelphia Chronicle*. There, Sarah helped him to manage the business until her death on 5 January 1770.

See also Franklin, Ann Smith; Goddard, Mary Katherine; Green, Ann Catherine Hoof; Timothy, Ann Donovan.

Godey's Lady's Book

Founded by Louis A. Godey in 1831, *Godey's Lady's Book* was a heavily illustrated monthly that took its articles from popular English women's magazines, until it merged with *American Ladies' Magazine* in 1837. Godey bought *American Ladies Magazine* in order to get its editor, Sarah Josepha Hale, who used the new magazine to highlight books written by and for women. She also wrote editorials supporting better education for women and girls and commissioned articles on women's history. Although more conservative than the journals of the women's rights movement, *Godey's Lady's Book* promoted women's issues to middle-class women.

See also Hale, Sarah Josepha.

Goldman, Emma (1869–1940)

Anarchist Emma Goldman was one of the most riveting female lecturers in American history. She was an advocate of birth control, women's rights, free speech, and sexual liberation. Born 27 June 1869 in an area of

Russia that is now Lithuania, Emma Goldman was living in St. Petersburg, Russia, in 1885, when she decided to emigrate to the United States rather than submit to an arranged marriage. In the United States, she obtained work in clothing factories, first in Rochester, New York, and later in New Haven, Connecticut. She found working conditions oppressive and became a public critic of capitalism. In 1889 she moved to New York City, where she joined radicals Johann Most and Alexander Berkman in the anarchist movement. Berkman was imprisoned from 1892 to 1906 for his attempt to assassinate Carnegie Steel's Henry Clay Frick during the bitter Homestead strike of 1892. (Goldman had collaborated with Berkman in preparing for the murder but was not present when the attempt was made.) Goldman was imprisoned in 1893 for delivering an inflammatory speech to unemployed men in New York's Union Square. Upon her release she lectured in the United

Anarchist Emma Goldman, photographed in 1906

137

States and Europe. When Berkman was freed, they founded and edited the journal *Mother Earth* (1906–1917).

Although she thought the demand for the vote was trivial compared to the need for economic reform, she did lecture against the traditional role of women in marriage and argued for a reduction in family size and voluntary motherhood. For speaking out in favor of birth control in 1916 she spent more time in jail; in 1917 she was sentenced to two years in prison for opposing conscription. She was released in 1919, immediately declared a subversive alien, and deported to Russia with Berkman and 247 other radicals. She remained there only two years, later recalling her experiences in *My Disillusionment in Russia* (1923). She continued to lecture in Europe and wrote an autobiography, *Living My Life* (1931). Joining the antifascists in Spain during the civil war, Goldman was organizing on their behalf in Canada when she died in Toronto on 14 May 1940. Her other books include *Anarchism and Other Essays* (1911), and *The Social Significance of the Modern Drama* (1914).

See also Birth Control; Contraception; Sanger, Margaret.

Gordon, Kate M. (1861–1932)

Kate M. Gordon and her sister, Jean Gordon, were among the South's few suffragists. Kate Gordon was born 14 July 1861 in New Orleans, Louisiana. In 1896, she founded the Era Club (Era for equal rights association) to work for women's suffrage. The organization soon espoused a variety of reforms. In 1898, the Era Club gained for female taxpayers the right to vote on tax issues. One of its most important achievements was mobilizing the new voters to support better water and sewer systems for the city of New Orleans. Gordon entered the national suffrage movement in 1900, when she spoke at a National American Woman Suffrage Association convention. The following year she was elected corresponding secretary of that organization. From 1904 to 1913 she led the Louisiana state suffrage association, also organizing

the Southern States Woman Suffrage Conference to work for suffrage on a state-by-state basis. Gordon succeeded in influencing the Democratic National Convention of 1916 to endorse state suffrage in its platform. In 1921, she helped to create the first permanent juvenile court in New Orleans, and she later assisted in the establishment of the New Orleans Hospital and Dispensary for Women and Children. Gordon died 24 August 1932, in New Orleans.

See also Merrick, Caroline.

Granger Movement

In 1867, a socioeconomic movement began to help farmers, which also opened doors for women. Known as the Farmer's Movement, it was led by a secret fraternal organization called the National Grange of the Patrons of Husbandry. Because local chapters of the organization were called *granges*, the movement is frequently called the Granger Movement. The Patrons of Husbandry immediately opened its membership to women, and early in the 1870s a few women held higher office. In 1895, Sarah G. Baird became master of the Minnesota State Grange, a position she held for 17 years. No other agricultural organization provided for women's participation and leadership to the extent that the Patrons of Husbandry did during this period. At first, the Patrons of Husbandry did not address women's suffrage. However, local granges, beginning with the California State Grange in 1878, adopted resolutions supporting equal suffrage. Eventually, the National Grange, which supervised the local granges, adopted an equal suffrage resolution.

Grant, Zilpah Polly (1794–1874)

Educator Zilpah Grant was born 30 May 1794 in Norfolk, Connecticut. From the age of 15 she taught school. In 1820 Grant enrolled in the Rev. Joseph Emerson's female seminary in Byfield, Massachusetts, to further her own education. The next year she became a teacher at the school, and for the next few years she taught throughout

New England. In 1824 Grant became the first director of the Adams Female Academy of Londonderry, New Hampshire, where she established a rigorous curriculum. One of the academy's teachers was Mary Lyon, future founder of Mount Holyoke College, which also established high standards for women. In 1828, because of a conflict with the academy's trustees, Grant left for Ipswich, Massachusetts, where she founded the Ipswich Female Seminary. There she appointed Mary Lyon assistant principal. The school provided the model for Mount Holyoke Seminary. Grant married William B. Banister in 1841 and, in 1852, became a member of the board of managers of Catharine Beecher's American Woman's Educational Association, which recruited and trained teachers in the Midwest. In 1856, she published *Hints on Education*, and thereafter devoted herself to religious activities. Grant died 3 December 1874 in Newburyport, Massachusetts.

See also Beecher, Catharine; Lyon, Mary; Mount Holyoke College.

Great Awakening

The Great Awakening was, in the words of historian Arthur Schlesinger, "the first universal and spontaneous movement in the history of the American people." It consisted of a series of religious revivals that swept colonial America from the late 1730s to the 1760s, centering in New England from 1740 to 1743. The word *awakening* was perhaps first used by the famous revivalist Jonathan Edwards in Northampton, Massachusetts (1734). The leaders of the movement were George Whitefield, the internationally known Anglican preacher from England who had been preaching in Savannah, Georgia; Whitefield's follower, Gilbert Tennent; and, perhaps best remembered, Edwards. Some local clergymen, including Congregationalists, Presbyterians, and Baptists, supported the cause.

Preaching in an emotional and dramatic manner, the itinerant preachers so impressed their listeners with the reality of sin and the promise of redemption that men and women alike wept, shrieked, and even fainted in a frenzy of ecstatic emotional cleansing, which was interpreted as the evidence of salvation. Women and men, many of them adolescents, followed these traveling preachers, turning their spiritual focus inward and embracing the emotional conversion experience.

The revival sparked much debate in both secular and religious circles. The revivalists attacked as heretics clergymen who took a scientific, rationalistic approach to Christianity. The rationalistic approach found expression in the doctrine of free will, or the idea that people could use rational thought to ascertain the will of God and through their actions attain or forfeit salvation. That was a sterile faith, the revivalists charged, and the clergy who preached it were emotionally dead. For their part, the rationalistic preachers condemned the revivalists for making religious devotion a matter of passion rather than thought.

The revival came to an end in Massachusetts when the General Court of Massachusetts required itinerant preachers to obtain permission to preach from the local pastor. Between 1744 and 1745 Whitefield discovered that most pulpits in New England were closed to him.

Many of the sects that formed as a result of the Great Awakening declined, but churches that embraced emotional evangelism, such as the Baptists and Methodists, were poised to become great popular denominations of the future.

Following the Great Awakening, religious experience in America was increasingly emotional, and this may have created greater sympathy for women. In the years following the revival, the number of convictions for infanticide dropped, marriage was more often based on love than on parents' choice, and divorce for alienation of affection became more common.

See also Second Great Awakening.

Greeley, Horace (1811–1872)

Editor and statesman Horace Greeley gave favorable publicity to the women's rights

139

movement in his newspaper, the *New York Tribune,* and generally supported women's rights. He was born 3 February 1811, near Amherst, Massachusetts. At the age of 14, Greeley was apprenticed to the *Northern Spectator* of East Putney, Vermont. There, he became interested in politics and gradually took over editing most of the newspaper. After the paper ceased publication in 1830, Greeley traveled by foot and canal boat to New York City. Employment was hard to find because Greeley, in poorly fitting clothes with only ten dollars to his name, looked like a runaway apprentice. In 1833 Greeley and Francis V. Story pooled $150, bought some type on credit, and began printing New York City's first inexpensive newspaper, the *Morning Post.* It failed after three weeks, and Story died the following year. In 1834, Greeley and another partner (the deceased Story's brother-in-law, Jonas Winchester) brought out the first issue of the *New Yorker,* which brought Greeley distinction. During this time, he also edited the *Jeffersonian* (Albany, New York), a Whig publication, and, by 1840, was editing *The Log Cabin.*

Overextended and practically penniless, Greeley's reputation allowed him to obtain a loan from a friend to launch *The Weekly Tribune,* and, in 1841, he announced he would begin publication of a daily newspaper called the *Tribune.* The New York *Tribune* is remembered for its aggressive discussion of the vital issues of the day, among them equal rights for women. During its first year of publication, the *Tribune* published many of Elizabeth Cady Stanton's essays. In 1845 Margaret Fuller became the paper's literary critic, and the first woman on its staff. In "Women and Work," published in the 1 September 1852 issue, Greeley summed up his ideas about the economic inequality of women: "Before all questions of intellectual training or political franchises for women . . . do I place the question of enlarged opportunities for work." He favored practical steps to enable more women to work, but he did not support women's suffrage because he thought most women did not want it. He believed in

the sanctity of marriage and opposed easy divorce, a position that put him into conflict with both Robert Dale Owen and Elizabeth Cady Stanton.

Greeley is best remembered as a leading abolitionist who educated the North about slavery and contributed to the election of President Abraham Lincoln.

Horace Greeley

In 1867, Greeley and most other newspaper publishers in the East dropped demands for women's suffrage to devote their efforts to win the Fourteenth Amendment, which guarantees that all persons born in any state of the United States are citizens of that state and of the United States and are guaranteed the privileges and immunities due to citizens of the United States and equal protection under the laws. Penalizing states when "the right to vote . . . is denied to any of the *male* inhabitants," the Amendment introduced gender restriction into the Constitution for the first time. When Elizabeth Cady Stanton turned to her old allies, urging them to withdraw support for the Fourteenth Amendment unless it was modified to include women, they refused.

Greeley published a great many books, including *Hints toward Reforms* (1850),

140

Glances at Europe (1851), *History of the Struggle for Slavery Extension* (1856), *Overland Journey to San Francisco* (1860), *The American Conflict* (two volumes, 1864–1866), *Recollections of a Busy Life* (1868), *Essays on Political Economy* (1870), and *What I Knew of Farming* (1871).

Greeley was the 1872 Liberal Republican candidate for president, and later presidential candidate of the Democratic Party, losing to Ulysses S. Grant. Greeley died soon after the election, on 29 November 1872.

See also Fuller, Margaret; Owen, Robert Dale; Smith, Gerrit; Stanton, Elizabeth Cady.

Green, Anne Catherine Hoof (c. 1720–1775)

Anne Green, one of the colonies' first female printers, published tracts that furthered the cause of the American revolutionaries. She was born about 1720, probably in the Netherlands. When she was a child, her family immigrated to America and settled in Philadelphia. In 1735 she married printer Jonas Green, who was employed by Benjamin Franklin and other notables. Ten years later he founded the *Maryland Gazette*, one of the colonies' earliest newspapers. His wife must have helped in the printing shop, for upon his death in 1767, she continued the paper's publication without missing an issue. That year she also published the volumes of *Acts* and *Votes and Proceedings* of the provincial assembly, later printing almanacs, political tracts, and a book on probating wills and administering estates. Her newspaper was the province's main source of news in the period before the American Revolution. By publishing early accounts of colonial protest against Great Britain, Green furthered the revolutionary cause. She died 23 March 1775, probably in Annapolis.

See also Franklin, Ann Smith; Goddard, Mary Katherine; Goddard, Sarah Updike; Timothy, Ann Donovan.

Gregory v. Paul

In 1818, the Massachusetts Supreme Court recognized a married woman's right to control her own property in the event of desertion by her spouse. In the case of *Gregory v. Paul*, Deborah Gregory's husband had deserted her. She supported herself as an independent businesswoman, or *feme sole* trader. The court decided that, by deserting her, her husband relinquished all rights to her services; furthermore, the court held that Deborah Gregory had to have a means of supporting herself. Therefore, although married, she was permitted to receive an inheritance and otherwise own property in his absence.

See also *Coutts v. Greenhow*; *Feme Covert*; *Feme Sole* Trader; *Flanagan's Lessee v. Young*; *Gregory v. Paul*; *Helms v. Franciscus*.

Griffith v. Griffith

In 1798 the Maryland court of appeals decided an important case for women. Mrs. Griffith had inherited real property from her husband. She wanted her dower right (a life estate to which a wife is entitled upon the death of her husband) extended to his personal property as well. The other heirs contested this. The court decided in Mrs. Griffith's favor, thereby granting widows dower rights to personal as well as real property and giving them a more equal share in family wealth.

See also Dower; *Garlick v. Strong*; *Kempe's Lessee v. Kennedy et al.*

Grimké, Angelina Emily (1805–1879)

Angelina Grimké, with her sister, Sarah Grimké, was a leading speaker on behalf of abolition and equal rights for women. She was born 20 February 1805 in Charleston, South Carolina. Her father, John Faucheraud Grimké, was an officer in the Continental army, a jurist, and a slave-owner. His daughters, Angelina and Sarah, were opposed to slavery. In 1829, Angelina left the South to join Sarah in Philadelphia, where they became Quakers.

In 1834, Angelina witnessed riots in Philadelphia and New York in which the homes of 45 African-American families were destroyed. When abolitionist William

Lloyd Garrison condemned the rioters in a series of articles in his paper, *The Liberator*, Angelina wrote him a sympathetic letter (8 August 1835). Unknown to her, Garrison published the letter. Angelina was flooded with criticism from the Quaker community and her family. Nevertheless, that year she joined the Philadelphia Female Anti-Slavery Society, meeting women who were selling pamphlets that promoted abolition and circulating petitions. The petitions protested the admission of slave states to the Union, the presence of slavery in the nation's capital, and interstate trade in slaves. In 1836 Angelina Grimké produced the influential pamphlet, *An Appeal to the Christian Women of the South*, which was printed by the American Anti-Slavery Society. This document stands alone as the only antislavery appeal ever written *by* a southern woman *for* southern women. When copies of the pamphlet reached Charleston, the postmaster publicly burned them. Angelina was warned by the police, through her family, not to return to Charleston.

The pamphlet earned Angelina an invitation to work as an agent for the American Anti-Slavery Society. She was trained for the task by the fearless agitator Theodore Weld, whom she later married (1838). Soon, she and Sarah were speaking on behalf of the society to small private gatherings in New York. In 1837 Angelina began to speak to mixed audiences of women and men. She made a speaking tour of New England, a highly unusual undertaking for a woman at the time. In Massachusetts the sisters addressed crowds in large halls.

This was too much for some of the New England clergy. In July 1837 a group of Congregational ministers issued "Pastoral Letter of the General Association of Massachusetts to the Congregational Churches under Their Care." The intent of the letter was to close the doors of Congregational churches to female speakers. The letter was read in orthodox churches throughout the state. It argued that when a woman "assumes the place and tone of a man as public reformer . . . her character becomes unnatural." There followed two clerical appeals

that attacked the sisters and their sponsor, Garrison. John Greenleaf Whittier ridiculed the church's position in his poem *The Pastoral Letter*.

Thus, Angelina fought not just slavery but the exclusion of women from reform circles. Responding to Catharine Beecher's *An Essay on Slavery and Abolitionism with Reference to the Duty of American Females*, which was addressed to Angelina, she discussed the question of women's position in society in a series of letters to *The Liberator*. The letters were published in a pamphlet in 1838. Far from curtailing her activities, on Wednesday, 21 February 1838, Angelina delivered a speech to the Massachusetts legislature, becoming the first woman in history to address a U.S. legislative body. Attendance was enormous. The aisles and lobby were packed. People who had waited for hours were turned away at the door. Even members of the legislature had to fight their way to their seats. It was a speech worth waiting for. In it, Angelina made the connection between the fight for abolition and the fight for women's rights. She declared,

> . . . because it [slavery] is a political subject, it has often been said, that women had nothing to do with it. Are we aliens because we are women? Are we bereft of citizenship because we are mothers, wives, and daughters of a mighty people? Have women *no* country—no interests staked in public weal—no liabilities in common peril—no partnership in a nation's guilt and shame? . . . If so then we may well hide our faces in the dust, and cover ourselves with sackcloth and ashes. This dominion of women should be resigned—the sooner the better; in the age which is approaching she should be something more—she should be a citizen. (*The Liberator*, 2 March 1838)

Angelina's second appearance was scheduled for Friday, 23 February. This time when she rose to speak, hisses greeted her. She was interrupted three times, but when she finished, Angelina reported that even

"The chairman was in tears almost the whole time I was speaking." (*Weld-Grimké Letters*, II)

Angelina's marriage to Theodore Weld in 1838 marked the end of her public activities. Two days after their marriage she made her last public address at the Anti-Slavery Convention of American Women, held in Philadelphia. While she spoke an angry mob raged outside the hall; the next day the mob set fire to it. In 1839, Angelina and her sister worked with Weld on the influential book *American Slavery as It Is: Testimony of a Thousand Witnesses.* She died 26 October 1879 in Hyde Park (now Boston).

See also Abolition Movement; American Anti-Slavery Society; Garrison, William Lloyd; Grimké, Sarah; Pastoral Letter; Weld, Theodore Dwight.

Grimké, Sarah Moore (1792–1873)

Sarah Grimké, though less vocal and public than her younger sister, Angelina Grimké, was an abolitionist who championed equal rights for women. She was born 26 November 1792 in Charleston, South Carolina. Sarah was 13 years older than Angelina and was also the younger girl's godmother. As a young woman she wanted to become a lawyer; her father, John Faucheraud Grimké, was a jurist and her older brother, Thomas Grimké, was a lawyer and state senator. However, she was not allowed to attend college, so she secretly studied Greek, Latin, law, and philosophy. Living in a slaveholding family, she privately deplored this practice, secretly teaching the enslaved girl who served as her personal servant to read. This alienated her from the rest of her family, and in 1821 she left the South, never to return.

In 1821 Sarah left the Episcopal church because of its conservative position on slavery. She joined the Society of Friends (Quakers), but left that church in August 1836 because of its discriminatory treatment of women. She moved to New York, where, in November, she attended a course for abolitionist agents held by Theodore Weld, whom Angelina would marry in 1838. As a result of this meeting, Sarah was inspired to write *Epistle to the Clergy of the Southern States,* published that year by the American Anti-Slavery Society. It was a widely read work that denied the argument that the existence of slavery in Biblical times justified its existence in the present. As agents of the American Anti-Slavery Society, the sisters gave talks on slavery, first in private and then in public, to increasingly larger audiences. In 1837, a series of lectures to large audiences of men and women in Massachusetts prompted Congregational ministers to issue a pastoral letter decrying the women's actions and exhorting churches to close their doors to female speakers. Sarah, remembering how discrimination had curtailed her education and disrupted her relations with the Society of Friends, wrote a series of articles for the Boston *Spectator* on the topic "The Province of Woman." She also wrote a pamphlet, *Letters on the Equality of the Sexes, and the Condition of Woman* (1838), that refuted arguments in the pastoral letter. These writings planted the seeds of the women's rights movement in the United States.

Sarah worked with Angelina and her husband Theodore Weld on the influential book *American Slavery as It Is: Testimony of a Thousand Witnesses* (1839). At the age of 62 she remained eager to study law or medicine, and at 75 she translated and abridged Lamartine's life of Joan of Arc. At the age of 79, she and Angelina joined women in a symbolic effort to vote in Hyde Park. Sarah died there two years later, on 23 December 1873.

See also Abolition Movement; Grimké, Angelina; Garrison, William Lloyd; *Letters on the Equality of the Sexes, and the Condition of Women;* Pastoral Letter; Weld, Theodore Dwight.

Griswold v. Connecticut

Griswold v. Connecticut (1965) prompted a major Supreme Court decision striking down two Connecticut laws that made it illegal to use or give information about contraceptives. The Supreme Court recognized the fact that a married couple had a right to privacy that could not be infringed upon by the state laws. The case emerged after Estelle T. Griswold, executive director of the Planned Parenthood League of Connecticut (PPLC), opened a family planning clinic on 1 November 1961. On 18 November, Griswold and a physician who worked at the clinic were arrested for violating the Connecticut laws. Although they had given information on contraception to a married couple, Griswold and her associate were convicted and fined $100 each. The state appellate courts upheld this decision. But Griswold appealed to the Supreme Court on the grounds that the statutes violated the Fourteenth Amendment.

By a 7 to 2 vote, with several different opinions, the Court found that the laws were unconstitutional. The court decided that a married couple was entitled to a right of privacy implied in several Bill of Rights guarantees (the First, Third, Fourth, Fifth, and Ninth Amendments). It held that the regulation of a marital relationship by the state was an invasion of this implied right to privacy and that the means of enforcing such laws (outlawing the use of birth control devices rather than their sale and manufacture) could harm the relationship of a married couple. In the plurality opinion, Justice William Douglas asked, "Would we allow the police to search sacred precincts of marital bedrooms for telltale signs of the use of contraceptives?"

After the judicial branch made this landmark decision, the legislative and executive branch began to strengthen and support the ruling. In 1966, President Lyndon B. Johnson endorsed public funding for family planning and the government soon followed by subsidizing services for low-income families.

See also Eisenstadt v. Baird.

Hadassah

With more than 385,000 members, Hadassah (the Hebrew name for Queen Esther, meaning "myrtle") is the largest women's volunteer organization in America. It was founded by Henrietta Szold, the daughter of Hungarian immigrants. A teacher and writer, Szold was deeply involved in Zionism. On 24 February 1912 with the women of her Hadassah Study Circle in New York City, she formed the Hadassah Chapter of Daughters of Zion. The organization was renamed Hadassah at its first national convention. Szold, its first president, initiated aid programs for Palestine, sending two nurses to the region to promote public health. In 1916, through the work of Justice Louis D. Brandeis and Judge Julian W. Mack, Szold received funds that permitted her to leave her job at the Jewish Publication Society and devote her life to Zionist work.

In 1918 Szold led the effort to organize the American Zionist Medical Unit. The group was sponsored by Hadassah, the Zionist Organization of America, and the American Jewish Joint Distribution Committee. It sent 44 doctors, nurses, and other health workers and 400 tons of equipment to Palestine. In 1922 the organization was renamed the Hadassah Medical Organization; a gift from Macy's department store chief Nathan Straus allowed the project to continue operation until more secure financial backing could be found. Szold resigned as president of Hadassah in 1925, becoming its honorary president. Hadassah's activities have extended far beyond its original aims. In 1934 Hadassah established a relief movement for children, which has relocated refugees from all over the world, and its hospitals in the Middle East serve all faiths. Its educational publishing includes books and magazine;

Hadassah Magazine has the largest circulation of any Jewish publication in the United States.

See also Voluntarism.

Hale, Sarah Josepha Buell (1788–1879)

Sarah Josepha Hale was the first female editor of a major magazine for women, She was born 24 October 1788 in Newport, New Hampshire, and educated at home. She married David Hale in 1813; during their marriage, she reared their five children and wrote a few poems. Her husband's death in 1822 left her with little money. So Hale began to write for publication, producing *The Genius of Oblivion* (1823), a collection of poems, and *Northwood, a Tale of New England* (1827), a novel. These publications brought her name to the public eye and she received an offer to edit a new Boston-based magazine, *Ladies' Magazine* (1828). She wrote and edited most of the publication, using its pages to promote the Boston Ladies' Peace Society and professional and educational advances for women. The magazine changed its name in 1834 to *American Ladies' Magazine*.

In 1837, Hale became the editor of the most influential and best-selling women's magazine in the country, the 100-page, monthly *Godey's Lady's Book* (after its merger with *American Ladies' Magazine*). In 1860 *Godey's Lady's Book* had a circulation of 150,000. Harriet Beecher Stowe, Ralph Waldo Emerson, Henry Wadsworth Longfellow, and many other men and women of letters wrote for the magazine. In its pages, Hale expressed concern for the welfare of children and called for more female teachers and the founding of more women's colleges. Her support helped to accomplish the founding of Vassar College. Hale did not join any women's rights groups, and she rejected the idea that women should involve themselves in public affairs, which she considered demeaning.

Although Hale is best remembered for her poem "Mary Had a Little Lamb," published in 1830, her most significant work in book form is *Woman's Record, or Sketches of Distinguished Women* (1853, 1869, and 1876). In all, 36 volumes of these women's biographical profiles were completed. Hale retired from *Godey's Lady's Book* in 1877 at the age of 89. She died 30 April 1879 in Philadelphia.

See also Godey's Lady's Book; Vassar College.

Hansberry, Lorraine (1930–1965)

Playwright and civil rights activist Lorraine Hansberry was born 19 May 1930 in Chicago. She was the daughter of middle-class African-American parents who moved into a European-American neighborhood despite threats of violence. The move led to a lawsuit, sponsored by the National Association for the Advancement of Colored People, in which the Supreme Court ruled that one race does not have the right to exclude another from a neighborhood (*Hansberry v.*

Lorraine Hansberry

Lee, 1940). Hansberry's parents, both active Republicans, believed in sending their children to public schools despite their ability to pay for private schools. Hansberry's school system was segregated, and her school was open to African Americans for only half-day sessions. Nonetheless, Hansberry pursued her interests in writing and theater, enrolling at the University of Wisconsin in 1948. She remained there two years, later briefly attending the Art Institute of Chicago and Roosevelt University. In 1950 Hansberry moved to New York City, where she worked for the African-American liberation paper, *Freedom*, took part in the civil rights and peace movements, and studied at the New School for Social Research. On 20 June 1953, she married Robert Nemiroff, a playwright and graduate student at New York University. They divorced in 1964.

By 1958 Hansberry had raised enough money to begin the production of her first play, *A Raisin in the Sun.* On 11 March 1959—after successful runs in Philadelphia, Chicago, and New Haven, Connecticut—the play became the first by an African-American woman to be staged on Broadway. The story of an African-American family in Chicago, it was an immediate success. It ran until 1960, was made into a movie (1961), and won the New York Drama Critics' Circle Award, making Hansberry the only African-American woman to receive this award. Her civil rights activities inspired her next play, *The Sign in Sidney Brustein's Window*, which opened in 1964. During its run, Hansberry learned she had cancer. While she was hospitalized, the play ran for a total of 101 performances. Hansberry, one of the nation's most inspiring playwrights, died at the age of 34 on 12 January 1965. Her sketches and writings were later published in *To Be Young, Gifted, and Black* (1969), edited by her former husband, Robert Nemiroff.

Harper, Ida A. Husted (1851–1931)

Writer Ida Harper was press secretary for women's suffrage campaigns, official biographer of Susan B. Anthony, and a significant contributor to the multivolume *History of Woman Suffrage*. She was born 18 February 1851 in Fairfield, Indiana. After the age of ten, she was reared in Muncie, Indiana. She attended the University of Indiana for one year before becoming principal of a high school in Peru, Indiana. In 1871 she married lawyer Thomas W. Harper, and they settled in Terre Haute, Indiana. The following year, against his wishes, she began to write articles for local newspapers. Her column, "A Woman's Opinions," was initially published under a male pseudonym in the *Terre Haute Saturday Evening Mail,* and it ran for 12 years. From 1884 to 1893 Harper edited a section of the *Locomotive Firemen's Magazine,* and in 1887 she became secretary of a state women's suffrage society. In 1890, the year that she divorced her husband, she became editor in chief of the *Terre Haute Daily News.* She soon moved to Indianapolis, joining the editorial staff of the *Indianapolis News.* In 1893 Harper moved to California to attend Stanford University; she attended for two years but did not graduate. In 1896, Susan B. Anthony selected Harper to direct a public relations campaign for the drive for a suffrage amendment to the California constitution. After the drive failed, Anthony asked Harper to become her official biographer. Harper moved to Rochester, New York, where she lived with Anthony for a number of years. Harper wrote the three-volume *Life and Work of Susan B. Anthony* (1898 and 1908). During this time she also worked with Anthony on the fourth volume of *History of Woman Suffrage* (1902) and served as chairman of the press committee of the International Council of Women (1899–1902). Harper edited a women's column in the New York *Sunday Sun* (1899–1903) and the women's page of *Harper's Bazaar* (1909–1913). In 1916, Harper also spearheaded the National American Woman Suffrage Association's publicity campaign for the Nineteenth Amendment. After the amendment's passage, Harper wrote the fourth and fifth volumes of *History of Woman Suffrage* (1922). Harper died 14 March 1931 in Washington, D.C.

See also Anthony, Susan B.; *History of Woman Suffrage;* International Council of Women; National American Woman Suffrage Association.

Harris v. Forklift Systems

Teresa Harris was the plaintiff in a major sexual harassment case, eventually heard before the U.S. Supreme Court. While working as a manager for Forklift Systems, Inc., of Nashville, Tennessee, Harris was sexually harassed on various occasions by Charles Hardy, her boss and the owner of the company. After repeated occasions of verbal abuse and sexual innuendos, Harris expressed her discontent to Hardy. Ignoring her wishes, Hardy continued to subject Harris to an abusive, hostile work environment. Harris finally quit her job on 1 October 1987 and sued Hardy.

From 1987 through 1992, various lower courts ruled against Harris. Although the courts agreed that remarks and actions made by Hardy were offensive, they ruled that the remarks and actions did not create an environment sufficiently poisoned to make it an intimidating or abusive place to work. Court decisions heard previously on similar matters concluded that women only had a case if they were traumatized to the point of having a mental breakdown or suffered from severe medical problems.

Harris's case ultimately went before the U.S. Supreme Court in October 1993. It took only four weeks for the high court to reach a decision. Based on the interpretation and reasoning of the 1964 Civil Rights Act, Justice Sandra Day O'Connor delivered the court's unanimous ruling on 9 November 1993. Giving a simple and forthright explanation, O'Connor wrote that a workplace environment that "would reasonably be perceived, and is perceived, as hostile or abusive" because of sexual harassment is a form of sex discrimination prohibited by federal law. Citing the "broad rule of workplace equality" and federal laws against job discrimination, the court stated that no single factor is necessary; if the environment is violated or becomes abusive from any number of sources, this constitutes illegality. This significant decision enabled Justice

O'Connor to provide broad principles for lower courts to follow in future sexual harassment cases.

Hart, Nancy (1735?–1830)

Nancy Hart is remembered for her defense of the Whigs in the British colony of Georgia during the American Revolution. She is believed to have been born in 1735, in either Pennsylvania or North Carolina. Her given name was Ann but she was commonly known by the more familiar form, Nancy. She married Benjamin Hart, and the couple moved to South Carolina and then to Wilkes County, Georgia (1771). During the American Revolution, her most famous exploit was the capture of five Tories who arrived at her cabin demanding food. As she roasted a turkey, she surreptitiously sent her daughter for help and hid the soldiers' rifles. When the soldiers discovered what she was up to, she used one of their rifles to kill one and wound two others. When help arrived she insisted that the invaders be taken into the forest and hanged. Hart is also said to have taken great risks to spy on the enemy, at one point crossing the Savannah River on a raft of logs lashed with grapevines to gather information. Hart died in Clark County, Georgia, in 1830. Hart County and its seat, Heartwell, are named in her honor.

Harvey and Wife v. Pecks

In 1810, Virginia jurists voided the sale of a wife's property made by Harvey and Lydia Pecks in 1745. The wife's heirs argued she had been coerced into the sale. The court ruled that, because Lydia Pecks did not sign the deed of sale executed by her husband, nor was there proof of a private examination by a judge, coercion had to be assumed. Thus the court voided the mortgage of the wife's property to pay her husband's bills.

See also Coercion; *Ewing v. Smith; Watson v. Bailey.*

Hayden Rider

The Hayden rider was a clause added to a version of the equal rights amendment that was approved by the Senate in 1950 and 1953. Proposed by Carl Hayden, an Arizona Democrat, the rider would have fundamentally changed the spirit of the amendment by preserving state protective legislation that regulated the hours and wages of female workers. Historian William Chafe recalls Hayden boasting, "My amendment is a revolving door. . . . We come in one side and go out the other." One Washington reporter wrote that Hayden "could put a rider on the Ten Commandments and nullify them completely." Although passed by the Senate in 1953, the ERA was not approved by Congress until the late 1970s because of the rider's effectiveness in robbing the ERA of any real value.

See also Equal Rights Amendment.

Health Care Providers

In colonial America more women than men may have practiced medicine, serving as nurses, apothecaries, unlicensed doctors, and midwives. Only surgery (that is, amputation) was reserved for men. Tradition and the shortage of formally trained doctors forced people to turn to housewives, family friends, and enslaved females for medical help. Women with a particular medical skill were paid for their services, as were women who sold medicines, tonics, and syrups made from herbs.

One midwife and healer, Martha Ballard, recorded in her diary a total of 814 births she attended between 1785 and 1812. Walking in waist-deep snow, fording deep rivers, riding alone on horseback, she covered a large territory surrounding Hallowell, Maine, and Augusta, Maine. In addition to attending births, she treated persons suffering from colic, scarlet fever, and other ills. At this time, midwifery was the only area of medicine that required a license. Colonial midwives served lengthy apprenticeships, observing hundreds of births before they received their certification.

With the professionalization of medicine and the establishment of medical schools and hospitals during the nineteenth century, men came to dominate medicine. Women practitioners were kept out of medical schools, in part by inferior preparatory education. This had ramifications for midwives. In the late eighteenth century, midwives attended almost all births in the United States; by 1910 they attended only about half of all births, and over the next few decades the practice almost disappeared.

The nineteenth century women's movement helped to make medical careers available to some women. When, in 1847, Elizabeth Blackwell began to seek admission to medical school, the leading schools rejected her because of her gender. When she was finally admitted to Geneva (New York) Medical College, the townspeople and male students shunned her; she was even barred from a classroom demonstration. Despite the adversity, in January 1849 Blackwell ranked first in her class as she became the first woman to graduate from medical school in the United States. To provide more opportunities for women, female medical colleges were founded in the latter half of the nineteenth century. When women were denied residencies in hospitals, they founded their own. Gradually they began to be accepted in the men's schools, and the need for separate institutions diminished.

By the turn of the century, women made up 4–5 percent of American doctors, a figure that remained fairly constant until the 1960s. More recently the number of women in medical schools has increased. According to the American Association of Medical Colleges, during the 1991–1992 academic year, women made up 38.1 percent of medical students in the United States.

See also Blackwell, Elizabeth; Woman's Hospital.

Helms v. Franciscus

The 1818 *Helms v. Franciscus* decision illustrates one way in which some American courts protected married women's property rights. In this case, the Maryland chancellor was convinced that Lewis Helms had married Anna Wandelohr only for her money. Because Helms was insolvent, the court allowed his wife to keep all of the real property that she had recently inherited from a relative. Thus she was allowed to own her own property even during marriage.

See also Common Law; *Coutts v. Greenhow; Flanagan's Lessee v. Young; Gregory v. Paul.*

Henry Street Settlement

Founded in New York City in 1893 by Lillian Wald (1867–1940), the Henry Street Settlement originally provided nursing services to the poor. That year, Lillian Wald dropped out of medical school (New York Woman's Medical College) to move to the Lower East Side to offer her services as a nurse. Two years later, with help from banker Jacob H. Schiff, she opened the Nurses Settlement, which grew from two nurses in 1893 to more than 250 by 1929. Services soon expanded to include training of nurses and educational and youth clubs. A few years afterwards, the Henry Street Settlement was established, becoming a source of new ideas in relief work for years to come. The Neighborhood Playhouse was opened there in 1915, and residents included Sidney Hillman, Adolf A. Berle, Jr., and other luminaries.

In 1902, the settlement, in an experimental program, moved the nursing program into a local public school and, as a result of its success, the board of health instituted a citywide public nursing program, which was the first of its kind in the world.

Settlement workers, especially Wald, advocated laws to curb the workday for children, improve working conditions, and implement other reforms. Wald resigned as the head of the Henry Street Settlement in 1933 and was replaced by Helen Hall, who served until 1967. Today, the Henry Street Settlement, located on Grand Street, provides day care, youth employment, and home care services.

Heterodoxy

Founded in 1912, Heterodoxy was a feminist society founded in New York's Greenwich Village by Marie Jenny Howe.

149

Members, all of whom were strong advocates of women's suffrage, aired their radical opinions in private meetings. Membership included Crystal Eastman, Charlotte Perkins Gilman, Inez Gillmore Irwin, and Henrietta Rodman. No minutes of the meetings were kept because the women feared ridicule.

Over the years the group held talks on various feminist topics, which were open to the public. In 1914 Margaret Sanger presented her ideas about the importance of birth control, but the group rejected Sanger's attempt to unite women for the cause of birth control. However, a few of the women attending this meeting went on to organize the National Birth Control League, a coalition of reformers led by Mary Ware Dennett, whose goal was to repeal the state and federal Comstock (antiobscenity) laws.

Heterodoxy held its last meeting in 1942.

See also Eastman, Crystal; Gilman, Charlotte Perkins; Irwin, Inez Leonore Haynes Gillmore; National Birth Control League; Sanger, Margaret.

Higginson, Thomas Wentworth Storrow (1823–1911)

Thomas Wentworth Higginson—teacher, pastor, soldier, and candidate for Congress—was one of the leading women's rights advocates of the nineteenth century. Born 22 December 1823 in Cambridge, Massachusetts, he graduated from Harvard in 1841, leaving to teach school for two years before returning to the college. In 1846 he enrolled in Harvard's divinity school, graduating the following year. Higginson was pastor of the First Religious Society (Unitarian) of Newburyport, Massachusetts (1847–1850), and of the Free Church at Worcester, Massachusetts (1852–1858). In 1850 he unsuccessfully ran for Congress on the Free Soil ticket. Three years later he was indicted, with reformers Wendell Phillips and Theodore Parker, for helping to release the fugitive slave Anthony Burns in Boston. After the Kansas–Nebraska bill was passed in 1854, he worked to make Kansas a free state. During the Civil War, he was captain of the

51st Massachusetts Volunteers and, later, colonel (1862–1864) of the 1st South Carolina Volunteers, the first Union regiment recruited from former slaves. Higginson described his experiences with the regiment in *Army Life in a Black Regiment* (1870).

Higginson argued eloquently for the equal treatment of women, writing in *Women and the Alphabet: A Series of Essays* (1859) that women's equality depended primarily on education, rhetorically asking, "What sort of philosophy is that which says, 'John, being a man, shall learn, lead, make laws, make money; Jane, being a woman, shall be ignorant, dependent, disenfranchised, underpaid?'" In a later book, *Women and Men* (1888), he again put forward the case for equal opportunity for females. Later he edited the *Woman's Journal* with suffragist Lucy Stone and Henry Blackwell (1870–1884). Higginson's many books include *Life of Margaret Fuller Ossoli* (1884). He died on 9 May 1911.

See also American Woman Suffrage Association; Fuller, Margaret.

Hill, Anita
See Anita Hill Case.

History of Woman Suffrage

Compiled by Susan B. Anthony, Elizabeth Cady Stanton, Matilda Joslyn Gage, and Ida Husted Harper, *History of Woman Suffrage* is a six-volume, 5,703-page history of the struggle to win the vote for women in the United States. Volumes 1, 2, and 3 were edited by Stanton, Anthony, and Gage; the first two volumes were published in 1881 and 1882, the third in 1886. Volume 4, by Susan B. Anthony and Ida Husted Harper, was published in 1902. Harper wrote volumes 5 and 6, both published in 1922. Unfortunately, Lucy Stone, of the more conservative American Woman Suffrage Association, would not send information on her wing of the suffrage movement to the editors of volumes 1–3 because they belonged to the more radical National Woman Suffrage Association, so that the final product is one-sided. However, the work is invaluable for its early history of the struggle for suffrage, including records of women's rights conventions, newspaper articles, letters, petitions, speeches, and biographies of key suffrage leaders.

See also Anthony, Susan B.; Blatch, Harriot Easton Stanton; Gage, Matilda Joslyn; Harper, Ida A. Husted; Stanton, Elizabeth Cady; Stone, Lucy.

Hobby, Oveta Culp (1905–)

Oveta Culp Hobby was the first director of the Women's Army Auxiliary Corps (WAAC) and the first secretary of Health, Education and Welfare (1953). Born 19 January 1905, in Killeen, Texas, she attended private primary and secondary schools. She studied at Mary Hardin-Baylor College and the University of Texas Law School, but the only degrees she received were honorary ones. At the age of 20 she was parliamentarian of the Texas House of Representatives. She held this position until her marriage to the former governor of Texas, William Pettus Hobby, in 1931. During the 1930s Hobby worked for her husband's newspaper, the *Houston Post*, where she initiated a number of women's features. She became executive vice-president of the company in 1938. She wrote a book on parliamentary law, *Mr. Chairman* (1937), and for two short periods resumed her position as parliamentarian in the Texas legislature (1939 and 1941).

In 1941, President Franklin D. Roosevelt appointed Hobby head of the women's division of the public relations bureau of the war department. She went on to help create the Women's Army Auxiliary Corps (1942). After the corps became a regular branch of the army (1943), the word *auxiliary* was dropped from its name. Hobby was director of the corps until July 1945, with the relative rank of major; she was later promoted to colonel. Under her direction the corps grew to its maximum strength of 100,000 women during World War II. Of these, 17,000 members served overseas. For her work with the corps, Hobby was awarded the U.S. Army Distinguished Service Medal (1945).

She was the first woman to receive this award.

After the war Hobby returned to the *Houston Post*, where she became coeditor and publisher. She also became president of the Southern Newspaper Publishing Organization (1949) at the same time serving as a director of KPRC, radio and television broadcast stations. Hobby helped to organize the Democrats for Eisenhower in 1952. After Eisenhower took office in 1953, he appointed her head of the Federal Security Administration (FSA). In April 1953, when the FSA was given cabinet status (under the new name Department of Health, Education and Welfare), Hobby became its secretary. Thus she became the second woman in American history (after Frances Perkins, Roosevelt's labor secretary) to serve in the cabinet.

Hobby resigned in 1955 to become president and editor of the *Houston Post*; in 1965 she became chairman of the board. In 1968 she was made a director of the Corporation for Public Broadcasting, and in 1970 she became chairman of the board of Channel Two TV Company. From 1978 to 1983 Hobby was chairman of the board of H&C Communications, Inc. Since then, she served as chair of its executive committee.

See also Perkins, Frances Coralie.

Home Industry

Home industry refers to the manufacture of goods within the home for household use or sale. During the colonial period, the household served as home, factory, and school. The family produced most of the goods that its members used: Women spun and wove cloth, sewed clothes and linens, and made soap, medicine, candles, and foodstuffs. In 1787, having earned $150 from the sale of farm products, one New England farmer wrote, "I never spent more than ten dollars a year which was not for salt, nails, and the like. Nothing to eat, drink, or wear was bought, as my farm provided all."

When American industry was young, merchants tapped women's home production of yarn, cloth, and the like for sale in their shops. By the early nineteenth century, mechanized factories required a large, full-time work force, and entire families were recruited to work outside the home. Between 1825 and 1855, home production for personal use dropped sharply, with women preferring to buy rather than make yarn, cloth, and other items. As women changed from home-based producers to consumers, their status declined. Factory worker Harriet Robinson recalled in 1883, "The law took no cognizance of woman as a money spender. She was a ward, an appendage, a relic."

In 1860 home manufacture was performed only by women, and it constituted a small part of the national product. Near the turn of the century, manufacturers assigned certain steps in the manufacturing process to women working at home. Working-class and some middle-class housewives continued to provide a cheap source of seasonal labor—seasonal workers being the first to be fired when business slowed down. These home workers, known as outworkers, were usually immigrant women. They did piecework for cigar manufacturers, artificial flower companies, the garment industry, and other concerns. Isolated from one another, they rarely tried to unionize and were badly exploited.

Home production was replaced by the "sweating system," in which women and small children worked in small shops (often called "sweatshops" because of their poor working conditions). By the end of the nineteenth century, most ready-made clothing and other products produced by outworkers came from these shops.

See also Piecework.

Hooker, Isabella Beecher (1822–1907)

Suffrage leader Isabella Beecher Hooker was born on 22 February 1822 in Litchfield, Connecticut, a daughter of the Rev. Lyman Beecher and his second wife, Harriet Porter. She was a half sister of Henry Ward Beecher, Catharine Beecher, and Harriet Beecher Stowe. She received most of her education in schools founded by Catharine Beecher. In 1841 she married John Hooker, a law student. The two lived in Farmington, Connecticut for ten years, then moved to Hartford.

Isabella Hooker began to take an interest in the legal position of women when her husband read to her from the commentaries of the English jurist Sir William Blackstone, who wrote that, under common law, married women had no legal existence apart from their husbands. She was further influenced in 1861 by John Stuart Mill's essay, "The Enfranchisement of Women" and in 1864 by Mill's *The Subjection of Women.*

Soon Hooker became associated with Susan B. Anthony, Elizabeth Cady Stanton, Paulina Wright Davis, and other feminist leaders. In 1868 she helped to found the New England Woman Suffrage Association. The following year, she arranged the convention in Hartford that resulted in the formation of the Connecticut Woman Suffrage Association. She assumed the presidency of the organization, serving until 1905. Hooker wrote "A Mother's Letters to a Daughter on Woman's Suffrage," which were published in *Putnam's Magazine* in 1868 and as a pamphlet in 1870. That year she came to national prominence because of her speech at the second convention of the National Woman Suffrage Association (NWSA).

Hooker made plans to organize and finance a convention in Washington, D.C., to lobby Congress for a federal suffrage amendment, but Victoria Woodhull had independently submitted a suffrage petition to Congress and was asked to address the House Judiciary Committee on the same day that Hooker's convention was to meet. Dragged by Susan B. Anthony to hear Woodhull speak, Hooker was so impressed that she immediately became an ally of her rival. Her loyalty cost her the support of her family when *Woodhull and Claflin's Weekly* published a scandalous account of Henry Ward Beecher's adulterous affair with Elizabeth Tilton, wife of reformer Theodore Tilton. Hooker took Woodhull's side;

Beecher publicly labeled his sister insane, and family relations were never the same.

Woodhull interested Hooker and her husband in Spiritualism. In 1876 Hooker came to believe that she would, within a year, become the head of a matriarchal government of the United States and the world. Her future role was to be communicated by the spirits on New Year's Eve; to usher in the event, Hartford's most prominent mediums assembled in the Hooker home.

Despite her eccentricities, Hooker made substantial contributions to the suffrage movement. She published *Womanhood: Its Sanctities and Fidelities* (1874) and lobbied effectively for the passage of a woman's property bill in Connecticut, which passed in 1877. She was active in NWSA, speaking at its conventions and at Congressional hearings. In 1892 Hooker left the NWSA because of its support for state, rather than federal, suffrage. That year she endorsed Olympia Brown's Federal Suffrage Association. Also that year she was one of two Connecticut representatives on the Board of Lady Managers of the World's Columbian Exposition in Chicago. Hooker died 25 January 1907 in Hartford, Connecticut.

See also Beecher, Catharine; Brown, Olympia; National Woman Suffrage Association; Woodhull, Victoria.

Horney, Karen Danielsen (1885–1952)

Psychiatrist Karen Danielsen Horney, an early feminist, rejected much of Freud's male-oriented psychology. She was born 16 September 1885 in Hamburg, Germany. Against the wishes of her father she attended college, receiving a medical degree from the University of Berlin in 1911. Two years before graduating, she married Oscar Horney, a lawyer. After practicing medicine for a time, she became interested in psychoanalysis, studying from 1913 to 1915 under Karl Abraham, a disciple of Freud.

She took her first clients for psychoanalysis in 1919, began lecturing on women's topics at the Berlin Psychiatric Clinic and Institute in 1920, and eventually became the clinic's training and supervising analyst. Horney's writings during the 1920s and 1930s focused more and more on female psychology as she came to doubt Freud's notions of penis envy and the castration complex. In a series of articles, including "The Flight from Womanhood" (1926), "Inhibited Femininity" (1926), "Distrust between the Sexes" (1931), and "The Dread of Woman" (1932), she reasoned that women's psychological problems were caused by male domination. She argued that women's reproductive capacities are so powerful that it is men, not women, who experience envy of the opposite sex.

In 1932 Horney became assistant director of the Chicago Institute for Psychoanalysis and began to emphasize the role of culture in shaping female psychology. In 1934, she started teaching at the New York Psychoanalytic Institute and New School for Social Research, at the same time building a private practice. Three years later she and Oscar divorced. In 1939, Horney published *New Ways in Pyschoanalysis*, a book that was considered so outside the mainstream in its criticism of Freudian psychology that it contributed to her being disqualified as an instructor by the New York Psychoanalytic Institute. With colleagues Harry Stack Sullivan, Clara Thompson, and Erich Fromm she immediately organized the Association for the Advancement of Psychoanalysis and its institute, the American Institute for Psychoanalysis.

Other aspects of Freudian theory that Horney rejected are its emphasis on the instincts and the primary roles of the libido and death wish. Horney considered women's ability to both rear children and pursue careers an asset. Throughout her life she struggled to promote the freedom to do both. Her other books are *The Neurotic Personality of Our Time* (1937), *Self-Analysis* (1942), *Our Inner Conflicts* (1945), and *Neurosis and Human Growth* (1950). She was founder and editor of the *American Journal of Psychoanalysis*. Horney died 4 December 1952 in New York City. That year the Karen Horney Foundation was established, leading to the creation in 1955 of the Karen

Horney Clinic. Her papers were collected and published under the title *Feminine Psychology* (1966).

Hospitals
See Woman's Hospital.

Howe, Julia Ward (1819–1910)
Julia Ward Howe, author of "Battle Hymn of the Republic" (1862), was the first woman elected to the American Academy of Arts and Letters. She was born 27 May 1819 in New York City, and educated in private schools. In 1843 she married Samuel Gridley Howe and moved to Boston. Her first books of poems, *Passion-flowers* (1854) and *Words for the Hour* (1857), were published anonymously. They sold poorly, as did the subsequent *Leonora, or the World's Own* (1857) and *A Trip to Cuba* (1860). The Howes published the antislavery newspaper *Commonwealth,* one of their few collaborations; Samuel Howe strongly disapproved of his wife's involvement in public life. Despite her feelings, recorded in her journal in 1863, that she had never known her husband to approve of any of the activities that she herself valued, Julia Howe continued to write and to participate in public life.

A member of the women's department of the New England Sanitary Commission during the Civil War, Howe visited an army camp near Washington, D.C., in 1861, where she became inspired to write her poem, "Battle Hymn of the Republic." The poem was published the following year in *The Atlantic Monthly.* Soon it was put to the tune of "John Brown's Body" and became the unofficial song of the Union army.

After the war Howe became a leader of many women's clubs and suffrage associations. In 1868, she founded the New England Women's Club and joined Lucy Stone in forming the New England Woman Suffrage Association; she served as the association's president from 1868 to 1877 and 1893 to 1910. In 1869, when the woman's suffrage movement divided into two factions, Howe became president of the American Woman Suffrage Association. She was also a member of the board that negotiated the reunion of the suffrage movement in 1890. She served as president of the Massachusetts Woman Suffrage Association (1870–1878 and 1891–1893). In 1870 she was one of the founders of the *Woman's Journal,* to which she contributed as writer and editor for 20 years. The following year, she served as the first president of the American branch of the Woman's International Peace Association. She helped to organize the Association for the Advancement of Women (1873) and the General Federation of Women's Clubs (1890). She was the first to direct the Massachusetts Federation of Women's Clubs, founded in 1893.

Howe published a number of books, including *From the Oak to the Olive* (1868), *Sex and Education* (1874), *Modern Society* (1880), *Margaret Fuller* (1883), *Is Polite Society Polite?* (1895), *From Sunset Ridge: Poems Old and New* (1898), *Reminiscences* (1900), and *At Sunset* (1910). In 1908, she became the first woman elected to the American Academy of Arts and Letters. Howe was one of the most honored women in the United States at the time of her death, 17 October 1910 in Newport, Rhode Island.

See also American Woman Suffrage Association; General Federation of Women's Clubs; Sanitary Commission.

Hull House
See Addams, Jane.

Human Rights for Women, Inc.
Radical feminist Ti-Grace Atkinson and lawyers Mary Eastwood, Sylvia Ellison, and Caruthers Berger founded Human Rights for Women, Inc. (HRW) in 1968, in Washington, D.C. HRW was a nonprofit corporation dedicated to the advancement of women's rights. Its main contribution was in the area of legal aid, although the original intention was for it to devote its time to research and education as well. Now inactive, the organization provided legal counsel in a variety of high-profile cases, such as

Bowe v. Colgate-Palmolive Co. (1969), *Phillips v. Martin-Marietta Corp.* (1971), *Rosenfeld v. Southern Pacific* (California, 1968), and *United States v. Vuitch* (1971).

See also Bowe v. Colgate-Palmolive Co.; Phillips v. Martin-Marietta; United States v. Vuitch.

Hunter College

Hunter College in New York City was the first educational institution to offer a free college education to all women in the United States. The college opened in 1870, with Thomas Hunter as its president, and

Julia Ward Howe in 1908

admitted both black and white students, although New York's elementary schools were still segregated. Hunter College was originally called the Female Normal and High School, two months later renaming itself the Normal College of the City of New York. As its name suggests, the college's purpose was to train teachers. Its first class was made up of 1,095 female "teacher-pupils," who studied for five months in order to become teachers. The four-year teacher-training program was instituted in 1879 and, nine years later, Hunter became the first degree-granting, tuition-free college in the United States. By the start of the twentieth century, it was serving as a liberal arts college as well as a professional school. It became part of the City University of New York in 1961, granting doctoral degrees, and became coeducational in 1964.

See also Education.

Hurston, Zora Neale (1903–1960)

African-American anthropologist and writer Zora Neale Hurston was born 7 January 1903 in Eatonville, Florida. After her mother's death in 1910, she was, in her words, "passed around the family like a bad penny," finally leaving home at the age of 14. After supporting herself as a domestic worker, she attended Baltimore's Morgan College (1917) and Howard University (1921–1924). A writer of essays and short fiction, she received a scholarship to Barnard College, studying under renowned anthropologist Franz Boas. She became the college's first African-American graduate, receiving a B.A. in 1928. Hurston continued her graduate studies at Cornell University on a fellowship for two years, then conducted fieldwork among African Americans in the South until 1932, working in labor camps to write her ethnographies of rural life. Her marriages to Herbert Sheen (1927) and Albert Price (1939) both ended in divorce. Although she was a Guggenheim Fellow for ethnographic research in both 1936 and 1937, Hurston preferred the life of a writer, completing the books *Jonah's Gourd Vine* (1934), *Mules and Men* (1935), *Their*

Eyes Were Watching God (1937), *Tell My Horse* (1938), *Moses, Man of the Mountain* (1939), her autobiography *Dust Tracks on the Road* (1942), and *Seraphy and Suwanee* (1948). It was *Moses, Man of the Mountain* that firmly established her reputation. Hurston was on the faculty of North Carolina College for Negroes (now North Carolina Central University) in Durham in 1939, and wrote for Warner Brothers movie studio. She was also on the staff of the Library of Congress. Hurston was a public critic of integration, which she thought would weaken African-American culture. One of the most widely published African-American writers of her time, Hurston died in poverty and obscurity 28 January 1960 in Fort Pierce, Florida.

Hutchinson, Anne Marbury (1591–1643)

Anne Hutchinson was the first woman to dissent against the Puritans, to preach to women, and to start her own religious sect. Her trial (1636–1638) was one of the most important conflicts of the seventeenth century. Hutchinson was born in Alford, Lincolnshire, England, probably in the spring of 1591, to a family of dissenting Puritans. She was the daughter of a minister who had been silenced by church authorities for criticizing the clergy. In 1634 she immigrated to Boston with her family and husband, William Hutchinson, whom she had married in 1612, and with whom she had 12 children by 1630, nine of them surviving. By 1636, three more children were born.

In Boston, Hutchinson became a nurse and midwife. She also organized regular meetings in her home in which she preached first to women, then to both sexes, including city merchants and ministers. She took issue with the orthodoxy of the Massachusetts Puritans, favoring the ideas of Puritan minister John Cotton, whom she had followed to Massachusetts. She believed in a "covenant of grace," arguing that it was faith alone that was necessary for salvation and challenging the Puritan notion of a "covenant of works."

Sides were quickly drawn in what came to be called the Antinomian Controversy. Deputy governor John Winthrop and the clergy under the Rev. John Wilson lined up against Hutchinson. Behind Hutchinson stood her brother-in-law, the Rev. John Wheelwright (who was charged with sedition for his preaching); Governor Henry Vane (a political opponent of John Winthrop); and Cotton. In 1637, when Winthrop became governor, a synod of churches denounced Hutchinson and her followers, and Cotton signed a document against her interpretations of his doctrines, which were more radical than his own. A general court tried Hutchinson in 1637, during which Winthrop and several clerics verbally challenged her and suffered a skillful rebuttal from her that almost won the case. Winthrop responded, "We do not mean to discourse with those of your sex," and Hutchinson was convicted of heresy and sedition for "traducing the ministers," which meant undermining authority with falsehood. Hutchinson was excommunicated by the Boston Anglican Church and banished from the colony.

In 1638, Hutchinson and her family moved, with about 70 followers, to the island of Aquidneck, now Rhode Island. Soon after this move, Hutchinson suffered a midlife pregnancy that was aborted, according to Emery Battis in *Notable American Women*, into a "hydatidiform mole." Puritans interpreted this "monstrous birth" as divine justice. Hutchinson challenged the power of the Rhode Island magistrates, and, with the death of her husband in 1642, she was forced to move to the Pelham Bay area of Hutchinson River, New York (on what is now Long Island). There, she and five of her children were killed during a raid by Native Americans in August 1643. Only one daughter survived the massacre.

See also Dyer, Mary.

Immigrant Protective League (IPL)

The Immigrant Protective League (IPL) was founded in Chicago in 1908, by a committee of the Women's Trade Union League, after it was determined that about one-fifth of immigrant women traveling alone from Ellis Island to Chicago never arrived at their destination. Presumably, many were led into prostitution. Members of the IPL accompanied immigrant women to their new homes from Ellis Island, helped with language skills, and found jobs for the women. Leaders of the league were Jane Addams, Sophia Breckinridge, and Grace Abbott. After World War I, as the number of immigrants declined, so did the need for the IPL's services. By 1921 the league had only two paid members working in Chicago. Today it is part of that city's Traveler's Aid Society.

See also Addams, Jane; Immigrant Women.

Immigrant Women

Between 1820 and 1920, about 35 million Europeans immigrated to America. Of these, one-third were women. The first group came from northern Europe—Ireland, Scandinavia, and Germany. A second wave of eastern and southern Europeans began to arrive in 1880. By 1920 about 20 million Poles, Italians, Jews, Slovaks, Bohemians, Greeks, and Armenians had arrived. Most of these women had no legal existence apart from the men in their families. They worked in mills and factories that produced clothes, food, and appliances. Daughters, who could not afford to leave home until they married, worked by the time they were 12 or 13, often doing piecework at home. Ethnic groups tended to dominate specific occupations: German and Bohemian women rolled cigars; Italian women made artificial flowers, paper boxes, and trimmings for hats; Italian and Jewish women made coats, dresses, hats, shirtwaists, and underwear. Married women did this work at home until it was banned at the turn of the century. Single women worked in factories, where they came into contact with trade unionists. There, working 12 hours a day, 6 or 7 days a week, they joined unions to fight for better working conditions. Many immigrants lived in neighborhoods where only their native language was spoken. They became more assimilated only when their children learned English at school and taught it to their parents.

See also Immigrant Protective League.

Indentured Servitude

Indentured servitude was a form of labor that originated early in the seventeenth century and provided a means for poor English men and women to pay for transportation to America. Indentured servants agreed to repay their debt by working four to seven years for shipmasters, merchants, or planters. Some received a stipend after serving their term. The term *indentured servant* derives from the contract between master and servant, which was written in duplicate on a large piece of paper and divided along an indented edge.

During the colonial period, one in three immigrants to Virginia were women, most of whom were indentured. In 1619, according to historian Eleanor Flexner, one ship arrived in Virginia with 90 women to be "sold with their own consent to settlers as wives, the price to be the cost of their own transportation."

Indentured servants were a major presence in the English colonies. According to labor historian Alice Kessler-Harris, during the colonial period, between one-half and two-thirds of all white immigrants entered the colonies as indentured servants. Indentured servants were present in all of the

159

English colonies, particularly Virginia, Maryland, and Pennsylvania. They made up three-fourths of Virginia's settlers in the seventeenth century.

Most indentured servants came to the colonies voluntarily in the hope that, after their period of service, they would find better opportunities than were available in their countries of origin. And, once free, most were better off than they had been in their homelands.

A minority came as the result of kidnapping, fraud, or force of law. Homeless people and children were sold to shipmasters for £1 or £2, to be resold in the colonies. Political prisoners were exiled from the British Isles. The largest group of indentured servants consisted of male and female convicts, who were forced to chose between jail or exile. About 30,000 convicts arrived in the eighteenth century, one-fourth of them women. Their Atlantic passage was grueling: according to historian Arthur Schlesinger, of 400 Germans shipped to Pennsylvania in 1745, 350 died; out of 200 in 1752, 181 died.

Upon their arrival in the colonies, indentured servants were often auctioned by their ship's captain. Husbands and wives might be sold to different masters, and children could be separated from their parents. Masters decided whether servants could marry. One result was that women bore children out of wedlock, which punishments, such as increasing the length of servitude, could not control.

During the eighteenth century German, Scottish, and Irish immigrants joined the English as indentured servants. By 1775 approximately 350,000 indentured servants had immigrated to America. Gradually the practice came to an end, disappearing altogether by the 1830s.

See also Domestic Service.

Industrial Workers of the World (IWW)

In 1905, radicals in the conservative American Federation of Labor left to form a new union called the Industrial Workers of the World (IWW), or the Wobblies. Organized by William Haywood, Eugene V. Debs, and Daniel De Leon, this was the most militant union in U.S. history. Until 1912 the Wobblies concentrated their efforts on organizing miners, lumbermen, and migrant farm workers in the West. But after mill workers in Lawrence, Massachusetts—most of whom were women and children—went on strike in January 1912 to protest a de facto wage cut that followed the passage of a law shortening hours from 56 to 54 hours per week, the IWW saw an opportunity to organize industrial workers. No union before the IWW had tried to organize workers of so many nationalities, but union head William "Big Bill" Haywood and 21-year-old Elizabeth Gurley Flynn did so in Lawrence, seizing command of the strike activity. Working women were helped by the Wobblies, which attempted to organize textile workers (in New York and in the South) and domestics (in Chicago, Salt Lake City, Denver, and Seattle). The union also championed birth control and equal pay for equal work. IWW members included several outstanding female leaders, such as Mother Jones (Mary Harris Jones) and Elizabeth Gurley Flynn.

See also Flynn, Elizabeth Gurley; Jones, Mary Harris; Lawrence (Massachusetts) Mill Workers' Strike; Sanger, Margaret; Strikes.

Institute To Coordinate Women's Interests

The Institute To Coordinate Women's Interests, founded in 1925, was one of the earliest attempts to reconcile women's homemaking responsibilities with the pursuit of a meaningful career. The institute addressed the concerns of educated women and attempted to redefine homemaking chores or arrange them around working women's needs. Some of the institute's experiments included joint shopping trips and communal nurseries, laundries, and kitchens. By addressing working women's challenges, the institute anticipated issues that would become publicized with the second wave of twentieth-century feminism, beginning in the 1960s. Ethel Puffer Howe, a former professor at Wellesley College, was the head of the institute, which lasted until 1931.

See also Smith College.

International Alliance of Women
See International Woman Suffrage Alliance.

International Council of Women
Susan B. Anthony helped organize and chaired the first meeting of the International Council of Women, in an attempt to unite the women's movement. At the first conference, held in 1888 in Washington, D.C., 49 delegates from nine countries agreed to work for the opening of all educational institutions to women, equal pay for equal work, and similar standards of morality for women and men. Countries represented included England, France, Denmark, Norway, Finland, India, Canada, and the United States. In 1904, dissension in the International Council of Women led to the formation of the International Woman Suffrage Alliance, later called the International Alliance of Women.

See also International Woman Suffrage Alliance.

International Ladies' Garment Workers' Union (ILGWU)
Predominantly female, the International Ladies' Garment Workers' Union (ILGWU) was one of the earliest examples of the successful unionization of women. It was founded in 1900 to unite women who worked in the Triangle Shirtwaist factory and to upgrade conditions in the sweatshops. In 1909 female shirtwaist makers went on strike in New York City. It was thought that only 3,000 workers would join the strike against the Triangle Shirtwaist Company, but 20,000–30,000 young women flooded the streets of the Lower East Side. As a result, wages were raised. More important, the strike showed that union activity got results, and the idea of a general

strike became more acceptable in the United States. As a result of this Uprising of the 20,000, as it was called, the workers changed the insignificant ILGWU into a union with tens of thousands of members. More women were organized than ever before in American history.

A member of the International Ladies' Garment Workers' Union works as a cutter, one of the most skilled and highly paid occupations in the garment industry.

The ILGWU organized workers of an entire industry, instead of those of one particular craft. Together with the Amalgamated Clothing Workers of America (ACWA), it organized almost 50 percent of all female clothing workers by 1920. Although it experienced setbacks in the 1920s, pro-union New Deal legislation helped the ILGWU to firmly establish itself in the 1930s.

See also Amalgamated Clothing Workers of America; "Protocol in the Dress & Waist Industry;" Triangle Shirtwaist Fire; Uprising of the 20,000.

International Woman Suffrage Alliance (IWSA)

Led by Carrie Chapman Catt until 1923, the International Woman Suffrage Alliance (IWSA), later the International Alliance of Women, emerged from a division in the International Council of Women at its 1904 meeting. Dominated by Americans, the founders of the IWSA championed women's suffrage as their first priority, a goal that other members of the International Council of Women considered too radical. In the early years of the alliance, member societies were located in Canada, Great Britain, Germany, Sweden, and Norway. Later, societies were started in many other countries. Throughout its existence, the IWSA suffered from divisions among those whose primary goal was universal suffrage and others who thought the vote should go only to educated women.

See also International Council of Women.

Irwin, Inez Leonore Haynes Gillmore (1873–1970)

Inez Leonore Haynes Gillmore Irwin was a writer, historian of the women's movement, and suffragist. She was born 2 March 1873 in Rio de Janeiro, Brazil, where her family had moved from New England, hoping to prosper in the coffee business. She attended school in Boston, graduating from Boston Normal School in 1892. In 1897 she married Rufus Hamilton Gillmore, a reporter, and the same year she enrolled in Radcliffe College (1897–1900). There, among students who did not care about suffrage, she became a suffragist and supporter of women's rights. In 1900 she and Maud Wood Park co-founded the College Equal Suffrage League, which soon became a national organization. In 1908 her first novel, *June Jeopardy*, was published. By 1911, she had moved to Greenwich Village and become the first fiction editor of Max Eastman's magazine, *The Masses*. She was one of the earliest members of Heterodoxy, a group of feminists with radical views that was founded in Greenwich Village in 1912, and also joined Query, another feminist society. Through these groups she met many prominent feminists. In 1913 she divorced Gillmore; three years later she married journalist Henry Irwin. During World War I the two reported on the war from France and Italy. Inez Irwin later joined the National Advisory Council of the National Woman's Party. An effective historian and publicist of the women's movement, Irwin wrote a history of the suffrage battle, *Story of the Woman's Party* (1921), and an account of the role of women's organizations in public policy, *Angels and Amazons: A Hundred Years of American Women* (1933). Irwin also wrote children's books and novels; her story "The Spring Flight" won the O. Henry Award for the short story in 1924. Irwin served as the president of a number of literary organizations, including the Authors Guild and the Authors' League of America. She also served as vice-president of the New York chapter of P.E.N., an international writers organization committed to preserving the freedom to write. A lifelong suffragist and feminist, Irwin died 25 September 1970 in Norwell, Massachusetts.

See also Heterodoxy; National Woman's Party; Park, Maud May Wood.

Jane

In 1969, the Chicago Women's Liberation Union began running an abortion referral program that had been started by a University of Chicago student who called herself Jane. Eventually the women began performing abortions, although they lacked formal medical training. Women who sought abortions contacted the organization by telephone and were given counseling and an explanation of the abortion procedure, before being taken to a well-concealed location where the abortion was performed. In 1973, after the group had performed thousands of successful abortions, the police were tipped off as to the group's whereabouts. Some members of Jane were arrested but the charges were dropped. Jane became inactive after 1973.

See also Abortion.

Jane Club

In 1891, Jane Addams and Mary Kenney O'Sullivan founded this cooperative apartment house for women in Chicago. The project marked a change for Addams, from philanthropist to social activist. The Jane Club, which was part of Hull House, provided inexpensive housing for young women who might be left on the streets if they lost their jobs. Mary Kenney O'Sullivan, who had organized the first bookbinders union for women in Chicago, was 27 years old when she took over the administration of the Jane Club. She looked to the Jane Club to help strikers to withstand the demands of their employers. Residents paid $3 per week for room and board. At first the Jane Club had only 15 members, but after a few years it had 50 members. Members created regulations and assigned responsibilities for the building's upkeep. In 1898, a large donation made possible the purchase of a new building. In 1938, after the death of Jane Addams,

Charlotte E. Carr took over Hull House and changed the Jane Club from a cooperative to low-cost housing.

See also Addams, Jane; Bookbinding.

Janeway, Elizabeth Hall (1913–)

Elizabeth Janeway is one of the most admired writers of the women's movement. She was born 7 October 1913 in Brooklyn, New York. After completing her education she married economist Eliot Janeway in 1938 and five years later published her first novel, *The Walsh Girls* (1943). But it was not until the publication of *Man's World, Woman's Place* (1971) that Janeway became an influential feminist. The book brings together research on psychology, sociology, anthropology, and history as it pertains to the theory of separate spheres, arguing that women bargained away their freedom when they accepted the power of the domestic sphere in return for giving men power in the public arena. Janeway continued her reasoning in *Between Myth and Morning* (1974) and *Powers of the Weak* (1980), concluding that the exchange of power is responsible for women's lower status. In the latter book, which analyzes power in terms of the weak, she argues that "women are the oldest, largest, and most central group of human creatures in the wide category of the weak and ruled." Yet, she continues, many tools are available to the seemingly powerless, and it is men's childhood experience of weakness in comparison to the powerful mother that makes some men hate women. Janeway's other nonfiction works include *Women: Their Changing Role*, which she edited in 1972, and *Cross-Sections from a Decade of Change* (1982). Besides *The Walsh Girls*, her novels include *Daisy Kenyon* (1945), *The Question of Gregory* (1949), *Leaving Home* (1953), *The Third Choice* (1959), *Accident* (1964), and *Improper*

Behavior (1987). Janeway has also written five children's books. She has served as a director of the Authors Guild and a trustee of Barnard College. She and her husband live in New York City.

Johnson, Sonia Harris (1936–)

Sonia Johnson defied the Mormon church to support the Equal Rights Amendment. She was born 27 February 1936 in Malad City, Idaho, and was raised a Mormon. She received a B.A. from Utah State University in 1957, where, as a graduate student, she met her future husband, Rick Johnson. The two were married in 1959. After her marriage, Sonia Johnson continued her graduate studies while rearing the couple's two children. She received a Ph.D. from Rutgers University in 1965. Soon, the Johnsons began traveling to southeast Asia to teach and do missionary work. Upon their return to the United States, they moved to Virginia, where Johnson became interested in the women's movement. At this time she came to believe that the Mormon church erred in its emphasis on patriarchal traditions and in its opposition to the Equal Rights Amendment (ERA). Johnson founded a group called Mormons for the ERA, which participated in the 1978 march in Washington, D.C., to extend the ERA's ratification deadline. In 1979 she was excommunicated by Mormon leaders for her political activities. Her husband, who had supported her activities before the excommunication, filed for a divorce, and Johnson continued her reform activities alone, publishing *From Housewife to Heretic* in 1981. In 1984, she became the first third-party candidate to qualify for federal matching campaign funds. Campaigning for president on the Citizens Party ticket, she won 1 percent of the vote.

See also Equal Rights Amendment.

Johnson v. Thompson

The South Carolina Court of Appeals decision in *Johnson v. Thompson* (1814) illustrates how courts in the early nineteenth century interpreted the "doctrine of intentions" in determining the legal technicalities surrounding the bestowal of separate estates upon married women. In the case of *Johnson v. Thompson*, a father gave a gift to his married daughter. Her husband sold it. After her death, her children sued their father, claiming that the gift was a separate estate belonging to their mother, not to their father, according to the intent of their grandfather. The court ruled that the document that conferred the gift had to be carefully scrutinized to ensure the correct legal language had been used, but it did indicate that the grandfather had meant the gift to be a separate estate. Later, in *Lowndes v. Champneys* (1821), the South Carolina court held that it was "immaterial" in what form or language a trust for a wife was set up—what was important was the intent or desire of the person leaving the estate.

See also Doctrine of Intentions.

Johnson v. Transportation Agency of Santa Clara County, California (1987)

In *Johnson v. Transportation Agency of Santa Clara County, California* (1987), the Supreme Court upheld the constitutionality of voluntary affirmative action programs for women in fields from which women had previously been excluded, even if there was no evidence that the specific employer had participated in discriminatory practices. Paul Johnson applied for a position as a road dispatcher with Santa Clara County, which had adopted an affirmative action program in 1978. Partly because of the affirmative action program, the county chose Diane Joyce, who, although she was judged qualified for the job, earned slightly less than Johnson on an interview test score. The Supreme Court ruled that the county's policy of taking into account the gender of job applicants was not a violation of Title VII.

See also Title VII of the 1964 Civil Rights Act.

Jointure

Jointure, a form of marriage settlement during the colonial period, was an alternative to dower. Jointure was a contract between wife and husband that designated what property the woman would receive in place of dower rights. Dower rights entitled a widow to at least one-third of her deceased husband's real property. Jointure guaranteed that widows would receive specific property but took away their stake in the size of the family fortune. Jointure settlements were made as compensation for the loss of property women endured at marriage, and gave them no powers of control while their husbands were still alive.

See also Dower.

Jones, Jane Elizabeth Hitchcock (1813–1896)

Jane Elizabeth Jones was an abolitionist and feminist. She was born 13 March 1813 in Vernon, New York, an area that saw many reform and revival movements. In the 1840s she met abolitionist Abby Kelley Foster, who interested her in the antislavery movement headed by William Lloyd Garrison. With Foster she lectured throughout New England and eastern Pennsylvania. In 1845 she moved with a group of antislavery lecturers to Salem, Ohio, becoming coeditor of the new *Anti-Slavery Bugle* (until 1849) and managing an antislavery book agency. In 1846 she married one of her fellow speakers, Benjamin Smith Jones, giving birth in 1848 to their daughter. That year her children's book, *The Young Abolitionists*, was published. A strong supporter of women's rights, Jones spoke at the first women's rights convention in Ohio, which was held in Salem in April 1850. A member of the Ohio Woman Rights Association, she lectured about reforming laws that pertained to married women's property and child custody rights. Her address to the Woman's Rights Committee of the Ohio legislature in 1861 facilitated passage of a married woman's property law. With the advent of the Civil War, Jones ended her reform activities, returning to Vernon in the 1860s. She died there 13 January 1896.

See also Married Women's Property Acts.

Jones, Mary Harris (1830–1930)

Labor leader and radical Mary Jones, better known as Mother Jones, was born 1 May 1830 in Cork, Ireland. Her father came to the United States in 1835, later making arrangements for his wife and children to follow him. Mary went to school in Toronto, Ontario. She taught school in Monroe, Michigan, and later opened a dressmaking business in Chicago. Going to Memphis to resume her teaching career, she met and married, in 1861, a member of the Iron Molders' Union. Only his last name, Jones, is known. Six years later Jones's husband and their four children died of yellow fever. Nursing others until the epidemic subsided, she then moved back to Chicago to reopen her dressmaking business. In 1871, she lost her business and all of her personal possessions in the Chicago Fire, which prompted

Labor leader and radical Mary Jones became known as Mother Jones.

165

her attendance at meetings of the Knights of Labor, whose quarters had also been partially destroyed in the disaster. The Knights of Labor meetings helped to focus her growing resentment against the low pay and long hours of the working poor. Over the next 50 years she organized working people. She was in Pittsburgh during the railroad strike of 1877; in Chicago during the Haymarket riot of 1886; in Birmingham in 1894; with the coal workers of Pennsylvania in 1900–1902; in the Colorado coal fields in 1903–1906; and in a copper mine strike in Idaho in 1906. In 1905 Jones supported the establishment of the Industrial Workers of the World. Throughout these years she gave speeches, led marches, and unionized workers. Following the 1913 United Mine Workers strike in West Virginia, she was convicted of conspiracy to commit murder, but she was imprisoned only a short time before a new governor took office and freed her. After the 1914 massacre of miner's families in Ludlow, Colorado, she lobbied President Woodrow Wilson to influence the mine owners to compromise with the union. From 1915 to 1916, she worked with the garment workers and streetcar workers of New York City, and in 1919 she traveled throughout the country to aid the national steel strike. Into her nineties, Mother Jones addressed West Virginia miners about the inequities of their economic situation, embracing other causes as well, including the plight of child laborers and the conditions of prisoners. At a party on her one-hundredth birthday, the fiery agitator received a congratulatory telegram from her old enemy, John D. Rockefeller, Jr. She died six months later, on 30 November 1930, in Silver Spring, Maryland.

See also Industrial Workers of the World; Strikes.

Jones v. Porter

In 1740, a Virginia court voided the transfer of a married woman's property because no court officer had noted in writing that a private judicial examination of the woman had taken place. Courts required such examinations to ensure that husbands did not coerce their wives into giving up their property. This case illustrated how seriously Virginia (as well as Maryland and South Carolina) safeguarded the interests of married women when it came to the conveyance of their property, unlike the northern colonies, especially the Quaker and Puritan colonies of Pennsylvania and Connecticut.

See also Coercion.

Jong, Erica Mann (1942–)

Erica Jong is perhaps the most widely read novelist and poet of the women's movement. She was born 26 March 1942 in New York City. She attended Barnard College, receiving a B.A. in 1963. Two years later she received an M.A. from Columbia University, going on to do postgraduate work at the Columbia School of Fine Arts (1969–1970). After a brief marriage to Michael Werthman, she married child psychiatrist Allan Jong in 1966. The couple divorced in 1975. Jong's novel of sexual liberation, *Fear of Flying* (1973), was a best-seller. Her poetry includes *Fruits and Vegetables* (1971), *Half-Lives* (1973), *Loveroot* (1975), *At the Edge of the Body* (1979), *Ordinary Miracles* (1983), and *Becoming Light* (1991). Her novels include *How To Save Your Own Life* (1975), *Parachutes and Kisses* (1984), *Fanny: Being the True Adventures of Fanny Hackabout-Jones* (1980), *Megan's Book of Divorce: A Kid's Book for Adults* (1984), *Serenissima: A Novel of Venice* (1987), and *Any Woman's Blues* (1990). *Witches* (1981) contains both nonfiction and poetry. Jong's heroines are lusty, liberated women whom some see as reflections of their witty and passionate author. Jong married writer Jonathan Fast in 1977; they divorced in 1983. Their daughter lives with her mother in Connecticut.

Juries

During the early American period and continuing until the late 1800s, jury duty had been reserved for white males. This criterion was established under common law. The only exception was in a specific case when all-women panels listened to testimony from female claimants. In 1879, the views of the Supreme Court sparked the beginning of change when it stated that forbidding African-American men to serve as jurors denied them equal protection and due process under the guidelines of the Fourteenth Amendment. The court did, however, retain its original belief that the Fourteenth Amendment applied only to race—not to gender.

In 1884, in *Rosencrantz v. Territory of Washington*, a woman who had been indicted by a grand jury in Washington insisted that the presence of a married woman on the jury was unconstitutional. The territorial supreme court's decision said that a woman with a right to vote in her territory and control property (under the local married women's act) was obviously a householder and a capable elector. Judge Turner, however, was in strong disagreement with this decision. Three years later, in 1887, this same court overruled its original decision and refused to allow women to sit upon juries. It joined other states and regions, who at that time chose only men for jury duty.

At the end of World War I, with the passage of the Nineteenth Amendment, the question concerning the status of female jurors arose once again. Following the guidelines of most state statutes, women could vote and were considered capable and qualified electors. However, states were slow to accept female jurors. Several cases were heard before the Supreme Court during the next three decades. By the early 1940s, 28 states admitted women to sit upon juries, with 15 states giving women the right to claim exemption because of their gender. The remaining 20 states refused to allow women to serve on juries.

After the passage of the Civil Rights Act in 1957, women were guaranteed the right to serve on federal juries. Lower courts in 21 states, however, still refused to consider women on juries. In 1961, the Supreme Court indicated that women did not have a constitutional right to serve upon juries. However, in *Hoyt v. Florida*, Gwendolyn Hoyt demanded to have a jury of both male

and female participants after having been convicted by an all-male jury of murdering her husband. Justice John Marshall Harlan disagreed. He thought gender discrimination was irrelevant to a fair jury decision and that the blanket excuse of all women from jury service should be upheld. Harlan cited an earlier decision in the 1884 reversal of *Rosencrantz v. Territory of Washington*, remarking "Granted that some women pursue business careers, the great majority constitute the heart of the home . . . the state legislature has permitted the exemption in order not to risk disruption of the basic family unit. Its action was far from arbitrary." The court upheld Florida's practice of restricting jury service to men unless women registered separately to serve as jurors.

With the passage of the Federal Jury Selection and Service Act of 1968, the courts were finally able to provide a fair representation of the community—jurors of every race, creed, sex, natural origin, and economic status. In 1973, all 50 states accepted women on juries, but 19 states still allowed individual exemption clauses, based on gender (pregnancy, needing to care for minor children, and so on). In 1975, the Supreme Court finally overruled the *Hoyt* decision in *Taylor v. Louisiana* (1961). The high court stated that a law denying a male defendant a trial by a jury composed of a cross-section of participants violated the defendant's rights under the Sixth Amendment. Though the decision did not use exact terms relating to gender classification concerning juries, it did revoke any remaining state laws that restricted jury duty on the basis of gender. In its 1975 *Taylor* decision, the court quoted a 1946 opinion of William O. Douglas (*Ballard v. United States*). Douglas, responding to the claim that an all-male jury represented a cross-section of the community, asked, "Who would claim that a jury was truly representative of the community if all men were intentionally and systematically excluded from the panel?"

Through the 1970s and 1980s, feminists continued to fight for female jury members on an equal rights basis. In a significant 1986 case *(Batson v. Kentucky)* involving an African American murder defendant, a court ruling stated that prosecutors could not exclude potential jurors based on race. The justices have widened this protection in other cases.

A November 1993 decision in an Alabama Paternity case promises to affect the jury-selection process nationwide. A Supreme Court hearing will determine if the Batson case will be broadened to include sex discrimination. Many women's groups, along with the Clinton administration, stand in support of this. Ruth Bader Ginsburg, the newest justice of the high court, has tried to win the same constitutional protections for women that now exist for racial minorities.

See also Taylor v. Louisiana.

Kansas Campaign

The Kansas campaign of 1867 marked the point at which the women's suffrage movement began to divide. After the Civil War, abolitionists and women's rights advocates were at loggerheads about who should be enfranchised first: African-American men or women and men of all races. Many abolitionists felt that the post–Civil War era was "the Negroes' hour," a point no women's rights activist could ignore.

Early in 1867, the Kansas legislature announced a November election in which voters would decide whether to extend suffrage to women and African-American men. The issues were to be decided separately. Lucy Stone and Henry Blackwell, leaders in both the abolition and suffrage movements, traveled to Kansas shortly after the election was announced. Women's suffrage supporters transported them around the state, and they spoke to large, enthusiastic audiences.

Elizabeth Cady Stanton and Susan B. Anthony traveled to Kansas later in 1867. Arriving in September, they discovered the Republicans had interpreted the American Equal Rights Association's stand on universal suffrage to apply to men only and had formed an Anti-Female Suffrage Committee. Suddenly women's suffrage in Kansas seemed doomed. Then, George Train, a Democrat, offered to campaign for women's suffrage. When Anthony and Stanton accepted his offer, an outcry ensued. The Republicans objected to Train not only because he was a Democrat but also because he was a racist who opposed African-American suffrage under any circumstances. When Stone learned that Train's appearances with Anthony were represented as American Equal Rights Association events, she printed cards denying the connection. Because Anthony and Stanton accepted Train's help, they too were accused of racism, a charge they denied. That fall, both women's and African-American suffrage were defeated. By that time, Anthony and Stanton had alienated Republicans across the country as well as many of their friends and colleagues. The split widened when Train gave Anthony the funds to start a newspaper, *The Revolution*, which began publication 8 January 1868.

In February 1869 the Fifteenth Amendment, which guarantees men's right to vote regardless of "race, color, or previous condition of servitude," was proposed. Stanton and Anthony heatedly addressed the American Equal Rights Association at a meeting in May 1869. Immediately after the meeting, they founded an organization devoted exclusively to women's suffrage, the National Woman Suffrage Association (NWSA). Stone did not join them, concluding, "There are two great oceans; in one is the black man, and in the other is the woman. But I thank God for that XV Amendment, and . . . will be thankful in my soul if *any* body can get out of the terrible pit."

See also American Equal Rights Association; Anthony, Susan B.; Bloomers; National Woman Suffrage Association; Stanton, Elizabeth Cady; Stone, Lucy.

Kelley, Florence (1859–1932)

Born on 12 September 1859 in Philadelphia, Florence Kelley was named Florence Molthrop Kelley, but dropped the use of her middle name. A social reformer and feminist, she was known for her energetic approach to many varied social and political issues and was the general secretary of the National Consumers' League for years.

Kelley followed a family tradition of public service. Her father, William, active in politics, set an inspiring example that she chose to follow. Except for short periods, Kelley received her early education at home. Graduating from Cornell University in

1882, she traveled to Zurich to study government and law. While there she met her future husband, Lazure Vishnevetsky, an East European medical student. They had two children, but Kelley was physically abused by her husband and they were divorced in 1891. Kelley then became a resident of Hull House in Chicago, one of the first social settlements in the United States. While living at Hull House, she earned her law degree from Northwestern University and worked as the first woman factory inspector for the state of Illinois. Kelley was responsible for the passage of a state anti-sweatshop bill. The bill contained a significant eight-hour-workday clause.

Kelley moved from Chicago and became part of New York City's Henry Street Settlement in 1899. She soon became the general secretary of the National Consumers' League and traveled extensively throughout the United States to establish local consumers' leagues. She actively supported laws to protect women and children and was an avid industrial reformer. Kelley's views were published in her books, *Ethical Gains through Legislation* (1905) and *Modern Industry* (1913). One of the highlights of her career was the establishment of a ten-hour-workday law for women that was upheld in the 1908 Supreme Court ruling in *Muller v. Oregon.* She and the Oregon leagues were instrumental in the defense of this case, persuading Louis D. Brandeis to join them and writing up the medical and cultural studies used in his brief.

Kelley was active in the woman suffrage movement and a pacifist during World War I and remained active in legislative struggles until her death on 17 February 1932 at Naskeag Point, Maine.

See also Addams, Jane; Henry Street Settlement; National Consumers' League.

Kemble, Frances Anne (1809–1893)

Fanny (Frances) Kemble was said to be the first woman to wear an outfit that would inspire the creation of the Bloomer costume and was the first actress of stature to perform in the United States. She was born 27 November 1809 in London, into an English theatrical family. Her father was part owner of the renowned Covent Garden theater. Kemble was educated in France and showed no interest in acting until her father's impending bankruptcy necessitated her debut at Covent Garden in 1829. Her portrayal of Juliet in Shakespeare's *Romeo and Juliet* was an immediate success and it saved her family financially. Three years later, the theater fell on hard times again, and Fanny Kemble's father arranged for her to tour the United States. She gave her first performance in New York City in 1832. In 1834 she married a Philadelphia gentleman and planter, Pierce Butler, and turned to writing. When she moved with Butler to his plantation in Georgia, she was horrified to see how enslaved people were treated. This set her on a path that eventually led her out of the South and the United States, and to her separation from her husband, who was granted a divorce on grounds of abandonment in 1849. One of Kemble's most widely read works emerged from a diary she kept while living on the plantation in 1838 and 1839. *Journal of a Residence on a Georgian Plantation* (1863), which contained penetrating observations about the cruel treatment of slaves, was used to turn British opinion against slavery during the Civil War.

In the 1840s Kemble returned to acting in Rome and London; in 1848 she began to give public readings from Shakespeare. About this time, she was credited with being the first woman to wear a pantaloon outfit that inspired Elizabeth Smith Miller to design the so-called Bloomer costume. She lived intermittently in the United States, in Lennox, Massachusetts (1849–1862), and Pennsylvania (1867–1877). She returned to England in 1877. Kemble wrote several plays and books, including *A Year of Consolation* (1847), *Record of a Girlhood* (1878), *Records of Later Life* (1882), *Notes on Some of Shakespeare's Plays* (1882), and *Further Records* (1890). She died 15 January 1893 in London.

See also Bloomer, Amelia Jenks; Bloomers; Miller, Elizabeth Smith.

Kempe's Lessee v. Kennedy et al.

An 1809 lawsuit involving dower rights sheds light on marital relations in the United States at the beginning of the nineteenth century. Before the American Revolution, Grace Kempe had been married to John Tabor Kempe, the king's attorney general for New York City. She brought to the marriage land she owned in New Jersey. At the time of the American Revolution her husband was forced into exile in England. She went with him, and the land was confiscated. Later, the land was sold by New Jersey. After her husband died, Grace Kempe tried to get the land back. The case was originally tried in the Inferior Court of Common Pleas for Hunterdon County, New Jersey, which decided against her. It came before the Supreme Court on appeal. Kempe's lawyer, John Stockton, argued that, as a married woman, Grace Kempe had no choice but to remain with her husband during the war. He also pointed out that she did not help the British when they occupied New York City but was merely passive. He claimed, "It [the confiscation of her land] supposes a *free will*, a *volition*, an election to go or stay; but a *feme covert* [married woman], in the presence of her baron, has no will; and on the subject of residence, she can have no will different from his." Stockton argued that, even if Grace Kempe had known her husband was a traitor, she had not committed treason by remaining with him. Although Chief Justice John Marshall implied his sympathies lay with Grace Kempe, he allowed the lower court decision against her to stand on a technicality. While Grace Kempe did not regain her lands, the case was the first to contest the forfeit of a woman's dower right to come before the Supreme Court.

See also Dower; *Garlick v. Strong; Griffith v. Griffith.*

King, Billie Jean Moffitt (1943–)

Professional tennis player Billie Jean King, founder of World Team Tennis and the Women's Professional Softball League, is perhaps best known for defeating male tennis professional Bobby Riggs in the 1973 publicity stunt "The Battle of the Sexes." Although the event made King's name a household word, it is only one of her many important efforts to build public respect for and improve the status of female professional athletes. Billie Jean Moffitt was born 22 November 1943 in Long Beach, California. In 1958, she won the Southern Championship and, by the age of 17, she was the United States's fourth-ranked player. In 1961, at the age of 18, she became the youngest player ever to win a Wimbledon doubles championship (with Karen Hantze). In 1965 she married Larry King. The following year she won her first singles title at Wimbledon. In 1967 King became even more famous when she won the single, doubles, and mixed doubles Wimbledon titles. Eventually she amassed 20 Wimbledon titles—6 singles, 10 doubles, and 4 mixed doubles—more than any woman before her. King used her fame to promote women's tennis and to establish the first Virginia Slims Tournament in 1971. That year she was the first woman athlete to earn more than $100,000 in a single year. On 20 September 1973, she defeated Bobby Riggs in "The Battle of the Sexes." The match drew an audience of 30,400, the largest ever to watch a tennis match. King has worked tirelessly for women's sports, founding the Women's Professional Softball League in 1975 and World Team Tennis in 1976. With her husband she established *Womensports* magazine and the Women's Sports Foundation (1974). Among her many world tennis titles are the U.S. Singles, U.S. Doubles, U.S. Indoor Championships, French Open, and Australian Open. Her autobiography, *Billie Jean*, was published in 1982.

King, Coretta Scott (1927–)

Widow of the assassinated civil rights leader Martin Luther King, Coretta Scott King has spent the years since his death struggling to advance the cause they both cared so much about. Born 27 April 1927 in Heiberger, Alabama, she graduated first in her class from Lincoln School (Marion, Alabama) in

1945. She earned an A.B. degree in music and education from Antioch College in 1951, and a degree in music (1954) from the New England Conservatory of Music. While in Boston she met the young philosophy student Martin Luther King, whom she married 18 June 1953. The following year they went to live in Montgomery, Alabama. There, she raised four children and worked with her husband in the nonviolent civil rights movement. In 1962 King was a delegate to the General Disarmament Convention held in Geneva, Switzerland, as part of the Women Strike for Peace. That year, she began to teach music at Morris Brown College in Atlanta, where the Kings had moved two years earlier. In 1964, King accompanied her husband to Oslo, Norway, where he accepted the Nobel Peace Prize. After her husband was assassinated in 1968, Coretta Scott King became a speaker in her own right, lecturing on racism and poverty. She served on the board of directors of the Southern Christian Leadership Conference and helped create the Martin Luther King, Jr., Center for Non-Violent Social Change in Atlanta, Georgia. In 1993, King published *My Life with Martin Luther King, Jr.*

Kirchberg v. Feenstra

In *Kirchberg v. Feenstra* (1981), the Supreme Court unanimously overturned a Louisiana statute that gave husbands the privilege of disposing of joint marital property without their wives' consent, describing a husband as the "head and master" of such property. Seven justices drew on the principle for dealing with gender-based discrimination formulated in the *Craig v. Boren* decision (1976) and subsequent related decisions. In the *Craig* case, the Supreme Court established a new standard by which gender-based or discriminatory laws must be judged. According to the standard, gender classifications must be "substantially related" to an "important government objective." The other two justices articulated an alternative equal protection test to the one set forth in the *Craig* decision: these justices expressed concern over the unequal treatment of people acting in essentially the same capacity or role. The law overturned in the *Kirchberg* decision exemplified the type of law that did not meet even the minimum standards for being judged constitutional under the *Craig* test or alternative equal protection tests of justices of all ideological persuasions.

Knight, Sarah Kemble (1666–1727)

Born 19 April 1666 in Boston, diarist Sarah Kemble received a good education for the time. She married Richard Knight before 1689. After the death of her father, a Boston merchant, she took over his business. In October 1704 she traveled alone by horseback from Boston to New Haven, Connecticut, and then on to New York, returning to Boston in March. She kept a journal of her river crossings, night rides, and other adventures. Her diary was kept in the family and was first published in 1825 as *The Journal of Madam Knight*. It has since become a much-loved account of eighteenth-century New England life. Knight died 25 September 1727 in New London, Connecticut.

Knights of Labor

The first attempt in the United States to organize workers on a general or universal basis, instead of by trade or craft, was made by the Noble Order of Knights of Labor of America. The group was founded on Thanksgiving Day 1869 in Philadelphia by Uriah S. Stephens and six other men, originally as a secret society of tailors. The Knights of Labor emerged from the 1868 dissolution of the garment-cutters union, which had failed to maintain acceptable wages. In its place, Stephens planned a new organization that would include "all branches and honorable toil." The first local assembly was held in 1873 in Philadelphia. In January 1878 the first general assembly was held; at this time membership was a few thousand men. Five years later the membership had climbed to 50,000. At its fifth session, in 1881 in Detroit, the union made two decisions that sparked a decade of rapid growth. At that session the assembly announced that, after 1 January 1882, the union would go public as the Knights of Labor and would admit women on an equal basis with men. At the next general assembly, in 1882 in New York, the new constitution was adopted. From this point forward, the union tried to organize women and men, blacks and whites, skilled and unskilled labor. Within five years, it chartered 113 women's affiliated groups and gained 50,000 female members. Like the male members, women joined the national assembly as delegates and participated in strikes. The union's membership peaked in the years 1883–1886, when membership totaled one million. Shortly after, its membership began to decline. In part, this was a result of the Haymarket Square bombing, an outbreak of violence in Chicago on 4 May 1886 during a demonstration for the eight-hour workday staged by anarchists. When police tried to break up a crowd of 1,500, a bomb exploded. Adversaries of organized labor tried to use the incident to discredit the Knights of Labor, which was already in decline. The union's membership dropped to 130,000 in 1900. With its demise, working women lost one of their strongest supporters. In its place emerged the conservative American Federation of Labor, which was only interested in organizing skilled workers. By 1900, many people felt that the unskilled laborer could be helped only by radical change in the economic and social system of the United States.

See also American Federation of Labor.

KNOW

One of the first feminist publishing houses, KNOW was created in the fall of 1969 to meet the growing demand for information about feminism. Under female ownership and operation, KNOW initially devoted most of its efforts to reprinting academic articles. On a larger scale, because many fledgling feminist organizations could afford to produce only mimeographed newsletters, KNOW became the first official publisher of many essays that had previously appeared only as mimeographed copies.

See also The Feminist Press.

Kreps, Juanita Morris (1921–)

Juanita Kreps was the first woman to be appointed secretary of commerce. She was born 11 January 1921 in Lynch, Kentucky, and graduated from Berea College (Kentucky) in 1942. She earned an M.A. (1944) and a Ph.D. (1948), both in economics, from Duke University. She joined the faculty of Denison University as an economic instructor in 1945, continuing as an assistant professor from 1947 to 1950. In 1944 she married economist Clifton H. Kreps. She taught economics at Denison University (Granville, Ohio), Hofstra College (Hempstead, New York) and Queens College (Queens, New York) from 1945 to 1955, before returning to Duke in 1955. There, she became a full professor in 1968 and James B. Duke professor of economics in 1972, also serving as assistant provost (1969–1972) and vice-president of the university (1973–1977). In 1977, Kreps became President Jimmy Carter's secretary of commerce, a post she held until 1979. She became the first woman to serve as director of the New York Stock Exchange Board of Directors (1972), serving on the board until 1977. Her books include *Principles of Economics* (with Charles E. Ferguson, 1962), *Automation and Employment* (1964), *Taxation, Spending, and the National Debt* (1964), *Lifetime Allocation of Work and Leisure* (1971), *Sex in the Marketplace: American Women at Work* (1971), *Contemporary Labor Economics* (with other contributors, 1974), *Sex, Age and Work: The Changing Composition of the Labor Force* (1975), *Economics of Stationary Populations* (1977), and *Contemporary Labor Economics and Labor Relations* (1980). Kreps has edited several other collections, including *Women and the American Economy* (1976).

Kuhn, Maggie (1905–)

Gray Panther founder Maggie Kuhn was born 3 August 1905, in Buffalo, New York. Her family moved to Cleveland, Ohio, where she graduated from West High School (1922). In 1926, she received a B.A. degree in English from Case Western Reserve and went to work as publications editor for the New York City branch of the YWCA. She also worked for the United Presbyterian Church, editing a church publication called *Social Progress.* She helped organize the Consultation of Older and Younger Adults for Social Change, which came to be known as the Gray Panthers. Kuhn urged the church to fight discrimination against the elderly, called "ageism." This issue was particularly important to her as she herself faced mandatory retirement in 1970. With the Gray Panthers, she lobbied for better conditions in nursing homes and for legislation to help the hearing impaired. She twice addressed Congress (1973 and 1977). In 1978, more than 350 delegates attended the second biennial convention of the Gray Panthers in Chevy Chase, Maryland. That year Kuhn won the Humanist of the Year award. Through the late 1980s, Kuhn was an active public speaker for reform.

La Follette, Belle Case (1859–1931)

Belle La Follette, wife of Progressive leader Robert La Follette, never held a political office, but she was, nonetheless, a Progressive leader in her own right. She was born 21 April 1859 in Summit, Wisconsin. Graduating from the University of Wisconsin in 1879, she married classmate and future governor La Follette two years later. She attended law school while rearing their first child. In 1885 La Follette became the first woman to receive a law degree from the University of Wisconsin Law School. She was a leader of the Progressive cause in Wisconsin and served as her husband's assistant during his three congressional terms (1885–1891), with Rebecca Felton, one of the first women to play such an active role in her husband's political life. After her husband was defeated in 1890, La Follette pursued her own political issues, speaking on behalf of women's suffrage and protective legislation for women and children.

When her husband became governor of Wisconsin in 1900, La Follette helped him launch the legislative reforms that came to be known as the Wisconsin Idea, or Progressivism. She advocated child welfare and an end to segregation and other positions considered advanced for their day. In 1906, Robert La Follette was elected to the Senate, and the family returned to Washington, D.C. In 1909 the couple launched *La Follette's Weekly Magazine*, which soon had a national readership. Writing a column on women and education, Belle La Follette combined news and political commentary to advocate reform. She also wrote a column for the North American Press Syndicate (1911–1912). Her skill as a speaker and her distinguished reputation made her a much-loved lecturer, and she used her platform to advance the cause of women's suffrage. She aided the suffrage campaigns in Wisconsin, Oregon, Nebraska, and North Dakota and spoke before the Senate Committee on Suffrage in June 1913.

In 1921 La Follette helped organize the National Council for the Prevention of War. She also was a leader in the Women's Committee for World Disarmament, which called for the first disarmament conference in world history. La Follette helped her husband campaign for the presidency in 1924. When he died the following year, many groups and individuals—including women, members of the Wisconsin legislature, and labor—urged her to serve out his Senate term. Yet, she refused. Although there is no doubt she would have won if she had run for election, thus becoming the first woman to win a Senate seat, she chose to become associate editor of the monthly *La Follette's Magazine*, (formerly *La Follette's Weekly Magazine*) and to write a biography of her husband. La Follette died 18 August 1931, in Washington, D.C.

See also Felton, Rebecca Ann Latimer; Progressive Party.

Ladies' Home Journal Sit-In

On 19 March 1970, to dramatize their objections to the conservative viewpoint represented by the *Ladies' Home Journal*, feminists from various organizations arranged a sit-in at the office of John Mack Carter, then editor in chief and publisher of the magazine. As part of the heavily publicized protest, the feminists distributed a press release in which they complained about the lack of attention the *Journal* paid to practical issues, such as employment, child care, and abortion, and its failure to present nontraditional lifestyles. The feminists demanded appointment of a female editor in chief and establishment of an employee child care facility and a training program for secretaries. Their major demand was the opportunity to publish an issue of the magazine, which they would call *Women's Liberated Journal.* By the end of the day Carter agreed to negotiate. Eventually, he agreed to publish an eight-page supplement to be written by a feminist collective. The supplement, when it was published, included articles entitled "Women and Work" and "How To Start Your Own Consciousness-Raising Group," and it referred readers to feminist groups. Although many readers did not like the supplement, the sit-in may have influenced future changes at *Ladies' Home Journal* and other publications.

Ladies Magazine and Repository of Entertaining Knowledge

Founded in 1792 by William Gibbons, the *Ladies Magazine and Repository of Entertaining Knowledge* marked the advent of women's magazine publishing in the United States. It published essays that emphasized women's educational and spiritual growth as well as excerpts from other works, including *A Vindication of the Rights of Women* by Mary Wollstonecraft. The magazine ceased publication one year after its founding.

Laidlaw, Harriet Burton (1873–1949)

Harriet Laidlaw was one of the leading speakers for women's suffrage in America. Born 16 December 1873 in Albany, New York, she attended public schools. She received a bachelor's degree in pedagogy from Albany Normal College (now New York State College for Teachers) in 1895 and received the school's first master of pedagogy degree the following year. In 1902 she received an A.B. degree from Barnard College. She married James Lees Laidlaw three years later. Harriet Laidlaw gave her first speech advocating women's suffrage in 1893 in Albany. Thereafter she became one of the most active and eloquent speakers in the women's rights movement. She worked for the New York Woman Suffrage Association and became its vice-chairman. With the party she campaigned successfully for the

passage of the state's suffrage amendment in 1917. A director of the National American Woman Suffrage Association, she edited *Organizing To Win*, a guide for suffragists on how to organize. After passage of the Nineteenth Amendment, Laidlaw became a leader in the peace movement. From 1946 until her death, she was a member of the executive committee of the American Association for the United Nations. Laidlaw died 25 January 1949 in New York City.

See also National American Woman Suffrage Association.

Lanham Act

The Lanham Act of 1943 provided money to build facilities for defense-related industries. However, because states and communities were unable to build child care facilities for female war workers, the federal government did so under the act. A year after the law was enacted, only 10 percent of the children of working mothers attended the centers, and most mothers had to struggle to meet their obligations to their children and their country.

Larcom, Lucy (1824–1893)

Lucy Larcom was a poet, teacher, and editor. She was born 5 May 1824 in Beverly, Massachusetts. She spent ten years of her youth working in the Lowell textile mills, an experience she described in several of her works, including "Among Lowell Mill-Girls: A Reminiscence," which appeared in *The Atlantic Monthly* (1881); a long poem, *An Idyl of Work* (1875); and the book for which she is known, *A New England Girlhood* (1889). Larcom first published in the *Lowell Offering*, a factory operatives' magazine. As early as 1849 she was included in Rufus W. Griswold's *Female Poets of America*. Leaving the mill town, she acquired a college education at the Montessori Seminary in Godfrey, Illinois (1849–1852). In 1854 Larcom began to teach at the Wheaton Seminary in Massachusetts, where she remained for almost eight years. After leaving the school, she began to contribute creative writing to

176

magazines. She edited the periodical *Our Young Folks* from 1865 to 1873. Her other books include *Similitudes from Ocean and Prairie* (1854), *The Sunbeam and Other Stories* (1860), *Poems* (1869), *Childhood Songs* (1873), *Wild Roses of Cape Ann, and Other Poems* (1881), *Easter Gleams* (1890), *As It Is in Heaven* (1891), *The Unseen Friend* (1892), and *At the Beautiful Gate and Other Songs of Faith* (1892). Larcom died 17 April 1893 in Boston.

Law Enforcement
See Policewomen.

Lawrence (Massachusetts) Mill Workers' Strike
The Lawrence Strike proved that unskilled, ethnically diversified workers, many of them women and children, could unite when their self-interest was at stake. On 12 January 1912 in Lawrence, Massachusetts, textile workers went on strike. The state had recently reduced the workweek from 56 to 54 hours, and employers responded by speeding up the looms and cutting wages. The operatives had no leaders until Local 20 of the Industrial Workers of the World (Wobblies) sent in Joe Ettor, Arturo Giovannitti, Elizabeth Gurley Flynn, and Big Bill Haywood. For the first time a national union tried to organize immigrant workers of diverse backgrounds, including Jews and Catholics, Poles and Italians. More than 10,000 workers picketed. The women's chant, "We Want Bread, and Roses Too" formed the basis of a well-known song and poem. Police fought the strikers with brutality against the women on the picket line and trumped-up murder charges against the Wobblies. To gain sympathy for the strike and to save money, Elizabeth Gurley Flynn and birth control advocate Margaret Sanger sent a number of strikers' children to be looked after in various cities, an act that created a great deal of publicity for the union cause. Through passive resistance and solidarity among skilled and unskilled workers of 27 ethnic groups, the strikers prevailed. The company yielded 1 March.

The strikers' succeeded despite the opposition of the American Federation of Labor (AFL). At the start of the strike, the Women's Trade Union League (WTUL) and the Lawrence Central Labor Union opened a relief center for strikers. The center fed and clothed 8,000 workers. But two weeks after the start of the strike, the AFL, which did not sanction the strike (believing that women could not be organized), ordered United Textile Workers chief John Golden to close the relief center. The WTUL had to comply, following its policy of working only for AFL-approved strikes. Although workers eventually won a 5 percent wage increase, the breach between the AFL and its female allies was not healed for years.

See also American Federation of Labor; Flynn, Elizabeth Gurley; Immigrant Women; Industrial Workers of the World; Sanger, Margaret; Strikes; Women's Trade Union League.

League of Women Voters (LWV)
In 1919, Carrie Chapman Catt conceived of the idea of an organization to unite women once they were enfranchised, and, in February 1921, the National League of Women Voters (LWV) was formed at a convention celebrating the suffrage victory of its parent organization, the National American Woman Suffrage Association (NAWSA). Roughly 5 percent of NAWSA became members of LWV. Originally, the LWV's priorities included more than five dozen items, which were grouped into seven categories: improvement of the electoral process, citizenship education, women's legal status, the condition of women working in industry, child welfare, social hygiene, and food supply. In 1923, its goals were redefined as the following: (1) women's legal rights; (2) the promotion of pacifism; and (3) effective government handling of social welfare objectives.

Many feminist historians have noted with a degree of resentment that the concept behind the founding of LWV implied that women were, in comparison to men, deficient in the understanding of political matters; however, in practical terms, the birth of the league could simply be attributed to the desire of an existing body of activists, the suffragists, to continue their work combining the two elements: women and the issue of voting. Initially, the league did in fact adopt a frankly feminist approach, stressing the potential power of a women's voting bloc. (By voting as a bloc and having their votes make a recognizable difference in elections, women would have had a tool for forcing their demands to be taken seriously.) However, to the dismay of some feminists, it was, in a few years, intimidated into abandoning that position because of the hostility to it from members of the establishment who felt threatened by an unfamiliar and therefore uncontrollable political tactic. Those individuals declared that any basis for organizing individuals (such as gender) apart from the two-party system was inherently un-American.

The approach adopted by the league in place of militant feminism was one that emphasized improvement in government as its chief overall aim, with the political education of women as merely a means to that end. This shift was, ironically, somewhat more—although not entirely—consistent with Carrie Chapman Catt's original conception of the organization: namely, that it would not attempt to steer women away from the major political parties or make them shun working with men, but would lead them to participate in the political process on an *individual* basis, entering the existing political parties and working for their improvement. (Though the league made the decision not to compete ideologically with the political parties, it is interesting to note that, whether or not this was intentional, it often competed with them for the energies of women active on political issues.)

For many years, the league actually devoted more attention to issues such as disarmament, wages and working hours, and child labor than to women's rights, such as the right to use birth control, divorce law reform, equal pay, and the right for women to serve on juries. (Even after the suffrage victory, some additional persuasion was required for states to allow women to serve on juries; furthermore, although most states granted this right following the ratification of the Nineteenth Amendment, many states did not, for many decades, call women for jury service unless they requested it.) Despite its middle- and upper-class membership, the league was determined to reach as many types of women as possible. It was careful to create a strong consensus among its members before proceeding with any decision. As part of its effort to be nonsectarian and nonpartisan, it avoided, for the most part, candidate endorsements. To promote unity with other women, the league joined nine other women's organizations in the Women's Joint Congressional Committee to lobby for feminist goals. The committee was responsible for the Sheppard-Towner Maternity and Infancy Protection Act (1921), which provided health care funds, and the Cable Act (1922), which granted married women citizenship that was not fully dependent on (although still not fully independent of) their husbands' status.

Out of a desire to express support for working women, the LWV endorsed protective laws. For this reason, it often came into conflict with the staunchly feminist National Woman's Party, which opposed protective legislation because of its interference with the principle of a comprehensive ban on all sex discrimination in the form of an equal rights amendment. Moreover, some feminist groups accused the LWV of emphasizing patriotism over women's rights to the point of complacency on the latter subject. LWV's determination to effect change through the use of the right to vote may have been mistaken by some feminists as settling merely for equal suffrage; also, the fact that it favors an incremental approach to achieving women's rights may have contributed to the perception that it lacked passion for feminist causes.

In the second wave of twentieth-century feminism, though LWV no longer occupied a central role in the women's movement, it served as a valuable ally for the new groups.

See also Cable Act; Catt, Carrie Clinton Lane Chapman; Park, Maud May; National Woman's

178

Party; Sheppard-Towner Act; Women's Joint Congressional Committee.

Leser v. Garnett

In *Leser v. Garnett*, the Nineteenth Amendment was accepted as a legitimate exercise of the amending power of the Constitution. *Leser v. Garnett* was argued before the Supreme Court on 23 and 24 January 1922. The decision was read on 27 February 1922, with Justice Louis D. Brandeis delivering the majority opinion of the court.

With the ratification of the Nineteenth Amendment on 26 August 1920, women were granted the right to vote. Some states, however, did not ratify the amendment, challenging it on the premise that it had greatly expanded the electorate and undercut the political autonomy of these states. On 12 October 1920, two Maryland women, Cecelia Streett Waters and Mary D. Randolph, applied for and were granted registration as qualified voters. Oscar Leser petitioned to have their names removed from the voter registration list and took his complaint to the court of common pleas. His grounds were that the applicants were women, and Maryland, at that time, had limited suffrage to men. The case finally appeared before the U.S. Supreme Court in 1922.

The Supreme Court firmly decided that the Nineteenth Amendment affected the electorate no more than the Fifteenth Amendment had (where voting discrimination was forbidden due to race, color, or previous condition of servitude). The court also noted that the latter amendment had been considered valid and enforced by law for more than 50 years.

See also Nineteenth Amendment.

Letters on the Equality of the Sexes, and the Condition of Woman

Letters on the Equality of the Sexes, and the Condition of Woman is one of the earliest arguments for women's rights published in the United States. As editor Miriam Schneir notes, their major theme is "Woman's equal moral responsibility with man to *act* for the good of humanity." The letters also damn a society that denies equal pay for equal work and equal access to education. Written by Sarah Grimké in 1837 to Mary S. Parker, president of the Boston Female Anti-Slavery Society, the 15 letters were later published in newspapers and in pamphlet form (1838). They were a response to the pastoral letter of the New England Congregationalist Church, which had attacked the Grimké sisters for lecturing to audiences of women and men. In the letters, Sarah Grimké claimed that God meant women to be equal to men. She wrote, "I ask no favors for my sex. . . . All I ask of our brethren is, that they will take their feet from off our necks and permit us to stand upright on that ground which God designed us to occupy."

See also Grimké, Angelina; Grimké, Sarah.

Liberal Feminism

Liberal Feminism refers to the mainstream, least controversial component of the twentieth-century women's movement. Taking an extremely practical approach, liberal feminism emphasizes the gradual achievement of rights and opportunities—especially economic ones—that men enjoy. In other words, it does not seek a complete restructuring of society but presses for change within the existing society.

See also National Organization for Women.

The Lily

Founded by Amelia Bloomer in January 1849, *The Lily*, a six-page monthly, was the organ of the Ladies Temperance Society of Seneca Falls, New York. Originally it carried little information about women's rights. But in the spring of 1849, soon after *The Lily* started publication, the Tennessee legislature decided that, because women have no souls, they could not own property. Amazed, Mrs. Bloomer stated in the next issue of *The Lily*, "[It is] high time that women should open their eyes and look where they stand. It is quite time that their rights *should be discussed*, and that woman herself should enter the contest." The paper's masthead was changed to include the slogan Devoted to the Interests of Women. Later, the slogan was changed to The Emancipation of Woman from Intemperance, Injustice, Prejudice, and Bigotry. Bloomer also provided a room where women could meet and discuss their concerns.

The Lily championed women's causes, from suffrage to dress reform. Elizabeth Cady Stanton wrote articles for it under the pen name Sun Flower. In one article she complained that excessive decoration is useless: "What use is all the flummery, puffing, and mysterious folding we see in ladies' dresses? What use in ruffles on round pillow cases, night caps, children's clothes?" *The Lily* attacked the senseless restrictions of corsets and stays, promoting what became known as the Bloomer costume, with its loose waist, knee-length skirt, and long pantaloons. Bloomer herself began wearing the outfit, because "it seemed proper that I should practice as I preached," as did Elizabeth Cady Stanton, Susan B. Anthony, and other feminists. Immediately after Bloomer announced that she was going to try the outfit, hundreds of women wrote asking how to obtain patterns for it. Bloomer supplied them with sewing instructions, and people began to call the outfit the Bloomer costume. The circulation of *The Lily* skyrocketed from 500 to 4,000 per month.

When the Bloomer family moved to Mt. Vernon, Ohio, Bloomer continued to publish *The Lily*, but after settling in Council Bluffs, Iowa, in 1855, she was forced to sell the newspaper to Mary Birdsall because of difficulties in distribution. Birdsall continued publishing it until 1856.

See also Bloomer, Amelia Jenks; Bloomers; Kemble, Frances Anne.

Lindbergh, Anne Spencer Morrow (1906–)

Author Anne Morrow Lindbergh is the first woman to qualify for a glider's license and the first to receive the National Geographic Society Hubbard Gold Medal. Born 22 June 1906 in Englewood, New Jersey, she attended Miss Chapin's School in New York City and graduated from Smith College (1928). The following year she married Charles Lindbergh. She had met Lindbergh at the American embassy in Mexico City where her father was the U.S. ambassador. Lindbergh's fame for crossing the Atlantic in 1927 soon embraced her as well, and she began to travel with him on all of his flights. The year of their marriage they pioneered the Transcontinental Air Transport route from New York to Los Angeles. In 1930 they broke the transcontinental speed record, flying from Glendale, California, to Roosevelt Field, Long Island, in 14 hours and 23 minutes. Anne Morrow Lindbergh earned a private pilot's license the following year. In 1933, she received the National Geographic Society's Hubbard Medal for acting as her husband's copilot and radio operator during a 40,000-mile flight over five continents. The tragic kidnapping of their baby son in 1932 and the sensational murder trial of the kidnapper, Bruno Hauptman (1934–1935), drove the couple to England. There Lindbergh published her first book, *North to the Orient* (1935). Many books followed, including *The Wave of the Future* (1940), *The Steep Ascent* (1944), the best-selling *Gift from the Sea* (1955), *The Unicorn and Other Poems* (1956), *Dearly Beloved: A Theme and Variations* (1962), *Earth Shine* (1969), *Bring Me a Unicorn* (1972), *Hour of Gold, Hour of Lead* (1973), *Locked Rooms and Opened Doors* (1974), *The Flower and the Nettle* (1976), and *War within and Without* (1980). After her husband's death in 1974, Lindbergh retired to Connecticut.

List of Demands to the National Conference for a New Politics

The women's liberation movement—the more radical element of twentieth-century feminism—got its start when most radical females realized that the male-dominated New Left would never fight for women's rights. The final break came at the 1967 National Conference for a New Politics.

The conference brought together various New Left radicals but ended with division among them. At the conference women discovered that radical men, like society in general, treated women's issues with contempt. Women's concerns ranked low on the agenda of the New Left, despite the movement's goal of radical social change and empowerment of people excluded from full participation in society.

Before the conference, Heather Booth and Naomi Weisstein led a women's seminar at the Center for Radical Research, a free university program at the University of Chicago. The seminar led to the formation of a small group of women who considered attending the conference to air their grievances. This group was probably the first independent radical feminist group. Some of the women did attend the conference, where they joined other female attendees to form an ad hoc radical women's caucus. The caucus proposed a resolution on women's civil rights, including equal pay and abortion rights. The conference deliberately avoided discussing the resolution, agreeing to hear only a more conservative resolution on women's pacifism. Male attendees belittled women's concerns and refused to recognize them as political issues.

Among the members of the caucus were Jo Freeman and Shulamith Firestone, who later founded feminist groups in Chicago and New York. The confrontation at the conference exposed the futility of working for women's concerns within the New Left, and many radical women broke away to become part of an independent women's liberation, or radical feminist, movement.

Lockwood, Belva Ann Bennett McNall (1830–1917)

Belva Lockwood was the first woman to be admitted to practice before the Supreme Court and a founder of the first suffrage group organized in Washington, D.C. (1867). She was born 24 October 1830 in Royalton, New York. She graduated from Genesee College (forerunner of Syracuse University) in 1857, taught in New York state until 1866, and then moved to Washington, D.C., to open a school. There, she began to study law. She married Ezekiel Lockwood in 1868, who then took over the school. In 1871, after being refused admission to Georgetown University, Howard University, and Columbian College (now George Washington University), Lockwood enrolled in National University Law School. She graduated in 1873 and was admitted to the District of Columbia bar in the same year. As a lawyer she wrote bills and petitions and addressed Congress, all on behalf of women's rights. She drafted a bill for equal pay for women in government jobs, which became law in 1872. That year she also supported Victoria Woodhull's candidacy for president.

Belva Lockwood

In 1876 Lockwood was denied permission to practice before the Supreme Court. In response she pushed through legislation that enabled women to practice before the Court, and she was the first female to do so in 1879. She was active in the National Woman Suffrage Association from the

1870s through the 1900s. In 1884 she ran for president on the National Equal Rights Party ticket. Her reform platform won 4,149 votes in six states. She ran again in 1888 but received fewer votes. Lockwood attended peace conferences in Europe in 1889, 1906, 1908, and 1911. She helped to secure passage of laws that guaranteed equal property rights and equal guardianship of children for married women in the District of Columbia (1896). She also wrote suffrage amendments to the bills requesting statehood for Oklahoma, New Mexico, and Arizona (1903). Lockwood held positions of leadership in many reform organizations before her death on 19 May 1917 in Washington, D.C.

Longshore, Hannah E. Meyers (1819–1901)

Hannah Longshore was the first female faculty member of a medical school in the United States and Philadelphia's first woman doctor. She was born 30 May 1819 in Sandy Spring, Maryland, and was reared in Washington, D.C., and Columbiana County, Ohio. She lacked the money to study medicine and in 1841 married Thomas E. Longshore, a teacher. They moved to Attleboro (now Langhorne), Pennsylvania, in 1845. At the age of 31 and as the mother of two children, Longshore joined the first class of the Female (later Woman's) Medical College of Pennsylvania, which was founded by her brother-in-law, Joseph S. Longshore. She received a medical degree in 1851 at a commencement ceremony that was guarded by police because of threats from male medical students. Amid much ridicule she slowly built up her medical practice. Partly because of her success in giving public lectures on hygiene and physiology, her practice eventually extended to about 300 families. Her accomplishments paved the way for the acceptance of women physicians in Philadelphia by the last decade of the century. Longshore died 18 October 1901 in Philadelphia.

See also Health Care Providers; Woman's Hospital.

Lowell Female Labor Reform Association (LFLRA)

The Lowell Female Labor Reform Association (LFLRA), a labor organization of female textile workers in Lowell, Massachusetts, was formed in December 1844 to fight for a ten-hour workday, in response to the longer hours and wage cuts imposed by mill managers. The LFLRA, an auxiliary of the New England Workingmen's Association, was the first of many local Female Labor Reform Associations. Sarah Bagley, who helped organize the group, was its first president.

During the next year, the LFLRA collected 2,000 signatures on petitions demanding the shorter workday and presented the petitions to the Massachusetts House of Representatives Committee on Manufacturing. On 13 February 1845, the first U.S. government investigation of labor conditions began, with Sarah Bagley and other operators testifying that working conditions had worsened their health. Despite their testimony, the committee recommended that no ten-hour-day legislation be initiated. In response the LFLRA, whose motto was Try Again, successfully campaigned against the chairman of the committee in his bid for reelection. Bagley went on to organize branches of the LFLRA in Waltham and Fall River in Massachusetts and Manchester, Dover, and Nashua in New Hampshire.

In 1846, the LFLRA and the New England Workingmen's Association conducted another petition drive for the ten-hour workday, and again the legislature refused to act. It was 1874 before Massachusetts law mandated the ten-hour workday.

By the late 1840s poor immigrant girls were replacing native-born operatives. Wages fell and factories became more mechanized. As a result, the LFLRA changed its name and its nature in 1847. Under the new name, the Lowell Female Industrial Reform and Mutual Society, the group became less spirited but more practical, providing relief to the poor and ill.

See also Bagley, Sarah; Factory System; Female Labor Reform Associations; Immigrant Women; *Lowell Offering*; Unions; *Voice of Industry*.

Lowell Offering

The characters and personalities of the early female employees, called operators or operatives, of the textile mills at Lowell, Massachusetts, can be seen in their periodical, the *Lowell Offering* (1840–1845). Published monthly, it was organized by the Rev. Abel Charles Thomas, who was pastor of the First Universalist Church. From October 1840 to March 1841 it comprised articles prepared for the workers' literary circles, or self-improvement groups. Later, the magazine broadened its scope, publishing poetry, letters, and stories written by operatives. In August 1841 it merged with the *Operatives Magazine*. From October 1842 to December 1845 it was edited by two former operatives, Harriot F. Curtis, whose pen name was

The cover of the August 1845 Lowell Offering, *a monthly periodical that showcased writings by women textile workers in Lowell, Massachusetts.*

Mina Myrtle, and Harriet Farley, who became the magazine's manager and owner. The publication sought to showcase the culture and talents of the workers, and Farley selected letters, stories, and poems that best illustrated the workers' virtue and gentility. Famous contributors to the magazine were Harriet Hanson, who wrote *Early Factory Labor in New England* (1883), and Lucy Larcom, who wrote *A New England Girlhood* (1889).

During the labor unrest in the mid-1840s, the *Lowell Offering* took no position on wages and board. Ignoring the growing turmoil, it was replaced in 1845 by more progressive magazines such as *The Voice of Industry* and, a year later, *Factory Girls' Album and Operatives' Advocate*, which sought to portray the actual working conditions in the mills. Farley later published selections from the *Lowell Offering* under the titles *Shells from the Strand of the Sea of Genius* (1847) and *Mind among the Spindles* (1849). In September 1847 Farley revived the magazine as the *New England Offering*, but in March 1850 it ceased publication.

See also Bagley, Sarah; *Factory Girls' Album and Operatives' Advocate;* Factory System, Farley, Harriet; Female Labor Reform Associations; *Operatives' Magazine; Voice of Industry.*

Luce, Clare Boothe (1903–1987)

Clare Boothe Luce was the first woman to represent the United States as ambassador to a major power. She was born 10 April 1903 in New York City and graduated at the top of her class from The Castle in Tarrytown, New York (1919). After briefly studying drama, she worked as secretary to the millionaire suffragist Alva Belmont. An early marriage to George T. Brokaw in 1923 ended in divorce six years later.

Following the divorce she went to work for *Vogue* (1930–1931) and *Vanity Fair* (1931–1934), where she became managing editor. In 1931 her first book, *Stuffed Shirts*, was published. In 1935 she married Henry Luce, creator of *Fortune, Life*, and *Time* magazines. That year her first play, *Abide with Me*, opened on Broadway. In 1936 her satirical play, *The Women*, was staged. It is a

183

Clare Boothe Luce with husband Henry Luce

sharp criticism of a group of rich, self-indulgent women who contribute nothing to society. Luce commented in 1973, when the play was revived, "My play shows what I didn't like—idle, parasitical women. I didn't approve then and I don't approve now. The women who inspired this play deserved to be smacked across the head with a meat ax and that, I flatter myself, is exactly what I smacked them with." Luce went on to write the screenplays for the movies *Kiss the Boys Goodbye* (1938) and *Margin for Error* (1940). As a *Life* magazine correspondent, she wrote an eyewitness account of the 1939 German invasion of Belgium, *Europe in the Spring* (1940). Luce returned to the theatrical world late in life, writing a feminist play, *Slam the Door Softly* (1971).

In 1942 Luce was elected to the House of Representatives (Fourth District of Connecticut). She was reelected in 1944, the year her only daughter died in an automobile accident. During her two terms in Congress she served on the Military Affairs Committee. However, still mourning the loss of her daughter, she left politics in 1946. She returned to political life as a delegate to the 1952 Republican National Convention. The following year President Dwight D. Eisenhower appointed her ambassador to Italy. In 1956 she again returned to private life, writing and traveling. Nominated ambassador to Brazil in 1959, her anticommunist views created such controversy that she resigned the post shortly after surviving bitter confirmation hearings. Luce seconded Barry Goldwater's nomination for president at the Republican national convention in 1964.

In 1973 Richard Nixon appointed her to the President's Foreign Intelligence Advisory Board. He thought she was "a lead-pipe cinch to become the first woman president" were she younger. In 1983 President Ronald Reagan awarded her the Presidential Medal of Freedom. Throughout her life Luce was

184

dogged by questions about whether, as a woman, she was fit to hold office, but she proved that gender was no hindrance to excellence. Luce died 9 October 1987 in Washington, D.C.

Lyon, Mary Mason (1797–1849)

Mary Mason Lyon was the founder of Mount Holyoke Female Seminary. She was born 28 February 1797 in Buckland, Massachusetts, and in 1814 began teaching school to pay for her education. Between 1817 and 1821, she attended the Sanderson Academy (Ashfield), Amherst Academy, and the Reverend Joseph Emerson's school in Byfield. There, she became friendly with Zilpah Grant, who was one of her teachers. In 1824 Lyon opened a school in Buckland; during its summer recess she taught under Grant at the Adams Female Seminary in New Hampshire. When Grant opened the Ipswich Female Seminary in Massachusetts, Lyon joined her there. During the following year, she came to the belief that more had to be done for the education of women. Under Grant's leadership, the Ipswich Female Seminary devised a challenging curriculum that Lyon would use at Mount Holyoke. In 1834, Lyon participated in planning the Wheaton Female Seminary in Norton, Massachusetts, single-handedly raising funds for its establishment. The seminary (now Wheaton College) opened the following year. In 1836 she obtained a charter for the Mount Holyoke Female Seminary (now Mount Holyoke College), one of the first institutions for the higher education of girls. The school opened in November 1837 with 80 students. The school's goal was that it should be accessible to middle-class girls. By 1838 Mount Holyoke was so popular that 400 applicants had to be rejected for lack of space. Lyon was the school's principal for 12 years. She died 5 March 1849 in South Hadley, Massachusetts.

See also Grant, Zilpah; Mount Holyoke College.

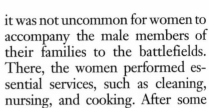

McAuliffe, Sharon Christa (1948–1986)

Christa McAuliffe was the first U.S. citizen to be a passenger (as opposed to a crew member) on a space mission. The ride ended tragically, only seconds after it began, when the space shuttle *Challenger* exploded. She was born 2 September 1948 in Boston. In high school she was an all-star softball player. She attended Framingham State College in Framingham, Massachusetts, receiving an M.A. in American history and secondary education (1970). In 1978 she received an M.Ed. from Bowie College in Bowie, Maryland. She went on to become a social studies teacher at Concord High School in Concord, New Hampshire. There, she created a course called "The American Women." On 19 July 1985, she was chosen from among 11,000 applicants to ride on the shuttle. This was in response to President Ronald Reagan's announcement that he wanted to send a teacher into space. McAuliffe planned to teach science lessons during the flight; the lessons were to be broadcast via public television to schools. On 28 January 1986, at Cape Canaveral, Florida, the space shuttle exploded shortly after takeoff, killing all seven passengers.

McCauley, Mary Ludwig Hays (1754–1832)

Mary McCauley, better known as Molly Pitcher, was the first woman to receive a military pension from a state government. She was born 13 October 1754 in Trenton, New Jersey. She lived on a dairy farm until 1769, when her father sent her to be a servant for William Irvine, a doctor in Carlisle, Pennsylvania. She married John Hays soon after. During the American Revolution, John Hays joined the 7th Pennsylvania Regiment, headed by Dr. Irvine. During the American Revolution, unlike the Civil War, it was not uncommon for women to accompany the male members of their families to the battlefields. There, the women performed essential services, such as cleaning, nursing, and cooking. After some delay, Molly Hays joined her husband at the regiment's New Jersey encampment, where she nursed and cooked. She won her nickname during the battle of Monmouth on 28 June 1778, when she is said to have brought pitchers of water to the soldiers. When her husband fell from heat exhaustion, she took over his battle station, loading his cannon until the fighting ended. After the war the Hayses returned to Carlisle, where they lived quietly until his death in 1789. In 1792 she married John McCauley, another veteran. In 1822, the Pennsylvania legislature passed a law granting her a pension of $40 per year for her services during the war. She died 22 January 1832 in Carlisle.

McDowell, Anne Elizabeth (1826–1901)

Anne McDowell was the first woman in the United States to publish a newspaper that was completely financed and put out by women. She was born 23 June 1826 in Smyrna, Delaware, but spent her childhood in Philadelphia. In 1855 she founded the *Woman's Advocate*. It was the only publication in the nation that was completely owned and produced by women, from writing through typesetting and printing. Although its principal energies were directed toward encouraging women to enter the work force, its pages offered arguments for and against other reform issues of the day, from slavery to suffrage. After the weekly ceased publication (about 1860), McDowell continued to write for various newspapers and to work for the causes of women and labor. She died on 30 September 1901 in Philadelphia.

McDowell, Mary Elisa (1854–1936)

Mary McDowell was a founder of the National Women's Trade Union League and the Woman's Bureau in the U.S. Department of Labor. Born 30 November 1854 in Cincinnati, Ohio, McDowell moved with her family to Chicago at the end of the Civil War. Her first experience with social work was helping people and families who were made homeless by the Chicago Fire of 1871. She worked with Jane Addams at Hull House in 1890. In 1894, McDowell helped University of Chicago faculty members establish the University of Chicago Settlement in the Evanston stockyards. While there, she established a nursery, library, park, clubs, and other services for immigrant stockyard workers and their children. McDowell successfully pressured the city to build solid-waste-reduction plants and to stop dumping garbage in open pits that surrounded the yards. She also helped organize the first women's union in the stockyards. A letter she wrote to President Theodore Roosevelt helped persuade the federal government to investigate conditions in the stockyards. In 1903 McDowell worked to establish the National Women's Trade Union League, serving as president of its Chicago branch from 1904 to 1907. In 1907, she prodded the federal government into investigating the role of women and children in industry, later working on behalf of wages and hours laws in Illinois and other states. And in 1920 she worked for the creation of the U.S. Department of Labor's Women's Bureau. In addition, McDowell was active in the League of Women Voters, the Immigrants' Protective League, the National Association for the Advancement of Colored People, and the Urban League. Known as "the Angel of the Stockyards" for her support of the Chicago Stockyard Strike of 1904, McDowell retired as director of the University of Chicago Settlement in 1929. She died 14 October 1936 in Chicago.

See also Addams, Jane; Women's Bureau; Women's Trade Union League.

Madison, Dolley Payne Todd (1768–1849)

Dolley Madison, the wife of the fourth president of the United States, James Madison, also acted as the White House hostess for her husband's predecessor, Thomas Jefferson. Born 20 May 1768 in Guilford County, North Carolina, she lived until the age of 15 on a plantation near Hanover, Virginia. In 1783, under the influence of Quaker values, her father freed his enslaved workers and moved the family to Philadelphia. There Dolley married John Todd, Jr., in 1790; when he died three years later, she was left with two small children. The following year she married James Madison, an over-40 congressman from Virginia who was several inches shorter than she. The two lived in Orange County, Virginia, from 1797 to 1801, when James Madison became secretary of state under President Thomas Jefferson. Because President Jefferson was a widower, Dolley Madison acted as First Lady. She was especially known for giving dinners that brought together men of the opposing Federalist and Republican parties. Her guest lists were sometimes criticized for their democratic leanings, a senator from Massachusetts sniping that she "mixed all classes of people . . . from the Minister from Russia to underclerks of the post office." When her husband won the presidency in 1809, she became first lady. Her warm sociability helped to diminish the strains of political warfare. Because of her evenhandedness, James Blaine, who later tried to become president himself, credited her with part of her husband's 1812 victory.

In 1814, when the British burned the president's mansion, she single-handedly spirited away state papers and historic documents, as well as a Gilbert Stuart painting of George Washington. Historian Betty Boyd Caroli writes that Dolley Madison had been warned that the enemy was stronger than had been expected, yet when a friend came to hurry her to safety, she consented to go only "as soon as the large picture of George Washington is secured. . . . I have ordered the frame to be broken and the canvas taken out." The Madisons left Washington in 1817, returning to Orange County, where they lived until James Madison's death in 1836. Dolley Madison then returned to Washington, D.C., where she was a leading socialite until her death on 12 July 1849.

Mann, Horace (1796–1859)

Educational reformer and advocate of co-education, Horace Mann was born into poverty 4 May 1796 in Franklin, Massachusetts. Early hard manual labor weakened his health. Using the local library, founded by Benjamin Franklin, he educated himself. At the age of 20 he enrolled in Brown University, graduating with highest honors in 1819. He studied law briefly at Wrentham, Massachusetts, tutored (1820–1822), and then worked as a librarian (1821–1823). After earning a law degree from the Litchfield Law School under Judge James Gould at Litchfield, Connecticut, Mann was admitted in 1823 to the Northfolk (Massachusetts) bar. For 14 years he practiced law, while serving a total of ten years in the Massachusetts legislature, first in the house (1827–1833) and then in the senate (1835–1837). In 1837, Mann became secretary of the newly formed state board of education and began the work for which he would become famous, revolutionizing the common (public) school system of Massachusetts and influencing the schools of other states. Mann worked for coeducation, believing it to be mutually advantageous to men and women. In 1848, he resigned from the state school board and ran for the House of Representatives seat of the deceased John Quincy Adams. He was elected as an antislavery Whig and was reelected in 1849, serving until 1853. That year, he became president of the newly opened Antioch College in Yellow Springs, Ohio, after an unsuccessful bid for governor of Massachusetts.

Mann proved to be one of the most able champions of abolition and equal rights for women of his day. At the founding of Antioch College in 1854, in a speech entitled

"Dedication of Antioch College and Inaugural Address," Mann remarked,

That female education should be rescued from its present reproach of inferiority, and advanced to an equality with that of males, is a conviction which has already taken fast hold of the best minds in society. . . . Such segregation [of the sexes in institutions of higher learning] is obviously unnatural, and if it be necessary for the preservation of sexual purity, it is time that the whole community should take the alarm and hasten to devise a less monstrous remedy.

Mann was president of Antioch from its founding until his death on 2 August 1859 in Yellow Springs.

See also Education.

Married Women's Property Acts

During the colonial period under common law all the property, both real and personal, belonging to a woman became her husband's to manage upon their marriage. She could neither sue, make contracts, transfer property, nor keep the wages she earned. Legal scholars differ about how much the American Revolution changed this. Joan Hoff writes that the revolution had little direct effect on the legal status of married women, except for small, isolated improvements in the property rights of women in South Carolina and Connecticut. But Marilynn Salmon thinks that daughters (including those who were married) did gain more rights to family property as the result of the new nation's emphasis on equality. For example, courts rejected the British law of primogeniture and the old colonial rules of double shares for eldest sons in cases of intestacy. Other gains evolved gradually, usually as modifications of existing laws within each state. These gains date from the late eighteenth and early nineteenth centuries. In the judicial arena, the most important gains were greater tolerance for divorce and legal separation; the enforcement of direct contracts between married women and their husbands; and stricter enforcement of the requirement that judges question wives privately to prevent coercion by husbands in the sale or transfer of the wives' property. Laws provided other gains as well: a 1787 Massachusetts law recognized *feme sole* traders; a 1792 South Carolina law made more equal the inheritance rights of women and men; and an 1809 Connecticut law gave married women the right to make a will.

However, on one point most historians do agree: Between 1839 and 1895, a series of married women property acts permanently changed women's status under the law. The 1830s saw the enactment of the first married women's property acts, which guaranteed women the right to control their separate estates (meaning the property they brought with them into marriage). Mississippi was the first state to pass such legislation, in 1839, although it dealt primarily with slaveholdings.

New York passed an act in 1848 that would be a model for other states, offering an example of how women secured such legislation. In 1836, Polish immigrant Ernestine Rose introduced a petition for a married woman's property law to the state legislature. This law would have given married women the right to own and control any property that was theirs before marriage. Rose's petition carried only six signatures and was easily defeated. The following year Thomas Herttell (1771–1849) addressed the state house assembly to argue for similar legislation. In "The Right of Married Women To Hold and Control Property Sustained by the Constitution of the State of New York: Remarks in the House of Assembly of the State of New York in the Session of 1837 To Restore to Married Women 'The Right of Property' as Guaranteed by the Constitution of This State," Herttell pointed out that existing laws protected the rights of single women to acquire, manage, and dispose of real and personal property, but the

. . . wife's personal property, whether acquired by will, deed, inheritance, or her own industry, becomes vested in her husband, and she is as fully deprived of her title to it, and her right to use or dispose of it, or to control the management of it, as if she instead of being *married,* had been sold a *slave* to a *master.* Nor is she divested of her personal property only; she is also deprived of the *use* of her *real estate;* the rents, issues and profits of which, go to the husband during coverture [marriage].

Herttell concluded that if women, like men, were born free and equal, then they were entitled to own and control their own property.

Ernestine Rose circulated and presented her petition every year after 1836, in 1840 joining with Paulina Wright Davis and Elizabeth Cady Stanton to collect signatures and speak before a committee of the legislature in Albany, New York. In 1843 and 1845, Elizabeth Cady Stanton again unsuccessfully lobbied the New York legislature. Finally, on 6 April 1848, the legislature passed the Married Woman's Property Act—the most important of its time—which states in part:

The real and personal property of any female who may hereafter marry, and which she shall own at the time of her marriage, and the rents, issues and profits thereof, shall not be subject to the disposal of her husband nor be liable for his debts and shall continue her sole and separate property as if she were a single female.

In 1855, a solitary Susan B. Anthony traveled New York State to gather signatures on petitions asking the state legislature to expand the Married Woman's Property Act of 1848. Her petitions urged that women be allowed to assume custody of their children in case of divorce, control their own earnings, and vote. On 14 February 1855, Stanton appeared before a joint judicial committee of both houses of the New York legislature—the first woman to do so—arguing for the extended bill. Her words failed to move the lawmakers. The following year Anthony presented her petitions to the legislature, and by 1857 the New York Married Woman's Property Act was amended. In 1860 it was expanded again (An Act Concerning the Rights and Liabilities of Husband and Wife).

During the Civil War, as women were being widowed in unprecedented numbers, the legislature in 1862 replaced key portions of the married woman's property act of 1860. A mother's hard-won right to equal custody of her children and her right to use a deceased husband's estate for the benefit of her children were abolished. "Well, well," Anthony wrote to her friend Lydia Mott, "while the old guard sleep the young 'devils' are wide-awake, and we deserve to suffer for our confidence in 'man's sense of justice,' and to have all we have gained thus snatched from us."

Despite Anthony's cynicism, married women's property laws were enacted and expanded throughout the United States. The Homestead and Exemption laws, which contained provisions for the wife and family of a homesteader, also strengthened married women's property rights. Under the Homestead Act of 1862, any citizen who was head of a family or 21 years old—or younger persons who had fought for the Union for 14 days or more—could apply for 160 acres or less of unappropriated public lands. If the homestead belonged to a married couple, the signatures of both were required to mortgage it. By the mid-1870s, every northern state had passed a married woman's property act, and by 1900 southern states had followed suit.

See also Common Law; Equity Law; *Feme Covert; Feme Sole;* New York Married Woman's Property Act (1848); New York Married Woman's Property Act (1860).

Martin, Anne Henrietta (1875–1951)

Anne Henrietta Martin, the first woman to run for the Senate, was born 30 September 1875 in Empire City, Nevada. She received a B.A. from the University of Nevada (1894), a second B.A. from Stanford University (1896), and an M.A. from Stanford (1896). In 1897 she founded and headed the history department at the University of Nevada. She went to England in 1909 and there joined suffragists under the leadership of Emmeline Pankhurst. She and 30 other women were arrested for disturbing the peace on 18 November 1910 by order of then–home secretary Winston Churchill. She returned to Nevada in 1911, where she was elected president of the Nevada Equal Franchise Society (1912). Under her leadership Nevada women won the right to vote on 3 November 1914. After 1914 Martin worked in national suffrage politics, serving on executive committees of the National American Woman Suffrage Association and the Congressional Union. When the National Woman's Party was organized in 1916, Martin became its first vice-chairman. Arrested on 14 July 1917 for picketing the White House, she served a short sentence in a workhouse. After her release she decided to run for the Senate (1918), the first woman in the nation to do so. Although she failed to win in either 1918 or in 1920, she was a pioneer for women in politics, supporting an equal rights amendment and urging women to vote as a group. Martin moved to Carmel, California, in 1921, where she became a freelance magazine writer specializing in women's topics. There, she was influential in the Women's International League for Peace and Freedom. Martin championed the greater participation of women in politics, criticizing the National Woman's Party for remaining satisfied with lobbying male politicians for legal reform, instead of running for office directly. Similarly, she condemned Carrie Chapman Catt for leading the League of Women Voters toward an educational role, instead of one of direct political participation. Martin attended several world conferences and participated in many international organizations before her death on 15 April 1951 in Carmel.

Martin v. Commonwealth

In 1805, the Massachusetts Supreme Court decided an important case that involved the political relationship of women to the state. William Martin and Anna Martin were British loyalists. They owned land that Anna Martin had originally brought into their marriage. But when they fled to Britain during the American Revolution, the state confiscated their property, later selling it in 1781. In 1801 the Martins' son, William, returned to claim the land. He petitioned a lower court to return the property on the grounds that his father had only a lifetime interest in the property and his mother was its rightful owner. (At this time, under common law, husbands were permitted to manage but not sell their wives' property.) As a married woman, or *feme covert*, he argued, his mother had been compelled to reside wherever her husband wished. The court decided that Martin had a legitimate claim to the property because his mother had "no *political* relation to the *state* any more than an *alien*."

Federalist lawyer Theophilus Parsons, arguing for William Martin, explained that the Massachusetts confiscation law applied to every "inhabitant and member" of the state—meaning that it applied only to those who were both inhabitants *and* members of the state. As a *feme covert*, Parsons argued, Anna Martin was not a member of the state, only an inhabitant. Massachusetts solicitor general Daniel Davis, defending the state's right to confiscate the property, argued, "cannot a *femme covert* [married woman] levy war and conspire to levy war?" If a woman had such rights and abilities, then Anna Martin had a will of her own. Parsons was left no choice but to argue, "Infants, insane, *femmes coverts*, all of whom the law considers as having no will, cannot act *freely*." The state supreme court agreed.

See also Feme Covert; Feme Sole.

A Matter of Simple Justice

A Matter of Simple Justice is the December 1969 report of the Task Force on Women's Rights and Responsibilities, created by President Richard Nixon. Nixon created the task force in response to pressure from female legislators and Washington columnist Vera Glaser. The group's purpose was to develop ideas for Nixon's 1970 state of the union message. The task force, which comprised ten women and two men, was headed by Virginia Allen, the executive vice-president of a drug store chain and ex-president of the National Federation of Business and Professional Women's Clubs.

Because of the absence of the task force recommendations from the state of the union address, and because of a six-month delay in issuing the report, many women's rights activists accused the Nixon administration of trying to conceal the report's bold proposals. Released in June 1970, during the fiftieth anniversary celebration of the labor department's Women's Bureau, the report had a much more militant tone than any previous government report, but it made no revolutionary proposals. The report recommended that an Office of Women's Rights and Responsibilities be established and that the White House sponsor a conference on women's rights honoring the fiftieth anniversary of the adoption of the Nineteenth Amendment. In addition to asking that more women be appointed to high-ranking positions within the administration, the report asked the executive branch to take a number of steps to fight sex discrimination, including suggestions from the president, action by the attorney general, and guidelines from the U.S. Department of Labor. Finally, the report recommended passage of the Equal Rights Amendment (ERA). The report's greatest achievement appears to be that it brought women's concerns to the attention of administration officials and legislators.

Mead, Margaret (1901–1978)

Anthropologist Margaret Mead, one of the twentieth century's most accomplished women, was born 16 December 1901 in Philadelphia, the daughter of an economist and a sociologist. She studied for one year at DePauw University (1919) before transferring to Barnard College in New York City, from which she graduated in 1923. That year she married Luther Cressman, a student who later became a sociologist. Mead continued her studies at Columbia University under the renowned anthropologists Franz Boas and Ruth Benedict, receiving an M.A. in psychology in 1924.

With Cressman she made the first of several trips to the South Seas (1925–1926), working on the island of Tau in Samoa. There, she gathered material for her landmark book *Coming of Age in Samoa* (1928). Upon her return to New York, Mead was appointed assistant curator of ethnology at the American Museum of Natural History. In 1929 she and Cressman divorced, and Mead married fellow anthropologist Reo Fortune. She received a Ph.D. in anthropology from Columbia University the following year.

Mead traveled to the Admiralty Islands in the western Pacific (1928–1929) to conduct fieldwork among the Manus children. From this emerged her classic *Growing Up in New Guinea* (1930). Her third trip to New Guinea (1931–1933) led to her study of the Mountain Arapesh, the Mundugumor, and the Tchambuli, described in another classic work, *Sex and Temperament in Three Primitive Societies* (1935).

Mead divorced Fortune in 1935, marrying English scientist Gregory Bateson in 1936. She published *Cooperation and Competition among Primitive Peoples* in 1937. Two years later she gave birth to her only child, Mary Catherine Bateson. (Bateson later became a well-known linguist.) With her husband, Mead developed a strong interest in Balinese culture. Together they published several works, including *Balinese Character: A Photographic Analysis* (1942). In 1942 Mead turned to the examination of American cultural values, which she described in *And Keep Your Powder Dry*. Also in 1942 she became the second woman, after Amelia Earhart, to be honored with the gold medal of the Society of Women Geographers. Possibly Mead's most influential book was *Male and Female: A Study of the Sexes in a Changing World* (1949), in which she examined areas

of socialization, such as how sex-role behavior is learned and how different peoples view marriage. Mead and Bateson divorced in 1950.

Margaret Mead

Perhaps because of her fame, her skill in public speaking, and her readable books, she was the target of some criticism for overpopularizing anthropology. Nonetheless, during the 1950s, she wrote more than ever before. In 1951 she produced *Growth and Culture: A Photographic Study of Balinese Childhood* (with Frances MacGregor), *The School in American Culture*, and *Soviet Attitudes toward Authority*. Other books produced in the 1950s include *Cultural Patterns and Technical Change* (1954), *New Lives for Old* (1956), and *People and Places* (1959). She edited *An Anthropologist at Work: Writing of Ruth Benedict* (1959). Later works were *Continuities in Cultural Evolution* (1964), *Anthropology: A Human Science* (1964), *Family* (with K. Heyman, 1965), *Anthropologists and What They Do* (1965), *Culture and Commitment: A Study of the Generation Gap* (1970), *A Way of*

193

Seeing (with Rhoda Metraux, 1970), and *A Rap on Race* (with James Baldwin, 1971). Her autobiography, *Blackberry Winter*, appeared in 1972.

In 1973 Mead, still making field trips, was elected to the National Academy of Science. Other honors included the presidency of the World Federation of Mental Health (1956–1957), the World Society for Ekistics (1969–1971), the Scientists' Institute for Public Information (1970–1973), the Society for Research in General Systems (1972–1973), and the American Association for the Advancement of Science (1975). Mead taught as an adjunct professor at Columbia University from 1951, although she never was made a full professor in the anthropology department. At Fordham University, she chaired the social sciences division from 1968 to 1971. She also maintained an active office at the American Museum of Natural History in New York City. Despite her own example of liberated womanhood, Mead could be critical of feminism and warned of a violent male backlash if women made too many demands. She died 15 November 1978 in New York City.

Men Allied Nationally for the Equal Rights Amendment (M.A.N. for the E.R.A.)

Founded by Barry Shapiro in 1978, Men Allied Nationally for the Equal Rights Amendment (M.A.N. for the E.R.A.) organized rallies, marched with women in ERA demonstrations, and campaigned in many states for ratification of the amendment. M.A.N for the E.R.A. also counseled men about violence toward women. Other groups, such as the California Anti-Sexist Men's Political Caucus and the National Organization for Men against Sexism, have also worked toward supporting the reforms advocated by feminists.

See also Equal Rights Amendment.

Men's League for Woman Suffrage

In 1910, several influential men in New York joined socialist editor Max Eastman in forming the Men's League for Woman Suffrage. They included Oswald Garrison Villard, publisher of the *New York Evening Post;* philosopher John Dewey; and Rabbi Stephen Wise. This was the nation's first men's feminist organization. With 30 chapters in various states and additional branches abroad, its goal was to publicize and otherwise help women in their struggle for the vote.

Meritor Savings Bank v. Mechelle Vinson

In the landmark *Meritor Savings Bank v. Mechelle Vinson* (1986), the Supreme Court ruled that sexual harassment is illegal under federal antidiscrimination law, thus upholding a standard setting guidelines for the handling of Title VII adopted by the Equal Employment Opportunity Commission in 1980. The Court also made employers responsible for making efforts to prevent their supervisory personnel from sexually harassing employees. Vinson was an employee of the Meritor Savings Bank from 1974 until 1978, when she was fired. She claimed that her supervisor repeatedly made sexual demands over the four-year period that she worked at the bank and that she submitted to the demands out of fear of being fired. The Court found that the supervisor's behavior constituted sexual harassment because it created an atmosphere of hostility in the workplace. Sexual harassment, the Court ruled, was contrary to Title VII of the 1964 Civil Rights Act, which applies to both tangible and intangible forms of discrimination.

See also Title VII of the 1964 Civil Rights Act.

Merrick, Caroline Elizabeth Thomas (1825–1908)

Caroline Merrick, woman's suffrage and temperance leader, was born 24 November 1825 in East Feliciana Parish, Louisiana. Educated by governesses at home, at the age of 15 she married Edwin Thomas Merrick, moving with him to New Orleans. At the age of 52, her life changed when she told her husband that a relief organization of which she was secretary had been denied an inheritance because the donor's will was witnessed solely by women. At her husband's urging, she promptly petitioned the Louisiana constitutional convention of 1879, demanding the removal of women's legal disabilities and the granting of at least partial suffrage to women. She, Elizabeth Lyle Saxon, and Dr. Hariette Keating were invited to address the convention, and they became the first women to speak publicly in Louisiana about the equal rights of women. Merrick became president of the National Woman's Christian Temperance Union in 1882. In 1888, while in Washington, D.C., to attend the first meeting of the International Council of Women, Merrick testified for suffrage before a Senate committee. In 1892 she organized the Portia Club, a society devoted to the study of politics, particularly the legal rights of women and children. In 1896, the Portia Club joined with the Era Club to form a state suffrage association, which in 1898 gained for female taxpayers the right to vote on tax issues. Merrick published an autobiography, *Old Times in Dixie Land: A Southern Matron's Memories* (1901). She died 29 March 1908 in New Orleans.

See also Gordon, Kate.

Mexican-American Women's National Association (MANA)

The Mexican-American Women's National Association (MANA) is a feminist organization that includes members from many Hispanic backgrounds. The group is based in Washington, D.C., and has chapters and members in a number of states. It was created in 1974 to give Hispanic women recognition they could not find in existing women's or Mexican-American organizations. The group seeks to link Hispanic women, consolidate their influence, publicize their concerns, and help women to achieve equality with men within the Hispanic community. It enjoys great influence, and a number of causes have benefited from its effective lobbying. Particularly interested in family issues and education, MANA started the *Hermanitas* (little sisters) program to aid in the educational process of Hispanic girls. Despite the fact that many of its members are Roman Catholic, MANA favors legalized abortion. However, the group emphasizes that many other issues, for example, sterilization abuse, must be addressed in the drive for reproductive freedom.

Midwifery
See Health Care Providers.

Miller, Elizabeth Smith (1822–1911)

Elizabeth Smith Miller designed the famous Bloomer costume in 1850 after she saw actress Fanny Kemble wearing a similar outfit in Europe in 1849. Elizabeth Smith was born 20 September 1822 near Geneseo, New York. The daughter of reformer Gerrit Smith (a cousin of Elizabeth Cady Stanton), her family's home in Peterboro, New York, was a center of activism. In 1843 she married Charles D. Miller. The couple lived in Cazenovia, New York (1843–1846), and Peterboro (1846–1869) before settling in Geneva, New York. Both signed the call for the first National Woman's Rights Convention in Worcester, Massachusetts (1850). Disgusted with the clumsiness of her long skirts when gardening, she designed an outfit that came to be known as the Bloomer costume. It consisted of a knee-length dress worn over full Turkish pantaloons. Miller wore the outfit while visiting Elizabeth Cady Stanton in Seneca Falls, New York, in the winter of 1850–1851. Both Stanton and Amelia Bloomer adopted the costume. Bloomer praised the outfit in her women's rights paper, *The Lily*, and thousands of requests for sewing instructions poured in. Thus the outfit was dubbed the Bloomer costume. The dress was widely criticized in the press, and some women who wore it were ridiculed in the street. Yet Miller continued to wear the outfit many years after other women had given it up. In 1875 Miller published *In the Kitchen*, a best-selling cookbook. She died 22 May 1911 in Geneva.

See also Bloomer, Amelia Jenks; Bloomers; Kemble, Frances Anne; Stanton, Elizabeth Cady.

Millett, Kate (1934–)

Writer, sculptor, and leading theoretician of the modern feminist movement, Kate Millett was born 14 September 1934 in St. Paul, Minnesota, where she attended parochial schools. She graduated from the University of Minnesota magna cum laude and Phi Beta Kappa in 1956, later studying literature for two years at Oxford University, where she received a First. Millett taught English at Barnard College in 1968, and received her Ph.D. in English and comparative literature from Columbia University (1970). An activist during the civil rights battles of the 1960s, in 1966 Millett became a charter member of the National Organization for Women. In 1969, she wrote *Sexual Politics*, which analyzed the methods used by patriarchal societies to marginalize women, and which became one of the most influential books of the women's movement. In it Millett wrote, "Groups who rule by birthright are fast disappearing, yet there remains one ancient and universal scheme for the domination of one birth group by another—the scheme that prevails in the area of sex." The book was originally written as her Ph.D. thesis for Columbia University, but was published as a general trade book by Doubleday. In the first month, it sold 80,000 copies. Millett's work then took on an international scope. She was expelled from Iran in 1979 because of her work on behalf of women there and their rights. Millett's other works include *Flying* (1974), *The Prostitution Papers* (1976), *Sita* (1977), *The Basement: Mediation on a Human Sacrifice* (1979), *Going to Iran* (1982), and *The Loony Bin Trip* (1990).

Minimum Wage

From 1912 to 1938 minimum-wage laws for women and children ranked high on the agendas of consumers' groups, feminists, and other reformers. Massachusetts was the first to pass such protective legislation in 1912; the following year, 13 states followed suit. Employers and male unionists opposed the laws and succeeded in winning Supreme Court decisions against them based on the argument that the laws interfered with the freedom to contract labor. At issue, writes legal historian Robert E. Cushman, was the question "Does the due process clause of the Fourteenth Amendment guarantee to employers, as an essential part of their freedom of contract, the right to pay women and children starvation wages?" In *Adkins v. Children's Hospital* (1923) and *Morehead v. New York ex rel. Tipaldo* (1936), the Supreme Court struck down minimum-wage laws. In the Adkins case, the majority opinion was similar to that of *Lochner v. New York:* there is no connection between women's wages and their health or morals that justifies the legal abolition of freedom of contract. In *Morehead*, which held New York's minimum-wage law for women and children invalid, the court held that *any* minimum-wage law was a denial of due process. In *West Coast Hotel v. Parrish* (1937) the Court ruled that the public interest was more important than freedom of contract. This led to the Fair Labor Standards Act of 1938, which guaranteed a minimum wage to workers of both sexes.

See also Adkins v. Children's Hospital; Fair Labor Standards Act; *Morehead v. New York ex rel. Tipaldo; West Coast Hotel v. Parrish.*

Minor, Virginia Louisa (1824–1894)

Virginia Minor founded the Woman Suffrage Association of Missouri, the first U.S. organization devoted solely to women's suffrage. She was also plaintiff in the Supreme Court case *Minor v. Happersett.* Born 27 March 1824 in Caroline County, Virginia, very little is known of her childhood. In 1843 she married Francis Minor, settling in 1844 in St. Louis, Missouri. When the Civil War broke out, Virginia Minor joined the St. Louis Ladies Union Aid Society, which became the largest branch of the Western Sanitary Commission. The experience helped shape her belief that women should have political equality. In 1865, while the public controversy about suffrage for former male slaves raged, Minor was the first woman to speak out for women's rights in her state. In 1867, she petitioned the Missouri legislature to include women in a proposed constitutional amendment to enfranchise African-American men. When the effort failed, she and others formed the Woman Suffrage Association of Missouri. She was president of the group from its founding in 1867 until 1871. That year, when the organization voted to join the American Woman Suffrage Association (AWSA), Minor resigned her position and aligned herself with the National Woman Suffrage Association (NWSA). After the Fourteenth Amendment was adopted, Minor unsuccessfully attempted to vote, insisting that, as citizens, women were covered by the amendment. With her husband (women could not bring legal action on their own), Minor sued the voter registrar for keeping her from voting. The case, *Minor v. Happersett*, was heard by the Supreme Court in 1874. In a unanimous decision, the Court found that women were not entitled to the vote under the Fourteenth Amendment. In 1879 the NWSA organized a St. Louis branch, and Minor became its president. When the NWSA merged with the AWSA in 1890, Minor was elected president of the Missouri branch of the new National American Woman Suffrage Association. She held the position for two years, until poor health forced her to resign. She died 14 August 1894 in St. Louis.

See also Fourteenth Amendment; *Minor v. Happersett*; National Woman Suffrage Association.

Minor v. Happersett

For women in the nineteenth century, the question of suffrage was settled by the Supreme Court decision of *Minor v. Happersett* (1874). In this case, Virginia Minor was not allowed to register to vote in St. Louis, Missouri, because she was a woman. With her husband (women were not allowed to initiate legal action independent of their husbands) Minor brought suit against Reese Happersett, the registrar, claiming that the Missouri law conflicted with the Constitu-

tion. "Being unanimously of the opinion that the Constitution of the United States does not confer the right of suffrage upon any one, and that the Constitutions and laws of the several States which commit that important trust to men alone are not necessarily void," the Court decided that even the Fourteenth Amendment's provision safeguarding citizens' rights did not extend the vote to women. Not until 1971, with *Reed v. Reed*, did the Supreme Court find sex discrimination to be a violation of the Fourteenth Amendment's equal protection clause.

See also Bradwell v. State of Illinois; Fourteenth Amendment; Minor, Virginia Louisa.

Miss America Protest

The protest of the 1968 Miss America contest is probably one of feminism's best-known demonstrations. The protest, which involved 200 women on the Atlantic City boardwalk, was the brainchild of New York Radical Women. Rejecting the conventional emphasis on physical attractiveness was a major theme among feminists, and the Miss America protest gave that theme its most dramatic expression. The demonstrators compared the pageant to animal judging at a county fair by crowning a sheep Miss America. They also threw various items of restrictive clothing, including lingerie, into a garbage can. When the media falsely reported that the garbage can had been lit, the derogatory term *bra burners* was born.

See also New York Radical Women.

Mitchell, Maria (1818–1889)

Maria Mitchell was the first woman admitted to the American Academy of Arts and Sciences. She was born 1 August 1818 on Nantucket Island, Massachusetts, the daughter of a Quaker schoolteacher and an astronomer. Her father let her assist him with rating chronometers for the Nantucket whaling fleet and taught her how to use his telescope. Mitchell quickly developed an interest in mathematics, and for 20 years worked as the librarian and informal teacher for the Nantucket Atheneum (1836–1856). She taught herself astronomy through nightly observations of the skies and by reading the library's science books. On 1 October 1847, Mitchell discovered the orbit of a new comet. This made her famous in scientific circles. The following year King Christian VIII of Denmark presented her with a gold medal. In 1848 the American Academy of Arts and Sciences elected her its first woman member. (She remained that organization's only female member until 1943.) Ten years later a group of women under the leadership of Elizabeth Peabody gave Mitchell a large telescope, and from that time forward, feminists helped to publicize her achievements.

Following a European tour (1857–1858), Mitchell moved with her widowed father to Lynn, Massachusetts, in 1861. In 1865, she was appointed the first professor of astronomy and director of the observatory at Vassar Female College, which had opened the previous year in Poughkeepsie, New York. There she became the school's most renowned teacher, although for a long time her male colleagues earned twice as much as she. While at Vassar she continued her own research, including the discovery of various nebulae, daily photographs of sun spots, observations of the surfaces of Jupiter and Saturn, and study of solar eclipses.

She was elected to the American Philosophical Society in 1869. Four years later, she and a group of women founded the American Association for the Advancement of Women to encourage the overall advancement of women. Mitchell served as the organization's president from 1875 to 1876. She believed in the potential of women, having been a pioneer in the male-dominated field of science. Mitchell wrote, "I wish we could give to every woman who has a novel theory dear to her soul for the improvement of the world, a chance to work out her theory in real life." She died 28 June 1889 in Lynn, six years after being elected into the Hall of Fame for Great Americans.

Morehead v. New York ex rel. Tipaldo

One of the most unpopular Supreme Court decisions in history was made when *Morehead v. New York ex rel. Tipaldo* was argued before the court on 28 and 29 April 1936. Originally heard before the New York Supreme Court, the case was of the manager of a laundry establishment who failed to obey a mandatory order of the state industrial commissioner prescribing minimum wages for women employees. The case eventually went before the U.S. Supreme Court and a ruling was made on 1 June 1936. A slender majority of the high court attacked a New York minimum-wage law for women and children, stating that minimum-wage laws were a violation of due process. Justice Butler argued for the court with four other justices sharing his opinion: James McReynolds, George Sutherland, Will Van Devanyer, and Owen J. Roberts. Justice Butler stated that "the right to contract for wages in return for work is part of the liberty protected by the due process clause of the Fourteenth Amendment." He went on to explain that a state government should not be allowed to interfere with any contracts for labor. Justices Louis D. Brandeis, Benjamin Cardozo, Charles Evans Hughes, and Harlan Fiske Stone were in dissent. Justice Stone stated that the majority had acted on the premise of their personal economic predilections, and said "there is a grim irony in speaking of the freedom of contract of those who, because of their economic necessities, give their services for less than is needful to keep body and soul together."

There were 344 editorials written on this case; of that number all but 10 attacked the *Morehead* decision. The 1936 Republican Party Platform struck down the decision, as well as the Supreme Court when its 1936 decision was overruled in *West Coast Hotel v. Parrish* in 1937. A court reversal was seen on 29 March 1936 when the court upheld the state of Washington's minimum-wage law for women and children workers. This was almost identical to the state law that was eradicated only ten months earlier in *Morehead v. New York ex rel. Tipaldo*. Other similar decisions concerning due process and minimum wages soon followed.

See also Adkins v. Children's Hospital; Fair Labor Standards Act; Minimum Wage.

Morgan, Robin (1941–)

Feminist theorist, journalist, and poet Robin Morgan was born in 1941 in Lakeworth, Florida. She produced the first anthology of feminist writings to become a best-seller, *Sisterhood Is Powerful* (1970). Her poetry collection, *Monster* (1972), was the first book of militant feminist poetry published in the United States by a major press (Random House). She is the author of two nonfiction books: *Going Too Far: The Personal Journalist of a Feminist* (1978) and *The Anatomy of Freedom* (1982). Her interest in international feminism led to the publication of *Sisterhood Is Global* (1984). Morgan's other titles include *Demon Lover: On the Sexuality of Terrorism* (1989), *Upstairs in the Garden: Selected and New Poems, 1968–1988* (1990), *The Mer-Child: A New Legend* (1991), and *The Word of a Woman: Poems 1968–1991* (1992). From 1990–1993 Morgan was the editor of *Ms.* magazine.

Morrill Land-Grant Act

See Education.

Morrison, Toni (1931–)

Novelist and essayist Toni Morrison won the 1993 Nobel Prize in Literature for her lyrical novels about the legacy of slavery in America, as seen mostly through the eyes of African-American women. The Swedish Academy awarded the prize to Morrison "who, in novels, characterized by visionary force and poetic import, gives life to an essential aspect of American reality." She is the first African American to win the prize, and only the eighth woman.

Morrison was born Chloe Anthony Wooford on 18 February 1931 in Lorain, Ohio, the second of four children of Alabama sharecroppers who migrated north. She received a B.A. in 1953 from Howard University (Washington, D.C.), and an M.A. in 1955 from Cornell. In 1957, she married Harold Morrison. She became a textbook editor at L. B. Singer and later a general book editor at Random House, where Robert Gottlieb, managing editor of the Knopf imprint, edited Morrison's own fiction.

Morrison's first novel, *The Bluest Eye* (1970) concerns the lives of African-American girls growing up in a small Ohio town, one of whom goes mad, imagining she has, at last, blue eyes. *Sula* (1973) traces the lives of two women who share a murderous secret. Other early novels include *Song of Solomon* (1977) and *Tar Baby* (1981). *Beloved* (1987), which won the 1988 Pulitzer Prize in fiction, tells the tragic consequences of slavery through the viewpoint of a mother who escapes slavery with her children, but who has murdered one daughter to keep her from being captured and returned to plantation life. In 1992, Morrison published a novel, *Jazz*, and a book of essays, *Playing in the Dark: Whiteness and the Literary Imagination*. In the latter, Morrison wrote, "My work requires me to think about how free I can be as an African-American woman writer in my genderized, sexualized, wholly racialized world. My project rises from delight, not disappointment." Morrison also wrote a play, *Dreaming Emmett*, which was first produced in 1986, but has not been published. She has been professor of humanities at Princeton University since 1989.

Mott, Lucretia Coffin (1793–1880)

Lucretia Mott, a Quaker minister, led the way for women in abolition and women's rights. She was born Lucretia Coffin on 3 January 1793 on the island of Nantucket, Massachusetts, the daughter of a sea captain. Raised in an atmosphere of female independence, she recalled in her diary,

I always loved the good in childhood, and desired to do the right. In those

199

early years I was actively useful to my mother, who, in the absence of my father on his long voyages, was engaged in the mercantile business, often going to Boston to purchase goods in exchange for oil and candles, the staple of the island. The exercise of women's talents in this line, as well as the general care which devolved upon them, in the absence of their husbands, tended to develop and strengthen them mentally and physically.

Many Nantucket men spent long periods of time at sea, leaving their wives to manage their families and their businesses. Mott's mother ran a shop and did her own bookkeeping, skills that, elsewhere, women were thought unable to master.

Lucretia Mott

Lucretia Coffin attended public schools in Boston after 1804 so that she could learn about democratic ideals. Later she attended a Quaker boarding school near Poughkeepsie, New York. After two years there, she became an unpaid teaching assistant, aware

that her male colleagues were paid for doing the same work. In 1811, Lucretia Coffin married a fellow teacher, James Mott. In about 1818 Lucretia Mott began speaking to religious gatherings, and in 1821, at the age of 28, she was accepted as a minister by the Society of Friends (Quakers). She dressed simply, as was the Quaker custom, with a white kerchief across her shoulders and a white cap and plain bonnet. People were drawn to her soft-spoken, attentive manner, but she had a will of steel. When, during the 1820s, the Great Separation divided the Society of Friends into two sects, Mott joined the more radical Hicksite group and followed its leader, Elias Hicks, in abstaining from using products of slave labor.

In 1833 Mott attended a convention, organized by William Lloyd Garrison, at which the American Anti-Slavery Society was organized. When it became clear that the society was not going to allow female members, Mott helped to create the Philadelphia Female Anti-Slavery Society. Later, when the American Anti-Slavery Society opened its membership to women, Mott was an active member of the national society and served on the executive committee of its Pennsylvania branch. She was among the women who, in 1837, organized the Anti-Slavery Convention of American Women. She was present at the second national female antislavery convention, which took place 15 May 1838 in Philadelphia's Pennsylvania Hall. Two days later she calmly waited as a mob, after burning the hall, headed toward her home. Fortunately, the mob dispersed before it reached its destination. In March 1840, at the age of 47, Mott was one of the American Anti-Slavery Society's delegates to the World's Anti-Slavery Convention in London. The convention refused to accept the credentials of Mott and the other female American delegates. This event prompted Mott and Elizabeth Cady Stanton to take up the cause of women's rights.

It was not until eight years later, however, that Mott, Stanton, and three other women met for tea and spontaneously organized the first-ever women's rights convention. The convention was held less than one week later, 19–20 July 1848, in Seneca Falls, New York. Because the women had no experience presiding over such meetings, they asked James Mott to act as chairman. Following the convention, Lucretia Mott became increasingly involved in the cause of women's rights, attending various conventions and writing *Discourse on Woman* (1852), which argued that the apparent inferiority of women stemmed from inferior opportunities for education and advancement.

In 1852 Mott was elected president of the third National Woman's Rights Convention in Syracuse, New York. In 1866, at the first convention of the American Equal Rights Association, she was named president. Three years later, when the association split into the American Woman Suffrage Association and the National Woman Suffrage Association, Mott tried to play the role of mediator between the two groups. In 1867, she joined Robert Dale Owen, Rabbi Jacob Wise, and others in organizing the Free Religious Association. After the Civil War she worked for suffrage for freedmen. Mott worked for free religion, women's rights, and peace until her death on 11 November 1880 near Philadelphia.

See also Abolition; American Anti-Slavery Society; American Equal Rights Association; Female Antislavery Societies; Philadelphia Female Anti-Slavery Society; Seneca Falls Convention; Society of Friends; World's Anti-Slavery Convention.

Mount Holyoke College

Founded by Mary Lyon in 1837 in South Hadley, Massachusetts, Mount Holyoke Female Seminary was one of the first institutions to offer higher education to girls of modest income. In 1893 the name was changed to Mount Holyoke College. Mary Lyon devised a method of controlling costs by paying low wages to teachers and assigning household tasks to each student. Although she was widely criticized for this practice, she provided higher education to thousands of young women who otherwise might not have had the opportunity to receive it. In 1861 a four-year course was introduced. Mount Holyoke became renowned for its training of female teachers and for its innovation. Students were required to write essays, which were read aloud by other students; sections of the same course were evaluated on merit; human anatomy lessons were illustrated as early as the 1840s by a mannequin with removable organs; and rote learning was discarded in favor of discussion of various subjects. College presidents and professors from other colleges visited Mount Holyoke, and the institution began to have an influence on other schools. Its low cost and educational initiatives established Mount Holyoke's reputation as a leader in women's education.

See also Grant, Zilpah; Lyon, Mary.

Ms.

Ms. was the first slick, stylish, monthly feminist magazine to gain nationwide circulation. The magazine was the brainchild of a group of New York women writers and editors, notably journalist Gloria Steinem and former *McCall's* editor Patricia Carbine, who objected to the media's treatment of the women's movement. A number of feminist publications existed, but they had little success reaching women who were not already involved in the women's movement. Under the sponsorship of *New York* magazine, the preview issue of *Ms.* was issued in January 1972 and was surprisingly successful. In April 1972, Warner Communications provided financial backing in an agreement that allowed the founding editors to retain editorial control. In July 1972 *Ms.* began regular publication. Over the years the format and ownership have changed several times. During 1989 and 1990 it ceased publication for a short time; it emerged in a new format, without advertisements and available by subscription only, under editors Robin Morgan (1990–1993) and Marcia Anne Gillespie (from 1993 on). By presenting itself as a mainstream magazine, *Ms.* gave feminist ideas broader reach and more appeal than was possible through academic journals.

Muller v. State of Oregon

In *Muller v. State of Oregon* (1908), the Supreme Court upheld the constitutionality of a maximum-hour law for women. The Court said that the childbearing capacity of women created a special societal need to protect them from stressful work that could interfere with the women's ability to bear children or with the health of their fetuses. On 19 February 1903, Oregon had passed a law establishing a ten-hour workday for women working in factories and laundries. When the law was challenged under the Fourteenth Amendment's equal protection clause, it went to the Supreme Court. The National Consumers' League supported the law, hiring Louis Brandeis to defend it before the Court. Brandeis argued that the "two sexes differ in structure of body, in the function to be performed by each, in the amount of physical strength [and] in the capacity for long-continued labor." These differences, he asserted, justified regulating the number of hours women could work. The court's decision, delivered 24 February 1908 by Justice David Brewer, agreed that "[w]oman has always been dependent upon man. . . . Even though . . . she stood as far as statutes are concerned, upon an absolutely equal plane with him, it would still be true that she . . . will rest upon and look to him for protection."

Prominent reformers held that women differed from men in terms of strength and physical make-up and therefore had to be protected by law from exploitation. Eleanor Roosevelt, for example, believed that protective legislation was more important than an abstract concept of equal rights under the law. Alice Paul and members of the National Woman's Party, as well as other feminists, believed that protective legislation discriminated against women. They pointed to restrictive state laws as proof that what women needed was an equal rights amendment to the Constitution. The debate became increasingly bitter despite the passage of the Fair Labor Standards Act (1938), which extended protective legislation to workers of both sexes.

See also Equal Rights Amendment; Fair Labor Standards Act; Fourteenth Amendment; National Woman's Party; Paul, Alice.

Murray, Judith Sargent (1751–1820)

Judith Murray, feminist and writer, was the first American woman dramatist to have a play staged professionally. She was born 1 May 1751 in Gloucester, Massachusetts, and was such a precocious student that she was permitted to participate in her brother's school lessons as he studied to enter Harvard. She began writing verse during the 1770s but turned to essays as the revolutionary period stimulated her to think about the rightful place of women in society. In 1779, she wrote an essay arguing that men and women are of equal intelligence and should be equally educated. In 1784, using the pseudonym Constantia, she wrote an essay in *Gentleman and Lady's Town and Country Magazine* in which she asserted that if women had more self-respect they would not marry early in life simply to gain status or avoid being single. A few other essays by Murray also appeared in the *Boston Magazine* under her pseudonym, earning the author the reputation of a feminist. The writer's first husband, John Stevens, whom she had married in 1769, died in 1786. Two years later she married John Murray, pastor of the first Universalist meeting house in the United States. In 1792, still under her pen name, Murray began to write a column, "The Gleaner," for *Massachusetts Magazine*. She wrote about politics, education, religion, and other topics until 1794, once commenting that women, capable of more than reflecting on the "mechanism of a pudding," should be allowed to earn a living, receive equal education, and be an equal companion to man. In 1795 her play, *The Medium, or A Happy Teaparty*, was staged at Boston's Federal Street Theatre, the first play by an American staged at that theater. She wrote another play, *The Traveller Returned* (1796), and in 1798 published *The Gleaner*, a three-volume collection of her columns. More of her poems were published between 1802 and 1805. Murray also compiled and edited a three-volume collection of her husband's writings, *Letters and Sketches of Sermons* (1812–1813). After her husband's death in 1815, Murray edited his autobiography, *Records of the Life of the Rev. John Murray, Written by Himself, with a Continuation by Mrs. Judith Sargent Murray* (1816). That year Murray left Boston to live with her daughter in Natchez, Mississippi, where she died 6 July 1820.

Nathan, Maud (1862–1946)

Maud Nathan was perhaps the first woman to give a speech in a synagogue in place of a sermon by a rabbi. In 1897 at Temple Beth-El in New York City, she lectured on "The Heart of Judaism," a call to Jews to obligate themselves to social justice. Nathan was born 20 October 1862 in New York City. She attended private schools in New York and a public school in Green Bay, Wisconsin, graduating from the latter in 1876. Four years later she married her cousin, Frederick Nathan. Maud Nathan became involved in community service shortly after her marriage. She worked with the New York Exchange for Women's Work and the Women's Auxiliary of the Civil Service Reform Association, also serving as a director of the nursing school of Mount Sinai Hospital in New York City. In 1890 she helped found the Consumers' League of New York, which mobilized consumers to bring about reforms in industry. Her first project was to improve the working conditions for sales clerks, most of whom were female. In 1897 Nathan became president of the Consumers' League of New York. Under her direction the league inspected factories and shops, published lists of employers whose working conditions met the group's standards, and lobbied lawmakers for protective legislation. Nathan was the first vice-president of the Equal Suffrage League of New York and was the chair for women's suffrage in Theodore Roosevelt's Bull Moose party. She served in an executive capacity on the boards of many women's suffrage and labor organizations and was active in the Woman's Municipal League of New York, the General Federation of Women's Clubs and its New York affiliate, the League of Women Voters, and the National Council of Jewish Women. She wrote *The Story of an Epoch-making Movement* (1926) and an autobiography, *Once upon a Time and To-day* (1933). Nathan died 15 December 1946 in New York City.

See also National Consumers' League.

Nation, Carry Amelia Moore (1846–1911)

Carry Nation was the country's best-known temperance agitator, infamous for attacking saloons with hatchets and bricks. Born Carry Moore on 25 November 1846 in Garrard County, Kentucky, she was educated intermittently in Kentucky, Missouri, and Texas, where her family lived at various times. In 1867, at the age of 20, she married an alcoholic, Charles Gloyd, who died of his addiction shortly after their marriage, leaving his wife with a child and a hatred of liquor. After securing a license to teach from the Missouri State Normal School (now Missouri State University), she taught in Holden, Missouri.

In 1877 she married David Nation, moving with him to Texas (1879) and to Medicine Lodge, Kansas (1879). There, she helped found a chapter of the Woman's Christian Temperance Union (1892). Although Kansas was a dry state, liquor interests operated behind flimsy fronts, and they had begun agitating for repeal of state prohibition. Nation held that saloons that broke the law were outside of the law. In 1899 she began her protest, first by singing temperance songs in saloons, later by wrecking them with a hatchet or bricks. In 1900 she attacked the Hotel Carey in Wichita, Kansas; the following year her husband divorced her for desertion. She lectured about her experiences, dressed as a deaconess, and sold small hatchets imprinted with "Carry Nation, Joint Smasher." She published the newsletters the *Smasher's Mail*, the *Hatchet*, and the *Home Defender*. Her autobiography, published in 1904, was titled *The Use and Need of the Life of Carry A. Nation*. Jailed repeatedly, sometimes physically attacked,

Temperance leader Carry Nation aboard a ship in 1904.

she nonetheless inspired other like-minded vigilantes. Her zany tactics publicized the cause of Prohibition like no other, but historians are divided over how much she contributed to the adoption of the Eighteenth Amendment, which enacted Prohibition. Nation died 9 June 1911 in Leavenworth, Kansas.

See also National Woman's Christian Temperance Union; Temperance.

National Abortion Rights Action League (NARAL)

The National Abortion Rights Action League (NARAL) is a political action group that tries to build and sustain backing for abortion as a constitutional right, as set forth in the 1973 *Roe v. Wade* decision legalizing abortion. The group was founded in 1969, and from that time until the *Roe* decision, it was called the National Association for the Repeal of Abortion Laws. The site of the group's founding was the First National Conference on Abortion Laws, a conference proposed by Lonny Myers, a leading Chicago abortion rights advocate. She sought to end the debate among various abortion rights groups about whether to repeal or merely reform antiabortion laws by uniting all of the groups behind the former position. At the conference, Larry Lader, author of the influential book *Abortion*, suggested that an organization be formed. He served as NARAL's first chair. Most of NARAL's activities revolve around Congress; the group lobbies, briefs members of Congress, testifies at hearings, and supports candidates who support legalized abortion. In addition, the group organizes local affiliates and trains field representatives.

See also Abortion; *United States v. Vuitch*.

National Advisory Committee on Women

Congresswoman Bella Abzug and Carmen Delgado Votow were cochairs of the National Advisory Committee on Women, which was created in 1978 by President Jimmy Carter. When the committee boldly criticized the potential consequences of Carter's 1980 budget proposals, Abzug was fired, and the committee's feminist contingent voluntarily stepped down. This was one of several incidents that contributed to worsening relations between the Carter administration and the feminist movement.

See also Abzug, Bella Savitzy.

National Advisory Council on Women's Educational Programs (NACWEP)

The purpose of the National Advisory Council on Women's Educational Programs (NACWEP) is to give women some input to the formulation of national education policy. The council was created by the Women's Educational Equity Act (1973). Although it consists of 20 presidential appointees, NACWEP is intended to be independent of the Oval Office. Bipartisan throughout the 1970s, the council became entirely conservative during the Reagan administration.

See also Women's Educational Equity Act.

National American Woman Suffrage Association (NAWSA)

The formation of the National American Woman Suffrage Association (NAWSA) in 1890 represented the start of a truly modern, nationwide women's rights movement. The group reunited two groups of the women's suffrage movement that had bitterly parted in 1869: the more radical National Woman Suffrage Association, founded by Elizabeth Cady Stanton and Susan B. Anthony in New York in 1869, and the more conservative American Woman Suffrage Association, established by Lucy Stone later that year in Cleveland, Ohio. Elizabeth Cady Stanton was the group's first president; Susan B. Anthony assumed the post in 1892. The organization was infused with the ideas of a younger generation of feminists who had attended college and had careers.

Over Anthony's objections, Alice Stone Blackwell influenced NAWSA in 1893 to convene outside Washington, D.C., every other year. But after Colorado women won the vote that year, Anthony joined the younger women in campaigning for state suffrage in New York (1894) and California (1896) to no avail. To gain more southern members, Anthony, to the chagrin of African-American coworkers such as Ida B. Wells, failed to make her personal fight against racism a public issue for suffragists. Anthony even distanced herself from the first man to publicly support women's suffrage, Frederick Douglass. When NAWSA went to Atlanta, Georgia, Anthony revealed "I myself asked Mr. Douglass not to come. . . . I did not want anything to get in the way of bringing the southern white women into our suffrage association." (Ida B. Wells, *Crusade for Justice.*)

In 1896, NAWSA disassociated itself from Elizabeth Cady Stanton's *Woman's Bible.* Four years later, Carrie Chapman Catt became president, guiding NAWSA in a state strategy to win suffrage. She was challenged by Alice Paul, who joined the group in 1912 and pushed for a national amendment. Paul established NAWSA's Congressional Committee, which attracted younger, more radical members who wanted to take more militant steps to win the vote. Paul left to found the National Woman's Party in 1916.

The political nature of NAWSA was illustrated by its support of President Woodrow Wilson during World War I. Members acquired positions in federal offices and won political IOUs, which debtors repaid by endorsing the Nineteenth Amendment. After the Nineteenth Amendment was ratified in 1920, the nonpartisan NAWSA became the League of Women Voters.

See also American Equal Rights Association; American Woman Suffrage Association; Anthony, Susan B.; Blackwell, Alice Stone; Catt, Carrie Clinton Lane Chapman; League of Women Voters; National Woman Suffrage Association; Nineteenth Amendment; Stanton, Elizabeth Cady; Stone, Lucy; Winning Plan.

National Association of Colored Women (NACW)

The National Association of Colored Women (NACW), founded in 1896, resulted from the merger of the National Fed-

eration of Afro-American Women and the Colored Women's League. The purposes of the NACW are philanthropic and educational, but it has supported a number of reform issues, including women's suffrage. Mary Eliza Church Terrell was NACW's first president. NACW still exists, under the name National Association of Colored Women's Clubs, but its membership, at 45,000, is about one-half what it was in the 1920s.

See also National Council of Negro Women; National Federation of Afro-American Women; Terrell, Mary Eliza Church.

National Association of Colored Women's Clubs

See National Association of Colored Women.

National Birth Control League (NBCL)

The National Birth Control League (NBCL), a coalition of reformers whose goal was to revise state and federal Comstock laws so that contraception information was not considered obscene, brought together upper- and middle-class women in the fight for birth control. The group was formed in 1915 under the leadership of Mary Ware Dennett. Other key members were socialist Rose Pastor Stokes, muckraker Lincoln Steffens, educator Lucy Sprague Mitchell, and labor activist Helen Marot. Although Margaret Sanger worked with the NBCL, it became more closely associated with the moderate ideas of Dennett, a former officer in the National American Woman Suffrage Association, whom Sanger disliked personally. The two were also divided on tactics, with Sanger promoting direct action, breaking the laws she disagreed with, and Dennett advocating working within the law for legislative reform. Although Dennett asked Sanger to serve on the executive board of the NBCL in 1916 and 1919, Sanger refused, and in doing so helped to divide the group's membership. However, in 1917 when Ethel

Byrne, Margaret Sanger, and Fania Mindell were on trial for violating antiobscenity laws in passing out birth control information, NBCL members calling themselves the Committee of 100 raised $700 for legal expenses, called a rally at Carnegie Hall, and took Margaret to appeal to New York Governor Charles Whitman. In 1919 the NBCL changed its name to the Voluntary Parenthood League.

See also American Birth Control League; Birth Control; Comstock Act; Contraception; Sanger, Margaret.

National Black Women's Health Project (NBWHP)

In 1981 Byllye Avery started the National Black Women's Health Project (NBWHP) to address the health problems of African-American women. The NBWHP, with 2,000 members, has combated specific illnesses, focused on the issue of pregnancy, and started numerous self-help groups. The organization, headquartered in Atlanta, Georgia, addresses the stress-related causes of health problems as well as the issue of affordable care. The project has inspired similar efforts among other ethnic communities.

National Coalition against Domestic Violence (NCADV)

The National Coalition against Domestic Violence (NCADV) is a coalition of approximately 1,250 local organizations and shelters that aid battered women. The coalition, formed in 1978 and based in Washington, D.C., advocates handling the problem of domestic violence at the community level. The independent organizations of the coalition provide practical assistance to victims and attempt to rebuild their self-esteem. However the NCADV firmly believes that domestic violence is a societal problem, with underlying causes rooted deep in the culture, and that the problem cannot be solved solely by efforts at an individual level.

See also Violence.

National Consumers' League (NCL)

The National Consumers' League (NCL), organized in 1898 to bring together a number of state and local consumers' leagues, substantially improved the conditions of women who worked as retail clerks or in the garment or food production industries. Under the leadership of Florence Kelley, who was general secretary from 1899 until 1932, and Maud Nathan, a member of the executive board and vice-president, the group published lists of employers whose working conditions met the NCL's standards. The so-called White Lists were used to encourage shoppers, mainly affluent women, to support approved businesses. The NCL lobbied lawmakers on both state and local levels to pass protective legislation to establish a maximum workday for women and children and a minimum-wage scale. The group supported court cases that upheld protective legislation, for example, the benchmark *Muller v. Oregon* (1908) on the maximum workday, in which Louis Brandeis acted as the NCL counsel. The NCL frequently argued that women's reproductive capabilities were harmed by long hours and poor conditions. The group was more successful in campaigning for maximum hours than for minimum wages. After World War I, the league's accomplishments were set back by a more conservative Supreme Court, which decided in *Adkins v. Children's Hospital* (1923) that minimum-wage laws were unconstitutional. The NCL fell into decline in the 1920s; as of 1992 it had about 8,000 members.

See also *Adkins v. Children's Hospital*; *Muller v. State of Oregon*; Nathan, Maud; Protective Legislation.

National Council of Negro Women (NCNW)

The National Council of Negro Women (NCNW) was established in 1935 by Mary McLeod Bethune with representatives of 14 African-American women's groups. Bethune believed the earlier National Association of Colored Women was too parochial

National Council of Negro Women founder Mary McLeod Bethune, right, *pickets for civil rights.*

National Displaced Homemakers Network

See Alliance for Displaced Homemakers/National Displaced Homemakers Network.

National Education Association (NEA)

The National Education Association, formerly the National Teachers Association, was founded in 1857. Women were first admitted in 1866, and by 1884 they constituted a majority of its membership. Until 1957, the group maintained a policy of taking public positions only on issues involving education. But from 1957 to 1979 the group became known for its strong advocacy of women's issues, including the Equal Rights Amendment, curriculum reform, and legalized abortion and planned parenthood. With two million members, the NEA is the largest professional organization in the world.

See also Education.

National Federation of Afro-American Women

Founded in 1895 by the New Era Club, the National Federation of Afro-American Women was the nation's first national organization of African-American women's clubs. Josephine St. Pierre Ruffin, the group's leader, convened the first conference in Boston. Representatives of 32 clubs attended; in total, 104 African-American women and a few men, such as reformers William Lloyd Garrison and Henry Blackwell. Margaret Washington, the wife of Booker T. Washington, was the group's first president.

African Americans who were excluded from white organizations in the North and the South also had different purposes in organizing at this time. Their goal was to establish relief organizations for the poor, sick, and elderly. The New Era Club (1893) also published a newspaper, the *Women's Era*, and endorsed educational and political reforms. Within one year of its founding,

in its interests to be a powerful national group. Bethune served as the organization's first president until 1949. Under her leadership, NCNW campaigned for the integration of African-American women in the military during the 1940s, lobbied against the persecution of Jews in Germany and launched relief programs for impoverished African Americans in the South during the 1960s. Among the latter were Project Home and Operation Daily Bread, both based in Mississippi. Although the organization has represented more than one million women, the group lost much of its force after Bethune resigned. She died in 1955. In 1992 the NCNW had 40,000 members.

See also National Association of Colored Women.

the National Federation of African-American Women joined the Colored Women's League to form the National Association of Colored Women.

See also Garrison, William Lloyd; National Association of Colored Women.

National Federation of Business and Professional Women's Clubs (BPW)

The National Federation of Business and Professional Women's Clubs (BPW), though not always considered a feminist organization, aims to help professional women. Located in Washington, D.C., the organization concentrates its efforts at the federal level, with emphasis on equal rights legislation. The BPW was founded in 1919 as the result of a federal effort, in conjunction with the Young Women's Christian Association (YWCA), to encourage women to undertake office work during World War I. After the war, BPW turned its attention to helping professional women. It has endorsed the right of women to take civil service exams and has supported minimum-wage laws, better Social Security benefits, and equal pay. Since 1937 the BPW has been a staunch supporter of an equal rights amendment and has worked with members of Congress for its passage. The BPW has continually encouraged presidents' administrations to appoint more women and, in the process of suggesting applicants, has developed relationships with the administrations. In 1956, to give working women greater educational opportunities and to express its support of scholarship on women's issues, BPW created the Business and Professional Women's Foundation, which provides research grants and scholarships and runs a women's library. In 1962–1963 the organization campaigned to establish state commissions on the status of women.

The feminist commitment of BPW has sometimes been belittled because of the organization's reluctance to follow up on a suggestion to accept a role as an NAACP-type organization for women. (The desire to act upon this suggestion was eventually one of the reasons for the founding of the National Organization for Women.) BPW's dedication to women's rights, however, has been clear on a number of issues. BPW's efforts, particularly its lobbying and financial support, were a critical factor in the congressional passage of the ERA in 1972 and the subsequent drive for ratification by the states. In 1970 BPW had orchestrated a campaign to send enormous numbers of telegrams to members of Congress; this was directly responsible for getting the amendment out of the House Judiciary Committee and onto the floor of the House. The fact that Marguerite Rawalt, a leading ERA advocate, had been a president of BPW had helped to reinforce the organization's ties to ERA efforts. Because of their lobbying on the ERA and other issues, BPW lobbyists have become a fixture on the Washington political scene.

See also Young Women's Christian Assocation.

National Institute for Women of Color

In 1981 Sharon Parker and Veronica Collazo formed the National Institute for Women of Color, a feminist organization for women from various ethnic backgrounds. Among its achievements is a widespread change in terminology: The term *women of color* is commonly used in place of the older term, *minority women*, which implies inferiority or powerlessness. The institute, located in Washington, D.C., is an umbrella group that links several thousand organizations, to which it supplies information and support. Among other things, it links groups dealing with issues or concerns of mutual interest, encourages the appointment of women of color to boards and commissions, and ensures that women of color are speakers at major women's conferences.

National Judicial Education Program To Promote Equality for Women and Men in the Courts (NJEP)

The National Judicial Education Program To Promote Equality for Women and Men in the Courts (NJEP) combats sex bias in the courtroom. The NJEP was formed in 1980 by the National Organization for Women Legal Defense and Education Fund (LDEF) and the National Association of Women Judges. The program has received a mixed response from the judiciary. The NJEP conducts seminars throughout the country in an effort to prove to judges that bias against women exists and to foster greater appreciation of women's concerns. Evidence of bias discovered by the NJEP includes apathy, complacence, and pervasive negative views of women.

See also National Organization for Women.

National Labor Union (NLU)

The National Labor Union (NLU), founded in 1866, attracted women's suffragists and then rebuffed them. The political arm of the post–Civil War labor reform movement, the NLU was a loose federation of city trade assemblies, national trade unions, and reform organizations. The latter included anarchists, socialists, and women's suffragists. At its first convention, the union resolved, "We pledge our individual and undivided support to the sewing women, factory operatives, and daughters of toil in this land." The union believed that political action was the appropriate means of protecting female workers. At the time of the first convention (1866), unemployment was widespread. War industries were closing their plants, and demobilized soldiers were only slowly being reabsorbed into the peacetime economy.

In 1868, the year it won the eight-hour workday for employees of the federal government, the NLU caught the attention of feminists like Elizabeth Cady Stanton and Susan B. Anthony. To them the union seemed to have captured the spirit of reform to a greater extent than either the abolitionists or the Republicans, who turned their backs on suffragists after the war to concentrate their efforts on obtaining the vote for African-American men. In 1868 Susan B. Anthony's newspaper, *The Revolution*, called for a new party built on the reform issues of labor and women's suffrage. Her hope for

an alliance with labor were dashed at the third annual congress of the National Labor Union in September 1868. Several suffragists attended the meeting. Their most important victory was the admission of Susan B. Anthony, Elizabeth Cady Stanton, Mary Kellogg Putnam, and Mary McDonald as regular delegates. However, a minority of NLU members, most of them delegates of the building trades, threatened to leave the NLU unless Stanton's credentials were withdrawn because she represented women's suffrage, not labor. The men failed to unseat Stanton but persuaded the congress to renounce women's suffrage. The suffragists left the NLU soon after. Although the congress renounced suffrage, it did come out in favor of the eight-hour workday for women, equal pay for equal work, and the founding of trade unions for working women. Thus the NLU became the first labor federation in the world to endorse equal pay for equal work. The economic depression brought on the demise of the NLU, which converted itself into the National Labor Reform in 1872.

See also Anthony, Susan B.; Stanton, Elizabeth Cady; Working Woman's Association.

National Latina Health Organization

The California-based National Latina Health Organization promotes the health care objectives of Hispanic women. It was founded in 1986 by Luz Alvarez Martinez. The organization's priorities include providing a place where women can discuss their experiences with abortion (a taboo subject in many Catholic households); addressing issues concerning reproductive freedom, such as excessive sterilization and the availability of birth control; increasing the accessibility of medical care to people who speak only Spanish; and providing medical support and information to Hispanic women.

National Organization for Women (NOW)

The National Organization for Women (NOW) sprang from feminists' frustration with the government's failure to fight sex discrimination. Richard Graham, a sympathetic commissioner on the unresponsive Equal Employment Opportunity Commission, told women leaders that they could neither win the war nor even wage a battle until they had a feminist equivalent of the National Association for the Advancement of Colored People (NAACP).

The organization was founded in June 1966, during the third National Conference of the State Commissions on the Status of Women. Although some people regarded the commissions as a satisfactory vehicle for achieving equality, frustration grew when the conference was unable to pass or act upon antidiscrimination resolutions. At a luncheon on the final day of the conference, NOW was formed. Dr. Kathryn Clarenbach, who headed the Wisconsin State Commission on the Status of Women, was named temporary chair. The fledgling group included Betty Friedan, who was in the capital researching a book. Several people had encouraged Friedan to organize a new women's group, and she had been consulting with women activists about it. The group's first endeavor concerned the EEOC's official tolerance of sex-segregated want ads, to which women's activists had objected for some time.

On 29 October 1966, NOW announced its incorporation at a press conference in Washington, D.C. The group comprised 300 male and female charter members. Officers were Betty Friedan, president; Kay Clarenbach, chair; and former EEOC commissioner Richard Graham, treasurer. On the very day of its founding, NOW named Marguerite Rowalt head of a committee that would offer legal aid to those challenging protective legislation in the courts.

The fundamental goal of NOW was to permit women to share the opportunities that men monopolized. It rejected the notion that women should be excluded from professional opportunities on the grounds that motherhood consumes all their energies and is incompatible with a career. Most feminist groups had shunned any attempt to redefine or change the perception of motherhood, but NOW boldly ventured to explain that motherhood does not require lifelong effort and that concepts of homemaking and child-rearing should be redefined to accommodate women's career goals. Furthermore, NOW sought to change the images of women in the media and society. Although NOW has directed its efforts at a wide variety of women's concerns, it is perhaps most closely identified with the goals indicated in its 1967 Bill of Rights for Women, which demanded passage of the Equal Rights Amendment, employment and education opportunities, child care, legalized abortion, and reproductive freedom, among other things.

At the time of its founding, NOW represented an unprecedented degree of militancy rejected by earlier organizations, such as the National Federation of Business and Professional Women's Clubs and the League of Women Voters. However, NOW's feminism has generally been regarded as mainstream, in the liberal feminist as opposed to the women's liberation–radical feminist tradition. Many of NOW's efforts in its early years were directed at employment-related areas: airline stewardesses who were fighting not to be forced to retire at 32 enjoyed support from NOW; NOW had pressured President Johnson into signing Executive Order 11375 (which banned discrimination by federal contractors and in the hiring of federal employees); NOW's legal committee achieved a series of impressive victories (such as *Weeks v. Southern Bell*) in the fight against protective laws (the committee also challenged bias against women in the criminal justice system in the successful *Commonwealth v. Jane Daniels* case); NOW picketed and eventually sued the EEOC for inept handling of sex discrimination cases; 1,300 of the largest American corporations were made to face sex discrimination charges because of a suit brought by NOW; and, besides lobbying for government funding for child care, NOW even offered some immediate help for working mothers (and mothers who wished to work) by actually starting a few NOW nurseries. In addition, NOW protested restrictions on women in other areas of life: for example, it held demonstrations against the exclusion of women from certain restaurants and bars. Some of NOW's tactics were particularly innovative, such as the awarding of the "Barefoot and Pregnant in the Kitchen" award for advertising that is degrading to women.

The history of NOW in the 1970s and 1980s was the history of the feminist movement of that time in miniature. The effects and presence of NOW's influence have been felt in virtually every area of feminist activity. Besides winning specific victories in the battle against sex discrimination, NOW has established a reputation as a heavyweight lobbying force in Washington, paving the way for other feminist organizations to enjoy similar status. Further evidence of NOW's savvy comes from its skill in attracting interest from the media.

Throughout the 1970s, NOW's greatest challenge was perhaps not in the field of sex discrimination but in its efforts to respond to the inadequacies of its own organizational structure. Although it embraced egalitarian views consistent with the concept of sisterhood among women, NOW also adopted an extremely pragmatic approach, in contrast to radical groups, and this pragmatism made direct participation of all members in all decisions impracticable. The astonishing growth of NOW during the mid-1970s also exacerbated the problems of maintaining good communication with local groups and individual members. Part of the strength of NOW has been its effectiveness in meeting the challenges presented by these organizational problems. While it maintains a hierarchical structure to function with maximum efficiency, over the years it has taken a number of steps to prevent any one party from gaining excessive control of the organization, to continue to offer opportunities for rank-and-file involvement, and to maintain close ties with local chapters.

Despite the perception of some radical feminists and women of color that NOW's attention is focused mainly on the objectives of mainstream professional women, NOW has struggled since the 1970s, over the angry objections of some contingents within the organization, to give adequate attention to groups of women whose needs have been the most poorly represented by all activists in the past, such as the poor, the elderly, lesbians, and women of color. The impetus for this desire for diversity came in part from two 1970s NOW presidents, Wilma Scott Heide and Aileen Hernandez, who sought to expand NOW sympathies and to heal divisions within the women's movement, both for reasons of principle and because divisiveness had been so damaging to the organization. NOW's concerns extended to areas previously not often associated with feminism in the past, such as prison reform; the position eventually assumed by NOW could be regarded as that of a *humanist*, not merely feminist, organization.

Since the mid-1970s, NOW has become involved in electoral politics to a much greater degree. Its success in this area has been notable, despite the fact that its members' views are generally considerably to the left of the mainstream. In some cases its political astuteness has been striking: even before Ross Perot publicized Americans' dissatisfaction with their political system, NOW had identified this dissatisfaction and formed the Commission for a Responsive Democracy to propose solutions in the political process.

See also Friedan, Betty; Liberal Feminism; National Judicial Education Program To Promote Equality for Women and Men in the Courts; Older Women's League; President's Commission on the Status of Women; Project on Equal Education Rights; Title VII of the 1964 Civil Rights Act.

National S.E.E.D. Project on Inclusive Curriculum

The National S.E.E.D. (Seeking Educational Equity and Diversity) Project on Inclusive Curriculum was designed to help teachers develop an inclusive curriculum, that is, a curriculum that pays adequate attention to the contributions and concerns of women, people of color, the poor, and others. The project grew out of a 1983 series of seminars that were conducted by Peggy

McIntosh for the Wellesley College Center for Research on Women. In 1987 McIntosh, with Emily Jane Style, started what came to be called the S.E.E.D. Project, which was intended to give the original program a broader audience. They trained teachers in one-week summer sessions; these teachers in turn trained other teachers in their home school. As of 1991, the National S.E.E.D. was still in existence.

National Woman Suffrage Association (NWSA)

In 1869, immediately following a stormy meeting of the American Equal Rights Association in which Elizabeth Cady Stanton and Susan B. Anthony were sharply criticized, the two women and several of their followers left the American Equal Rights Association to form the National Woman Suffrage Association (NWSA) in New York City. They left disgusted with Lucy Stone, Julia Ward Howe, and other Boston-based activists who would not split with male abolitionists, such as Wendell Phillips and William Lloyd Garrison, over whether women should wait for the vote until African-American men had won it. The disagreement over this issue is illuminated in a conversation that took place two years before the break between *Herald Tribune* editor Horace Greeley, and Elizabeth Cady Stanton and Susan B. Anthony, which is recorded in *History of Woman Suffrage*, Volume 2. Mr. Greeley begins:

"This is a critical period for the Republican party and the life of the Nation. The word 'white' in our Constitution at this hour has significance which 'male' has not. It would be wise and magnanimous [of] you to hold your claims, though just and imperative, I grant, in abeyance until the negro is safe beyond peradventure, and your turn will come next. I conjure you to remember that this is 'the negro's hour,' and your first duty now is to go through the State and plead his claims." "Suppose," we [Cady Stanton and An-

thony] replied, "Horace Greeley, Henry J. Raymond and James Gordon Bennett were disenfranchised; what would be thought of them, if before audiences and in leading editorials they pressed the claims of Sambo, Patrick, Hans and Yung Fung to the ballot, to be lifted above their own heads? With their intelligence, education, knowledge of the science of government, and keen appreciation of the dangers of the hour, would it not be treasonable, rather than magnanimous, for them, leaders of the metropolitan press, to give the ignorant and unskilled a power in government they did not possess themselves? To do this would be to place on board the ship of State officers and crew who knew nothing of chart of compass, of the safe pathway across the sea, and bid those who undestand the laws of navigation to stand aside. No, no, this is the hour to press woman's claims; we have stood with the black man in the Constitution over half a century, and it is fitting now that the constitutional door is open that we should enter with him into the political kingdom of equality. Through all these years he has been the only decent compeer we have had. Enfranchise him, and we are left outside with lunatics, idiots and criminals for another twenty years." "Well," said Mr. Greeley, "if you persevere in your present plan, you need depend on no further help from me or the *Tribune.*"

But other issues were bubbling beneath the surface of the two groups. One of them involved George Train. In 1867, Elizabeth Cady Stanton and Susan B. Anthony had traveled to Kansas, where the legislature had announced that the state's voters could decide in November whether or not to enfranchise women and/or African Americans. Arriving in September, they found that Republicans were interpreting the American Equal Rights Association's "Universal Suffrage" goal to mean universal suffrage for men only and that the party had formed an Anti-Female Suffrage Committee. Women's suffrage in Kansas seemed doomed. Suddenly, "at the auspicious moment," as Cady Stanton and Anthony later recalled it, George Train, a Democrat, offered to travel across Kansas and speak on behalf of women's suffrage. A Republican outcry followed the acceptance of that offer, for not only was Train a Democrat but he held racist views and was opposed to granting the vote to African Americans under any circumstances. When Lucy Stone found out that his appearances with Anthony were represented as American Equal Rights Associaton events, she printed cards stating the fact that the American Equal Rights Association was not responsible. Cady Stanton and Anthony were immediately accused of racism, a charge they denied. But by the time both woman and African-American suffrage were defeated in Kansas, Cady Stanton and Anthony had alienated Republicans across the nation and colleagues in the East. The split within the women's movement widened when Train gave Anthony the funds needed to begin a newspaper.

The first issue of the *Revolution* was published on 8 January 1868. Susan B. Anthony was its proprietor and Elizabeth Cady Stanton and Parker Pillsbury were its editors. Its publication in 1869 of the article "That Infamous Fifteenth Amendment" brought the growing split between the radicals and conservatives to a head. At the May 1869 meeting of the American Equal Rights Association, Cady Stanton's and Anthony's more extreme view on black male and women's suffrage was the subject of bitter debate. Immediately following the meeting, the two founded the National Woman Suffrage Association. Although Lucy Stone, at the AERA meeting, had shown some sympathy for the more radical views, and had gone so far as to tell abolitionist Frederick Douglass woman suffrage was more imperative than his own, she had ultimately decided, "There are two great oceans; in one is the black man, and in the other is the woman. But I thank God for the XV Amendment, and would be thankful in my soul if *any* body can get out of the terrible pit." She did not join Cady Stanton and Anthony in the National Woman Suffrage Association.

Later in 1869, Stone and the Boston-based activists retaliated by founding the American Woman Suffrage Association (AWSA). This division lasted 20 years. The AWSA concentrated on getting the vote for women on the state and local level. The NWSA worked for an amendment to the Constitution that would grant women suffrage, and it advocated broad liberal reform, connecting suffrage with other women's rights. In 1890 the groups were reunited in the National American Woman Suffrage Association.

See also American Equal Rights Association; American Woman Suffrage Association; Anthony, Susan B.; Garrison, William Lloyd; National American Woman Suffrage Association; *The Revolution*; Stanton, Elizabeth Cady; Stone, Lucy.

National Woman's Christian Temperance Union (WCTU)

Formed in 1874 in Cleveland, Ohio, the National Woman's Christian Temperance Union (WCTU) was the nation's first major women's organization. It encouraged women to venture out of their homes and into the larger world of public life at the end of the nineteenth century. Women marched, prayed, sang, and dumped barrels of whiskey to protest the sale of liquor. Throughout the nation, they demonstrated, lobbied legislators, and destroyed property. Quiet during the Civil War, the temperance movement eventually drew millions of women to temperance-oriented reform organizations.

The first president of the WCTU was Annie Wittenmyer, who served until 1879. She was succeeded by Frances Willard, who was a delegate at the Cleveland Convention that founded the group. Under Willard's leadership (1879–1898), the organization embraced not only abstinence and prohibition but women's rights demands. For example, during the 1880s, the WCTU was a force behind the drive to permit women to vote in municipal elections, because local elections determined whether liquor could be sold. When Willard died in 1898, Lillian M. Stevens was elected president of the WCTU, holding the position until 1914. She refocused the group on the push for national prohibition, reaching out to other temperance groups, such as the Anti-Saloon League, toward this end. After the passage of the Eighteenth Amendment in 1919, prohibiting the sale of liquor, the WCTU emphasized issues such as the welfare of children and assimilation of new immigrants. It fought the repeal of the Prohibition amendment during the 1920s and 1930s.

Today, the organization's headquarters are in Evanston, Illinois. It has 48 state and 4,000 local groups and, as of 1992, it had 50,000 members. It is affiliated with the World's Woman's Christian Temperance Union, which was also organized by WCTU leader Frances Willard.

See also Nation, Carry Amelia Moore; Temperance; Willard, Frances.

National Woman's Loyal League

On 1 January 1863, President Abraham Lincoln issued the Emancipation Proclamation, freeing slaves in the rebel states. Those in states loyal to the Union were still in bondage. This gave Susan B. Anthony and Elizabeth Cady Stanton a new political opportunity. They called a meeting of the "Loyal Women of the Nation" in New York City on 14 May 1863. Their goal was to express support for the Thirteenth Amendment to the Constitution, introduced by U.S. Senator Charles Sumner, which would end slavery not only in the states in rebellion but also in the Union slaveholding states of Maryland, Missouri, Virginia, Tennessee, Kentucky, and Delaware. Cady Stanton and Anthony hoped to collect one million signatures on a petition in favor of Sumner's bill to "emancipate all persons of African descent held to involuntary service or labor in the United States." At the New York gathering, the National Woman's Loyal League was formed, with Stanton as its president and Anthony as secretary. By the end of May, the women had

opened a small office in Cooper Union, New York, from which they labored for the next 15 months.

Suffrage leaders Ernestine Rose, Angelina Grimké, and Lucy Stone agreed to collect the million signatures petitioning Congress in support of the Thirteenth Amendment. Two thousand men, women, and children circulated petitions for the league, and 5,000 people eventually joined. Stanton enlisted her own and other children in the effort, offering a badge of honor to any child who brought in 100 signatures. Anthony lived on $12 per week during the campaign, spending 10 cents for lunch and walking long distances. By the time the league disbanded in August 1864, it had collected 400,000 signatures. On 9 February 1864, two African-American men carried the petition rolls, which were too heavy for the Senate pages, to the Senate chamber and placed them on the desk of Senator Sumner. Sumner presented the rolls to the Senate. The Thirteenth Amendment was ratified in 1865.

See also Anthony Susan B.; Stanton, Elizabeth Cady.

National Woman's Party (NWP)

The National Woman's Party (NWP) was founded by Alice Paul and Lucy Burns, who acted as chair and vice-chair of the National American Woman Suffrage Association's Congressional Committee in 1912. The committee influenced NAWSA's young Turks to work for a federal suffrage amendment instead of adhering to assocation president Carrie Chapman Catt's state-by-state strategy. In 1913, they formed a new organization, the Congressional Union for Woman Suffrage (CU). In 1917, this group merged with Woman's Party to form the National Woman's Party. Members of the militant NWP were the first U.S. citizens to claim political prisoner status. Imprisoned for picketing the White House in 1917, the women became national heroes, and their unjustified imprisonment provided the final impetus for passage of the Nineteenth Amendment.

Members of the NWP had been arrested beginning in June 1917 on charges of "obstructing traffic." Found guilty, Alice Paul, Lucy Burns, and 96 other suffragists served sentences of up to six months. Lucy Burns smuggled the following message out of prison on 16 November 1917:

I was seized and laid on my back, where five people held me, a young colored woman leaping upon my knees, which seemed to break under the weight. Dr. Gannon then forced the tube through my lips and down my throat, I gasping and suffocating with the agony of it. I didn't know where to breathe from and everything turned black when the fluid began pouring in. I was moaning and making the most awful sounds quite against my will, for I did not wish to disturb my friends in the next room. Finally the tube was withdrawn.

The women claimed political prisoner status. Although no court responded to the argument, the women at least had the satisfaction of hearing a District of Columbia Court of Appeals declare their arrests to be "invalid" in 1918. The public outcry over the arrests, combined with the more practical "Winning Plan" of NAWSA, convinced Woodrow Wilson to support the women's cause in 1918. But the Senate voted the amendment down, and as a result the NWP opposed President Woodrow Wilson's bid for reelection in 1918, pursuing a strategy of opposing the party in power until a federal suffrage amendment was passed. In addition, the NWP punished the Democrats by opposing all of their candidates for Congress, regardless of their position on suffrage. Despite the NWP's opposition, Wilson won ten of the 12 suffrage states, and the NWP had little effect on congressional elections.

From 1919 to 1920, the NWP had 35,000–60,000 members. But after the passage of the Nineteenth Amendment, the NWP went into a decline, with only 152 paid members in 1921. At the national convention in 1923, the leadership proposed an Equal Rights Amendment (ERA), which was introduced into Congress by Senator Charles Curtis of Kansas on 10 December of that year. It said simply, "Men and women shall have equal rights throughout the United States and every place subject to its jurisdiction." In 1943, the wording of the ERA was revised to read: "Equality of rights under the law shall not be denied or abridged by the United States on account of sex." The change was made to bring it into line with the Nineteenth Amendment.

The NWP newsletter *Equal Rights*, founded in 1923, exemplified the high intellectual standards to which members of the NWP held themselves. It tracked legislative victories and other milestones for women, exposed discriminatory practices and their underlying social causes, and published essays on women's issues.

The NWP still exists, and *Equal Rights* remains the name of its newsletter. The organization advocates ratification of an equal rights amendment and maintains the NWP Equal Rights and Suffrage Art Gallery and Museum in the Sewall-Belmont House, a national historic landmark in Washington, D.C.

See also Belmont, Alva; Burns, Lucy; Congressional Union for Woman Suffrage; Equal Rights Amendment; Equal Rights Party; Nineteenth Amendment; Paul, Alice; Strikes.

National Women's Conference

Some historians consider the first National Women's Conference, held in Houston, Texas, in November 1977, a milestone in the history of the feminist movement. It represented the beginning of a stage at which second-wave feminism had come out of its formative years and had reached a certain level of maturity. Feminism as a movement would be treated with a new degree of seriousness and would be regarded as a force relevant not merely to "women's issues" but in reforming all areas of life. Antifeminists also became aware of the possibility that feminism could fundamentally change American society, and they became more aggressive in their efforts to create, encourage, and organize opposition to women's rights; objections to the ideas of the conference and related efforts to fight feminist goals were a sign of a coming era of political reaction. The Plan of Action adopted at the conference, with its planks on the Equal Rights Amendment, abortion rights, the rights of women of color, lesbian rights, the problems of domestic violence and of rape, as well as women's economic interests, has been considered a definitive statement about feminist thinking of the time, and an influence on feminist activity in the years that followed. A number of the nation's most notable women, including Rosalynn Carter, Betty Ford, and Lady Bird Johnson, attended the four-day conference. Although for the most part the conference reflected mainstream feminist views, radical feminists and even antifeminists participated to some degree.

The planning of the conference, beginning in 1975, was a two-year effort that highlighted deep divisions among different contingents within the feminist movement. Bella Abzug had introduced a bill into Congress in January 1975 that would require that the celebrations for the American Bicentennial include a women's conference. The National Commission on the Observance of International Woman's Year (IWY Commission), which had been established by executive order by President Gerald Ford as the U.S. government's attempt to honor the International Woman's Year (IWY) sponsored by the United Nations, would be responsible for planning the conference. The planning process involved convening state conferences that elected delegates and wrote preliminary drafts for a national plan of action on women's issues.

The involvement of the federal government and women of various ideologies created considerable public interest. The interest became even more intense because the press publicized the conflicts among feminists on several issues, which were revealed by the conference planning process. That, coupled with a barrage of attacks from antifeminist forces, yielded such a large degree of negative publicity that public confidence in the conference's chances for success began to be undermined. In an attempt to put a more dignified face on the process, the American Association of University Women created a Women's Conference Network of 40 organizations. The network sought to counter the success of antifeminists in tarnishing the images of the conference that were being presented through the media. Network press conferences gave feminists an opportunity to expose antifeminist tactics and to offer evidence of the merits of the program of the IWY Commission.

Among other things, the conference mandated the establishment of the National Women's Conference Committee (originally called the Continuing Committee of the National Women's Conference). The committee's purpose is to mobilize grassroots support for the conference's national Plan of Action in the areas of legal, economic, and social change. With a small membership and a budget of less than $25,000, the group maintains a speaker's bureau, publishes a semiannual newsletter, and sponsors an annual conference.

National Women's Education Fund
The National Women's Education Fund works to increase the presence of women in politics by conducting local seminars (funded with tax-deductible money) to instruct women on involvement in the political process and by supplying information about political women. The group was founded in the early 1970s by Margot Polivy, a former aide to Congresswoman Bella Abzug, and Ellen Sudow, a member of the House Democratic Study Group and former editor of the *WEAL Washington Report*.

National Women's Health Network
Created in 1975, the National Women's Health Network (NWHN) comprises hundreds of feminist and health groups and thousands of individuals. The network unites all elements of the feminist health

movement. In addition to serving as an information clearinghouse, NWHN monitors legislative proposals and various government agencies. It has combated high-dose birth control pills, the Dalkon shield, and sterilization abuse. In addition, NWHN supports efforts of women of color to establish their own health groups.

See also National Black Women's Health Project; National Latina Health Organization.

National Women's Political Caucus (NWPC)

Founded in July 1971, the National Women's Political Caucus (NWPC) was formed to put women in positions of power at all levels of government, to increase women's political activism, and to end legal inequities. Early members of the NWPC were Bella Abzug, Shirley Chisholm, Shana Alexander, Liz Carpenter, Betty Friedan, and Gloria Steinem. Efforts by the NWPC have resulted in increased percentages of female delegates to both the Democratic and Republican national conventions. The group also works with the National Organization for Women on select projects, such as the Coalition for Women's Rights.

The Coalition for Women's Appointments, founded in 1972 as a division of the NWPC, sought to increase the number of women appointed to federal positions. The coalition enjoyed considerable success during the Carter administration, during which time it was instrumental in placing an unprecedented number of female appointees. It is now inactive.

See also Chisholm, Shirley; Friedan, Betty; Steinem, Gloria.

National Women's Trade Union League

See Women's Trade Union League.

Neal, John (1793–1876)

John Neal was one of the first men to champion the vote for women before the Seneca Falls Convention of 1848. A Quaker, Neal was born 25 August 1793 in Portland, Maine. He had little formal schooling but educated himself at law and earned a living as a writer. He was a founding vice-president of the New England Woman Suffrage Association (1868) and regularly wrote articles for *The Revolution*, the newspaper of the National Woman Suffrage Association. At Margaret Fuller's request, he lectured to her classes in Providence, Rhode Island, about the destiny of women.

Neal wrote about the need to reform laws governing property rights so that women could own and control their property after marriage. Further, he argued that female dependency was caused by male oppression and that even clothing fashions (such as petticoats) were used by men to subjugate women. In an editorial entitled "Rights of Women" (1813), Neal compared the condition of women in the United States to that of slaves,

. . . to be taxed without their own consent; to be governed by laws, made not by themselves, nor by their representatives, but by people, whose interests instead of being identical with theirs, [are] directly opposed to theirs. . . . No vote can she give—no office can she hold. . . . All her personal property goes to her husband, or her husband's creditors. . . . Add to this, that while no part of the husband's earnings belong to the wife, all her earnings belong to him; *that she is bound to personal service during marriage*, and may be treated by him, like a servant, a child, or an apprentice, and actually beaten, if beaten moderately, . . . if she falters in her allegiance.

Neal was a lifelong spokesman for the equal rights of women and a committed activist before women themselves organized to fight for their rights. Neal's many books include *Seventy-Six* (1823); *Rachel Dyer* (1828), which concerns the witchcraft trials of Salem, Massachusetts; and an autobiography, *Wandering Recollection of a Somewhat Busy Life* (1869). Neal died 20 June 1876 in Portland, Maine.

New Directions for Women

One of the best-selling feminist periodicals, *New Directions for Women* was founded in New Jersey in 1972 under the name *New Directions for Women in New Jersey*. It began as a mimeographed newsletter for local feminists. Only 2,000 copies of the first 14-page issue were printed, and most of those were delivered to libraries. The Ford Foundation provided a grant to expand the newsletter's circulation. *New Directions* eventually assumed a position second only to *Ms.*, with a national circulation in the tens of thousands.

New Era Club

See National Federation of Afro-American Women.

New York Married Woman's Property Act (1848)

In 1848, three months before the Seneca Falls gathering, New York passed a law giving women control over the property they owned at the time of their marriage. The bill—the most comprehensive of its time—was originally introduced in the New York legislature in 1836 and was reintroduced every year thereafter. Ernestine Rose, Paulina Wright Davis, and Elizabeth Cady Stanton collected signatures on petitions throughout the state for its passage. Yet it took 12 years—from 1836 to 1848—for the bill to pass.

The act specifically stated:

1. The real and personal property of any female who may hereafter marry, and which she shall own at the time of her marriage, and the rents, issues and profits thereof, shall not be subject to the disposal of her husband nor be liable for his debts and shall continue her sole and separate property as if she were a single female.

2. The real and personal property and rents, issues and profits thereof of any female now married shall not be subject to the disposal of her husband; but shall be her sole and separate property as if she were a single female except so far as the same may be liable for the debts of her husband heretofore contracted.

3. It shall be lawful for any married female to receive by gift, grant device or bequest, from any person other than her husband and to hold for her sole and separate use, as if she were a single female, real and personal property and rents, issues and profits thereof, and the same shall not be subject to the disposal of her husband, nor be liable for his debts.

4. All contracts made between persons in contemplation of marriage remain in full force after such marriage takes place.

Although the law protected a married woman's real and personal property from creditors, it did not give women control of their wages; money earned by married women still belonged to their husbands. Amended in 1857, the act was enlarged in 1860. After the passage of the act, Elizabeth Cady Stanton remarked, "This was the death-blow to the Blackstonian code for married women in this country." She also noted in an 1854 speech to the New York state legislature that the right of property would, in time, lead to women's right to vote and hold elective office. History would prove her right.

See also Common Law; *Feme Covert*; Married Women's Property Acts; New York Married Woman's Property Act (1860).

New York Married Woman's Property Act (1860)

In 1860, New York passed an "Act Concerning the Rights and Liabilities of Husband and Wife," commonly called the New York married woman's property act. The bill gave married women the right to control their wages as well as their other property. Also for the first time, a wife's inheritance legally became hers when her husband died. Under the 1860 law, a wife could make contracts with her husband's consent—or, if he were an alcoholic, a convict, or insane, without his consent. In addition, the law made the wife a joint guardian of her children. Later, other states in the Northeast and Midwest passed similar laws, but New York's was the most comprehensive of its time.

See also Common Law; *Feme Covert*; Married Women's Property Acts; New York Married Woman's Property Act (1848).

New York Radical Feminists (NYRF)

New York Radical Feminists (NYRF) was formed in response to growing public interest in the feminist movement. Although some radical feminist groups considered themselves elite, vanguard groups, NYRF believed that mass membership would help the women's movement. As it grew, NYRF became an umbrella group of local, nonhierarchical groups of about 15 women. The groups fostered close personal relations among their members; the groups usually were referred to as brigades and were named after great feminists.

The group was founded in 1969 by Shulamith Firestone, previously of the Redstockings and New York Radical Women, and Anne Koedt, previously of The Feminists. Firestone and Koedt sought to merge elements of various feminist theories and to eliminate their common defects. *Politics of the Ego*, the manifesto of NYRF, describes the system of male supremacy as a result of demands made by the male ego, independent of all class conflicts and historical conditions. The group held that women internalize sexist values (i.e., are brainwashed) and must seek change on a personal level. The group placed even greater emphasis on fundamental change in social organizations. The group's 1971 speak-out and conference on rape were among its best-known events; they did a great deal to raise public awareness of the full dimensions of the problem of rape. Firestone and Koedt eventually left the group because of controversy about the status of the Stanton-Anthony founding brigade within NYRF.

Firestone and Koedt felt that the newer brigades needed more commitment to social change and not merely improvement of individual lives; newer members, on the other hand, objected to the supremacy of the Stanton-Anthony Brigade, as well as a lengthy initiation period during which members-to-be assumed a subordinate position.

See also New York Radical Women; Radical Feminism; Redstockings.

New York Radical Women (NYRW)

New York Radical Women (NYRW) was formed in 1967 by women who had a degree of exposure to the New Left movement. Shulamith Firestone and Pam Allen organized the group, which attracted prominent feminist theorists such as Kate Millett and Robin Morgan. NYRW introduced consciousness-raising, which the Redstockings later made extremely popular, and in 1968 they published the highly influential book *Notes from the First Year*, which introduced revolutionary feminist concepts and represented the first stages of radical feminist thinking.

The group included women who had opposing ideas about the status of the women's movement in relation to the broader radical movement, and ideological disagreements among members caused considerable factionalism in the group. Eventually, members of the NYRW argued about the appropriateness of activities intended to gain attention by shocking the public. A dispute over the wisdom of the staging of the protest of the 1968 Miss America pageant led to the dissolution of the group. Firestone went on to organize the Redstockings and New York Radical Feminists the following year.

See also Miss America Protest; New York Radical Feminists; Radical Feminism; Redstockings.

Nichols, Clarina Irene Howard (1810–1885)

Clarina Nichols was a women's rights leader, writer, and editor. She was born

25 January 1810 in West Townshend, Vermont. From 1830 to 1843 she was married to Justin Carpenter and lived in Herkimer, New York, where around 1835 she may have opened a girls' school.

In 1839 she returned to Vermont, where she began to write for the Brattleboro *Windam County Democrat*. In 1843 she divorced her husband, married the *Democrat*'s publisher, and became editor of the newspaper. Under her editorship, the newspaper became more radical, advocating abolition, Prohibition, and other reforms. At the same time, Nichols became active in the women's rights movement, writing a series of articles on the need for reform in women's legal and property rights (1847). Her pressure led to the passage of a married woman's property law in Vermont in 1847. With her support, expansions of the law were enacted in 1849 and 1850. In 1852, Nichols petitioned the Vermont legislature to grant women the right to vote in school elections.

Nichols was in much demand as a lecturer on women's topics, particularly at women's rights conventions. In 1853 the family moved to Kansas, and Nichols canvassed for the Kansas Woman's Rights Association. Her activities prompted the delegates of the Kansas constitutional convention to assure women equal rights to education in state schools, suffrage in school elections, and custodial rights to their children. In 1861, as a representative of the Kansas Woman's Rights Association, Nichols addressed a joint session of the first state legislature about the need for a married woman's property law, which was enacted in 1867. In 1863 Nichols (a widow since 1855) moved to Washington, D.C., where she worked as a clerk in the Quartermasters Department. In 1865 she became a matron in a home operated by the National Association for the Relief of Destitute Colored Women and Children. In 1866 Nichols returned to Kansas. She joined Susan B. Anthony the following year in the unsuccessful campaign for women's suffrage in Kansas. Nichols moved to California in 1871, where she wrote for the *Mendocino County Rural Press.*

She died 11 January 1885 at Potter Valley, California.

See also Fowler, Lydia Folger; Married Women's Property Acts.

Nichols, Mary Sargeant Neal Gove (1810–1884)

Mary Nichols, a leader in health reform, was perhaps the first woman in the United States to lecture about anatomy, physiology, and hygiene. Born 10 August 1810 in Goffstown, New Hampshire, the future health expert was a sickly child. Shy and with limited schooling, she was an enthusiastic reader and eventually became an accomplished public speaker. At the age of 18, she was teaching, publishing stories and poems in local newspapers, and studying medical texts in secret. By the age of 21 she had married Hiram Gove, a poorly educated milliner whose marginal business made it necessary for her to do needlework to support the family. The family expanded to three with the birth of a daughter in 1832. That year, despite her husband's opposition, she began giving cold-water treatments to overworked local women. Based on her reading, she believed that water contained electricity that united with the body's warmth to enhance energy.

Approximately five years later, the family moved to Lynn, Massachusetts, where Mary Gove opened a girls' school. This was perhaps the first school in the United States to teach scientific topics to girls, and its leader became one of the nation's first women to lecture on anatomy, physiology, and health. In 1838 she gave a series of lectures to the Ladies Physiological Society of Boston. She gave her earnings to her husband as required by law; nonetheless, she had launched her career as a health reformer, and she began to pursue it in earnest. Following the regimen of Sylvester Graham, she taught women in the Northeast about the virtues of whole-wheat bread, vegetarianism, regular exercise, fresh air, cleanliness, daily cold-water baths, and abstinence from liquor, tea, and coffee. By 1840 she was editing the Worcester, Massachusetts, *Health Journal* and Advocate of Physiological Reform and later wrote Lectures to Ladies on Anatomy and Physiology (1842).

Hiram and Mary Gove, long separated, divorced sometime between 1847 and 1848. In 1847 she met Thomas Low Nichols, a fellow writer who supported equal rights for women, and a year later they were married. Their only child, born in 1850, died at 13. The Nicholses published the Water-Cure Journal. In addition, they opened a water-cure business in New York City (1851) and girls' summer school in Port Chester, New York (1852). However, the Nicholses were too radical for other reformers: They believed in free love and the right of every woman to choose the father of her child. In 1856, Mary Nichols underwent a spiritual awakening and founded a school requiring confession, chastity, and penance.

In their many individual and joint works, husband and wife declared marriage the root of all evil. Under the pseudonym Mary Orme, Mary Nichols wrote stories for the widely read Godey's Lady's Book. She also wrote several novels, including Uncle John: or, "It Is Too Much Trouble" (1846), Agnes Morris: or, The Heroine of Domestic Life (1849), The Two Loves: or, Eros and Anteros (1849), Uncle Agnes (1864), and Jerry: A Novel of Yankee American Life (1872). Her autobiographical novel, Mary Lyndon, appeared in 1855.

In 1861 Mary Nichols and her husband moved to England, where they operated a water-cure establishment in the spa town of Malvern. Nichols died 30 May 1884, and was buried in London.

Nineteenth Amendment
(Equal Suffrage Amendment)

The Nineteenth Amendment, also called the Equal Suffrage and Anthony Amendment, guarantees women the right to vote. The amendment is the product of several decades of activism on the part of reformers. Although suffrage amendments were introduced in the Senate and House annually, beginning in 1868, it was not until 1919, after many narrow margins, that Congress finally approved the Nineteenth Amendment. By 26 August 1920, the required 36 states had ratified the amendment and it was adopted.

The first measure to introduce such an amendment was proposed in 1868. Ten years later, Senator Aaron A. Sargent introduced another measure, which without any change in wording would become the Nineteenth Amendment.

On 10 January 1918, the suffrage amendment came up for a vote in the House. During the floor battle, a New York congressman left his suffragist wife's deathbed to vote for the amendment; another congressman had to be carried into the House on a stretcher. The final vote of the House, 274 to 136, was one vote more than the two-thirds necessary for passage.

The Senate battle proved just as close. Probusinessmen from the northern states led the fight against the suffrage amendment. They were allied with the antisuffrage southern Democrats, who raised the argument of states rights, wanting to preserve white dominance by keeping black women from voting. Senator Borah of Ohio said, "Do you propose to put the South under Federal control as to elections? . . . Nobody intends that the two and a half million negro women of the South shall vote. . . ." A stand-off ensued, which blocked the vote for an entire year. Finally, on 18 September 1918, President Woodrow Wilson appeared before the Senate, with only a half-hour warning. He said, "We have made partners of women in this war; shall we admit them only to a partnership of suffering and sacrifice and toil and not to a partnership of privilege and right?" Despite this, arguments such as the following by Senator McCumber helped win the day for the antisuffragists: "Whether the child's heart pulses beneath his own breast or throbs against her breast, motherhood demands above all tranquillity, freedom from contest, from excitement, from the heart burnings of strife." One day after President Wilson spoke, the suffrage amendment was defeated 62 in favor (split equally between Democrats and Republicans), 34 opposed. Two votes kept the amendment from passing.

Women's groups immediately went to work, retiring some of the antisuffrage senators and reducing the majorities of others. They passed referenda on suffrage at state level. Finally, on 20 May 1919, a new Congress, the Sixty-Sixth, repassed the suffrage amendment 304 to 89 in a special session called by Wilson for this purpose. On 4 June 1919, the Senate approved the amendment, 66 to 30. It took another 18 months for the states to ratify the amendment. On 18 August 1920 Tennessee became the thirty-sixth state to vote for ratification. The deciding vote was cast by 24-year-old Harry Burns, whose mother had sent him this telegram: "Hurrah! and vote for suffrage. . . . Don't forget to be a good boy and help Mrs. Catt put 'Rat' in ratification." On 26 August 1920, the amendment was officially adopted. The 72-year struggle had come to an end.

The amendment reads as follows:

"Section 1: The right of citizens of the United States to vote shall not be denied or abridged by the United States or by any State on the account of sex.

"Section 2: Congress shall have power to enforce this article by appropriate legislation."

See also Catt, Carrie Clinton Lane Chapman; National American Woman Suffrage Association; National Woman's Party; Paul, Alice.

Norton, Eleanor Holmes (1937–)

Eleanor Holmes Norton, now a congresswoman, was the first female chair of the Equal Employment Opportunity Commission (EEOC). She was born 13 June 1937 in Washington, D.C. After graduating from Dunbar High School, she received a B.A. from Antioch College in 1960, an M.A. from Yale University in 1963, and an L.L.B. from Yale in 1964. From 1965 to 1970, Norton was assistant legal director of the American Civil Liberties Union (ACLU), specializing

in First Amendment cases. Her first Supreme Court case defended the right of white supremacists to hold a rally. After five years with the ACLU, Norton became chair of the New York City Commission on Human Rights (1970). In 1977 President Jimmy Carter appointed Norton chair of the EEOC, an office she held until 1981, when the Republicans won the White House. When she arrived at the EEOC, 130,000 cases awaited her. She cut by half the case backlog and increased EEOC productivity by 65 percent.

Norton taught law at Georgetown University Law Center until 1990, when she was elected as a nonvoting delegate to the House of Representatives for the District of Columbia. She was serving in that capacity as of 1993.

Noyes, John Humphrey (1811–1886)

John Humphrey Noyes, founder of the Oneida Community in New York, held many radical and egalitarian views about women. One of his most controversial ideas was the complex marriage, in which each member of his utopian community was, in theory, married to every other community member of the opposite sex. Noyes was born 3 September 1811. After studying at Dartmouth, Andover, and Yale, he began to preach in New Haven, Connecticut, in 1833. One year later his license to preach was revoked because of his novel religious ideas. In 1845 he formed the Putney Corporation, or the Association of Perfectionists. This was the precursor of the Oneida Community (1848). In the pamphlet *Bible Communism* (1848), Noyes held that true Christianity rejected exclusiveness with regard to money, property, or persons: "Our communities are families as distinctly bonded and separated from promiscuous society as ordinary households. The tie that binds us together is as permanent and sacred, to say the least, as that of common marriage, for it is our religion." Noyes felt that monogamous marriage, compulsory sex, and too many children made slaves of

225

women. His solution was complex marriage and continence, a form of intercourse in which the man does not ejaculate. Noyes placed the burden of preventing pregnancy entirely on men and raised the hope of equality for women at a time when few others lent their support to sexual or political parity of the sexes. The Oneida Community existed in upstate New York for 25 years before public sentiment roused against its unconventional sexual practices. In 1879, facing legal action, Noyes told his followers that they would have to give up complex marriage. He left New York for Canada, where he died 13 April 1886.

See also Utopian Communities.

Oberlin College

Oberlin was the first college in the United States to practice coeducation, and among the first to offer women an education comparable to men, and admit African Americans. Oberlin was founded in 1833, chartered in 1834 as Oberlin Collegiate Institute, and renamed Oberlin College in 1850. It began admitting both sexes to its full course in 1837. Located in Lorain County, Ohio, southwest of Cleveland, the school was named in honor of clergyman and philanthropist Jean Frederic Oberlin.

The college opened a Theological Seminary in 1835. That year 40 students, led by Theodore Weld, transferred to Oberlin from the Lane Theological Seminary in Cincinnati, Ohio, after Lane's directors forbade the discussion of slavery. The students were not the only ones to transfer; Asa Mahan, a member of Lane's board of directors who strongly disapproved of the ban, became Oberlin's first president. A station on the Underground Railroad, Oberlin became an important center of antislavery sentiment. In a famous fugitive slave case, the runaway Littlejohn was taken at Oberlin in September 1858 by a federal marshal but was rescued at Wellington. Several of the rescuers, among them Professor Henry Everard Peck of Oberlin, were imprisoned for several months.

The first three women to receive undergraduate degrees from Oberlin were Caroline Rudd, Mary Hosford, and Elizabeth Prall. Although the school advocated equal education, it did not advocate equal rights or standing for men and women. Its female students were expected to set a moral example and to serve men in the traditional manner, washing their clothes, serving them meals, and silently listening to them speak. Women's rights advocates Lucy Stone and Antoinette Brown (Blackwell) combated these rules. Stone went so far as to draft a commencement address, which she was forbidden to read. Nonetheless, Oberlin's coeducational experiment influenced religious colleges throughout the Midwest and set an example of reform for many other colleges in the United States.

See also Blackwell, Antoinette Louisa Brown; Education; Stone, Lucy.

O'Connor, Sandra Day (1930–)

Sandra Day O'Connor became the first female associate justice of the U.S. Supreme Court in 1981. Born 26 March 1930, in El Paso, Texas, she attended private girls' schools and later graduated from Austin High School. In 1950 she graduated cum laude from Stanford University with her B.A. in economics; two years later, she received an L.L.B., also from Stanford. She was third in her law class and an editor of the *Stanford Law Review*. In 1952, she married fellow law student John J. O'Connor III, with whom she would raise three sons.

Despite her outstanding academic accomplishments, O'Connor was unable to get a job in a private law firm in the 1950s because of gender discrimination. She applied for many jobs, but her only offer was a job as a legal secretary. Therefore, in 1952–1953, O'Connor worked as the deputy county attorney in San Mateo County, California. From 1954 to 1957 she lived in Frankfurt, Germany, where she worked as a civilian lawyer for the Quartermaster Corps. In 1959 O'Connor opened a law practice in Arizona, and from 1965 to 1969 served as Arizona's assistant attorney general. In 1969 she was appointed to the state senate seat of Senator Isabel A. Burgess, who was selected for a job in Washington, D.C., winning the seat in her own right in 1970 and 1972. In 1972, she became the first female majority

Sandra Day O'Connor

leader in any state senate. She helped to change laws that discriminated against women and voted for the Equal Rights Amendment. In 1975 O'Connor was elected a superior court judge of Maricopa County, Arizona, and four years later Governor Bruce Babbitt appointed her to the Arizona Court of Appeals. In 1981, President Ronald Reagan chose her to be the first female associate justice to the U.S. Supreme Court, replacing Justice Potter Stewart and joining Justice William H. Rehnquist, the valedictorian of O'Connor's Stanford law class.

O'Connor's decisions indicate she is a centrist on many issues. She opposes affirmative action remedies unless there is clear evidence of systematic or intentional discrimination against women or minorities, dissenting in cases such as *United States v. Paradise* (1987), when the Court ordered Alabama to promote an African-American state trooper for every white trooper to compensate for past discrimination. In *Casey v. Pennsylvania* (1992), she is credited with pulling together a moderate majority that kept the Court from overturning *Roe v. Wade.* Since O'Connor joined the Court, it has decided that sexual harassment and stereotyping are illegal forms of gender discrimination, and O'Connor has voted with the majority in these cases. While O'Connor has written that some disparities between men and women are due to women's "late start," others are because of cultural barriers. She writes, "Despite the encouraging and wonderful gains and changes for women that have occurred in my lifetime, there is still room to advance and to promote correction of the remaining deficiencies and balances." A second female associate justice to the Supreme Court—Ruth Bader Ginsburg—was appointed by President Bill Clinton in 1993.

See also Ginsburg, Ruth Bader.

Older Women's League (OWL)

The Older Women's League (OWL), an outgrowth of the Older Women's League Educational Fund (OWLEF), works for reform in the areas of pensions, Social Security, and health insurance—areas in which gender-based inequalities contribute to the increasing impoverishment of elderly women. In 1978 Laurie Shields and Tish Sommers, formerly of the Alliance for Displaced Homemakers, founded OWLEF to investigate and collect data on the concerns of older women. In 1980 they formed the more narrowly focused OWL to deal with those concerns. With chapters nationwide, OWL's headquarters are in Washington,

D.C. OWL's activism was a factor leading to the congressional enactment of several laws in the 1980s to ameliorate the financial condition of older women.

Among these laws was a law that established a precedent, setting guidelines for division of pensions among divorcing couples in which one spouse was a member of the Foreign Service or military; the Retirement Equity Act; and a bill allowing divorcing women to have coverage continued on their husbands' health policies on a short-term basis (if they can pay the premiums).

See also Alliance for Displaced Homemakers/National Displaced Homemakers Network; Retirement Equity Act.

Olsen, Tillie (1912–)

Tillie Lerner was born 14 January 1912 in Omaha, Nebraska, and graduated from high school. She married Jack Olsen in 1936 and would later write one of the most respected works of feminist literary theory, *Silences* (1978), a study of literature and its relation to sex, race, and class. Olsen is also a writer of working-class themes and situations. A Guggenheim Fellow (1975–1976), Olsen has received many awards and honors, including the 1961 O. Henry award for the short story *Tell Me a Riddle* (1961) and honorary degrees from several colleges and universities, including the University of Nebraska. The 1973 edition of Rebecca Harding Davis's *Life in the Iron Mills* (1861), for which Olsen wrote the biographical afterword, was published by The Feminist Press in its series of feminist literary classics. Olsen's titles include *Yonnondio from the Thirties* (1974), *The Word Made Flesh* (1984), and *Mothers to Daughters, That Special Quality* (1989). Olsen lives in California with her husband.

Oneida Community
See Utopian Communities.

Operatives' Magazine
In April 1841, in Lowell, Massachusetts, several young, female textile mill workers

who belonged to an improvement circle headed by the Rev. Thomas Thayer decided to follow the lead of fellow factory workers who had started a magazine called the *Lowell Offering* (1840). The second group called its publication the *Operatives' Magazine*. First edited by Lydia S. Hall and Abba A. Goodard, the latter was written and edited only by women. However, it did not publish exclusively for or about women but requested articles, poems, and essays from operatives of both sexes. In July 1841 the publication changed its name to *Operatives' Magazine and Lowell Album*. In August 1842 it merged with the *Lowell Offering*.

See also Factory System; *Lowell Offering*.

Organization of Pan Asian American Women (Pan Asia)

Formed in 1976, the Organization of Pan Asian Women, known in briefer form as Pan Asia, seeks to strengthen the influence of Asian and Pacific Islands (API) women by giving them a unified voice. Pan Asia tries to fill the legislative void created when the stereotype of the successful Asian caused Asian women's interests to be neglected. In addition to applauding and participating in the most familiar feminist efforts and events, Pan Asia has a number of unique concerns: accurate and distinct census counting for API women; health insurance, language, and other programs for factory workers; and the practice of bringing mail order brides into the United States and the living conditions of those women.

Our Bodies, Ourselves

See Boston Women's Health Book Collective.

Ovington, Mary White (1865–1951)

Mary Ovington, a founder of the National Association for the Advancement of Colored People (NAACP) in 1909, was one of the organization's few white members. She was also one of the few white members of W. E. B. DuBois's Niagara Movement, an African-American organization that was more militant than the NAACP. Born 11 April 1865 in Brooklyn, New York, she attended Packer Collegiate Institute (1888–1891) and Radcliffe College until 1893. That year, the depression forced her to leave college, but she found a job as registrar at Pratt Institute in Brooklyn, and then head social worker at Greenpoint Settlement (1895–1903). In 1903 a speech by Booker T. Washington motivated her to work at another settlement house, Greenwich House. She studied the lives of African Americans in New York City, writing about her work in *Half a Man: The Status of the Negro in New York* (1911). In 1905 she joined the Socialist party. In 1919 she became chairman of the board of the NAACP, a position she held until 1932. That year she resigned the presidency and became treasurer of the organization. Her many contributions to the organization include fund raising, lobbying Congress on such issues as an antilynching bill, and smoothing relations between differing factions. However, perhaps her most important service came in 1923, when she refocused the NAACP toward obtaining federal financial aid for both black and white schools. She worked tirelessly for black women's suffrage, school desegregation, and the end of the occupation of Haiti. Ovington wrote several books and novels, but her most significant work was with the NAACP, from which she retired in 1947. Ovington died 15 July 1951 in Newton Highlands, Massachusetts.

Owen, Robert Dale (1801–1877)

Owen, a political figure, reformer, and U.S. minister to Naples, was an advocate of equality between women and men. Born 9 November 1801 in Scotland, Owen came to the United States with his father (Robert Owen) in 1825. From 1826 to 1827, he helped his father run the socialist New Harmony community in Indiana, returning there briefly in 1848. There, with Frances Wright, whom he accompanied to the Nashoba, Tennessee, community for liberated African Americans the year before, he edited the *New Harmony Gazette*.

In a widely read treatise, *Moral Physiology; Or, a Brief and Plain Treastise on the Population Question* (1830), Owen proposed limiting the size of families. He advocated contraception and "complete withdrawal, on the part of the man, immediately previous to emission." With Wright he launched the *Free Enquirer*, a magazine that advocated more liberal divorce, among other reforms. Owen served as a member of the Indiana house of representatives (1836–1839) and served two terms in the U.S. House of Representatives (1844–1847), where he drafted the bill for the founding of the Smithsonian Institution.

In 1850, Owen was elected a member of the Indiana constitutional convention and was instrumental in securing for married women and widows the right to control their own property, a highly unpopular idea at the time. He made it clear at his wedding that he rejected laws giving him control over his wife's property. In his 1832 marriage contract with Mary Jane Robinson, Owen wrote, "Of the unjust rights which in virtue of this ceremony an iniquitous law tacitly gives me over the person and property of another, I can not legally, but I can morally, divest myself." Owen was responsible for the adoption of a common free school system in Indiana. Owen thought women's status at home as well as their status in society had to be raised, and he remained a staunch advocate of women's equality until his death on 24 June 1877.

See also Birth Control; Coercion; Common Law; Contraception; *Feme Covert*; Utopian Communities; Wright, Frances.

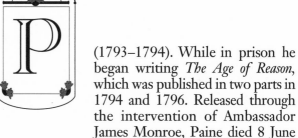

Paine, Thomas (1737–1809)

Thomas Paine, best known as a political leader of the American Revolution and author of the tract *Common Sense*, wrote compassionately about the rights of women at a time when few American intellectuals considered it an important issue. Born 29 January 1737 in Norfolk, England, Paine came to America in 1774. In *An Occasional Letter on the Female Sex* (1775), he surveyed the status of women throughout the world, acknowledging that, in most places, females were severely oppressed by men. According to Paine, if a woman were to state her case without fear to a man, she would say, "How great is your injustice? If we have an equal right with you to virtue, why should we not have an equal right to [public] praise? The public esteem ought to wait upon merit." Most radical intellectuals of the day were, like Paine, principally concerned about the American Revolution, and Paine's *Common Sense* sold 120,000 copies within three months of its publication on 10 January 1776. During the American army's retreat across New Jersey, Paine wrote the famous opening lines of his *Crisis* papers (1776–1783): "These are the times that try men's souls. The summer soldier and the sunshine patriot will, in this crisis, shirk from the service of their country." Read to the revolutionary troops, it revived the spirits of many undecided colonists, including many women who traveled with their male relatives' regiments or cared for homesteads in the men's absence. Paine returned to Europe in 1787. In *Rights of Man* (1791–1792), Paine defended republican government; for this he was tried for treason in England and banned from Great Britain. In 1792 he became a French citizen. One year later the party with which he was allied, the Girondins, fell from power. Paine was stripped of his French citizenship and imprisoned for a year (1793–1794). While in prison he began writing *The Age of Reason*, which was published in two parts in 1794 and 1796. Released through the intervention of Ambassador James Monroe, Paine died 8 June 1809 in New York City.

Park, Maud May Wood (1871–1955)

Maud May Wood Park led the effort to involve young women in the suffrage movement and, after the Nineteenth Amendment was adopted, she became the first president of the League of Women Voters. She was born 25 January 1871 in Boston. After she graduated as valedictorian from her high school in 1887, she taught school to earn money to attend Radcliffe College, which she entered in 1895. At Radcliffe she met her lifelong friend Inez Haynes Gillmore. Both women joined the Massachusetts Woman Suffrage Association (MWSA) when such action was uncommon among students. In 1897 she married Charles Park, but kept the marriage a secret until the following year, when she graduated from Radcliffe summa cum laude.

In 1900 Park was elected to chair the MWSA, and the following year she became executive secretary of the Boston Equal Suffrage Association for Good Government (BESAGG). At a 1900 meeting of the National American Woman Suffrage Association (NAWSA), she found herself the youngest delegate. To attract more young members, she and Gillmore organized the College Equal Suffrage League (CESL). The CESL began as a Massachusetts group, but in 1907 Park resigned from the MWSA to work on the national expansion of the CESL. One year later the NAWSA agreed to support a national CESL. Park became vice-president, a position she held until the group disbanded in 1916.

233

Charles Park had died in 1904; in 1908 Maud Park married Robert Hunter, a marriage that was never made public. After spending 18 months abroad studying women, Park returned to Boston in 1910 to work with BESAGG. In 1917, the year after CESL disbanded, Park went to Washington, D.C., to help implement Carrie Chapman Catt's "Winning Plan," which was a systematic campaign of political action to pressure Washington for a federal suffrage amendment, while at the same time agitating on a state-by-state level.

Three years later Park became the first president of the League of Women Voters (LWV). The league's purpose was to educate new voters, but Park used her position to promote issues of immediate concern to women, such as education and protective legislation for children and working women. As part of the Women's Joint Congressional Committee, the LWV worked for passage of the Sheppard-Towner Act of 1921 and the Cable Act of 1922, which granted married women citizenship independent of their husband's status. Park remained involved in various reform causes until her death on 8 May 1955.

See also Catt, Carrie Clinton Lane Chapman; Irwin, Inez Leonore Haynes Gillmore; National American Woman Suffrage Association.

Parker, Theodore (1810–1860)

Theodore Parker was a theologian, scholar, and author who worked for both abolition and women's suffrage. Born 24 August 1810, Parker graduated from Harvard Divinity School in 1836 and was ordained the following year at the Unitarian Church in West Roxbury, Massachusetts. Parker believed that women should participate in public affairs, a point he made best in "A Sermon of the Public Function of Women—Preached at the Music Hall, March 27, 1853." In this speech, Parker said that men and women have gender-based characteristics to bring to family, community, church, and state, but "[b]y nature, woman has the same political rights that man has—to vote, to hold office, to make and administer laws. These she has as a

matter of right." Parker believed that, in some respects, women would exercise such rights in a more humane and moral manner than men would.

Among Parker's other reform activities was abolition. He wrote *A Letter to the People of the United States Touching on the Matter of Slavery* (1848), among other works, and secretly supported John Brown's raid at Harpers Ferry. Parker's health deteriorated in 1857 and in 1859 he retired from public life, traveling to Europe. He died 10 May 1860 in Florence, Italy.

Parton, Sarah Willis Payson (1811–1872)

Sarah Willis Payson Parton, who used the pseudonym Fanny Fern, was a leader in journalism in the United States and one of America's first female columnists. She was born Grata Payson in Portland, Maine, on 9 July 1811. Educated at Catharine Beecher's Seminary in Hartford, Connecticut, she became the country's first newspaper columnist and among the highest paid journalists of her day. She also authored the best-selling novel *Ruth Hall*. Fern originated the epigram "The way to a man's heart is through his stomach" but also wrote about serious, controversial subjects such as venereal disease, prostitution, prison reform, contraception, and divorce. As a columnist for the *New York Ledger*, she favored progressive issues such as children's rights. After the death of her first husband in 1846, she remarried in 1849, leaving her second husband after three years. In 1856, Fern, by now a celebrity, married biographer James Parton, who was 11 years her junior, and their marriage was a long one. Fern died 10 October 1872 in New York City. According to her biographer, Joyce W. Warren, she has been lost to history because of society's ambivalence toward "the aggressive assertions of the female voice."

Pastoral Letter

In 1837, the Congregational ministerial association of Massachusetts issued a pastoral letter that condemned Angelina and Sarah

Grimké for speaking against slavery to mixed audiences of men and women. The letter described the sisters as unnatural, declaring "If the vine, whose strength and beauty it is to lean up on the trelliswork, and help conceal its clusters, thinks to assume the independence and the overshadowing nature of the elm, it will not only cease to bear fruit, but fall in shame and dishonor into the dust." The pastoral letter, citing the New Testament, set the tone for antifeminist writing in the nineteenth century. After its publication some churches closed their doors to the Grimkés, and it became more difficult for them to rent halls. Nevertheless the Grimkés continued to lecture throughout New England, with free speech, freedom of assembly, and women's rights as their key topics.

Paul, Alice (1885–1977)

Alice Paul, a pivotal figure in the passage of both the Nineteenth Amendment and the Equal Rights Amendment, is credited with introducing militant measures to the U.S. women's suffrage movement. She was frequently involved in hunger strikes and pickets, and was one of a group of women who were the first U.S. citizens to claim political prisoner status.

Born 11 January 1885 in Moorestown, New Jersey, Paul was a Quaker who attended private schools as a child, and graduated from Swarthmore College in 1905. In 1906, she did graduate work at the New School of Philanthropy, then went to England, where she did settlement work. While in England, Paul participated in several women's suffrage demonstrations organized by suffragist leader Emmeline Pankhust; Paul was arrested and imprisoned three times. Continuing her graduate studies at the University of Birmingham and the University of London, she received a master of arts in absentia from the University of Pennsylvania in 1907. After her return to the United States, she earned a Ph.D. at the University of Pennsylvania (1912).

Paul chaired the congressional committee of the National American Woman Suffrage Association (NAWSA) in 1912. In 1913, she and other radical members of that committee founded the Congressional Union for Woman Suffrage, which would use more militant tactics in the pursuit of a federal suffrage amendment rather than organize on a state-by-state level, as was NAWSA's method at the time. That year, the two organizations came to Washington, D.C., meeting with Mary Beard and Crystal Eastman, and planned a march of 5,000 women for the day before President Woodrow Wilson's inauguration. When Wilson reached Washington the streets were bare; he was told the people were out watching the suffrage parade. Paul chaired the national Congressional Union until 1917, when the Congressional Union merged with the Woman's Party to form the National Woman's Party (NWP). Paul served as chair of the national executive committee of the NWP from 1917 to 1921, remaining a dominant presence in the organization for 30 years.

Beginning 17 January 1917, Paul and Lucy Burns led the NWP's famous picket of the White House, which lasted for many months. Beginning in June, NWP members were regularly arrested for obstructing traffic. Paul and 96 other suffragists were found guilty and served up to six months in Virginia's infamous Occoquan workhouse. The women were held in solitary confinement, and when Alice Paul, Burns, and Dorothy Day refused to eat, they were force-fed. Rose Winslow wrote, "The women are so magnificent, so beautiful. Alice Paul is as thin as ever, pale and large-eyed."

On scraps of paper some of the women wrote a document in which they claimed political prisoner status, managing to pass it from woman to woman for signing. It was the first time any U.S. citizen had claimed such status. Although the District of Columbia Court of Appeals found the arrests invalid in 1918, it never responded to the women's claim of political imprisonment.

After ratification of the Nineteenth Amendment in 1920, Paul earned several law degrees, including one from the Washington College of Law (1922). She also

Alice Paul toasts a success at the Washington, D.C., headquarters of the National Suffrage Association.

earned further master's (1927) and doctorate (1928) degrees from American University. She continued to agitate for women's rights. Through her efforts an equal rights amendment was introduced in Congress in 1923, but it, like its many successors, was defeated. Some historians credit Paul with passage of the Equal Rights Amendment in 1970. The ERA, though approved by Congress, failed to be ratified by the states.

In addition to domestic concerns, Paul advocated an international equal rights treaty; from 1927 to 1937 she chaired the Woman's Research Foundation and from 1930 to 1933 she served on the Nationality Committee of the Inter-American Commission of Women. Paul was a member of the Women's Consultative Committee on Nationality of the League of Nations, a founder of the World's Women's Party (also called the World Party for Equal Rights for Women), and was an instrumental voice in persuading the framers of the United Nations charter to include a reference to sexual equality in the charter's preamble. Paul stubbornly believed that wars occurred because women were denied representation in the political process, specifically arguing that World War II might not have happened had women been allowed to participate in the Versailles peace conference. One of the most respected leaders of the women's rights movement, Paul died 10 July 1977 in Moorestown.

See also Beard, Mary; Burns, Lucy; Catt, Carrie Clinton Lane Chapman; Congressional Union for Woman Suffrage; Equal Rights Amendment; National Woman's Party; Nineteenth Amendment; Protective Legislation.

Pay Equity
See Comparable Worth.

Pennsylvania Divorce Statute of 1785
The Pennsylvania Divorce Statute of 1785 granted more options for separation and divorce than any other law at the time. The law allowed married women who were separated from their husbands to receive ali-

mony, but husbands who were granted absolute divorce had no further obligations. Men and women could obtain divorce for adultery, four-year desertion, bigamy, sexual incapacity, and, in some circumstances, cruelty. The law reflected the general trend toward more liberal divorce laws after the American Revolution.

See also Divorce.

People v. Belous
Even before the 1973 *Roe v. Wade* Supreme Court decision legalized abortion nationwide, some states decided to adopt abortion laws that were somewhat more liberalized than existing laws. California was one such state. The *People v. Belous* decision in 1969 was one in which the California Supreme Court threw out the state's old (more restrictive) abortion law, thereby strengthening abortion rights. The court ruled that marriage and reproductive privacy rights should be free from state interference. Moreover, the ruling allowed physicians, in deciding whether to permit an abortion, to weigh the risks of childbirth against those of an early abortion; because early abortions are safer than childbirth, the law indirectly justified all early-term abortions. The comments made by the justices in their opinions even appeared to indicate that the reformed law was not liberal enough. All of this increased public confidence in the legality of abortion and thus made safe abortion in California easier to obtain. (Also, with more facilities willing to perform abortions, greater competition resulted, and this in turn made abortions more affordable.) *Belous* was an important pre-*Roe* victory for abortion rights.

See also *Doe v. Bolton; Roe v. Wade.*

Perkins, Frances Coralie (1882–1965)
Frances Perkins was the first female secretary of labor and the first female member of a U.S. president's cabinet. She was born 10 April 1882 in Boston. She attended public schools in Worcester, Massachusetts, and was a 1902 graduate of Mount Holyoke

College. After graduating she taught intermittently before accepting a full-time position teaching biology and physics in Lake Forest, Illinois. She volunteered at Hull House in Chicago, working with Jane Addams. Later resuming her studies at the Wharton School of Finance and Commerce of the University of Pennsylvania and at

Frances Perkins

Columbia University, she received an M.A. from the latter institution in 1910. That year Perkins also became executive secretary of the Consumers' League of New York, holding this position for two years. Under the leadership of Maud Nathan, she directed studies of labor conditions of women and children. She helped to secure passage of New York's 1912 law mandating the 54-hour workweek and championed workers' health and safety laws. Perkins also worked on behalf of women's suffrage. Park was executive secretary of the New York Committee on Safety (1912–1917) and executive director of the New York Council of Or-

ganization for War Service (1917–1919). In 1919, Governor Alfred E. Smith appointed Perkins to New York's State Industrial Commission, making her the first woman to hold the position. With a salary of $8,000, she was the highest paid state employee. In 1923 Perkins served on the State Industrial Board (formerly Industrial Commission), becoming its chair in 1926. Governor Smith's successor, Franklin D. Roosevelt, appointed Perkins the state's industrial commissioner in 1929. When he became president, Roosevelt named her secretary of labor. It was a controversial appointment because of her gender, but Perkins served for 12 years. Among her many achievements as secretary of labor were the Social Security Act, Federal Relief Act, Fair Labor Standards Act, and National Industrial Recovery Act. She left the cabinet in 1945 but was later appointed by President Harry S Truman to the Civil Service Commission (1946–1953). Her books are *People at Work* (1934) and *The Roosevelt I Knew* (1946). Perkins died 14 May 1965 in New York City.

See also Addams, Jane; Camp Jane Addams; Fair Labor Standards Act; Hobby, Oveta Culp; Nathan, Maud; Protective Legislation.

Personnel Administrator of Massachusetts v. Feeney

In *Personnel Administrator of Massachusetts v. Feeney* (1979), the Supreme Court upheld a Massachusetts law giving veterans, most of whom were male, an advantage when applying for civil service jobs. Because there were few female veterans, women as a group were at a disadvantage and all of the high civil service positions in Massachusetts were filled with male veterans, who made up one-fourth of the state's total population. Helen Feeney, who was not a veteran, repeatedly failed to be hired for civil service jobs even though she had impressive scores (second or third in the state) on civil service exams. Despite its indirect detrimental effect on women, the Supreme Court upheld the law, citing the lack of evidence that it was intended to discriminate against women. *Personnel Administrator of Massachusetts v. Feeney* shows how even gender-neutral laws can harm women, but also illustrates the new willingness of women to challenge such discriminatory laws.

Petitions

Petitions did not exist as a political tool for women before the 1770s. But, in 1774, amid growing numbers of female Anti-Tea Leagues, whose members refused to buy or drink "the pestillent herb" as a symbol of American resistance, 51 women in Edenton, North Carolina, announced they would no longer buy tea or cloth from Britain. They drew up a document, called the Edenton Proclamation, asserting that they had a right and duty to participate in the political events of their time, a refreshing idea at a time when women had few political rights of any sort. Their act met with much ridicule in England.

By the 1830s circulating petitions had become commonplace among female reformers, especially those in antislavery societies. Their effectiveness was unmistakably demonstrated in the 1834 campaign to abolish slavery in Washington, D.C. William Lloyd Garrison's American Anti-Slavery Society initiated the petition drive. The drive was phenomenally successful; hundreds of petitions flooded Congress. In response, southern congressmen effectively denied citizens the right to petition Congress about slavery by passing a series of resolutions, called Gag Rules, which required all petitions relating to slavery to be laid on a table without being referred to committee or printed. The first of these resolutions, passed in 1836, was the Pinckney Resolution, named for its sponsor, Henry Pinckney of South Carolina. This resolution was readopted at each succeeding session of Congress until it was repealed in 1844.

Congressman John Quincy Adams, the 70-year-old former president, raised the first opposition to the gag rule. At first he simply defended the right of his own constituents to petition Congress. When word of his sympathy spread, antislavery petitions from across the North flooded his desk. A great number of these petitions came from female antislavery societies. Congressman Howard of Maryland argued that the departure of the female petitioners from their proper domestic sphere discredited not only the North but the entire nation. Women had no right to petition because they had no right to vote, Howard said.

As Adams would later recall in his "Speech . . . Upon the Rights of the People, Men and Women, to Petition" (1838),

> [Congressman Howard] . . . thought that these females could have a sufficient field for the exercise of their influence in the discharge of their duties to their fathers, their husbands or their children, cheering the domestic circle and shedding over it the mild radiance of the social virtues, instead of rushing into the fierce struggles of political life. He felt sorrow at this departure from their proper sphere. . . .

Over a period of four days (26–30 June 1834), Adams delivered a series of speeches reminding the House of women's role in the American Revolution and asking why women could not engage in politics or vote. Although only a small group of congressmen initially supported Adams, by 1844 the gag rules were abolished.

By 1837 systematic petitioning was the prevailing antislavery activity, in large part because of the great number of women in the movement and the fact that it was the only method of political expression open to them. Boxes in the National Archives in Washington, D.C. hold thousands of antislavery petitions, yellowed, patched together, and laboriously collected.

Petitioning became popular among feminists campaigning for women's rights. In 1836 Ernestine Rose had circulated a petition asking the New York legislature to enact a law expanding married women's property rights. In *History of Woman Suffrage* (Volume I) she recalled,

> I sent the first petition to the New York State Legislature to give a married

239

woman the right to hold real estate in her own name, in the winter of 1836 and '37 to which after a great deal of trouble I obtained five signatures. Some of the ladies said the gentlemen would laugh at them; others, that they had rights enough; and the men said the women had too many rights already.... I continued sending petitions with increased numbers of signatures until 1848 and '49, when the Legislature enacted the law which granted women the right to keep what was their own. But no sooner did it become legal than all the wom[e]n said: "Oh! that is right! We ought always to have had that!"

Susan B. Anthony headed a famous petition drive for women's rights in 1855. Her petition urged that women be allowed to assume custody of their children in case of divorce, control their own earnings, and vote. Anthony left home on Christmas Day 1854 with $50 in her pocket. Alone, she traveled New York State to gather petitions asking the legislature to extend the Married Woman's Property Act of 1848. She made her own traveling arrangements at a time when women who traveled alone might be refused service in a dining room. In the 1850s couples traveling by train ate separately. Men would leave the train and go into the station to eat a hot meal, while women remained in the car with cold food they brought from home. Anthony was one of the few women of her day who would leave the train and walk up and down the platform for exercise. Holding her first meeting in Mayville, Chautauqua County, she noted in her expense journal: "56 cents for four pounds of candles to light the courthouse." It was one of the snowiest winters on record. Snow blocked the roads and chilled Anthony's feet. At times she had to be helped onto the stage from which she gave her speech, often to people who had never heard a woman speak publicly before. Many towns were some distance from the railroad and could be reached only by sleigh. After a long trip, Anthony would arrive in

an unheated room and have to break the ice in a pitcher in order to bathe. Despite many hardships, Anthony held a meeting every other day, gathering signatures at each of them.

By 1 May 1855, she had organized the canvassing of 54 counties. On February 1856 she presented her petitions to the state legislature. The petitions were referred to the state senate's judiciary committee, chaired by the distinguished lawyer Samuel G. Foote. He scoffed at them. In a notorious statement received with "roars of laughter," according to the *Albany Register*, he quipped,

The Committee is composed of married and single gentlemen. The bachelors, with becoming diffidence, have left the subject pretty much to the married gentlemen. They have considered with the aid of the light they have before them and the experience married life has given them. Thus aided, they are enabled to state that the ladies always have the best place and choicest tidbit at the table. They have the best seat in the cars, carriages and sleighs; the warmest place in winter and the coolest place in summer. They have their choice on which side of the bed they will lie, front or back. A lady's dress costs three times as much as that of a gentleman; and at the present time, with the prevailing fashion, one lady occupies three times as much space in the world as a gentleman. It has thus appeared to the married gentlemen of your committee . . . that if there is an inequality of oppression in this case, the gentlemen are the sufferers.

The petitions failed to move the lawmakers, but the women persevered. In 1857 the New York Married Woman's Property Act was amended, and in 1860 it was expanded again.

See also Abolition Movement; Adams, John Quincy; Anthony, Susan B.; Daughters of Liberty; Female Antislavery Societies; Married Women's Property Acts; New York Married Woman's Property Act (1848); New York Married Woman's Property Act (1860); Rose, Ernestine.

Philadelphia Female Anti-Slavery Society

In 1833 Lucretia Mott and several other women founded the Philadelphia Female Anti-Slavery Society after being excluded from full participation in the American Anti-Slavery Association because of their sex. (The women were allowed to attend meetings and speak publicly from the floor but not to join the association.) Unsure of their organizational skills, the women asked a freedman to chair their first meeting.

From 1833 to 1870 the society worked to abolish slavery and to aid freed men and women. Perhaps the first women's political organization in America, the group's members included Lucretia Mott, Sarah Grimké, Angelina Grimké, and other advocates of abolition and equal rights for women. Following its lead, other female antislavery societies were formed across the country. The interracial group disbanded after the passage of the Fourteenth Amendment in 1868.

See also American Anti-Slavery Society; Female Antislavery Societies; Mott, Lucretia; Petitions.

Phillips v. Martin-Marietta Corp.

Phillips v. Martin-Marietta Corp. (1971) was the first case dealing with the sex discrimination aspect of Title VII of the 1964 Civil Rights Act to reach the U.S. Supreme Court. Ida Phillips could not get a job as a trainee at Martin-Marietta because she had small children. Company policy was not to consider young mothers for certain positions. The underlying principle of this policy came to be known as the sex-plus theory. Under the sex-plus theory, gender alone was insufficient to deny a woman a job, but gender plus another factor was sufficient reason to do so. Based on this reasoning, the federal district court (Maryland, Florida) and the U.S. Court of Appeals for the Fifth Circuit upheld the company policy. The Supreme Court objected to the sex-plus theory. It ruled that the company could not have different hiring policies for men and women and could not add distinctions based on sex. In other words, the company could not refuse to hire mothers of small children unless it also refused to hire fathers of small children. Although it struck down the sex-plus theory, the Court angered women's rights groups by leaving open the possibility that sex might be considered a bona fide occupational qualification if parenting could be shown to have a lesser impact on a man's job performance than on a woman's.

See also Bona Fide Occupational Qualification; Title VII of the 1964 Civil Rights Act.

Piecework

The piecework, or price-rate, system, coupled with the sexual division of labor, made women the cheapest laborers in the United States in 1900. Most female factory workers were paid by the piece, in place of weekly wages. One consequence was that working women in the late nineteenth and early twentieth century earned one-third to one-half what men did. Few women dared to challenge their employers when the time came to compute payment. A woman might hand in 20 items but be paid for only 15. She might be fined for flawed work, tardiness, talking, or even laughing. Fines for less than perfect work ran 300 to 400 percent above the cost of material. Some industries charged women for their supplies and even the electricity used. Nonetheless piecework enabled some mothers to work from home and contribute income that was indispensable to a working-class family's support.

See also Home Industry; Pin Money; Sexual Division of Labor.

Pierce, Sarah (1767–1852)

Sarah Pierce was an early educator of women. Born 26 June 1767 in Litchfield, Connecticut, she attended schools in her home town and in New York City. In 1792 she started a small school in Litchfield, teaching composition, geography, history, needlework, painting, and dance, and encouraging physical exercise. By 1798 word of her school was so widespread that the town bought her a building, which was eventually incorporated into the nationally recognized Litchfield Female Academy (1827).

Between 1811 and 1818 Pierce produced four textbooks in a series entitled *Sketches of Universal History Compiled from Several Authors. For the Use of Schools.* In 1814 Pierce hired her nephew, John B. Brace, to teach logic, philosophy, and the sciences. In 1825 Pierce made Brace principal of the school. She continued to teach history until she retired in 1833. The academy, which at its peak enrolled 130 students, closed in 1842. With Tapping Reeve's famous Litchfield Law School, it made the town a center of education in America. Pierce died 19 January 1852 in Litchfield.

See also Education; Reeve, Tapping.

Pin Money

In the nineteenth and early twentieth centuries, employers viewed men as the principal wage earners in their families. Employers justified paying women less than men by claiming that women worked only for pin money, or money to buy nonessential items. Yet many families relied on the wives' or daughters' incomes to buy necessities, and single women had no other income to rely on. The idea that women were amply provided for and worked only for pleasure or a little extra spending money implied that women were not serious, steady workers. This view of female workers undermined efforts to win wage increases and better treatment in the workplace and may have contributed to the reluctance to organize women workers on the part of major labor unions, which may have feared that to do so would appear to trivialize their efforts and destroy their credibility. Evidence to the contrary was presented in various studies, including studies by the labor department's Women's Bureau. Nevertheless, the belief persisted and was even sanctioned by other government reports. Even during the second wave of twentieth-century feminism (beginning in the 1960s), feminists tended to emphasize women's right to seek employment *as a form of self-fulfillment*, which, although legitimate, did little to counter the notion that women do not need to work out of sheer financial necessity. In the late 1970s, there was recognition of the phenomenon of the "feminization of poverty," that is, that poor adults were mostly women, and that there appeared to be a link between single motherhood and the impoverishment of women; the recognition of this problem may have had, ironically, the illuminating effect of demonstrating the fact that many women needed their jobs to pay basic living expenses.

See also Feminization of Poverty.

Pinckney, Elizabeth Lucas (1722–1793)

Elizabeth Lucas Pinckney experimented with and eventually produced indigo on her South Carolina plantation. She was born 28 December 1722, in the West Indies and came to the colonies with her family in 1738. In 1739 the management of the family's plantation passed to her, and she began experimenting with various crops. In 1739 she recorded in her journal the results of her trials with indigo, ginger, cotton, and other plants. She continued to experiment for several years, until by 1744 she had grown a fine crop of indigo, six pounds of which were sent to England. The dye made from American indigo was better than that made from the French indigo plant. In addition, the British resented having to purchase indigo from the French islands. These two factors combined to create a market for American indigo in England. Indigo seed was distributed to other growers as well. In 1776 South Carolina planters shipped 40,000 pounds of the plant to England; in 1777 they exported 100,000 pounds. For the next 30 years, indigo sales sustained the colony's economy. An avid and cultivated letter writer, Pinckney's collection of letters is one of the largest of the period. After her marriage to Charles Pinckney (1744), she reared the couple's four children and managed seven estates. She died 26 May 1793 in Philadelphia, where she had gone to seek treatment for cancer. Her death was widely mourned, and George Washington was a pallbearer at her funeral.

Pitcher, Molly
See McCauley, Mary Ludwig Hays.

Pittsburgh Press v. Human Relations Commission
Pittsburgh Press v. Human Relations Commission ended the practice of running sex-segregated want ads in newspapers. In 1969, the Pittsburgh Human Relations Commission issued an administrative order that forbade sex discrimination, at the urging of future National Organization for Women (NOW) president Wilma Scott Heide. NOW had been on a campaign against sex segregation of want ads since the time of its founding, and in October 1969 the local NOW chapter used the ordinance as the basis for a lawsuit against the *Pittsburgh Press* over the want ads issue. In 1973 the case reached the Supreme Court, where the justices assumed that segregated ads could only lead to discriminatory hiring practices. The Court upheld the city's order on the grounds that it is not unconstitutional to prevent the *Press* from contributing in advance to an illegal situation.

Planned Parenthood Federation of America (PPFA)
In 1942 the American Birth Control League changed its name to Planned Parenthood Federation of America (PPFA) in the belief that the new name would be more acceptable to the public. At the same time, the group began to expand its activities beyond distributing contraceptive information.

In 1948 representatives from more than 20 nations attended the International Conference on Population and World Resources in Relation to the Family, which led to the formation of the International Planned Parenthood Committee. At a 1952 conference in Bombay, India, PPFA helped launch the International Planned Parenthood Federation (IPPF) to promote birth control around the world. In 1972 PPFA established its own international division, Family Planning International Assistance (FPIA), which became the largest U.S. nongovernmental provider of family planning services to developing countries. In 1984 the administration of President Ronald Reagan announced the "Mexico City policy," which would bar nongovernmental foreign recipients of U.S. governmental family planning funds from using private funds to support abortion. The policy, which became effective in 1985, met resistance from the PPFA, which refused to comply and joined a lawsuit against the U.S. Agency for International Development in 1986. That year the U.S. District Court for the Southern District overturned the Mexico City policy. In 1987 President Reagan proposed a gag rule that prevented federally funded clinics from discussing abortion with a client, which rule the PPFA opposed in *Rust v. Sullivan* (1991). In that case, the gag rule was upheld.

Today, PPFA offers help with abortion, infertility, birth control, sterilization, menopause, and other areas of male and female reproductive health. It also supports medical and demographic research.

See also American Birth Control League; National Birth Control League; *Planned Parenthood of Central Missouri v. Danforth; Planned Parenthood of Southeastern Pennsylvania v. Casey*; Sanger, Margaret.

Planned Parenthood of Central Missouri v. Danforth
The 1976 Supreme Court ruling in *Planned Parenthood of Central Missouri v. Danforth* found a number of provisions in a Missouri abortion statute to be unconstitutional. These provisions required that parents consent to abortions performed on unmarried minors and that spouses consent to abortions performed on married women; outlawed saline abortions; and required that physicians attempt to preserve the life of any fetus, including a nonviable fetus. The decision was viewed as a victory for abortion-rights activists, although the Court did uphold the less burdensome provisions of the Missouri law, including a requirement

243

that women sign a written consent for an abortion, a vague definition of the viability of a fetus, and record keeping requirements.

See also Planned Parenthood of Southeastern Pennsylvania v. Casey; Webster v. Reproductive Health Services.

Planned Parenthood of Southeastern Pennsylvania v. Casey

On 19 June 1992, in the case of *Planned Parenthood of Southeastern Pennsylvania v. Casey*, the Supreme Court, while reaffirming the essence of the constitutional right to abortion established by *Roe v. Wade* (1973), permitted Pennsylvania to impose restrictions on a woman seeking an abortion. These restrictions, created by the state's Abortion Control Act, included a 24-hour waiting period, presentation of material intended to change a woman's mind, and the permission of one parent or a judge for girls under 18. The law also required doctors to submit statistical reports to the state. In a five-to-four decision, the Court affirmed that *Roe v. Wade* established a "rule of law and a component of liberty we cannot renounce." However, in upholding the law, the Court applied for the first time a new standard that considers whether a state regulation imposes an undue burden on women seeking an abortion. In applying this standard, the court said a state must not construct a "substantial obstacle in the path of a woman seeking an abortion before the fetus attains viability." The Court struck down the part of the Pennsylvania law that required a married woman seeking an abortion to notify her husband but let the other restrictions stand. Justice Sandra Day O'Connor, reading the joint decision, said, "Our obligation is to define the liberty of all, not to mandate our own moral code." The decision, a disappointment to some, came as a relief to others who feared the high court might have used the case to overturn completely *Roe v. Wade.*

See also O'Connor, Sandra Day; Planned Parenthood of Central Missouri v. Danforth; Webster v. Reproductive Health Services.

Plath, Sylvia (1932–1963)

Poet Sylvia Plath has come to be hailed as a prophet of the women's liberation movement. She was born 27 August 1932 in Boston. Plath published her first poem at the age of eight, the year that her father died of complications from the amputation of his leg. Her mother moved the family to Wellesley, Massachusetts, to live with her parents. In 1950, after graduating from Bradford High School, Sylvia entered Smith College as a scholarship student. In 1953 she spent one month in New York as editor at *Mademoiselle*, but instead of the period being a joyous experience for the young perfectionist, it left Plath depressed. After she returned home she attempted suicide and underwent psychiatric hospitalization. Plath was able to return to Smith in 1954, where the next year she graduated summa cum laude. She soon received a Fulbright fellowship to study at Newnham College in Cambridge, England.

In Cambridge Plath met the working-class English poet Ted Hughes. They were married in 1956, envisioning a partnership dedicated to the service of poetry. The following year the couple came to the United States where Plath taught at Smith and Hughes at the University of Massachusetts. It was during this time that Plath, with Anne Sexton and other young poets, enrolled in poetry seminars given by Robert Lowell at the University of Massachusetts. While teaching in the United States, however, Plath and Hughes concluded that academic life interfered with their writing.

In 1959 Hughes and Plath returned to England, where the following year Plath gave birth to a daughter, Frieda Rebecca, and also published her first book of poetry, *The Colossus*. In 1961 the family moved to Devon, and Plath received a grant to work on *The Bell Jar*, her only novel, which she published under the pseudonym Victoria Lucas. The novel is largely autobiographical in nature and deals with the efforts of its young heroine to avert compulsive suicidal tendencies. In January 1962 she gave birth to a son, Nicholas Farrar, and in the months that followed wrote a verse-play, *Three Women.*

In July of that same year, Plath learned that Hughes was having an adulterous relationship with Assia Wevill, and when he left her in October, Plath became enraged, unable to eat or sleep and running high fevers. It was during this period of intense emotional turmoil that Plath, in the space of about eight months, wrote the poems on which her reputation rests. As divorce proceedings progressed, she produced "Stings," "Daddy," "Mystic," "Edge," and other poems of unusual intensity, imagination, and forcefulness.

In December 1962 Plath and her children moved to the William Butler Yeats house of Fitzroy Road, London. There, on 11 February 1963, she committed suicide by inhaling the gas inside her oven; her preparations included sealing off the openings of her children's bedroom and leaving them a plate of bread and mugs of milk. Eight months later, ten of her poems were published in *Encounter* magazine to widespread acclaim. Two years later, her late poems were collected in the book *Ariel.* Several additional volumes of Plath's poetry were published posthumously, including *Crossing the Water* (1971), *Winter Trees* (1972), and *Selected Poems* (1985), edited by Hughes. Plath's reputation has steadily grown, stimulating numerous biographies, collections, and critical studies. Approximately one-third of Plath's journals lie in the Neilson Library at Smith College.

Policewomen

A career as a policewoman was difficult to achieve before the early twentieth century. Most people felt that to work successfully as a law enforcement officer, a candidate must be well above average in height and physical strength. This view eliminated most female applicants, but the view has been proven false throughout the years.

Women began working in police departments as early as 1776, most of them holding positions as matrons or "gaolers." In 1845 New York was the first state to hire a woman

as a prison matron. Marie Owens, a widow of a police officer, became a member of Chicago's police force in 1893. Although she held the post for more than 30 years, she was never officially sworn in on the force. The first woman to be officially sworn in as a police officer was Alice Stebbins Wells, in Los Angeles, California, on 10 September 1910.

By 1912 three other women were sworn in on the Los Angeles force. Wells made a six-month national speaking tour on the subject of women and law enforcement. Her appearances were evidently influential, because by 1918, more than 200 city police forces had hired women.

In 1930 Massachusetts became the first state to hire female state troopers. In the late 1950s, Miami, Florida, was the first city to hire female plainclothes detectives. In 1971 the Secret Service hired its first female agents and the following year the FBI hired its first female agent.

By 1970 there were nearly 6,000 women working in law enforcement positions, but there was a major discrepancy. Only 135 of them were assigned to the same duties as the male officers. Most women officers were assigned to cases involving women or children. During the 1970s Congress passed anti–sex discrimination laws that helped women achieve full-fledged law enforcement postings throughout the country, and by 1978, 9,000 female officers held such positions, performing regular police duties in the same manner as male officers. Federal Bureau of Justice figures for 1992 tallied 53,577 female law enforcement officers—excluding federal and special police officers—which represented about 10 percent of the total force.

Many women police officers still encounter prejudice. In recent accomplishments, however, the Texas Rangers permitted women to apply for positions on their esteemed crime-fighting force. In June 1993 the Texas Department of Public Safety announced that Cheryl Campbell Steadman, 32, and Marie Reynolds Garcia, 38, would be the newest Texas Rangers. They are the first women to become Rangers.

Opportunities for women to become police chiefs also exist. Mary F. Rabadeau was named chief of police in Elizabeth, New Jersey, in December 1992, the first woman to head a major police department in the state of New Jersey.

Pregnancy Discrimination Act (PDA)

The Pregnancy Discrimination Act (PDA), enacted in 1978, identifies discrimination based on pregnancy as a type of sex discrimination and requires that pregnancy be treated by employers as a temporary disability. Before the act was passed, pregnant women were frequently fired or demoted, or they lost their seniority. The act was passed under pressure from women's groups and other groups that were enraged by the 1976 Supreme Court decision in *General Electric Co. v. Gilbert*. In that case, the Court ruled that pregnancy discrimination was not a type of sex discrimination. The PDA, which was an amendment to Title VII of the 1964 Civil Rights Act, did not force companies to grant maternity leaves or provide maternity benefits.

See also Title VII of the 1964 Civil Rights Act.

President's Commission on the Status of Women

The President's Commission on the Status of Women, created 14 December 1961 by President John F. Kennedy, represented the U.S. government's first attempt to deal with women's issues since the passage of the suffrage amendment in 1920. Its purpose was to study conditions that interfered with women's rights. The commission comprised 13 women and 11 men from public and private spheres and was headed by former first lady Eleanor Roosevelt. Despite her limited support for the Kennedy administration, Roosevelt served as head of the commission until her death in November 1962.

Roosevelt's friend, Esther Peterson, was the commission's executive vice-president, and she was responsible for most of its undertakings. Peterson had been a Kennedy campaign worker and labor lobbyist, and had been appointed by Kennedy to head the labor department's Women's Bureau. One factor that led Kennedy to create the commission was a 1957 study by the National Manpower Council, titled *Womanpower*, which suggested that women were an underused resource. Another factor was Peterson's urging. Some historians have suggested that political considerations also motivated Kennedy. By creating the commission he could expand support among women voters and compensate individual women who had campaigned for him but were not appointed to important political posts. In addition, by delegating the issue of women (and, by extension, the issue of an equal rights amendment) to a commission, Kennedy could extricate himself from a difficult position between two groups of supporters—women and labor, which opposed an equal rights amendment.

The commission's proposals were released 11 October 1963 in a report, *American Women*. The proposals were not far-reaching, reflecting a desire by members of the commission to maintain women's homemaking role to some extent. But the report undeniably contributed to a climate favorable to women's activism. *American Women* included recommendations from seven committees on the topics of civil and political rights, education, federal employment, private employment, home and community, Social Security and taxes, and protective labor legislation. The commission also identified four areas of study in which it would seek the input of outsiders: private employment opportunity, new patterns of volunteer work, portrayal of women by the mass media, and the problems of African-American women.

American Women did not contain all of the recommendations provided by the commission's committees. Instead the report adopted a moderate tone to avoid immediate political rejection. The report cited statistics without analysis and made only extremely specific recommendations. Reports of individual committees—which also were made public—offered more detail and analysis and were more militant than the commission's report. By releasing both the general report and the committee reports, the commission made available a considerable body of information and feminist opinion.

Two of the commission's recommendations were enacted during its life span. The first was the opening of high-level positions in the federal government to women. This was achieved through a 1962 presidential directive that reversed an interpretation of an 1870 law that had been used to exclude women from such jobs. The second was the Equal Pay Act (1963).

The commission recognized the challenges facing women in the area of employment opportunites and made specific suggestions for combating discrimination, but advocated a moderate approach. The commission suggested that Kennedy issue an executive order endorsing equal opportunity for women in employment, but it advocated avoiding active enforcement in favor of relying on employers to cooperate. The commission refused to equate sexual and racial discrimination, declaring that women and minority groups faced obstacles of a different nature (perhaps reflecting the philosophy of the *Womanpower* report, which stressed women's potential usefulness and refused to recognize their status as victims of discrimination).

The commission intensely scrutinized state and federal laws dealing with women (for example, marriage, property rights, child custody, Social Security, and jury service). It favored maintaining state protective legislation, such as that regulating hours and working conditions. The commission also suggested that government enact legislation to prevent states from making women ineligible for jury service; remove laws prohibiting married women from owning property, conducting business, and controlling their income; and recognize the full value of homemaking and raising children. The commission declared that an equal rights amendment to the Constitution was not necessary because other amendments to the Constitution could be used to achieve equality and that the latter alternative offered flexibility in dealing with women's issues. The commission recommended counseling for girls to encourage them to explore nontraditional roles. It suggested that child care be available to families at all income levels and that working mothers' child care expenditures be tax-deductible. The commission suggested two types of government bodies that could be formed to advance women's rights farther: the Citizens' Advisory Council on the Status of Women and the State Commissions on the Status of Women. The commission's contribution to the formation of these bodies, particularly the state commissions, is widely regarded as its greatest achievement.

See also Citizens' Advisory Council on the Status of Women; Equal Pay Act; *Womanpower.*

President's Task Force on Women's Rights and Responsibilities
See A Matter of Simple Justice.

Price Rate.
See Piecework.

Professional Women's Caucus (PWC)
The Professional Women's Caucus (PWC) was created 11 April 1970 at a conference of academic and professional women held in New York City. Dr. Jo-Ann Evans Garner, a behavioral scientist, and Doris Sassower, an attorney, organized the conference to bring together women from various fields to discuss ways to improve the condition of women. They focused on practical issues to attract women who were not interested in consciousness raising. The conference offered information about education, the arts, and law. Although PWC is a mainstream organization, its nonhierarchical structure

247

reflects leftist influences. The group seeks to change not only external conditions but the attitudes that create them.

Progressive Party

In 1912 the Republican national convention renominated William Howard Taft for president. Reformers, including Jane Addams, responded by organizing the Progressive party (Bull Moose party), and nominating former president Theodore Roosevelt as its presidential candidate. The group's platform advocated suffrage for women; an eight-hour workday and a six-day workweek; federal insurance covering old age, accidents, and unemployment; protective regulation of female labor; a lower tariff; and a ban on hiring children younger than 16 years old. This platform foreshadowed the New Deal of the 1930s, in which women had a stronger voice in policymaking than ever before. The Progressive party maintained its organization until 1916, when most progressives supported the Republican ticket. In 1924 another Progressive party nominated Robert M. La Follette for president. Again the platform called for social and economic reforms. La Follette won five million popular votes but only 13 electoral votes, and the election went to Republican Calvin Coolidge. The party continued in Wisconsin until 1946. A third Progressive party ran Henry A. Wallace in the 1948 presidential contest, but he lost to Harry S Truman. The party won no electoral votes and only one million popular votes. Despite their losses, Progressive parties highlighted women's issues, giving many feminists more of a choice in the political process.

Project on Equal Education Rights (PEER)

The Project on Equal Education Rights was created by the National Organization for Women in 1974 (using funds from foundations) to oversee the enforcement of Title IX of the 1972 Higher Education Act, which bans discrimination in education. Four years later PEER issued a report, *Stalled at the Start*. The report drew attention to the poor handling of Title IX issues by the Department of Health, Education, and Welfare (HEW) and to HEW's lack of commitment to Title IX. A companion project, which originated in Michigan, encourages grassroots participation in the process on enforcing Title IX regulations.

See also National Organization for Women; Title IX of the 1972 Higher Education Act.

Project on the Education and Status of Women

The Project on the Education and Status of Women, created by the Association of American Colleges in 1971, contributed to the recognition of academic sex discrimination as a serious issue. Because the sponsoring association included men and women, the project did not encounter the contempt that was directed at many feminist organizations that were attempting to raise sex discrimination issues. Initially directed by Bernice Sandler, the purpose of the project was to educate the academic community about women's issues as a first step in bringing about change. The project provided educational institutions and women's groups with information about how women might achieve equality in education. It dealt with issues ranging from integration to sexual harassment. Its newsletter, *On Campus*, was a progress report on women in education.

See also Title IX of the 1972 Higher Education Act; Women's Educational Equity Act.

Project on the Psychology of Women

The Project on the Psychology of Women studied the self-confidence of adolescent girls from 1981 to 1984. The study was conducted by Dr. Carol Gilligan of Harvard. Funding came from the Geraldine Rockefeller Dodge Foundation, hence the common name of the project, Dodge Study. Gilligan and her colleagues studied girls between the ages of 7 and 16 at the Emma Willard School in Troy, New York. They found that, at age 11, the girls were most confident, but by age 15 or 16, they had lost a large measure of that confidence. Gilligan concluded that, as girls move through adolescence, they undergo a crisis of confidence caused by a culture that encourages them to ignore the absence of women in key roles in society. The results of the Dodge Study are summarized in *Making Connections: The Relational Worlds of Adolescent Girls at Emma Willard School* (1989). Among the study's goals was intervening in a positive way in girls' adolescent development.

See also Gilligan, Carol.

Protective Legislation

Beginning in the nineteenth century, reformers campaigned for state laws that would regulate the hours and working conditions of female workers. Initially, they tried to pass laws that would cover men, too, but the courts ruled that such legislation interfered with men's right to make contracts. Gradually, the contention that women possess distinctive attributes, such as physical weakness and a capacity to bear children, took hold. In 1852 Ohio passed the first law regulating the maximum number of hours a woman could work. Other states followed. In 1908 the Supreme Court decided in *Muller v. Oregon* that such laws were constitutional. Most reformers agreed with the Court's decision, and by 1920 most states had passed laws limiting the number of hours a woman could work and prohibiting night work in many industries. Other laws banned women from selling liquor, carrying mail, working in foundries or mines, or operating elevators; still others required employers to provide women with a clean, safe workplace, rest periods, and good ventilation and light.

The labor department's Women's Bureau, organized labor, and most women's groups supported protective legislation. Reformers, such as the members of the National Consumers' League (NCL), asserted that women were not equal to men physically, economically, or socially, and therefore should be treated as a separate class. Only a few feminists, such as members of the National Woman's Party (NWP), thought that protective legislation would limit employment for women. These feminists preferred to lobby for passage of an equal rights amendment to the Constitution that would give women absolute equality with men in all areas of public policy. The NWP filed a legal brief in *Adkins v. Children's Hospital* (1923) asking the Supreme Court to invalidate Washington, D.C.'s minimum-wage law for women. The NWP filed another legal brief 13 years later in a New York State minimum-wage case, *Morehead v. New York ex rel. Tibaldo*. In both cases the court seemed to endorse the NWP's argument that the laws interfered with women's freedom to make contracts.

By the 1930s the women's movement had become so polarized over these issues and the passage of the ERA that it could not fight discrimination in an organized way. Reformers called the NWP a "small but militant group of leisure class women," and the NWP called the reformers Tories who would oppose for themselves the workplace restrictions imposed on working women. In 1938 Congress passed the Fair Labor Standards Act. It established a precedent for providing wage and hour legislation for workers of both sexes. Yet the conflict continued. Reformers would see many of their social welfare programs adopted by the New Deal administration of President Franklin D. Roosevelt. This left the reformers with the negative goal of defeating the women who were campaigning for an equal rights amendment. Not until the 1970s did the courts finally rule that protective legislation violates the ban on sex discrimination in employment under Title VII of the 1964 Civil Rights Act.

See also Adkins v. Children's Hospital; Equal Pay Act; Equal Rights Amendment; Fair Labor Standards Act; *Morehead v. New York ex rel. Tipaldo; Muller v. State of Oregon;* National Woman's Party; Title VII of the 1964 Civil Rights Act; Women's Bureau.

"Protocol in the Dress & Waist Industry"

In 1913 the International Ladies' Garment Workers' Union signed the first contract between labor and management arbitrated by outside negotiations. The contract, called the "Protocol in the Dress & Waist Industry," formalized the division of labor that existed in the industry. By this written agreement, the more lucrative, skilled jobs went to men, the less skilled to women. The result was that the lowest paid man earned more than the highest paid woman, with men earning more than women when their jobs were identical.

See also International Ladies' Garment Workers' Union; Unions.

Proulx, E. Annie (1936–)

E. Annie Proulx is the first woman to be named as winner of the PEN/Faulkner Award for Fiction, which she received for her first novel, *Postcards.* The announcement was made 20 April 1993 by Robert Stone, chairman of the PEN/Faulkner Foundation in Washington, D.C.

The oldest of five children, Proulx was born in Connecticut in 1936. Since 1947 she has lived most of her life on farms in Vermont. She dropped out of Colby College, escaped two bad marriages, and as a single mother raised her three sons. She returned to college and graduated cum laude from the University of Vermont in 1969. Proulx went on to receive her master's degree from Montreal's Sir George Williams College in 1975.

A talented journalist, Proulx has written both fiction and nonfiction. She has investigated migrant farm labor in California and has been on archaeology digs in the Southwest. She has traveled from Newfoundland to the Pacific Northwest exploring the effects of deforestation. She is a frequent contributor to *Organic Gardening* and *Vermont Life* magazines.

Proulx's fiction is noted for its realism and skillful use of dialog. In addition to *Postcards,* her works include short stories collected in

Heart Songs and her newest novel, *The Shipping News.* A forthcoming book, *Forests,* deals with logging. Proulx lives outside of Vershire, Vermont.

Pugh, Sarah (1800–1884)

Abolitionist and women's rights activist Sarah Pugh was born 6 October 1800 in Alexandria, Virginia. She was reared as a Quaker and educated at a Quaker boarding school in Westtown, Pennsylvania. In 1821, she began teaching in the Friends' School of the Twelfth Street Meeting House in Pennsylvania. She resigned in 1828, after a split between the liberal and traditional Quakers. In 1829 she founded an elementary school, where she taught for the next ten years. Pugh was also an abolitionist and women's suffragist. In the mid-1830s she joined the Philadelphia Female Anti-Slavery Society. She was presiding officer of the organization for many years. When a mob burned down Pennsylvania Hall in 1838, the second National Female Anti-Slavery Convention met in Pugh's schoolhouse. In 1840 Pugh traveled with Lucretia Mott, Mary Grew, and others to the meeting of the World Anti-Slavery Convention in London. When the women were denied participation in the meeting, Pugh protested in writing. She returned to the United States and continued to circulate petitions and attend antislavery conventions. After her mother's death in 1851, Pugh returned to England, where she lectured about American antislavery efforts. Eighteen months later, Pugh returned to Philadelphia, where she worked for the improvement of the freedmen's situation and for women's rights after the civil war. After 1864 Pugh lived in Germantown, Pennsylvania, with her brother and sister-in-law. There she died of a fall 1 August 1884.

See also Female Antislavery Societies; Society of Friends.

Quakers
See Society of Friends.

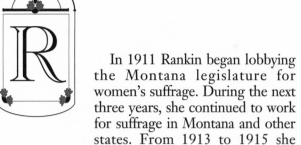

Radical Feminism

Radical feminism is an ideology that supports a fundamental change in the character of society rather than merely correcting specific instances of discrimination. Many radical feminists scorn association with men and call for an immediate and complete end to the existing social order, which they consider patriarchal. Radical feminists have been aligned, to some extent, with other left-wing movements, but sexism within those movements has contributed a great deal to the growth of radical feminism. Radical feminists often endorse separatism as a strategy for liberating women and as an expression of their philosophy. In the belief that this would maximize the egalitarian nature of their groups and reflect their values, many of these groups have favored a nonhierarchical style of organization.

See also Atkinson, Ti-Grace; The Feminists; New York Radical Feminists; New York Radical Women; Redstockings.

Rankin, Jeannette Pickering (1880–1973)

Jeannette Rankin was the first woman elected to the House of Representatives and the only member of Congress to vote against U.S. participation in both World War I and World War II. She was born 11 June 1880 on a ranch near Missoula, Montana. She attended public schools and graduated from the University of Montana in 1902 with a degree in biology. Following training at the New York School of Philanthropy (1908), she worked briefly as a social worker. She then enrolled in the University of Washington, where she was introduced to the state campaign for woman suffrage. Her work in the Washington State suffrage campaign proved successful; in a 1910 referendum, voters granted women suffrage. She said later that the experience changed her life.

In 1911 Rankin began lobbying the Montana legislature for women's suffrage. During the next three years, she continued to work for suffrage in Montana and other states. From 1913 to 1915 she served as the field, or legislative, secretary for the National American Woman Suffrage Association (NAWSA). Her efforts in Montana bore fruit in 1914, when women of the state won suffrage.

Because Montana women were able to vote, Rankin was effectively able to run for Congress before adoption of the Nineteenth Amendment in 1920. In 1916 she campaigned as a Republican for the House of Representatives and on 2 April 1917 became the first female member of Congress. Rankin worked for a women's suffrage amendment to the Constitution and legislation to help women and children. Believing that suffrage and peace were entwined, she voted against U.S. involvement in World War I. Her pacifism caused her defeat in the Senate race of 1918.

In 1919 Rankin accompanied Florence Kelley and Jane Addams to Zurich, Switzerland, for the second International Congress of Women, which became the Women's International League for Peace and Freedom. (Rankin later became a board member of the league.) After returning to the United States, Kelley appointed Rankin field secretary of the National Consumers' League. Rankin fought for the passage of the Sheppard-Towner Act, which, in 1921, authorized $1.25 million annually to fight disease in mothers and children. She was also active in other reform causes, including protective legislation for working women and pacifism. From 1929 until 1939, she served as a lobbyist and organizer for the National Council for the Prevention of War.

Rankin left the council to run for Congress in 1940. She was elected to the House of Representatives. On 8 December 1941,

Jeannette Rankin

she cast the single vote against U.S. entry into World War II. The vote cost her reelection, but she continued her opposition to war. She inspired the Jeannette Rankin Brigade, which demonstrated against the Vietnam War in 1968. Rankin was a student of Gandhi's nonviolent resistance and an advocate of global peace when these ideas were unpopular in both her party and society. She was preparing to run for a third term in Congress at the age of 88 when she underwent surgery and had to withdraw. Rankin died 18 May 1973 in Carmel, California.

See also Addams, Jane; Sheppard-Towner Act.

Rape
See Violence.

Ray, Dixy Lee (1914–1994)
Dixy Lee Ray was the first woman sworn into a full five-year term on the U.S. Atomic Energy Commission and the second woman to be elected governor on her own merits. She was born Margaret Ray on 3 September 1914 in Tacoma, Washington and later renamed herself after a favorite region and Civil War general. She graduated from Mills College, earning a bachelor's degree

in zoology (1937) and an M.A. in zoology (1938). After receiving her Ph.D. from Stanford (1945), she taught zoology at the University of Washington, becoming an assistant professor (1947) and associate professor (1957). Ray published a number of research papers on marine biology and edited one book, *Marine Boring and Fouling Organisms* (1959). She campaigned for more research to understand the dangers posed to ecosystems by chemical manufacturing, waste disposal, and other hazardous materials. From 1960 to 1962 she was a consultant to the National Science Foundation, and in 1963 she was appointed director of the Pacific Science Center in Seattle. That year she was also special assistant to the director of the National Science Foundation. Ray served on President Richard Nixon's task force on oceanography in 1969. In 1972 President Nixon named her to head the Atomic Energy Commission; she was the first woman to serve a full five-year term. In 1973 she succeeded James R. Schlesinger as chair of the commission, a job that made her the most powerful woman in government. She worked to improve employment opportunities for minorities and to increase research on the safety of nuclear reactors. Ray moved to the state department as assistant secretary of oceans and international environmental affairs in 1974. She left the federal government the following year to run for governor of Washington State as a Democrat, at the age of 62, commenting "I guess I'm a late bloomer." Her victory made her the second woman (after Ella Grasso of Connecticut) to win a state governorship without being preceded by her husband. Ray served for four years but lost her bid for reelection in 1980, after which she lectured on environment issues and wrote two books criticizing the environmental movement, *Trashing the Planet* (1990) and *Environment Overkill* (1993). Ray died on Fox Island on 3 January 1994.

Red Cross, American (National)
Feminist Clara Barton founded the American National Red Cross in 1881, serving as

its president for 23 years. She learned of the International Committee of the Red Cross (founded by Swiss banker Jean Henri Dunant in 1863) in 1869, while on a trip to Switzerland. Established by the Treaty of Geneva, the International Committee of the Red Cross enabled wounded soldiers and ambulance and sanitary personnel to be treated as neutral parties under a white flag with a red cross, a reversal of the Swiss flag. By 1864, 11 countries had ratified this treaty. Clara Barton was instrumental in getting the U.S. Congress to also ratify it in 1882. She wrote and spoke on the need for a relief organization to help victims of natural disasters, accidents, and diseases, and it was this argument that gained American support rather than earlier appeals for a Red Cross to help out during wartime. While lobbying for the United States to sign the Treaty of Geneva, Barton organized the American Association of the Red Cross (1881), chartered in Washington, D.C., as the American National Red Cross (1893).

Barton worked tirelessly for the organization from 1881 to 1904, providing relief in 21 disasters in America and abroad. She refused government money, preferring her organization to be a voluntary one, and used her own funds to carry on her activities rather than accept a salary. In almost every disaster that required Red Cross help, Barton herself went to the site. During the Ohio and Mississippi floods (1881), she chartered riverboats to carry emergency aid and materials for rebuilding homes and barns after the disaster. In a hurricane emergency in Galveston, Texas (1900), the Red Cross, under Barton's close supervision, provided 1.5 million strawberry plants to destitute farmers so that they could support themselves.

During World War I (1914–1918) the American Red Cross established hospitals, recruited nurses, and procured ambulances for the U.S. Army. Red Cross volunteers also made dressings, provided transport, and ran canteens. By the war's end, the Red Cross had expanded to provide aid to veterans and their families, and had established a Junior Red Cross. During the 1920s, it de-veloped a public health program providing education in safety, home nursing, accident prevention, and nutrition.

During World War II (1939–1945) the organization provided overseas relief aid. Ninety percent of the nurses who served in the armed forces were recruited by the Red Cross, which also trained more than 200,000 nurse aides. One of the organization's greatest achievements was the initiation of the first national blood bank in U.S. history. By 1945, 13 million pints of blood had been donated by volunteers for use in the field. By 1947, the Red Cross was supplying blood for civilians without charge, and during the Korean War it supplied blood for the armed services. The American Red Cross is a voluntary membership organization, which, as of 1994, had 2,700 chapters in the United States. Elizabeth Dole is now head of the organization.

Redstockings

Founded by Shulamith Firestone and Ellen Willis in 1969, the Redstockings became one of the best-known groups in the radical contingent of the women's movement. The Redstockings devoted themselves exclusively to feminist purposes rather than adopting the agenda of the entire radical movement. They were responsible for promoting consciousness raising and speak-outs, and they participated in activities to publicize women's issues. They interrupted the New York legislature's hearings on abortion in 1969 and organized a ground-breaking abortion speak-out in the same year. (A speak-out is a public forum that raises awareness about a problem by having individuals discuss their personal experiences with that problem.)

The Redstockings, while they did not accept the content of Marxist teaching, found it appropriate to borrow the Marxist style of analysis in discussing women's issues. They attributed the perpetuation of the inferior status of women not to long-term social conditioning or brainwashing but to practical control exercised by men on a daily basis. The Redstockings focused on unity among women more than on achievement of rights for women as individuals; they argued that the bonds of sisterhood could help women survive the daily strain of living with discrimination. The Redstockings had great tolerance of many various feminist ideologies and of nonfeminist women. They viewed feminism as a force that transcends class and racial barriers; they urged women as a class to confront men as a class. The Redstockings reinforced the argument for female unity by describing all men—not only those in the establishment—as beneficiaries of, and therefore participants in, a sexist system. They adopted the position that social institutions are not themselves ultimately responsible for sexism but are merely vehicles for sexist control—for which men as individuals cannot avoid taking responsibility. Although internal conflicts led to the dissolution of the Redstockings in the fall of 1970, the group left an indelible mark on the course of the radical feminist movement.

See also Consciousness Raising; New York Radical Feminists; New York Radical Women; Radical Feminism.

Reed, Esther De Berdt (1746–1780)

Esther Reed cofounded the first relief organization to benefit Continental soldiers during the American Revolution. She was born 22 October 1746 in London, and came to America with her husband in 1771. Soon she became active in the revolutionary movement, hosting many of the delegates to the First Continental Congress (1774). Reed organized one of the most-remembered acts of political involvement conducted by women during the revolutionary period: the Philadelphia campaign to raise funds for George Washington's army. She joined forces with Sarah Franklin Bache, daughter of Benjamin Franklin, and 35 other women. They knocked on doors, mostly in Philadelphia and Germantown, to collect money. Loyalist Rebecca Rawle Shoemaker wrote to her friend Catherine Livingston on 10 June 1782, "Of all the absurdities, the ladies going about for money exceeded everything; they were so

extremely importunate that people were obliged to give . . . something to get rid of them." By 4 July 1780, $7,500 in gold had been collected and used to buy linen for making shirts. When Reed died of sudden dysentery in Philadelphia on 18 September 1780, Bache took over, delivering to Washington's army a total of 2,005 shirts, many of them sewn in Bache's house.

See also Bache, Sarah Franklin; Daughters of Liberty.

Reed v. Reed

In *Reed v. Reed* (1971), argued by Ruth Bader Ginsburg, the Supreme Court established that the law cannot automatically favor men simply because it is convenient. Sally Reed and Cecil Reed were a divorced couple with a son, Richard, who had been in the custody of his father since his early teens. When Richard committed suicide at the age of 19, both parents sought the right to administer his estate. Idaho law stated that when a male and a female with the same relation to the deceased apply to be administrator of an estate, the court must automatically appoint the man. The Idaho law was defended on the grounds that it avoided the necessity of probate court hearings.

The *Reed* decision had broad constitutional significance that went beyond the realm of the subject matter of the decision. *Reed* demonstrated the effectiveness of the use of the Equal Protection Clause of the Constitution in the battle against sex-specific laws, and encouraged its further use in other cases. The judges did not formally establish a basis for examining laws that discriminated against women with greater scrutiny than necessary for ordinary laws, but it was apparent from their reasoning that they endorsed such a practice. Because of *Reed*, the irrational and unfair use of gender for classifying individuals in place of more relevant types of classification was discouraged. In later cases, the judges referred to the unarticulated standard of *Reed* and used it to overturn other gender-based discrimination statutes. The standard still did not require, however, that gender classifications be scrutinized with maximum intensity, as was required by race classifications. In the *Craig v. Boren* case of 1976, the method manifested in *Reed* for judging gender classifications was formally established.

See also Craig v. Boren; Ginsburg, Ruth Bader.

Reeve, Tapping (1744–1823)

A Connecticut Supreme Court judge and author of the first treatise on domestic relations published in the United States, Tapping Reeve wrote *The Law of Baron and Feme, of Parent and Child, of Guardian and War, of Master and Servant, and of the Powers of Courts of Chancery* (1816). Reeve was born in Brookhaven, Long Island, New York, in October 1744. He graduated from the College of New Jersey (now Princeton) in 1763 and opened his law practice in Litchfield, Connecticut. Tapping Reeve's view of common law and women's legal status after marriage were unusual. He challenged the argument of British legal theorist William Blackstone that, under the law, a married couple was one person, that person being the husband. Reeve thought that the legal term of *one person* was a figurative expression rather than a legal one, and that various legal doctrines recognized the separate legal existence of married women, for example, the right to inherit real property. According to Reeve, only the fear of male coercion made the courts reluctant to recognize contracts made by women. Reeve is also remembered for the law school he started in 1784, the Litchfield Law School, preceded only by the law department at the College of William and Mary. Litchfield became the leading law school in the United States, graduating John C. Calhoun, Horace Mann, and other leaders. In 1798, after Reeve became a judge, he recruited a former student, James Gould, to run the school, to whom its continued excellence was credited.

See also Common Law; *Feme Covert.*

Reno, Janet (1938–)

Veteran Miami prosecutor Janet Reno is the first female attorney general of the United States. She was appointed in 1993 by President Bill Clinton after he withdrew the nominations of his first two choices, Aetna lawyer Zoë Baird and Judge Kimba M. Wood. Before her appointment, Reno was the state's attorney in Dade County, Florida, for 15 years. She became well known for her prosecution of cases involving police corruption, racial violence, and child abuse.

Reno was born 21 July 1938 in Miami, one of four children of Jane Wood Reno and Danish immigrant Henry Reno. Her mother was a reporter who wrestled alligators, hunted, and kept peacocks and snakes as pets. Her father was a police reporter for the *Miami Herald.* The family lived on a remote 21-acre homestead near Florida's Everglades National Park, where they built a rustic home that became a local landmark. Reno attended Dade County public schools and was the state debating champion in high school. She attended Cornell University, where she earned an undergraduate degree in chemistry and served as president of the women's student government. In 1963 Reno earned a law degree from Harvard, where she was one of only 16 women in a class of more than 500 men.

In 1978 she was appointed state's attorney for Dade County. In that position, she won praise for reforming the juvenile justice system and establishing a special court for drug cases, among other initiatives. Single and with no children, Reno was supported by female activists throughout the country for the justice department's top job. When asked by a reporter if she was a feminist, the attorney general replied, "My mother always told me to do my best, to think my best and to do right, and to consider myself a person."

Republican Motherhood

In the 1780s, the concept of "republican motherhood" provided the rationale for women's political activities. It also initiated a debate on women's education and led to the first female academies. The term recalled Thomas Paine's ideal of the republican as an independent, mature person

257

dedicated to the good of society. It reflected women's newfound patriotism, which developed during the American Revolution. Republican mothers had a dual responsibility: to educate sons to be good citizens and to promote the communal good. Throughout the nineteenth century, women used the rhetoric of republican motherhood to justify their political activities, saying they could not be good mothers unless they could vote to keep wrongdoers out of public office.

Retirement Equity Act

In 1984, in response to complaints from women's groups about gender-based inequities in retirement benefits, Congress passed the Retirement Equity Act. Under the act, both spouses must give written consent before a worker may refuse survivor benefits, a wife must be paid benefits even if her husband does not live to reach retirement, and the coverage of workers who must take time away from a job to care for small children must be continued.

The Revolution

The Revolution (1868–1870) was a feminist weekly that contributed to the split between the National Woman Suffrage Association and the American Woman Suffrage Association in 1869. It was financed by politician George Train. Susan B. Anthony was its proprietor, and Elizabeth Cady Stanton and Parker Pillsbury were its editors. Its motto was "Men Their Rights and Nothing More; Women Their Rights and Nothing Less." Its first issue was published on 8 January 1868. In successive issues, the 16-page paper covered every aspect of women's lives, such as clothing, marriage, motherhood, health, and work. It urged women to become economically independent and to educate themselves, and it called for suffrage as a means of gaining other rights for women. The newspaper used only one criterion in its evaluation of proposed legislation and other issues: Whether the measure under consideration would have a positive or negative effect on women. Thus, when the Fifteenth

Amendment, guaranteeing the voting rights of all *men* regardless of "race, color, or previous condition of servitude," was proposed in February 1869, the *Revolution* immediately responded with an article entitled "That Infamous Fifteenth Amendment." The article and Train's racism prompted a bitter debate at the May 1969 meeting of the American Equal Rights Association. Immediately afterwards, Cady Stanton and Anthony founded the National Woman Suffrage Association, devoted to Women's rights only.

Train, an eccentric Democrat and racist, traveled to Ireland, became involved in supporting nationalists there, and was arrested. Anthony, $10,000 in debt, sold the paper for a dollar to Laura Curtis Bullard and Theodore Tilton in 1870. The *Revolution* continued under the editorship of Bullard, with Edwin Studwell as publisher, until on 17 February 1872 it was sold to the *New York Christian Enquirer.*

See also Anthony, Susan B.; National Woman Suffrage Association; Stanton, Elizabeth Cady.

Rich, Adrienne (1929–)

Poet, essayist, and critic Adrienne Rich was born 16 May 1929 in Baltimore, Maryland. In 1951 she received a B.A. cum laude from Radcliffe. Her first volume of poems, *A Change of World* (1951), was chosen by W. H. Auden for the Yale Younger Poets Award. In *Snapshots of a Daughter-in-Law* (1963) Rich began speaking in the more political voice of her later books. By the 1970s her poetry reflected a strong commitment to feminism, and she became a much admired poet of the women's and lesbian feminist movements. In 1974 she received the National Book Award for *Diving into the Wreck* (1973); she refused to accept the $25,000 award as an individual, accepting it on behalf of all women. With the publication of *Twenty-One Love Poems* (1975) and *The Dream of a Common Language: Poems 1974–1977* (1978), her work became recognized as lesbian as well as feminist. Her many writings include essays on motherhood, female consciousness, forgotten female writers, and other topics. During the 1980s Rich was coeditor of the lesbian feminist quarterly publication *Sinister Wisdom.* Her books include *The Will To Change* (1971), *Of Woman Born* (1976), *On Lies, Secrets and Silence* (1979), *A Wild Patience Has Taken Me This Far* (1981), *Blood and Bread Poetry* (1986), *Times Power Poems 1985–1988* (1989), and *An Atlas of the Difficult World, 1988–1991* (1991). Rich was awarded the first Ruth Lilly Poetry Prize and a Brandeis University Creative Arts Medal. She lives in California.

Ride, Sally K. (1951–)

Sally Ride, one of the first women selected for the U.S. space shuttle program, is the first American woman astronaut in space. She was born 26 May 1951 in Los Angeles. A young athlete, she was ranked eighteenth in the nation's junior tennis circuit. Ride studied at Westlake School for Girls in Los Angeles, graduating in 1968. She enrolled in Swarthmore College, intending to major in physics, but she left college to play tennis. In 1970 she enrolled at Stanford, graduating

Sally Ride in 1984.

three years later with two bachelor's degrees, one in English and one in physics. In 1978, while Ride was working toward a doctorate in astrophysics at Stanford, NASA chose her to be one of six women to undergo astronaut training. Ride served as capsule commander for the space shuttle missions STS-2 and STS-3 in 1981 and 1982. The latter year she was selected to be a mission specialist and flight engineer for the *Challenger*'s seventh flight. On 18 June 1983, aboard the *Challenger*, she became the first American woman astronaut in space. After the explosion of the *Challenger* in 1986, Ride was assigned the task of investigating the accident. After the investigation she was appointed special assistant to the administrator for long-range planning. She left NASA in 1987, becoming a science fellow at the Stanford University Center for International Security and Arms Control. She lives in Texas with her husband, astronaut Steven Hawley.

Rideout Case

People v. Rideout was instrumental in encouraging many states to reform their rape laws to cover forced sex in marriage. In 1978 John Rideout was tried for raping his wife, Greta, under an Oregon law that did not make a marital exemption for rape. The law had been passed in 1977. Before this law, rape, by definition, could not occur in a marriage. Although Greta Rideout in her testimony described a devastating experience with her husband, he was acquitted. Contemporary press reports were unsympathetic to Greta Rideout and critical of the Oregon law, but the publicity generated by the case drew attention to the need for reform.

"The Rights and Conditions of Women"

In 1840 the Rev. Samuel J. May spoke to a New York audience about the recent convention to frame the New York State constitution, at which no women were present. In "The Rights and Conditions of Women," he pointed out that women were neither permitted to vote for the document nor to have their interests reflected in it. May argued, "The entire disenfranchisement of females is as just as the disenfranchisement of the males would be, for there is nothing in their moral, mental or physical nature, that disqualifies them to understand correctly the true interests of the community." He went on to claim that women were not fairly compensated for their labor, were encouraged by popular magazines and newspapers to marry too young, and acted as domestic slaves to their husbands. Responding to his own rhetorical question about whether, under these circumstances, men could ever feel respect for women, he said, "Yes, about as much as the slaveholders feel for the slaves."

Rind, Clementina (c. 1740–1774)

Born about 1740, Rind took over as editor of the *Virginia Gazette* in 1773 upon the death of her husband. The Williamsburg paper was popular among women because of its literary pieces, and it also covered news about science, shipping, and politics. Rind was appointed the colony's public printer in 1774 and thereafter printed the colony's official documents. Rind died 25 September 1774 in Williamsburg.

Rochester Convention

On 2 August 1848, only two weeks after the first women's rights convention at Seneca Falls, New York, a second convention was held in Rochester, New York. Organized by Amy Post, Sarah D. Fish, Sarah C. Owen, and Mary H. Hallowell, it marked the first time a woman presided over a convention. At Seneca Falls, because none of the women felt equal to the task, Lucretia Mott's husband, James Mott, had presided. The Rochester convention was opened by Amy Post, who proposed Abigail Bush for president of the convention, although, according to *History of Woman Suffrage* (Volume I), "Mrs. [Lucretia] Mott, Mrs. [Elizabeth] Cady Stanton, and Mrs. [Elizabeth] McClintock thought it a most hazardous experiment to

have a woman president, and stoutly opposed it." The *History of Woman Suffrage* continues

"To write a Declaration and Resolutions, to make a speech, and debate, had taxed their powers to the uttermost; and now, with such feeble voices and timid manners, without the slightest knowledge of Cushing's Manual, or the least experience in public meetings, how could a woman preside? They were on the verge of leaving the Convention in disgust, but Amy Post and Rhoda De Garmo assured them that by the same power by which they had resolved, declared, discussed, debated, they could also preside at a public meeting, if they would but make the experiment. And as the vote of the majority settled the question on the side of a woman, Abigail Bush took the chair, and the calm way she assumed the duties of the office, and the admirable manner in which she discharged them, soon reconciled the opposition to the seemingly ridiculous experiment."

Afterward, all approved the Seneca Falls Declaration of Sentiments. They adopted even stronger resolutions than those adopted at Seneca Falls. For instance, in Clause 5, it was resolved "that those who believe the laboring classes of women are oppressed ought to do all in their power to raise their wages, beginning with their own household servants." Like the Seneca Falls convention, the Rochester convention approved a resolution calling for women's suffrage; the resolution garnered more support in Rochester than it had in Seneca Falls. Eighteen months later a third women's rights convention was held in Salem, Ohio.

See also Declaration of Sentiments; Salem (Ohio) Convention; Seneca Falls Convention.

Rockford Female Seminary

Called the Mount Holyoke of the West, the Rockford (Illinois) Female Seminary was founded in 1847. President Anna Sill tried to provide the students with the same quality of education provided by eastern men's schools. Perhaps the school's most famous graduate was Jane Addams, who enrolled in 1877. The school became a college in 1882 and became coeducational in 1958. Rockford has retained its religious mission, reflecting the goals of its founders, an alliance of Presbyterian and Congregational churches.

Roe v. Wade

Roe v. Wade was the 1973 landmark Supreme Court case that legalized abortion. More properly, the decision relegalized abortion, because abortion had been legal until the late 1800s. Norma McCorvey, who was called Jane Roe to conceal her identity, was a poor, young, pregnant Texan who participated in a test case orchestrated by attorneys Linda Coffee and Sarah Weddington. Henry Wade, the defendant, was the Dallas County district attorney. Coffee and Weddington challenged an 1857 state law that prohibited abortion except to save the life of the mother. A lower court overturned the law too late to help Norma McCorvey. She had the child and gave it up for adoption.

Before the Supreme Court, Weddington described the hardships caused by the inaccessibility of abortion. She based her argument on the idea that women have certain fundamental rights and on the universal right to privacy, which stems from the Ninth Amendment's provision that citizens have rights in addition to those specifically enumerated in the Constitution. The opposing argument (in *Doe v. Bolton* as well) defended the state's interest in restricting abortion and stated that the case was moot because Roe was no longer pregnant, and declared that pregnant women are inherently incapable of victory in legal battles over abortion because it takes more than nine months for a case to progress through the courts; therefore, no pregnant woman who filed a suit would still be pregnant by the time the case reached the Supreme Court. In a seven-to-two decision, the Supreme Court overturned the Texas law on the grounds that such laws violate the Fourteenth Amendment, which guarantees due process.

The Court established a trimester-based framework for regulating abortions. In the first trimester, the state cannot interfere with a physician's decision to abort a fetus. In the second trimester, the state can regulate abortion only to protect the woman's health. In the third trimester, because the fetus is viable, the state may prohibit abortion unless the pregnancy threatens the woman's life or health. The Court viewed abortion as a medical issue, that is, it did not view abortion in terms of reproductive rights so much as a health issue that should be handled by a woman's doctor. The Court did not speculate on the religious or philosophical question of when life begins. However, it did note that, because abortion was legally available when the Constitution was written, the term *person* in the Constitution does not refer to a fetus. Because the *Doe v. Bolton* case was decided on the same day and was also part of the relegalization of the majority of abortions, the term "Roe v. Wade" is occasionally used to refer to both cases.

See also Abortion; Blackmun, Harry A.; *Doe v. Bolton; People v. Belous; Planned Parenthood of Central Missouri v. Danforth; Planned Parenthood of Southeastern Pennsylvania v. Casey; United States v. Vuitch; Webster v. Reproductive Health Services.*

Roosevelt, Eleanor (1884–1962)

Eleanor Roosevelt was the first first lady to take controversial stands on important issues, to hold a press conference, to travel by air to a foreign country, and to be appointed a delegate to the United Nations after she had left the White House. Born 11 October 1884 in New York City, she was orphaned at the age of ten. She was educated in England, later spurning the world of the debutante to do settlement work. In 1905 she married a cousin, Franklin D. Roosevelt. She nurtured his political career while rearing the couple's six children, becoming particularly supportive of him after he suffered an attack of polio in 1921. She became a champion of equal rights for women, African Americans, the poor, and other disadvantaged groups. She was an especially active member of the Woman's Trade Union League and the Democratic party. From 1927 she was part owner and vice-principal of the Todhunter School in New York City, where she taught sociology, government, and economics.

With her husband's election as president in 1932, Roosevelt began her 12 years as first lady. In 1933, she held a press conference for a small group of female reporters on the subject of the country's economic crisis and its effect on women. It was the first press conference ever held by a first lady; thereafter, Roosevelt held them on a regular basis. In 1934 she became the first first lady to travel by air, visiting Haiti, Puerto Rico, and the Virgin Islands to study social conditions. Roosevelt was a popular writer. Her newspaper column, "My Day," began syndication in 1936. At first the column discussed women's affairs, but its focus changed to public affairs. In 1939 Roosevelt announced in the column that she had resigned from the Daughters of the American Revolution because the group prevented African-American singer Marian Anderson from performing at Constitution Hall in Washington, D.C. Roosevelt helped to secure the opera singer's performance at the Lincoln Memorial before 75,000 people. In 1941 Roosevelt began another column, "If You Ask Me," in the *Ladies' Home Journal.*

Roosevelt is remembered for influencing her husband's New Deal policy, for advocating women's integration into the war effort, and for helping Jewish refugees. Because her husband was confined to a wheelchair, she carried out much of the ceremonial work of the presidency, especially the inspection of government work projects. During World War II, she visited almost every front to support American soldiers. As a delegate to the United Nations' Charter Commission, a post she assumed shortly after her husband's death in 1945, she helped shape policy during the organization's early years. As chair of the U.N. Commission on Human Rights from 1946, Roosevelt was a central figure in drafting the Universal Declaration of Human Rights in 1948. She resigned from the United Nations in 1952 and spent the next ten years traveling and promoting the work of the United Nations. In 1961, President John F. Kennedy named Roosevelt to chair the President's Commission on the Status of Women. Among her many books are: *This Is My Story* (1937), *My Days* (1937), *The Moral Basis of Democracy* (1940), *This I Remember* (1949), *On My Own* (1958), *You Learn by Living* (1960), and *The Autobiography of Eleanor Roosevelt* (1961). Roosevelt died 7 November 1962 in New York City.

See also Camp Jane Addams; President's Commission on the Status of Women.

Rose, Ernestine Sismondi Potowski (1810–1892)

Ernestine Rose wrote one of the first petitions for a law granting married women the right to own property. She was born 13 January 1810 in the ghetto of Piotrkow, in Russian Poland. In 1826 her mother died, leaving her daughter certain property. Her father arranged her marriage to a man of his own age, using the inheritance as dowry, as was customary. At 16, Ernestine took her father to court and won back her inheritance. After living in Germany, Holland, and France, she went to England (1830), where she met reformer Robert Owen. In 1836 she married one of his disciples, William E. Rose, and the couple moved to the United States.

After they settled in New York, Rose wrote and circulated the state's first petition for a married women's property act (1840) and spoke before a legislative committee in Albany, New York. The petition carried only five signatures, yet Rose circulated it every year. The state legislature did not pass a married women's property act until 1848. In 1843 the Roses established a short-lived utopian community in Skaneateles, New York. Beginning in the 1850s Rose was active in the women's rights, temperance, and antislavery movements. During the Civil War, she worked with Elizabeth Cady Stan-

262

ton and Susan B. Anthony in the National Woman's Loyal League; after the war she was active in the American Equal Rights Association. In 1869 Rose helped Stanton and Anthony found the National Woman Suffrage Association. Also that year she sailed with her husband to England, where she gave speeches on various reforms. An effective writer, Rose was for 50 years a contributor to the *Boston Investigator*. She died 4 August 1892 in Brighton, England.

See also Married Women's Property Acts; New York Married Woman's Property Act (1848); Petitions.

Ross, Betsy (1752–1836)

Legend has it that Betsy Ross was the designer and maker of the first U.S. flag. Born 1 January 1752 in Philadelphia, she was raised a Quaker and educated in Quaker schools. The Quakers disowned her when she married John Ross, an Episcopalian, in 1773. After his death, in 1776, she took over his Philadelphia upholstering business. According to a paper given before the Historical Society of Pennsylvania in 1870, Ross was visited in 1776 by George Washington, Robert Morris, and George Ross, her late husband's uncle, who were members of a secret committee of the Continental Congress. The team commissioned her to design a flag for the new nation. Ross is said to have suggested the use of a six-point star instead of a five-point star on the flag. However, no contemporary evidence exists for this story. Ross married Joseph Ashburn in 1777. He died in 1782, and she married John Claypoole a year later. Her daughter took over the profitable upholstery business in 1827. She died 30 January 1836 in Philadelphia.

Rowlandson, Mary White (c. 1635–c. 1678)

Mary Rowlandson wrote the first published account of a New Englander captured by Native Americans. Born about 1635 in England, she came with her parents to America as a child. She lived in Salem, Massachusetts, until 1653, at which time the family moved to Lancaster. In 1656 she married the Rev. Joseph Rowlandson and lived quietly for the next 20 years. But in 1676 she found herself in the middle of King Philip's War. Five tribes—the Wampanoags, Mohegans, Narragansetts, Poduncks, and Nipmucks—felt the pressure of New England settlers' expansion. When Philip became chief of the Wampanoags (1662), tension mounted between the tribes and the settlers. On 9 September 1675, the New England Confederation declared war on the tribes. The war continued until 1676. In February of that year, Rowlandson's house was attacked in retaliation for the massacre of more than 600 Narragansetts at their winter home in the swamps of central Rhode Island the previous November. "At length," Rowlandson wrote, "they came and beset our House, and quickly it was the dolefullest day that ever mine eys say." She later wrote, "Some in our House were fighting for their Lives, others wallowing in their Blood; the House on fire over our Heads, and the bloddy Heathen ready to knock us on the Head if we stirred out." Rowlandson, her three children, and 20 other captives were taken prisoner. In a forced march west, her young daughter died of starvation and a bullet wound. Rowlandson's sewing skills may have saved her own life; she was given some measure of respect and eventually was ransomed back to her husband. Her captivity narrative became a classic of captivity and colonial literature, contributing a great deal of information about her captors. In the second edition it was titled *The Soveraignty & Goodness of God, Together, with the Faithfulness of His Promises Displayed: Being a Narrative of the Captivity and Restauration of Mrs. Mary Rowlandson.* Rowlandson died after 1678; the place of her death is unknown.

See also Duston, Hannah.

Rowson, Susanna Haswell (c. 1762–1824)

Susanna Haswell Rowson was the first best-selling novelist in the United States. Born about 1762 in Portsmouth, England, she came to America in 1768, where she lived in

Nantasket Beach, Massachusetts. She became an actress and wrote many of her own productions. Her first novel, *Victoria*, was published in 1786. Her second, *Charlotte* (1791), was read on both sides of the Atlantic and went into 200 printings. Rowson founded a Young Ladies Academy in Boston, one of the first to educate girls after elementary school (1797–1822). She wrote many of her own texts as well as articles and novels in which she protested the low position of women. Rowson died 2 March 1824 in Boston.

RU-486 Controversy

The RU-486 controversy, which began in the 1980s, adds a new dimension to the abortion debate. RU-486 is a French drug that, when used in conjunction with another drug, can induce an abortion, thus eliminating the need for surgery. Because it seems to offer easier access to abortion, antiabortion groups have threatened to boycott any company marketing the drug. The Food and Drug Administration ruled that the drug could not be brought into the United States by any means. Feminists have continued to press for release of the drug for use under medical supervision. Many physicians have noted the drug's other potential uses, for example, the treatment of Cushing's disease and endometriosis.

See also Abortion; Birth Control; Contraception.

Rush, Benjamin (1746–1813)

Physician and educator Benjamin Rush advocated equal education for women. He was born 4 January 1746 near Philadelphia. A pioneer in the scientific treatment of the mentally ill, he received a medical degree

from the University of Edinburgh in 1768. A friend of Benjamin Franklin, Rush represented Pennsylvania at the second Continental Congress in 1776 and signed the Declaration of Independence. John Adams appointed him treasurer of the U.S. mint in 1797. An advocate of reform in many areas, in 1774 Rush and James Pemberton founded the first antislavery society in America. Rush attacked the evils of drink, argued for an end to capital punishment, advocated the establishment of new and better schools, and championed improvements to women's education.

Rush gave the 18 July 1787 commencement address at the Young Ladies Academy of Philadelphia. The address was titled "Thoughts upon Female Education, Accommodated to the Present State of Society, Manners, and the Government of the United States." In it Rush carefully presented the case for equal education. He stated that American women required much better education than British women to be better guardians of their husband's property, better instructors of their children, and better supervisors of household servants, who were more independent than their British counterparts. He believed women should not be confined to a narrow range of subjects but should study grammar, writing, math, bookkeeping, history, geography, astronomy, natural philosophy, music, dancing, and religion. Rush's writing covered topics from capital punishment and smoking to the study of Latin and Greek to the use of medicine among Native Americans. His five-volume work, *Medical Inquiries and Observations* (1789–1798), includes the first American treatise on the scientific treatment of mental illness. Rush died in 1813 in Philadelphia.

Sacajawea (c. 1786–1812)

Born about 1786, in either western Montana or eastern Idaho, Sacajawea became famous as the interpreter for the explorers Meriwether Lewis and William Clark. She was a member of the Snake tribe of the Shoshone. At the age of 13, she was forcibly taken by a group of Hidatsas to their camp in what is now North Dakota. She was then sold to Toussaint Charbonneau, a fur trapper, who married her in 1804. In that same year, the Lewis and Clark Expedition wintered in the area and hired the couple as guides for their travels to the Pacific Coast. Sacajawea's knowledge of various languages and her relationship to the chief of the Lemhi Shoshone (who was her brother) helped the explorers secure passage across the Continental Divide. Sacajawea died 20 December 1812 near present-day Omaha, Nebraska.

Salem (Ohio) Convention

The third women's rights convention in the United States was held 19–20 April 1850 at the Second Baptist Church in Salem, Ohio. (The first convention was in Seneca Falls, New York; the second in Rochester, New York.) According to the *History of Woman Suffrage* (Volume 1), the convention had a particular characteristic: it was officiated entirely by women. "*Never did men so suffer.* They implored just to say a word; but no; the President was inflexible—no man should be heard." The women leaders even refused men the right to vote or sit on the platform. The men, well aware that women experienced the same exclusion at male-dominated gatherings, suffered the insults with dignity and "generously endorsed all the ladies had said and done." The convention called for the first national women's rights convention, held later that year in Worcester, Massachusetts. Over the next decade women's rights conventions were held annually, except in 1857. The officers of the Salem Convention were: Betsey M. Cowles, president; Lydia B. Irish, Harriet P. Weaver, and Rana Dota, vice-presidents; Caroline Stanton, Ann Eliza Lee, and Sallie B. Grove, secretaries; and six other members of the Business Committee.

Salem Witch Trials

In 1692, in the town of Salem Village, now Danvers (Massachusetts Bay colony), 14 women and five men were hung for practicing witchcraft. (A sixth man, Giles Corey, was pressed to death for refusing to plead to the indictment.) The witchcraft hysteria that spread through the town and neighboring areas is the most serious example of the disintegration of an American community in the 1600s.

It began when two girls in a pastor's household repeated to a teenage companion the accounts of Barbadian voodoo told to them by the family's servant, Tituba. The girls fell to the ground in "fits," presumably because of witches, who also pinched and stuck pins in them. An inflammatory sermon, preached by a visiting preacher, aroused suspicions of the devil. The children joined forces and began accusing adults of practicing black magic upon them. Soon, the civil magistrate became involved, and a court was appointed by the governor. Between May and September, hundreds were arrested, 19 executed, and many others jailed. Among the accused were Sarah Nurse, old and deaf and a newcomer to the colony; other older or aggressive women; and a bawdy woman who gave loud parties and dressed in red. Some of the accused women had inherited money, upsetting the traditional male-dominated system of inheritance. Others were suspected of being imperfect Puritans. By 1693, all those

265

arrested had been released, as the community resisted the further rise of mass hysteria. The Salem witch trials were one of the most important instances of social and political conflict in the seventeenth century and have been used by some historians to illustrate the power of gossip as a means of social control during this period.

Sampson, Deborah (1760–1827)

Deborah Sampson was the first woman to impersonate a man in battle and then lecture on her military experiences. She was born 17 December 1760 in Plympton, Massachusetts. In 1782 she walked to Boston, and on 20 May she enlisted in the revolutionary army as Robert Shurtleff. Four months later, the First Baptist Church of Middleborough, Massachusetts, which Sampson had joined two years earlier, excommunicated her for dressing as a man, enlisting in the army, and for long-term behavior that was "loose and unchristian like." Sampson fought in several skirmishes and was wounded in Tarrytown, New York. When she was hospitalized for a fever, her gender was discovered, and in 1783 she was discharged. In 1805, Congress granted Sampson a veteran's disability pension and, after 1818, a full pension. She returned to Massachusetts, where she married and raised three children. Beginning in 1802 she became the first woman to give public lectures on her military experience. Sampson died 29 April 1827 in Sharon, Massachusetts.

Samuelson, Joan Benoit

See Benoit (Samuelson), Joan.

Sanger, Margaret Higgins (1883–1966)

Margaret Sanger, founder of the American birth control movement, was jailed at least nine times for campaigning for the right of women to use birth control. Sanger was born Margaret Louise Higgins on 14 September 1879 in Corning, New York. One of 11 children, she would later attribute her

Margaret Sanger

mother's early death in 1899, at age 49 or 50, to her frequent pregnancies. The family was poor, with a neighbor recalling that one brother had to wear his sister's clothes while his mother pressed his trousers. In spite of poverty, Higgins attended Claverack College in New York's Catskills, then taught school. The death of her mother may have focused her attention on medicine and birth control, for she soon after entered the White Plains Hospital in New York, where she completed two years of nurse's training, working in a drafty 12-bed hospital with no plumbing or central heating. There she became head nurse of the women's ward. In 1902 she married William Sanger; their wedding was a quick one so that Margaret could report for her 4:30 A.M. shift the next day. She retained his surname after their divorce 18 years later, but the couple was separated long before, Margaret unwilling to fulfill Bill's wish for a "real home" with Margaret in it as "presiding queen." The couple had three children.

Sanger worked as a home nurse in New York City, ministering primarily to maternity patients in the slums of the Lower East Side. There, she witnessed the high rate of infant mortality, unplanned pregnancies, and self-induced abortions. The Sangers had befriended numerous socialists and radicals. During 1910 and 1911, Margaret lectured to Socialist party women on sexuality, her popularity leading to an invitation to write articles about female sexuality, sexual liberation, and birth control in a column called "What Every Girl Should Know" in the Socialist party's paper, *The Call*. In one column she explicitly condemned conventions that forced women to rely on men for support. Though later collected in two books, *What Every Girl Should Know* (1916) and *What Every Mother Should Know* (1917), the articles caused a furor in 1913, prompting the U.S. Postal Service to refuse to mail *The Call*, judging one of the essays, on syphilis, to be obscene according to the criteria of the 1873 Comstock Act, which classified information about birth control and contraception obscene and prohibited use of the post office for mailing such information.

Margaret joined the Industrial Workers of the World in their efforts to unionize the textile workers in the Northeast, particularly during 1912–1913. With Elizabeth Gurley Flynn, she helped evacuate the workers' children during the "Bread and Roses" strike in Lawrence, Massachusetts. Gradually, Sanger distanced herself from her radical male friends because, unlike her, their agenda did not emphasize birth control.

By 1912, Sanger had given up nursing to devote her life to birth control, a term coined by Otto Bobstein in 1914. In 1913, she traveled to Scotland and France, gathering information. When she returned in 1914, she launched a monthly radical magazine, *The Woman Rebel*, which was intended to challenge the Comstock law. In March it was published from Sanger's dining table. When the term *birth control* appeared in the publication, and with it the promise to provide women with contraceptive advice, the post office once again cited the 1873 Comstock Act and refused to mail the magazine, threatening Sanger with arrest if she continued to attempt to mail the *Rebel*. She did so nonetheless and in August 1914 was arrested for violating the postal code. Sanger left for

Europe the day before her trial, having been charged on four criminal counts carrying a maximum sentence of 45 years. In Europe she continued her study of birth control, attending Dutch classes in how to fit diaphragms and visiting Dutch birth control clinics. Before leaving New York, Sanger wrote the pamphlet "Family Limitation," which explained with diagrams methods of birth control. Once outside the United States, she cabled New Jersey printer Bill Shattoff to publish 100,000 copies of "Family Limitation." IWW locals helped distribute the pamphlet and by 1917, 160,000 copies had been sold.

In 1915, Sanger returned to the United States, where charges against her were soon dropped. On 16 October 1916, using a $50 donation, Sanger opened, according to Ellen Chesler, the country's first birth control clinic, an act of civil disobedience. The clinic occupied two rooms on the ground floor at 46 Amboy Street, near Pitkin Avenue in the Brownsville section of Brooklyn. Announcements of the opening were printed in English, Yiddish, and Italian. The staff consisted of Sanger; her sister, Ethel Byrne; and a Yiddish-speaking woman, Fania Mindell. In the ten days before police closed the clinic, almost 500 women visited the clinic to get information about birth control and contraceptive devices. Mindell was fined for selling copies of *What Every Girl Should Know*. Byrne was sentenced to 32 days imprisonment (later reversed); she went on a hunger strike until she was carried out of jail on a stretcher. Sanger was sentenced to 30 days in prison for creating a public nuisance. Her appeal to the New York Court of Appeals resulted in a ruling that allowed doctors to advise their married patients about birth control for health purposes, which she later interpreted as grounds to start doctor-staffed or legal birth control clinics (1923). Restrictions would loosen even more in 1936, when doctors were allowed to import and prescribe contraceptive devices (*United States v. One Package*).

Around the time of her release, Sanger began publication of *The Birth Control Review*. Slowly the efforts of the birth control movement showed results. During World War I, the United States distributed condoms and copies of Sanger's *What Every Girl Should Know* to soldiers. In 1921 Sanger founded the American Birth Control League, serving as its president until 1928. In 1923, she founded the Birth Control Clinical Research Bureau in New York City, which was America's first doctor-staffed or legal contraceptive clinic. In 1927 she organized the First World Population Conference. Four years later, she founded the national Committee on Federal Legislation for Birth Control.

In 1939, the American Birth Control League merged with the education department of the Birth Control Research Bureau. Three years later the group changed its name to Planned Parenthood Federation. Sanger was honorary chair of the organization. In 1953, she became founder and first president of the International Planned Parenthood Federation. Among Sanger's many books are *The Case for Birth Control* (1917), *The Pivot of Civilization* (1922), *Women, Morality and Birth Control* (1922), *Women and the New Race* (1923), *Happiness in Marriage* (1926), and *Motherhood in Bondage* (1928). She also published two autobiographies, *My Fight for Birth Control* (1931) and *Margaret Sanger: An Autobiography* (1938). In 1935, she began writing *Journal of Contraception*, later titled *Human Fertility*. Sanger died 6 September 1966 in Tucson, Arizona.

See also American Birth Control League; Birth Control; *Birth Control Review*; Comstock Act; Contraception; Industrial Workers of the World; Flynn, Elizabeth Gurley; National Birth Control League; Planned Parenthood Federation of America; *Woman Rebel*.

Sanitary Commission

The efforts of America's first female physician, Elizabeth Blackwell, led to the formation of the Sanitary Commission, a relief agency that enabled women to help soldiers during the Civil War. It coordinated the care of soldiers, staffed and supplied hospitals, supplemented soldiers' diets, instituted standards of cleanliness, and provided medi-

cal attention to the wounded. Women created order and cleanliness in the field hospitals and established hospital ships and convalescent homes.

History of Woman Suffrage (Volume II) records that Dr. Elizabeth Blackwell first called the meeting that conceived the organization. Held at the New York Infirmary for Women and Children on 25 April 1861, the group took the name Ladies Central Relief. The next day, at the Cooper Union, a public meeting was held, "its object being to concentrate scattered efforts by a large and formal organization." The organization was then named the Women's Central Relief Association of New York, and Louisa Lee Schuyler was elected its president.

Believing there was a need to affiliate with the federal government, Schuyler had an address sent to the secretary of war from the Woman's Central Relief Association, the Advisory Committee of the Board of Physicians and Surgeons of the hospitals of New York, and the New York Medical Association for furnishing medical supplies. As a result, the Sanitary Commission was founded on 9 June 1861.

Although "The Sanitary," as it was called, was a government organization, it was not sustained at taxpayers' expense but by individual women. The rules under which it was founded were:

1. The system of sanitary relief established by army regulations was to be adopted; the Sanitary Commission was to acquaint itself fully with those rules and see that its agents were familiar with all the plans and methods of the army system.

2. The commission was to direct its efforts mainly to strengthening the regular army system and work to secure the favor and cooperation of the Medical Bureau.

3. The commission was to know nothing of religious differences or state distinctions, distributing without regard

A member of the Sanitary Commission rides to aid Union soldiers during the Civil War.

to the place where troops were enlisted, in a purely national spirit.

So, under these rules, the commission raised $92 million to aid the sick and wounded Union soldiers. The organization received the affection of men in the field, "who, in tents or hospitals, hailed the approach of medicine and delicacy, with an affectionate, 'How are you, Sanitary?' "

In wars prior to the Civil War, four soldiers died of disease for every one who died in battle or of wounds received there. The Sanitary Commission, "by reducing the mortality of our troops by disease . . . to two to one," remarked Josiah H. Benton in a Memorial Day Speech on 30 May 1894, "saved more than one hundred and eighty thousand lives."

Besides its medical contributions, the Sanitary Commission enabled northern women, who made up most of its workers, to become involved in public life, encouraging some to become activists in the struggle to win the vote.

Schneiderman, Rose (1882–1972)

Rose Schneiderman's prominent role in the development of trade unionism throughout the United States spanned more than 50 years. Born Rachel Schneiderman on 6 April 1882 in Russian Poland, she and her Jewish family immigrated to the United States in 1890 and lived on the Lower East Side of New York City, where Schneiderman attended Hebrew as well as American schools. Her father died in 1892, leaving her mother to raise four young children, but Deborah Schneiderman was a resourceful and confident woman. Rose began working at age 13, helping her family to survive financially. Working as many as 70 hours per week for as little as two dollars total pay, she early on became familiar with industry work and union conditions.

Schneiderman's career as a union organizer began in 1903, when she and two other women established the first female local of the Jewish Socialist United Cloth Hat and Cap Makers' Union, for which Schneiderman became a dynamic spokesperson. The

Union organizer Rose Schneiderman speaks on behalf of the Book-keeper's, Stenographer's and Accountant's Union.

union's membership grew steadily to include several hundred people; Schneiderman herself was to remain a lifelong member. In 1910 she began to focus her attention on the Women's Trade Union League (WTUL), serving as president of the New York chapter from 1918 to 1949. She helped to organize the garment workers' strike (1909 through 1914) and was instrumental in establishing the International Ladies' Garment Workers' Union. Schneiderman was an active supporter and effective speaker for the National American Women's Association from 1913 on and she helped to establish the International Congress of Working Women in 1919.

At the end of World War I, Schneiderman supported legislation for education, minimum wage, and protective work laws. She was president of the national WTUL from 1926 until its disbanding in 1950. Her friendship with Eleanor Roosevelt led to a position in President Franklin Roosevelt's National Recovery Administration (where she was the only woman to serve) between 1933 and 1935. Another significant achieve-ment was her position as Secretary of the New York State Department of Labor from 1937 to 1943.

Schneiderman retired from public life in 1955. She died 11 August 1972 in New York City.

Schroeder, Patricia Scott (1940–)

Patricia Schroeder was the first woman Colorado ever sent to Congress and she has been a U.S. Representative from the state's first district for more than 20 years. As a Democratic candidate, her first term began after her 8 November 1972 victory over Republican incumbent James D. ("Mike") McKevitt.

Schroeder was born Patricia Scott on 30 July 1940 in Portland, Oregon, where she went to public school. She attended the University of Minnesota, receiving her B.A. degree in 1961. She completed her education at Harvard Law School, where she received a J.D. degree in 1964. While there, she met James White Schroeder, whom she married on 18 August 1962. The Schroeders moved to Colorado, where she was hired as a field attorney for the National Labor Relations Board. While raising two children, Schroeder worked as a lawyer in private practice. In 1971, Schroeder was named hearing officer for the Colorado Department of Personnel, while at the same time she served as legal counsel for Planned Parenthood of Colorado.

Schroeder's husband was partly responsible for her 1972 congressional race. James Schroeder was then a professional campaign manager who was casting about for a viable Democratic candidate to face the incumbent McKevitt. Pat Schroeder decided to run, basing her campaign on social welfare issues and opposition to wasteful defense spending and to the Vietnam War. She won the primary race against Clarence Decker by 4,000 votes and went on to beat McKevitt, earning 51.6 percent of the vote.

During her freshman term Schroeder encountered some anticipated male chauvinism. In a *People* magazine interview, she related that when asked by a fellow member of Congress how she could possibly be the "mother of two small children and a member of Congress at the same time," she replied "I have a brain and a uterus and I use them both."

Hoping to work toward curbing unnecessary defense spending, Schroeder maneuvered herself onto the Armed Services Committee in 1973, despite the opposition of Chairman F. Edward Hébert. Feeling that defense issues affected everyone, including women and children, Schroeder called for better ways to protect people than building military bases or creating bigger, more deadly weapons.

On the House floor, Schroeder focused on environmental, consumer, and social welfare issues. As chair of the National Task Force on Equal Rights for Women, Schroeder endorsed federal payment for abortions. She also criticized the Supreme Court's ruling that allowed firms to deny sick pay for pregnancy as "gender-based discrimination."

In 1993 Schroeder introduced much legislation of special interest to women. In-

cluded were: the Contraception and Infertility Research Centers Act of 1993; the Violence against Women Act of 1993; the Gender Equity in Education Act of 1993; the Women's Health Equity Act of 1993; and the Federal Prohibition of Female Genital Mutilation Act of 1993.

Schuyler, Catherine Van Rensselaer (1734–1803)

Catherine Van Rensselaer Schuyler acted bravely and patriotically during the Revolutionary War. She was born 4 November 1734 in Claverack, Columbia County, New York. In 1755, she married Philip Schuyler, who, in 1775, became one of George Washington's four major generals. Her husband was away from home when, two years later, British General John Burgoyne and his troops marched down the Hudson Valley. Catherine Schuyler—who managed the estate in her husband's absence—risked her life by approaching the British columns in order to burn her husband's fields so they could not be used to provide food for the enemy. With only one guard to accompany her, she met refugees who beseeched her to return home, but she continued on and carried out her duty successfully. Schuyler died 7 March 1803 in Albany, New York.

Seaman, Elizabeth Cochrane (1865–1922)

Elizabeth Seaman is better known as Nellie Bly, the name under which she wrote for the *Pittsburgh Dispatch*. She was born 5 May 1865, although some sources cite the year as 1867. Her place of birth, Cochran's Mills, Pennsylvania, was named for her father, Michael Cochran, and Elizabeth would later add the last "e" to her name. Although she had little formal schooling, Elizabeth was a prolific writer. She got her job at the *Pittsburgh Dispatch* in 1885, after writing an angry letter to the newspaper in response to an editorial that opposed women's suffrage. There, she covered the conditions of working women in Pittsburgh, life in the slums, and similar topics. Her byline, Nellie Bly, was chosen after a Stephen Foster song. In the winter of 1886 she traveled in Mexico, sending the *Dispatch* articles on official corruption and poverty. Although she was expelled from the country, her articles were collected in *Six Months in Mexico* (1888).

In 1887 Cochrane went to work for Joseph Pulitzer, publisher of the New York *World*. She immediately convinced Pulitzer to expose the neglect of the mentally ill by committing her to a public asylum. Her articles were published in the *World* and collected in *Ten Days in a Mad-House* (1877). Her work prompted a grand jury investigation and improvements in the care of residents. She also wrote about jails, sweatshops, and the legislature, where she exposed bribery among lobbyists. Reforms followed her investigative journalism, and a new style of undercover reporting was born. As a journalistic stunt, she became the first woman to circle the globe alone (1889–1890). The trip was a race against the record set by the fictional Phineas Fogg in Jules Verne's *Around the World in Eighty Days*. She completed the trip in 72 days, 6 hours, 11 minutes, and 14 seconds, using only commercial transportation, including steamship, train, rickshaw, and sampan. In 1895 Cochrane married Robert L. Seaman and retired from journalism. In 1919 she returned to newspapers, writing for the *New York Journal*. She died 27 January 1922 in New York City.

Second Great Awakening

During the first quarter of the nineteenth century, a Second Great Awakening, reminiscent of the first, began. Once again, the goal was to rekindle enthusiasm among churchgoers. Women had long made up the majority of church members; with the Second Great Awakening, their numbers increased even more. Women frequently converted independently of their families. Records from western New York indicate a disproportionate conversion rate among women. Historian Catharine Clinton cites the example of Utica, New York. Although half the population of Utica was female,

during a Baptist revival there in 1838, almost three-fourths of the converts were women.

Perhaps women converted in such great numbers because of the autonomy the Church allowed them. Women began playing greater roles within the Church, even doing missionary work. Certainly, the Second Great Awakening encouraged women to participate in more public activities, specifically social reform. Within the churches, women began to organize voluntary groups, such as sewing circles and charitable associations. The revival also spawned moral reform societies, Bible groups, and social welfare organizations, the most famous of which worked for abolition and temperance. In all of these movements, women were increasingly active, first in female organizations and, after the 1830s, in mixed groups of men and women. By midcentury, the number of women who had joined churches resulted in what historians have called the feminization of American religion. Some of this energy would be transferred to the social and political reforms.

See also Great Awakening.

Seneca Falls Convention

The Seneca Falls Convention was the first women's rights convention in U.S. history. In 1848 Elizabeth Cady Stanton received an invitation to tea at the home of Jane Hunt in Waterloo, New York. There, she became reacquainted with abolitionist leader Lucretia Mott and also met Martha Wright and Mary Ann McClintock. Cady Stanton confessed her long-standing discontent about the status of women and found that the other women shared her complaints. She and Mott recalled holding their first discussion about a women's rights convention in 1840, as they walked arm in arm in London, while attending the World Anti-Slavery Convention. "Sitting around the tea-table," the four women drafted a notice for the local paper, the *Seneca County Courier*.

"Women's Rights Convention.—A Convention to discuss the social, civil, and religious condition and rights of woman, will be held in the Wesleyan Chapel, at Seneca Falls, N.Y., on Wednesday and Thursday, the 19th and 20th of July, current; commencing at 10 o'clock A.M. During the first day, the meeting will be exclusively for women, who are earnestly invited to attend. The public generally are invited to be present on the second day, when Lucretia Mott, of Philadelphia, and other ladies and gentlemen, will address the convention."

On Sunday morning, they once again met in McClintock's parlor to write a declaration and resolutions and select topics for speeches. (The antique mahogany center-table on which the documents were written would later be put on display at the Smithsonian Institution.) They had only three days before the meeting, and "no experience in the *modus operandi* of setting up conventions, nor in that kind of literature. . . . On the first attempt to frame a resolution, to crowd a complete thought, clearly and concisely into three lines, they felt as helpless and hopeless as if they had been suddenly asked to construct a steam engine."

History of Woman Suffrage (Volume I) records the "humiliating fact" that "before taking the initiative step, these ladies resigned themselves to a faithful perusal of various masculine productions. The reports of Peace, Temperance, and Anti-slavery conventions were examined, but all alike seemed too tame and specific for the inauguration of a rebellion such as the world had never seen before."

After much give and take, one of the four took up the Declaration of Independence, reading aloud with much emotion. Immediately, the group decided to pattern their own declaration on it, substituting "all men" for "King George." Noting that the founding fathers had 18 grievances, they pored over law books and other sources, aided by some of their male friends, until their case was made, and the 18 grievances were drafted.

On 19–20 July 1848, the convention convened at the Wesleyan Methodist chapel in Seneca Falls, New York. When the organizers arrived the door was locked, but "an embryo professor of Yale College was lifted through an open window to unbar the door," and the church quickly filled.

About 300 people attended the convention, which was chaired by Lucretia Mott's husband James. Lucretia Mott, Elizabeth Cady Stanton, and Elizabeth and Mary McClintock spoke to the assembly. Finally, Cady Stanton read The Declaration of Sentiments, which began, "When in the course of human events," and went on to declare that "men and women are created equal." The 18 grievances that followed included the lack of the vote, right to wages, and equal custody of children. After the assembly passed the Declaration, they also adopted 12 resolutions—the ninth of which, calling for the vote, barely passed. Cady Stanton, the principal writer of the group, insisted that the ninth resolution be included over the objections of Mott. Henry Stanton, who generally supported women's rights, objected so strongly to the ninth resolution that he left town and stayed away until the convention was over. Much hard discussion focused on this resolution, which held "That it is the duty of women of this country to secure to themselves their sacred right to the elective franchise." Many of the convention attendees feared that the demand for the vote would work against the other resolutions and make the whole movement appear ridiculous. But Cady Stanton and Frederick Douglass argued persistently until the ninth resolution was approved. By the end of the convention, 68 women and 32 men had signed the Declaration of Sentiments.

After the convention the women faced a storm of criticism from the press. One editorial called the meeting "the most shocking and unnatural incident ever recorded in the history of womanity." The *Worcester Telegraph* (Massachusetts) opined, "The list of grievances which the *Amazons* exhibit, concludes by expressing a determination to insist that women shall have 'immediate admission to all rights and privileges which belong to them as citizens of the United States.' . . . This is *bolting* with a vengeance."

Only a few papers, such as Horace Greeley's *New York Tribune* and Frederick Douglass's *North Star*, supported the women. The negative press caused many of the 100 people who had signed the declaration to withdraw their names.

A second convention was held two weeks later at Rochester, New York. After 18 months, as news spread of the Seneca Falls convention, preparations began for conventions in other states, including Massachusetts, Ohio, Pennsylvania, and Indiana. With a program and leadership established, the women's movement in the United States had officially begun.

See also Anthony, Susan B.; Declaration of Sentiments; Douglass, Frederick; Greeley, Horace; Mott, Lucretia; Stanton, Elizabeth Cady.

Separate Estate

Under English common law and the early law of the colonies, single women were equal to men before the law and were able to own property. Once a woman married, however, she lost legal standing and the right to own property. A woman could retain some degree of independence if she brought her own real property to the marriage and if her husband consented to her separate ownership. *Separate estate* is the term for the property brought by a wife to her marriage.

See also Common Law; Dower; *Feme Covert.*

Separatist Feminism

See Radical Feminism.

Settlement House Movement

The settlement house movement began in England when Anglican clergyman Samuel A. Barnett and several Oxford University students founded Toynbee Hall in an undesirable section of East London in 1884. Their concept was to enable university men to establish themselves in a working-class neighborhood so they could experience poverty at close hand and then help to alleviate it.

The settlement idea soon reached the United States. Stanton Coit was the first to establish a U.S. settlement house with the 1886 opening of the Neighborhood Guild on the Lower East Side of New York City. Three years later, Jane Addams and Ellen Starr began Hull House on the West Side of Chicago. The settlement house concept spread quickly and by 1900 there were more than 100 houses throughout the country.

A common goal of the houses was to teach middle-class values to the poor. There were, of course, differences between the English and U.S. houses. Women became more actively involved as leaders of the U.S. establishments. The most significant difference was that the U.S. centers worked with more diverse cultural groups. In some instances, immigrants were helped to adjust to their new country's way of life. With guidance, African-American communities began neighborhood settlements, and Hull House played a key role in the founding of the National Association for the Advancement of Colored People.

Settlements were organized to preserve human values in a rapidly industrializing age. They often began with the organization of clubs, lectures, or classes on various topics, then expanded services to include boardinghouses, day nurseries, and dispensaries. Settlements also provided their own workers an avenue for expanding their careers in politics and social leadership. Progressive women's leaders such as Florence Kelley, Julia Lathrop, and Grace Abbott were such workers. Alice Hamilton left Hull House to accept a position as the first woman professor at Harvard Medical School in 1919. The settlement house movement also led to the growth of social work as a profession for women, many of whom played a key role in the New Deal.

Throughout the years, settlements went through periods of change and reform. By 1980, there were still 800 official settlements, many of them now called neighborhood centers. Though it is no longer traditional for workers to live at the centers, they continue to provide valuable services to senior citizens, troubled youths, and abused women and children.

See also Addams, Jane; Henry Street Settlement; Kelley, Florence.

Settlements, Marriage or Antenuptial

Under common law in colonial America, a married woman could not own property; any land that a single woman owned was managed by her husband after marriage. A wife's only protection was to withhold her consent for the transfer of her lands. The land that a woman owned before she was married was called her separate estate. Equity law provided ways for a married woman to own and control her separate estate. Paramount among these was the marriage or antenuptial settlement. At first, equity courts enforced only marriage settlements that were in the form of a trust. Under this arrangement, a third party administered the wife's separate estate for her. By the end of the eighteenth century, marriage settlements existed in several forms

Sex Equity

See Comparable Worth.

Sexual Division of Labor

The division of labor by sex—encouraged by sex-segregated want ads—was a key reason women constituted the cheapest labor pool in America in 1900. In 1870 there were 1.3 million nonagricultural women workers, 70 percent of whom were domestics. Shoe making, clothing, and textile production accounted for 24 percent of the nonagricultural women workers. By the end of the nineteenth century, according to the U. S. census, 360 of 369 industries employed women—most of them in unskilled, segregated jobs, earning one-half to one-third the wages of male workers. Piecework was a corollary factor in suppressing women's wages. In the late twentieth century, sexual division of labor results in a majority of women (by some estimates 80 percent) being concentrated in too few job categories, called pink-collar industries. These jobs,

making up 20 of 427 government categories, include teaching, nursing, clerical, and retail work. Comparable worth, or equal pay for comparable work, has been touted as the means to end pay inequities caused by the sexual division of labor.

See also Comparable Worth; Piecework.

Sexual Politics
See Millett, Kate.

Shakers
See Utopian Communities.

Shaw, Anna Howard (1847–1919)

Anna Howard Shaw was a clergywoman, physician, and suffragist. Born 14 February 1847, in Newcastle-on-Tyne, England, her family settled in Massachusetts in 1851. Because her father was away from home for extended periods of time and her mother suffered from a psychiatric collapse, Anna was forced to concern herself with family survival at the age of 12, clearing land, planting crops, and carrying on for her family. Thus, she grew up knowing that she could not rely on marriage for security. When Shaw was a young woman, the Methodist church began to license female ministers. Shaw became a preacher, delivering her first sermon in 1870. At the age of 26 she enrolled in Albion College (Michigan), paying her way by preaching and lecturing on the evils of drink. In 1876 she enrolled in Boston University's divinity school, graduating in 1878. That same year, she assumed responsibilities for a church in East Dennis, Massachusetts, but the New England Conference of the Methodist Episcopal church refused to allow Shaw to administer the sacraments; when she appealed its decision to the General Conference, the group revoked her license to preach. At last, in 1880, she was ordained by the Methodist Protestant church as their first female minister. Deciding she could help women more by practicing medicine

275

than by preaching, she earned an M.D. from Boston University in 1886.

At about this time Shaw began to lecture about women's suffrage. In 1885 she became a lecturer for the Massachusetts Woman Suffrage Association, and from 1888 to 1892 she served as superintendent of the franchise department of the Woman's Christian Temperance Union. She became a national lecturer for the National American Woman Suffrage Association (NAWSA) in 1891 and vice-president of NAWSA in 1892, serving until 1904, when she succeeded Carrie Chapman Catt as president. Shaw stepped down in 1915 because she lacked the support of the group and because of the growing split with Alice Paul's Congressional Union. At the age of 70, at the start of World War I, Shaw was appointed to chair the Woman's Committee of the U.S. Council of National Defense, a post that she held until 1919. Although she intended to resume lecturing on behalf of the Nineteenth Amendment, former president William Howard Taft convinced her to speak for the League of Nations. During her lecture tour she became ill. She died 2 July 1919 in Moylan, Pennsylvania.

See also National American Woman Suffrage Association.

She-Merchant

By the mid-eighteenth century the female shopkeeper, or she-merchant, was an established figure in New York society. A letter to John Peter Zenger, editor of the *New York Journal* (21 January 1733), makes this clear: "We, the widows of this city . . . are House Keepers, Pay our Taxes, carry on Trade, and most of us are she Merchants, and as we in some measure contribute to the Support of Government, we ought to be Intitled to some of the Sweets of it." Female shopkeepers were common throughout the northern colonies. As early as 1643, a Mrs. Goose in Salem, Massachusetts, sold groceries, as probate records of Joanna Cummins's will indicate: Cummins owed Goose for one pound of sugar. She-merchants sold a vari-

ety of goods, including liquor, window glass, clothes, dry goods, groceries, and seeds. She-merchants also kept tobacco stores, eyeglass shops, apothecaries, bookstores, import houses, and a colonial version of the hardware store, which also carried cutlery and other goods. Some women went into partnerships with men unrelated to them. The proportion of she-merchants doing business in the colonies before 1776 was probably higher than in 1900, according to historian Elizabeth Anthony Dexter, who puts the figure at 9.5 percent and 4.3 percent, respectively.

Colonial women also did business as innkeepers. If no one wanted to be the town's innkeeper, the selectman assigned the job to someone who had a large house. This is one way that widows with large houses became innkeepers. It is possible that, as in the case of shopkeepers, there were more female innkeepers during the colonial period than there were early in the twentieth century.

See also Feme Sole Trader.

Sheppard-Towner Act

One of the few laws of its time that dealt with women's issues, the Sheppard-Towner Act (1921) required that $1.25 million be spent annually to improve the health of mothers and infants. In spite of criticism from opponents of the bill over what they perceived as excessive government interference in what was considered essentially a family matter, the act won the endorsement of President Warren G. Harding and passed both houses of Congress without considerable dissent. Its passage was one of the major successes of the Women's Joint Congressional Committee, and has been attributed to lawmakers' fear that women voters would retaliate if the bill failed to pass. Documentation showed that the lack of funds for mother and infant health care caused hundreds of thousands of deaths each year. There was considerable anxiety about the undiscovered potential of the new women's vote, especially because the Sheppard-Towner Act was clearly the type of compassionate legislation that women were said to favor.

See also Women's Joint Congressional Committee.

Signs

Catherine Stimpson, a pioneer in the field of women's studies, was the editor of *Signs: A Journey of Women in Culture and Society*, the best-known women's studies journal introduced in the 1970s. First published in 1975, *Signs* provided an important forum for the exchange of feminist ideas before the publication of large numbers of books in the field. The quarterly became one of the best-selling journals of the University of Chicago Press. As of 1994, *Signs* was still in circulation.

Smith, Abby Hadassah (1797–1878), and Smith, Julia Evelina (1792–1886)

Reformers Abby and Julia Smith came to suffrage late in life. They were born in Glastonbury, Connecticut: Abby on 1 June 1797, and Julia on 27 May 1792. Both sisters were educated at home, and for a few years Julia taught at the Troy Female Seminary. Both were active in temperance and abolition work. William Lloyd Garrison, barred from all Hartford churches, held his abolition meetings on the lawn of their home. In 1869, when Abby was 72 years old and Julia was 77, they attended their first women's suffrage meeting in Hartford, Connecticut. Four years later Julia attended the first meeting of the Association for the Advancement of Women in New York. In November 1873 the sisters became angry about what they considered unfair property taxes. They attended a Glastonbury town meeting, where Abby read a protest against the taxation of women who were denied the vote. From that time forward, she and Julia refused to pay taxes because they were not allowed to vote in the town meetings. In January 1874 seven of their cows were seized by the town and sold to pay the sisters' taxes. At a town meeting in

April they confronted the men. When Abby was denied permission to speak at the meeting, she climbed on a wagon parked outside the building and delivered her speech to the crowd. As the Smiths refused to pay any taxes, in June officials seized 15 acres of their land, valued at $2,000, to pay $50 of what was due. After a prolonged legal battle, the sisters succeeded in having the sale of the land set aside. They bought back their cows, but the animals, now known as the Glastonbury Cows, were sold twice more for back taxes. The sisters became famous, and their case was described in a pamphlet edited by Julia, *Abby Smith and Her Cows, with a Report of the Law Case Decided Contrary to Law* (1877). In 1876, Julia published a translation of the Bible in an attempt to display the intellectual ability of women. The sisters spoke at many suffrage meetings and before governmental bodies. In January 1878 Julia addressed the Senate and, in March of that year, Abby testified before a committee of the Connecticut legislature. Abby Smith died 23 July 1878. The next year Julia married and moved to Hartford, where she died 6 March 1886.

Smith, Gerrit (1797–1874)

Born in 1797, Gerrit Smith was a social reformer and ally of the women's suffrage movement. A cousin of Elizabeth Cady Stanton, he inspired her with his reform ideas. He managed the family fortune and dispensed much of it to philanthropies for the poor. He supported the temperance, women's rights, and abolition causes. In 1840, he helped found the antislavery Liberty party and was its candidate for governor of New York that year. Gerrit Smith's daughter, Elizabeth Smith Miller, is credited with seeing the Bloomer outfit in Europe and, with Amelia Bloomer and Elizabeth Cady Stanton, introducing it to American women in the 1850s. In 1853 Smith was elected to the House of Representatives on an abolition ticket. Beginning in 1858 he gave financial support to John Brown and may have known about

Brown's 1859 raid on the arsenal at Harper's Ferry. In 1872 Smith was a delegate to the Republican National Convention. He died in New York City in 1874.

See also American Anti-Slavery Society.

Smith, Hannah Whitall (1832–1911)

Hannah Smith was a leading preacher and author of religious tracts. Born 7 February 1832 in Philadelphia, she was raised as a Quaker and educated at the Friends' School. In 1851 she married Robert P. Smith, also a Quaker, and they moved to Germantown, Pennsylvania. In 1865 they moved to Millville, New Jersey. There they were influenced by the Methodist holiness movement, which taught that sanctification comes through faith and the experience of salvation. Soon Robert Smith began preaching at meetings and publishing the periodical *Christian's Pathway to Power*. Hannah Smith contributed to the periodical and began to preach. In 1873 her husband went to England; in 1874 she followed. The Smiths became the dominant figures in the interdenominational Higher Life movement that was popular in England from 1873 to 1875. Hannah Smith was called the "angel of the churches" because of her eloquent speaking style. Their prominence ended when Robert Smith was implicated in a scandal, and the two returned to Philadelphia. After 1875 Hannah Smith spoke at many women's suffrage conventions. She was a well-known advocate of college education for women, influencing her niece, Martha Carey Thomas, who later became president of Bryn Mawr and the founder of a preparatory school, the Bryn Mawr School for Girls. Smith helped found the Woman's Christian Temperance Union, and in 1883 became the first superintendent of its national evangelistic department. She wrote a number of books. *The Record of a Happy Life; Being Memorials of Franklin Whitall Smith*, a memoir of her late son, was privately published in 1873. *The Christian's Secret of a Happy Life* (1875) sold two million copies around the world. Her other works include *John M. Whitall: The Story of His Life* (1879), *Every-Day Religion; or, the Common-Sense Teaching of the Bible* (1893), *The Unselfishness of God and How I Discovered It* (1903), and *Walking in the Sunshine* (1906). The Smiths returned to England in 1888. Hannah Smith died 1 May 1911 in Effley, England.

See also Education; National Woman's Christian Temperance Union.

Smith, Sophia

See Smith College.

Smith College

Smith College, founded in 1875 in Northampton, Massachusetts, was one of the first institutions of higher learning in New England to offer women an education equal to that offered men. It is also the first women's college for which funds were provided by a woman. Smith was founded by the will of Sophia Smith, who bequeathed $393,105 "for the establishment and maintenance of an institution for the higher education of young women, with the design to furnish them means and facilities for education equal to those which are afforded in our colleges for young men." The idea for the college originated with the Rev. John Morton Greene, who advised Smith on how to dispose of her fortune. Initially, the concept was opposed by the presidents of Amherst, Harvard, Willams, and Yale, whom Greene consulted. But, by 1868, Sophia Smith decided on her course of action. Smith's will specified Northampton as the site of the college and named its trustees. The college was chartered in 1871 and opened in 1875. Smith's wish that women maintain conventional feminine standards led to the establishment of the house system of living, which organized students into familylike quarters. Smith College, the largest independent women's college in the world, saw its endowment grow from the original $393,105 to nearly $80 million in the 1970s.

See also Institute To Coordinate Women's Interests.

Society of Friends

Colonial American women were discouraged from participating in public affairs, and since the time of the religious leader Anne Hutchinson were expected to be silent in church. Only one denomination, the Society of Friends, permitted women to preach, prophesy, or speak in meetings. Other denominations used the writings of St. Paul in the New Testament of the Bible to forbid women to preach or participate in church governance.

The Society of Friends originated in England during the seventeenth century. The founder, George Fox, who began to preach in 1647, believed that a person could find spiritual guidance through an Inner Light. The believers rejected weapons, the taking of oaths, and social or official titles. They dressed simply and used the forms of address "thee" and "thou." Members of the Society of Friends were called Quakers because they trembled with emotion during their meetings.

The Quakers were persecuted in New England. In 1656, Mary Fisher reached Boston but was deported by the Puritans, who banned further Quaker immigration. Despite fines and floggings, other Quakers came to the Bay Colony. In 1659–1661, four Quakers were hung in Boston. Yet the Quakers found safe harbor in Rhode Island and in a colony created for them by William Penn (the founder of Pennsylvania). Quakers also became established on Cape Cod (1657), Long Island (1657), Maryland (1656), and Virginia (1657). By 1676, they inhabited sections from New England to the Carolinas. By the nineteenth century, they were also living on the Pacific Coast. In 1827–1828 the Friends split (the "Great Separation") and formed two groups: the Hicksites under Elias Hicks, who stressed inner guidance, and an orthodox group, which preferred guidance by the scriptures. Many women and reform-minded Quakers sided with the Hicksites.

Lucretia Mott was ordained a Quaker minister in 1821, when she was 28 years old. Of the five organizers of the Seneca Falls convention in 1848, four were Quakers: Lucretia Mott, Mary Ann McClintock, Martha Wright, and Jane Hunt. The Quakers were active in the abolition, temperance, and women's suffrage movements and were the first organization in history to ban slaveholding. They valued education, including higher education for women. Bryn Mawr was founded in 1885 by a group of Pennsylvania and Baltimore Quakers. Suffrage leader Alice Paul was one of the church's most active members in the realm of politics. The National Woman's Party, founded by Paul, included many Quakers, who were its most active members and leaders. In 1947 the American Friends Service Committee, which was organized in 1917 to help Quakers substitute noncombatant work in place of military service, and the Service Council of the British Society of Friends were jointly awarded the Nobel Peace Prize. Still active in the causes of peace and justice, the Society of Friends has one of the longest and most honorable traditions of activism in America.

See also Mott, Lucretia; Paul, Alice.

SPARS

In 1942 the U.S. Coast Guard created a women's corps. The corps was named SPARS after the coast guard motto, Semper Paratus ("Always Ready"). During World War II, about 13,000 women were members of SPARS. Their service freed men for front-line duty. Reporting to the Department of Transportation, the U.S. Coast Guard is not prohibited from training women for combat roles. For this reason, combat experience being important for promotion in the other armed services branches, women have had more opportunity for advancement in the coast guard than in other branches of the armed forces.

Stanton, Elizabeth Cady (1815–1902)

Elizabeth Cady Stanton was the spirit behind the first women's rights convention at Seneca Falls, New York, and the first woman to address the New York legislature. She was also the cofounder of the National Woman Suffrage Association, over which she nearly continuously presided from 1869 until 1890. Elizabeth Cady was born 12 November 1815 in Johnstown, New York, one of five daughters of the tall, queenlike horsewoman Margaret Livingston and lawyer Daniel Cady. A friend once described her as the girl with "the joyous laugh, the merry joke, the smile, the kind word." She was lively, sociable, and a bit of a prankster. However, she thought that her father's hopes and ambitions rested with her brother Eleazer, "a fine, manly fellow, the very apple of my father's eye," she wrote. When Eleazer died at the age of 20, Elizabeth threw her arms around her father's neck and promised she would try to be "all my brother was." She studied Greek, learned to ride horseback, and became the only girl to study math and Latin at Johnstown Academy. Despite her efforts, she believed that her father did not value her accomplishments. Years later she would write that Eleazer "filled a larger place in his affections and future plans than the five girls altogether." Until she died she remembered the day she ran home to show him a top prize she had earned in Greek, only to hear him sigh, "Ah, you should have been a boy."

At the age of 15, Elizabeth wanted to go with her male classmates to Union College in Schenectady, New York. At that time no college in America admitted girls, so she was forced to attend Emma Willard's Troy Female Seminary, from which she graduated in 1832. Although it was the most advanced school for girls of its day, the Troy Female Seminary could not match the standards of the men's colleges, and she was unhappy there.

In 1839 Elizabeth met Henry Stanton, a 24-year-old abolitionist, at the home of her cousin, reformer Gerrit Smith (father of Amelia Bloomer). One month later Stanton proposed, despite the fact that he was already betrothed. She stalled, but when he said he was going to London as a delegate to the World's Anti-Slavery Convention, she immediately made her decision. The two were married 10 May 1840, Elizabeth insisting that the word *obey* be struck from the ceremony. Two days later, the newlyweds were aboard the ship *Montreal* en route to England.

On the ship, Elizabeth Cady Stanton formed her first impression of the Quaker minister Lucretia Mott: Strolling on deck she listened as the Liberty party's presidential candidate, James G. Birney, described Mott and the other female delegates as women "who had fanned the flames of dissention, and had completely demoralized the anti-slavery ranks" by attending the convention. Stanton went on to recall in her eulogy at Mott's memorial service (19 January 1881), "As my first view of Mrs. Mott was through his prejudices, no prepossessions in her favor biased my judgment." At the conference Stanton saw the American female delegates excluded because of their gender. She sat with them behind a curtained partition, unable to participate in the meetings. She would never forget the humiliation, and she spent many hours walking with Mott through the streets of London, planning a new movement of women to fight for equality.

After returning to the United States, the Stantons lived with the Cady family. While Henry Stanton studied law with his father-in-law, Elizabeth Cady Stanton cared for their family, reading law and economics in her spare time. Henry opened a law practice in Boston in 1842, and the following year Elizabeth joined him, where the two enjoyed city life among their antislavery colleagues and reform-minded friends. In 1843 and 1845 she lobbied the New York legislature for a married women's property act, which was defeated in 1836 and 1840. Passed by the legislature in March 1848, the law granted married women the right to own and control property they brought to their marriages.

In 1847 the Stantons moved to Seneca Falls, New York. There, Elizabeth Cady Stanton's spirits plummeted. She was 31, with three adventurous boys to care for and a husband away on business much of the time. Running a household in Seneca Falls was more difficult than it had been in Boston, and she missed lectures, churches, theaters, concerts, and temperance meetings.

Because Seneca Falls was a malarial region, she found herself continually nursing children and servants. To add to her burdens, the house at 32 Washington Street was on the outskirts of town, serviced by muddy roads without sidewalks. "My duties were too numerous and varied and none sufficiently exhilarating or intellectual to bring into play my higher faculties. I suffered with mental hunger, which, like an empty stomach, is very depressing."

In 1848 Stanton received an invitation to tea from Jane Hunt, who lived in the nearby town of Waterloo. There, on 13 June 1848, she was greeted by Hunt, Mott, Martha C. Wright, and Mary Ann McClintock, all liberal Quakers. Depressed since her move to Seneca Falls, Stanton poured out her heart to the women, who were sympathetic. They wrote an announcement calling a meeting of women to be held 19–20 July at the Wesleyan Methodist chapel in Seneca Falls. The announcement was published 14 June 1848 in the *Seneca County Courier*. The meeting was the first women's rights convention ever held in the United States.

Stanton wrote the convention's Declaration of Sentiments, modeled after the Declaration of Independence and including the statement "men and women are created equal." Although Mott objected and Henry Stanton left town in protest, Stanton appended to the declaration a resolution calling for women's suffrage. Thus, she became the first person to publicly demand the vote for women. Although 11 of the 12 resolutions appended to the declaration were unanimously approved by the convention, the suffrage resolution won approval by only a small margin.

In 1851, Stanton met the woman who would be her friend and ally for the next 50 years. Amelia Bloomer had invited Susan B. Anthony, a temperance activist, to her home in Seneca Falls. Anthony and Stanton met on a street corner one March evening, Anthony rushing from a temperance meeting, Stanton dressed in her Bloomer outfit. The two women liked each other immediately and began a lifelong collaboration in the women's movement. In 1854, Stanton re-

ceived an unprecedented invitation to address the New York legislature on the need for an expanded married women's property law. Passed in 1860, it gave women ownership of their wages and the right to custody of their children. That year, Stanton shocked many of her supporters by championing liberalized divorce laws, including drunkenness as grounds for divorce. With Anthony she formed the National Woman's Loyal League (1863), which petitioned Congress for an amendment to the Constitution to immediately end slavery. The women collected more than 300,000 signatures on their petitions.

In a test of women's constitutional right to hold office, Stanton ran for Congress in 1866 as an independent. She received only 24 of the 12,000 votes cast. In 1867 she and Anthony made an exhausting tour of Kansas to campaign for a proposed women's suffrage amendment. The amendment was defeated in a general election. Stanton and Anthony opposed the Fourteenth Amendment and the Fifteenth Amendment because they excluded women. In 1868, Stanton advocated a sixteenth amendment to guarantee universal suffrage regardless of color, race, or sex. Soon, Stanton became coeditor of *The Revolution*, a weekly women's suffrage paper that Anthony published from 1868 to 1870.

In 1869 Stanton and Anthony founded the National Woman Suffrage Association, of which Stanton was president for 21 years. They had founded the organization after a heated discussion at the American Equal Rights Association over a variety of issues, including whether the group should put its energies into winning the vote for women or formerly enslaved men. When that organization merged with its rival, the American Woman Suffrage Association, Stanton was elected president of the new National American Woman Suffrage Association (1890); she served for two years.

Stanton persuaded Senator Aaron A. Sargent of California to sponsor a federal suffrage amendment (1878), which was introduced in every session of Congress thereafter. The language of the Nineteenth

Amendment, approved by Congress in 1919, was virtually unchanged from this version. With Anthony and Matilda Joslyn Gage, Stanton compiled the first three volumes of *History of Woman Suffrage* (1881 and 1886). She also published *The Woman's Bible* (1895), and her reminiscences, *Eighty Years and More* (1898). Stanton died 26 October 1902 in New York City.

See also American Equal Rights Association; Anthony, Susan B.; Declaration of Sentiments; *History of Woman Suffrage;* Kansas Campaign; Mott, Lucretia; National American Woman Suffrage Association; National Woman Suffrage Association; National Woman's Loyal League; New York Married Woman's Property Act (1860); Seneca Falls Convention; *The Woman's Bible;* World's Anti-Slavery Convention.

State Commissions on the Status of Women

State commissions on the status of women provided one of the first means of organizing feminists for the contemporary women's movement. A number of forces worked to create the commissions: a recommendation from the President's Commission on the Status of Women, a campaign by the National Federation of Business and Professional Women's Clubs, and the efforts of political women at the state level. The commissions were established in every state to study laws as they affected women. Most of the members of the commissions belonged to women's organizations and represented various degrees of feminist sentiment. The state commissions fostered networking and unity among women within the commissions. Widespread publicity of the commissions' activities fostered ties among the commissions and outside groups. The Interdepartmental Committee on the Status of Women and the Citizens Advisory Council on the Status of Women joined forces with the state commissions and furthered the networking process. The commissions' research called attention to issues involving sex discrimination and fostered support for battling sex discrimination with legislative and other means. Many of the commissions were more militant than the President's Commission on the Status of Women. Many endorsed state equal rights amendments despite the fact that members' status as political appointees made them particularly vulnerable to the influence of party politics. The merits of these commissions notwithstanding, many feminists became disillusioned with them. Because many appointments were political (frequently they were a way of rewarding campaign workers), some members of the commissions were antifeminists, who, even in small numbers, could hinder progress. The formation of the National Organization for Women (NOW) came in part in response to the deficiencies of the commissions. Many of the state commissions continue to function.

See also Citizens' Advisory Council on the Status of Women; President's Commission on the Status of Women.

Steinem, Gloria

Feminist, writer, and editor Gloria Steinem was born on 25 March 1934 in Toledo, Ohio. She graduated from high school in 1952 and in 1956 graduated magna cum laude with a major in government from Smith College in Massachusetts. Steinem then studied in India for two years on a Chester Bowles fellowship, eventually abandoning studies she considered "pointless" to travel throughout India with a group called the Radical Humanists.

Upon her return to the United States in 1958, she worked as a researcher in Cambridge, Massachusetts, and in 1960 moved to New York City, where she supported herself as a freelance writer. Steinem worked for one month as a hostess ("bunny") in the Playboy Club in New York in order to write an exposé about the club. The resulting article created a sensation and soon she was writing for numerous magazines and for NBC-TV as a scriptwriter. Steinem wrote the column "The City Politic" for *New York* magazine and contributed to *Esquire, Life, Cosmopolitan, Vogue,* and other periodicals. From 1964 to 1965 she wrote the NBC series "That Was the Week That Was." In 1963 Steinem published *The Beach Book* and

Gloria Steinem

in 1964 *James Baldwin: An Original.* In 1968 she became a contributing editor to *New York* magazine and, from 1969 to 1970, was a consulting editor to *Seventeen* and the periodical *Shows.*

In 1970, Steinem joined Betty Friedan to organize the Women's Strike for Equality, which was organized to celebrate the fiftieth anniversary of the Nineteenth Amendment. That same year, she joined with Shirley Chisholm and Bella Abzug to found the National Women's Political Caucus. In 1971 she also helped found the Women's Action Alliance.

The achievement for which Steinem is perhaps best known came about in 1972 when, with Patricia Carbine, she founded the feminist *Ms.* magazine. Also in 1972, *McCall's* magazine named Steinem Woman of the Year. In 1984 Steinem published *Outrageous Acts and Everyday Rebellions* and two years later cowrote with George Barris *Marilyn: Norma Jean.* She published *Bedside Book of Self-Esteem* in 1989 and her autobiographical book *Revolution from Within* (1992), in which she explored once more the issue of self-esteem, was on the *New York*

Times best-seller list for many weeks. Throughout her career, Steinem has worked for the passage of the Equal Rights Amendment, reproductive choice, and other issues critical to the feminist movement of the second half of the twentieth century.

See also Women's Strike for Equality.

Stone, Lucy (1818–1893)

Lucy Stone was the first woman to debate and speak publicly at Oberlin Collegiate Institute and the first woman arrested in the United States for an act of civil disobedience. She founded the feminist *Woman's Journal,* which she edited for 47 years. Called the morning star of the women's movement, she was a brilliant extemporaneous public speaker. She was born 13 August 1818 in West Brookfield, Massachusetts, the eighth of nine children. Her mother worked hard; she milked eight cows the night before she gave birth to Lucy. On the Stone farm women not only helped with farm chores but wove cloth, nursed children, and cooked and washed clothes for family and fieldhands. The women also made shoes for sale; Lucy Stone was expected to produce nine pairs each day. She wanted a better life than her mother's, but her father did not believe in educating girls. When he heard that she wanted to go to college, he asked, "Is the child crazy?" Although he paid for his sons' schooling, only reluctantly did he lend his daughter money to help finance her education.

Stone worked intermittently until she was almost 30 years old before she earned her undergraduate degree. She studied at Mount Holyoke Female Seminary for a time and enrolled at Oberlin in 1843. When she graduated with honors in 1847, she became the first woman from Massachusetts to earn a college degree. To earn money for tuition, she held many jobs, including kitchen work, for which she was paid 3 cents per hour, and teaching, which paid less than 13 cents per hour—much less than what male teachers were paid. She spent almost 50 cents per week for food and was too poor to travel home to visit her family. According to writer Miriam Gurko, when Stone's father died, he left all of his money and property to his sons, except that "each of his surviving daughters was to receive $200."

Lucy Stone

Stone was considered a radical at Oberlin. Antoinette Brown (Blackwell), who would become the first female ordained minister in the United States, was warned by an Oberlin trustee to avoid Stone because of her dangerous opinions. Despite the trustee's advice, Brown went out of her way to meet Stone at the earliest opportunity. The two worked together for the equality of women at Oberlin. One of their courses was rhetoric, in which the boys debated and the girls listened. When the two women demanded that girls be allowed to debate, their professor, James Thorne, allowed the girls to debate each other. Enraged officials forbade women to debate altogether, so the women met in the house of a former slave.

After graduating from Oberlin, Stone began lecturing for the American Anti-Slavery Society. She spoke about women's rights during the week and about abolition on weekends, becoming the only woman in America to make a career out of lecturing on women's rights. The newspapers, unused to hearing a woman speak publicly, described her as loud and brassy, a "she hyena" who smoked cigars and wore boots. Actually she was petite, soft-spoken, unassuming, and neatly dressed. In the spring of 1850 she attended an antislavery convention in Boston. There she heard an announcement asking attendees who wanted to hold a women's rights convention to meet afterward. Stone went to the meeting, and her name later appeared on a list of people calling for a national women's rights convention. Later that year she would be among those who called the first national convention on women's rights in Worcester, Massachusetts.

In 1855, despite having resolved never to marry, she married Henry Brown Blackwell, brother of Elizabeth Blackwell, the country's first female physician, and Samuel Blackwell, who later married Antoinette Brown. She insisted on keeping her maiden name, and thereafter married women who retained their maiden names were called Lucy Stoners. The marriage was performed by Thomas Wentworth Higginson and featured a protest by the bride and groom against traditional marriage vows.

After presiding over the seventh National Woman's Rights Convention in 1856 in New York, Stone retired from politics to care for her only daughter, Alice Stone Blackwell, born in 1857. In 1858 the family moved from Cincinnati to Orange, New Jersey, where Stone refused to pay property taxes, protesting women's lack of the franchise. As a result, she became the first woman in the United States to be arrested for an act of civil disobedience. During the Civil War, she supported the National Woman's Loyal League. In 1866, she was a founder of the American Equal Rights Association and served on its executive committee. In 1867, while living in Boston, she was president of the New Jersey Woman

Suffrage Association and campaigned for suffrage in Kansas and New York. In 1868 she was a founder of the New England Woman Suffrage Association.

In 1869 a conflict erupted within the women's movement. Susan B. Anthony and Elizabeth Cady Stanton wanted women to oppose the Fifteenth Amendment unless it was modified to include women. They also wanted broad reforms, including liberalized divorce laws. They formed the National Woman Suffrage Association in May. Lucy Stone, Julia Ward Howe, and others were alarmed by this move and by the support the association solicited from the racist George Train and writer and freethinker Victoria Woodhull. In response, the Boston women, as they were called, formed the American Woman Suffrage Association in November. When the two factions reunited in 1890 to form the National American Woman Suffrage Association, Stone was chairperson of the group's executive committee. Stone's last lectures were given at the World's Columbian Exposition in Chicago in 1893. She died 18 October 1893 in Boston.

See also American Equal Rights Association; American Woman Suffrage Association; Blackwell, Alice Stone; Blackwell, Antoinette Louisa Brown.

Stowe, Harriet Beecher (1811–1896)

Harriet Beecher Stowe wrote *Uncle Tom's Cabin*, a novel that polarized public opinion on the issue of slavery. She was born 14 June 1811 in Litchfield, Connecticut, into one of the country's most accomplished families. Her father was pastor Lyman Beecher; her brothers, clergyman Henry Ward Beecher and educator Edward Beecher; and her sister, educator Catharine Beecher. Harriet attended Sarah Pierce's school in Litchfield (1819–1824) and for three years Catharine Beecher's Hartford Female Seminary. She taught at her sister's school from 1827 to 1832. In 1832 she and Catharine accompanied their father to Cleveland, Ohio. There, Harriet taught at the Western Female Seminary; her father became president of Lane Theological Seminary. In 1836 she married

Calvin E. Stowe, helping to support the family by writing short stories, some of which were collected in *The Mayflower* (1843). In 1850 the Stowes moved to Brunswick, Maine.

Stowe's reading and her personal experiences in Ohio and Kentucky acquainted her with the cruelties and abuse of slavery, and her novel about its evil effects was to make her famous. *Uncle Tom's Cabin* was published serially from 1851 to 1852 and in book form in 1852. Instantly popular, the book brought Stowe prosperity in the North and ridicule in the South, where owning a copy could be dangerous. The book influenced public opinion more than any previous novel, polarizing opinion on both sides of the issue.

Beginning in 1852 Stowe made her home in Andover, Massachusetts, while traveling widely in the United States and Europe. In 1853 she visited England, where she was warmly received. In 1853 she wrote *A Key to Uncle Tom's Cabin*, which provided documentary evidence for the abuse depicted in her best-selling novel. Moving to Hartford, Connecticut, in 1854, she published a reminiscence of her travels, *Sunny Memories of Foreign Lands*. A less hopeful antislavery novel, *Dred: A Tale of the Great Dismal Swamp*, appeared in 1856. In 1864 she moved to Hartford, Connecticut, where she continued to write steadily, particularly for *The Atlantic Monthly*. In an article published in *The Atlantic Monthly* (1869) she claimed that Lord Byron engaged in an incestuous affair with his half sister; the article created a furor in England, and Stowe suffered much criticism. Stowe's other works include *The Minister's Wooing* (1859), *The Pearls of Orr's Island* (1862), *The Ravages of a Carpet* (1864), *Religious Poems* (1867), *Oldtown Folks* (1869), *Pink and White Tyranny* (1871), *Sam Lawson's Oldtown Fireside Stories* (1872), *Old Palmetto Leaves* (1873), *We and Our Neighbors* (1875), *Poganuc People* (1878), and *A Dog's Mission* (1881). She remained one of the country's most popular writers and lecturers until her death. She died 1 July 1896 in Hartford.

See also Beecher, Catharine; *Uncle Tom's Cabin*.

Strikes

The first strike in the United States involving female factory workers took place in 1824 at the textile mills of Pawtucket, Rhode Island. There, 102 women joined with male workers to protest a wage cut and extended workday. That was only the beginning. Four years later the first all-female strike took place at a Dover, New Hampshire, cotton mill. Approximately 400 women walked off their jobs to protest fines for tardiness. In 1834 female workers in Lowell, Massachusetts, demanded the right to join unions. A strike began when a woman was punished for protesting a wage cut of 25 percent. She tossed her bonnet in the air to signal other workers to leave their looms. Rallying, one of the strikers climbed on the town pump and made a rousing speech about the rights of women. Almost 1,000 women and girls walked out.

In 1836, strikers again marched through Lowell, singing,

> Oh, isn't it a pity
> that such a pretty girl as I
> Should be sent into the factory
> to pine away and die?

Although these strikes were broken, the women's dormitories became places of organization, leading to the formation of the Lowell Female Reform Association (1845), whose leader was Sarah Bagley. The union fought unsuccessfully against speedups on the looms and for the ten-hour workday and other reforms. Many similar strikes took place throughout New England, each lasting only a few days. After the news of a wage cut or work speedup passed from one operator to another, the women would walk off their jobs, hold a meeting, pass a resolution, and then drift back to work.

By 1857 the budding labor movement had almost collapsed under the pressure of recession. After the Civil War, however, the movement gained momentum. As more and more women joined the work force, their union activity increased. The number of female factory workers increased from 225,922 in 1850 to 323,370 in 1870. Many of the men who left the work force to fight in the Civil War were too badly injured to return to work after the war. To fill the gap, women entered various trades, such as sewing, printing, and cigar making. Following the Civil War, high prices, demands for higher wages, and the introduction of labor-saving machinery led to the formation of the first national unions.

The first two national unions to allow women to join were the cigar makers (1867) and the printers (1869). They were quickly followed by the shoemakers of Lynn, Massachusetts, who in 1869 formed the first national union of working women, called the Daughters of St. Crispin. Within three years, the Lynn branch of the union defeated a wage cut. Although the unions of this period were short-lived, they were examples of how working women helped to build the first nationally organized unions.

The next gain for women in labor occurred in 1882, when the Knights of Labor, a secret fraternal labor organization, went public and began to accept female members. It was during this period that the eight-hour-day movement caught fire. The movement protested long workdays, often 12–16 hours, for all workers—women, children, and men. Thousands of female workers joined Eight Hour Leagues. On 1 May 1886, now called International Workers Day, 350,000 workers across the nation put down their tools and walked off their jobs. Thousands won reduced hours.

The first unions composed mainly of women developed during the period 1903–1917. They originated in the garment business, which gave birth to the International Ladies' Garment Workers Union in 1900 (earliest locals). One of these women's unions initiated the first major strike in the history of working women, the 1909–1910 shirtwaist makers' walkout in New York and Philadelphia. A small number of shirtwaist makers in two shops, the Triangle Shirtwaist Company and Leiserson & Company, had been on strike since September, when a mass meeting of the workers was called at Cooper Union on 22 November 1909 to vote on taking new action. Margaret Dreier Robins

Woolworth workers strike for a 40-hour workweek.

of the New York Women's Trade Union League, labor leader Samuel Gompers, and other notables took the floor. But it was a teenager, Clara Lemlich, who galvanized the workers. She cried, "I am tired of listening to speakers who talk in general terms.... I offer a resolution that a general strike be declared—now!" The chairman was moved

287

to demand that the workers take an old Jewish oath: "If I turn traitor to the cause I now pledge, may this hand wither from the arm I now raise!" Every worker in the hall rose to swear the oath.

Thousands more workers, three-fourths of them women, walked off their jobs the next day. It was the first modern, general strike. The strike was called the Uprising of the Ten, Twenty, or Thirty Thousand, depending on which account one reads. What is known is that during the 13-week strike, the women suffered physical attacks, more than 600 arrests were made, and some of the women went on hunger strikes. The strikers won a few gains, such as shorter hours and higher wages, negotiated on a shop-by-shop basis; the women's largest gain, however, was to bring the International Ladies' Garment Workers' Union (ILGWU) into more than 300 shops. Helped immeasurably by the Women's Trade Union League, which publicized the striker's cause and bailed out the strikers, the strike also proved to male unionists that women could be effectively organized.

The shirtwaist makers' strike led to the next wave of strikes, this time in the men's garment business in Chicago, and again without long-lasting results. It began in the same way as the shirtwaist strike, with a few unorganized workers going on strike, leading to a mass action of 45,000 men and women. Aided by the Women's Trade Union League, the workers were out for 14 weeks, with disappointing results.

On 12 January 1912, female weavers in Lawrence, Massachusetts, also walked out, protesting a pay cut. They adopted the battle cry, "Better to starve fighting than to starve working!" By the end of the month more than 23,000 workers were on strike, half of them women and children. The Lawrence strikers asked for help from the Industrial Workers of the World (IWW). Among the IWW organizers was 21-year-old Elizabeth Gurley Flynn, who, with Margaret Sanger, helped organize an evacuation of workers' children, which won them much publicity. After two months the workers returned to

work with a 20 percent pay raise. Throughout New England, other textile mill owners granted pay raises in fear of more strikes.

In 1919, the United States was swept by a wave of protest in opposition to postwar unemployment and low wages. Especially important was the strike of 8,000 telephone workers, who walked out on 15 April of that year and picketed around the clock for six days. The operators persuaded the linemen to help them tie up service throughout New England. In 1926–1927 women in the Fur and Leather Workers' Union protested postwar price hikes and cuts in jobs and wages, which occurred as veterans returned to the work force and war production tapered off. Women went on strike in industry after industry, winning wage increases and other benefits. In 1933 about 18,000 Mexican and Chicana women struck the cotton fields in Pixley, California, when growers cut wages from a dollar to 40 cents per 100 pounds of cotton. Vigilantes shot and killed two workers, but after 24 days the strikers forced wages back up, setting an example for farm workers.

In 1937, when auto workers staged a sit-down strike against General Motors in Flint, Michigan, their wives led the support activity. They picketed days and nights and brought food to the strikers in the plants. The strikers won. The Flint strike inspired other industrial workers to organize. For example, the steel workers, supported by their wives, went on strike in 1937. That year, the mostly female Woolworth Retail Clerks Local 1250 also went on strike, winning a 40-hour workweek and a $20 minimum weekly wage. In 1951, during the Empire Zinc Strike in Silver City, New Mexico, an injunction was brought against mostly Chicano and Mexican miners, prohibiting them from blocking a road to the mine. Their wives formed picket lines for nine months, and the strikers won.

In 1973, about 700 textile operators, most of them women, struck the Oneita Knitting Mills in South Carolina, winning union recognition and seniority rights. That year miners in Brookside, Kentucky, voted the

United Mine Workers into the eastern part of the state. Their wives were essential to their victory, getting up at 4:30 every morning to picket for 11 months. In 1974 the longest strike of Chinese immigrant workers took place, lasting until 1975. During the strike, 135 women workers picketed the Great American Sewing Company for higher wages and better working conditions.

Over the past 25 years the proportion of unionized workers in relation to the labor force has declined, and with it the number of significant labor strikes. However, a potential victory for airline workers occurred in November 1993 when the Flight Attendants Union went on strike citing wage and security issues at American Airlines, prompting the intervention of President Bill Clinton, who insisted on negotiations.

See also Abortion; Bagley, Sarah; Factory System; Flynn, Elizabeth Gurley; Industrial Workers of the World; International Ladies' Garment Workers' Union; Knights of Labor; Lowell Female Labor Reform Association; National Woman's Party; Paul, Alice; Triangle Shirtwaist Fire; Uprising of the 20,000.

Student Non-Violent Coordinating Committee
See Casey Hayden–Mary King Paper

Suffrage, Women's
In colonial America most positions of power outside the family were available only to men. Propertyless women and men could not attend town meetings and assemblies where decisions were made. After the American Revolution, female taxpayers voted in some areas, such as New Jersey, which allowed women to vote until 1807. At the first women's rights convention, held in 1848 in Seneca Falls, New York, Elizabeth Cady Stanton shocked her colleagues when she asked the assembly to vote on a resolution demanding suffrage.

After the Civil War, Stanton, Susan B. Anthony, and other feminists became concerned that Congress would not give women the vote in return for women's support of the war effort. The Fourteenth Amendment, which gives African-American men the vote, was discussed during the summer of 1865 and proposed in April 1866. Congressman Robert Dale Owen of Indiana sent a draft of the amendment to the National Woman's Loyal League. By penalizing states when "the right to vote . . . is denied to any of the male inhabitants," the amendment introduced gender restriction to the Constitution. To Anthony and Stanton, this was not "Negro suffrage" but expanded male suffrage. They immediately opposed it. Cady Stanton urged her male allies to withdraw their support unless the amendment was modified to include women, arguing: "Do you believe the African race is composed entirely of males?" Stanton prepared a petition requesting an amendment to the Constitution prohibiting states "from disenfranchising any of their citizens on the ground of sex." But male abolitionists who supported women's suffrage during the war seemed surprised, even indignant, that women objected to the amendment, and most of them refused to sign the petition.

Not until 1868 was a women's suffrage amendment to the Constitution introduced in Congress by Senator Samuel Pomeroy of Kansas. In 1877, the National Woman Suffrage Association resolved to collect signatures for a petition supporting a federal suffrage amendment. The responsibility for organizing the drive was turned over to Susan B. Anthony. After collecting 10,000 signatures from 26 states, she presented them to the Senate. The response was loud laughter. One newspaper reported that "the entire Senate presented the appearance of a laughing school sidesplitting." In 1878, Elizabeth Cady Stanton persuaded a friend of Susan B. Anthony, Senator Aaron A. Sargeant of California, to introduce what is now called the "Anthony Amendment." More than 40 years later, without any change in the language, the amendment was approved by Congress (21 May 1919, by the House of Representatives; 4 June 1919, by the Senate). The Nineteenth Amendment was adopted 26 August 1920. The last challenge to women's right to vote was defeated when the Supreme Court upheld the Nineteenth Amendment in *Leser v. Garnett* (1922).

See also Anthony, Susan B.; Fourteenth Amendment; National Woman's Loyal League; Nineteenth Amendment; Owen, Robert Dale; Stanton, Elizabeth Cady.

Swisshelm, Jane Grey Cannon (1815–1884)

Jane Swisshelm was an abolitionist, newspaper publisher, and advocate of women's rights. She was born 6 December 1815 in Pittsburgh. She became a schoolteacher at the age of 14 and married James Swisshelm at the age of 20. In 1838, the two moved to Louisville, Kentucky, where Jane, observing the practice of slavery firsthand, decided to devote her life to the abolitionist cause. Jane had a corset-making business, which she dropped in 1839 to nurse her aging mother. In 1840, her mother died, and James tried to sue the older woman's estate to compensate Jane for the time she had spent nursing her mother. This action, which Jane herself opposed, focused her attention on the legal inequities faced by married women. She left her husband, but returned to him in 1842,

and the two moved to Pittsburgh, Pennsylvania. In 1848 Swisshelm launched an antislavery paper, the *Saturday Visitor*, which for ten years published articles advocating abolition and women's rights. Her editorials advocating reform of women's property rights may have influenced the governor of Pennsylvania to support a reform bill, which was passed in 1848. In 1857, Swisshelm left her husband for good, becoming editor of the *St. Cloud Visitor* in Minnesota. Her abolitionist ideas alienated the leader of the state Democratic party, who wrecked her press and type, then sued her, eventually causing the paper to cease publication. Swisshelm immediately launched the *St. Cloud Democrat* and began lecturing about reform throughout the state. She sold the paper in 1863 and in 1865 she began to publish the *Reconstructionist*, which folded one year later after she criticized President Andrew Johnson. She continued to work for reform and was a delegate to the National Prohibition party convention in 1872. Her autobiography, *Half a Century*, was published in 1880. Swisshelm died 22 July 1884 near Pittsburgh.

Take Back the Night

This 1980 collection of writings and reports against pornography was edited by Laura Lederer. Its contributors include Gloria Steinem, Robin Morgan, Susan Brownmiller, Adrienne Rich, and Alice Walker. The title is a slogan used in the 1970s by women opposed to pornography, including Women against Pornography, a group that demonstrated in San Francisco in 1978. These women consider pornography a form of hate literature against women.

Tarbell, Ida Minerva (1857–1944)

Ida Tarbell was one of a group of young reformers who, through their writings, exposed corruption in American life. The group included Lincoln Steffens, Ray Stannard Baker, Thomas W. Lawsen, and David Graham Phillips. Born 5 November 1857 in Erie County, Pennsylvania, Tarbell grew up in Titusville, where she attended public schools. She entered Allegheny College in 1876, where she was one of five females, and graduated in 1880. She then taught for two years at Poland (Ohio) Union Seminary, before joining the staff of the *Chautauquan* magazine in Meadville (1883–1891). In 1891, Tarbell left for Paris, where she studied the role of women in the French Revolution. On her return, Tarbell supported herself by writing for *Scribner's* and *McClure's*. Her journalism brought her fame, and articles she wrote about Napoleon Bonaparte and Abraham Lincoln were collected in two popular books. Another series of articles was the basis of the critical book *The History of the Standard Oil Company*, which caused an uproar in 1904. Two years later, Tarbell helped to buy the *American Magazine*, jointly editing it with fellow muckrakers until 1915. There, she wrote a series of articles attacking the high tariff, which would also later form the basis of a book. When the magazine was sold in 1915, Tarbell became a lecturer on topics such as peace and unemployment, and served on several government committees, including the Woman's Committee of the U.S. Council of Civil Defense in World War I.

Although Tarbell's life was an inspiration for many women of her day, she disagreed with feminists such as Anna Howard Shaw and Carrie Chapman Catt over the value of women's suffrage, sadly suspecting she had given up too much (in terms of family) in pursuit of her career. Ida Tarbell's books include *A Short Life of Napoleon Bonaparte* (1895), *Life of Madam Roland* (1896), *Life of Abraham Lincoln* (1900), *Recollections of the Civil War* (1898), *The Tariff in Our Times*

Ida Tarbell

291

(1911), *New Ideals in Business* (1916), *The Life of Elbert H. Gary* (1925), *Owen D. Young* (1932), *The Business of Being a Woman* (1912), and *All in a Day's Work*, her 1939 autobiography. Ida Tarbell died in Bridgeport, Connecticut, on 6 January 1944.

See also Catt, Carrie Clinton Lane Chapman; Shaw, Anna Howard.

Taussig, Helen Brooke (1898–1986)

Physician Helen Taussig, the first president of the American Heart Association, was born 24 May 1898 in Cambridge, Massachusetts. She attended Cambridge School for Girls and, in 1917, entered Radcliffe as one of the college's first students. Two years later she transferred to the University of California at Berkeley, graduating in 1921. Taussig began her medical studies that year at Harvard's medical school, unofficially, as women were not then admitted to full status as students, later transferring to the Boston University medical school, and then to Johns Hopkins University, where she continued to specialize in the study of the heart. Taussig received an M.D. from Johns Hopkins in 1927. In 1930 she was named director of the university's pediatrics department, the Children's Heart Clinic of the Harriet Lane Home. In addition to teaching and practicing medicine, she conducted research. One area of research concerned newborns suffering from cyanosis, called "blue babies." Taussig theorized that the condition was caused by a constriction of the pulmonary artery leading from the heart to the lungs. In May 1945, she and vascular surgeon Dr. Alfred Blalock published an article in the *Journal of the American Medical Association* that described a new operation for cyanosis. Their research paved the way for the successful treatment of "blue babies." In 1946 Taussig became associate professor of pediatrics at the Johns Hopkins University medical school. Taussig later foresaw the dangers of Thalidomide, a sleep-inducing drug that causes birth defects, and she did research on rheumatic fever and congenital heart malformations. Her book *Congenital Malformations of the Heart* was published in 1947. In 1959 she was appointed the first female full professor at Johns Hopkins, and in 1963 she was made professor emeritus. Taussig was the first woman to serve as president of the American Heart Association (1965), and the first woman to be admitted to the Association of American Physicians. Her many honors and awards include the French Legion of Honor (1947), the Albert Lasker award (with Blalock in 1954), the Eleanor Roosevelt Achievement Award (1957), and the Medal of Freedom (1964). Taussig died 20 May 1986 in Kennett Square, Pennsylvania.

Tavern Keeper
See She-Merchant.

Taylor v. Louisiana

The 1975 Supreme Court decision in *Taylor v. Louisiana* prohibited states from excluding women from jury pools. Billy Taylor, who had been convicted of kidnapping in 1972, requested a retrial on the grounds that the all-male jury that heard his case did not fairly represent the community of his peers. Louisiana had adopted the widespread practice of calling women for jury duty only if they asked to serve. In previous cases (*Hoyt v. Florida*, 1961) that policy, as well as gender-based jury-selection practices, had been upheld by the Supreme Court based on the supposition that greater demands were made of women in the home. In this case, however, the Court agreed that the presence of women is necessary to create a jury that reflects a community's composition. The majority ruling cited a 1946 opinion of Justice William O. Douglas: "Who would claim that an all female jury was truly representative of the community if all men were intentionally and systematically excluded from the panel?"

Temperance

The first temperance society in America was organized in 1808 in Saratoga County, New

York, under the leadership of Dr. Billy J. Clark. Clark was inspired by the writings of Benjamine Rush (1784). His members swore to use no spirits, except under doctor's orders. In 1810–1811, Lyman Beecher, similarly influenced by Rush, preached against drink in East Hampton, Long Island, and Litchfield, Connecticut, arguing against the "rum-selling, tippling folk, infidels and ruff-scruff." In the years that followed, anti-liquor societies sprang up throughout New England. In 1826, the American Society for the Promotion of Temperance was formed in Boston. By 1836 chapters were in every state. The drive to ban the sale of liquor began in earnest in the East in 1840 and in the West in the early 1870s. Protestant churches and women, who were frequently the victims of family violence, were in the forefront of the battle to stop the sale of alcoholic beverages. Over the years the movement had changed into a drive for government prohibition. In Maine, Neal Dow became convinced that family violence, crime, etc. were the result of drunkenness and convinced the legislature to pass a regulatory law in 1851. Thirteen of the 31 states that then made up the Union had similar laws by 1855.

The issue took hold when women in the West began their attacks on demon rum in the 1870s. Armies of women closed thousands of saloons. Carry Nation (1846–1911), the most famous of these women, marched into saloons with an ax or bricks to smash bars and bottles. Spreading from Ohio in 1873, the movement was unique in American history. In 1874 the Woman's Christian Temperance Union (WCTU) was founded. The first widely supported national women's organization, it attracted hundreds of thousands of members. As the meeting places for local political bosses, saloons were the heart of the urban Democratic political machine, which excluded women. Hence, the vehemence with which the women of the temperance movement challenged them. Educator Frances Willard (1839–1898) was one of the most effective leaders of the WCTU. Under the guise of temperance she pushed through reforms to help women and children. These included women's suffrage, establishment of kindergartens, restrictions on child labor, and protective legislation. By forming alliances with the WCTU, the women's suffrage movement alienated the liquor interests, which fought against giving women the vote. In 1895, leaders of the Anti-Saloon League of America began influencing primary elections, identifying for their membership candidates who were "dry." In the years that followed these politicians were supporting women's suffrage. By 1916 saloons were illegal in 21 states. In 1917, Congress sent the Eighteenth Amendment to the states, which ratified it in 1919. The Volstead Act followed in 1920 and, as a result, liquor consumption generally declined. (The Volstead Act was repealed on 20 February 1933 when Congress passed the Twenty-First Amendment.) The act marked a long campaign—in large part supported by women—to end the traffic and consumption of liquor.

See also Nation, Carry Amelia Moore; National Woman's Christian Temperance Union; Willard, Frances.

Terrell, Mary Eliza Church (1863–1968)

Mary Eliza Church Terrell, an African-American suffragist, was president of the National Association of Colored Women, a charter member of the National Association for the Advancement of Colored People, and the first African-American woman to become a member of the American Association of University Women (at the age of 85). She was born 23 September 1863 in Memphis, Tennessee. She taught in the District of Columbia until she married (District of Columbia regulations required married women to stop teaching). Terrell led demonstrations against lynching and segregation and for the rights of women and African Americans. It is a reflection of her courage that she asked for clemency for Ethel Rosenberg, who was executed in 1953 for conspiracy in passing atomic secrets. Terrell died at the age of 105 on 24 July 1968 in Annapolis, Maryland.

Textile Mills
See Factory System.

Thomas, Martha Carey (1857–1935)

Educator Martha Carey Thomas was the first female college faculty member to become a dean, and she offered the first graduate scholarships for foreign students in the United States. She was born 2 January 1857 in Baltimore, Maryland and attended Quaker schools in Baltimore and Ithaca, New York. Thomas's father did not want her to attend college, but she overrode his opposition. She graduated from Cornell in 1877. She enrolled at Johns Hopkins University but was forced to study privately under a professor because women were not allowed to attend classes. After one year she left Johns Hopkins to travel to Europe, where she pursued graduate studies in linguistics. After studying at the University of Leipzig for three years she was refused a graduate degree because of her gender. At the time only the University at Zurich and the Sorbonne in Paris admitted women to study for higher degrees. Thomas went to Zurich, where she received a Ph.D. summa cum laude (1882). She was the first woman and first foreigner to earn a degree from the university. She completed one more year of study at the Sorbonne before returning to the United States.

After returning to the United States in 1884, Thomas was appointed dean and professor of English at Bryn Mawr, which opened in 1885. She established both undergraduate and graduate courses of study, making Bryn Mawr the first women's college to offer a graduate program of any kind. In 1885 Thomas, with Mary Garrett and other women, cofounded a college preparatory school, the Bryn Mawr School for Girls, in Baltimore, Maryland. In 1889, Thomas led a group of women who convinced Johns Hopkins to open its medical school to women, threatening to withhold funds for the new institution unless it did so. Thomas organized the first graduate scholarships for foreign (that is, European) students in the United States. In 1894 Thomas

succeeded Bryn Mawr's retiring president, James E. Rhodes, serving as president and dean until 1908 and as president until 1922. She insisted that Bryn Mawr enforce entrance exams as rigorous as those of the top men's colleges.

Thomas championed women's suffrage and worked to pass the Nineteenth Amendment. She was president of the National College Women's Equal Suffrage League from 1908 to 1913. In 1900 she helped found the Association To Promote Scientific Research by Women and the International Federation of University Women. Thomas died 2 December 1935 in Philadelphia.

Thomas, Mary Frame Myers (1816–1888)

Physician and feminist editor Mary Frame Myers Thomas was born 28 October 1816, in Bucks County, Pennsylvania. She was educated at home and, after the family moved to New Lisbon, Ohio, she attended local schools. In 1839 she married Owen Thomas. They lived in Salem, Ohio, for the next ten years. In 1845 she attended a speech given by Quaker minister Lucretia Mott, which stimulated her interest in women's rights. In 1849, after the birth of their first child, the family moved to Fort Wayne, Indiana, where Thomas began to study medicine. In 1853, after sewing enough clothes to last the family six months and arranging for the care of her children, she left to study medicine in Philadelphia. She enrolled in the first session of the female department of Penn Medical University. Although her studies were interrupted by the long illness and death of her oldest daughter, Thomas obtained an M.D. from Penn Medical in 1856. That year Thomas moved with her family to Richmond, Indiana, and began her medical practice. During the Civil War, she worked with the Sanitary Commission, nursed the wounded, and helped bring supplies to the battlefield by ship.

Thomas was active in suffrage activities. In 1855 she became vice-president of the

Indiana Woman's Rights Society. She edited *The Lily*, Amelia Bloomer's women's rights newspaper (1857), and was associate editor of the *Mayflower*, an Indiana suffrage paper (1861). In 1859, she petitioned the Indiana legislature for a married women's property law and a women's suffrage amendment to the state constitution. After the Civil War, she participated in the reorganization of the women's movement by forming an Indiana branch of Lucy Stone's American Woman Suffrage Association (AWSA). She was elected president of the AWSA in 1880. Thomas died 19 August 1888 in Richmond.

See also American Woman Suffrage Association; *The Lily*; Married Women's Property Acts; Mott, Lucretia; Sanitary Commission; Stone, Lucy.

Tiernan v. Poor

In *Tiernan v. Poor* (1829), the Maryland Court of Appeals ruled that Deborah Poor held the powers of a single woman with regard to her separate estate. That meant she could sell or mortgage the property she brought to her marriage. The property had been conferred on Poor by a trust before her marriage. She had mortgaged the property to provide security for her husband's $600 debt. When she lost the property, she went to court. Although the terms of her original trust settlement permitted Poor to transfer the property, her lawyer argued that as a *feme covert*, or married woman, she could mortgage it only after undergoing a judicial examination. Private questioning by a judge was a legal precaution against a husband's coercion in cases involving the wife's property. Poor's lawyer said that because no examination had been conducted, the deed of mortgage was not valid. The opposing lawyer reasoned that, with regard to the separate estate Poor was a *feme sole*, and the court had no right to restrict her activities through private judicial examination. The court upheld the mortgage deed, ruling that Poor did have the powers of a *feme sole* over her separate estate. In the opinion of the court, Poor "was never intended to be placed in a state of pupilage with regard to her property." This decision advanced women's property rights in Maryland.

See also Coercion; Common Law; *Feme Covert*; *Feme Sole*.

Timothy, Ann Donovan (c. 1727–1792)

Ann Timothy was the second woman in South Carolina, after her mother-in-law, Elizabeth Timothy, to publish a newspaper. She is believed to have been born about 1727 in Charleston, South Carolina. She married Peter Timothy in 1745. He became publisher of the *South-Carolina Gazette*. The *Gazette*, the first permanent paper in the colony, was previously published by Timothy's father and, after his father's death, by his mother. Ann Timothy bore perhaps 15 children, seven of whom died young. Her husband died in 1782. In 1783 Ann Timothy resumed publishing the paper, which had been renamed the *Gazette of the State of South Carolina*. She became the state's official printer in 1785. After her death in 1792, her son, Benjamin Timothy, took over the paper and maintained it until 1802.

See also Franklin, Ann Smith; Goddard, Mary Katherine; Goddard, Sarah Updike; Green, Anne Catherine Hoof; Timothy, Elizabeth.

Timothy, Elizabeth (?–1757)

Printer and publisher Elizabeth Timothy became one of the first colonial woman to publish a newspaper, the *South-Carolina Gazette*. She was born in Holland and immigrated with her husband, Lewis Timothy, and their four children to Philadelphia in 1731. In 1737 the family moved to Charleston, South Carolina. There, with Benjamin Franklin as his partner, Lewis Timothy became publisher of the colony's first permanent newspaper, the *South-Carolina Gazette*. Lewis Timothy died in 1738; without missing an issue, his wife continued to publish the paper. Although Elizabeth Timothy was the owner of the paper, she published it under the name of her 14-year-

295

old son, Peter. Franklin claimed that she was a better business manager than her husband. Her son, Peter Timothy, took over the business in about 1846. Elizabeth Timothy established a bookshop and through good business sense left her children well provided for. Peter Timothy continued to publish the paper after Elizabeth's death in Charleston in 1757.

See also Franklin, Ann Smith; Goddard, Mary Katherine; Goddard, Sarah Updike; Green, Anne Catherine Hoof; Timothy, Ann.

Title VII of the 1964 Civil Rights Act

Title VII of the 1964 Civil Rights Act (which actually took effect beginning 2 July 1965), known as the Equal Employment Opportunity section, forbids discrimination by private employers, employment agencies, and unions on the basis of race, color, religion, national origin, or sex. In its original form, the act did not cover academic institutions or government itself, with the exception of the U.S. Employment Service and federally assisted local employment agencies. Nor did it cover sex discrimination. The provision banning sex discrimination was added by Representative Howard Smith (D-VA). Smith opposed the bill and thought he could lessen its chances of passage by adding what he thought was a preposterous proposal.

The Equal Employment Opportunity Commission (EEOC) was created to oversee the administration of Title VII, and subsequent legislation gave the commission authority to enforce its decisions. The commissioner of the EEOC is named by the president. Title VII does not prohibit sex discrimination entirely, because it does permit a narrow category of exemptions for cases in which sex is a bona fide occupational qualification (BFOQ), that is, when there is a genuine need to have a worker of one particular sex perform a job. For example, sex can be considered a BFOQ for modeling women's clothes or acting in female roles because, realistically, a man could not be expected to be suitable for such work. Over the years the courts have given an increas-

ingly narrow interpretation, as feminists would favor, to the BFOQ exception.

See also Bona Fide Occupational Qualification.

Title IX of the 1972 Higher Education Act

Title IX of the Higher Education Act, enacted in 1972, bans sex discrimination in educational programs that receive federal funds. Because of pressure from some Ivy League schools, Title IX contains an exemption for undergraduate admission to private colleges. This exemption notwithstanding, the bill addresses discrimination in athletics, where the law evoked particularly strong opposition; admission to specific university classes; and pregnant students' maternity leave and their rights to continue their education. Title IX regulations were released in 1974 and revised in 1975. The Office of Civil Rights at the Department of Health, Education and Welfare (HEW) was responsible for Title IX administration but lacked resources and was inefficient. HEW's deficient handling of Title IX complaints forced feminist groups to bring a lawsuit against HEW and the Department of Labor to ensure proper enforcement of Title IX. In 1974, funds from foundations were used by the National Organization for Women (NOW) to create the Project on Equal Education Rights (PEER) to monitor Title IX enforcement. Critics charged that enforcement was uneven because of unenthusiastic handling by HEW. This problem became pronounced during the 1980s, under the administration of President Ronald Reagan. In 1984, the Supreme Court, in *Grove City College v. Bell*, declared that educational institutions can in fact receive federal funding, even if they practice discrimination, so long as the funding did not go to the specific programs that were discriminatory. This significantly reduced Title IX's effectiveness. The 1988 Civil Rights Restoration Act was passed by Congress to legislatively reverse the *Grove City* decision; however, in 1989, the Court

The nationally ranked Colorado Buffs play the University of Wyoming Cowgirls. Athletic programs for women improved following the passage of Title IX of the 1972 Higher Education Act.

renewed its insistence on narrow definitions of Title IX antidiscrimination regulations.

See also American Association of University Women.

A Treatise on Domestic Economy

Written by Catharine Beecher in 1841, *A Treatise on Domestic Economy* was an attempt to bring scientific principles to bear on housework. In keeping with the idea of male (public) and female (domestic) spheres popular in the nineteenth century, Beecher believed a woman's place was in the home. However, Beecher sought to reinforce and enlarge women's domestic role. Her book offered advice on building, plumbing, gardening, room arrangement, child care, medicine, cooking, and countless other topics. A best-seller for years, *A Treatise on Domestic Economy* was revised and retitled *The American Woman's Home* (1869) and *The New Housekeeper's Manual* (1873).

See also Beecher, Catharine.

Triangle Shirtwaist Fire

The Triangle Shirtwaist Fire of 1911 greatly strengthened contemporary pro-union sentiments by demonstrating the legitimacy of the demands made by workers on strike. Specifically, it helped spur the efforts of the International Ladies' Garment Workers' Union to organize the workers of the Triangle factory. Public outrage was so great over the tragedy that a state commission was formed to investigate the factory and sweatshop conditions generally, and called for reforms. The first major strike by working women had taken place among the shirtwaist makers in New York and Philadelphia from 1909 to 1910. The strike had lasted 13 weeks and resulted in gains for some workers. One of the companies targeted during the strike was the Triangle Shirtwaist Company. On 25 March 1911, a fire broke out in a building that housed the company. Of the 500 workers who were trapped on the top floors of the ten-story building, 146 died. The causes of the fire were in fact grievances about which workers had been protesting in the strike: namely, the company's negligence in failing to provide fire escapes or sprinkler systems and its policy of locking doors between floors to keep employees from leaving with materials. The public reacted with outrage, and strikes across the nation increased. The owners of the company were acquitted of negligence and fined $20. However, in 1914, a statement called for widespread changes. New laws imposed strict building codes and inspections.

See also International Ladies' Garment Workers' Union; Strikes; Uprising of the 20,000.

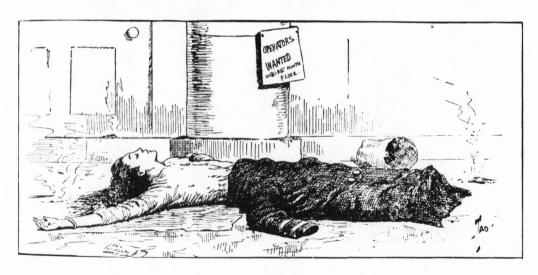

An editorial cartoon following the 25 March 1911 Triangle Shirtwaist Factory fire asked, "Is anyone to be punished for this?"

Troy Female Seminary

By 1821 the town council of Troy, New York, had raised $4,000 in tax money to build a girls' school. The Troy Female Seminary opened in September of that year under the direction of Emma Willard. An all-female committee supervised the school, which offered women advanced instruction at a time when colleges would not admit them. The school pioneered the teaching of science, math, and social studies. Willard thought that women had a major contribution to make to the new republic. In addition to fulfilling the ideal of the republican mother (that is, raising patriotic sons), Willard argued that women were needed to teach virtuous students of both sexes. Between 1821 and 1872, more than 12,000 women enrolled in Willard's seminary. The students created a network of female friendships from New England to the Deep South and went on to establish many schools of their own. Willard was head of the school until 1838; in 1895 the school was renamed the Emma Willard School.

See also Education; Republican Motherhood; Willard, Emma.

Truth, Sojourner (c. 1797–1883)

Born in Ulster County, New York, about 1797, Sojourner Truth was an abolitionist and reformer. Originally named Isabella, she was born in slavery to a Dutch family in New York, and she was reared speaking Dutch. From 1810 to 1827 she was owned by the Dumont family of New Paltz. During this time she gave birth to five children. Two of the four surviving children were sold to other families. In 1827 she ran away and was taken in by Isaac and Maria Van Wagener, whose name she adopted. In about 1829 she moved to New York City, where she worked as a domestic, preaching religion to prostitutes in her spare time. In 1843, her mystic visions inspired her to take the name Sojourner Truth and to become an itinerant preaching about the love of God. Truth then became an abolitionist and embarked on a tour of the country speaking against slavery.

Her autobiography, *Narrative of Sojourner Truth*, was published in 1850.

Truth supported women's rights and temperance. On 28–29 May 1851, women activists held a convention in Akron, Ohio. A greater number of men attended the meeting than ever before, but many were clergymen who had come to heckle. Neither President Frances D. Gage nor her colleagues could silence the hecklers. Suddenly Truth came forward. As Gage recalled in *History of Woman Suffrage* (Volume I), she was nearly six feet tall, with a proud carriage and a gaze that made her seem to Gage "like one in a dream." She wore a gray dress and white turban covered by a bonnet. Although the women could not know it, her back was covered with the scars she received from beatings by plantation owners. The leaders trembled as they watched her walk up the aisle. Members of the audience whispered "Woman's rights and niggers!" and "Go to it, darky!" Truth crouched against the wall on the corner of the pulpit stairs while fearful members of the audience begged Gage not to recognize her, with one member claiming "Every newspaper in the land will have our cause mixed up with abolition and niggers, and we shall be utterly denounced." But the next day, despite hissing opposition, Gage recognized Truth. There was a hush as she went to the pulpit. She turned her attention to a clergyman who had mocked the women as being too helpless to be trusted with the vote. She said, "The man over there says women need to be helped into carriages and lifted over ditches, and to have the best places everywhere. Nobody ever helped me into carriages, or over puddles, or gives me the best place—and ain't I a woman?" By the time she was finished, the ridicule was drowned out by a roar of approval, with many members of the audience in tears.

In the mid-1850s, Truth moved to Battle Creek, Michigan. During the Civil War, she raised donations of food and clothes for the Negro volunteer regiments. In 1864, President Abraham Lincoln welcomed her to the White House. In 1870, Truth petitioned President Ulysses S. Grant to ask that freed slaves be given western lands on which to

Sojourner Truth

live. Though the suggestion did not catch on, it encouraged many freed men and women to migrate to Kansas and Missouri. Into old age, Truth continued to travel throughout the East, lecturing on behalf of suffrage, abolition, and temperance. She retired to Battle Creek, Michigan, in 1875, where she died on 26 November 1883.

See also Akron Convention; Gage, Frances.

Tubman, Harriet (c. 1820–1913)

Harriet Tubman, called the "Moses of people of color," was the first woman to run an Underground Railroad, or a route to lead runaway slaves to the North. Originally named Araminta, she was born about 1820 in Dorchester County, Maryland, to parents who had been brought to the United States in chains. Later, she adopted her mother's first name. As a child she was made to work as a fieldhand and domestic servant. When she was 13 years old, she suffered a fractured skull when an overseer struck her with a two-pound weight. The physical effects lingered throughout her life. After 1844 she married John Tubman, a freedman. Between 1847 and 1849, Tubman worked for Anthony Thompson. When he died she feared she would be sold, so she ran away. She escaped to Philadelphia, then went farther north to Saint Catharines, Ontario. In 1850 she began her practice of freeing slaves. First, she led a sister and her two children out of Maryland. The following year she led out her brother and his family, then she led a larger group that included another brother and his family. In 1857 she helped her elderly parents escape.

In 1858 or 1859, Tubman moved to a farm near Auburn, New York. During a period of ten years, she made 19 trips into Maryland, rescuing between 60 and 300 slaves. At one time the reward for her capture was as high as $40,000. Tubman had intended to participate in John Brown's raid of Harpers Ferry, but an illness prevented her from doing so. For three years during the Civil War, she acted as a scout and a spy for the Union army, extracting information from African Americans who lived in the South; she also served as a nurse. After the war, she began the Harriet Tubman Home for Indigent Aged Negroes on her New York farm. The home continued for several years after her death on 10 March 1913.

Turner, Eliza Sproat Randolph (1826–1903)

Eliza Turner was an author and a social reformer. She was born 20 June 1826 in Philadelphia. A member of the Philadelphia Female Anti-Slavery Society before the Civil War, she later devoted her life to improving the situation of women. In December 1869 she helped to form the Pennsylvania Woman Suffrage Association. She served as the organization's corresponding secretary and wrote *Four Quite New Reasons Why You Should Wish Your Wife To Vote* (1875). After 1876, Turner edited and contributed to the newspaper *New Century for Women*, which was run entirely by women. In 1877 she helped found the New Century Club, a women's improvement society that also did civic work. In 1881, she became chair of the club's committee that organized evening classes for working women and girls. Turner died 20 June 1903 at her Chadds Ford farm outside Philadelphia.

The Una

Founded by Paulina Wright Davis in 1853, *The Una* was the first women's suffrage newspaper in the United States. The paper was published in Providence, Rhode Island. In it appeared some of the most recognized feminist writers in the country, including Elizabeth Cady Stanton and Lucy Stone. The paper ceased publication after three years.

Uncle Tom's Cabin

Harriet Beecher Stowe's *Uncle Tom's Cabin, or Life among the Lowly*, appeared in installments in the *National Era* from June 1851 through April 1852. Published in book form in 1852, the work sold 300,000 copies in the United States during its first 12 months of publication. Since then it has been translated into 20 languages. Fanning the flames of the abolition movement, the novel was intended to both critique slavery and condemn its effects on family life. Stowe showed how the laws, in particular the Fugitive Slave Law of 1850, separated families and destroyed Christian values. *Uncle Tom's Cabin* is still in print and remains the most widely read antislavery book ever written.

See also Stowe, Harriet Beecher.

Unions

Women have tried to organize for better hours, pay, and working conditions from the time the first factories were established in New England in the 1820s and 1830s. Despite repeated attempts throughout the nineteenth century, women failed to build lasting unions. The Lowell (Massachusetts) Female Labor Reform Association (1845–1848), led from 1845 to 1846 by Sarah Bagley, was perhaps the first significant women's trade union in the United States. The association, an auxiliary of the New England Workingmen's Association, gradually spread to other New England mill towns such as Manchester, Waltham, Dover, Nashua, and Fall River.

During a period of rapid industrial growth stimulated by the Civil War, the cigar makers (1867) and printers (1869) organized the first two national unions in the United States. They were the first national unions to admit women, who constituted many of the workers in these trades. The best-known women's union during this time was the Troy Collar Laundry Union (TCLU). Located in Troy, New York, by 1863 these makers of separate collars for men's shirts had seen their trade develop into a major industry. In 1863 the workers, who toiled long hours in temperatures of almost 100 degrees, waged a successful strike for higher pay. By 1866, the union treasury was full enough to permit it to contribute $1,000 to the striking Iron Molders' Union, for which its president, William Sylvis, was grateful. That year, at its first convention, the National Labor Union, a federation of national unions led by Sylvis, pledged to support "sewing women and daughters of toil." By 1868 Sylvis had named TCLU president Kate Mullaney assistant secretary of the National Labor Union. In 1869 the collar ironers went on strike for higher wages, and the starchers joined them. A cooperative laundry operated by union members was formed to pressure manufacturers. The action coincided with the death of Sylvis. Without his support, financial and otherwise, and under attack from management, both the TCLU and its newly formed Co-Operative Collar Company went into swift decline; the union was abolished in 1870. Another factor contributing to its demise was the introduction of paper collars.

On 28 July 1869, the female shoemakers in Lynn, Massachusetts, formed a local chapter. It held annual conventions through

303

1872. That year, when manufacturers tried to cut wages, 900 workers successfully fought back. Yet, during the depression of 1873–1878, the union vanished.

The 1880s saw rapid industrial growth, and female workers were in demand for low-paying jobs. According to historian Eleanor Flexner, in 1880, 2,647,000 women were in the labor force; ten years later the number had risen to 4,005,500, an increase from 15.2 percent to 17.2 percent of the total work force. Though the demand for labor was high, increased immigration kept wages low, provoking the first successful attempts to build national unions. During this decade, many of the female workers who had participated in the short-lived local unions of the 1860s and 1870s joined the Knights of Labor. The Knights chartered its first women's assemblies in 1881 and 1882. Women—including waitresses, printers, tailoresses, domestics, tobacco workers, writers, music teachers, and cooks—joined in record numbers. By 1886 a total of 113 assemblies had been chartered. In 1883 one female delegate attended the Knights' general assembly. The following year only two women delegates appeared. Of the 600 delegates at the 1886 meeting, 16 were women, more than ever before. The union's attempts to organize women ended in 1890, when the organization itself started to decline because of its failure to unite workers.

The American Federation of Labor (AFL) in 1881 chartered women's local chapters in certain trades. However, the AFL concentrated on craft workers, or skilled laborers such as carpenters and plumbers, all of whom were male. During the 1890s and early 1900s, women continued to attempt to organize, setting up sporadic unions in the meat packing, glove making, printing, millinery, and tobacco industries.

The twentieth century has seen the growth of the first women-dominated unions. These originated in the garment industry, with the earliest local chapters of today's International Ladies' Garment Workers' Union beginning in 1900. Since the late 1960s and early 1970s, the United States has witnessed growth in the organizations of teachers (National Education Association (National Education Association and American Federation of Teachers), government workers (American Federation of State, County and Municipal Employees), hospital workers (American Nurses Association), office workers (Office and Professional Employees International), and other service workers (Retail, Wholesale and Department Store Union and Service Employees International Union). The International Ladies' Garment Workers' Union had 175,000 members in 1990, and the United Textile Workers of America had 26,000 members that year. All of these organizations, many of which have grown with the service sector of the economy, are dominated by women.

See also American Federation of Labor; Bagley, Sarah; Collar Trade; Female Labor Reform Associations; International Ladies' Garment Workers' Union; Knights of Labor; Lowell Female Labor Reform Association; National Education Association; National Labor Union; Strikes; United Auto Workers Women's Department.

United Auto Workers Women's Department

The United Auto Workers (UAW) has been one of the nation's leading advocates of women's rights during this century, owing in large part to the influence of its Women's Department. Created in 1944 to handle the influx of women workers during World War II, the department has done research to help UAW determine policy regarding women and has been instrumental in the passage of staunchly feminist resolutions at the union's national conventions. As early as 1941, the UAW encouraged the U.S. government to follow the union's example of nondiscrimination—including the rejection of sex discrimination—in the awarding of contracts and in other areas. In 1949, it endorsed a national equal-pay law and opposed the limitation of maximum-hour laws on only women. After UAW's women's department studies revealed that protective legislation usually hurts women, the union abandoned its long-standing support of state protective legislation in favor of Title VII of the 1964 Civil Rights Act. The UAW was the first major union to call for Equal Employment Opportunity Commission guidelines that clearly indicate that Title VII takes precedence over states' protective legislation. In 1970, the union's advocacy of women's rights extended to support of the Equal Rights Amendment, child care centers, and abortion law reform.

See also Protective Legislation; Unions.

United States v. Libbey-Owens, United Glass and Ceramic Workers of North America, AFL-CIO Local #9

United States v. Libbey-Owens, United Glass and Ceramic Workers of North America, AFL-CIO Local #9 (1970) was the Justice Department's first sex discrimination suit filed under Title VII of the 1964 Civil Rights Act. Libbey-Owens and the unions were accused of hiring women for only one of the company's five glass plants in Toledo, Ohio, and with assigning women to the less attractive jobs in that plant. Libbey-Owens said it was unable to comply with Title VII because Ohio laws mandated that women be treated differently from men. The company pointed to the maximum-hour workday law and a limitation on weight lifting. The Justice Department demanded a change in the company's hiring policy and back pay for women who were adversely affected by the hiring policy. The case, settled by a consent agreement, offered no conclusive resolution of the conflict between Title VII and state protective legislation. For this reason, and because the court failed to award back pay, many women's rights groups viewed the case with a degree of disappointment. However, Libbey-Owens did agree to promote some women immediately, to consider women for more types of jobs, and to educate women about job opportunities.

See also Protective Legislation; Title VII of the 1964 Civil Rights Act.

United States v. One Package

United States v. One Package took place in the District Court of New York in 1936 when physicians challenged the federal Comstock law. At issue was Section 305 of the Tariff Act of 1930, which originated from the Comstock Act of 1873. In an attempt to protect public morals, the statute prohibited the importation into the United States of any device used to prevent conception or induce abortion. Dr. Hannah M. Stone, a licensed gynecologist, imported rubber pessaries from a physician in Japan in order to conduct experiments testing the devices' reliability. She testified that she prescribed the pessaries in cases where it was not desirable for a patient to become pregnant. A number of physicians testified on her behalf, saying that from a medical standpoint, it was necessary to prescribe a contraceptive to prevent or cure diseases. Directed to return the pessaries, Dr. Stone appealed to the court on 7 December 1936 and received the following decision: "Statutes forbidding importation of articles for prevention of conception or causing unlawful abortion held NOT to bar articles employed by physician in practice of profession for preventing conception to protect patients' health or save them from infection." This exemption was made law in December 1936.

United States v. Vuitch

Before the *Roe v. Wade* (1973) decision legalizing abortion, some abortion rights advocates suggested that merely repealing existing antiabortion laws would be sufficient to guarantee the right to an abortion. The aftermath of *United States v. Vuitch* (1971) made it apparent that the mere absence of antiabortion laws, without legislation or court decisions actually upholding abortion rights, was inadequate. In *United States v. Vuitch*, a Washington, D.C., court overturned a local abortion law restricting abortion and left the district without any law on abortion. The public hospital on which most of the district's poor residents relied, D.C. General, soon virtually stopped giving abortions. Private hospitals were similarly restrictive. The National Abortion Rights Action League (NARAL), in conjunction with the American Civil Liberties Union

(ACLU), sued D.C. General Hospital twice and obtained two court orders that forced the hospital to perform more abortions. This experience convinced many abortion rights advocates working for the repeal of abortion laws that the route they had chosen was problematic. Because of the controversy surrounding abortion, hospitals generally lacked the confidence to perform abortions unless there were clear, specific, and concrete guidelines about the types of circumstances under which they could perform them. The overturning of the original D.C. law restricting abortion meant that hospitals had to assume that all abortions were legal in order to perform them, whereas hospitals felt that the burden of proof was on abortion seekers to prove that abortion was legal (in the circumstances in which they were seeking it). Laws restricting abortion to a certain set of circumstances not only prohibited abortion in some cases, they also had the less obvious feature of making it clear that abortion was legal in other cases. For this reason, the Supreme Court's 1971 overturning of *U.S. v. Vuitch* and upholding of the original D.C. law restricting abortion ironically yielded greater access to abortion in Washington, D.C.

See also Doe v. Bolton; National Abortion Rights Action League; *Roe v. Wade.*

Uprising of the 20,000

The 1909–1910 garment workers' strike in New York City, which came to be known as the Uprising of the 20,000 (also known as the 10,000 or 30,000, depending on the account), was one of the most significant efforts of the early women's labor movement. The strike officially began 22 November 1909 at a meeting of shirtwaist makers called by the International Ladies' Garment Workers' Union (ILGWU) in Cooper Union in New York, although local chapters had been on strike earlier. Tension had been growing among workers and employers because of low wages and the fact that workers had to provide their own supplies. Although the meeting was not organized to call a strike, remarks made by a teenager, Clara Lemlich, stirred up the members of the group and motivated them to walk out. She interrupted the speech making of the famous labor leaders—Samuel Gompers, president of the American Federation of Labor, and Margaret Dreier Robins of the New York Women's Trade Union League—to announce, "I am tired of listening to speakers who talk in general terms. What we are here for is to decide whether or not we shall strike. I offer a resolution that a general strike be declared—now!" The following day between 18,000 and 25,000 workers, most of them women, went on strike. The strikers generated a great deal of public support and received contributions from wealthy persons who were angered by reports of police violence. Although the strikers did not achieve their goal of manufacturers' universal recognition of the union, many of the workers did win better wages, hours, and working conditions in shop settlements. One of the consequences of the strike was the increase in the size of the ILGWU and workers' confidence in it.

See also International Ladies' Garment Workers' Union; Knights of Labor; National Labor Union; Strikes; Triangle Shirtwaist Fire.

Upton, Harriet Taylor (1853–1945)

Harriet Taylor Upton was a suffragist and writer. She was born 17 December 1853 in Ravenna, Ohio, the daughter of Ezra Booth Taylor, who served in Congress for 13 years. She grew up in an intellectually stimulating household and was educated in the public schools of Warren, Ohio, where her family moved in 1861. Enthusiastic about science, she successfully protested the Warren High School rule that prohibited girls from entering the chemistry laboratory. Her father disapproved of a college education for her, but she traveled with him during his tenure as a circuit court judge, learning a good deal about politics. In her later teenage years and early twenties, she served as secretary of the Woman's Christian Temperance Union. At that time she was a strong opponent of women's suffrage. But in about 1889, after meeting Elizabeth Cady Stanton and Susan

B. Anthony, and while gathering information and interviewing people for an antisuffrage article, her viewpoint changed. In 1890 she joined the National American Woman Suffrage Association (NAWSA). In 1894 she was elected treasurer of NAWSA, an office she held until 1910. From 1902 until 1910 she edited the monthly suffrage newspaper, *Progress.* Upton was president of the Ohio Woman Suffrage Association for 18 years (1899–1908 and 1911–1920). After ratification of the Nineteenth Amendment, she remained involved in politics. She was vice-chair of the Republican National Executive Committee for four years (1920–1924). Upton wrote many political articles that emphasized the role women played in American history. She also published a children's book and two historical works, *A Twentieth Century History of Trumbull County, Ohio* (1909) and *History of the Western Reserve* (1910). Taylor retired from public life in 1931 and moved to Pasadena, California, where she died on 2 November 1945.

Utopian Communities

Beginning in the late eighteenth century, hundreds of utopian communities flourished throughout the country. Their living and working arrangements challenged the customs of the rest of the nation. Some societies expanded the role of women. One of these, the American sect of the United Society of Believers in Christ's Second Appearing, founded by (Mother) Ann Lee in 1774, when she came to the United States from England, was referred to as the Society of Shakers, or Shaking Quakers because of the way its members shook with emotion during prayer meetings. Spiritually, the group believed in a dual deity, or mother and father God, confession, and a messiah. The Shakers settled first in Albany, New York, and later moved to New Lebanon, New York (1784). Between 1787 and 1794, 11 communities grew up in New England, and in the first quarter of the nineteenth century, seven more flourished in Ohio, Kentucky, and Indiana. By 1822 their numbers had

reached 4,000. The Shakers developed an economy and social structure similar to a seventeenth-century village, favoring communal work over specialized duties of men and women. Shakers viewed their work as a way of praising God. To this end, men and women working side by side made simple but beautiful furniture and canned goods, and the profits were shared by all. The role of the housewife was abolished, and both sexes shared domestic labor. Because they were pacifists, the Shakers were carefully watched during the American Revolution, and some were jailed. Shaker women wore simple gowns and caps and vowed celibacy (as did Shaker men). The few children who lived in the communities were separated from their parents and reared by members of both sexes. The devotional spirit of the Shakers lives on in their few remaining, sparsely populated communities, and in their finely crafted household items, which now have become collectors' items.

By the 1820s, followers of Robert Dale Owen were planning cooperative societies in which men and women would live in harmony. At Owen's socialist community at New Harmony, Indiana, domestic chores such as cooking, washing, and heating rooms were done by both sexes. Owen advocated withdrawal as a form of birth control. He advocated birth control because he believed that if they were able to have fewer children, women could be more equal with men—a goal that ultimately he failed to achieve.

Perhaps the nation's most radical communal society was the Oneida Community in Oneida, New York. This community was founded in 1848 by John Humphrey Noyes, who believed in the egalitarianism of women. Noyes promoted equality among men and women in their sexual relations. He devised the complex marriage, which replaced monogamous relationships with regulated promiscuity. Under complex marriage, every member of the community was, in theory, married to every other community member of the opposite sex. Mutual consent to sex was required. Men were responsible for birth control, mostly through

307

the practice of continence, or intercourse without ejaculation. The community, like that of the Shakers, resembled a seventeenth-century village in its economy and social organizion. Traditional male and female roles were abolished. Instead, men and women working side by side produced food, medicines, silverware, brooms, furniture, and other commodities. The profits were shared by all. Women wore shirts and pantaloons and kept their hair short. Tobacco, liquor, profanity, and obscenity were banned. The community's diet consisted mostly of fruits and vegetables. At first the community devoted itself to agriculture and raising fruit, but it had little financial success until it began to manufacture steel traps. The manufacture of steel chains for use with the traps and the canning of fruits and vegetables soon followed (1854). In 1866 the community began sewing and embroidering silk. For 25 years the community prospered undisturbed, until several ecclesiastical bodies in New York lobbied for legislative action against it. On 14 February 1879, resolutions were passed denouncing the community, and legal action was recommended. Noyes told his followers on 20 August 1879 that they would give up complex marriage in deference to public opinion. The community ultimately transformed itself into the Oneida Community, Limited, a cooperative joint stock company.

See also Noyes, John Humphrey; Owen, Robert Dale.

Van Duyn, Mona (1921–)

Born on 9 May 1921 in Waterloo, Iowa, Mona Van Duyn won the 1991 Pulitzer Prize in poetry for her collection *Near Changes* (1990). She was named the nation's first female poet laureate on 14 June 1992, becoming the nation's sixth poet laureate. She has stated that before the position of poet laureate was created in 1985, the position of poetry consultant to the Library of Congress was held by few female poets: 25 men compared to 6 women. The recipient of a National Book Award (1971) and Guggenheim fellowship (1972), Van Duyn commutes to Washington, D.C., from St. Louis, Missouri. Van Duyn's other books are: *A Time of Bees* (1964), *Merciful Disguises* (1973), *Letters from a Father and Other Poems* (1982), and *If It Be Not I: Collected Poems, 1959–1982* (1993).

Vassar College

Founded in 1861 by Matthew Vassar at the suggestion of seminarian Milo Jewett and with support from Sarah Josepha Buell Hale, who called for more women's colleges and faculty in the magazine *Godey's Lady's Book*, Vassar College is a private college for women in Poughkeepsie, New York. It was incorporated in 1861 as Vassar Female College; the word *Female* was dropped in 1867. Matthew Vassar, a brewery owner, selected the board of trustees and donated $400,000 and 200 acres of land to the college. Building began in June 1861, and the college opened four years later (September 1865), dedicated to the belief that women and men have the same right to intellectual attainments. Its first principal was Hannah W. Lyman, who oversaw a faculty of eight professors and 20 instructors and teachers. The student body consisted of 353 pupils. Because of controversy about whether women should be awarded bachelor's degrees, the first four graduates (1867) received certificates awarding them "the First Degree of Liberal Arts." The next year the certificates were replaced by A.B. diplomas. Vassar's student body was the largest of any women's college of its day. Although the board of directors and president were at first all male, the noted astronomer Maria Mitchell joined the staff in 1865, training the first generation of women who went on to scientific and professional careers. A chapter of Phi Beta Kappa was founded at Vassar in 1898, and the college built an outstanding reputation in physics, astronomy, chemistry, and psychology. In 1969 Vassar became coeducational.

See also Hale, Sarah Josepha Buell; Mitchell, Maria; Vassar School of Euthenics.

Vassar School of Euthenics

Founded in 1924, the Vassar School of Euthenics represented the effort of a feminist school to accommodate a growing demand for women's schools to prepare women for domestic life. "Euthenics" refers to attempts to improve the physical quality of the human race through improvements in living conditions; in effect, it elevated homemaking to a science. Vassar and other leading women's schools tried to offer the same intellectual rigor as the all-male Ivy League schools. The School of Euthenics, however, combined studies from various fields to teach women homemaking and child rearing. Some of the courses offered included "Husband and Wife," "Motherhood," and "The Family as an Economic Unit." Other schools started similar programs, despite feminists' protests.

See also Vassar College.

Violence

American women are injured more often by the men in their lives than by car accidents and street crime combined. In 1992 the

309

American Medical Association, backed by the U.S. surgeon general, declared that violent men constitute a major threat to women's health. In 1991 alone, four million women were beaten and 1,320 were murdered in domestic attacks. The National League of Cities estimates that as many as half of all women will experience violence in their marriages. Of all the women who are treated in emergency rooms, 22–35 percent are treated for injuries from domestic assaults. Between one-third and one-half of all female murder victims are killed by their spouses or lovers, compared with 4 percent of male victims.

Psychologist Gus Kaufman, Jr., cofounder of Men Stopping Violence, a clinic in Atlanta, Georgia, believes that violence against women is "as old an institution as marriage." He thinks that as long as women were considered men's legal property, police and the courts were unable to prevent or punish domestic assaults. Holly Maguigan, a law professor at New York University, traces wife beating to the traditional "rule of the thumb" that restricted a man's right to use a weapon against his wife: He couldn't use a rod that was thicker than his thumb. In the nineteenth century, North Carolina became one of the first states to limit a man's right to beat his wife. Until the 1970s, aggravated assault against a stranger was a felony under the law, but assaulting a spouse was a misdemeanor. This distinction still exists in most states, although, according to the Boston Bar Association, domestic attacks are at least as dangerous as 90 percent of felony assaults.

The question of why women remain in threatening situations has perplexed social scientists. In 1984 Denver psychologist Lenore Walker coined a term for this behavior: *battered woman syndrome*. Walker conducted a study that traced the cycle of violence in battering households: first a period of tension; then a violent episode, often fueled by drugs or alcohol; and, finally, a stage of remorse. Women occasionally strike back and are tried for their crime of violence. Psychologist Charles Ewing compared a group of 100 battered women who

had resorted to violence with those who had not. He found that those who resorted to violence were most isolated, most badly beaten, had children who had been abused by the man in their life, and were living with men who were addicted to drugs or alcohol. In 1992 President George Bush signed legislation that calls for the development of training materials to help defendants and their lawyers use expert testimony in some domestic violence cases. However, as of 1993, only nine states had passed laws permitting expert testimony about the battered woman syndrome in trials of women who have struck back.

Individual states and the federal government have attempted to intervene to protect women. On the state level, Minnesota serves as a model. In 1981 Duluth became the first city to institute mandatory arrests in domestic disputes. Since then, half the states have followed suit. Since 1990, at least 28 states have passed stalking laws that make it a crime to threaten, follow, or harass someone. Congress has also attempted to solve the problem. On 14 January 1991, Senator Joseph R. Biden, Jr., introduced the Violence against Women Act. The law would classify rape as a gender-based hate crime, punishable under federal civil rights statues as well as state criminal law. The law would increase penalties for violence against women, and it would grant $300 million to police, prosecutors, and the courts to combat violence against women. Endorsing the bill before the Senate Judiciary Committee, Biden said, "There's something wrong, something terribly wrong, when over the last 15 years, violence against young men has decreased by 12 percent while violence against young women in America has increased 50 percent. Something is wrong." He cited statistics showing that, since 1974, the number of murders has decreased 5.6 percent for older males but increased 29.9 percent for older females. Biden went on to address the problem of jurors who think that victims invite rape.

Consider this: If I walk from here, out across the mall to the Capitol, waving

310

2,000 dollar bills in front of everyone for all to see, and someone comes and grabs them out of my hand and runs. The young woman or man who grabbed the 2,000 dollar bills that I was waving and flaunting in front of the public cannot say in court, "By the way, he invited it—Biden was walking down the street waving 2,000 dollar bills." They cannot use that as a defense. So even if a woman . . . walked in the most promiscuous and inviting manner from here to the Capitol across the way, no one under any circumstance has any right, for any reason, to violate her physically.

As of this writing, the act is being debated by Congress.

See also Family Violence Prevention and Services Act; Rideout Case.

Voice of Industry

The *Voice of Industry* was the most widely read labor paper of the 1840s. Originally published in Fitchburg, Massachusetts, its first issue was produced 19 May 1845 by an association of workingmen under the editorship of William F. Young. On 3 July 1845, the *Voice of Industry* criticized another operatives' paper, the *Lowell Offering*, for ignoring the real problems of factory women. In October 1845, the magazine combined with two other papers, moved to Lowell, Massachusetts, and asked Sarah D. Bagley, the country's first woman labor leader, to serve on its publication committee with Young and Joel Hatch. On 7 November 1845, the *Voice of Industry* carried the notice

We cordially invite the Factory Girls of Lowell, and the operatives and working people generally, whether they agree with us or not, to make the *Voice* a medium of communication; for it is your paper, through which you should be heard and command attention. The Press has been too long monopolized

by the capitalist non-producers, party demagogues and speculators, to the exclusion of the people, whose rights are as dear and valid.

By May 1846 women in the mills took over the publication, which had been bought by the Lowell Female Reform Association, and Bagley became its chief editor. Although the *Voice of Industry* carried poetry, stories, and advice, it was much more militant than the papers that preceded it, including the *Lowell Offering* and the *Operatives' Magazine*. It published bitter attacks against the factory system and arguments on behalf of the ten-hour workday. The *Voice of Industry* ceased publication in 1848.

See also Bagley, Sarah; Farley, Harriet; Lowell Female Labor Reform Association; *Lowell Offering*.

Voluntarism

Women's voluntary societies have traditionally consisted of benevolent or charity organizations and reform societies. The years following the American Revolution witnessed the founding of the first of these organizations. The earliest were church sewing circles that raised funds to support charities. Later, societies emerged such as the Female Association for the Relief of Women and Children in Reduced Circumstances, the Newark Female Charitable Society, and the Boston Female Asylum. The treasurers of these groups were usually single women. (This prevented husbands from taking possession of the funds, which they were legally entitled to do.) The groups helped women to acquire the organizational and political skills essential to the coming women's movement.

From 1820 to 1845 the nation experienced a growth of voluntary associations. Among the women's groups, many were educational. For example, throughout the 1820s the Smithfield (Rhode Island) Female Improvement Society met each week to read books and its members' original writings. During the 1830s, free African-American women formed literary societies in Philadelphia, Boston, and other eastern cities. The Ohio Ladies Education Society was formed to establish education for African-American children in the state. In 1833 the Philadelphia Female Anti-Slavery Society was formed by 20 women. Uncertain of their ability to conduct a meeting, they asked a freedman to serve as chair. In 1834, a few women met at the Third Presbyterian Church in New York City to form an organization to fight prostitution and the double standard in sex. By 1844 more than 400 chapters of the American Female Reform Society existed, collectively publishing a newspaper, the *Advocate*, to promote the groups' views.

Through voluntarism, women expanded their sphere of influence beyond the confines of the home. They built schools, raised money, worked for education, gathered petitions, helped the poor, and worked to develop the social infrastructure of the nation. Class limitations may have prevented many middle-class and upper-class women from comprehending the real struggles of African-American and working-class women, yet women scholars believe they acknowledged the problems of the oppressed more than traditional male politicians. The settlement house movement clearly illustrates middle-class concern for the disadvantaged. Organizations like Hull House performed services that earlier voluntary associations had assumed, but on a broader lever, calling it "social work." And a "social worker" such as Jane Addams had a higher level of education.

Eventually, women realized that the social problems they were trying to solve could be handled only by legislation. For example, Julia Lathrop, the first director of the Children's Bureau, documented the abuse of children who lived in cities, lobbying for government assistance. As women realized that formal political action was needed to provide solutions to problems associated with the domestic sphere, they worked through government channels to find solutions, eventually becoming part of activist administrations, such as those of President Franklin D. Roosevelt and President Lyndon B. Johnson.

See also Benevolent Societies.

Voluntary Parenthood League

Founded by Mary Ware Dennett in 1918, the Voluntary Parenthood League had as its goal the repeal of the Comstock Act that prohibited the use of the U.S. post office for mailing information about birth control. Dennett considered voluntary parenthood as fundamental a right as free speech. She believed that contraceptives should be available to everyone. Her views conflicted with those of Margaret Sanger, who thought that only doctors should be able to distribute contraceptive information. Dennett worked to make birth control widely available, but the topic was too controversial for her time, and Congress failed to enact laws to decriminalize contraception.

See also American Birth Control League; Comstock Act; Sanger, Margaret.

Walker, Alice Malsenior (1944–)

Alice Walker is the first African-American woman to win a Pulitzer Prize for fiction. The daughter of a sharecropper and a domestic worker, she was born 9 February 1944 in Eatonton, Georgia. An injury at the age of eight left her blind in one eye. Partly because of this disability, she was offered a special scholarship to Spelman College in Georgia (1961–1963). She transferred to Sarah Lawrence College, graduating in 1965, and became a civil rights activist. In 1964 she traveled to Africa; her experiences there inspired poems that were collected in *Once* (1968). In 1967 she married Melvyn R. Leventhal. The couple moved to Mississippi, where Walker was a writer in residence at several colleges between 1968 and 1971. The poet and essayist won the Rosenthal Foundation Award in 1974 from the American Institute of Arts and Letters for *In Love and Trouble: Stories of Black Women* (1973). Her book *Revolutionary Petunias* (1973) won the Lillian Smith Award of the Southern Regional Council. In 1974 Walker and her husband moved to New York City, where she became a contributing editor of *Ms.* Two years later Walker and her husband divorced. In 1982 Walker's third novel, *The Color Purple*, became a best-seller. In 1983, it won both the Pulitzer Prize and the American Book Award; two years later it was made into a successful movie. Walker's works reflect her social activism on behalf of African Americans and women. She continues her political and creative work in San Francisco. *Possessing the Secret of Joy*, a book about women's genital mutilation, was published in 1992.

See also Womanism, Womanist, Womanish.

Wallace, Zerelda Gray Sanders (1817–1901)

Zerelda Wallace was a temperance and women's suffrage reformer. She was born 6 August 1817 in Millersburg, Kentucky. A prominent member of the National Woman's Christian Temperance Union (WCTU), she organized an Indiana branch and twice served as its president (1874–1877 and 1879–1883). In 1875, at the WCTU's national convention, she proposed a resolution for women's suffrage, arguing that it was essential to the temperance movement. The resolution was approved. In 1878 she and May Wright Sewall formed the Indianapolis Equal Suffrage Association. She also founded the Indiana Woman Suffrage Association. Wallace spent her last years in Cataract, Indiana, where she died 19 March 1901.

Walters, Barbara (1931–)

Barbara Walters is the first woman to co-anchor a national daily television evening news program and the first to be honored by the American Museum of the Moving Image. She was born 25 September 1931 in Boston. After attending both public and private schools, she continued her studies at Sarah Lawrence College, from which she graduated in 1954. She was hired by NBC in 1961 to write for the "Today" show. Walters began her on-air career at NBC in 1965, when she was asked to stand in on the "Today" show. In 1970 she published *How To Talk with Practically Anybody about Practically Anything*. Four years later she became coanchor of the "Today" show. In 1976, Walters became television's highest paid reporter when she accepted an annual salary of $1 million to anchor ABC's primetime evening news show. That year she began to

313

host ABC's occasional series, "The Barbara Walters Special." Walters became a regular on the popular magazine program "20/20" in 1979. She has received many broadcasting awards, including broadcaster of the year (1975). In a 1990 *Ladies' Home Journal* article, Walters stated, "When I first started out, there was a period when people called me pushy, while a Mike Wallace would be called authoritative. Or my questions were bitchy, while someone else's were courageous." Walters persevered in the face of much criticism, blazing the trail for women in television news. In 1992 she became the first woman to be honored by the American Museum of the Moving Image.

Waltham System
See Factory System.

War Manpower Commission
The War Manpower Commission, founded in 1942, recruited female workers for the defense industry in 1942 and 1943. One of the group's strategies was asking newspaper editors to use pictures of female defense workers on their front pages. The commission also sponsored films, radio announcements, and posters to encourage women to enter the work force. The commission called attention to the need for women to mobilize during wartime.
See also Women's Advisory Committee.

Watson v. Bailey
In *Watson v. Bailey* (1808), the Pennsylvania Supreme Court strengthened the court's protection of women in the conveyance of property jointly held by husband and wife. A 1770 statute required justices of the peace to interrogate women to learn if they were acting voluntarily or involuntarily in selling lands with their husbands. In this case the court reviewed a deed that transferred property held by a married couple. The deed had been witnessed by a justice of the peace, who recorded that the wife had told him in private that she wanted to sell the property.

However, the justice had not complied with the law, as he had not questioned the wife to ascertain whether of her own free will and with full understanding of her actions she did, in fact, agree with her husband. The court's sloppiness in such matters was commonplace as, in Pennsylvania, the property rights of married women had traditionally been held to be of little value. The state supreme court declared the deed invalid because the justice of the peace had recorded the wife's agreement to the conveyance too haphazardly. As a result, Pennsylvania courts had to be more conscientious in enforcing the law with regard to property transactions involving *femes coverts. Watson v. Bailey* became a guide for future cases in Pennsylvania.
See also Ewing v. Smith; Feme Covert; Harvey and Wife v. Pecks.

Waves
The feminist movement has frequently been divided by historians into two separate and distinct time periods or phases, which are labeled "waves." The first wave, which focused for the most part on political rights, culminated in the victory of the passage of the suffrage amendment in 1920. The next four decades are usually regarded as a lull in feminist activity, indeed a period of retreat rather than advance in the field of women's rights. (Very recently, some historians have begun to question this interpretation of history, arguing that women continued their activism on various social issues relevant to the feminist agenda, such as pacifism and social welfare, through the vehicle of their own organizations.) With the 1961 establishment of the President's Commission on the Status of Women, the federal government paid significant attention to women's issues for the first time since the suffrage amendment was passed. However, it was the 1963 publication of Betty Friedan's bestseller *The Feminine Mystique,* which challenged the limitation of women to homemaking roles, that launched the second wave of feminist activity. The second wave pressed not only for greater legal rights

for women but also for a reexamination of women's social roles and the societal pressures that had been forcing women to accept a fixed set of confining lifestyle choices. There is some debate among historians about the status of the second wave. Some say that it essentially came to a conclusion with the end of the 1970s, by which time the period of greatest activity (especially legal activity) was over. These scholars describe the 1980s as an antifeminist period and points to the setbacks caused by the lack of sympathy to feminist goals on the part of the administration of President Ronald Reagan. Those on the other side of the debate maintain that, because many of the cultural changes that feminists had sought (such as the acceptability of women's employment) had already become incorporated into society by the late seventies, feminism merely lost some of its distinct identity, but survived.

Today new voices are represented by such writers as Susan Faludi, whose *Backlash* postulates a negative reaction from white males to the gains of the women's movement, though this appears to be cast in doubt by the Gallup Poll's David Moore, who documents much more of a "cultural war" among women themselves. Writers Camille Paglia and Naomi Wolf have stirred new controversy among feminists in books critical of the women's movement. The one area of general consensus is that the 1990s represent a renewed interest in feminist theory.

Webster v. Reproductive Health Services

In *Webster v. Reproductive Health Services* (1989), the Supreme Court upheld a Missouri law restricting abortion. The law outlaws the use of public money, facilities, and employees to perform abortions not necessary to save the woman's life. It also forces physicians to determine whether the pregnancy has lasted more than 20 weeks. The law affects all hospitals that receive public money, which includes almost every hospital in the state; thus, the law affects the availability of abortion in general. The pre-

amble, which declares that life begins at conception, appears to many to be an unconstitutional legal endorsement of a particular religious view. The Court allowed the preamble to stand; this decision could have an impact on other reproductive health issues. Four of the justices ruling on the case favored undoing *Roe v. Wade* altogether. In the wake of the *Webster* decision, many state legislatures proposed antiabortion laws; however, the anger generated by opposition to the ruling served to revitalize the reproductive freedom movement in America.

See also Blackmun, Harry; *Roe v. Wade*.

Weddington, Sarah (1945–)

Sarah Weddington, as a young lawyer just out of college, argued the landmark case *Roe v. Wade* (1973) and won for women the constitutional right to an abortion. The daughter of a Methodist minister, she was born 5 February 1945 in Abilene, Texas. As a high school student, she was president of the Future Homemakers of America. She worked several part-time jobs to pay her way through law school. In *Roe v. Wade*, Weddington challenged a Texas law prohibiting abortion. Working without pay, she represented a group of women who had established an abortion referral service at the University of Texas. Norma McCorvey, the Jane Roe of the case, was a waitress with a tenth-grade education who was barely able to pay her bills and was unable to travel to another state to pay for an abortion. On her behalf Weddington filed the lawsuit against Henry Wade, the Dallas County district attorney. She argued that the law violated McCorvey's right to privacy, which is protected under the First, Fourth, Fifth, Eighth, Ninth, and Fourteenth amendments. In June 1970 a panel of three Supreme Court justices declared the law unconstitutional. Another case, brought on behalf of Mary and John Doe, was dismissed for lack of standing.

On 13 December 1971, Weddington first argued the case of *Roe v. Wade*; on 22 January 1973, the Supreme Court decided in her favor. Weddington is the author of a book on the case, *A Question of Choice* (1992). She works as a lawyer, author, and lecturer.

See also Abortion; *Doe v. Bolton; Roe v. Wade.*

Weeks v. Southern Bell Telephone and Telegraph Co.

Weeks v. Southern Bell Telephone and Telegraph Co. (1968) is considered a landmark case in the area of protective legislation for women. Because a Georgia law limited the amount of weight that women could lift on the job, Southern Bell refused to promote Lorena Weeks to a job for which she applied. A district court upheld the law, but, before an appellate court could hear the case, the law was repealed. The issue at hand evolved into a conflict between a state law and a federal law (Title VII of the 1964 Civil Rights Act) as to whether a company could describe sex as a bona fide occupational qualification (BFOQ) for jobs requiring the lifting of more than a certain amount of weight (it was only by demonstrating that sex was a BFOQ that sex discrimination could be permissible under Title VII). The appellate court ruled that Southern Bell did not demonstrate that sex was a BFOQ for the job. This ruling has broad significance because it places the burden of proof on the employer. This means that whenever an employer restricts a particular job to men, the employer must prove that there is a rational reason to believe that almost all women are unable to perform the restricted job. By setting forth this standard for judging BFOQ exceptions in their opinions, the judges established a precedent that was an important addition to the legal arsenal and that could be used against state protective legislation, although the court had not actually ruled on that subject. In addition to placing the burden of proof on the employer, the court rejected the paternalistic attitude exhibited by the weight limitation as being fundamentally contrary to Title VII.

See also Bona Fide Occupational Qualification; Title VII of the 1964 Civil Rights Act.

Weld, Theodore Dwight (1803–1895)

Theodore Weld was a leading abolitionist and supporter of women's suffrage. He was born 23 November 1803 in Hampton, Connecticut. In 1825 he entered Oneida Institute in Whitesboro, New York, to prepare for the ministry. There, he worked for temperance and became one of the movement's most powerful advocates. In 1832, he convinced philanthropists Arthur Tappan and Lewis Tappan to support the Lane Theological Seminary, then under construction in Cincinnati, Ohio. Weld joined the school but was dismissed in 1834 for organizing antislavery debates in which male and female students participated. After his dismissal, Weld led much of the student body to Oberlin Collegiate Institute in Oberlin, Ohio.

In 1834 Weld began training agents for the American Anti-Slavery Society. By 1836, the success of these agents was so great that the abolitionists abandoned their pamphlet campaign and devoted all their resources to speakers, whose numbers had reached 70. One of the speakers was Angelina Grimké, whom Weld married on 14 March 1838.

Weld lobbied for abolition in Washington, D.C., and assisted John Quincy Adams in his campaign against slavery in the House of Representatives. Weld's most famous publications are *The Bible against Slavery* (1837) and *American Slavery as It Is: Testimony of a Thousand Witnesses* (1839). He died 3 February 1895 in Boston.

See also Abolition; American Anti-Slavery Society; Grimké, Angelina; Oberlin College.

Wellesley College

From the date of its founding in 1875, Wellesley College benefited women in two ways: It offered high-quality education to students as well as teaching opportunities to college-trained scholars. Henry F. Durant, who believed in offering women the same quality education offered to men, founded Wellesley College near Boston in 1875. Because of its costly tuition, the college attracted a number of older and well-to-do students. It offered the opportunity to learn from the nation's first college-trained female scholars. These scholars found job opportunities at Wellesley that they were denied at men's colleges. Today Wellesley is a coeducational institution.

See also Education.

Wells-Barnett, Ida Bell (1862–1931)

Ida Bell Wells-Barnett was a founder of the first African-American women's suffrage club, a journalist, and a feminist. She was born into slavery on 16 July 1862 in Holly Springs, Mississippi, and attended Shaw University (now Rust University), a freedman's school in Holly Springs. When she was 14, both of her parents and three of her siblings died of yellow fever, and she began to teach school to support herself and the remaining five children. Finding an old woman who had been a friend of her mother's to stay with the younger children, Wells took a job as schoolteacher six miles out of town, earning $25 per month. In her autobiography she wrote, "I came home every Friday afternoon, riding the six miles on the big back of a mule. I spent Saturday and Sunday washing and ironing and cooking for the children and went back to my country school on Sunday afternoon."

In 1884 Wells moved to Memphis, Tennessee, where she taught in Shelby County. One day while riding the train back to school, she took a seat in the ladies' coach as usual. Ever since the Supreme Court repealed the Civil Rights Act of 1883, there had been efforts all over the South to separate the races on railroads. The conductor on Wells's train tried to put her in the smoking car, dragging her out of her seat. She bit his hand, and he returned with two other men to help him, as whites stood up on the seats to look on. She got off the train and sued the railroad and was awarded $500 by Judge Pierce, an ex-Union soldier. The *Memphis Daily Appeal* covered the story on 25 December 1884 under the heading "A Darky Damsel Obtains a Verdict for Dam-

ages against the Chesapeake & Ohio Railroad!"

Wells also attended summer classes at Fisk University, where she prepared to be a city teacher to earn more money. In 1887 the Tennessee Supreme Court, reversing a lower court decision, ruled against her in her suit against the Chesapeake & Ohio Railroad. Wells described the incident in an article for her church newspaper and soon began writing for African-American newspapers under the pseudonym Iola. Because she publicly criticized the inferior education offered to African-American children, the Memphis school system did not renew her teaching contract in 1891. Before the year's end, she purchased a one-third interest in the *Memphis Free Speech* newspaper. She wrote, "We printed the *Free Speech* on pink paper to make it distinctive to a great many people who could not read."

Ida Wells-Barnett

In 1892 three of her friends were lynched. By now a half-owner of the *Memphis Free Speech*, she began a crusade against lynching.

317

The articles she published so angered some readers that the newspaper's offices were destroyed. She then moved to New York City, first working as a writer for the *New York Age*, then lecturing and organizing groups to oppose lynching. She established antilynching societies and black women's clubs wherever she went. Her 100-page statistical study of lynching during a three-year period, entitled *A Red Record*, was published in 1895. An account of lynchings since the Emancipation Proclamation, *A Red Record* was the only documentation of lynching in the United States. Also that year, Wells married Chicago lawyer Ferdinand L. Barnett and adopted the name Wells-Barnett. She moved to Chicago, where she became active in local affairs and contributed to her husband's newspaper, the *Conservator*. In 1901 they were the first African-American family to own a home east of State Street, where they were subjected to much racial hostility. From 1913 to 1916, she was a probation officer for the Chicago municipal court system.

Wells-Barnett helped found the first black women's suffrage association, called the Alpha Suffrage Club and the Ida B. Wells Club, Chicago's first African-American women's civic club. She served as secretary of the National Afro-American Council (1892–1902) and chaired the Chicago Equal Rights League, which she had joined in 1913. In 1909, she also took part in the Niagara meeting that led to the founding of the National Association for the Advancement of Colored People (NAACP). However, after its founding, she spurned the NAACP because it was not radical enough.

Wells-Barnett took part in the 1913 Washington, D.C., suffrage parade. The National American Woman Suffrage Association asked her to march with a segregated African-American contingent. Ignoring the request, Wells-Barnett marched with the Illinois contingent. Three years later she led Alpha Suffrage Club members in a parade in Chicago. Wells-Barnett died 25 March 1931 in Chicago. In 1950 the city designated her as one of the 25 outstanding women in the city's history.

West Coast Hotel v. Parrish

In *West Coast Hotel v. Parrish* (1937), the Supreme Court overturned a previous Supreme Court decision (*Adkins v. Children's Hospital*, 1923) to permit a minimum-wage law for women. The state of Washington had on its books a law that created a board to set minimum wages for women and children. Elsie Parrish, an employee of the West Coast Hotel Company, went to court seeking enforcement of the law and back pay. In deciding in her favor, the Court said the states should have the power to regulate such matters, that women need special protection, and that all workers should not be at risk of being exploited.

See also Adkins v. Children's Hospital.

Wharton, Edith Newbold Jones (1862–1937)

Edith Wharton was the first woman to receive the Pulitzer Prize in fiction, the first woman to be a grand officer in the Legion of Honor, and the first to receive an honorary degree from Yale. She was born 24 January 1862 in New York City. She was educated by private tutors in New York and Europe, where the family lived for six years during the Civil War. She married Edward Wharton, a Boston banker, in 1885. During the 1890s she began writing in earnest, contributing poems and stories to *Scribner's*, *Harper's*, and other magazines. After overseeing the remodeling of a house in Newport, Rhode Island, she collaborated with architect Ogden Codman, Jr., on *The Decoration of Houses* (1897). Her short stories were collected in *The Greater Inclination*, (1899) *Crucial Instances*, (1901) and *Xingu and Other Stories* (1916). Her first novel, *The Valley of Decision* (1902), a novel about eighteenth-century Italy, was followed by *The House of Mirth* (1905), her first major work, which satirized New York society—a theme she would return to often. She moved permanently to Europe in 1907, but continued to write about American society. Her 1911 novel *Ethan Frome*, set in New England, is considered by many her least typical and best work. In 1913, she wrote *The Custom of the Country*, followed in 1920 by *The Age of Innocence* (1920), for which she won the Pulitzer Prize in fiction in 1921. In 1923 she became the first woman to receive an honorary doctorate from Yale University. Also that year she became the first female grand officer of the Legion d'Honneur, having earlier (1916) received the Cross of the Legion d'Honneur for her work in organizing U.S. relief for refugees during World War I. Her books *The Marne* and *A Son at the Front* recall her wartime experiences.

Wharton was a friend and admirer of Henry James, whom she remembered fondly in her autobiography *A Backward Glance* (1934). In all, she wrote about 50 books, including 20 novels, 10 short-story collections, and several travel books and works of criticism. In 1934 Wharton became a member of the American Academy of Arts and Letters. She died 11 August 1937 near Paris.

Wheatley, Phillis (c. 1753–1784)

Poet Phillis Wheatley, born about 1753 in Senegal, Africa, was kidnapped at the age of eight and brought to America on a slave ship. Boston tailor John Wheatley bought her at a slave market to be a personal servant to his wife. The Wheatleys treated her with kindness. In two years they taught her English, and she went on to learn Greek and Latin. She was well known among Boston scholars for her translation of a tale from Ovid. At the age of 13, she began to write poetry. Her best-remembered works are "To the University of Cambridge in New England," "To the King's Most Excellent Majesty," and "On the Death of Rev. Dr. Sewall." The first of her poems to be published was "An Elegiac Poem, on the Death of the Celebrated Divine . . . George Whitefield" (1770). Her work was so well known that, on a trip to London with Mrs. Wheatley's son in 1773, she was a guest of the Countess of Huntington. That year, the countess arranged for publication of Wheatley's first book, *Poems on Various Subjects Religious and Moral.* Wheatley left England after learning that Mrs. Wheatley was ill. Both Mr. and Mrs.

Wheatley died soon thereafter, leaving Phillis Wheatley free. George Washington met with her after her return to America. In 1778 Wheatley married John Peters, a freedman, who abandoned her. The poet died in poverty 5 December 1784 in Boston, leaving three small children. Her own copy of her poems, held at Harvard College, was sold after her death to pay her husband's debts. Several years after her death her works were collected in two books, *Memoir and Poems of Phillis Wheatley* (1834) and *Letters of Phillis Wheatley, the Negro Slave-Poet of Boston* (1864). Abolitionists cited her work as proof of the intellectual equality of Africans.

White House Conference on the Emergency Needs of Women

Eleanor Roosevelt organized the White House Conference on the Emergency Needs of Women in November 1933, in response to the inadequate handling of the problems of unemployed women. She announced that if work could not be found for women, then money must be spent to create jobs for them. Among the 50 leading social workers who attended the conference was Roosevelt's own contingent of female appointees and social reformers. Harry Hopkins, who was in charge of federal relief efforts, expressed his desire to provide work for 3,000–4,000 women. Ellen Woodward, who was in charge of women's projects at the Federal Emergency Relief Administration and Civil Works Administration, proposed types of work she considered suitable for women, including sewing, canning, providing child care in emergency nursery schools, and participation in projects in the fields of public health, historical research, and music. The conference could not undo all the bias and limitations that existed against women in employment, and women received only a small percentage of the available jobs; nonetheless, by the standards of the day, the numbers were sufficient to impress contemporary feminists, and the White House Conference may have contributed to any gains that were made in emergency employment then.

Senegalese-born and brought to America as a slave, Phillis Wheatley's poetry was published in London and Boston.

Willard, Emma Hart (1787–1870)

Emma Willard founded the first institution of higher learning for women. Born 23 February 1787 in Berlin, Connecticut, she was the sixteenth of 17 children. Her father encouraged her to seek an education far beyond that of many farm girls, and she enrolled in the Berlin Academy, which was her first school, in 1802. She was so precocious that by 1804 she was teaching at the school, and by 1806 took charge of it for one term. In 1807 she was hired as an assistant at an academy in Westfield, Massachusetts. She then became preceptress of a girls' school in Middlebury, Vermont. There she met Dr. John Willard; they married in 1809.

After the marriage, John Willard's nephew, who attended Middlebury College, lived with the Willards. Reading his textbooks, Emma Willard recognized the huge gap between men's and women's education. Fired by her discovery, she opened the Middlebury Female Seminary in her home. Her goal was to offer an education comparable to that offered by men's colleges, especially in classical and scientific subjects. In 1819 she wrote *An Address to the Public; Particularly to the Members of the Legislature of New-York, Proposing a Plan for Improving Female Education*. Both Thomas Jefferson and John Adams praised the work, but it did not persuade the legislature to fund schools for women. In 1819 Willard moved to Waterford, New York, where she opened a school. In 1821, after hearing that the city of Troy, New York, had raised funds to establish a girls' school, she moved there. She opened the Troy Female Seminary in 1821, introducing some courses that were more advanced than those offered by men's colleges. In 1825 her husband died, but Willard continued to build the school. By 1831 more than 100 boarders and 200 day students attended the school, which became one of the most influential schools in the United States. She remained head of the Troy Female Seminary until 1838, when she married Christopher Yates. The couple divorced in 1843. Willard published several textbooks, including *History of the United States, or Republic of America* (1828) and *A System of Universal History in Perspective* (1835). She also published a collection of poems, *The Fulfilment of Promise* (1831). Her later books include *A Treatise on the Motive Powers which Produce the Circulation of the Blood* (1846), *Guide to the Temple of Time* and *Universal History for Girls* (1849), *Last Leaves of American History* (1849), *Astronography; or Astronomical Geography* (1854), and *Morals for the Young* (1857). Willard died 15 April 1870 in

Troy. Her school was renamed the Emma Willard School 25 years later.

See also Troy Female Seminary.

Willard, Frances Elizabeth Caroline (1839–1898)

Frances Willard was president of the National Woman's Christian Temperance Union (WCTU) for almost 20 years. She was born 28 September 1839 in Churchville, New York. Her family moved to Ohio, then Wisconsin. She began teaching in 1859 and became the dean of women at Northwestern University in 1873. The following year she resigned to join the growing crusade against liquor, becoming corresponding secretary of the WCTU. In 1879 she became president of the WCTU, a position she held until her death. She was influential in the Prohibition party and the Populist party but was disappointed in her attempts to merge the two. In 1883 she organized the World's Woman's Christian Temperance Union and became its first president. Willard advocated women's suffrage as well as temperance. She was elected president of the National Council of Women in 1888. She wrote many articles and several books,

Frances Willard

321

including *Woman and Temperance* (1883), the autobiographical *Glimpses of Fifty Years* (1889), *How To Win* (1886), and *A Great Mother* (1894). She coedited *A Woman of the Century* (1893) with Mary Livermore. Willard died 17 February 1898 in New York City.

See also National Woman's Christian Temperance Union.

Willingbam v. Simons

In *Willingbam v. Simons* (1792) a South Carolina court allowed a married woman to receive payment intended for her husband. In this case, the court decided her husband had given tacit consent to his wife's receipt of money owed him for the sale of slaves. Under common law, payment to a wife was illegal, but when a man seemed to support his wife's actions on his behalf by not immediately objecting to them, he legitimized them. In effect, the wife was acting as her husband's agent, a legal concept upheld by the courts in South Carolina from then on.

See also Common Law.

Winnemucca, Sarah (c. 1844–1891)

Born about 1844 in Humboldt Sink, Nevada, Sarah Winnemucca, whose tribal name was Shell-Flower, was a leader among the Nevada Paiute. Her father was the Paiute chief, and her grandfather was said to have led John Frémont across the Sierra Nevada to California (1845–1846). Her grandfather's dying request was that she attend school at St. Mary's Convent in San Jose, California. She did attend the school for three weeks, but the protests of wealthy parents forced the school to expel her. This ended her formal education, although she was fluent in both English and Spanish.

She grew into a beautiful young woman who dedicated her life to the betterment of her people. In 1860 the movement of settlers into western Nevada brought about frequent battles with the Paiute during which several of Winnemucca's relatives were killed, including a young brother. Yet Winnemucca assumed the role of negotiator, and between 1868 and 1871 was an inter-

preter at Camp McDermitt in northeast Nevada. In 1871 she married an officer and shortly after that she married a Paiute, but left them both for mistreatment.

In 1872 she moved to a new reservation, the Malheur, in Oregon. In 1875 she became an interpreter for Samuel Parrish, an agent for the reservation. The next year Parrish was replaced by the abusive Major William V. Rinehart. When Winnemucca reported his conduct, he dismissed her, and Winnemucca left the reservation. Other Paiutes left the reservation at the same time because of harsh treatment, and some joined Idaho's Bannock tribe. When war broke out between the Bannocks and the United States in 1878, Winnemucca began working for the army. Upon hearing that her father was a member of a group of Paiutes that were being forced to join the Bannock, she rode without sleep for hundreds of miles through Idaho and Oregon, discovered that her father and his allies were surrounded by the Bannock, and spirited them away to safety. She then worked as a guide and interpreter for General Oliver O. Howard.

The press was impressed by the beautiful Paiute advocate and gave wide publicity to the speeches she would make periodically against the civilian agents. In 1880 Winnemucca met with President Rutherford B. Hayes and Secretary of the Interior Carl Schurz, who agreed to permit the Paiute to return to the Malheur and to give them an allotment of land. However, the civilian agents opposed this action, fearing the Indians would be killed en route from Yakima Reservation back to Malheur, and Schurz's order was not carried out.

Winnemucca taught for one year at an Indian school in Washington, then married L. H. Hopkins in 1881 and embarked on a lecture tour. Her lectures formed the basis of *Life among the Piutes* (1883). She collected thousands of signatures on petitions that asked Congress to grant the individual allotments of land held in reservation for the Paiutes. Although Congress passed the bill in 1884, it was not executed by the secretary of the interior. During the next few years, Winnemucca opened and ran a Paiute school in Lovelock, Nevada. But after her husband's death in 1886 she retired, going to live with a sister in Monida, Montana. There she died 16 October 1891. She was remembered by whites as "the princess" and by Paiutes as "mother."

Winning Plan

In 1916 in an attempt to match the vigor of the Congressional Union for Woman Suffrage, the National American Woman Suffrage Association (NAWSA) redoubled its efforts. As part of its restructuring, it made Carrie Chapman Catt leader of its principal strategy. She devised the Winning Plan (kept secret for years), which was based on the idea that state and federal victories would interlock, that is, state victories would encourage the representatives and senators from the states' regions to support a federal suffrage amendment. Catt placed great emphasis on destroying the united opposition of the South and Northeast by winning one key southern state and New York. Catt complemented these strategies by energizing the entire suffrage campaign and establishing friendly relationships with legislators and President Woodrow Wilson. She believed that to be successful, the plan would require

> . . . a constructive program of hard, aggressive work for six years, money to support it, and the cooperation of all suffragists. It will demand the elimination of the spirit of criticism, back-biting and narrow-minded clashing of personalities which is always common to a stagnant town, society or movement, and which is beginning to show itself in our midst. Success will depend less on the money we are able to command, than upon our combined ability to lift the campaign above this sordidness of mind, and to elevate it to the position of a crusade for human freedom. ("Report of Survey Committee to National Board of NAWSA.")

See also Catt, Carrie Clinton Lane Chapman; Congressional Union for Woman Suffrage; National American Woman Suffrage Association; Nineteenth Amendment.

Woman in the Nineteenth Century

Margaret Fuller's *Woman in the Nineteenth Century* (1845) raised many of the issues regarding suffrage, property rights, child custody, and equal education that later were championed by the nineteenth-century women's rights movement. The work first appeared as an essay titled "The Great Lawsuit. Man *versus* Men, Woman *versus* Women" in *The Dial* (July 1843). Fuller wrote, "Those who think the physical circumstances of Woman would make a part in the affairs of national government unsuitable, are by no means those who think it impossible for negresses to endure field work, even during pregnancy, or for sempstresses to go through their killing labors." *Woman in the Nineteenth Century* was the first full-length feminist document published in the United States.

See also Fuller, Margaret.

Woman Rebel

Conceived aboard a ship sailing from New York to France in 1914 by reformer Margaret Sanger, *Woman Rebel* was a monthly publication for working women. It was emblazoned with the Industrial Workers of the World slogan "No Gods, No Monsters." In the first issue, Sanger challenged women "To look the whole world in the face with a 'go-to-hell' look in the eyes; to have an ideal; to speak and act in defiance of convention." Although it did not give specific information about contraception, it advocated the use of birth control. It also advocated a wide variety of radical policies. The *Woman Rebel*, which was produced solely by Sanger (the first issue from her dining table), was intended to provoke confrontation with government authorities by deliberately violating New York's 1869 Comstock law, which defined information about birth control as obscene. Breaking the law was a common tactic among radicals because it generated valuable publicity. When the U.S. Postal Service tried to stop distribution of the *Woman Rebel* and to prosecute Sanger, arresting her in August 1914, her cause gained widespread recognition. Sanger fled the country one day before her trial, and eventually the government dropped the charges against her because it did not want her prosecution to enhance her stature in the eyes of her followers.

See also Industrial Workers of the World; Sanger, Margaret.

Womanism, Womanist, Womanish

Author Alice Walker coined the term *womanist* in 1983 to identify African-American feminists. Although many African-American women had feminist values and were sympathetic to feminist goals, they were somewhat reluctant to identify with the mainstream women's movement, which they perceived as dominated by whites and not entirely related to their own agenda. As Walker defines the term, *womanist* means "a black feminist or a feminist of color." She describes womanist behavior as "outrageous . . . courageous or willful. . . . Responsible. In charge. Serious. . . . " Walker states that the term originated from "the black folk expression of mothers to female children, 'You acting womanish,' i.e., like a woman."

See also Walker, Alice Malsenior.

Womanpower

The report *Womanpower* was issued by the National Manpower Council in 1957. The report suggested that a commission be formed to study the condition of women. This recommendation influenced President John F. Kennedy's decision to form the President's Commission on the Status of Women four years later. The report was not prepared from a feminist perspective and did not argue that women should be considered a class that experienced discrimination. Instead, it described women as a resource that could benefit the nation. This attitude carried over to the President's Commission on the Status of Women and was reflected in some of its proposals.

See also President's Commission on the Status of Women.

The Woman's Bible

In 1895 and 1898, Elizabeth Cady Stanton, working with a committee of feminists, published in two volumes a critique of the Old Testament called *The Woman's Bible*. This work analyzed parts of the scripture considered derogatory toward women. Stanton thought the Bible was biased and contributed to women's subjugation. For example, she objected to the idea that woman (Eve) was created from man (Adam's rib). A firestorm of protest erupted from clergymen and feminists alike. In 1896, the National American Woman Suffrage Association (NAWSA) passed a resolution stating that it had no connection with the "so-called woman's Bible." Stanton—who then stopped working for NAWSA—continued to write *The Woman's Bible* until her death in 1902.

See also Stanton, Elizabeth Cady.

Woman's Christian Temperance Union (WCTU)

See National Woman's Christian Temperance Union.

Woman's Committee for Political Action (WCPA)

The Woman's Committee for Political Action (WCPA), formed in the spring of 1923, represented the far left of the feminist ideological spectrum. The group included some of the most notable feminists of the day, including Charlotte Perkins Gilman, Harriot Stanton Blatch, and Freda Kirchway. The group espoused pacifism and prolabor economic principles, although its members were divided on the equal rights amendment. By 1924 the WCPA had members in almost every state and had chapters in more than 25 states. The WCPA helped to maintain contact and good relations between female reformers and the Progressive movement. When Wisconsin senator Robert La Follette entered the 1924 presidential race on the Progressive party ticket, the WCPA allowed itself to be absorbed into the women's division of the La Follette campaign.

See also Progressive Party.

Woman's Hospital

The first hospital created exclusively for the treatment of women's diseases was the Woman's Hospital in New York City. It was founded by 30 women on 10 February 1855, and opened 4 May of that year. Originally located on Madison Avenue at East 29th Street, the hospital had one surgeon, one nurse, and two matrons for 40 beds. Later, the hospital moved to East 49th Street between Lexington Avenue and Park Avenue. Finally, the hospital moved to West 114th Street between Columbus Avenue and Amsterdam Avenue. It is now part of St. Luke's Hospital.

Woman's Journal

See American Woman Suffrage Association.

Woman's Medical College of Pennsylvania

The Woman's Medical College of Pennsylvania, one of the first medical schools to admit women, opened in 1850. The college was one of the few in the United States to admit women of every race, religion, and ethnic group. By doing so, it offered professional training to generations of women who were refused entrance into all-male medical schools. The college opened a dispensary in 1858 and a hospital in 1861. The school is still in existence, but the word *Woman's* has been dropped from its name.

Woman's Peace Party

Crystal Eastman, Florence Kelley, Jane Addams, Charlotte Perkins Gilman, and Carrie Chapman Catt were some of the distinguished women leaders attracted to the Woman's Peace Party, founded in 1915. Promoting peace had been a constant theme in the women's movement for several de-

cades, but the Woman's Peace Party was the first women's organization devoted entirely to pacifism. Its members declared that peace was of special importance to women, especially mothers, and that women had a much greater capacity than men for preserving it. The participation of all major women's groups attested to the universality of the party's appeal. Catt headed the group's first meeting in 1915 in Washington, D.C., at which 86 delegates developed the Woman's Peace Party platform. By the following year, the Woman's Peace Party had 25,000 members. American entry into World War I was a temporary setback for the organization, but it regained its strength in the 1920s, by which time it had become part of the Women's International League for Peace and Freedom.

Woman's Sphere

Nineteenth-century writers wrote at length about the man's sphere and the woman's sphere. They characterized men and women as polar opposites: women as passive, dependent, and weak; men as independent, tough, and strong. In the 1700s women were seen as brave, strong, daring, or adventurous, but by the 1800s only men were thought to possess these qualities. Home and church were supposed to be woman's natural sphere of action; politics, commerce, and work outside the home were man's. Some historians have argued, however, that by granting women dominance in their "sphere," which came to include charitable, religious, and reform organizations, full participation in public activities followed.

See also Benevolent Societies; Voluntarism.

Women against Pornography

The New York–based group Women against Pornography was created to express feminist objections to pornography as material that glorifies violence, abusiveness, and sexism, and that, despite its label as erotic entertainment, really constitutes a type of hate literature. The group's methods for combating pornography have included conducting tours for women of Times Square in New York City, a center of pornography; arranging demonstrations; producing information to educate the public; and encouraging boycotts and petitions. It was particularly successful in attracting members in the 1970s. The group has, somewhat ironically, encountered opposition from other feminists, who view the suppression of pornography as censorship.

See also Take Back the Night.

Women Air Force Service Pilots (WASPs)

Demand for pilots during World War II led to the formation, in August 1943, of the Women Air Force Service Pilots (WASPs). This noncombat corps expanded the opportunities for female pilots, although its main responsibility was to transport aircraft, a job even previously performed by civilian female pilots. The WASPs flew bombers and fighter planes from the factories where they were made to various air bases and finally to distribution points. They helped test planes by taking practice flights in model planes, testing the instruments while flying. They also flew engineering-related flights and assisted in antiaircraft gunnery practice. The WASPs drew an enthusiastic response from the public, notwithstanding male pilots' hostility. In a close vote, the House of Representatives defeated a proposal to permanently incorporate WASPs into the army air corps. The WASPs corps was abolished in late 1944, when a sufficient number of male pilots was available. In 1979 the WASPs were retroactively granted military status and veterans' benefits.

Women United

The Washington, D.C., group Women United served as a link among pro-ERA organizations in the 1970s and was particularly successful in generating nationwide support for the ERA. Woman United was a coalition of women's organizations, which announced its formation in 1971 with the stated purpose of serving as a clearinghouse for all matters pertaining to the Equal Rights Amendment (ERA) on the congressional and, during the ratification process, state levels. The group included women from a number of different organizations representing wide-ranging political viewpoints. The coalition did not represent its member organizations in an official capacity, which allowed it to act freely. The coalition came to an end in 1982 with the defeat of the ERA.

See also Equal Rights Amendment.

Women's Action Alliance

In 1971, Gloria Steinem and Brenda Feigen Fasteau founded the Women's Action Alliance as an information service in New York. It was financed by *Ms.* magazine and has published several books, such as *A Practical Guide to the Women's Movement* (1975) and *Women's Action Almanac* (1980). The alliance assists feminists with fund raising, holding conferences and workshops, and educating the public on women's issues. The organization is still active.

See also Ms.; Steinem, Gloria.

Women's Advisory Committee (WAC)

The Women's Advisory Committee (WAC) was created during World War II by President Franklin D. Roosevelt as a sister organization to the War Manpower Commission (WMC). The official reason for its establishment was to address the concerns of women workers, but the real purpose—at least in part—was to keep women out of the WMC, as the male members of that body desired. Despite its members' wishes, the WAC was merely symbolic. The government never gave the WAC the resources to investigate and evaluate the conditions of working women, and its advice on women's problems was never sought or heeded. In spite of its limited ability, the WAC attempted to have more child care facilities built during the war. After the war, it tried to preserve the gains women had achieved during the war.

See also War Manpower Commission.

Women's Army Corps (WAC)

The Women's Army Corps (WAC), originally named the Women's Army Auxiliary Corps, was created in 1942 to enlist women for noncombat duty during World War II. Newspaperwoman Oveta Culp Hobby was its first director and Sgt. Mabel Carney was its first member to land in Normandy after the 6 June 1944 invasion. WACs, who numbered 100,000 by 1945, served in the United States and overseas as secretaries, medical assistants, and cartography clerks. Although enlistment ended in 1945, shortages in army hospitals and personnel centers forced the war department to ask for reenlistments in 1946. The WAC was established as a regular part of the army in 1948 and remained in existence until 1979, when women were integrated into the army.

See also Hobby, Oveta Culp.

Women's Bureau

The Women's Bureau, a branch of the labor department, was founded in 1920 to collect information about women in industry and to improve their opportunities and working conditions. The bureau developed out of the Women's Division of the Ordnance Department, which, during World War I, regulated conditions of female workers in ordnance and munitions plants. The Women's Bureau was first headed by union leader Mary Anderson. Although it has

Four World War II pilots, recent graduates of the four-engine school at Lockbourne Field, Ohio, walk past a B-17 in 1944.

sought better opportunities for women, the Women's Bureau for several decades favored preserving the role of women as homemakers, and it did not encourage young mothers to work outside the home unless necessary. It also favored protective legislation. The pro-labor activism of the trade union contributed, in a broad sense, to the existence of the Women's Bureau, although feminists have regarded the trade union movement as male-oriented, and were dismayed by the bureau's association with it. When Title VII of the 1964 Civil Rights Act began to undo most protective legislation, the bureau adopted many positions more appealing to some feminists. The bureau is still in existence and frequently publishes analyses of statistics it has compiled.

See also McDowell, Mary Eliza.

Women's Clubs

During the last decades of the nineteenth century, millions of women participated in reform politics through women's clubs or civic associations. They improved drinking water; upgraded schools; and supported orphanages, libraries, and homes for wayward girls. The clubs were one of three kinds: garden clubs and associations devoted to educational pursuits; national public-service organizations, such as the General Federation of Women's Clubs; and reform groups, such as the Woman's Christian Temperance Union. These groups brought about child welfare laws, improved working conditions for women, and other progressive legislation. Although the proliferation of women's groups from 1880 to 1920 is often used to indicate active feminism, in fact, the organizations did little to push equality for women. By then the clubs had become bastions for conservative middle-class housewives.

See also Benevolent Societies; Voluntarism.

Women's Committee, Council of National Defense

The Women's Committee was established during World War I by the Council of National Defense to organize and expand women's roles in the war effort. Women were registered by the committee and then were studied by that body and recommended for different types of work. The committee's leader, Anna Howard Shaw, urged women to be productive, frugal, and resourceful, suggesting they work, sell government bonds, conserve fuel, grow their own food, and eat less.

Women's Educational Equity Act (WEEA)

The Women's Educational Equity Act (WEEA) was passed in 1973 as a noncontroversial part of a broader Senate education bill. The bill created the National Advisory Council on Women's Educational Programs (NACWEP), an advisory council within the Department of Health, Education and Welfare, to monitor women's status in education. The act also funds a variety of programs, including women's studies programs, projects to eliminate sexism from textbooks, and attempts to sensitize teachers to issues of sex discrimination in education. A number of WEEA programs have been designed to meet the needs of women of color. Although the WEEA's allocation was small, the Reagan administration devoted considerable effort to control the NACWEP by packing it with antifeminists and by attempting to undo its programs altogether. Both efforts failed when Congress rewrote the WEEA legislation in 1984. The new legislation prohibits the program managers from making fundamental changes in its character; it also continues the program's funding on a smaller scale.

Women's Equity Action League

The Women's Equity Action League (WEAL) fights sex discrimination on many fronts. The group was founded in 1968 in Cleveland, Ohio, by lawyer Elizabeth Boyer. According to some founding members of NOW, WEAL was formed by NOW members who were reluctant to take a stand on the controversial issue of abortion. In its early years, the group concentrated its efforts on fighting sex discrimination in employment, de facto tax inequities, and, especially, education. It was particularly active in advocating the Equal Rights Amendment. Its other activities include combating sex discrimination by labor unions, collecting information for lawyers who are preparing to argue sex discrimination cases, and maintaining a speakers bureau for businesses and schools.

See also National Organization for Women.

Women's Joint Congressional Committee (WJCC)

The Women's Joint Congressional Committee (WJCC) was formed in 1920 to provide a means for women to coordinate the exercise of their right to vote. It was a coalition of some existing women's groups; among its ten charter members were the League of Women Voters, the Women's Trade Union League, Business and Professional Women, the National Consumers' League, and the Woman's Christian Temperance Union. The WJCC lobbied Congress on issues that concerned a number of its member organizations. Among its earliest triumphs are the Sheppard-Towner Bill (1921) and the Cable Act (1922).

See also Cable Act; League of Women Voters; Sheppard-Towner Act.

Women's Joint Legislative Committee (WJLC)

The Women's Joint Legislative Committee (WJLC) was a coalition of groups in favor of an equal rights amendment (ERA). The coalition was created by the National Woman's Party in the 1940s. Although the National Woman's Party remained extremely exclusive, the size of the WJLC, with its membership of five to six million, succeeded in demonstrating the strength of pro-ERA sentiment.

See also Equal Rights Amendment.

Women's Political Union

See Congressional Union for Woman Suffrage; Equality League of Self-Supporting Women; Woman's Peace Party.

Women's Review of Books

Formed in 1983 by the Wellesley College Center for Research on Women, the monthly *Women's Review of Books* reviews books by and for women. The goal of the publication is to promote diversity in feminist perspectives. It seeks to represent a wide range of women's publications.

Women's Rights Conventions

The first women's rights convention was held 19–20 July 1848 at Seneca Falls, New York. Two weeks later, on 2 August a second meeting was held at Rochester, New York. No meetings were held for more than a year afterward. But on 19–20 April 1850, reform-minded women and men met in Salem, Ohio. There, William Lloyd Garrison, Gerrit Smith, and Wendell Phillips called for the first *national* women's convention to be held in Worcester, Massachusetts, that same year. National conventions were held annually through 1860, except in 1857. From February 1861 to May 1866, no national women's rights conventions were held in the United States, enabling women to devote their time and effort to the Civil War.

See also Douglass, Frederick; Garrison, William Lloyd; Mott, Lucretia Coffin; Seneca Falls Convention; Stanton, Elizabeth Cady; Smith, Gerrit.

Women's Rights Project

See American Civil Liberties Union.

Women's Rights Project of the Center for Law and Social Policy (CLASP)

The Center for Law and Social Policy (CLASP) is a law firm committed to public interest issues. In 1974 the center founded the Women's Rights Project. Based in

Washington, D.C., CLASP has devoted considerable attention to women's health issues as well as the administration of Title IX regulations, which prohibit discrimination in higher education. Women's groups that lack the resources to undertake or sponsor legislation have benefited from the center's skill in encouraging the enforcement of antidiscrimination regulations.

The Women's Room
Published in 1977, Marilyn French's novel *The Women's Room* is, perhaps, the most widely read novel of the women's movement. French chronicles the disappointments and hard-won liberation of a middle-class suburban woman. In portraying the life of a housewife from the 1950s to the early 1970s, the novel is perceptive and relentless in its criticism. Other works by Marilyn French are: *The Bleeding Heart* (1980), *Shakespeare's Division of Experience* (1981), *Beyond Power: On Women, Men and Morals* (1985), *Her Mother's Daughter* (1987), *The War against Women* (1992), and *Our Father* (1994).

Women's Strike for Equality
In 1970, to celebrate the fiftieth anniversary of the adoption of the Nineteenth Amendment, feminist Betty Friedan proposed a national strike. Local chapters of the National Organization for Women (NOW) acted as strike committees, and new strike committees were established around the country. Around-the-clock child care, legalized abortion, and equal employment and educational opportunities were the strikers' key demands. In addition to striking and holding protest marches, women participated in teach-ins and theater skits on Strike Day, 26 August 1970. The mayors of some cities proclaimed Strike Day a day to honor women's rights. To the delight and surprise of many, the women's strike for equality was the largest and most visible demonstration for women's equality to date. Its success was due to the fact that it united or appeared to

unite women who represented many different ideologies.

See also Friedan, Betty; National Organization for Women.

Women's Studies
Women's studies is an interdisciplinary academic field that developed in the 1970s. Women's studies has challenged every aspect of traditional academic teaching. It not only demands that attention be paid to the experiences of women, it has reshaped the male-oriented perspective from which women's experiences have been viewed. This has involved revising a considerable amount of history, and the material for this has not only come from a reexamination of leaders in history but from a study of the lives of ordinary people throughout history.

Women's Trade Union League (WTUL)
The National Women's Trade Union League was organized as a result of the failure of the American Federation of Labor (AFL) and its affiliates to organize female workers. Indeed, the group got its start during the 1903 AFL convention, when William E. Walling proposed the idea to Mary

The logo of the Women's Trade Union League from the 1924 Convention.

Kenney O'Sullivan. A series of meetings were held with AFL officials, labor leaders, and settlement house workers. Membership was open to anyone who was willing to help trade unions that had female members or to organize new women's unions. As a coalition of working- and middle-class women, the WTUL sought to improve working conditions, win equal pay for equal work, get the vote, and mandate an eight-hour workday and a minimum wage. Following the model of the Progressive party, the league collected information and publicized its findings. The league's support of strikes fostered good relations with the labor movement.

The original three leagues were located in Boston, New York, and Chicago. Membership on the executive board was to be divided between women trade unionists, who were in the majority, and nonunionists or "allies" who were sympathetic to the cause. This division was not achieved until 1907, when new leaders came from the ranks of workers. One of those leaders, Maud Swartz of the typographers union, became the WTUL's first working woman president in 1921.

The league supported the largest strike of women workers in the United States, the shirtwaist makers' strike of 1909, also called The Uprising of the 20,000. The New York Women's Trade Union League was poorly prepared and had little experience when the strike began in November, but it grew in strength as the struggle continued. The league organized pickets of thousands, raised bail, organized strike relief, and provided welfare. In New York the league rented 24 halls for meetings and obtained speakers who could address workers in Yiddish, Italian, and English. It publicized the strikers' case, enlisting contributions from wealthy women who were horrified at the brutal treatment the strikers suffered. The strikers—75 percent of whom were women—held out for 13 weeks, until the strike was called off 15 February. Results were mixed, with settlements made on a shop-by-shop basis. But that strike led to several other women workers' strikes, and the WTUL assisted with most of them.

Male unionists had claimed that women were not worth organizing; the women were proving them wrong.

In 1909 the WTUL produced guidelines for achieving labor-reform legislation, including the eight-hour workday, a minimum wage, and the elimination of night work. By 1911 the WTUL had branches in 11 cities; that year it began publishing the monthly *Life and Labor.*

On the surface the WTUL and the AFL were amicable, holding conventions at the same time and place. However, the league served as an unpleasant reminder that the AFL had not done enough to bring women into the ranks of the already organized trades. Ultimately, the league failed to generate solid public support because of widespread distrust of unions. However the group worked for social reform through the 1950s.

See also American Federation of Labor; Strikes; Unions; Uprising of the 20,000.

Woodhull, Victoria Claflin (1838–1927)

Victoria Claflin Woodhull was the first woman to run for president of the United States. She was born 23 September 1838 in Homer, Ohio, to a poor, transient family that staged a traveling medicine and fortune-telling show. She was prone to trances as a child, and her sister, Tennessee Claflin, soon learned to stage séances for her. At the age of 15, she married Dr. Canning Woodhull. The couple was separated for several years and divorced in 1864. The two sisters traveled throughout the Midwest, conducting séances and lecturing on spiritualism. By 1866 Woodhull had met and perhaps married Col. James H. Blood, but she continued to use the name Woodhull, and at certain times Victoria, Canning, and James all lived together. The sisters moved to New York City in 1868, where they met Cornelius Vanderbilt. Vanderbilt was interested in spiritualism, and he helped the sisters establish a stock brokerage, Woodhull, Claflin & Company. The firm opened in 1870 and became a success as the first woman's stock brokerage firm. With their profits the sisters founded *Woodhull & Claflin's Weekly*, which advocated women's rights, free love, legalized prostitution, dress and tax reform, and other causes.

In 1871 Woodhull appeared before the House of Representatives judiciary committee to speak for women's suffrage. She declared that suffrage was an implied right under the Constitution by virtue of the Fourteenth Amendment and Fifteenth Amendment. Despite their earlier misgivings, Elizabeth Cady Stanton and Susan B. Anthony immediately invited her to speak at a convention of the National Woman Suffrage Association. In her speech at the convention, Woodhull threatened to set up a new government unless Congress gave women the vote. In another speech in New York that year, she declared, "We mean treason, we mean secession, and on a thousand times grander scale than was that of the South. We are plotting revolution." As a result of her speech, the NWSA endorsed reforms in every area of government, even passing a resolution in support of Victoria Woodhull's pet cause, free love.

In May 1872 Woodhull called a convention of a new political party, the Equal Rights party. The party chose her to be its presidential candidate and named abolitionist Frederick Douglass to be her running mate. Douglass declined. In 1872 Woodhull became the first woman to run for president of the United States. However, she was without funds and was widely ostracized for her views on free love. Her by that time former husband, Dr. Canning Woodhull, had returned to live with her and Blood, fueling public hostility. She felt that she was being punished for openly supporting what many people did privately. To challenge what she saw as hypocrisy, she revealed the details of an affair between the most famous preacher of the day, Henry Ward Beecher, and Elizabeth Tilton, one of Beecher's parishioners and the wife of suffrage supporter Theodore Tilton. On 2 November 1872, Woodhull publicized the affair in a special edition of *Woodhull & Claflin's Weekly*. It was the biggest scandal of the nineteenth cen-

tury. Yet the revelation backfired. Woodhull and her sister were arrested for violating the Comstock Act, which prohibited using the U.S. post office to distribute obscene literature. They were acquitted.

Woodhull and her sister emigrated to England in 1877. Woodhull married John B. Martin in 1883 and continued her career as a lecturer and author. Her books include *Stirpiculture, or the Scientific Propagation of the Human Race* (1888), *Garden of England: Allegorical Meaning Revealed* (1889), *The Human Body: the Temple of God* (1890), and *Humanitarian Money: The Unsolved Riddle* (1892). With her daughter, Woodhull published *Humanitarian* magazine from 1892 to 1901. Victoria remained in England for the rest of her life. She died in Tewkesbury on 10 June 1927.

See also Claflin, Tennessee; Hooker, Isabella Beecher.

Worcester (Massachusetts) Convention

In 1850 suffrage leaders held the first National Woman's Rights Convention in Worcester, Massachusetts, at Brinley Hall. This convention brought together the most famous feminist leaders in the United States: Paulina Wright Davis, Ernestine Rose, Angelina Grimké, Abby Kelley Foster, and Lucretia Mott. It introduced them to new faces in the movement, including Lucy Stone and Sojourner Truth. Lucy Stone, Abby Kelley Foster, and Paulina Wright Davis organized the conference, which they had called a year earlier. Among the 89 signatures on the "call" were those of Wendell Phillips, William H. Channing, William Lloyd Garrison, Gerrit Smith, and Bronson Alcott. Lucy Stone's name headed the list. More than 1,000 people were admitted and many were turned away. Resolutions were passed in favor of legal, social, educational, and industrial rights for females. The conference influenced the British women's rights movement, yet the *New York Herald* called those in attendance "that motley gathering of fanatical radicals, of old grannies, of fugitive slaves and fugitive lunatics." The Worcester conference was followed by national women's conferences every year (except 1857) until 1860.

See also Foster, Abigail Kelley; Garrison, William Lloyd; Stone, Lucy; Smith, Gerrit; Truth, Sojourner.

Working Woman's Association (WWA)

In 1868 Susan B. Anthony and a group of working women founded the Working Woman's Association (WWA). It was established to give Anthony credentials to attend the 1868 convention of the National Labor Union. Although it only lasted one year, the organization was a pioneering attempt to unite wage-earning women in a challenge to male-dominated labor unions and employers, both of which oppressed and excluded women. No other organization had attempted to unite women against both political and economic injustice. The group split because of class differences. The suffragists recruited middle-class women like themselves. These middle-class women dominated the WWA's positions of leadership, raised its dues, and moved its meeting place out of the Cooper Union neighborhood of New York City. Working-class women soon dropped out, and by 1869 the membership was completely middle class. Its collapse was marked by the National Labor Union's refusal to recognize Anthony as a delegate to its 1869 convention. Male unionists argued that the WWA was no longer a bona fide labor organization but a suffrage group. And female union members opposed her for not sufficiently supporting strikers. The result of this split was the growth in organization of middle-class women committed less to their laboring sisters than to their own equality and freedom, and would lead to the development of the first independent feminist movement in America.

See also National Labor Union.

World's Anti-Slavery Convention

The seeds of the first women's rights convention (the Seneca Falls Convention of 1848) probably were sown during the World's Anti-Slavery Convention of 1840. In October 1836 the British and Foreign Anti-Slavery Society invited all "friends of the slave" to meet in London 12–20 June 1840. In February 1840, realizing that the word *friends* might be interpreted to include women, the group revised its invitation to change *friends* to *gentlemen friends*. One month before the convention, the American Anti-Slavery Society split in two, in part because of what some members considered the "insane innovation" of letting women serve as speakers and officers (and in part because the group's leader, William Lloyd Garrison, was considered too unpolitical). The dissident members, led by James Birney, who was not antiwoman, formed a new organization, the Liberty party. The Tappans, who were antiwoman, formed the American and Foreign Anti-Slavery Society. The latter group was favored by the British and Foreign Anti-Slavery Society.

Because the first conference announcement made no mention of gender, several U.S. antislavery societies sent female delegates. Garrison's American Anti-Slavery Society sent five delegates, including one woman, Lucretia Mott. Mott also represented the Philadelphia Female Anti-Slavery Society. She was accompanied by women representing the Massachusetts Anti-Slavery Society and the Boston Anti-Slavery Society. Another American Anti-Slavery Society delegate was Henry Stanton. His wife of two days, Elizabeth Cady Stanton, accompanied him to the convention. Garrison, anticipating trouble, wrote to his wife, "It is, perhaps, quite probable that we shall be foiled in our purpose; but the subject cannot be agitated without doing good." In another letter he wrote, "With a young woman [Queen Victoria] placed on the throne of Great Britain, will the philanthropists of that country presume to object to the female delegates from the United States, as members of the Convention, on the grounds of their sex?"

Early on the first day of the convention, the American women arrived at London's Freemasons' Hall. They immediately became embroiled in a dispute with other delegates about whether the female delegates should be seated. Abolitionist Wendell Phillips, an ally of Garrison, moved that a committee prepare a roster of all delegates from any accredited antislavery society. The discussion lasted for hours, with most of the delegates loathe to seat the women. As Stanton later recalled in *History of Woman Suffrage* (Volume I), the opponents declared the women were constitutionally unfit for public office. The Rev. Eben Galusha declared, "I have no objection to woman's being the neck to turn the head aright, but do not wish to see her assume the place of the head." Other delegates believed that to try to settle the woman question would weaken a convention dedicated to abolishing slavery. When it was proposed that all accredited delegates be seated regardless of sex, there were shouts of, "Turn out the women!" Finally, the gauntlet was thrown by the Rev. C. Stout, who cried, "shall we be divided on this *paltry question* and suffer the whole tide of benevolence to be stopped by *a straw*. No! You talk of being men, then be men!"

The vote went against the female delegates, who were led to a curtained-off gallery to observe the proceedings. Garrison joined the women, declaring, "After battling so many long years for the liberation of African slaves, I can take no part in a convention that strikes down the most sacred rights of all women." Stanton later wrote that she and Mott decided then and there to hold a convention to discuss women's inequality when they returned to the United States. A new circle of reformers was beginning to coalesce. Eight years later the first women's rights convention gave birth to one of the great revolutionary struggles of the modern era.

See also Garrison, William Lloyd; Mott, Lucretia; Seneca Falls Convention; Stanton, Elizabeth Cady.

Wright, Frances (1795–1853)

Born 6 September 1795 in Dundee, Scotland, Frances Wright was a writer and reformer, who created an uproar by speaking before mixed audiences of men and women. Her father was a radical merchant who circulated the writings of Thomas Paine. When she was two years old, her parents died, leaving a fortune to Frances and her sister. The two girls were raised by conservative relatives in London and Devon, England. At the age of 21, Wright returned to Scotland to live with a grand-uncle, continued her self-education, and wrote *A Few Days in Athens* (1822). In 1818 Wright and her sister sailed to the United States for a visit. During their stay, her play *Altorf*, which concerned Swiss independence, was produced in New York City. Upon her return to England in 1820, a series of letters she had written during her stay in the United States were collected in *Views of Society and Manners in America* (1821). In 1824, with the Marquis de Lafayette, she toured the United States, joining him in meetings with Thomas Jefferson and James Madison. When Lafayette returned to France in 1825, Wright remained in America.

In 1825 Wright published *A Plan for the Gradual Abolition of Slavery in the United States without Danger of Loss to the Citizens of the South*, the broad outlines of which she had discussed with Jefferson and Madison. The book proposed that the U.S. Congress use public lands for slave labor, using the profits to buy the workers' freedom. When the proposal was ignored, Wright established a 640-acre community near Memphis, Tennessee, named Nashoba. Her popularity vanished overnight. When the community failed in 1828, Wright joined idealist Robert Dale Owen in the utopian community in New Harmony, Indiana, founded by Owen's father.

By 1829 Wright had moved to New York City, where she and Owen published the *Free Enquirer*. That year Wright began to give public lectures about reform and the legal rights of women. She gave the lectures in a small church on Broome Street, which she purchased and turned into a "Hall of Science." She was subjected to bitter criticism by the press and pulpit. Particularly enraged by her suggestion that women practice birth control, they dubbed her The

Great Red Harlot of Infidelity. That year her book, *Address on the State of the Public Mind,* which advocated educational reforms at a time when fewer than half of the children of New York City were enrolled in school, was received favorably. In the book, Wright suggested the establishment of a national system of free boarding schools supported by a progressive property tax. Her interest in educational reform led to her involvement in the city's emerging working-class movement. She helped to form the Association for the Protection of Industry and for the Promotion of National Education, which opponents called the Fanny Wright party. With *Free Enquirer* supporters, the association won a seat in the state legislature.

In 1830, two years after the failure of the Nashoba community, Wright arranged for its residents to emigrate to Haiti. Wright moved to France in 1831, where she married Guillaume Sylvan Casimir Phiquepal D'Arusmont. In 1835 the couple moved to Cincinnati, Ohio, where Wright was active in politics, supporting the Democratic party in 1836 and 1838. Wright and her husband divorced in 1850. The reformer died 13 December 1852 in Cincinnati.

See also Owen, Robert Dale; Utopian Communities.

Wright, Martha Coffin Pelham (1806–1875)

Martha Wright, sister of abolitionist and women's rights activist Lucretia Mott, was one of the five planners of the first women's rights convention. She was born 25 December 1806 in Boston, Massachusetts, and attended Kimberton Boarding School near Philadelphia for three years. In 1824 she left to marry Peter Pelham, who died in 1826. In 1829 she married David Wright. Wright's reform activities began in 1848 when she joined Mott, Elizabeth Cady Stanton, and others in organizing the first women's rights convention, held in Seneca Falls, New York, that summer. She was secretary of the third National Woman's Rights Convention at Syracuse in 1852, vice-president of the Philadelphia conven-

tion in 1854, and president of conventions in Cincinnati, Saratoga, and Albany in 1855. Wright was also a member of the New York State Woman's Rights Committee, serving as president of its convention in New York City in 1860. A chief advisor to Susan B. Anthony and Stanton, Wright advocated they adopt a gradual approach to woman's rights, beginning with married rights and property rights on the state level before proceeding to suffrage on the national level. In 1866 she joined Anthony and Stanton in forming the American Equal Rights Association; three years later she helped them form the National Woman Suffrage Association (NWSA). In 1874 she was elected president of the NWSA. Wright died 4 January 1875 in Boston.

See also Anthony, Susan B.; Seneca Falls Convention; Stanton, Elizabeth Cady; Winning Plan.

Wright, Susanna (1697–1784)

Born 4 August 1697 in England, Susanna Wright was a poet who lived the arduous life of a frontier woman. In 1714, Wright's family decided to move to America and, after completing her education, Susanna joined them in Chester, Pennsylvania. Later, they moved to Hempfield, Pennsylvania, where, after the death of her mother in 1722, Wright took charge of all domestic duties. As part of her responsibilities, she manufactured silk from her own cocoons, which numbered at least 1,500, the largest number in Philadelphia at the time. She served as an unofficial lawyer, writing wills and deeds, and was widely admired for her many accomplishments. Only a few of her poems exist at the present time. Wright died on 1 December 1784, and was buried in Columbia, Pennsylvania.

Wyoming Territory

The first victory of the women's suffrage movement was in Wyoming Territory in 1869, the same year that the eastern suffrage movement split into two camps. Esther Morris, a milliner from New York, was largely responsible for the law's passage. She convinced Wyoming lawmakers that if suffrage passed, more families would come to Wyoming and that women could help win law and order in the rough new territory. At the first session of the territory's legislature, the lawmakers passed a bill that gave the vote to all women, property rights to married women, and equal pay to male and female teachers. Edward M. Lee claimed he wrote the bill. Other supporters were William H. Bright and Governor John A. Campbell, who had attended a women's rights conven-

tion in Salem, Ohio, 20 years earlier. On 6 September 1870, Wyoming women voted for the first time. When Wyoming was admitted to the United States in 1890, it became the first state since New Jersey to include women's suffrage in its state constitution. New Jersey had allowed women's suffrage in the years 1776–1807. Three months after the Wyoming law was passed, a similar law was passed in Utah Territory.

See also Cullom Bill; Salem (Ohio) Convention.

Yalow, Rosalyn Sussman (1921–)

Rosalyn Sussman Yalow was the first woman to win the Albert Lasker award (1976) in her name alone and the second to win the Nobel Prize in physiology or medicine (1977). In accepting the latter, Yalow spoke about the problems women face in a society that expects them to remain at home rather than win career success. She was born 19 July 1921 in the Bronx, New York City and graduated from Hunter College in 1941. In 1943 she married A. Aaron Yalow. The only woman on the engineering faculty of the University of Illinois-Urbana, she received a Ph.D. in physics from that institution in 1945. From 1946 to 1950, she taught physics at Hunter College in New York City and consulted in nuclear physics at the Bronx Veterans Adminstration Hospital. Becoming assistant head of the radioisotope service and the hospital in 1950, Yalow developed, with Dr. Solomon A. Berson, the radioimmunoassay (RIA) technique used to calculate the amount of insulin in humans. Subsequently, RIA was used for many other purposes, e.g., to screen the blood in blood banks for the hepatitis virus and to determine the correct dosage levels of drugs and antibiotics. Named chief of the radioisotope service in 1968, Yalow became chief of the RIA reference laboratory the following year, and head of nuclear medicine in 1970. In 1973, she became director of the Solomon A. Berson laboratory after her colleague's death. From 1968 to 1974 Yalow also worked as a research professor at Mount Sinai School of Medicine. In 1976 she received the Albert Lasker prize for basic medical research, and the following year, she shared the Nobel Prize in physiology or medicine with Roger C. L. Guillemin and Andrew V. Schally for research on the role of hormones in the chemistry of the human body. She was the second woman to win the prize after Gerty T. Cori. In 1979 she declined the *Ladies' Home Journal* Woman of the Year Award because it is gender based. A member of the National Academy of Sciences and the American Academy of Arts and Sciences, Yalow has also served on the President's Study Group on Careers for Women, beginning in 1966.

The Yellow Wallpaper
See Gilman, Charlotte Perkins.

The Young Ladies Academy of Philadelphia

In 1787 The Young Ladies Academy of Philadelphia opened its doors, its mission to offer to girls an education similar to the education offered to boys, with math, grammar, speech, and geography as the basic curriculum. Respected men taught at the school, and it soon became famous. The school changed the way men thought about women in terms of education, that is, that women were worthy of equal education. Benjamin Rush, speaking to the students in July 1787, challenged them to demonstrate "that the female temper can only be governed by reason and that the cultivation of reason in women is alike friendly to the order of nature and to private as well as public happiness."
See also Rush, Benjamin.

Young Women's Christian Association (YWCA)

The Young Women's Christian Association (YWCA) was founded in 1855 in London, England, and opened in New York City in 1858 as the Ladies' Christian Association. In 1866, the Young Women's Christian Association of Boston was founded, and two years later it opened its own boardinghouse. In

337

1871, an International Conference of Women's Christian Associations took place in Hartford, Connecticut, and in 1886 a National Association of YWCAs was formed. The YWCA began as a religious voluntary organization, but, by 1911, it was addressing the many problems of the period and helping to unite women of separate classes. The YWCA worked with the federal government to increase the presence of women in the job force; one of the products of this endeavor was the formation of The National Federation of Business and Professional Women's Clubs (BPW), one of the largest organizations of professional women. It was a YWCA-sponsored conference for businesswomen during World War I that led to the formation of BPW. When the spirit of the Progressive Era swept the organization during the 1930s, the YWCA organized a Federation of Industrial Clubs to aid working women, supported protective legislation for women and children, and made alliances with other reform groups to advance their progressive agendas. The industrial clubs were critical in organizing black and white working women, particularly textile workers in the South. The clubs educated women and encouraged them to express their grievances at legislative hearings. In addition, some club members participated in summer schools for workers, such as the Bryn Mawr Summer School for Workers. During the 1970s the YWCA was one of many older, traditional women's groups that showed increased concern for women's rights. The YWCA's National Women's Resource Center was established to help reshape society's view of women and to promote women's understanding of their role in society. The center educated poor young women about their options in life, and it collected films, tapes, literature, and information for various types of studies.

See also Bryn Mawr; Business and Professional Women.

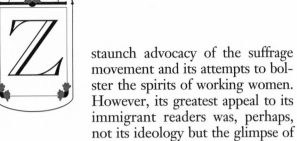

Zemsky Listy

Zemsky Listy was a Bohemian paper based in Chicago in the early twentieth century. It had a circulation of about 6,000, and most of its readers were immigrants. All of the editorial and printing tasks associated with its publication were handled by women. *Zemsky Listy* had a feminist perspective, exemplified in its staunch advocacy of the suffrage movement and its attempts to bolster the spirits of working women. However, its greatest appeal to its immigrant readers was, perhaps, not its ideology but the glimpse of the American lifestyle that it provided, especially through its advertisements.

Chronology

1619 Ninety women reach Virginia and are sold by their own consent to settlers as wives in return for the cost of their transportation.

1632 Virginia enacts legislation allowing freedom of choice in marriage without parental consent, a departure from English custom.

1636 The Plymouth colony enacts a law establishing that land set aside for a wife and children is inviolate, protecting it from the creditors of a deceased husband.

1646 Massachusetts protects orphan girls from having to marry for money by requiring that their marriages be approved by a majority of the selectmen of their towns.

1654 A Maryland court upholds the validity of antenuptial agreements, contracts made between engaged couples protecting the property of the woman so that she can retain it in her own name and dispose of it as she chooses.

1660 Seventeen women meet at the home of Dean Ephraim Bowen in Providence to spin and weave in the aftermath of the Stamp Act. Groups like this one, called "Daughters of Liberty," will multiply, providing support for the growing sentiment for independence.

1664 Plymouth law requires a wife to consent formally to the sale of houses or lands.

1667 A Plymouth court upholds the legality of antenuptial agreements. Connecticut and New York will follow suit in 1673 and 1683, respectively.

1685 At William Penn's suggestion, Pennsylvania passes a law requiring a basic elementary education for both girls and boys.

1691 The provincial charter granted by King William allows women who hold property to vote for all elective offices, a practice continued until 1780, the date of the adoption of Massachusetts' constitution. Women with property will appear on polling lists in Boston, Cambridge, and elsewhere.

1692 The Massachusetts General Court writes into law that an unmarried or widowed woman has the right to buy and sell, to sue or be sued, to act as an administrator or executor of an estate, to have power of attorney, and to sign and receive documents. In short, single women are granted *"feme sole* trader" status.

1695 Dinah Nuthead becomes the first woman to operate a printing shop in the colonies.

341

1712 South Carolina passes a law entitled "An Act for Better Securing the Payment of Debts," requiring single women in business to be responsible for their own debts.

1718 The Pennsylvania General Assembly passes "An Act Concerning Feme-Sole Traders," allowing married women whose husbands did not support them to act as single women when it came to trade.

1724 Vermont includes the names of women property owners on its polling lists.

1734 Anna Zenger publishes her husband's newspaper, the *New York Weekly Journal*, from November 1734 until August 1735, while her husband is in prison for libeling William Cosby, governor of New York.

1736 The Maryland case of *Carroll v. Warren* upholds the use of a private judicial examination of a married woman to protect her against male coercion in the transfer of her property.

1738 Elizabeth Timothy takes over publication of the *Gazette*, South Carolina's first permanent newspaper, which she publishes for ten years.

1740 In *Jones v. Porter* a Virginia court voids the transfer of a married woman's property by her husband because the legal technicalities are not met, thereby protecting women from the threat of coercion by their husbands.

1742 Cordelia Bradford takes over the publication of the *American Weekly Mercury* after the death of her husband, becoming one of the first female journalists and printers in the colonies.

1744 Anna Franklin is the first woman in America to have her imprint on the title page of a book: The Charter Granted by His Majesty King Charles

II to…Rhode Island and Providence Plantations….

1747 Under a female pseudonym, Benjamin Franklin writes "The Speech of Polly Baker" for the *London General Advertiser*, protesting prejudice toward women.

1765 Philadelphia newspapers report that women have joined the boycott of British goods.

The Blackstone Code (1765–1769) strikes a blow at the rights of married women in America. Sir William Blackstone argues that "the very being or legal existence of the woman is suspended during the marriage…."

1767 Upon the death of her husband Jonas Green, Anne Green continues to publish the *Maryland Gazette* without missing an issue. It is one of the first newspapers in the colonies.

1770 Over 400 Boston women sign an agreement to avoid drinking tea until the repeal of the tea tax.

1771 New York enacts "An Act to confirm Certain Conveyances and directing the Manner of proving Deeds to be recorded," requiring a married woman to sign a deed and tell a judge she agrees with her husband's sale or mortgage of her separate estate.

1774 Clementina Rind is appointed public printer in Williamsburg, Virginia.

Mary Goddard moves to Baltimore, Maryland, to take over Baltimore's first newspaper, the *Maryland Journal*, making her one of the colonies' earliest women newspaper publishers.

In Boston, Margaret Draper begins publication of the Tory paper *Massachusetts Gazette and Boston News Letter*. Lasting until 17 March 1776, it is the oldest and last pro-Tory paper in America.

1775 Mary Goddard becomes the first woman postmaster for Baltimore, Maryland.

Thomas Paine writes an article for *Pennsylvania Magazine* proposing women's rights. It is called "An Occasional Letter on the Female Sex" and argues that women are "surrounded on all sides by judges who are at once their tyrants and seducers."

Fifty-one women meet in Edenton, North Carolina, to produce the Edenton Proclamation, stating they have a right and duty to participate in the politics of their time, and supporting the Non-Importation Association resolves of 1774.

The first shots of the American Revolution are exchanged at Lexington, Massachusetts. Approximately 20,000 women will soon follow their husbands and companions to war (a woman will follow one out of every ten soldiers to camp).

1776 Congress proclaims the Declaration of Independence on 4 July. The document states that "all men are created equal." Seventy years later at Seneca Falls, New York, Elizabeth Cady Stanton, Lucretia Mott, and others will amend this to "all men and women are created equal" in their "Declaration of Rights and Sentiments."

Margaret Corbin accompanies her husband to Fort Washington near New York City, takes over his battle post when he is wounded, and is herself wounded and permanently disabled. She will become the first American woman to receive a military pension from Congress.

1777 Abigail Adams writes that women "will not hold ourselves bound by any laws in which we have no voice."

Mary Goddard prints the first copy of the Declaration of Independence to include the names of the signers in the *Maryland Journal*.

1778 Mary McCauley, nicknamed "Molly Pitcher" for carrying pails or pitchers of water to the troops, takes over her husband's battle station at the Battle of Monmouth, loading his cannon and helping to win victory for the Americans.

1782 In *Flanagan's Lessee v. Young*, Maryland jurists decided that the transfer of a married woman's separate property by her husband was invalid because the proper legal technicalities had not been followed. This protected the woman from her husband's coercion in the sale or mortgage of her property.

1783 The Treaty of Paris is signed ending the American Revolution. There follows a liberalization of divorce and other laws affecting women, and a new spirit of equality is felt by women under the new republic.

1810 In *Harvey and Wife v. Pecks*, Virginia jurists void a sale of a wife's property made by Harvey and Lydia Pecks in 1745, assuming the she was coerced into the sale by her husband because neither was her signature on the deed, nor was she privately examined by a judge.

1811 In the Virginia case of *Coutts v. Greenhoe*, jurists view marriage as "sufficient consideration" for a husband to provide his wife with a settlement.

The *Ewing v. Smith* decision protects a married South Carolina woman from the threat of coercion by her husband in the transfer of her own property.

1813 Francis Cabot Lowell's Boston Manufacturing Company establishes the first large textile mill in America, in Waltham, Massachusetts, and rapidly recruits women as workers.

1814 The Supreme Court case of *Johnson v. Thompson* makes it easier for men to bestow separate estates on women.

The first power-driven loom is established in Waltham, Massachusetts, operated by Deborah Skinner.

1818 In *Helms v. Franciscus* the Maryland chancellor, convinced that Lewis Helms married Anna Wandelohr only for her money, allows Wandelohr to control her separate property during marriage.

In *Gregory v. Paul* the Massachusetts Supreme Court recognizes a married woman's right to hold property in the event her husband abandons her.

The Reverend Joseph Emerson opens a female seminary in Bufield, Massachusetts, introducing new teaching techniques such as topical study and discussion instead of rote learning.

1819 Emma Willard presents Governor DeWitt Clinton of New York *An Address to the Public; Particularly to the Members of the Legislature of New York, Proposing a Plan for Improving Female Education.*

1821 Frances Wright publishes *Views of Society and Manners in America.*

Emma Willard establishes the Troy Female Seminary in New York.

1822 Zilpah Grant establishes the Adams Academy for Girls in Derry, New Hampshire, the first U.S. school to award diplomas to female students.

1824 The earliest known strike of women factory workers takes place in Pawtucket, Rhode Island, where women join men in protesting a wage cut and longer hours.

The first public school for girls in the United States opens in Worcester, Massachusetts.

1828 Francis Wright, in the face of great hostility, becomes the first woman to speak in public before audiences of both men and women.

1829 In *Tiernan v. Poor* the Maryland Court of Appeals decides that Deborah Poor can act as a single woman and control her own separate estate, allowing her to mortgage her own property to pay off a husband's debt.

1832 In *Garlick v. Strong* New York's Chancery Court decides that women have the right to withhold their consent to the transfer of their property.

1833 Oberlin College, the nation's first coeducational college, is established in Ohio.

The American Anti-Slavery Society is organized in Philadelphia, but denies membership to women. Lucretia Mott establishes the Philadelphia Female Anti-Slavery Society.

1836 The Married Woman's Property Act is introduced in the New York state legislature. Ernestine Rose circulates a petition in support of it, but gathers only six signatures.

Angelina Grimké writes "An Appeal to the Christian Women of the South."

1837 Harriet Martineau publishes *Society in America.*

The first National Anti-Slavery Society convention meets in New York.

The first National Convention of American Anti-Slavery Women is held in New York City.

Angelina and Sarah Grimké give anti-slavery speeches before audiences of men and women. Angelina Grimké debates two men on the issue of slavery. The women are attacked and called "unchristian" in July by the Congregationalist Church of Massachusetts in a pastoral letter. The letter is followed by two clerical appeals attacking William Lloyd Garrison and female antislavery activists who engage in public speaking.

Mary Lyons opens Mount Holyoke Female Seminary (now Mount Holyoke College).

1838 Harriet Martineau publishes *How To Observe Manners and Morals*, the first book on sociological methods.

Angelina Grimké speaks before the Massachusetts state legislature, the first woman ever to make such an appearance.

1839 Margaret Fuller begins a series of famous "conversations," or discussion groups, for women in Boston. These were, in Elizabeth Cady Stanton's words, "a vindication of woman's right to think."

1840 Margaret Fuller joins Ralph Waldo Emerson in producing and editing *The Dial*, a transcendentalist journal.

The American Anti-Slavery Society splits over the issue of allowing women to speak and vote in the organization. The association's leader, William Lloyd Garrison, is upheld in his support for equal rights for women. A formal vote is taken on the appointment of Abby Kelly to a business committee and is sustained by a majority in favor. Two of the men on the committee ask to be excused from serving. The anti-Garrison minority walks out and later forms the American and Foreign Anti-Slavery Society. Henry Stanton becomes executive secretary of the new group.

The World's Anti-Slavery Convention is held in London. Female delegates, including Lucretia Mott, are denied recognition by majority vote.

1841 Oberlin College becomes the first college in the United States to award an academic degree to a woman student.

Catharine Beecher writes *A Treatise on Domestic Economy*, later published as *The American Woman's Home* (1869), giving housewives practical information to fulfill better their domestic obligations.

1843 Margaret Fuller publishes "The Great Lawsuit: Man versus Men, Woman versus Women" in *The Dial*; it is republished a year later as *Woman in the Nineteenth Century*.

1845 Dorothea Lynde Dix writes *Remarks on Prisons and Prison Discipline in the United States*, which paves the way for prison reforms.

1846 Three members of the Lowell Female Labor Reform Association, along with five men, become directors of the New England Labor Reform League.

1847 Newspaper editor Clarina Howard Nichols begins to write on the need to reform women's legal rights. Her work leads to the married woman's property law in Vermont.

1848 The Married Woman's Property Act is passed in New York.

The Seneca Falls Convention, often regarded as the birth of the movement for women's rights, meets in Seneca Falls, New York; 68 women and 32 men sign the Declaration of Rights and Sentiments.

1849 Harriet Tubman escapes slavery for freedom in Philadelphia, Pennsylvania; she will organize an escape route for other fugitive slaves, the "underground railroad."

Elizabeth Blackwell becomes the first woman to receive a medical degree in the United States, from Geneva College in New York.

1850 Antoinette Brown (Blackwell) completes the theological course at Oberlin but is not permitted to graduate because of her sex.

Sojourner Truth's autobiography, *Narrative of Sojourner Truth*, (with Olive Gilbert) is published.

A Woman's Rights Convention is held in Salem, Ohio, the first in the state. Women bar men from any vocal participation.

The first National Woman's Rights Convention is held in Worcester, Massachusetts. Women's movement leaders are brought into national prominence.

1851 Harriet Beecher Stowe begins serial publication of *Uncle Tom's Cabin*.

First school to train girls as teachers opens in Washington, D.C. It will close in 1859.

Bloomer costume, created by Libby Smith Miller, makes its appearance. It is first known as the "Turkish dress."

Sojourner Truth electrifies the audience at the National Woman's Rights Convention in Akron, Ohio, with her "And Ain't I a Woman?" speech.

1852 Susan B. Anthony is turned out of a Sons of Temperance meeting for trying to speak; she organizes a woman's meeting where Elizabeth Cady Stanton gives her first speech.

Catharine Beecher establishes The American Woman's Educational Association.

Clarina Howard Nichols petitions the Vermont legislature for women's right to vote in school meetings.

1853 The *Una*, edited by Paulina Wright Davis, begins publication. Elizabeth Cady Stanton writes monthly essays for the magazine.

Antoinette L. Brown (Blackwell) becomes the first ordained female minister of a recognized U.S. denomination at the First Congregational Church in Wayne County, New York.

1854 The Married Woman's Property Bill passes in Massachusetts.

Mary Ann Shadd Cary is the first black woman to publish a newspaper, *The Provincial Freeman*, in Windsor, Ontario.

1857 Dr. Elizabeth Blackwell opens the New York University Infirmary, staffed entirely by women.

1859 The Indiana legislature passes a divorce reform bill that establishes desertion, drunkenness, and cruelty as grounds for divorce.

1860 An expansion of the Married Woman's Property Act of 1848 is passed in New York. It is called "An Act Concerning the Rights and Liabilities of Husband and Wife."

A new bill for the enlargement of the Married Woman's Property Act is introduced and passed by the New York state legislature. Women are granted rights to their wages and guardianship of their children, but the right to vote is withheld. Some of the rights contained in the bill will be repealed in 1862.

1861 Vassar Female College (later Vassar College) is chartered by the state of New York. It will not open until after the Civil War.

Women in Kansas are granted "school suffrage."

1863 Wisconsin State University admits women to its normal school training course.

The Woman's National Loyal League is formed.

1864 Anna E. Dickinson addresses President and Mrs. Lincoln, justices of the Supreme Court, and members of Congress in the Senate chamber.

1865 The Freedmen's Bureau is created. Josephine Griffing is later given credit for its initiation.

1866 Women delegates attend the General Assembly of the Knights of Labor.

Lucy B. Hobbs graduates from the Cincinnati Dental College and becomes the first female dentist in America.

The Eleventh National Woman's Rights Convention resolves itself into the American Equal Rights Association.

Elizabeth Cady Stanton declares herself the first woman candidate for Congress.

1867 The New England Women's Club is founded by Julia Ward Howe, Caroline Severance, and others.

The Working Woman's Association is founded.

1868 The Fourteenth Amendment to the Constitution is ratified. It guarantees full rights of citizenship to "all persons born or naturalized in the United States."

1869 The Iowa bar, acting in violation of state statutes, admits Arabella Mansfield, the first woman admitted to the bar in the United States.

Women's suffrage is granted in Wyoming and Utah territories.

The Woman Suffrage Amendment is proposed as the Sixteenth Amendment to the Constitution, but is not ratified.

A schism in the American Equal Rights Association leads to the founding of the National Woman Suffrage Association by Elizabeth Cady Stanton and Susan B. Anthony and to the formation of the American Woman Suffrage Association, organized by Lucy Stone.

Daughters of St. Crispin, a union of female shoe workers, is founded in Massachusetts. A year later, the members will pass a resolution demanding equal pay for equal work.

1871 Victoria Woodhull addresses Congress, declaring that women's suffrage is an implied right under the Constitution.

1872 Nine hundred working women of Lynn, Massachusetts, join together to protest pay cuts and change employment rules in boot and shoe trades.

1873 Julia Ward Howe calls the first convention of women preachers in America.

1874 The National Woman's Christian Temperance Union is formed in Cleveland, Ohio.

1875 Michigan and Minnesota grant suffrage, on school issues only, to widowed mothers of school children.

Smith College, endowed by Sophia Smith of Hatfield, Massachusetts, opens. It is the first American college to be endowed by a woman.

1878 A constitutional amendment to grant full suffrage to women is introduced in Congress; it will be reintroduced every year until its ratification as the Nineteenth Amendment in 1920.

1879 Belva Lockwood becomes the first woman lawyer admitted by the U.S. Supreme Court to its bar.

1880 Vermont and New York grant school suffrage to women.

1882 The Society for the Collegiate Instruction of Women (the "Harvard Annex") is founded.

Both houses of Congress appoint select committees on women's suffrage.

1883 Washington Territory grants women's suffrage.

1884 The first Working Girls' Club is founded in New York City by Grace Dodge and 12 factory workers.

1885 The Association of Working Girls' Societies is founded to unite Working Girls' Clubs across the country.

Bryn Mawr College opens; it will later become the first U.S. college to offer graduate studies to women.

1887 Congress passes the Edmunds-Tucker Act, forbidding polygamy and disenfranchising women in Utah Territory.

The "age of protection" for girls is raised from 10 to 14 years in Wisconsin; violation is made punishable by life imprisonment. The legislation, however, will be weakened two years later.

1889 Women's suffrage is defeated in a Washington state referendum.

1890 The General Federation of Women's Clubs is founded.

The American Federation of Labor declares support for a national women's suffrage amendment.

The National Woman Suffrage Association and the American Woman Suffrage Association merge; officers of the new National American Woman Suffrage Association (NAWSA) are Elizabeth Cady Stanton, Susan B. Anthony, Lucy Stone, and Alice Stone Blackwell.

Wyoming is admitted to the Union; women's suffrage is included in its constitution.

1891 The medical school of Johns Hopkins University becomes the first in the country to open its doors to men and women together.

1892 Elizabeth Cady Stanton resigns the presidency of the National American Woman Suffrage Association. Susan B. Anthony is elected president.

1894 The *Boston Woman's Era*, a monthly newspaper devoted to publishing the work of "representative colored women" from all parts of the United States, is founded; Josephine St. Pierre Ruffin is editor.

1895 The National Federation of Afro-American Women is founded.

Utah is admitted to statehood; women are enfranchised under the new state's constitution.

The National Association of Colored Women is founded, merging the National Federation of Afro-American Women and the Colored Women's League of Washington.

1897 The National Congress of Mothers is founded.

1900 Carrie Chapman Catt is elected to replace Susan B. Anthony as president of the National American Woman Suffrage Association.

Sister Julia McGroaty establishes Trinity College, the first Roman Catholic college for women in the country.

Elizabeth Cohn, seconding William Jennings Bryan's nomination for president of the United States, becomes the first woman delegate to make a seconding speech at the Democratic National Convention.

1901 The College Equal Suffrage League is founded by Maud Wood Park in Massachusetts.

1903 Maggie Lena Walker becomes the nation's first bank president, taking over the St. Luke Penny Savings Bank in Richmond, Virginia.

1906 Nora Stanton Blatch becomes the first woman to be admitted to the American Society of Civil Engineers.

The first class at Simmons College, a women's technical school, graduates in Boston, Massachusetts.

1908 In *Muller v. Oregon* the Supreme Court upholds the constitutionality of a maximum-hour law for women.

The National College Women's Equal Suffrage League is formed. Smith, Radcliffe, Barnard, Bryn Mawr, Mount Holyoke, and the universities of Chicago, California, and Wisconsin are represented by faculty and graduates.

The National Association of Colored Graduate Nurses is founded. In 1950, the American Nursing Association will open its membership to both black and white nurses, and the National Association of Colored Graduate Nurses will be dissolved.

The Nurse Corps is set up by the Navy with Esther Voorhees Hanson as its first superintendent.

1910 Congress is petitioned by 404,000 women requesting women's suffrage.

The first women's suffrage parade, organized by the Women's Political Union, is held in New York City.

Congress passes the Mann Act, which prohibits interstate or foreign transportation of women for immoral acts.

A. S. Wells, America's first female police officer, is appointed in Los Angeles.

1911 A fire at the Triangle Shirtwaist Company in New York City kills 146 workers, mostly women. Public outrage at the sweatshop conditions that prevailed in the factory before the fire lead to much-needed labor reforms.

The Feminist Alliance drafts a letter to President Woodrow Wilson for passage of a constitutional amendment prohibiting job discrimination on the basis of sex.

Therese Hubbell West becomes the first woman president of the American Library Association.

Harriet Quimby becomes the first licensed woman airplane pilot.

1912 The Progressive Party supports women's suffrage; Jane Addams seconds the nomination of Theodore Roosevelt.

Marie Jenny Howe founds the feminist group Heterodoxy.

The Girl Guides (later Girl Scouts) is founded by Juliette Gordon Low.

1913 Alice Paul organizes a suffrage parade in the nation's capital on the day preceding Woodrow Wilson's inauguration.

Clara Munson becomes the first woman elected the mayor of a city west of the Rockies: Warrington, Oregon.

1914 Alice Gertrude Bryant and Florence West Duckering become the first

women elected to the American College of Surgeons.

The first woman prosecutor, Annette Abbott Adams, is appointed. She becomes attorney general for the Northern District of California.

1915 A petition of 500,000 names supporting a women's suffrage amendment is delivered to President Woodrow Wilson. It is carried by Sara B. Field from San Francisco to Washington.

Mary Ware Dennett forms the National Birth Control League.

1916 America's first birth control clinic is opened in Brooklyn by Margaret Sanger.

1917 Mary Frances Lathrop becomes the first woman admitted to the American Bar Association.

1918 President Wilson declares himself in support of the national women's suffrage amendment.

Opha May Johnson becomes the first woman to join the Marine Corps.

Members of the Union of Streetcar Conductors strike in Cleveland to protest the employment of women.

1919 National Federation of Business and Professional Women's Clubs is founded.

Mary Evelyn Beatrice Longman is elected the first woman member of the National Academy of Design.

A women's suffrage amendment passes in Congress and goes to the states for ratification.

1920 The Women's Bureau is founded as a branch of the Labor Department.

The National League of Women Voters is established.

The Women's Joint Congressional Committee is founded.

Marie Luhring is elected the first woman member of the Society of Automotive Engineers.

The Nineteenth Amendment is ratified by the states. Women of the United States are enfranchised.

1921 For the first time a woman chairs the House of Representatives; she is Alice Robertson, a Republican from Oklahoma.

Margaret Sanger establishes the American Birth Control League.

The Sheppard-Towner Act, providing funding for mothers and infants, becomes law.

1922 The Cable Act is passed, granting most married women independent status in regard to their citizenship.

Rebecca Felton becomes the first woman to occupy a seat in the U.S. Senate, following her husband's death.

The Government Printing Office begins paying men and women equally for the same work.

The Department of State appoints its first woman Foreign Service employee, Lucile Atcherson Curtis.

1923 A minimum wage for women and children is declared unconstitutional by the Supreme Court.

1924 Lena Jones Springs becomes the first woman nominated for vice-president, receiving 18 votes at the Democratic National Convention.

Nellie Tayloe Ross of Wyoming is elected the first woman governor in America. Fifteen days later Miriam Ferguson becomes the governor of Texas, the nation's second woman governor.

1928 Genevieve Cline becomes the first woman associate federal justice, in the U.S. Customs Court, New York City.

1929 Ruth Peterson and Evelyn Southworth, testifying during a tariff debate in the U.S. Senate, are the first women, other than members of Congress, to be permitted on the Senate floor.

1930 Jessie Daniel Ames founds the Association of Southern Women for the Prevention of Lynching.

The International Ladies' Garment Workers' Union is formed.

1931 The Nobel Peace Prize is awarded to Jane Addams, the first American woman to receive this honor.

Mary T. Norton becomes the first woman to chair a congressional committee; she will head the District of Columbia Affairs Committee until June 1937.

1932 Hattie Wyatt Caraway is elected to the U.S. Senate. She is the first woman to win a Senate election and becomes the first woman to preside over the Senate.

The chair of the board of the Pittsburgh Pirates is Florence Wolf Dreyfuss.

Amelia Earhart completes a transatlantic solo flight and a transcontinental flight, both firsts for a woman pilot.

Frances Elizabeth Willis is named the first woman chargé d'affaires, serving at the American legation in Stockholm, Sweden.

1933 Passage of the National Economy Act results in the dismissal of many women from government jobs.

The White House Conference on the Emergency Needs of Women is organized by Eleanor Roosevelt.

Camp Jane Addams is one of 28 special camps for women formed following Eleanor Roosevelt's White House Conference on Resident Schools for Unemployed Women.

Frances Perkins is appointed U.S. secretary of labor, becoming the first woman cabinet member.

President Franklin D. Roosevelt names Ruth Bryan Owen envoy to

Denmark and Ireland. She is the first woman ambassador to represent the United States abroad.

Nellie Tayloe Ross is named director of the U.S. Mint.

1935 Amelia Earhart is the first to make a solo flight from Hawaii to North America.

Laura Ingalls becomes the first woman to make a nonstop, east-west transcontinental airplane flight.

Gretchen B. Schoeleber becomes the first woman member of the New York Stock Exchange.

1937 Supreme Court's decision in *West Coast Hotel v. Parrish* permits a minimum-wage law for women.

1939 Ruth Hanna McCormick Simms becomes Thomas Dewey's presidential campaign comanager. She is the first woman given authority on a presidential campaign.

1940 The National Woman's Party fights against legal discrimination by conducting an extensive campaign for an equal rights amendment to the Constitution.

1941 In Washington, the National Woman's Party dedicates the world's first feminist library on the 126th anniversary of Elizabeth Cady Stanton's birth.

1942 The War Department urges industries to hire women.

Lieutenant Commander Dorothy Constance Stratton becomes the head of the Coast Guard Woman's Reserve (SPARS).

1943 The Women Air Force Service Pilots (WASPS) is founded.

President Roosevelt signs a law creating the Women's Army Corps (WACS).

In Vice-President Henry A. Wallace's absence, Hattie Wyatt Caraway

presides as president pro tem of the U.S. Senate.

1944 The U.S.S. *Sanctuary* becomes the first "mixed" Navy ship, with two women officers and sixty enlisted women on board.

1945 Secretary of Labor Lewis Schwellenbach addresses the Senate regarding payment of "uniformly lower wages" to women. He urges legislation to ban wage differentials because of sex and claims that discrimination "depresses the whole wage structure."

1947 Senators Claude Pepper and Wayne Morse introduce a bill that would require equal pay for male and female factory workers.

Florence Blanchfield, superintendent of Army Services, is the first regularly commissioned woman officer in the U.S. Army.

1948 Freida Barkin Hennock becomes the first woman to be sworn in as a member of the Federal Communications Commission.

The first six women to enlist under the Women's Armed Services Integration Act are inducted into the Navy.

1949 Margaret Chase Smith is elected to the Senate and becomes the first woman to have served in both houses of Congress.

Georgina Neese Clark is confirmed by the Senate as the first woman treasurer of the United States.

1950 The U.S. Senate passes the proposed Equal Rights Amendment by a vote of 63–19, and it is passed on to the House of Representatives.

Anna M. Rosenberg becomes the first woman assistant secretary of defense. She previously was a director of the National Recovery Administration and a Social Security board member. She also held a seat on the War Manpower Commission.

The *Wall Street Journal* reports that the number of working wives has increased 90 percent in the past decade.

1951 The Labor Department reports that 18,846,000 women are in the U.S. labor force.

1952 The Republican Party includes a plank supporting the Equal Rights Amendment, adopted by acclamation.

1953 Clare Boothe Luce is sworn in as ambassador to Italy, having been nominated by President Dwight D. Eisenhower.

Oveta Culp Hobby becomes the second woman to hold a cabinet post when she is sworn in as the country's first secretary of the Department of Health, Education, and Welfare.

Jacqueline Cochran becomes the first woman to fly faster than the speed of sound, piloting an F-86 fighter at Edwards Air Force Base, California.

Frances E. Willis is named U.S. ambassador to Switzerland; she is the first woman career diplomat advanced to the rank of ambassador.

1954 In a dispute with American Airlines, the Airline Stewards and Stewardesses Association appeals for mediation regarding the company's policy that stewardesses must retire at age 32.

1955 The General Assembly of the Presbyterian Church approves the ordination of women as ministers.

1956 President Eisenhower calls for "equal pay for equal work without discrimination because of sex" in his State of the Union message.

1959 The American Law Institute suggests in its Model Penal Code that abortions be permitted in certain situations.

1961 A Florida law exempting women from jury duty unless they volunteer is upheld by the Supreme Court. Florida is one of 18 states that allow this practice. Alabama, Mississippi, and South Carolina bar women from juries altogether.

President John F. Kennedy issues Executive Order 10980 to form the President's Commission on the Status of Women; Eleanor Roosevelt is named chair.

1963 The Equal Pay Act is passed by Congress.

Betty Friedan's *The Feminine Mystique* is published.

1965 The Planned Parenthood League of Connecticut challenges a state law prohibiting the use of birth control for family planning. In the case, *Griswold v. Connecticut*, the Supreme Court finds that the law interferes with the right to marital privacy.

1966 The National Organization for Women is founded with Betty Friedan as its first president.

In Montgomery, Alabama, a federal court rules that state laws excluding women from jury service will be considered null and void after 1 June 1967 because they "deny to women the equal protection of the laws in violation of the 14th Amendment."

The U.S. Department of Health, Education, and Welfare approves the distribution of birth control instruction and contraceptives to all U.S. women who request them.

1967 In Atlantic City, New Jersey, a group of women picket at the site of the Miss America Pageant, arguing that the contest is offensive to women.

The organization New York Radical Women is formed.

1968 The Women's Equity Action League is founded by Elizabeth Boyer.

To express their opposition to the Vietnam War, the Jeanette Rankin Brigade, a network of antiwar organizations for women, holds a demonstration and convention in Washington.

Federally Employed Women (FEW) is founded by Daisy Fields to gain equality and equal opportunities for women in the federal government.

Roxanne Dunbar founds Cell 16, regarded as the most militant group within the women's liberation movement.

1969 The Interstate Association of State Commissions on the Status of Women is organized.

The Bread and Roses organization is formed in Boston to link small feminist collectives. Their attention is focused not only on women's rights, but also on protests against the Vietnam War, feminist theater projects, and efforts to spread the ideas of the women's liberation movement.

The Feminists is created by Ti-Grace Atkinson in opposition to the National Organization for Women.

A Washington, D.C., court overturns the local abortion law as a result of the *Vuitch* case.

The National Abortion Rights Action League is founded at a conference proposed by Dr. Lonny Myers.

Bowe et al. v. Colgate-Palmolive overturns weight-lifting restrictions as applied only to women.

President's Task Force on Women's Rights and Responsibilities, established by Richard M. Nixon, issues a militant report, "A Matter of Simple Justice."

In *People v. Belous*, the California Supreme Court throws out the state's abortion law.

Founded by Shulamith Firestone and Ellen Willis, the Redstockings become one of the best-known groups in the radical contingent of the women's movement.

Representative Shirley Chisholm takes her place in the 91st Congress, the first African-American woman elected to Congress.

In Charles Town, West Virginia, Barbara Jo Rubin becomes the first woman jockey in America to win at a thoroughbred race track with parimutuel betting.

1970 The Department of Labor establishes official guidelines to prohibit sex discrimination in the workplace.

The Boston Women's Health Book Collective is formed; it becomes one of the leading forces in the feminist health movement.

Elizabeth Duncan, director of the Women's Bureau, announces that companies with government contracts of $50,000 or more, or companies with 50 employees or more, must follow federal guidelines against sex discrimination.

A law permitting abortions during the first 24 weeks of pregnancy takes effect in New York City.

A five-year federal program is authorized by Congress to provide family planning services and population research. The program's goal, according to President Nixon, is to serve the 5 million U.S. women in need of family planning services.

1971 The Supreme Court rules that companies may not deny employment to women with small children unless they do so to men also.

The Civil Service Commission rules that sex specification in federal jobs must be eliminated.

The National Women's Political Caucus is formed by 200 women in Washington, D.C.

The Supreme Court lets stand a U.S. circuit court ruling that company pension plans requiring women to retire before men is a violation of federal civil rights law.

1972 Title IX of the Higher Education Act, which calls for equal opportunities for male and female students, is passed. It bans sex discrimination in educational programs receiving federal funds.

Ms. magazine is founded by Gloria Steinem and Pat Carbine.

The Center for the American Woman in Politics is organized at Rutgers University to analyze the treatment of women in political life.

Eisenstadt v. Baird challenges the "crimes against chastity" law that makes it illegal to dispense contraceptives to unwed people. The law was found to be in violation of the Fourteenth Amendment because it discriminated against the unmarried.

The Equal Rights Amendment is approved by the Senate by a vote of 84–8 and is sent to the states for ratification.

The Supreme Court rules that unwed fathers have a right to prove themselves as fit parents, just as unwed mothers do. This must be taken into consideration before they can be denied custody of their children.

Nina Kuscik is the first woman officially to run in the Boston Marathon. She finishes before 800 male runners and 8 other women.

Alene B. Duerk, director of the Navy Nurse Corps, is named the first woman admiral in U.S. history.

Sally J. Priesand is ordained in Cincinnati, Ohio, as the first woman rabbi in the United States and the second in the history of Judaism.

A Board of Education ruling requiring pregnant teachers to take a six-month leave of absence without pay after their fifth month of pregnancy is overturned by a Chicago district court.

1973 Congress passes the Women's Educational Equity Act to finance women's studies programs and help eliminate sexism from all aspects of education.

The Supreme Court, in *Frontiero v. Richardson*, strikes down as unconstitutional a law that prohibits female officers from receiving extra money for housing and extra medical benefits unless they can prove that their husbands are dependents.

Pittsburgh Press v. Human Relations Commission ends the practice of running sex-segregated want ads in newspapers.

Emily Howell, an employee of Frontier Airlines, becomes the first woman pilot to work for a scheduled U.S. carrier.

The Supreme Court rules in *Roe v. Wade* that a woman's right to privacy "is broad enough to encompass a woman's decision whether or not to terminate her pregnancy."

Dixy Lee Ray becomes the first woman to chair the Atomic Energy Commission.

Women are barred from membership in the Jaycees.

The Federal Home Loan Bank Board ends discrimination against women when granting mortgage loans.

1974 The Equal Credit Opportunity Act is passed, making it unlawful to deny credit on the basis of sex or marital status.

The First Woman's Bank is founded in New York City.

The National Organization for Women creates the Project on Equal Education Rights to oversee the enforcement of Title IX.

Katherine Graham, publisher of the *Washington Post*, becomes first woman to be named to the 18-member Associated Press Board.

The League of Women Voters decides to allow full membership to men.

President Gerald Ford signs a law making the Federal Deposit Insurance Company responsible for prohibiting credit discrimination on the basis of gender.

1975 *Signs*, the woman's studies journal, is founded by Catherine Stimpson.

The Supreme Court rules in *Taylor v. Louisiana* that the Louisiana law excluding women from jury duty is unconstitutional.

The National Women's Health Network is founded.

A part of the Social Security law that provides widows and children with survivors' benefits, but denied these benefits to men who had lost their spouses, is unanimously struck down by the U.S. Supreme Court.

Antidiscrimination rules issued by the Department of Health, Education, and Welfare are aimed toward implementing Title IX of the 1972 Higher Education Act.

Congress passes a bill to allow women to gain admittance to the nation's military academies beginning in 1976.

The U.S. Coast Guard Academy becomes the first service academy to admit women.

1976 The Organization of Pan Asian American Women is formed.

The Supreme Court decides in *Craig v. Boren* that a gender-based drinking law in Oklahoma is unconstitutional.

Sarah Caldwell becomes the first woman to conduct an opera at the Metropolitan Opera in New York City.

Barbara Walters becomes the first woman to anchor a network television news program and the highest-paid journalist in history by accepting ABC's offer of a five-year contract at $1 million annually.

Kentucky's Commission on Human Rights orders two coal companies to hire women as miners, and also orders them to pay $29,000 in back wages to two women who had been denied employment.

Women win 13 of 32 Rhodes Scholarships awarded to Americans, the first time the scholarships have been open to women.

1977 The Committee for Abortion Rights and Against Sterilization Abuse (CARASA) is organized in New York City.

1978 National Coalition Against Violence is founded to help battered women.

Margaret Brewer is named the first woman general in the U.S. Marine Corps.

A law barring U.S. Navy women from duty on ships other than hospital and transport vessels is found to be unconstitutional by U.S. District Court Judge John Sirica.

The ratification deadline for the Equal Rights Amendment is extended to 30 June 1982 by a Senate vote of 60–36.

1979 The Supreme Court rules that members of Congress can be sued for sex discrimination.

Lieutenant Susan Ingalls Moritz becomes the first woman to command a Coast Guard ship on a regular patrol.

Sonia Johnson, an outspoken leader of Mormons for the Equal Rights Amendment, is excommunicated by the Church of Jesus Christ of Latter-Day Saints.

1980 The National Judicial Education Program to Promote Equality for Women and Men in the Courts is formed to combat sex bias in the courtroom.

The Defense Department extends full military veteran status to 16,000 women who served in the Women's Auxiliary Army Corps during World War II.

Equal Employment Opportunity Commission chair Eleanor Holmes Norton issues regulations that prohibit sexual harassment of workers by supervisors in government and private industry.

Former federal judge Shirley Hufstedler becomes the first U.S. secretary of education.

The Ford Motor Company agrees to pay $23 million in settlement of a job discrimination case to develop special job training programs for women and minority employees. This settlement also states that women will be hired for 30 percent of openings for nonskilled workers.

1981 The National Black Women's Health Project is formed by Byllye Avery to address the health problems of African-American women.

Sharon Parker and Veronica Collazo form the National Institute for Women of Color to unite women from a variety of ethnic backgrounds.

The Massachusetts Supreme Court decides that the state is required to pay for all medically necessary abortions for women on welfare, whether or not their lives may be in danger.

The Supreme Court rules that a doctor must inform the parents of a dependent teenage girl before performing an abortion.

A Supreme Court ruling states that women can sue their employers for wage discrimination even if their jobs vary from those of their male coworkers.

The U.S. Supreme Court rules in the case of *Rostker v. Goldberg* that the Constitution permits excluding women from draft registration and from the military draft itself.

A strike by municipal workers in San Jose, California, ends when the city agrees to bring women's pay up to the level of men's for comparable work.

The Equal Employment Opportunity Commission reports that women's earnings lag 60 percent behind those of men.

Sandra Day O'Connor is sworn in as the first woman member of the U.S. Supreme Court.

1982 United Airlines is ordered by a federal district court judge to rehire 1,800 female flight attendants who lost their jobs when they married. In a separate case the Supreme Court rules that Trans World Airlines flight attendants who were fired prior to 1971 because of pregnancy are entitled to back pay and retroactive seniority.

National Women's History Week is established by President Ronald Reagan.

The Equal Rights Amendment fails, falling three states short of the necessary 38 for ratification.

Waterfront employers and the International Longshoreman's and Warehouseman's Union agree to hire women at rates that will make them 20 percent of the job force by 1997.

1983 The Supreme Court overturns Ohio abortion restrictions.

Sally Ride becomes the first American woman sent into space. She spends six days as a crew member aboard the *Challenger.*

1984 Congress passes the Family Violence Prevention and Services Act.

The U.S. Supreme Court rules that women cannot be excluded from full membership in the Jaycees.

A bill signed by President Ronald Reagan requires states to pass laws requiring employers to withhold wages from parents falling one month behind in child support payments.

At the Democratic National Convention, Geraldine A. Ferraro is nominated by acclamation as the vice-presidential candidate to run on the ticket with Walter F. Mondale.

The Retirement Equity Act is signed by President Reagan to make it easier for women to earn retirement benefits under private pension plans.

President Ronald Reagan signs a bill that will allow former spouses of federal employees to receive survivor benefits.

1985 Commodore Roberta Hazard is named the first woman commander of the country's largest naval training facility: the U.S. Naval Training Center in Great Lakes, Illinois.

Geri B. Larson becomes the first woman forest supervisor in the U.S. Forest Service. She is in charge of Tahoe National Forest in northern California.

Penny Harrington becomes the first woman to head a major city's police department when she is sworn in as chief of police in Portland, Oregon.

The Equal Employment Opportunity Commission rejects any cases of job discrimination based on comparable worth.

Wilma Mankiller is sworn in as principal chief of the Cherokee Nation of Oklahoma and becomes the first woman in history to head a major Native-American tribe.

1986 In *Meritor Savings Bank v. Vinson* the Supreme Court defines sexual harassment as a type of discrimination illegal under federal law.

The National Latina Health Organization is formed in California to promote the healthcare objectives of Hispanic women.

The U.S. Supreme Court rules in *Babbitt v. Planned Parenthood* that Arizona cannot deny state funding to a private family planning group that provides abortions and abortion counseling.

1987 In the case of *Johnson v. Transportation Agency* the Supreme Court upholds the constitutionality of voluntary affirmative action programs for women in employment fields where they had previously been excluded.

The U.S. Supreme Court upholds a California law requiring employers to grant women disability leave for pregnancy and childbirth.

A unanimous decision of the Supreme Court allows states to retain the right to deny unemployment benefits to

women who leave work because of pregnancy.

1989 The Supreme Court upholds a Missouri law in *Webster v. Reproductive Health Services* restricting abortion.

1990 Legislators introduce a job-bias bill into both houses of Congress stipulating that any employment decisions based on gender, race, ethnicity, or religion are illegal.

The American Bar Association votes for the first time to support a constitutional right to abortion.

John Van de Kamp, California's attorney general, proposes that California permit testing of the French abortion pill, RU-486.

A panel commissioned by the American Psychological Association finds legal abortions performed in the first trimester of pregnancy cause little long-term mental distress.

The Church of Jesus Christ of Latter-Day Saints drops rituals offensive to women.

The Supreme Court in *Hodgson v. Minnesota* upholds a provision that minors must wait 48 hours for an abortion after notifying their parents; however, the Court blocks an absolute two-parent requirement. In a separate decision, *Ohio v. Akron Center for Reproductive Health*, the Court upholds an Ohio law requiring minors to notify one parent or to seek permission from a court in order to have an abortion.

Secretary of Health and Human Services Louis Sullivan selects cardiologist Bernadine P. Healy to become the first woman to head the National Institutes of Health.

The Food and Drug Administration approves Norplant, the first major new form of contraception in over 20 years.

The Blue Cross and Blue Shield Association announces that it will finance experimental breast cancer treatment. This is the first time a private health insurance company has agreed to finance an experimental treatment. The company will spend $10 million to study 1,200 women to see if temporary removal of bone marrow and injection of cancer-fighting drugs will improve survival rates.

1991 The Supreme Court, in declining to hear the case of *Tiger Inn v. Frank*, lets stand a New Jersey Supreme Court ruling that required an all-male Princeton eating club to admit women.

1992 The Supreme Court rules in *United Automobile Workers v. Johnson Controls* that employers cannot bar pregnant women from jobs where they might be exposed to hazardous materials.

The House of Representatives approves a defense budget that includes a provision to allow women in the Air Force, Navy, and Marine Corps to fly combat aircraft for the first time. The bill also authorizes abortions in military hospitals for servicewomen and dependents.

University of Oklahoma law professor Anita Hill publicly accuses Supreme Court nominee Clarence Thomas of sexual harassment. Following widely publicized hearings, the Senate confirms Thomas as an associate justice.

1993 The Florida Supreme Court orders John E. Santora to step down as chief judge of the state's Fourth Judicial Circuit. The order is given after Santora makes remarks considered racist, sexist, and anti-Semitic. He remains as a district court judge.

The Supreme Court rules that Title IX of the 1972 Higher Education Act entitles students receiving federal funds at school the right to sue for monetary damages if they are victims of sexual harassment.

The State Farm Insurance Company agrees to pay a total of $157 million to 814 past and current female employees to settle sex discrimination charges.

Bibliography

Addams, Jane. *Twenty Years at Hull House.* New York: Signet, 1981.

Adelman, Clifford. *Women at Thirtysomething: Paradoxes of Attainment.* Washington, D.C.: U.S. Department of Education, June 1991.

Ames, Mary. *From a New England Woman's Diary in Dixie.* Norwood, Massachusetts: Plimpton Press, 1906.

Anderson, John Q. *Brokenburn: The Journal of Kate Stone, 1861–1868.* Baton Rouge: Louisiana State University Press, 1955.

Andrews, Eliza Frances. *The War-Time Journal of a Georgia Girl, 1864–1865.* New York: D. Appleton, 1908.

Anthony, Katharine. *Susan B. Anthony: Her Personal History and Her Era.* Garden City, New York: Doubleday, 1954.

Aptheker, Herbert, ed. *A Documentary History of the Negro People in the United States.* Vol. 1, *From the Colonial Times through the Civil War.* New York: Carol Publishing, 1951.

Archer, Jules. *Breaking Barriers.* New York: Viking, 1991.

Avary, Myrta Lockett. *A Virginia Girl in the Civil War, 1861–1865.* New York: D. Appleton, 1903.

Bacon, Margaret Hope. *Valiant Friend: The Life of Lucretia Mott.* New York: Walker, 1980.

———, ed. "Lucretia Mott Speaking: Excerpts from the Sermons & Speeches of a Famous Nineteenth Century Quaker Minister & Reformer." Pamphlet 234. Wallingford, Pennsylvania: Pendle Hill, 1980.

Ballou, Patricia K. *Women: A Bibliography of Bibliographies.* Boston: Hall, 1980.

Barnes, Gilbert H., and Dwight L. Dumond, eds. *Letters of Theodore Dwight Weld, Angelina Grimké Weld and Sarah Grimké, 1822–1844.* Gloucester, Massachusetts: Peter Smith/American Historical Association, 1965.

Barry, Kathleen. *Susan B. Anthony: A Biography of a Singular Feminist.* New York: New York University Press, 1988.

Baxandall, Rosalyn, Linda Gordon, and Susan Reverby. *American Working Women.* New York: Random House, 1976.

Beard, Mary R. *Woman as Force in History.* New York: Macmillan, 1946.

Benton, Josiah H., Jr. "What Women Did for the War, and What the War Did for Women." Memorial Day speech before the Soldier's Club, Wellesley, Massachusetts, 30 May 1894. Microfilm. Woodbridge, Connecticut: Research Publications, 1977.

Berkin, Carol Ruth, and Mary Beth Norton. *Women of America: A History.* Boston: Houghton Mifflin, 1979.

Bird, Caroline. *Born Female.* New York: Pocket Books, 1969.

Blackwell, Alice Stone. *Lucy Stone: Pioneer of Woman's Rights.* Detroit, Michigan: Grand River Books, 1971. First published, 1930.

Blackwell, Sarah Ellen. *A Military Genius: Life of Anna Ella Carroll of Maryland.* 2 vols. Washington, D.C.: Judd Detweiler, 1891–1895. Microfilm. Woodbridge, Connecticut: Research Publications, 1983.

Blatch, Harriot Stanton, and Alma Lutz. *Challenging Years: The Memoirs of Harriot Stanton Blatch.* New York: G. P. Putnam & Sons, 1940.

Bodry-Sanders, Penelope. *Carl Akeley: Africa's Collector, Africa's Savior.* New York: Paragon House, 1991.

Boumil, Marcia Mobilia, Joel Friedman, and Barbara Ewert Taylor. *Sexual Harassment.* Deerfield Beach, Florida: Health Communications, Inc., 1992.

Bowne, Eliza Southgate. *A Girl's Life Eighty Years Ago.* Women in America. New York: Arno Press, 1974.

Boydson, Jeanne, Mary Kelly, and Anne Margolis. *The Limits of Sisterhood: The Beecher Sisters on Women's Rights and Women's Sphere.* Chapel Hill: University of North Carolina Press, 1988.

Brock, Sallie. *Richmond during the War: Four Years of Personal Observation. By a Richmond Lady.* Alexandria, Virginia: Time-Life Books, 1983.

Brown, Dorothy M. *American Women in the 1920s: Setting a Course.* Boston: Twayne, 1987.

Brown, Lyn Mikel, and Carol Gilligan. *Meeting at the Crossroads: Women's Psychology and Girls' Development.* New York: Ballantine, 1992.

Brownmiller, Susan. *Against Our Will: Men, Women, and Rape.* New York: Simon & Schuster, 1975.

Buel, Joy Day, and Richard Buel, Jr. *The Way of Duty.* New York: W. W. Norton, 1984.

Burnett-Smith, A. *As Others See Her: An Englishwoman's Impressions of the American Woman in War Time.* Boston: Houghton Mifflin, 1919.

Cantor, Norman F., and Michael S. Werthman, eds. *The History of Popular Culture to 1815.* New York: Macmillan, 1968.

Caroli, Betty Boyd. *First Ladies.* New York: Oxford University Press, 1987.

Catt, Carrie Chapman. Papers. Manuscript and Archives Division, New York Public Library, New York.

Catt, Carrie Chapman, and Nettie Rogers Shuler. *Woman Suffrage and Politics.* New York: Charles Scribner and Sons, 1923.

Chafe, William Henry. *The American Woman: Her Changing Social, Economic, and Political Roles, 1920–1970.* New York: Oxford University Press, 1981.

———. *The Paradox of Change: American Women in the 20th Century.* New York: Oxford University Press, 1991.

Chesler, Ellen. *Woman of Valor: Margaret Sanger and the Birth Control Movement in America.* New York: Simon & Schuster, 1992.

Chesler, Phyllis. *Women and Madness.* New York: Harcourt Brace Jovanovich, 1989.

Chesnut, Mary. *Mary Chesnut's Civil War.* Edited by C. Vann Woodward. New Haven, Connecticut: Yale University Press, 1981.

Child, Lydia Maria. *Letters of Lydia Maria Child.* Biographical introduction by John G. Whittier. Appendix by Wendell Phillips. New York: Negro University Press, 1969.

———. *Selected Letters, 1817–1880.* Edited by Milton Meltzer and Patricia G. Holland. Amherst: University of Massachusetts Press, 1982.

Chodorow, Nancy. *The Reproduction of Mothering.* Berkeley: University of California Press, 1978.

Clark, Judith Freeman. *American Women in the 20th Century.* New York: Prentice Hall Press, 1987.

Clinton, Catherine. *The Other Civil War: American Women in the Nineteenth Century.* New York: Hill and Wang, 1984.

Cochran, Thomas C., and Wayne Andrew, eds. *Concise Dictionary of American History.* New York: Scribner's, 1962.

Conway, Jill K. et al. *The Female Experience in Eighteenth and Nineteenth Century America: A Guide to the History of American Women.* Princeton, New Jersey: Princeton University Press, 1985.

Costa, Marie. *Abortion.* Santa Barbara, California: ABC-CLIO, 1991.

Cott, Nancy F. *The Bonds of Womanhood: "Woman's Sphere" in New England, 1700–1835.* New Haven, Connecticut: Yale University Press, 1977.

———. *The Grounding of Modern Feminism.* New Haven, Connecticut: Yale University Press, 1987.

———. *Root of Bitterness: Documents of the Social History of American Women.* Boston: Northeastern University Press, 1972.

Cowan, Ruth S. *More Work for Mother: The Ironies of Household Technology from the Open Hearth to the Microwave.* New York: Basic Books, 1983.

Culley, Margo. *A Day at a Time: The Diary Literature of American Women from 1764 to the Present.* New York: Feminist Press, 1985.

Cushman, Robert E. *Leading Constitutional Decisions.* New York: Appleton-Century-Crofts, 1958.

Davis, Allen F. *American Heroine: The Life and Legend of Jane Addams.* New York: Oxford University Press, 1973.

Davis, Angela Y. *Women, Race and Class.* New York: Random House, 1981.

Davis, Flora. *Moving the Mountain: The Women's Movement in America since 1960.* New York: Simon & Schuster, 1991.

De Hart Matthews, Jane, and Linda K. Kerber, eds. *Women's America: Refocusing the Past.* New York: Oxford University Press, 1982.

Debs, Eugene V. Writings and Speeches of Eugene V. Debs. Cold Spring, Minnesota: Hermitage, 1948.

Dexter, Elizabeth Anthony. *Colonial Women of Affairs: A Study of Women in Business and the Professions in America before 1776.* Boston, New York: Houghton Mifflin, 1924.

Dickens, Charles. *American Notes for General Circulation.* New York: Penguin Books, 1989.

Diner, Hasia R. *Erin's Daughters in America: Irish Immigrant Women in the Nineteenth Century.* Baltimore, Maryland: Johns Hopkins University Press, 1983.

Dublin, Thomas. *Farm to Factory: Women's Letters, 1830–1860.* New York: Columbia University Press, 1981.

DuBois, Ellen Carol. *Elizabeth Cady Stanton/Susan B. Anthony: Correspondence, Writings, Speeches.* New York: Schocken Books, 1981.

———. *Feminism and Suffrage: The Emergence of an Independent Women's Movement in America, 1848–1869.* Ithaca, New York: Cornell University Press, 1978.

Duniway, Abigail Scott. *Path Breaking: An Autobiographical History of the Equal Suffrage Movement in Pacific Coast States.* Portland, Oregon: James, Kerbs & Abbot, 1914.

Duster, Alfreda M., ed. *Crusade for Justice: The Autobiography of Ida B. Wells.* Chicago: University of Chicago Press, 1970.

Echols, Alice. *Daring To Be Bad: Radical Feminism in America 1767–1974.* Minneapolis: University of Minnesota Press, 1989.

Ehrenreich, Barbara, and Deirdre English. *For Her Own Good: 150 Years of the Experts' Advice to Women.* Garden City, New York: Doubleday, 1989.

Eisler, Benita. *The Lowell Offering: Writings by New England Mill Women (1840–1845).* New York: Lippincott, 1977.

Elshtain, Jean Bethke. *Women and War.* New York: Basic Books, 1987.

Encyclopaedia Britannica: A Dictionary of Arts, Sciences, Literature and General Information. 29 volumes. Eleventh ed. New York: Encyclopaedia Britannica, 1911.

Epstein, Cynthia Fuchs. *Deceptive Distinctions: Sex, Gender, and the Social Order.* New York: Russell Sage Foundation, 1988.

———. *Woman's Place: Options and Limits in Professional Careers.* Los Angeles: University of California Press, 1970.

Evans, Sara M. *Born for Liberty: A History of Women in America*. New York: Free Press, 1989.

Faludi, Susan. *Backlash: The Undeclared War against American Women*. New York: Crown Publishers, 1991.

Faragher, John Mack, ed. *The Encyclopedia of Colonial and Revolutionary America*. New York: Facts on File, 1990.

Ferree, Myra Marx, and Beth B. Hess. *Controversy and Coalition: The New Feminist Movement*. Boston: Twayne, 1985.

Fetterley, Judith, ed. *Provisions: A Reader From 19th-Century American Women*. Bloomington: Indiana University Press, 1985.

Finch, Jessica Garretson. *How the Ballot Would Help the Working Woman*. New York: Equal Franchise Society of New York City, 1909.

Flexner, Eleanor. *Century of Struggle: The Woman's Rights Movement in the United States*. Rev. ed. Cambridge: Harvard University Press, 1975.

Foner, Philip S. *The Factory Girls*. Chicago: University of Illinois Press, 1977.

———. *Frederick Douglass on Women's Rights*. Westport, Connecticut: Greenwood Press, 1976.

———. *Women and the American Labor Movement: From Colonial Times to the Eve of World War I*. New York: Free Press, 1979.

Foner, Philip S., and John A. Garraty, eds. *The Reader's Companion to American History*. Boston: Houghton Mifflin, 1991.

Fox-Genovese, Elizabeth. *Feminism without Illusions: A Critique of Individuals*. Chapel Hill: University of North Carolina Press, 1991.

———. *Within the Plantation Household: Black and White Women of the Old South*. Chapel Hill: University of North Carolina Press, 1988.

French, Marilyn. *The Women's Room*. New York: Summit Books, 1977.

Friedan, Betty. *The Feminine Mystique*. New York: Dell, 1974.

———. *The Second Stage*. New York: Dell, 1991.

Frost, Elizabeth, and Kathryn Cullen-DuPont. *Women's Suffrage in America: An Eyewitness History*. New York: Facts on File, 1992.

Fuller, Margaret. *Woman in the Nineteenth Century*. New York: W. W. Norton, 1971.

Garrison, Wendell Phillips, and Francis Jackson Garrison. *William Lloyd Garrison 1805–1879* (vol. 2). New York: Arno Press and The New York Times, 1969.

Gates, Henry Louis, Jr., ed. *Six Women's Slave Narratives*. Introduction by William L. Andres. The Schomburg Library of Nineteenth Century Black Women Writers. New York: Oxford University Press, 1988.

Gelb, Joyce, and Marian Lief Palley. *Women and Public Policies*. Princeton, New Jersey: Princeton University Press, 1982.

Genovese, Eugene D. *Roll, Jordan, Roll: The World the Slaves Made*. New York: Vintage, 1976.

Gibson, Anne, and Timothy Fast. *The Women's Atlas of the United States*. New York: Facts on File, 1986.

Gifis, Steven H. *Law Dictionary*. Third ed. New York: Barron's, 1991.

Gilligan, Carol, Nona P. Lyons, and Trudy J. Hanmer. *Making Connections: The Relational Worlds of Adolescent Girls at Emma Willard School*. Cambridge: Harvard University Press, 1990.

Gilman, Charlott Perkins. *The Yellow Wallpaper*. New York: Feminist Press, 1973.

Goldstein, Leslie Friedman. *The Constitutional Rights of Women: Cases in Law and Social Change*. Madison: University of Wisconsin Press, 1988.

Grew, Mary. *Diary, 1840*. Microfilm. Woodbridge, Connecticut: Research Publications, 1983.

Griffith, Elisabeth. *In Her Own Right: The Life of Elizabeth Cady Stanton*. New York: Oxford University Press, 1984.

Grimes, Alan P. *The Puritan Ethic and Woman Suffrage*. New York: Oxford University Press, 1967.

Guernsey, Alfred H., and Henry M. Alden, eds. *Harper's Pictorial History of the Civil War*. New York: Fairfax Press, 1866.

Gurko, Miriam. *The Ladies of Seneca Falls: The Birth of the Woman's Rights Movement*. New York: Schocken Books, 1974.

Harper, Ida Husted. *The Life and Work of Susan B. Anthony* (vols. 1–3). Indianapolis, Indiana: Hollenbeck Press, 1898.

Harrison, Cynthia. *On Account of Sex: The Politics of Women's Issues 1945–1968*. Berkeley: University of California Press, 1988.

Hedrick, Joan D. *Harriet Beecher Stowe: A Life*. New York: Oxford University Press, 1994.

History of Woman Suffrage. Vol. 1 (1881), Vol. 2 (1882), and Vol. 3 (1886), edited by Elizabeth Cady Stanton, Susan B. Anthony, and Matilda Joslyn Gage. Vol. 4 (1902), edited by Susan B. Anthony and Ida Husted Harper. Vol. 5 (1922) and Vol. 6 (1922), edited by Ida Husted Harper. Reprinted. Salem, New Hampshire: Ayer, 1985.

Hoff-Wilson, Joan. *Law, Gender, and Injustice: A Legal History of U.S. Women*. New York: New York University Press, 1991.

Holt, Judith, and Ellen Levine. *Rebirth of Feminism*. New York: Quadrangle, 1971.

Hymowitz, Carol, and Michaele Weissman. *A History of Women in America*. New York: Bantam, 1978.

Jeffrey, Julie R. *Frontier Women: The Trans-Mississippi West, 1840–1880*. New York: Hill and Wang, 1979.

Jones, Jaqueline. *Labor of Love, Labor of Sorrow: Black Women, Work and the Family, from Slavery to the Present*. New York: Vintage, 1986.

Kahn, Ada P., and Linda Hughey Holt. *The A–Z of Women's Sexuality*. New York: Facts on File, 1990.

Kerber, Linda K. *Women of the Republic: Intellect and Ideology in Revolutionary America*. New York: W. W. Norton, 1986.

Kerr, Andrea Moore. *Lucy Stone: Speaking Out for Equality*. New Brunswick, New Jersey: Rutgers University Press, 1992.

Kessler-Harris, Alice. *Out To Work: A History of Wage-Earning Women in the United States*. New York: Oxford University Press, 1982.

Kimmel, Michael, and Thomas E. Mosmiller. *Against the Tide: Pro-Feminist Men in the United States, 1776–1990*. Boston: Beacon Press, 1992.

Klein, Ethel. *Gender Politics: From Consciousness to Mass Politics*. Cambridge: Harvard University Press, 1984.

Knappman, Edward W. *Great American Trials*. Detroit: Gale Research, 1993.

Koedt, Anne, Ellen Levine, and Anita Rapone, eds. *Radical Feminism*. New York: Quadrangle, 1973.

Kraditor, Aileen S. *The Ideas of the Woman Suffrage Movement, 1890–1920*. New York: W. W. Norton, 1981.

Lerner, Gerda. *Black Women in White America: A Documentary History*. New York: Vintage Books, 1973.

———. *The Majority Finds Its Past: Placing Women in History*. New York: Oxford University Press, 1979.

———, ed. *The Female Experience: An American Documentary*. New York: Oxford University Press, 1977.

Lifton, Robert J. *The Woman in America*. Boston: Beacon Press, 1967.

Lunardini, Christine A. *From Equal Suffrage to Equal Rights: Alice Paul and the National Woman's Party, 1910–1928*. New York: New York University Press, 1986.

Lynn, Naomi, ed. *Women, Politics and the Constitution*. New York: Harrington Park Press, 1990.

McFeely, William S. *Frederick Douglass*. New York: W. W. Norton, 1991.

McHenry, Robert, ed. *Famous American Women: A Biographical Dictionary from Colonial Times to the Present*. New York: Merriam, 1980.

MacKinnon, Catherine. *Feminism Unmodified: Discourses on Life and Law*. Cambridge: Harvard University Press, 1987.

———. *Sexual Harassment of Working Women*. New Haven, Connecticut: Yale University Press, 1979.

———. *Toward a Feminist Theory of the State.* Cambridge: Harvard University Press, 1989.

Mandle, Joan D. *Women and Social Change in America.* Princeton, New Jersey: Princeton Book Company, 1979.

Marberry, M. M. *Vicky: The Biography of Victoria C. Woodhull, Freelover, Indomitable Crusader for Human Rights, Who Precipitated the Great Reverend Henry Ward Beecher Scandal.* New York: Funk and Wagnalls, 1967.

Martin, Ralph G. *Henry and Clare: An Intimate Portrait of the Luces.* New York: Putnam, 1992.

Martineau, Harriet. *Society in America.* Edited by Seymour Martin Lipset. New Brunswick, New Jersey: Transaction Books, 1981.

Massachusetts Supreme Judicial Court. "Brief for Alice Stone Blackwell, et al., Petitioners under Bill, House No. 797, in Support of the Constitutionality of Said Bill, June 1917." Microfilm. Woodbridge, Connecticut: Research Publications, 1977.

Millett, Kate. *Sexual Politics.* New York: Aron Books, 1969.

Moers, Ellen. *Literary Women: The Great Writers.* Garden City, New York: Doubleday, 1976.

Moffat, Mary Jane, and Charlotte Painter, eds. *Revelations: Diaries of Women.* New York: Vintage Books, 1975.

Moore, Frank. *Women of the War; Their Heroism and Self-Sacrifice.* Hartford, Connecticut: Scranton, 1866.

Morgan, Robin, ed. *Sisterhood Is Powerful: An Anthology of Writings from the Women's Liberation Movement.* New York: Vintage Books, 1970.

Moritz, Charles, ed. *Current Biography: Who's News and Why, 1977.* New York: Wilson, 1978.

Morris, Richard B., ed. *Encyclopedia of American History.* New York: Harper and Brothers, 1953.

Morrison, Toni. *Racing Justice, Engendering Power.* New York: Pantheon Books, 1992.

Muccigrosso, Robert, ed. *Research Guide to American Historical Biography* (vols. 1–3). Washington, D.C.: Beacham, 1988.

Notable American Women. Vols. 1–3 (1971), edited by Edward T. James et al. Vol. 4. (1980), edited by Barbara Sicherman and Carol Hurd Green. Cambridge: Belknap Press of Harvard University Press.

O'Neill, Lois Decker, ed. *The Women's Book of World Records and Achievements.* New York: Da Capo Press, 1979.

O'Neill, William L. *Everyone Was Brave: A History of Feminism in America.* New York: Quadrangle, 1971.

Osborn, Thomas Ward. *The Fiery Trail: A Union Officer's Account of Sherman's Last Campaigns.* Edited by Richard Harwell and Philip N. Racine. Knoxville: University of Tennessee Press, 1986.

Papachristou, Judith. *Women Together.* New York: Knopf, 1976.

Paglia, Camille. *Sexual Personae.* New York: Vintage Books, 1991.

Payne, Elizabeth Anne. *Reform, Labor, and Feminism: Margaret Dreier Robins and the Women's Trade Union League.* Urbana: University of Illinois Press, 1988.

Payne, Karen. *Between Ourselves: Letters between Mothers and Daughters, 1750–1982.* Boston: Houghton Mifflin, 1983.

Planned Parenthood Federation of America, Inc. *A Tradition of Choice: Planned Parenthood at 75.* New York: Planned Parenthood Federation of America, 1991.

Pogrebin, Letty C. *Family Politics: Love and Power on an Intimate Frontier.* New York: McGraw-Hill, 1983.

Read, Phyllis J., and Bernard L. Witlieb. *The Book of Women's Firsts.* New York: Random House, 1992.

Reiter, Rayna R. *Toward an Anthropology of Women.* New York: Monthly Review Press, 1975.

Richardson, Dorothy. *The Long Day: The Story of a New York Working Girl as Told by Herself.* New York: Century, 1905.

Robinson, Harriet. *Loom and Spindle: Or Life among the Early Mill Girls.* Kailua, Hawaii: Press Pacifica, 1976.

Roe, Elizabeth A. *Recollections of Frontier Life.* New York: Arno Press, 1980.

Rossi, Alice S., ed. *The Feminist Papers.* Boston: Northern University Press, 1973.

Rothe, Anna, ed. *Current Biography: Who's News and Why, 1947.* New York: Wilson, 1948.

Rowbotham, Sheila. *Women, Resistance and Revolution: A History of Women and Revolution in the Modern World.* New York: Vintage Books, 1974.

Rozier, John, ed. *The Granite Farm Letters: The Civil War Correspondence of Edgeworth and Sallie Bird.* Athens: University of Georgia Press, 1988.

Rupp, Lelia, and Verta Taylor. *Survival in the Doldrums: The American Women's Rights Movement, 1945–1960s.* New York: Oxford University Press, 1987.

Ryan, Mary P. *Womanhood in America: From Colonial Times to the Present.* Second ed. New York: New Viewpoints, 1979.

Salmon, Marylynn. *Women and the Law of Property in Early America.* Chapel Hill: University of North Carolina Press, 1986.

Schlesinger, Arthur M. *The Almanac of American History.* New York: G. P. Putnam, 1983.

———. *The Birth of the Nation.* Boston: Houghton Mifflin, 1968.

Schlissel, Lillian. *Women's Diaries of the Westward Journey.* New York: Schocken Books, 1982.

Schmittroth, Linda, ed. *Statistical Record of Women Worldwide.* Detroit: Gale Research, 1991.

Schneider, Dorothy, and Carl J. Schneider. *American Women in the Progressive Era.* New York: Facts on File, 1993.

Schneiderman, Rose. "Miss Rose Schneiderman, Cap Maker, Replies to New York Senator." New York: Wage Earners' Suffrage League (n.d.). Microfilm. Woodbridge, Connecticut: Research Publications, 1977.

Schneir, Miriam. *Feminism: The Essential Historical Writings.* New York: Vintage Books, 1972.

Sherr, Lynn, and Jurate Kazickas. *The American Woman's Gazetteer.* New York: Bantam, 1976.

Sparhawk, Ruth M. et al. *American Women in Sport, 1887–1987: A 100-Year Chronology.* Metuchen, New Jersey, 1989.

Spruill, Julia C. *Women's Life and Work in the Southern Colonies.* New York: W. W. Norton, 1972.

Stacey, Judith, Susan Bereaud, and Joan Daniels, eds. *And Jill Came Tumbling After: Sexism in American Education.* New York: Dell, 1974.

Stanton, Elizabeth Cady, and the Revising Committee. *The Woman's Bible.* (Vol. 1, 1895; Vol. 2, 1898). Seattle, Washington: Coalition Task Force on Women and Religion, 1974.

Stanton, Theodore, and Harriot Stanton Blatch. *Elizabeth Cady Stanton.* (Vols. 1–2.) New York: Arno Press and The New York Times, 1969.

Stern, Madeleine B. *We the Women: Career Firsts of Nineteenth-Century America.* New York: Schulte, 1963.

Stevenson, Anne. *A Life of Sylvia Plath.* Boston: Houghton Mifflin, 1989.

Strasser, Susan. *Never Done: A History of American Housework.* New York: Pantheon Books, 1982.

Strong, Anna Louise. *I Change Worlds.* Seattle, Washington: Seal Press, 1979.

Switzer, Ellen. *The Law for a Woman: Real Cases and What Happened.* New York: Scribner's, 1971.

Tavris, Carol. *The Mismeasure of Women.* New York: Simon & Schuster, 1972.

Tierney, Helen, ed. *Women's Studies Encyclopedia.* New York: Peter Bedrick Books, 1991.

Tingley, Elizabeth, and Donald F. Tingley. *Woman and Feminism in American History: A Guide to Information Sources.* American Government and History Information

Guide Series, Vol. 12. Detroit, Michigan: Gale Research, 1981.

Tomalin, Claire. *The Life and Death of Mary Wollstonecraft.* New York: Harcourt Brace Jovanovich, 1974.

Tuttle, Lisa. *Encyclopedia of Feminism.* New York: Facts on File, 1986.

Ulrich, Laurel Thatcher. *A Midwife's Tale: The Life of Martha Ballard, Based on Her Diary 1785–1812.* New York: Knopf, 1990.

U.S. Congress. Senate. Subcommittee of the Committee on the District of Columbia. *Suffrage Parade Hearings.* 63d Cong., special sess. Washington, D.C.: Government Printing Office, 1913.

Van Doren, Charles, and Robert McHenry, eds. *Webster's American Biographies.* Springfield, Massachusetts: Merriam-Webster, Inc., 1974.

Wagner-Martin, Linda. *Sylvia Plath: A Biography.* New York: Simon & Schuster, 1987.

Wandersee, Winifred D. *On the Move: American Women in the 1970s.* Boston: Twayne, 1988.

Weatherford, Doris. *Foreign and Female: Immigrant Women in America, 1840–1930.* New York: Schocken Books, 1986.

Webster's New Biographical Dictionary. Springfield, Massachusetts: Merriam-Webster, Inc., 1988.

Weddington, Sarah. *A Question of Choice.* New York: G. P. Putnam's Sons, 1992.

Weiser, Marjorie P. K., and Jean S. Arbeiter. *Womanlist.* New York: Atheneum, 1981.

Welter, Barbara, ed. *The Woman Question in American History.* Hinsdale, Illinois: Dryden Press, 1973.

Wertheimer, Barbara Mayer. *We Were There: The Story of Working Women in America.* New York: Pantheon Books, 1977.

Wheeler, Leslie, ed. *Loving Warriors: Selected Letters of Lucy Stone and Henry B. Blackwell, 1853–1893.* New York: Dial Press, 1981.

Whittick, Arnold. *Woman into Citizen.* London: Athenaeum, 1979.

Who's Who in American History—Historical Volume 1607–1967. Rev. ed. Wilmette, Illinois: Marquis Publications, 1967.

Williams, Selma R. *Demeter's Daughters: The Women Who Founded America, 1587–1787.* New York: Atheneum, 1976.

Wollstonecraft, Mary. *A Vindication of the Rights of Women.* New York: W. W. Norton, 1975.

Woloch, Nancy. *Women and the American Experience.* New York: Knopf, 1984.

Woolf, Virginia. *A Room of One's Own.* New York: Harcourt Brace Jovanovich, 1929.

Wright, Frances. *Views of Society and Manners in America.* Edited by Paul K. Baker. Cambridge: Belknap Press of Harvard University Press, 1963.

Zinn, Howard. *A People's History of the United States.* New York: Harper and Row, 1980.

Zophy, Angela H., and Frances M. Kavenik, eds. *Handbook of American Women's History.* New York: Garland, 1990.

Illustration Credits

ii   Photograph by Gordon Parks. Library of Congress.

vii From a photograph of Margaret Dreier Robins, courtesy Department of Special Collections, University of Florida, Gainesville.

8   Courtesy The Nobel Foundation.

10   Jasper Yellowhead Museum and Archives, Jasper, Alberta.

20   New-York Historical Society 61900, New York City.

28   National Archives A46175.

32   Photograph by David Madison, Duomo Photography.

35   General Research Division, The New York Public Library, Astor, Lenox, and Tilden Foundations.

37   Library of Congress.

41   Seneca Falls Historical Society, Seneca Falls, NY.

44   Courtesy Margaret-Bourke White Estate. Margaret Bourke-White Papers, Syracuse University Library, Special Collections Department.

45   William L. Clements Library, University of Michigan.

50   Facing page 265 in *History of Woman Suffrage*, Vol. 2: 1861–1876. Elizabeth Cady Stanton, Susan B. Anthony, and Matilda Joslyn Gage, editors. New York: Fowler & Wells, Publishers, 1882.

51   Library of Congress.

61   Photograph by Donald Woodman. Courtesy Judy Chicago.

63   *Washington Post*; reprinted by permission of the D.C. Public Library, Washington, DC.

72   Library of Congress.

84   Frontispiece in *History of Woman Suffrage*, Vol. 2: 1861–1876. Elizabeth Cady Stanton, Susan B. Anthony, and Matilda Joslyn Gage, editors. New York: Fowler & Wells, Publishers, 1882.

87   Library of Congress.

90   Photograph by Charles Van Schaick. State Historical Society of Wisconsin WHi (V22) 1387.

93   *Oregonian* 4603; Oregon Historical Society, Portland

99   Library of Congress.

110 Photograph by Frances Benjamin Johnson. Library of Congress.

120 Drawing by John Held, Jr. Library of Congress.

121 Courtesy Industrial Workers of the World; from the Collection of the Labor Archives and Research Center, San Francisco State University.

133 Library of Congress.

136 Courtesy Girl Scouts of the U.S.A.

137 Chicago Historical Society DN 3882.

140 Library of Congress.

146 Springer/Bettmann Film Archive.

155 Library of Congress.

161 Photograph by Cara Metz. Courtesy International Ladies' Garment Workers' Union.

165 Library of Congress.

Index

Bolded page numbers refer to main entries on the subject; nonbolded page numbers are for references to the subject within other entries.

AAUW. *See* American Association of
     University Women
Abbott, Grace, 159, 274
ABCL. *See* American Birth Control League
Abolition movement, **3–4,** 114
     American Equal Rights Association, **16–17**
     National Woman's Loyal League, **217**
     Oberlin College and, 227
     petition drives, 239
     World's Anti-Slavery Convention, 14,
          131, 200, 250, 272, 280, **333–334**
     See also American Anti-Slavery Society;
          specific societies
Abolitionists
     Chapman, Maria Weston, **59–60**
     Child, Lydia Maria Francis, **61–62**
     Clarke, James Freeman, **66**
     Comstock, Ada Louise, **71**
     Davis, Paulina Kellogg Wright, **80**
     Dickinson, Anna Elizabeth, **83–84**
     Douglass, Frederick, **91–92**
     Foster, Abigail Kelley, **122**
     Garrison, William Lloyd, **130–131**
     Greeley, Horace, **139–141**
     Grimké, Angelina Emily, **141–143**
     Grimké, Sarah Moore, **143**
     Jones, Mary Harris, **165**
     Mann, Horace, **189**
     Pugh, Sarah, **250**
     Smith, Gerrit, **277–278**
     Stowe, Harriet Beecher **285**
     Swisshelm, Jane Grey Cannon, **290**
     Tubman, Harriet, **301**

     Weld, Theodore Dwight, **316**
     Wright, Frances, **334–335**
     See also Mott, Lucretia Coffin
Abortion, **4–5**
     access to clinics, 5
     ACLU activism, 16
     American Law Institute (ALI) abortion
          laws, **17–18,** 89
     antiabortion clause of Civil Rights
          Restoration Act, **22**
     *City of Akron v. Akron Center for
          Reproductive Health,* **65**
     Clergy Consultation Service on, **67**
     Committee for Abortion Rights and
          against Sterilization Abuse, **69–70**
     Doe v. Bolton, **89**
     Freedom of Choice Act, **125**
     Jane group, **163**
     Margaret Sanger and, 4
     Mexican-American National Association
          and, 195
     National Abortion Rights Action League,
          207
     People v. Belous, 237
     *Planned Parenthood of Central Missouri v.
          Danforth,* **243–244**
     *Planned Parenthood of Southeastern
          Pennsylvania v. Casey,* 5, 125, **244**
     potential birth defects and (Finkbine case),
          119
     Reagan's policies, 243
     Redstockings and, 255
     RU-486, **264**

369

Index

Civil Rights Act, Title VII of. *See* Title VII of the 1964 Civil Rights Act

Civil Rights Restoration Act, antiabortion clause of, **22**

Claflin, Tennessee Celeste, **65,** 72, 331

Clarenbach, Kathryn, 213

Clark, Billy J., 293

Clarke, James Freeman, **66**

Clay, Laura, **66**

Clergy Consultation Service on Abortion, **67**

Clerical work, **67**

Clinton, Hillary Rodham, **67–68**

Coast guard, 279

Code Napoléon, **68**

Coercion, 6, **68–69,** 32, 56, 106, 120, 148, 166, 190, 257. *See also* Property rights

Coffee, Linda, 261

Cohen, Judy. *See* Chicago, Judy

Collazo, Veronica, 211

College Equal Suffrage League, 233

Colleges. *See* Schools

Colored Women's League, 49

Committee for Abortion Rights and against Sterilization Abuse (CARASA), **69–70**

Common law, **70**
  abortion and, 4
  adultery and, 9
  Code Napoléon, **68**
  separate estate, **274**
  status of widows, 115
  See also Feme covert; Feme sole; Property rights

Commonwealth v. Addicks, 62

Commonwealth v. Jane Daniels, **70–71,** 213

Communist party, 120, 122

Comparable worth, 17, **71**
  Brown and Sharp Manufacturing case, **50**
  See also Occupation and employment; Pay equity

Complex marriage, 225–226, 307

Comstock, Ada Louise, **71**

Comstock, Elizabeth, **72**

Comstock Act, 33–34, 65, **72–73,** 150, 267, 305, 312, 332

Condoms, 74

Congress To Unite Women, **73**

Congressional Union for Woman Suffrage, 31, 40, 50, 52, **73,** 98, 217, 235

Connecticut Woman Suffrage Association, 152

Consciousness raising, **73,** 119

Contraband Relief Association, **73–74**

Contraception, **74**
  Griswold v. Connecticut, **143–144**

See also Abortion; Birth control; Comstock Act

Contracts, 222, 257
  doctrine of agency, **88**
  feme covert and, 115

Corbin, Margaret Cochran, **74**

Corset, **74**

Coutts v. Greenhow, **74–75,** 88

Coverture, 115

Cowles, Betsey, 265

Craig v. Boren, 75, 124, 172, 257

Crandall, Prudence, **75–76,** 101

Crater, Florence, 76

Crater's Raiders, **76**

Credit opportunities, 103–104

Crimes against Chastity law, 102

Criminal justice, *Commonwealth v. Jane Daniels,* **70–71**

Cullom Bill, **76**

Cult of domesticity, **76**

Curtis, George William, **77**

Curtis, Harriot F., 112, 183

Custody rights, 25, **62,** 70, 240

Cutler, Hannah, **77**

Dame schools, **79**

Daughters of Bilitis, **79**

Daughters of Liberty, **79**

Daughters of St. Crispin, **80,** 286

Daughters of Temperance, **80**

Davenport, Lacey, 117

Davis, Paulina Wright, 42, **80,** 190, 221

D.C. Women's Liberation Movement, **80–81**

Death penalty, for adultery, 9

Debs, Eugene Victor, **81**

Decker, Sarah Sophia, 132

Declaration of Rights for Women, **81–82**

Declaration of Sentiments, **82,** 260, 273, 281

Defense Advisory Committee on Women in the Services, **82–83**

Deloria, Ella Cara, **83**

Dennett, Mary Ware, 208, 312

Desertion, 88–89, 141

Dewey, John, **83**

Dickinson, Anna Elizabeth, **83–84**

Dickinson, Emily, **84–85**

Divorce, **85–86**
  adultery and, 9
  Pennsylvania Statute of 1785, **237**

Dix, Dorothea Lynde, **86–88**

Doctrine of agency, **88**

Doctrine of intentions, **88,** 164

Doctrine of necessities, **88–89**

Dodge Study, 132, **248–249**

Index

Index

Index

Index

Smith Miller, Elizabeth, 277
Snook, Neta, 97
Socialist feminists, 59
    Eastman, Crystal, **97–98**
    Flynn, Elizabeth Gurley, **120–122**
Socialist Party, 81
Society of Friends (Quakers), **279**
    Lucretia Mott and, 199–201
    persecution of, 94–95
    Sarah Grimké and, 143
    Shaking Quakers, 307
Society of Shakers, 307
Sojourner Truth. *See* Truth, Sojourner
Sommers, Tish, 12–13, 229
Southern States Woman Suffrage
    Conference, 66
SPARS, **279**
Spiritualism, 153
Stanton, Elizabeth Cady, **279–282**, 289
    American Equal Rights Association, **16–17**
    Bloomer costume, 41, 195
    criticism of Fifteenth Amendment, 258
    Declaration of Sentiments, **82**
    divorce laws and, 85–86
    Fifteenth Amendment and, 119
    Frederick Douglass and, 92
    Gerrit Smith and, 277
    Harriot Stanton Blatch and, 40
    History of Woman Suffrage, 150, 282
    Horace Greeley and, 140
    introduced to Susan B. Anthony, 21
    The Lily and, 180
    married women's property acts and, 190,
        221
    Martha Wright and, 335
    National Labor Union and, **212**
    National American Woman Suffrage
        Association and, **207–208**
    National Woman Suffrage Association
        and, **215–216**
    National Woman's Loyal League, **217**
    Nora Stanton Blatch Barney and, 27
    The Revolution and, **258**
    Seneca Falls Convention and, 272–273
    support from racists, 119, 169, 215–216
    Victoria Woodhull and, 332
    The Woman's Bible and, 24, 208, 282, **324**
    World's Anti-Slavery Convention and, 333
    See also National Woman Suffrage
        Association
Stanton, Henry, 333
Stanton v. Stanton, 124
State commissions on the status of women,
    282
Steadman, Cheryl, 245

Steinem, Gloria, 201, 220, **282–283**, 291,
    326
Sterilization abuse, 69
Stevens, Lillian, 217
Stimpson, Catherine, 277
Stokes, Rose Pastor, 208
Stone, Lucy, 119, **283–285**
    Alice Blackwell and, 37
    American Woman Suffrage Association, **18**
    Antoinette Brown Blackwell and, 38
    Bloomer costume, 42
    Hannah Cutler and, 77
    History of Woman Suffrage and, 150
    Kansas campaign, 127, **169**
    National Woman Suffrage Association
        and, 215
    Oberlin College and, 227
    petition for Thirteenth Amendment, 217
    See also American Woman Suffrage
        Association
Stone, Hannah M., 305
Stoneman, Abigail, 115–116
Stowe, Harriet Beecher, 30, **285**, 303
Strikes, 122, 160, **286–289**
    Lawrence mill workers, **177**
    Mary McDowell and, 188
    Mother Jones and, 166
    shirtwaist makers, 161, 286–287, 298, 331
    Uprising of the 20,000, 161, **306**, 331
    Women's Strike for Equality, 283, **330**
    See also Unions
Struck v. Secretary of Defense, 135
Student Nonviolent Coordinating
    Committee, 57
Style, Emily Jane, 215
Sudow, Ellen, 219
Suffrage, women's, **289–290**. *See also*
    American Woman Suffrage Association;
    Anthony, Susan Brownell; Fourteenth
    Amendment; Fifteenth Amendment;
    National American Woman Suffrage
    Association; National Woman Suffrage
    Association; Nineteenth Amendment;
    Stanton, Elizabeth Cady
The Suffragist, 52, 73
Surrogate mother cases, 25
Swartz, Maud, 331
Sweatshops, 152
Swisshelm, Jane Grey Cannon, **290**
Szold, Henrietta, 145
Take Back the Night, **291**
Talbot, Marion, 14
Tappan, Arthur, 13–14, 130, 131, 316
Tappan, Lewis, 13–14, 131, 316
Tarbell, Ida Minerva, **291–292**